www.wadsworth.com

wadsworth.com is the World Wide Web site for Wadsworth Publishing Company and is your direct source to dozens of online resources.

At *wadsworth.com* you can find out about supplements, demonstration software, and student resources. You can also send e-mail to many of our authors and preview new publications and exciting new technologies.

wadsworth.com
Changing the way the world learns®

PHILOSOPHICAL TRADITIONS
A Text with Readings

Second Edition

Louis P. Pojman
Clare Hall, Cambridge University

THOMSON
~TM

WADSWORTH

Australia • Canada • Mexico • Singapore • Spain
United Kingdom • United States

THOMSON

WADSWORTH

Publisher: Holly J. Allen
Philosophy Editor: Steve Wainwright
Assistant Editors: Lee McCracken, Barbara Hillaker
Editorial Assistant: John Gahbauer
Marketing Manager: Worth Hawes
Marketing Assistant: Andrew Keay
Advertising Project Manager: Laurel Anderson
Print Buyer: Doreen Suruki

Permissions Editor: Sarah Harkrader
Production Service: Ruth Cottrell
Copy Editor: Betty Duncan
Cover Designer: Yvo Riezebos
Cover Image: *School of Athens* by Raphael
Compositor: International Typesetting and Composition
Printer: Transcontinental Printing—Louiseville

Printed in Canada
1 2 3 4 5 6 7 08 07 06 05

For more information about our products, contact us at:
Thomson Learning Academic Resource Center
1-800-423-0563
For permission to use material from this text or product, submit a request online at
http://www.thomsonrights.com.
Any additional questions about permissions can be submitted by email to thomsonrights@thomson.com.

Library of Congress Control Number: 2004116652

ISBN 0-534-57042-9

Thomson Wadsworth
10 Davis Drive
Belmont, CA 94002-3098
USA

Asia
Thomson Learning
5 Shenton Way #01-01
UIC Building
Singapore 068808

Australia/New Zealand
Thomson Learning
102 Dodds Street
Southbank, Victoria 3006
Australia

Canada
Nelson
1120 Birchmount Road
Toronto, Ontario M1K 5G4
Canada

Europe/Middle East/Africa
Thomson Learning
High Holborn House
50/51 Bedford Row
London WC1R 4LR
United Kingdom

Latin America
Thomson Learning
Seneca, 53
Colonia Polanco
11560 Mexico D.F.
Mexico

Spain/Portugal
Paraninfo
Calle Magallanes, 25
28015 Madrid, Spain

Dedicated to my grandson, Theodore D. Pojman
May you become a philosopher, a lover of wisdom

Contents

Preface for Second Edition

Having use both single-authored texts and anthologies, sometimes one of each in introductory courses, I thought the idea of combining primary sources with analytic commentary might bring together the virtues of both types of textbooks. I wanted to put together a work that would serve students in learning about philosophy. I wanted a book that would, first of all, consider philosophy seriously and convey the wonder and vitality of the subject as it so richly deserves—hence the historical emphasis in this work. Philosophy was not invented yesterday. It has a rich heritage without which one cannot fully understand the discipline—hence the emphasis on the classical writing of Plato, St. Thomas Aquinas, René Descartes, David Hume, Immanuel Kant, John Stuart Mill, and others. However, I have also used those contemporary authors who set forth arguments and raise issues in new and interesting ways.

Second, I wanted a book that presented significant portions of classical and contemporary philosophical works. These are texts that the student should be able to analyze and use in developing his or her own considered views. Primary sources are invaluable; there is no substitute for them. They convey varieties of methods, interpretations, and styles, all pertinent in seeking understanding.

Third, I have gradually come to realize that philosophical tests, especially some of the classical or harder contemporary works, without commentary and analysis can be very difficult for beginning students. Thus, I have integrated commentary and analysis and questions with these primary sources.

This is mainly a work in Western philosophy, dealing with the classical questions raised therein (there are two readings from Eastern traditions). Philosophy as a rigorous use of reason and logic arose in the West, off the Greek isles, during the sixth century BCE. The ancient Greeks began something never before done (as far as we know). Other cultures wondered at the mysteries of the universe, but the Greeks sought to account for these mysteries by reason rather than myth or religion. They speculated and devised comprehensive systems but then subjected them to ruthless criticism. They invented both the analytic and dialectical methods (thesis and counterthesis based on counterexample and counterhypothesis). All the perennial and perplexing questions of philosophy arose with these amazing minds. Our tradition carried on these modes of thinking for over two millennia until the present time. It is a tradition we have reason to support, improve, and pass on to posterity.

Introductory material and nine major topics are considered in the thirty-four chapters of this work:

- Part I An Introduction
- Part II The Beginning of Philosophy: The Ancient Greeks—The Sophists, Socrates, Plato, and Aristotle
- Part III Philosophy of Religion: An Introduction
- Part IV The Theory of Knowledge
- Part V Metaphysics: Philosophy of Mind
- Part VI Freedom of Will and Determinism
- Part VII Ethics
- Part VIII Existentialism and the Meaning of Life

There is nothing sacred about this order. Part I should be read, and most teachers find it useful to go over the basic logic, but after that a lot of discretion is permitted. Because I think the history of the subject is important, I generally do Part II, "The Beginning of Philosophy," especially Chapters 3 and 4. Then I treat three or four other subjects during the semester, varying the topics each time I teach the course.

As additional aids to the student, I have included discussion questions ("For Further Reflection") at the end of each chapter, as well as a short annotated bibliography. An appendix ("How to Read and Write a Philosophy Paper") and a glossary follow the main text.

Besides revising several chapters, I have made several important additions for this new edition. I have added a chapter on Aristotle's philosophy, one on Kant's epistemology and metaphysics, and one on Arthur Schopenhauer, one of the most underrated philosophers in the history of philosophy.

I owe a debt of gratitude to Steve Wainwright and Lee McCracken who supported this revision and to Ruth Cottrell and Betty Duncan who did a marvelous job improving the style and format, bringing this work into production. The following reviewers of this work made important criticisms and suggestions that were valuable: Edward Slowik, Winona State University; Michael S. Valle, Scottsdale Community College; and Jay M. Van Hook, University of Central Florida. To all of these people, I am most grateful.

This book is dedicated to my grandson, Theodore (Petri) Pojman in the hope that he will come to love philosophy, the pursuit of wisdom, as much as his father, Paul, and I do.

I hope that this book will help you teach philosophy (if you are an instructor) or learn to do philosophy (if you are a student). I would be delighted to hear from you on your experience with it and to receive your suggestions for improvement. Please write to me at

Louis P. Pojman
Clare Hall
Cambridge University
Cambridge, UK
3CB 9AL

A Personal Word to the Student

Nothing worthwhile was ever accomplished without great difficulty.
Plato in *The Republic*

Philosophy is an exciting subject. I want very much that you come to love this subject as much as I do. If after working your way through significant parts of this book and you have acquired an appreciative understanding of this body of knowledge and method, I will have succeeded in my task. If you don't, I probably have failed. To prepare you for what is to come, to ensure success—or at least to make it more likely—a few words about what to expect may be in order.

Just about everyone who comes to philosophy—usually in college—feels a sinking sensation in his or her stomach when first encountering this very strange material, involving a different sort of style and method from anything else they have ever dealt with. It was certainly my first reaction as a student. Lured by such questions as "Is there a God? What can I truly know? What is the meaning of life? Is there life after death? Am I free or completely determined by antecedent causes? How shall I live my life?" I began to read philosophy on my own. My first books were Søren Kierkegaard's *Fear and Trembling,* a book part poetry and part philosophy about the nature of religious belief, and Bertrand Russell's *History of Western Philosophy,* which is much more than a history of the subject, more an analysis and evaluation of major themes in the history of Western philosophy. Kierkegaard's book had a devastating effect on me, forcing me to become totally dissatisfied with the mediocre life I had been living in college and drove me to depths of intensity and seriousness that I have still not recovered from.

Regarding Russell's work, though not a terribly difficult text, most of the ideas and arguments in it were new to me. Since he opposed many of the beliefs that I had been brought up with, I felt angry with him. But since he seemed to argue so persuasively, my anger gave way to confusion and then to a sense of defeat and despair. For a while Kierkegaard and Russell were juxtaposed in my mind as two opposing philosophies of life, both attractive. When I read a work of Kierkegaard, I'd conclude, "That's exactly right. What a persuasive case he makes." But then I'd read some more of Russell and reluctantly say the same thing about his work. Why couldn't I figure out what I believed and how to settle the conflicting viewpoints? I was perplexed, dissatisfied with my lack of ability to outargue these masters, and a bit angry at these figures for the state they left me in. Yet I felt compelled to go on with this "forbidden fruit," finishing Russell's long work and going on to read Plato's *Republic*, René Descartes' *Meditations*, David Hume's *Dialogues on Natural Religion*, selected writings of Immanuel Kant, John Stuart Mill's *Utilitarianism*, William James's *Will to Believe*, and finally contemporary readings by Albert Camus, Jean-Paul Sartre, Anthony Flew, R. M. Hare, John Hick, and Ludwig Wittgenstein. Gradually, I became aware that on every issue on which I disagreed with Hume or Russell, someone else—perhaps it was Kant or James or Hick—had a plausible counterargument. Eventually, I struggled to the place where I would see weaknesses in arguments (sometimes of those figures with whom I had agreed), and finally I came to the point where I could write out arguments of my own. The pain of the process slowly gave way to joy—addictive job, let me warn you—so that I decided to pursue an advanced degree in philosophy.

As I already mentioned, it was a gnawing worry about fundamental questions of existence that drew me to philosophy. Is there a God? What can I know for sure? What is the relationship of the mind to the body? Do I have a soul that will live forever? Am I truly free or simply determined by my heredity and environment? What is it to live a moral life? Are there objective moral truths, or is everything relative either to culture or the individual? If you have asked these questions and pondered alternative responses, this book will make sense to you. But if you haven't spent a lot of time thinking about this sort of subject matter, you might ask yourself whether these are important questions and outline your own present responses to them. For unless you've asked the questions, the proposed answers may sound like one end of a telephone conversation.

This text is meant to be suggestive of responses in order to stimulate you to work out your own position on the questions addressed herein. You will find many readings, over eighty, typically juxtaposing opposite views, interspersed with commentary and usually followed with analyses. I have endeavored to set forth the arguments on both sides of each issue as fairly as possible. Hopefully you, with your teacher's help, will be able to use this work as a guide, leading you to develop your own ideas and arguments, in order that you might work out your own philosophy of life.

I recommend that you first look over the table of contents in order to get a glimpse of what is to come and then read Chapter 1, "What Is Philosophy?" You might need to read it twice in order to let the ideas therein sink in. In fact, philosophical texts often do require two or more readings before one fully understands them. I have avoided technical jargon wherever possible, but some terms are necessary for a full grasp of the subject matter. There is a glossary at the end of the book, which may come in handy regarding these technical words.

Good luck, and I hope you enjoy your philosophical pursuit of wisdom and truth as much as I have. I would be glad to hear from you on any thoughts you might have on philosophical problems or on the material in this book. Please email me at

Lpojman@aol.com

PHILOSOPHICAL TRADITIONS
A Text with Readings

PART I
An Introduction

1 ❧ What Is Philosophy?

He that would seriously set upon the search of truth ought in the first place to prepare his mind with a love of it. How a man may know whether he be [a lover of truth] in earnest, is worthy of inquiry; and I think there is one unerring mark of it, namely, the not entertaining any proposition with greater assurance than the proofs it is built upon will warrant. Whoever goes beyond this measure of assent, it is plain receives not the truth in the love of it; loves not truth for truth's sake, but for some other bye-end.

John Locke[1]

Perennial and Perplexing Questions

The universe is vast, immeasurable, infinite, boundless; we are little, finite, infinitesimal specks of dust, limited by birth and death, time and place. Yet though tiny in stature and confined to a small planet in a small solar system in an undistinguished galaxy, we have the power to think—to wonder, investigate, reflect, deliberate, question, doubt, surmise, hypothesize, reason, argue, and systematize. Perhaps, within a certain limited domain, we can even begin to know—know even in a limited way about the unlimited.

We interrogate the universe: Where did I come from? Who or what is responsible for my being? Why am I here? Why is anything here? Why is there something and not just nothing? What is time? Space? Does the universe have a beginning, or is it eternal? Does it have boundaries, limits, ends after which they cease to be? Is this span of life all there is, or is there something more? What more? Is there life after life?

3

Is the universe essentially friendly, personal? The work of a benevolent intelligence? Or is it simply an intricate and complicated machine that accidentally cranked out a freak endowed with consciousness and reason in a tiny corner of the cosmos? Is there a God?

Who am I? Am I simply an animal with a more developed brain than a cockroach or mosquito? Or is there something divine, eternal, and precious within? Am I any more valuable, intrinsically, than a pig or ant or weed or rock? Am I free? Or am I completely determined by antecedent causes that even fool me into believing that I am free? Can I act against the sway of causal forces within and without? In what sense, if any, am I responsible for my actions, my self?

What, if anything, is my destiny? How should I live my life? Is there right and wrong, objective good and evil? Or is every act simply relative to an individual's feelings or the approval of one's peers, community, or culture? Is morality subject to time and place and social conditions? Is there a true morality, a right way to live?

What, if anything, can I know, can I be certain about? Can I be truly justified in my beliefs? Or is everything doubtful? Could I be systematically deceived about the simplest and most fundamental cognitive experiences? Is there Truth about reality, or are there only various and equally valid interpretations? If there is Truth, what is it and how can I apprehend it?

What, if anything, is the meaning of life? Is there objective purpose (a *telos*) to existence, or is each of us forced to invent our own reality, our own value, our own meaning to life?

These inquiries and others like them are the perennial questions of philosophy. They have been asked for as long as men and women reflected on their situation in the world. If you have asked them, you are already a philosopher, for **philosophy** is probing existence for its meaning, the search for truth and understanding, the hope of gaining, if not knowledge of the Truth, at least wisdom. If you have asked these questions already, this book will serve as a travel guide, assisting you in your pilgrimage through the perplexing paths and wondrous ways of life's myriad mysteries.

Philosophy is an exercise of reflection on life's perennial questions. It is speculative, wonder filled, critical, both *synthetic* (aiming at a comprehensive vision) and *analytic* (scrutinizing claims and arguments). It asks the big questions and explores big answers. It probes and counterprobes. It restlessly confronts the universe with its question: Why?

While recognizing the importance of desire and the emotions, philosophy is centered in reason—reason is its blood, its heart, its breath, its life, its glory. All things are subject to its blazing beam of light, even the question of the limits and uses of reason. Can reason discover its own limits? If it cannot, what else can? How else do we come to understand? Through intuition and experience? True, but even here reason must adjudicate between true and false intuitions, genuine and deceptive experiences.

Philosophy teaches us to think for ourselves: globally, deeply, critically, personally, systematically. It enables us to be autonomous individuals—not bound by unreflective authority, but as free rational individuals who are not easily sucked in by the intellectual fads of the day but who can stand alone against the prejudices and idols of popular culture, who comprehend deeply, who are ever growing in understanding of their own strengths and weaknesses, of their own fallibility.

The Love of Wisdom

Philosophy starts from an **assumption,** first announced by the founder of moral philosophy, Socrates (470–399 BCE), that the unexamined life is not worth living and that although hard thinking about important issues disturbs, it also consoles. Philosophy, as Aristotle (384–322 BCE) said over 2000 years ago, begins with wonder at the marvels and mysteries of the world. It begins in wonder in the pursuit of truth and wisdom and ends in a life lived in moral and intellectual integrity, in excellence in action and understanding. This is the classical philosophical ideal, beginning with the ancient Greeks down through Aquinas, Descartes, Locke, Hume, Kant, Kierkegaard, and Mill, to the present. Of course, this thesis about the worth of philosophy is to be subject to rational scrutiny. Let me expand on it.

Philosophy is the love of wisdom (etymologically from the Greek *philos,* meaning "lover," and *sophia,* meaning "wisdom"). It is the contemplation or study of the most important questions in existence with the end of promoting illumination and understanding, a vision of the whole. It uses reason, sense perception, the imagination, and intuitions in its activities of *clarifying concepts* and *analyzing and constructing arguments and theories* as possible answers to these perennial questions. It is revolutionary because its deliverances often disturb our common sense or our received tradition. Philosophy usually goes against the stream or the majority since the majority opinion is often a composite of past intellectual struggles or "useful" biases. There is often deeper truth, better and new evidence that disturbs the status quo and that forces us to revise or reject some of our beliefs. This experience can be as painful as it is exciting.

The pain may lead us to give up philosophical inquiry, and a great deal of emotional health may be required to persevere in this pursuit. We may retreat into unreason and obey the commandment of Ignorance: "Think not, lest thou be confounded!" Truth (or what we seem justified in believing) may not always be edifying. But in the end, the philosopher's faith is that the Truth is good and worth pursuing for its own sake and for its secondary benefits. Intelligent inquiry, which philosophy promotes, is liberating, freeing us from prejudice, self-deceptive notions, and half-truths. As Bertrand Russell (1872–1970) put it,

> The [person] who has no tincture of philosophy goes through life imprisoned in the prejudices derived from common sense, from the habitual beliefs of his age or his nation, and from convictions which have grown up in his mind without the co-operation or consent of his deliberate reason. . . . While diminishing our feeling of certainty as to

what things are, [philosophy] greatly increases our knowledge as to what they may be; it removes the somewhat arrogant dogmatism of those who have never travelled into the region of liberating doubt, and it keeps alive the sense of wonder by showing familiar things in an unfamiliar light.[2]

Philosophy should result in a wider vision of life in which the impartial use of reason results in an appreciation of other viewpoints and other people's rights and needs. There is no guarantee that this will occur. Some become radical skeptics with accompanying behavioral patterns, and some nasty people seem to be able to do philosophy quite well without being transformed by it. But for the most part, those who have had the vision of a better life and have worked through arguments on substantive issues relating to human nature and destiny have been positively affected by the perennial pilgrimage. They march to a different drummer and show in their lives the fruits of their travail. This ability to live by reflective principle in spite of and in the midst of the noise of the masses and a myriad of conflicting perspectives is a hallmark of philosophy. This is illustrated by one of its heros, Socrates, whom we will first encounter in Chapter 4 and then throughout this book.

We mentioned that one of the tasks of philosophy is clarifying concepts. Let me illustrate how this works with two different examples. The American philosopher and psychologist William James (1842–1910), brother to the novelist Henry James, was vacationing with friends in New England one summer. On returning from a walk, he found his friends engaged in a fierce dispute. The problem in question was this: Suppose a squirrel is clinging to the side of a tree and you are trying to see the back of the squirrel. But as you walk around the tree, the clever squirrel moves edgewise around the tree on its other side so that you never get a look at the squirrel. The question was, Did you go around the squirrel? Half the group contended that you did go around, and half contended that you did not. What do you think is the answer?

Here is what William James said:

Which party is right . . . depends on what you *practically mean* by "going around" the squirrel. If you mean passing from north of him to the east, then to the south, then to the west, and then to the north of him again, obviously the man does go around him, for he occupies these successive positions. But if on the contrary you mean being first in front of him, then on the right of him, then behind him, then on his left, and finally in front again, it is quite obvious that the man fails to go round him, for by the compensating movements the squirrel makes, he keeps his belly turned towards the man all the time, and his back turned away. Make the distinction, and there is no occasion for any further dispute.[3]

Here was a dispute over the concept "going around something." The philosopher is trained to look at the frame of reference of the phrase, to note its inherent ambiguity, and to unravel it, making things clearer. In this case, once James had pointed out the equivocation in the idea of "going around," all dispute ceased. The first step in philosophy is to make your ideas (concepts, notions) as clear as possible.

The hallmark of the philosophical method is *argument*. Philosophers clarify concepts and analyze and test propositions and beliefs, but their major task is analyzing and constructing arguments. Bertrand Russell said that one aim of philosophy is to begin with assumptions that no one would ever think of doubting and proceed through a careful process of valid reasoning to conclusions so preposterous to common sense that no one could help doubting. Indeed, in philosophy there is no "political correctness." No hypothesis, however outrageous to common sense or conventional thinking, is ruled out of court, *provided* only that you are seeking the truth and endeavor to support your claim with arguments, with good reasons. Otherwise, anything goes.

Philosophical reasoning is closely allied to scientific reasoning in that both look for evidence and build hypotheses that are tested with the hope of coming closer to the truth. However, scientific experiments take place in laboratories and have testing procedures through which to record objective or empirically verifiable results. The laboratory of the philosopher is his or her mind, where imaginative thought experiments take place; the study, where ideas are written down and examined; and wherever conversation about the perennial questions takes place, where thesis and counterthesis and counterexample are considered. Its instruments are imagination and the canons of logic. We will look more closely at this latter aspect in Chapter 2.

There is a joke that compares the equipment needs of the scientist, the mathematician, and the philosopher. The scientist needs an expensive laboratory with all sorts of experimental equipment. The mathematician needs only a pencil, paper, and a wastepaper basket. The philosopher needs only a pencil and paper! The truth embodied in this bit of humor is that it is not as easy to test philosophical theories as it is to test a mathematical theorem or a scientific hypothesis. Because philosophical questions are more speculative and metaphysical, one cannot prove or disprove most of the important theses. The relationship of philosophy to science is more complicated than the above suggests, for much of what theoretical scientists do could with justice be called philosophy. In general, the sciences have one by one made their way out of the family fold of philosophy to independence as they systematized their decision-making procedures. In the words of Jeffrey Olen,

> The history of philosophy reads like a long family saga. In the beginning there were the great patriarch and matriarch, the searchers for knowledge and wisdom, who bore a large number of children. Mathematics, physics, ethics, psychology, logic, political thought, metaphysics, . . . and epistemology . . .—all belonged to the same family. Philosophers were not *just* philosophers, but mathematicians and physicists and psychologists as well. Indeed, in the beginning of the family's history, no distinction was made between philosophy and these other disciplines. . . .
>
> In the beginning, then, all systematic search for knowledge was philosophy. This fact is still reflected in the modern university, where the

highest degree granted in all of the sciences and humanities is the Ph.D.—the doctor of philosophy.

But the children gradually began to leave home. First to leave were physics and astronomy, as they began to develop experimental techniques of their own. This exodus, led by Galileo (1564–1642), Isaac Newton (1642–1727), and Johannes Kepler (1571–1630), created the first of many great family crises. . . . Eventually, psychology left home.[4]

Major Subject Areas

The major areas of philosophy are *metaphysics* (concerned with such issues as the nature of ultimate reality, philosophy of religion, philosophy of mind, personal identity, freedom of the will, and immortality), *epistemology* (regarding the nature of knowledge), *axiology* (the study of values, including aesthetics, ethics, and political philosophy), and *logic* (having to do with the laws of thought and forms of argument). There are also secondary areas of philosophy, which work on conceptual and/or theoretical problems arising within first-order nonphilosophical disciplines. Examples of these are philosophy of science, philosophy of psychology, philosophy of mathematics, philosophy of language, and philosophy of law. Wherever conceptual analysis or justification of a theoretical schema is needed, philosophical expertise is appropriate. More recently, as technology creates new possibilities and problems, applied ethics (for example, biomedical ethics, business ethics, environmental ethics, and legal ethics) has arisen. History plays a dialectical role with regard to philosophy, for not only do philosophers do philosophy while teaching the history of philosophy, but they also involve themselves in the critical examination of the principles that underlie historical investigation itself, creating a philosophy of history.

We will touch on many of these areas in this work: a little logic and history of philosophy; philosophy of religion; epistemology; metaphysics, including the mind–body problem, personal identity, immortality, and free will and determinism; ethics; and the problem of the meaning of life. These are more than enough for an *introduction* to philosophy.

The Rapier of Reason

Philosophy, we noted, is centered in argument. It is a rational activity. You may have questions about just what this means. Sometimes students, especially in introductory classes, get annoyed, even angry, that their views are subjected to sharp critical scrutiny or that the views of philosophers of the past, who cannot defend themselves, get torn to pieces by their teacher. So they ask, "So what if [so and so's] argument is unsound. Why do we always have to follow the best reasons? Why don't philosophers respect leaps of faith or our nonrational beliefs?"

The initial response to this query is to ask whether the questioner wants a *rational* answer or a nonrational one. "Do you want a reason for justifying philosophical practice or just my own emotional prejudice?" Presumably, the former is wanted. Indeed, the question "Why?" implies a reason is called for, so even a question about the appropriateness of reason must be addressed by reason. If reason has limits, it is reason that discovers and explains this fact.

The teacher may go on and point out that reason does recognize the limits of reason. Immanuel Kant (1724–1804) tried to show these limits in order to make room for religious faith, and, more problematically, Søren Kierkegaard (1813–1855) used rational argument to show that sometimes it is rational even to go against reason. What does this mean?

Here we have to distinguish two kinds of reason: practical reason from theoretical reason. Practical reason has to do with *acting* in order to realize a goal. For example, you desire to be healthy and so carry out a regimen of exercise, good nutrition, and general moderation. You have a goal (something you desire), you ask what are the necessary or best means of reaching that goal, and then, if you are rational in the practical sense, you act on your judgment. Theoretical reason, on the other hand, has to do with *beliefs*. It asks, What is the evidence for such and such a proposition or belief? What is it rational to believe about the best way to stay healthy or the existence of God or the existence of ghosts or life after death?

Thus, we have two types of rationality: practical and theoretical, having to do with actions and beliefs. Sometimes these two types of reasons may conflict. For instance, I may have evidence that my friend has committed a crime. My evidence is substantial but perhaps not decisive. For practical reasons, I may ignore or dismiss the evidence against him, reasoning that to believe my friend is guilty would be an act of disloyalty or greatly damage our relationship (for I cannot hide my feelings very well). Or I may use theoretical reason to conclude that I should not use reason to analyze the best way to make baskets while I am playing basketball, for the act of shooting is more likely to succeed if I don't think too much about what I am doing, but just do it. Or when reading literature, I may want to turn off my critical faculties in order to more fully enjoy the story.

If all this is accurate, it is sometimes rational not to be rational. Paradoxical? Yes, but explainable and not contradictory. We are *practically* rational in not always using *theoretical* rationality when engaged in some activities. On one level, theoretical reason judges that we are justified in not using theoretical reason when engaged in practical activities but that we are practically rational in acting spontaneously, following our feelings, making leaps of faith.

These are cases, however, where theoretical reason is simply not an issue, where practical reasons are justified by theoretical reasoning. The more difficult question is, Is it ever right to allow ourselves to believe propositions where there is insufficient reason? Should practical reason sometimes *override* theoretical rationality? The British philosopher W. K. Clifford (1845–1879) said, "No, it is wrong always, everywhere, and for anyone, to believe anything upon insufficient evidence."

One problem with Clifford's absolute prohibition is that there seems to be insufficient evidence to support it, and if so, it is self-referentially incoherent (or self-refuting). Other philosophers—such as Blaise Pascal (1623–1662), Søren Kierkegaard, and William James—argue the reverse. Sometimes we are (practically) justified in getting ourselves to believe against the conclusions of (theoretical) reason, against the preponderance of evidence. We will examine some of these philosophers and arguments in Chapter 12. Here we need only point out that it is a live philosophical issue whether practical reason should override theoretical reason.

Thus, philosophy is a practice of giving reasons in support of one's beliefs and actions. Its ultimate goal is to arrive at a rationally justified position on one's beliefs about the important issues of life, including what is the best way to live one's life and organize society. Philosophy consists in the rational examination of worldviews, metaphysical theories, ethical systems, and even the limits of reason.

Although a clearer understanding of the nature of philosophy will only emerge while working through the arguments on the various issues you are going to study, I want to end this introduction with a set of guidelines for philosophical inquiry, "Ten Rules of Philosophy," which I hope will aid you in your own pilgrimage as you build your own philosophy of life. They embody what I take to be the classical philosophical perspective. You should test them, refine them, and possibly reject some of them or add better ones as you proceed on you own pursuit of wisdom.

Ten Rules of Philosophy

1. *Allow the spirit of wonder to flourish in your breast.* Philosophy begins with deep wonder about the universe and about who we are and where we came from and where we are going. What is this life all about?

2. *Doubt everything until the evidence convinces you of its truth.* Be reasonably cautious, a moderate skeptic, suspicious of those who claim to have the truth. Doubt is the soul's laxative. Do not fear intellectual inquiry. As Johann Goethe (1749–1832) said, "The masses fear the intellectual, but it is stupidity that they should fear, if they only realized how dangerous it really is."

3. *Love the truth.* "Philosophy is the eternal search for truth, a search which inevitably fails and yet is never defeated; which continually eludes us, but which always guides us. This free, intellectual life of the mind is the noblest inheritance of the Western World; it is also the hope of our future" (W. T. Jones).

4. *Divide and conquer.* Divide each problem and theory into its smallest essential components in order to analyze each unit carefully. This is the analytic method.

5. *Collect and construct.* Build a coherent argument or theory from component parts. One should move from the simple, secure foundations to the complex and comprehensive. As mentioned earlier, Bertrand Russell once

said that the aim of philosophical argument was to move from simple propositions so obvious that no one would think of doubting them via a method of valid argument to conclusions so preposterous that no one could help but doubt them. The important thing is to have a coherent, well-founded, tightly reasoned set of beliefs that can withstand the opposition.

6. *Conjecture and refute.* Make a complete survey of possible objections to your position, looking for counterexamples and subtle mistakes. Following a suggestion of Karl Popper, we can say that philosophy is a system of conjecture and refutation. Seek bold hypotheses and seek disconfirmations of your favorite positions. In this way, by a process of elimination, you will negatively and indirectly and gradually approach the Truth.

7. *Revise and rebuild.* Be willing to revise, reject, and modify your beliefs and the degree with which you hold *any* belief. Acknowledge that you probably have many false beliefs and be grateful to those who correct you. This is the *principle of fallibilism,* the thesis that we are very likely incorrect in many of our beliefs and have a tendency toward self-deception when considering objections to our position.

8. *Seek simplicity.* Prefer the simpler explanation to the more complex, all things being equal. This is the *principle of parsimony,* sometimes known as Occam's Razor.

9. *Live the Truth.* Appropriate your ideas in a personal way so that, even as the objective truth is a correspondence of the thought to the world, this lived truth will be a correspondence of the life to the thought. As Kierkegaard said, "Here is a definition of [subjective] truth: holding fast to an objective uncertainty in an appropriation process of the most passionate inwardness is the truth, the highest truth available for an existing individual."

10. *Live the Good.* Let the practical conclusions of a philosophical reflection on the moral life inspire and motivate you to action. Let moral Truth transform your life so that you shine like a jewel glowing in its own light amidst the darkness of ignorance.

Nondogmatically, pursue truth and wisdom, harken to the voice of wisdom, and aim at letting the fruits of philosophy transform your life. This is what Socrates meant when he said, "The unexamined life is not worth living." My hope is that philosophy will add a vital dimension to your life. Let's be on our way, then, with a brief look in Chapter 2 at the central method of philosophical discourse: logic.

Summary

Philosophy, as its etymology suggests, is the love of wisdom. It begins with wonder at the world, aims at truth and wisdom, and hopefully results in a life filled with meaning and moral goodness. It is centered in clarifying concepts and analyzing and constructing arguments regarding life's perennial and perplexing questions. In general, it involves hard thinking about the important issues in life. There is no subject or issue necessarily beyond its domain. Whatever seems vital to humankind is a candidate for philosophical examination. Virtually all the sciences arose from philosophy, which continues to ask questions wherever an empirical process is inadequate for a definitive answer.

FOR FURTHER REFLECTION

1. Consider the quotation by John Locke at the beginning of this chapter:

He that would seriously set upon the search of truth ought in the first place to prepare his mind with a love of it. How a man may know whether he be [a lover of truth] in earnest, is worth inquiry; and I think there is one unerring mark of it, namely, the not entertaining any proposition with greater assurance than the proofs it is built upon will warrant. Whoever goes beyond this measure of assent, it is plain receives not the truth in the love of it; loves not truth for truth's sake, but for some other bye-end.

Many people believe that philosophy, as reflected in this quotation, overemphasizes reason. "The heart has its reasons that reason knows nothing of," said Pascal, and Kierkegaard echoes his refrain (see Part 8). Reason has limits, they both contend. Do you agree? Discuss the matter. Ask yourself as you discuss it, "Am I using *reason* even in inquiring about the limits of reason?" That is, is even the contention that reason is limited a thesis that reason must adjudicate?

2. A man in one of Molière's plays discovered one day that he had been speaking prose all his life without knowing it. Similarly, all of us have been doing amateur philosophy all our lives. In a sense, philosophy is just hard thinking about the important issues of life. Mark Woodhouse illustrates how virtually every human activity has philosophical implications.

1. A neurophysiologist, while establishing correlations between certain brain functions and the feeling of pain, begins to wonder whether the "mind" is distinct from the brain.

2. A nuclear physicist, having determined that matter is mostly empty space containing colorless energy transformations, begins to wonder to what extent the solid, extended, colored world we perceive corresponds to what actually exists, and which world is the more "real."

3. A behavioral psychologist, having increasing success in predicting human behavior, questions whether any human actions can be called "free."

4. Supreme Court justices, when framing a law to distinguish obscene and nonobscene art forms, are drawn into questions about the nature and function of art.

5. A theologian, in a losing battle with science over literal descriptions of the universe (or "reality"), is forced to redefine the whole purpose and scope of traditional theology.

6. An anthropologist, noting that all societies have some conception of a moral code, begins to wonder just what distinguishes a moral from a nonmoral point of view.

7. A linguist, in examining the various ways language shapes our view of the world, declares that there is no one "true reality" because all views of reality are conditioned and qualified by the language in which they are expressed.

8. A perennial skeptic, accustomed to demanding and not receiving absolute proof for every view encountered, declares that it is impossible to know anything.

9. A county commissioner, while developing new zoning ordinances, begins to wonder whether the *effect* or the *intent* (or both) of zoning laws makes them discriminatory.

10. An IRS director, in determining which (religious) organizations would be exempted from tax, is forced to define what counts as a "religion" or "religious group."

11. A concerned mother, having decided to convert her Communist son, is forced to read the *Communist Manifesto* and to do some thinking about Marxist and capitalist ideologies.

We could continue this list of examples indefinitely. But already you can see that given a particularly relevant problem, even the nonphilosopher is lured into a modest amount of philosophical thinking. If the nonphilosopher fails to see any purpose in the discipline, try raising a philosophical problem of special relevance to his or her interests. In examining possible responses, that person will probably discover a commitment to certain philosophical theses.[5]

Find some examples in your life or in the newspaper that illustrate philosophical inquiry and discuss them.

3. As you read and work your way through this book, it will help if you can think of some puzzling philosophical problems that you would like to make progress in solving for yourself. Pick out a few and try to think about them every day. Ask your friends for their ideas on them and keep a journal on your own insights.

NOTES

1. John Locke, *An Essay Concerning Human Understanding* (1689).
2. Bertrand Russell, *The Problems of Philosophy* (Oxford, UK: Oxford University Press, 1912), 156.
3. William James, *The Writings of William James* (New York: Random House, 1967), 367.
4. Jeffrey Olen, *Persons and Their World* (New York: Random House, 1983), 3.
5. Mark Woodhouse, *A Preface to Philosophy* (Belmont, CA: Wadsworth, 1984).

FOR FURTHER READING

Copleston, F. C. *History of Philosophy*, 8 vol. New York: Doubleday, 1966. The most comprehensive work in the history of philosophy in English.

Edwards, Paul, ed. *Encyclopedia of Philosophy*, 8 vol. New York: Macmillan, 1996. Contains a rich and comprehensive set of essays on virtually every problem in philosophy.

Jones, W. T. *A History of Western Philosophy*, 5 vol. New York: Harper & Row, 1976. A lucid, accessible, reliable work.

Lawhead, William F. *The Voyage of Discovery*. Belmont, CA: Wadsworth, 1995. A very accessible, reliable history of philosophy.

Nagel, Thomas. *What Does It All Mean?* Oxford, UK: Oxford University Press, 1990. A succinct, thoughtful invitation to philosophical reflection.

Rosenberg, Jay. *The Practice of Philosophy*, 2nd ed. Englewood Cliffs, NJ: Prentice Hall, 1984. An excellent handbook to philosophy for beginners: concise, witty, and philosophically rich.

Russell, Bertrand. *The Problems of Philosophy*. Oxford, UK: Oxford University Press, 1912. Although a little dated, this marvelously lucid book, reputedly written in ten days, is a gold mine of ideas and pressing argument.

Woodhouse, Mark. *A Preface to Philosophy*. Belmont, CA: Wadsworth, 1984. This little gem is useful in discussing the purposes and methods of philosophical inquiry. It contains lively discussions of informal logic, reading philosophy, and writing philosophical papers.

2 ✴ A Little Bit of Logic

Philosophy is centered in the analysis and construction of **arguments.** We call the study of arguments **logic,** so let's devote a little time to the rudiments of logic. By *argument,* we do not mean a verbal fight but a process of supporting a thesis (called the *conclusion*) with reasons (called *premises*). An argument consists of at least two declarative sentences (sometimes called **propositions**), one of which (the conclusion) logically follows from the others (the premises). The connection by which the conclusion follows from the premises is called an **inference:**

Premise 1
Premise 2 (Inference)
Conclusion

Deductive and Inductive Reasoning

Deductive Arguments

A **valid deductive argument** is one that follows a correct logical form: If the premises are true, the conclusion must also be true. If the form is not a good one, the argument is invalid. We say that a valid deductive argument *preserves truth.* It does so in much the same way as a good refrigerator preserves food. If the food is good, a good refrigerator will preserve it; but if the food is already spoiled, the refrigerator will not make it good. The same is true with the premises of a valid argument. If the statements are true and the form is correct, the conclusion will be true; but if the premises are not true, a valid argument will not guarantee a true conclusion.

A classic example of a valid argument is the following:

1. Socrates is a man.
2. All men are mortal.
3. Therefore, Socrates is mortal.

To identify the form, let's look at conclusion 3 and identify the two major components: a subject (S) and a predicate (P). *Socrates* is the subject term, and *mortal* is the predicate term. Now return to the two premises and identify these two terms in them. We discover that the two terms are connected by a third term, *man* (or the plural *men*). We call this the *middle term* (M). The form of the argument is as follows:

1. S is M.
2. All M are P.
3. Therefore, S is P.

This is an example of a valid deductive form. If premises 1 and 2 are true, we will always get a true conclusion by using this form. But notice how easy it would be to get an invalid form. Change the order of the second premise to read "All P are M." Let the first premise read "My roommate is a mammal" and the second premise read "All dogs are mammals." What do you get?

1. My roommate, Sam Smith, is a mammal. (Premise)
2. Dogs are mammals. (Premise)
3. Therefore, my roommate is a dog. (Conclusion)

Regardless of how badly you might treat your roommate, the argument has improper form and cannot yield a valid conclusion; it is *invalid*. Every argument is either valid or invalid. Like a woman who cannot be a little pregnant, an argument cannot be only partly valid or invalid but must be completely one or the other. By seeking to find counterexamples for argument forms, we can discover which are the correct forms. (A full study of this would have to wait for a course in logic.)

Validity is not the only concept we need to examine. **Soundness** is also important, for an argument can be valid but still unsound. An argument is *sound* if it has a valid form and all its premises are true:

sound argument = valid argument + true premises

If at least one premise is false, the argument is *unsound*. Here is an example of a sound argument:

1. If Mary is a mother, she must be a woman.
2. Mary is a mother, for she has just given birth to a baby boy.
3. Therefore, Mary is a woman.

If Mary hasn't given birth, then premise 2 is false, and the argument is unsound.

You should be aware of four other deductive argument forms: *modus ponens, modus tollens, disjunctive syllogism,* and *reductio ad absurdum.* Here are their forms:

Modus Ponens
(MP, or affirming the antecedent)
1. If P, then Q.
2. P.
3. Therefore, Q.

Modus Tollens
(MT, or denying the consequent)
1. If P, then Q.
2. Not-Q.
3. Therefore, not-P.

Note in a hypothetical proposition (if P, then Q), the first term (the proposition P) is called the antecedent and the second term (Q) the consequent. Both affirming the antecedent and denying the consequent yield valid forms:

Disjunctive Syllogism
(DS, or denying the disjunct)
1. Either P or Q.
2. Not-Q.3.
3. Therefore, P.

Reductio ad Absurdum
*(RAA, or reducing to a **contradiction**)*
1. Suppose A (which you want to refute).
2. If A, then B.
3. If B, then C.
4. If C, then not-A.
5. Therefore, A and not-A.
6. But since a contradiction cannot be true, A must be false, and not-A must be true.

A **contradiction** both makes an assertion and denies that assertion. It claims P but also claims that not-P is the case: For example, God exists, and God does not exist. The one claim cancels out the other, so no assertion remains.

We have already given an example of a modus ponens:

1. If Mary is a mother, she must be a woman.
2. Mary is a mother, for she has just given birth to a baby boy.
3. Therefore, Mary is a woman.

Here is an example of a modus tollens:

1. If Leslie is a mother, she is a woman.
2. Leslie is not a woman (but a man).
3. Therefore, Leslie is not a mother.

Here is an example of a disjunctive syllogism (sometimes called "denying the disjunct"; a *disjunct* refers to a proposition with an "or" statement in it, such as "P or Q"):

1. John is either a bachelor or a married man.
2. We know for certain that John is not married.
3. Therefore, John is a bachelor.

Here is an example of a reductio ad absurdum. A little more complicated than the other forms, it is important especially in reference to the *ontological argument*. Suppose someone denies that there is such a thing as a self and you wish to refute the assertion. You might argue in the following manner:

1. Suppose that you're correct and there is no such thing as a self (not-A).
2. But if there is no such thing as a self, then no one ever acts (if not-A, then not-B).
3. But if no one ever acts, then no one can utter meaningful statements (if not-B, then not-C).
4. But you have purported to utter a meaningful statement in saying that there is no such thing as a self, so there is at least one meaningful statement (C).
5. Therefore, according to your argument, there is and there is not at least one meaningful statement (C and not-C).
6. Therefore, it must be false that there is no such thing as a self (not, not-A—which by double negation yields A). Thus, we have proved by reductio ad absurdum that there is such a thing as a self.

Before we leave the realm of deductive argument, we must point out two invalid forms that often give students trouble. To understand them, look back at forms MP and MT, which respectively argue by affirming the antecedent and denying the consequent. However, note that there are two other possible forms. You can also deny the antecedent and affirm the consequent in the following manner:

Denying the Antecedent (DA)	*Affirming the Consequent (AC)*
1. If P, then Q.	1. If P, then Q.
2. Not-P.	2. Q.
3. Therefore, not-Q.	3. Therefore, P.

Are these valid forms? Remember a valid form must always yield true conclusions if the premises are true. Try to find a counterexample that will show that these two forms are invalid. You might let premise 1 (if P, then Q) be represented by the proposition given earlier: "If Mary is a mother, then she is a woman." First, deny the antecedent. Does it necessarily yield a true conclusion? It says that Mary is not a woman, and that is false. There are many women who are not mothers. So DA is an invalid form:

1. If Mary is a mother, she is a woman.
2. Mary is not a mother.
3. Therefore, Mary is not a woman.

Take the same initial proposition and affirm the consequent "Mary is a woman." Does this in itself yield the conclusion that she is a mother? Of course not. She could be a woman without being a mother. The argument looks like this:

1. If Mary is a mother, she is a woman.
2. She is a woman.
3. Therefore, Mary is a mother.

Thus, whereas MP and MT are valid forms, DA and AC are not.

These are just simple examples of deductive argument forms. Often, alas, it is difficult to state exactly the author's premises.

Inductive Arguments

Let's turn our attention to inductive arguments. Unlike their counterpart (valid deductive arguments), **inductive arguments** are not truth preserving—that is, they do not guarantee that if we have true premises, we will obtain a true conclusion. They bring only *probability,* but in most of life that is the best we can hope for. David Hume (1711–1776) said that "probability is the guide of life." The wise person guides his or her life by the best evidence available, always realizing that one could be mistaken. We usually do not speak of inductive arguments as valid/invalid or sound/unsound but as strong or weak (or cogent or uncogent). In inductive arguments, the premises are *evidence* for the conclusion or hypothesis. In a strong inductive argument, if the premises are true, the conclusion is *probably* true. In a weak inductive argument, the premises fail to provide probable support for the conclusion.

An inductive argument has the following form:

1. A_1 is a B.
2. A_2 is a B.
3. A_3 is a B.
4. So probably the next A we encounter (A_4) will also be a B.

For example, suppose you are surrounded by four islands somewhere in the Pacific Ocean. You examine all trees on three of the islands but cannot get to the fourth. Nevertheless, you might make some predictions on the basis of your experience on the first three islands. For example, you note that all trees on islands A, B, and C are coconut trees. From this you predict that coconut trees will be on island D and that coconut is probably the only kind of tree found there.

We learn from induction. After a few experiences of getting burned by fire (or by people of a certain type), we learn to avoid fire (or people of a certain type). The human race has learned by inductive experience that cooperation generally produces more benefits than noncooperation, so we advocate cooperative ventures.

Sometimes, when we should know better, we generalize or make predictions from an inadequate sample. We call this *prejudice* a type of malformed induction. If a child infers from his only six bad experiences with people from Podunkville that all people in Podunkville are bad, that might be acceptable; however, if an adult, who could easily have evidence that a lot of good people live in Podunkville, still generalizes about the people of Podunkville and acts accordingly, we label this an irrational bias, a prejudice.

Abductive Reasoning

Abductive reasoning, or reasoning to the best explanation, was first formulated by the American philosopher Charles S. Peirce (1839–1914). Like inductive reasoning, **abduction** yields only probable truth, but whereas induction establishes general premises or probabilities about future occurrences, abduction provides explanatory hypotheses. It answers the question "Why is such and such the case?" The following example of Sherlock Holmes's reasoning in Arthur Conan Doyle's *The Red-Headed League* illustrates abductive reasoning.

THE RED-HEADED LEAGUE

The portly client puffed out his chest with an appearance of some little pride and pulled a dirty and wrinkled newspaper from the inside pocket of his greatcoat. As he glanced down the advertisement column with his head thrust forward and the paper flattened out upon his knee, I took a good look at the man and endeavored, after the fashion of my companion, to read the indications which might be presented by his dress or appearance.

I did not gain very much, however, by my inspection. Our visitor bore every mark of being an average commonplace British tradesman, obese, pompous, and slow. He wore rather baggy gray shepherd's check trousers, a not over-clean black frock-coat, unbuttoned in the front, and a drab waistcoat with a heavy brassy Albert chain, and a square pierced bit of metal dangling down as an ornament. A frayed top-hat and a faded brown overcoat with a wrinkled velvet collar lay upon a chair beside him. Altogether, look as I would, there was nothing remarkable about the man save his blazing red head and the expression of extreme chagrin and discontent upon his features. Sherlock Holmes's quick eye took in my occupation, and he shook his head with a smile as he noticed my questioning glances. "Beyond the obvious facts that he has at some time done manual labour, that he takes snuff, that he is a Freemason, that he has been in China, and that he has done a considerable amount of writing lately, I can *deduce* nothing else." Mr. Jabez Wilson started up in his chair, with his forefinger upon the paper, but his eyes upon my companion.

"How, in the name of good-fortune, did you know all that, Mr. Holmes?" he asked. "How did you know, for example, that I did manual labour? It's as true as gospel, for I began as a ship's carpenter."

"Your hands, my dear sir. Your right hand is quite a size larger than your left. You have worked with it, and the muscles are more developed."

"Well, the snuff, then, and the Freemasonry?"

"I won't insult your intelligence by telling you how I read that, especially as, rather against the strict rules of your order, you use an arc-and-compass breastpin."

"Ah, of course, I forgot that. But the writing?"

"What else can be indicated by that right cuff so very shiny for five inches, and the left one with the smooth patch near the elbow where you rest it upon the desk?"

"Well, but China?"

From: Arthur Conan Doyle, *The Red-Headed League* (New York: Harper & Bros., 1892).

> "The fish which you have tattooed immediately above your right wrist could only have been done in China. I have made a small study of tattoo marks and have even contributed to the literature of the subject. That trick of staining the fishes' scales of a delicate pink is quite peculiar to China. When, in addition, I see a Chinese coin hanging from your watchchain, the matter becomes even more simple."
>
> Mr. Jabez Wilson laughed heavily. "Well, I never!" said he. "I thought at first that you had done something clever, but I see that there was nothing in it, after all."

Philosophers appreciate Wilson's final remark, that Holmes's explanation makes so much sense that one wonders why one didn't think of it oneself. Holmes often chided Watson, "You see, but you do not observe." A good philosopher, like a good detective or scientist, observes while he or she sees.

There is a significant inaccuracy, however, in Holmes's description of what he does. He claims to be deducing the conclusions about Wilson from the tell-tale signs. Strictly speaking, he is doing no such thing. In deductive reasoning, if the form is correct and the premises are true, one cannot help but obtain a true conclusion, but such is not the case with Holmes's reasoning. For example, consider Wilson's arc-and-compass breastpin, which leads Holmes to conclude that Wilson is a Freemason. If the reasoning were deductive, the argument would go something like this:

1. Everyone wearing an arc-and-compass breastpin is a Freemason.
2. Mr. Wilson is wearing an arc-and-compass breastpin.
3. Therefore, Mr. Wilson is a Freemason.

Is this a valid argument? Of course not. Imagine that Wilson, who is not a Freemason, bought a similar arc-and-compass breastpin at a pawnshop and wore it, thinking it was a beautiful bit of Muslim design. In that case, premise 1 would be false. Not everyone wearing an arc-and-compass breastpin is a Freemason. Since it is possible that non-Freemasons wear that pin, the above is not a sound deductive argument.

What Holmes has really done is reason abductively—that is, reason to the best explanation of the facts. Like inductive reasoning, abduction does not guarantee the truth of the conclusions. Unlike induction, it is not simply about the probability of such and such being the case based on the evidence. Abductive reasoning attempts to offer explanations of the facts, why things are the way they are. The best explanation of Wilson's wearing the arc-and-compass breastpin is his belonging to the Freemasons. The best explanation of a child's having a fever and red spots is that she has the measles. The best explanation of the water covering our street is that it has recently rained.

The notion of the best explanation is fascinating in its own right. How do we discover the best explanation? What characteristics does it have? How do we rank various virtues of a good explanation? There are no definite answers to these questions, but it is generally agreed that such traits as predictability, coherence, simplicity, and fruitfulness are among the main characteristics. If a theory helps us predict future events, that is a powerful weapon. If it coheres well with everything or nearly everything else that we hold true in the field, that lends support to it. If it is simpler than its rivals, if it demands fewer **ad hoc,** or auxiliary, hypotheses, that is a virtue. If it leads to new insight and discoveries, that is also a point in its favor. But what if explanatory theory A has more of one of these features and theory B more of another? Which should we prefer? There is no decision-making procedure to decide the matter with any finality. In a sense, abduction is educated guesswork or intuition. Counterevidence counts strongly against a hypothesis, so if we can falsify our thesis, we have good reason to drop it; however, sometimes we can make adjustments in our hypothesis to accommodate the counterevidence.

Abduction has been neglected in philosophy, but it really is of the utmost importance. Consider the following questions: Why do you believe in God? Why do you believe in evolutionary theory? Why do you believe that there are universal moral principles? Why do you believe that all events are caused? In one way or another, the answer will probably be abductive—for you, it seems to be the best explanation among all the competitors. We will have opportunity to use abductive reasoning at several points during our course of study.

Some Applications

Let's apply these brief lessons of logic to reading philosophy. Because the key to philosophy is the argument, concentrate and even outline the author's reasoning. Find his or her thesis or conclusion. Usually, it is stated early on. After this, identify the premises that support or lead to the conclusion. For example, Thomas Aquinas (1224–1274) holds the conclusion that God exists. He argues for this conclusion in five different ways. In the second argument, he uses such premises as

1. There is motion.
2. There cannot be motion without something initiating the motion.

to reach his conclusion.

It helps to outline the premises of the argument. For example, here's how we might set forth Aquinas's second argument:

1. Some things are in motion. (Premise)
2. Nothing in the world can move itself but must be moved by another. (Premise)
3. There cannot be an infinite regress of motions. (Premise)
4. There must be a First Mover who is responsible for all other motion. (Conclusion of premises 1–3, which in turn becomes a premise for the rest of the argument)
5. This First Mover is what we call God (explanation of the meaning of God). (Premise)
6. Therefore, God exists. (Conclusion of second part of the argument, premises 4 and 5)

After you have identified the premises and conclusion, analyze them, looking for mistakes in the reasoning process. Sometimes arguments are weak or unsound but not obviously so. Then you need to stretch your imagination and think of possible counterexamples to the claims of the author. I found this process almost impossible at first, but gradually it became second nature.

Because philosophical arguments are often complex and subtle (and because philosophers do not always write as clearly as they should), a full understanding of an essay is not readily available after a single reading. So read it twice or even thrice. The first time I read a philosophy essay, I read it for understanding. I want to know where the author is coming from and what he or she is trying to establish. After the first reading, I leave the essay for some time, ruminating on it. Sometimes objections to the arguments awaken me at night or while I am working at something else. Then I go back a day or so later and read the essay a second time, this time trying to determine its soundness.

A few pointers should be mentioned along the way. Some students find it helpful to keep a notebook on their reflections on the readings. If you own the book, I suggest that you make notes in the margins—initially in pencil, because you may want to revise your impressions after a second reading. Finally, practice charity. Give the author the best possible interpretation in order to see if the argument has merit. Always try to deal with the most generous version of the argument, especially if you don't agree with its conclusion. The exercise will broaden your horizons and help you develop sharper reasoning skills.

Fallacies of Reasoning

Good reasoning depends on justified premises or reasons and valid logical form, but many arguments fail to satisfy these conditions. I have listed some of the main fallacies of reasoning. See if you can illustrate them with examples of your own.

- *Ad Hominem Argument* This is an argument "against the man." This argument attacks the person instead of the position—if I say to you, "You can't trust what Joan says about abortion, for she is an immoral person." But, of course, *her* argument for or against abortion, however, may be sound on independent grounds. Even the devil has true beliefs. The character of the person is irrelevant to the soundness of the argument.

- *Argument from Authority* Suppose we are arguing about the death penalty, and I tell you that we should believe in the death penalty because Plato believed in it. Since you don't know Plato's reasons (I may not either), it is not sufficient grounds for either of us to believe in the death penalty. We need positive arguments, not simply authority. Advertisements are notorious for subtly and sometimes not so subtly using this device. In a beer commercial, a famous athlete (nicely remunerated for the exercise) may be seen gratifying his thirst, proclaiming the ecstasy of the beverage, as if that were proof of its quality.

Of course, authority may sometimes be the best we can get and sufficient for justified belief as when a physicist tells us the conclusions of complicated physics research or a friend from Australia gives you pertinent information for your upcoming visit to that country. We sometimes do need to trust authority, but often it is an improper substitute for good reasoning.

- *Arguing in a Circle* This is sometimes referred to as "begging the question." Suppose I argue that you should believe that God exists. You ask why. I say, "Because the Bible says so." You ask, "Why should I believe what the Bible says?" I reply, "Because it's the Word of God." That is, I argue in a circle, using my conclusions as a premise to prove the conclusion. Note that all valid deductive arguments can appear as arguing in a circle, since the conclusion of such an argument is contained in the premises. The difference is that in a valid argument the conclusion brings out a nontrivial feature of the premises. Essentially, arguing in a circle is not invalid, just trivial and unconvincing, having no power to convince an opponent.

- *Argument from Ignorance* This kind of argument occurs when I claim that because you cannot prove a proposition is false, I am justified in believing it to be true. For example, because you can't prove God doesn't exist, I am free to believe that he does exist. Or because you can't prove that we do not have a soul, I am free to believe that we do.

- *False Dilemma* This happens when we reduce several possibilities to two alternatives. I once read of two travelers facing a swamp in which traveler A said to traveler B, "Since you admit you don't know the way through the swamp and there must be a way, follow me. I must know the way." Of course, neither may know the way. Similarly, someone may argue that since your answer to a problem isn't correct, his or hers must be. But, of course, both may be false.

- *Genetic Fallacy* This is arguing against a position or argument because its origins are suspect. Suppose I tell you not to believe in the principles of chemistry because they originated in superstitious alchemy or I tell you not to believe in an astronomical theory because it arose from astrological sources. The fact that a theory or position originated in discredited circumstances is irrelevant if the theory is supported by the evidence. For their theories, chemistry and astronomy can produce impressive evidence that is independent of the authority of alchemy and astrology. It doesn't matter where the truth comes from, as long as it is true.

- *Inconsistency* When we argue inconsistently, we argue from contradictory premises. Politicians when trying to win votes from one constituency sometimes contradict what they have said to other constituencies. For an illustration of this, consider some statements made by former President Reagan at different periods of his political career:

On Civil Rights

1. "I favor the Civil Rights Act of 1964 and it must be enforced at the point of a bayonet, if necessary" (October 19, 1965).
2. "I would have voted against the Civil Rights Act of 1964" (June 16, 1966).

On Redwood National Park

1. "I believe our country can and should have a Redwood National Park in California" (April 17, 1967).
2. "There can be no proof given that a national park is necessary to preserve the redwoods. The state of California has already maintained a great conservation program" (April 18, 1967—the next day).

On the Soviet Grain Embargo

1. "I just don't believe the farmers should be made to pay a special price for our diplomacy, and I'm opposed to [the Soviet grain embargo]" (January 7, 1980).
2. "If we are going to do such a thing to the Soviet Union as a full grain embargo, which I support, first we have to be sure our own allies would join us on this" (January 8, 1980—the next day).[1]

Of course, people change their minds and come to believe the opposite of what they formerly believed. That may show progress, but many of us are not aware of the inconsistencies in our own belief systems. For example, Fred may believe that morality entails universalizing principles ("what's good for the goose is good for the gander") but fail to note that his view on premarital sex—morally permissible for men but not for women—is inconsistent with that principle.

In Chapter 18 ("Truth, Rationality, and Cognitive Relativism"), I relate a story of an English professor who argues that inconsistency is all right and that logic, which rejects inconsistency, is "a phallologocentric instrument for the oppression of minorities." If inconsistency were acceptable, however, I could say that I'm both for and against oppression and still be making sense. But, of course, what I give with one side of my mouth, I bite back with the other. My utterance is meaningless.

- *Slippery Slope Fallacy* This is sometimes called the "edge of the wedge argument." Once you let the camel nose under the wedge of the tent, it will capsize the entire tent. Likewise, it will be argued, once we allow act A to occur, event B, which is evil, will occur. Robert Wright has argued that "once you buy the premise that animals can experience pain and pleasure, and that their welfare therefore deserves *some* consideration, you're on the road to comparing yourself with a lobster. There may be some exit ramps along the way—plausible places to separate welfare from rights—but I can't find any."[2] Others have argued that if we allow voluntary euthanasia, we are on the slippery slope to involuntary euthanasia, even eventually to a holocaust. Still others have argued that if we pass a national health care bill, it will inevitably lead to socialism and communism. The slippery slope fallacy ignores the truth that very often wise policy is a moderate stance between two extremes and that rational people can hold to a rational position without going to an extreme.

- *Straw Man Argument* This is an instance of misrepresenting an opponent's position. It occurs when someone ignores the evidence for a position and instead attacks an inferior version of the position. In the heat of debate on whether our nation should reduce its military spending, a militarist may argue that his opponent wants to leave our nation defenseless or a willing prey to communism. I once heard of a Russian tourist guide who claimed that she knew that God didn't exist, because if he did, he would announce his presence from heaven. The straw man argument is often a distortion of the other person's position. There is a tendency in all of us to attack a weaker—less plausible—version of our opponent's position. The principle of charity is the opposite of the straw man argument. It instructs us to give our opponent's position the very best form we can find—and then try to show it is unsound.

Summary

In a valid deductive argument, if the premises are true, the conclusion must be true by virtue of a logically necessary form. In a strong inductive argument, the premises make the conclusion probable but do not guarantee the truth of the conclusion. In a good abductive argument, the conclusion or hypothesis offers the best explanation of the data.

FOR FURTHER REFLECTION

1. Using the argument forms discussed in this chapter, construct an argument of your own for each form shown.

2. Explain the difference between deductive, inductive, and abductive reasoning.

3. Get a copy of your student newspaper or your local newspaper and analyze two arguments therein. Begin to look at the claims of others in argument form.

4. Philosophy can be seen as an attempt to solve life's perennial puzzles. Taking the material at hand, it tries to unravel enigmas by thought alone. See what you can do with the puzzles and paradoxes included here.

   a. There is a barber in Barberville who shaves all and only those barbers who do not shave themselves. Does this barber shave himself? (Who does shave him?)

   b. You are the sole survivor of a shipwreck and are drifting in a small raft parallel to the coast of an island. You know that on this island there are only two tribes of natives: Nobles, kind folk who *always* tell the truth, and Savages, cannibals who always lie. Naturally, you want to find refuge with the Nobles. You see a man standing on the shore and call out, "Are you a Noble or a Savage?" The man answers the question, but a wave breaks on the beach at that very moment, so you don't hear the reply. The boat drifts farther down along the shore when you see another man. You ask him the same question, and he replies, pointing to the first man, "He said he was a Noble." Then he continues, "I am a Noble." Your boat drifts farther down the shore where you see a third man. You ask him the same questions. The man seems very friendly as he calls out, "They are both liars. I am a Noble. They are Savages." The puzzle: Is the data given sufficient to tell you any man's tribe? Is it sufficient to tell you each man's tribe?

   c. Mrs. Smith, a schoolteacher, announces to her class on Friday that there will be a surprise test during the following week. She defines "surprise test" as one that no one could reasonably predict on the day of the test. Johnny, one of her students, responds that she may not give the test on pain of contradicting herself. Mrs. Smith asks, "Why not?" Johnny replies, "You cannot give the test on Friday because on Friday everyone would know that the test would take place on that day, and so it would not be a surprise. So the test must take place between Monday and Thursday. But it cannot take place on Thursday, for if it hasn't taken place by then, it would not be a surprise on Thursday. So the test must take place between Monday and Wednesday. But it cannot take place on Wednesday for the same reason that we rejected Friday and Thursday. Similarly, we can use the same reason to exclude Tuesday and Monday. On no day of the week can a surprise test be given. So the test cannot be given next week."

   Mrs. Smith heard Johnny's argument and wondered what the solution was. She gave the test on Tuesday, and everyone was surprised, including Johnny. How was this possible?

d. What follows from this puzzle?

It is sometimes said that space is empty, which means presumably, that there is nothing between two stars. But if there is *nothing* between stars, then they are not separated by anything, and, thus, they must be right up against one another, perhaps forming some peculiar sort of double star. We know this not to be the case, of course.[3]

NOTES

1. Marc Green and Gail MacCall, *There He Goes Again: Ronald Reagan's Reign of Error* (New York: Pantheon, 1983).
2. Robert Wright, "Are Animals People Too?" *New Republic* (March 12, 1990).
3. Jay Rosenberg, *The Practice of Philosophy* (Englewood Cliffs, NJ: Prentice Hall, 1978), 99.

FOR FURTHER READING

Copi, Irving. *Introduction to Logic,* 6th ed. New York: Macmillan, 1982. A widely used text, clear and concise.

Hurley, Patrick. *A Concise Introduction to Logic,* 4th ed. Belmont, CA: Wadsworth, 1991. An excellent work, clear and accessible.

Kahane, Howard. *Logic and Contemporary Rhetoric,* 7th ed. Belmont, CA: Wadsworth, 1995. Clear, concise, and entertaining.

Moore, Brooke, and Richard Parker. *Critical Thinking.* Mountain View, CA: Mayfield, 1992. A very good introduction to logical thinking.

Scriven, Michael. *Reasoning.* New York: McGraw-Hill, 1976. A rich presentation of the major topics in philosophical reasoning.

PART II

The Beginning of Philosophy:
The Ancient Greeks—The Sophists,
Socrates, Plato, and Aristotle

3 ⚓ The Rise of the Sophists

In the middle of the fifth century BCE, Athens flourished materially and culturally. Partly due to an unexpected and resounding victory over the Persians and partly due to exceptional leadership of the likes of Solon and Pericles, the founders of democracy, Athens became a prosperous economic force; in the arts it produced such dramatic geniuses as Aeschylus, Euripides, Sophocles, and Aristophanes. The Parthenon was built, and sculpture and the plastic arts reached their pinnacle. Because the city's prosperity depended on a large number of slaves, it allowed the citizens an unprecedented amount of leisure time to think and converse. The state religion, which was based on the Homeric gods, was scrutinized, tried, and found wanting by the brightest citizens, and secularism increased. Litigation also increased because the rising entrepreneurial class found it could tap into the wealth of the conservative aristocracy through the courts.

Sophistry: A New Profession

A new profession arose in fifth-century Athens, one bent on teaching citizens how to win cases in court. It was called *sophistry*, and its practitioners were called Sophists. The Sophists were secular relativists, cynical about religious and idealistic pretensions, aiming at material and political success in a democratic society by using rhetoric and oratory in persuading people. They rejected the quest of the pre-Socratic philosophers as useless speculation. If the big question of the pre-Socratics was "What is the nature of reality?", the Sophists' question was the more mundane "How can I succeed in the practical affairs of life" or "How can I play the game of life and win?" These are always appealing questions, and the Sophists made enormous sums of money selling their services to rich young men, teaching them how to win at litigation and use debating tricks to defeat their opponents.

The Sophists were prominent between 460 and 380 BCE. The older generation, Protagoras of Abdera (circa 490–420 BCE), Gorgias of Leontini in Sicily (485–380 BCE), Prodicus (460–399 BCE), and Hippias of Elis (fifth century BCE) were urbane, socially responsible, professional teachers, who even held political offices. Protagoras greatly influenced Pericles, the developer of Athenian democracy, and Gorgias was his friend. Being moral relativists, they took a pragmatic view toward social conventions and religious worship. Although they were skeptical about religion, they advised worship of the gods for socially prudent reasons. Laws and religious beliefs and rituals are the "glue" that holds society together. So even though they're probably human inventions, they are useful and should be valued for that reason.

The younger generation consisting of men like Callicles, Critias (Plato's uncle [480–403 BCE]), Antiphon, and Thrasymachus were much more hardened, not merely skeptical but cynical about religion, law, and moral conventions. For them, religion was a fraud, and conventional justice was simply a way of keeping the naturally superior from exercising their ability. Breaking with the older Sophists, who were moderates and held traditional values, these younger Sophists radicalized the ideas of their elders.

General Features of the Sophists

1. The Sophists were secularists—agnostic or atheist on religion, cynical of religion as a mechanism for social control. The gods are invented to function as an invisible, all-seeing police force. The Sophist Critias wrote:

> There was once a time when human life was chaotic,
> Brutal and subservient to force,
> When there was neither a reward for being decent
> Or any restraint on evil men.
> In consequence human beings
> Have enacted laws to be avengers
> So that justice might be ruler
> And keep violence in subjection;
> And if anybody did wrong he would be punished.
> After this, since the laws prevented people
> From doing violent deeds that could be seen,
> They committed them in secret, and it was then
> I think some man of clever well-compacted intellect
> Invented fear of the gods for mortal men so that
> It might be a kind of terror for wrongdoers
> Even if in secret they did or said or thought
> Some wrongful thing:
> Further to this he introduced the divine principle
> That there exists a spirit flourishing in life that
> Is free from decay,
> Hearing and seeing with its intelligence with supreme

Power of thought, applying its vast faculties and
Bearing a god-like nature, that will
Hear everything said amongst mankind and see their
Every act.[1]

2. The Sophists developed the art of *rhetoric,* the process of using language to persuade. Their chief tool was *eristic,* an argument used to win debates, not pursue truth and aimed at defeat rather than enlightenment. Aristotle called eristic "dirty fighting in argument."[2] What was needed was cleverness and ready speech, whereby to sway the passions of the mob and citizens. It was not without reason that they were accused of "making the worse argument seem better."

Another rhetorical tool was *antilogic*—arguing by means of contradictory propositions—leading to an *aporia,* a puzzle, possibly a dead end. They taught their students to argue both sides of the case and showed that, regarding any act, it could be seen as good, bad, or indifferent.

There is a story that Protagoras once offered to give a student lessons, deferring payment until he had won his first suit. After the first lesson, Protagoras sued his student for payment, arguing: (1) If the student wins, he must pay according to his agreement; (2) if I win, the student must pay according to the law. But the student counterargued: (1) If I lose, the agreement hasn't been fulfilled, so I don't have to pay; (2) but if I win, I shouldn't have to pay according to law, which now overrides the agreement. The jury ruled in favor of the student.[3]

3. They made education into a business. They were the first teachers to receive pay for their services, charging fees for teaching "wisdom" and "virtue." Their key question was, Can virtue be taught? They answered that it both could be taught and they were the ones skilled to teach it. Holding that virtue is relative to the culture, Protagoras taught that teachers and enlightened parents could train children to be good, law-abiding citizens.

4. The Sophists were pragmatists. Truth is what works for you. The Sophists were not speculative, systematic, or concerned with cosmology as the pre-Socratic philosophers were. However, they took the joint, mutually exclusive conclusions of the pre-Socratics to show that not even the best minds could know the nature of ultimate reality. Because knowledge is impossible, they embraced *skepticism* about ultimate reality and concentrated on that which is certain: Success in business, politics, and the practical life is very satisfying. Use common sense both in social and individual affairs.

The Sophist Gorgias exemplifies this pragmatic attitude better than anyone. He said,

1. Nothing exists.

2. But if something does exist, it can't be known.

3. But even if it can, it can't be communicated.

4. Therefore: Live by appearances. Practice prudence. Be practical! Avoid idle speculation. Seek practical education—that which has an optimum payoff.

As you might expect, Gorgias taught rhetoric to the wealthy young so that they might win political offices and court cases (which they could now confidently create: Sue Your Opponent if He Is Rich! might have been their motto).

5. The Sophists believed that egoism was both natural and right. Each of us must look out for himself. Hence, manipulation of others is permitted. Callicles argues that Socrates is either being naive or disingenuous in holding that moral law (*nomos*) is objectively true. Essentially, nature teaches that the superior should exploit and rule the weaker.

> You, Socrates, who pretend to be engaging in the pursuit of truth, are appealing to the popular and vulgar notions of right, which are admirable by convention, not by nature. Social convention and nature are generally opposed to one another. . . . The reason is that the makers of laws are the majority who are weak; and they make laws and distribute praise and censure with a view to themselves and to their own interests; and they terrify the stronger sort of men, and those who are able to get the better of them, in order that they may not get the better of them; and they say, that self-interested ambition is shameful and unjust, meaning, by the word injustice, the desire of a man to have more than his neighbors; for knowing their own inferiority, I suspect that they are only too glad of equality. And therefore the endeavor to have more than the many is conventionally said to be shameful and unjust, and is called injustice, whereas nature herself intimates that it is just for the better to have more than the worse, the more powerful than the weaker; and in many ways she shows, among men as well as among animals, and indeed among whole cities and races, that justice consists in the superior ruling over and having more than the inferior. For on what principle of justice did [the Persian King] Xerxes invade Greece, or his father the Scythians? Nay, but these men, I suggest, act in this way according to the nature of justice; yes, by Heaven, according to the law of nature, though not, perhaps, according to that law which we enact. We take the best and strongest of our fellows from their youth upwards, and tame them like young lions,—enslaving them with spells and incantations, and saying to them that with equality they must be content, and that the equal is the honorable and the just. But if there were a man born with enough ability, he would shake off and break through, and escape from all this. He would trample under foot all our formulas and spells and charms, and all our laws which are against nature. The slave would rise in rebellion and be lord over us, and the light of natural justice would shine forth.[4]

In sum: "Might makes right." Most people are sheep waiting and even wanting to be exploited by the cleverer and stronger egoist. These ideas were deemed plausible or even obvious by the Athenians when it came to war. In 416 BCE, when invaded by the Athenians, the people of Isle of Melos refused to give up their independence to the Athenians and argued that the Athenians were unjust to force them to become subservient to them. To this heroic celebration of freedom, the Athenian general responds:

This is not a law that was made by us nor were we the first to use it
when it had been made. We are merely acting in accordance with it
after finding it already in existence, and we shall leave it to exist for ever
in the future. We know that you or anyone else with the same power as
us would act in the same way.[5]

Justice is only applicable to equals, those with roughly equal power.
Otherwise, might makes right! In other words, the big fish eat the little fish.

The Sophists applied the logic of international relations to all of life. Isn't all
of nature a struggle for survival and power?

6. The Sophists were relativists, often of a subjectivist cast, contending that
each person is his own measure of truth, thus abandoning the idea of an independent reality apart from our consciousness. Truth is whatever you take it to
be, and, similarly, morality is whatever you believe to be good.

Perhaps the greatest Sophist of all was Protagoras of Abdera (circa 490–420
BCE), an exceptional man, who was renown for being able to argue either side
of a legal case successfully. He gave us the "Hymn to Relativism":

Man is the measure of all things:
Both of things that are,
Man is the measure that they are, And of the things that are not,
Man is the measure that they are not.

Protagoras was reacting against the distinction between sensation and
thought, which was held by the Eleatics as well as Heracleitus. Sensations are private, but thought is public. I cannot have your experience of the color green, but
we can both understand the concept (thought) of green, and can assent to the
proposition that nothing green can be red. According to the Eleatics, the senses
are untrustworthy, whereas *thought,* via reason, leads to truth, which is universal
and public. Protagoras denies the objectivity of reason as well as the universality
and public nature of truth. He subordinated thought under the same private
world as is appropriate to sensation. Each person is his own measure or standard
of what is true and false. What seems true to me is true. What seems true to you,
though it contradict what I believe, is true relative to you. In the same way, your
pain is true for you, and my pain is truly painful for me. *All* opinions are true.

Similarly, in ethics, whatever I deem morally right for me is right for me, and
whatever seems right for you is morally right to you. The Greek historian
Herodotus in his *Histories* gave an influential statement on this matter:

Thus it appears certain to me, by a great variety of proofs, that
Cambyses was raving mad; he would not else have set himself to make
a mock of holy rites and long-established usages. For if one were to
offer men to choose out of all the customs in the world such as seemed
to them the best, they would examine the whole number, and end by
preferring their own; so convinced are they that their own usages far
surpass those of all others. Unless, therefore, a man was mad, it is not
likely that he would make sport of such matters. That people have this
feeling about their laws may be seen by very many proofs: among
others, by the following. Darius, after he had got the kingdom, called

into his presence certain Greeks who were at hand, and asked— "What should he pay to them to eat the bodies of their fathers when they died?" To which they answered, that there was no sum that would tempt them to do such a thing. He then sent for certain Indians, of the race called Callatians, men who eat their fathers, and asked them, while the Greeks stood by, and knew by the help of an interpreter all that was said—"What he should give them to burn the bodies of their fathers at their decease?" The Indians exclaimed aloud, and bade him forbear such language. Such is men's wont herein; and Pindar was right, in my judgment, when he said, "Custom is the king o'er all."[6]

We may call this kind of relativism cultural or *conventional ethical relativism* (see Chapter 28), since it grounds moral rightness and wrongness in the culture. But some Sophists—such as Protagoras, Callicles, and Gorgias—were more radical, embracing *subjectivism*. Like beauty, virtue "is in the eye of the beholder." In this way, the Sophists anticipated contemporary moral relativists and subjectivists like Ernest Hemingway, who once said, "What is moral is what you feel good after and what is immoral is what you feel bad after."

Summary

The Sophists challenged the traditional values and opinions of Greek society. They undermined its religion and myths. They asserted that the state is founded on power, custom, and conventions, not eternal truth. They argued that there was no objective truth or right or wrong, unless it is the realistic adage that might makes right. Most important, they caused one of the most important events in the history of philosophy: To challenge their reliance on rhetoric, their businesslike pragmatism, their cynicism and relativism about values and morality, and their egoism, Socrates came forth and stood alone against the panoply of their ideas.

FOR FURTHER REFLECTION

1. What were the major doctrines of the Sophists? What was their role in Greek society?

2. Were the Sophists moral and cognitive relativists? Can you explain their views on these theories?

3. How does sophistry manifest itself in contemporary society? Can you find examples in advertising, legal reasoning, and political speeches?

NOTES

1. Diels and Kranz, *Fragments of the PreSocratics* 88b 25.
2. Aristotle *Sophistic Elenchi* 171b.
3. Although the story may be apocryphal, it illustrates sophistic reasoning. On the other hand, Protagoras seems to be one of the more honorable of Sophists, who remitted payment for anyone who did not benefit from his teaching.

4. Plato, *Gorgias,* in the *Dialogues of Plato,* ed. and trans. Benjamin Jowett (New York: Scribner, 1889), 73. I have slightly edited the translation.
5. Thucydides *The Peloponnesian War* Book 5.
6. Herodotus *Histories* III.

FOR FURTHER READING

Brumbaugh, Robert. *The Philosophers of Greece.* Albany, NY: SUNY Press, 1981. An easy-to-read, yet philosophically rich survey of classical Greek philosophy.

Guthrie, W. K. C. *The Sophists.* Cambridge, UK: Cambridge University Press, 1971. A clear, comprehensive, and scholarly work.

Kerferd, G. B. *The Sophistic Movement.* Cambridge, UK: Cambridge University Press, 1981. A cogently argued contemporary study, challenging many of the standard views about the Sophists.

4 ⚚ A Portrait of a Philosopher: Socrates

Ancient philosophy up to Socrates, who was taught by Archelaus the pupil of Anaxagoras, dealt with number and movement, and the source from which all things arise and to which they return; and these early thinkers inquired zealously into the magnitude, intervals and courses of the stars, and all celestial matters. But it was Socrates who first called philosophy down from the sky, set it in the cities and even introduced it into homes, and compelled it to consider life and morals, good and evil.

Cicero[1]

Life and Influence

A dramatic turn occurs in philosophical inquiry under the influence of Socrates (470–399 BCE). Before him, two intellectual groups dominated the Greek world, the cynical and egoistic Sophists and the speculative Cosmologists. The big question asked by early Cosmologists was, What is the nature of reality? Thales (585 BCE) had taught that the ultimate stuff of the universe was water; Anaximander (547 BCE), an infinite mixture; Anaximenes (520 BCE), air; and Heracleitus (480 BCE), fire. Parmenides (480 BCE) and Zeno of Elea (460 BCE) taught that the universe was a single, unmoving oneness, that all change was an illusion. Anaxagoras (460 BCE) posited a pluralistic universe with four essential elements (fire, air, water, and earth) under the direction of a great universal Mind (*Nous*). Socrates rejected both the cynicism and crass pragmatism of the Sophists and the ethereal speculation of the Cosmologists. As Cicero said, he was the first to call "philosophy down from the sky, set it in the cities and even introduced it into homes, and compelled it to consider life and morals, good and evil."

Socrates was born in 470 BCE in Athens. His father was a stonecutter and his mother a midwife. A stonecutter himself by profession, who also served his city as a soldier, Socrates was captivated by the philosophical quest. He spent his youth studying the philosophy of nature under the tutelage of Archelaus, the disciple of Anaxagoras. He abandoned the pursuit, however, for a more pressing concern, a philosophy of human nature, specifically a concern for how we ought to live. Perhaps he was spurred on to this study by the Sophists who claimed to make people wise or virtuous through their instruction. Perhaps Socrates saw that the problems that the Sophists were concerned with were the important issues, only they misunderstood them. They asked the right questions—How should I live? What is virtue? How can I succeed in life?—but lacked the passionate and disinterested love of truth, which was necessary in order to answer these questions. They seemed to accept an unexamined cynicism about higher truth in settling for shallow, relativist answers to these questions, substituting rhetoric for reason, oratory for logic, pragmatic success for objective truth. Socrates' genius was to transfer the rigorous truth-centered methods of scientific inquiry to questions of human nature and ethics. With him, ethical inquiry originates as a discipline worthy of regard. He is the father of moral philosophy.

What makes Socrates especially interesting with regard to ethics is that he apparently was an extraordinarily good person, one who was modest, wise, self-controlled, courageous, honest, and concerned about the true well-being of others. Stories abound that tell of Socrates in meditation, standing in one place all day and night, of his refusing to retreat in battle, of his refusing payment for his teachings, even though he was poor by Athenian standards. The renowned hero Alcibiades confessed that Socrates defended his life on the battlefield and deserved the distinguished medal which he, Alcibiades, won.

The Trial

We learn a great deal about his character and professional activity in Plato's report of one of the most famous trials of all history (399 BCE). Socrates is accused of religious heresy—that is, of not believing in the Olympian gods—and corrupting the youth. These are trumped-up charges. Though Socrates, like most of the educated, did not believe in the Olympian pantheon but was a monotheist, there was no law mandating such orthodoxy. What was important was the observing of the religious rituals and festivals of the city, and there is no evidence that Socrates went out of his way to disrupt these. With regard to the charge of corrupting the youth, Socrates was unfairly blamed by the bad behavior of his students, especially the betrayal by Alcibiades to the Spartan cause. It is closer to the truth that many of the leading citizens lost face before the youth of the city due to Socrates's relentless probing into their value system.

His opponents, Meletus and especially the moderate democrat Anytus, expected him to flee Athens, thus saving them the trouble of defending their charges, but instead Socrates chose to stand trial and face the unjust, trumped-up charges. He tells the jury of 500 that the real reason for his being brought to trial is his public ministry of trying to persuade his fellow citizens to place the care of their souls before the care of their fortunes. He sought wisdom and sought to get others to seek it too. In the process, he not only incurred poverty but also made powerful enemies. Let's turn to this trial. His accusers—Meletus, Anytus, and Lycon—have just charged him with not believing in the gods and with corrupting the youth of Athens; Socrates replies to these charges.

THE DIALOGUES

How you, O Athenians, have been affected by my accusers, I cannot tell; but I know that they almost made me forget who I was—so persuasively did they speak; and yet they have hardly uttered a word of truth. I will begin at the beginning, and ask what is the accusation which has given rise to the slander of me, and in fact has encouraged Meletus to bring this charge against me.

Socrates then repeats some of the charges brought against him, including those that he makes the worse argument appear the better, that he takes money for teaching, that he doesn't believe in the gods, and that he corrupts the youth.

With all these witnesses and charges, surely, one may be permitted to suspect, there must be something strange that Socrates has been doing. So Socrates explains both why he has the reputation with many for being wise and yet is hated by so many others. It started with his friend Chaerephon visiting the sacred Oracle at Delphi where he asked the god of Delphi, Apollo, a monumental question.[2]

Here, O men of Athens, I must beg you not to interrupt me, even if I seem to say something extravagant. For the word which I will speak is not mine. I will refer you to a witness who is worthy of credit; that witness shall be the God of Delphi—he will tell you about my wisdom, if I have any, and of what sort it is. You must have known Chaerephon; he was early a friend of mine, and also a friend of yours, for he shared in the recent exile of the people, and returned with you. Well, Chaerephon, as you know, was very impetuous in all his doings, and he went to Delphi and boldly asked the oracle to tell him whether—as I was saying, I must beg you not to interrupt—he asked the oracle to tell him whether any one was wiser than I was, and the Pythian prophetess answered, that there was no man wiser. Chaerephon is dead himself; but his brother, who is in court, will confirm the truth of what I am saying.

Why do I mention this? Because I am going to explain to you why I have such an evil name. When I heard the answer, I said to myself, What can the god mean? and what is the interpretation of his riddle? for I know that I have no wisdom, small or great. What then can he mean when he says that I am the wisest of men? And yet he is a god, and

From: Plato, *The Dialogues*, 3rd ed., trans. Benjamin Jowett (Oxford, UK: Clarendon Press, 1892).

cannot lie; that would be against his nature. After long consideration, I thought of a method of trying the question. I reflected that if I could only find a man wiser than myself, then I might go to the god with a refutation in my hand. I should say to him, "Here is a man who is wiser than I am; but you said that I was the wisest." Accordingly I went to one who had the reputation of wisdom, and observed him—his name I need not mention; he was a politician whom I selected for examination—and the result was as follows: When I began to talk with him, I could not help thinking that he was not really wise, although he was thought wise by many, and still wiser by himself; and thereupon I tried to explain to him that he thought himself wise, but was not really wise; and the consequence was that he hated me, and his enmity was shared by several who were present and heard me. So I left him, saying to myself, as I went away: Well, although I do not suppose that either of us knows anything really beautiful and good, I am better off than he is—for he knows nothing, and thinks that he knows; I neither know nor think that I know. In this latter particular, then, I seem to have slightly the advantage of him. Then I went to another who had still higher pretensions to wisdom, and my conclusion was exactly the same. Whereupon I made another enemy of him, and of many others besides him.

Then I went to one man after another, being not unconscious of the enmity which I provoked, and I lamented and feared this: But necessity was laid upon me,—the word of God, I thought, ought to be considered first. And I said to myself, Go I must to all who appear to know, and find out the meaning of the oracle. And I swear to you, Athenians, by the dog I swear!—for I must tell you the truth—the result of my mission was just this: I found that the men most in repute were all but the most foolish; and that others less esteemed were really wiser and better. I will tell you the tale of my wanderings and of the "Herculean" labours, as I may call them, which I endured only to find at last the oracle irrefutable. After the politicians, I went to the poets; tragic, dithyrambic, and all sorts. And there, I said to myself, you will be instantly detected; now you will find out that you are more ignorant than they are. Accordingly, I took them some of the most elaborate passages in their own writings, and asked what was the meaning of them— thinking that they would teach me something. Will you believe me? I am almost ashamed to confess the truth, but I must say that there is hardly a person present who would not have talked better about their poetry than they did themselves. Then I knew that not by wisdom do poets write poetry, but by a sort of genius and inspiration; they are like diviners or soothsayers who also say many fine things, but do not understand the meaning of them. The poets appeared to me to be much in the same case; and I further observed that upon the strength of their poetry they believed themselves to be the wisest of men in other things in which they were not wise. So I departed, conceiving myself to be superior to them for the same reason that I was superior to the politicians.

At last I went to the artisans, for I was conscious that I knew nothing at all, as I may say, and I was sure that they knew many fine things; and here I was not mistaken, for they did know many things of which I was ignorant, and in this they certainly were wiser than I was. But I observed that even the good artisans fell into the same error as the poets;—because they were good workmen they thought that they also knew all sorts of high matters, and this defect in them overshadowed their wisdom; and therefore I asked myself on behalf of the oracle, whether I would like to be as I was, neither having their knowledge nor their ignorance, or like them in both; and I made answer to myself and to the oracle that I was better off as I was.

This inquisition has led to my having many enemies of the worst and most dangerous kind, and has given occasion also to many calumnies. And I am called wise, for my hearers always imagine that I myself possess the wisdom which I find wanting in others: but the truth is, O men of Athens, that God only is wise; and by his answer he intends to show that the wisdom of men is worth little or nothing; he is not speaking of Socrates, he is only using my name by way of illustration, as if he said, He, O men, is the wisest, who, like Socrates, knows that his wisdom is in truth worth nothing. And so I go about the world, obedient to the god, and search and make enquiry into the wisdom of any one, whether citizen or stranger, who appears to be wise; and if he is not wise, then in vindication of the oracle I show him that he is not wise; and my occupation quite absorbs me, and I have no time to give either to any public matter of interest or to any concern of my own, but I am in utter poverty by reason of my devotion to the god.

Socrates' wisdom consisted in knowing one thing of which others were ignorant—that he knows nothing. Others falsely imagine that they know something when they do not. Socrates is ahead of them; he knows that he knows nothing.

Having exposed the ignorance of the leading citizens, poets, and artisans in front of the youth of the city, these citizens were furious with him. Not only had he exposed their pretensions to knowledge, but also he did it in front of their sons and fellow citizens. Such shame is not easy to endure. Such are the origins of the charge that he "corrupted the youth."

One may detect the renowned Socratic irony in the narration of his ignorance, for Socrates certainly did think he knew something of the meaning of virtue, that virtue is knowledge and can be attained. Socrates continues his defense. He takes up the charge of not believing in the gods. Let's join him in Athens.

Socrates asks Meletus whether he believes in some new gods, but not the right ones or whether he is an atheist.

MELETUS: I mean the latter—that you are an atheist.
SOCRATES: What an extraordinary statement! Why do you think so, Meletus? Do you mean that I do not believe in the godhead of the sun or moon, like other men?
MELETUS: I assure you, judges, that he does not: for he says that the sun is stone and the moon earth.
SOCRATES: Friend Meletus, you must think that you have Anaxagoras on trial, who holds such views, not me. Do you really think that I do not believe in any god?
MELETUS: I swear by Zeus that you believe absolutely in none at all.
SOCRATES: Nobody will believe you, Meletus, and I am pretty sure that you do not believe yourself. I cannot help thinking, men of Athens, that Meletus is reckless and impudent, and that he has written this indictment in a spirit of mere wantonness and youthful bravado. Has he not compounded a riddle, thinking to try me? He said to

himself:—I shall see whether the wise Socrates will discover my facetious contradiction, or whether I shall be able to deceive him and the rest of them. For he certainly does appear to me to contradict himself in the indictment as much as if he said that Socrates is guilty of not believing in the gods, and yet of believing in them—but this is not like a person who is in earnest.

I should like you, O men of Athens, to join me in examining what I conceive to be his inconsistency; and do you, Meletus, answer. And I must remind the audience of my request that they would not make a disturbance if I speak in my accustomed manner:

Did ever man, Meletus, believe in the existence of human things, and not of human beings? …I wish, men of Athens, that he would answer, and not be always trying to get up an interruption. Did ever any man believe in horsemanship, and not in horses? or in flute-playing, and not in flute-players? No, my friend; I will answer to you and to the court, as you refuse to answer for yourself. There is no man who ever did. But now please to answer the next question: Can a man believe in spiritual and divine agencies, and not in spirits or demigods?

He cannot.

How lucky I am to have extracted that answer, by the assistance of the court! But then you swear in the indictment that I teach and believe in divine or spiritual agencies (new or old, no matter for that); at any rate, I believe in spiritual agencies,—so you say and swear in the affidavit; and yet if I believe in divine beings, how can I help believing in spirits or demigods;—must I not? To be sure I must; and therefore I may assume that your silence gives consent. Now what are spirits or demigods? are they not either gods or the sons of gods?

Certainly they are.

But this is what I call the facetious riddle invented by you: the demigods or spirits are gods, and you say first that I do not believe in gods, and then again that I do believe in gods; that is, if I believe in demigods. For if the demigods are the illegitimate sons of gods, whether by the nymphs or by any other mothers, of whom they are said to be the sons—what human being will ever believe that there are no gods if they are the sons of gods? You might as well affirm the existence of mules, and deny that of horses and asses. Such nonsense, Meletus, could only have been intended by you to make trial of me. You have put this into the indictment because you had nothing real of which to accuse me. But no one who has a particle of understanding will ever be convinced by you that the same men can believe in divine and superhuman things, and yet not believe that there are gods and demigods and heroes.

Having reduced Meletus's argument to a contradiction, Socrates ends the first part of his defense, the negative part of answering the charges brought against him. Now he begins the positive part by describing the values for which he has lived and is prepared to die. He compares his present state to that of Achilles, as recorded in the *Iliad*, who altogether despised danger in comparison with disgrace. Knowing that if he fought on the morrow, he was fated to die, Achilles replies, "Let me die forthwith and be avenged of my enemy, rather than abide here by the beaked ships, a laughing stock and a burden of the earth." And so it has always been the dominant principle of my life, Socrates avers, not to put love of life before sense of duty. He relates two incidents to illustrate this. During the Peloponnesian War, after the disastrous battle of Arginusae in which Athens paid for a naval victory by losing twenty-five ships and 4000 men, the eight naval officers involved in the battle were tried for culpable negligence. Rather than being tried one by one in the presence of their accusers, they were condemned to death in absentia by a bloc vote. Socrates, at that time a member of the Senate, risked his life by rendering a lone, courageous protest against this illegal verdict. A few years later (403 BCE) after Athens had lost the Peloponnesian War and surrendered to Sparta, a violent, reactionary Commission of Thirty under the leadership of Critias, Plato's uncle, came to power in Athens. They forced the leading democrats to leave the city, executed some enemies, and confiscated their property. The oligarchy tried to implicate Socrates in their dealings and sent him with four others to arrest one of the wealthy democrats, Leon of Salamis, whose property they planned to confiscate. While the other men obeyed, Socrates exercised civil disobedience and refused to be a part of these nefarious proceedings. He would probably have been executed as a traitor for this act had not a democratic revolution overthrown the oligarchy.

When he was a soldier in the Battle of Potidaea, he was commanded by the generals to stay at his station even in the face of death. Now, as a philosopher, he has been commanded by God "to fulfill the philosopher's mission of searching into myself and other men" and must not forsake his duty in the face of death. If he flees his station now, he could legitimately be accused of denying the existence of the gods. It would also be a case of pretending to wisdom, of claiming to know that death is an evil to be avoided—something none of us knows. "The only thing I know is that injustice and disobedience to a better, whether God or man, is evil and dishonorable."

Therefore if you let me go now—if you say to me, Socrates, this time we will not mind Anytus, and you shall be let off, but upon one condition, that you are not to inquire and speculate in this way any more, and that if you are caught doing so again you shall die;—if this was the condition on which you let me go, I should reply: Men of Athens, I honour and love you; but I shall obey God rather than you, and while I have life and strength I shall never cease from the practice and teaching of philosophy, exhorting any one whom I meet and saying to him after my manner: You, my friend,—a citizen of the great and mighty and wise city of Athens,—are you not ashamed of heaping up the greatest amount of money and honour and reputation, and caring so little about wisdom and truth and the greatest improvement of the soul, which you never regard or heed at all? And if the person with whom I am arguing, says: Yes, but I do care; then I do not leave him or let him go at once; but I proceed to interrogate and examine and cross-examine him, and if I think that he has no virtue in him, but only says that he has, I reproach him with undervaluing the greater, and overvaluing the less. And I shall repeat the same words to every one whom I meet, young and old, citizen and alien, but especially to the citizens, inasmuch as they are my brethren. For know that this is the command of God; and I believe that no greater good has ever happened in the state than my service to the God. For I do nothing but go about persuading you all, old and young alike, not to take thought for your persons or your properties, but first and chiefly to care about the greatest improvement of the soul. I tell you that virtue is not given by money, but that from virtue comes money and every other good of man, public as well as private. This is my teaching, and if this is the doctrine which corrupts the youth, I am a mischievous person. But if any one says that this is not my teaching, he is speaking an untruth. Wherefore, O men of Athens, I say to you, do as Anytus bids or not as Anytus bids, and either acquit me or not; but whichever you do, understand that I shall never alter my ways, not even if I have to die many times. . . .

And now, Athenians, I am not going to argue for my own sake, as you may think, but for yours, that you may not sin against the God by condemning me, who am his gift to you. For if you kill me you will not easily find a successor to me, who, if I may use such a ludicrous figure of speech, am a sort of gadfly, given to the state by God; and the state is a great and noble steed who is tardy in his motions owing to his very size, and requires to be stirred into life. I am that gadfly which God has attached to the state, and all day long and in all places am always fastening upon you, arousing and persuading and reproaching you. You will not easily find another like me, and therefore I would advise you to spare me.

Socrates is found guilty by a vote of 281 to 220. The prosecutors propose the death penalty. Socrates is now expected to offer a penalty for his crime to match the prosecution's proposal. It was normal for the accused at this point to grovel before the jury, display his wife and children, and plead for mercy, lest they leave his children fatherless. Instead, Socrates refuses to admit guilt and proposes as a fitting "penalty" that he be given free, deluxe meals at the Prytaneum, the dining hall of the Olympian and military heroes.

And so the prosecution proposes death as the penalty. And what shall I propose on my part, O men of Athens? Clearly that which is my due. And what is my due? I who neglected my own affairs in order to persuade every man among you that he must seek virtue and wisdom before he looks to his private interests. What should be done to such a one? Surely some good thing. What would be a suitable reward for a poor man who is your benefactor? There can be no reward so fitting as maintenance in the Prytaneum, O men of Athens, a reward which he deserves far more than the citizen who won the prize at Olympia in the horse or chariot race.

He then rejects the suggestion of exile as a penalty, for he will very likely carry on the same mission, cause the youth to flock to him, thus antagonizing their elders.

Some one will say: Yes, Socrates, but cannot you hold your tongue, and then you may go into a foreign city, and no one will interfere with you? Now I have great difficulty in making you understand my answer to this. For if I tell you that to do as you say would be a disobedience to the God, and therefore that I cannot hold my tongue, you will not believe that I am serious; and if I say again that daily to discourse about virtue, and of those other things about which you hear me examining myself and others, is the greatest good of man, and that the unexamined life is not worth living, you are still less likely to believe me. Yet I say what is true, although a thing of which it is hard for me to persuade you. Also, I have never been accustomed to think that I deserve to suffer any harm.

Almost in mockery of the ordeal he is undergoing, Socrates finally offers to pay the equivalent of a few dollars. At this display of insolence, the jury becomes infuriated and votes for the death penalty: 361 to 140. Eighty jurors who voted that he was innocent now vote to execute him. Upon receiving the sentence, Socrates forgave his accusers: "I am not angry with my condemners, or with my accusers; they have done me no harm, although they did not mean to do me any good; and for this I may gently blame them."

When condemned to death and awaiting his execution, he was offered a safe plan of escape. The jailers had been bribed, and Socrates was assured of safe passage out of Athens to another city. Instead of jumping at the chance, he engaged in a discussion of civil disobedience and argued that it was proper for him to accept the decision of the court. His interpretation of the social contract demanded that he abide by the court's decision. To flee would not only support his enemies' judgment that he was a self-serving Sophist, but it also would be an act of disobedience to legitimate authority. So before his grieving, agonizing disciples, he dutifully drank the hemlock without a trace of repugnance and thus became the first philosophical martyr. A witness, Phaedo, summed up the consensus view of Socrates' followers: "Such was the end, Echecrates, of our friend, who was, I think, of all the men of our time, the best, the wisest, and the most just."

Scholars are divided on whether Socrates was right in refusing to escape, but that refusal was consistent with his notion of staying at one's station and not fleeing. It reflects his wider commitment to the pursuit of Truth and moral Goodness. Unlike the Sophists, with whom he was sometimes confused, he was committed to an ideal, not wealth. He refused to take money for his services and carried on his pilgrimage at great personal material sacrifice. The effect he had on others was phenomenal. Here, from the *Symposium*, is what one of the leading personalities of Greek society, the military hero Alcibiades, had to say of Socrates:

When I listen to him my heart leaps up much more than in a religious frenzy, his words move me to tears. I see this happening to many others too. When I listened to Pericles and other fine orators, I thought: they speak well. But nothing like this happened to me, my soul was not thrown into turmoil. I was not enraged at myself for living so like a slave. But this Marsyas* has often put me into a state where I felt that the life I lived was not worth living. He is the only man who ever made me feel ashamed.

---

*Marsyas: A satyr (a man with horns and who was a goat from the waist down) who challenged Apollo to a flute-playing contest and lost and was punished by being flayed alive.—Ed.

Socrates' Moral Philosophy: Virtue Is Knowledge

What were the distinguishing features of Socrates' ethics? What exactly did he believe about the good life? We can set forth five theses that he held. First, I will list these and then discuss them.

1. Care for the soul is all that matters.
2. Self-knowledge is a prerequisite for the good life.
3. Virtue is knowledge (no such thing as weakness of will—evil is ignorance).
4. You cannot harm the good person, but in trying to harm the other you harm yourself. The Good is good for you, and the Bad is bad for you.
5. The autonomy of ethics: To the dilemma set forth in the *Euthyphro,* is the Good good because God chooses it, or does God choose the Good because it is good? Socrates answers that God chooses it because it is good.

Let's elaborate these theses. We first examine the first two theses together:

1. Care for the soul (or inner self) is all that matters.
2. Self-knowledge is a prerequisite for the good life.

Socrates asks us the same question as Jesus in the Gospel of Matthew: "What good would it do me to gain the whole world and lose my own soul?" What good is knowledge of the heavens if I am unhappy or spiritually diseased or in despair? What good is it to live in a perfect society if I see no value in life itself or in my life? The one thing necessary is spiritual or psychological health. We need to discover the right sort of regimen to follow in order to promote excellence of soul. But this entails that we understand what the soul is. We need to scrutinize our values, measuring our lives by the highest possible standards. The unexamined life is not worth living.

How can we know the soul? Not necessarily through introspection but by understanding its function. Just as the function of a knife is to cut and the function of a ruler is to rule, the function of the soul is to attain virtue, to perfect itself in goodness and truth. In the *Phaedo,* Socrates describes this as the essence of philosophy, to prepare for death—that is, to purify one's soul through the attainment of wisdom that the soul will enter the next life worthy of blessedness:

> A craftsman can only do good work if he is in command of his tools and can guide them as he wishes, an accomplishment which demands knowledge and practice. Similarly, life can only be lived well if the *psyche* is in command of the body. It meant purely and simply the intelligence, which in a properly ordered life is in complete control of the senses and emotions. Its proper virtue is wisdom and thought and truth. This identification of the psyche with the self and the self with the reason might be said to have roots both in Ionian scientific thought and in Pythagoreanism, yet there was certainly novelty in Socrates' development of it.[3]

3. Virtue is knowledge.

Self-knowledge is a prerequisite for the good life. You cannot tend, care, or improve anything unless you know its nature. Knowing how must be preceded by knowing what. To know the good is tantamount to trying to do the good, for everyone wants to succeed, to flourish, to be happy, and goodness is good for us. Vice is simply the product of ignorance. Evil people simply do not know what is in their interest and so think that they are harming others, when they are mainly harming themselves. No wise person would ever do evil voluntarily.

Socratic ethics are thoroughly intellectualist. To know the Good is to do the good. There is no place for weakness of will. Evil is ignorance. "My own opinion is more or less this: no wise man believes that anyone sins willingly or willingly perpetuates any base or evil act; they know very well that every base or evil action is committed involuntarily"[4] Aristotle tells us that Socrates believed that the virtues are sciences, that doing well was analogous to knowing the truth of mathematics.

> Socrates believed that knowledge of virtue was the final aim, and he inquired what justice is, and what courage and every other kind of virtue. This was reasonable in view of his conviction that all the virtues were sciences, so that to know justice was at the same time to be just; for as soon as we have learned geometry and architecture we are architects and geometricians. For this reason he inquired what virtue is, but not how or from what it is acquired.[5]

Aristotle goes on to point out that while this relationship of knowing to being is true of the theoretical sciences, it is not so with the productive sciences in which knowledge is only a means to the further end. For example, knowledge of medicine is necessary but not sufficient for health. Knowledge of the good state is necessary but not sufficient for producing the good state.

Again Aristotle points out:

> The effect of [Socrates'] making the virtues into branches of knowledge was to eliminate the irrational part of the soul, and with it emotion and moral character. So his treatment of virtue was in this respect mistaken. After him Plato, rightly enough, divided the soul into the rational and irrational parts and explained the appropriate virtues of each.[6]

We are more likely to agree with Medea that sometimes people act against what they know to be good or with Milton's Satan,

> So farewell hope, and with hope farewell fear,
> Farewell remorse: all good to me is lost;
> Evil, be thou my good.

and with St. Paul that sometimes people suffer weakness of will and do not do the good that they would but the evil that they would not (Romans 7:19f).

Furthermore, Aristotle points out there is something deterministic about the Socratic theory of virtue:

> Socrates claimed that it is not in our power to be worthy or worthless men. If, he said, you were to ask anyone whether he would like to be just or unjust, no one would choose injustice, and it is the same with courage and cowardice and the other virtues. Evidently any who are vicious will not be vicious voluntarily. Neither, in consequence, will they be voluntarily virtuous.[7]

So what is the point of exhortation to seek the truth and the good if it is all determined? If we cannot help being virtuous or vicious?

It may well be that Socrates, the consummate rationalist, is harmed here by his own rationality. He apparently really would always choose according to the dictates of reason. He may have lacked a substantial degree of irrationality in the soul, and this may have blinded him to the fact that most people are less fortunate, that weakness of will and an evil will exist.

4. You cannot harm the good person, but in trying to harm the other you harm yourself. The Good is good for you, and the Bad is bad for you.

The classic illustrations of this are the story of Gyges' ring and the thought experiment of the two men, the seemingly bad good man who suffers injustice and the seemingly good bad man who enjoys the fruits of the virtuous, which are found in the second book of the *Republic*. Socrates argues that despite all appearances the tortured virtuous is really better off than the apparently happy evil man, for one has a healthy soul and the other a sick soul. Since it is the soul that truly defines our state of being, we can conclude that it always is better to suffer evil than to do evil!

This argument has been criticized by some who argue that unless there is life after death where justice rewards us according to our moral merit, it's hard to see why it isn't in our interest to act immorally when we can escape detection or punishment. Should Socrates have held to the idea of an afterlife, as his pupil Plato did? Socrates may be right in showing that virtue is a necessary condition for a fully flourishing life, but is it sufficient for happiness? Don't bad things happen to good people?

5. The autonomy of ethics: To the dilemma set forth in Plato's dialogue *Euthyphro* (see Chapter 32), is the Good good because God chooses it, or does God choose the Good because it is good? Socrates answers that God chooses it because it is good.

Socratic ethics lack a transcendental dimension. If there is an afterlife, well and good, it's icing on the cake, but it is not necessary for the justification of morality. Goodness has to do with the proper functioning of the soul and can be discovered through reason alone. There is no need for revelation, and if there are gods, they too must obey the moral law and keep their souls pure through following virtuous living. There is not even a hint that religion helps motivate people to virtuous living. Goodness is its own reward, and it is obviously so to anyone who knows what virtue is and how the soul functions. Religion is a fifth wheel, useless in the moral domain. The charge brought against him at his trial by Meletus that he didn't worship the gods of the city was not without some foundation. They certainly played no role in his moral theory.

We can sum up Socratic ethics by saying that it is based in a knowledge of human nature and proper functioning, that the self has a telos, or purpose, that involves living virtuously (that is, wisely and justly); that happiness is predicated on proper functioning, hence on living virtuously; that knowing the Good necessarily results in doing good; that we do not need religion to inform us of the Good or to motivate us to be virtuous.

Socrates' theory is programmatic. It is not hard to see how it might be modified in order to meet some telling objections. What's more, it has an existential thrust that is impressive. Here is a man who lived his ethic! One who not only sought the True and the Good with all his heart but displayed incredible endurance and self-control in that pursuit and in living in the light that he had.

Summary

The Sophists, who arose in fifth-century Athens, enabled the rising entrepreneurial class to succeed in litigation. Cynical about truth and religion, they were relativists, pragmatists, and egoists, and they were very successful in making money. Socrates appeared on the scene, disillusioned with the speculations of the early Cosmologist philosophers but possessed with their optimism and love of Truth. He opposed the Sophists at every point, developed the first thoroughgoing moral philosophy, centered in the idea that virtue is knowledge, and suffered the death of a martyr for philosophy.

FOR FURTHER REFLECTION

1. Explain the main ideas of the Sophists and show Socrates' response to each one. Is the debate between the Sophists and Socrates relevant for our own day? If so, in which ways?

2. Alcibiades, one of the Greek military heroes, who later was considered a traitor, said this of Socrates:

> When I listen to him, my heart leaps up much more than in a religious frenzy, his words move me to tears. I see this happening to many others too. When I listened to Pericles and other fine orators, I thought: they speak well. But nothing like this happened to me, my soul was not thrown into turmoil. I was not enraged at myself for living so like a slave. But this Marsyas has often put me into a state where I felt that the life I lived was not worth living. . . . He is the only man who ever made me feel ashamed. (Alcibiades in the *Symposium*)

Can you understand how people might feel this way about Socrates?

3. On the other hand, many people hated Socrates, thought of him as an elitist, who unkindly and unnecessarily showed up their weaknesses. I. F. Stone, in his book *The Trial of Socrates,* accuses Socrates of being antidemocratic, arrogant, and ultimately responsible for his own downfall. Along these same lines, the late eminent Greek scholar Gregory Vlastos argues that for all his dialectical skill,

Socrates lacked the virtue *agapē*, altruistic love, so prominent in Christianity some four centuries later.

How would you respond to the charges that Socrates was undemocratic and lacked sufficient love? Is it obvious that Socrates is less valuable for not believing in democracy and for not being as altruistic as Jesus or the Christian saints? Discuss your answer.

4. Discuss the five points in Socrates' moral philosophy. Is his philosophy cogent? Explain.

NOTES

1. Cicero *Tusculan Disputations* 5.4.10; quoted in W. K. C. Guthrie, *Socrates* (Cambridge, UK: Cambridge University Press, 1971), 98.
2. Except for the last, all remaining quotations in this section are from Plato, *The Dialogues*, 3rd ed., trans. Benjamin Jowett (Oxford, UK: Clarendon Press, 1892).
3. Guthrie, *Socrates,* 149.
4. Plato *Protagoras* 345d; *Meno* 78a; *Laws* 731c; *Republic* 589c.
5. Aristotle *Eudemian Ethics* 1216 b 2ff.
6. Aristotle *Magna Moralia* 1182 a 20.
7. Aristotle *Magna Moralia* 1187 a 7 and appendix.

FOR FURTHER READING

Guthrie, W. K. C. *Socrates.* Cambridge, UK: Cambridge University Press, 1971. A clear, accessible, scholarly work of the first order.

Guthrie, W. K. C. *The Sophists.* Cambridge, UK: Cambridge University Press, 1971. A clear, comprehensive study.

Plato. *Apology, Euthyphro, Crito, Protagoras, Gorgias, Republic,* and *Phaedo* are especially important for a firsthand account of Socrates.

Stace, W. T. *A Critical History of Greek Philosophy.* New York: St. Martin's Press, 1967. Chapters 9 and 10 are especially relevant for this chapter.

Stone, I. F. *The Trial of Socrates.* Boston: Little, Brown, 1988. A provocative investigative probe into the causes of the downfall of Socrates.

Vlastos, Gregory. *Socrates: Ironist and Moral Philosopher.* Ithaca, NY: Cornell University Press, 1991. A helpful book by a leading authority.

5 ⚘ The Philosophy of Plato: Knowledge and Reality

The safest general characterization of the European philosophical tradition is that it consists of a series of footnotes to Plato.

Alfred North Whitehead[1]

Plato (427–347 BCE) is generally recognized as the father of philosophy, the first systematic metaphysician and epistemologist, the first philosopher to set forth a comprehensive treatment of the entire domain of philosophy from ontology to ethics and aesthetics. He was born into an Athenian aristocratic family during the Periclean Golden Age of Greek democracy. During most of his life, Athens was at war with Sparta, the Greek city-state to the south. He was Socrates' disciple, systematized and developed his teacher's ideas, was the founder of the first university and school of philosophy (the Academy in Athens), and was Aristotle's teacher and an advisor to emperors. His goal was to found an ideal state where philosophers ruled with justice. Among his important works are *The Republic, Phaedo, Meno,* and *Phaedrus,* which will be examined in this book. Most of his books are dialogues in which Socrates is the key spokesman and interlocutor, who seeks an understanding of difficult concepts. In the early dialogues, such as the *Apology* and *Crito,* Plato may be reporting Socrates' own thoughts, but as Plato developed his own philosophy, he continued to use Socrates as his mouthpiece.

The Theory of Forms

What do all triangles or green objects have in common? Triangles come in different shapes and sizes. It is true that all triangles are closed plain figures with three sides and three angles adding up to 180 degrees, but the sides may be different sizes and the shape of the triangle may be isosceles or scalene. Even before we can articulate the definition of a triangle, we seem to know one when we see it. Regarding green objects, we cannot even define their common property—*green*. We cannot help a blind person understand what it is or even describe it to one who knows what green is. It is an unanalyzable simple property. All green things have this undefinable property in common. Now let's go from perceptual objects (triangles, colors, chairs, and tables) to abstract ideas: friendship, equality, justice, beauty, and goodness. What do all exemplars of each of these properties have in common? Plato's *theory of Forms* (sometimes referred to as his theory of Ideas) seeks to give us a satisfactory answer to this question.

Aristotle tells us how Plato first came upon this theory:

> The Theory of Forms occurred to Plato because he was persuaded of the truth of Heraclitus' doctrine that all things accessible to the senses are always in a state of flux, so that if knowledge or thought is to have an object there must besides things accessible to the senses be certain other entities which persist; for there is no knowledge of things which are in a state of flux. Socrates occupied himself with the moral virtues, and was the first to look for general definitions in this area. There are two things which may fairly be ascribed to Socrates, arguments by analogy and general definitions, both of which are concerned with the starting point of knowledge. But whereas Socrates made neither the universal nor the definition exist separately, others gave them a separate existence and this was the sort of thing to which they gave the name of Forms. So for them it followed by almost the same argument that there are Forms for everything to which general words apply.[2]

Whereas Socrates sought clear definitions of concepts in order to have a common basis for discussion (how can we even settle on an understanding of what a "just society" will be if we have different definitions of *justice*?), Plato went beyond *verbal* definitions and posited a comprehensive theory of reality.

According to Plato, every significant word (noun, adjective, and verb) and thing partakes of and derives its identity from a Form, or Forms. The Forms are single, common to all objects and abstract terms, perfect as the particulars or exemplars are not, independent of any particulars but their cause, having objective existence (they are the truly real, while particulars are only apparently so). While independent of the human mind, they are intelligible and can be known by the mind alone and not by sense experience. The Forms are a divine, eternal, simple, indissoluble, unchanging, and self-subsisting reality, existing outside space and time. They are the cause of all that is. Here, in a key passage from Plato's *Phaedo*, Socrates is instructing two disciples, Cebes and Simmias.

PHAEDO

SOCRATES: Well what I mean is this. As I am going to try to explain to you the theory of causation which I have worked out myself, I propose to make a fresh start from those principles of mine which you know so well—that is, I am assuming the existence of absolute Beauty, Goodness, Greatness and all the rest of the Forms. If you grant my assumption and admit that they exist, I hope with their help to explain causation to you, and to find a proof that the soul is immortal.

CEBES: Certainly I grant it. You need not lose any time in drawing your conclusion.

SOCRATES: Then consider the next, and see whether you share my opinion. It seems to me that whatever else beauty is apart from the Beautiful itself, it is beautiful because and only because it partakes in the Beautiful. Do you accept this kind of causality?

CEBES: Yes, I do.

SOCRATES: Well, now, that is as much as I can understand, for I cannot understand other ingenious theory of causation. If anyone tells me that what makes something beautiful is its having a gorgeous color or shape or any other such property, I dismiss these explanations, for I find them confusing. I simply cling to the explanation that the one thing that makes that object beautiful is the presence in it or association with it, in whatever way the relation comes about, of the Beautiful. All beautiful things become beautiful through the Beautiful. For this seems to me the safest answer to give to myself and to other people, and if I cling to this I cannot fall. Do you agree?

CEBES: I do.

SOCRATES: Then is it also through Largeness that large things are large and larger things larger, and by Smallness that smaller things are smaller?

CEBES: Yes.

SOCRATES: Suppose next that we add one to one. You would surely not say that the cause of our getting two is the addition, or in the case of a divided unit, the division? You would say that you know no other way in which an object can come into existence than by participating in the reality peculiar to its appropriate universal, and that in the cases which I have mentioned you recognize no other cause for the coming into being of two than participation in duality, and that whatever is to become two must participate in this, and whatever is to become one must participate in unity. You would dismiss these divisions and additions and other such niceties, leaving them for persons wiser than yourself to use in their explanations, while you, being nervous of your own shadow, as the saying goes, and of your inexperience, would hold fast to the security of your hypothesis and make your answer accordingly. If anyone should fasten upon the hypothesis itself, you would disregard him and refuse to answer until you could consider whether its consequences were mutually consistent or not.[3]

Plato's theory of the Forms is an instance of the idea of the *One and the Many*. What do the *many* similar things have in common? The *one* Form. All beautiful things have in common participation in the Form of the Beautiful; all good things have in common participation in the Form of the Good.

From: Plato, *Phaedo* 100–101, trans. Hugh Tredennick, in *Plato: The Collected Dialogues*, eds. Edith Hamilton and Huntington Cairns (Princeton, NJ: Princeton University Press, 1961). I have slightly revised the translation for pedagogical reasons.

Innate Ideas and the Theory of Recollection

In our next dialogue, *Meno*, Plato, through his spokesman Socrates, seeks to prove that we are born with **innate ideas** of the Forms. The dialogue begins with Meno raising a puzzle about learning: How do you know when you have found the answer to a question you are asking? Either (1) you don't know the answer and so won't know when you've found it or (2) you already know the answer, in which case why make an inquiry in the first place? Socrates sets about to solve this riddle about the impossibility of learning through the theory of recollection of knowledge. The specific question Meno raises is whether virtue can be taught.

MENO

MENO: O Socrates, I used to be told, before I knew you, that you were always doubting yourself and making others doubt; and now you are casting your spells over me, and I am simply getting bewitched and enchanted, and am at my wit's end. And if I may venture to make a jest upon you, you seem to me both in your appearance and in your power over others to be very like the flat torpedo fish, who torpifies those who come near him and touch him, as you have now torpified me, I think. For my soul and my tongue are really torpid, and I do not know how to answer you; and though I have been delivered of an infinite variety of speeches about virtue before now, and to many persons—and very good ones they were, as I thought—at this moment I cannot even say what virtue is. And I think that you are very wise in not voyaging and going away from home, for if you did in other places as you do in Athens, you would be cast into prison as a magician.

SOCRATES: You are a rogue, Meno, and had all but caught me.

Socrates now calls one of Meno's slaves, an uneducated boy. He will be the test case as to whether learning takes place through recollecting knowledge learned in a previous existence. I have illustrated the reasoning with diagrams.

…As to my being a torpedo, if the torpedo is torpid as well as the cause of torpidity in others, then indeed I am a torpedo, but not otherwise; for I perplex others, not because I am clear, but because I am utterly perplexed myself. And now I know not what virtue is, and you seem to be in the same case, although you did once perhaps know before you touched me. However, I have no objection to join with you in the enquiry.

MENO: And how will you enquire, Socrates, into that which you do not know? What will you put forth as the subject of enquiry? And if you find what you want, how will you ever know that this is the thing which you did not know?

SOCRATES: I know, Meno, what you mean; but just see what a tiresome dispute you are introducing. You argue that a man cannot enquire either about that which he knows, or about that which he does not know; for if he knows, he has no need to enquire; and if not, he cannot; for he does not know the very subject about which he is to enquire.

From: Plato, *Meno*, trans. Benjamin Jowett (Oxford, UK: Oxford University Press, 1896).

MENO: Well, Socrates, and is not the argument sound?

SOCRATES: I think not.

MENO: Why not?

SOCRATES: I will tell you why: I have heard from certain wise men and women who spoke of things divine that—

MENO: What did they say?

SOCRATES: They spoke of a glorious truth, as I conceive.

MENO: What was it: and who were they?

SOCRATES: Some of them were priests and priestesses, who had studied how they might be able to give a reason of their profession: there have been poets also, who spoke of these things by inspiration, like Pindar, and many others who were inspired. And they say—mark, now, and see whether their words are true—they say that the soul of man is immortal, and at one time has an end, which is termed dying, and at another time is born again, but is never destroyed. And the moral is, that a man ought to live always in perfect holiness. *"For in the ninth year Persephone sends the souls of those from whom she has received the penalty of ancient crime back again from beneath into the light of the sun above, and these are they who become noble kings and mighty men and great in wisdom and are called saintly heroes in after ages."* The soul, then, as being immortal, and having been born again many times, and having seen all things that exist, whether in this world or in the world below, has knowledge of them all; and it is no wonder that she should be able to call to remembrance all that she ever knew about virtue, and about everything; for as all nature is akin, and the soul has learned all things, there is no difficulty in her eliciting or as men say learning, out of a single recollection all the rest, if a man is strenuous and does not faint; for all enquiry and all learning is but recollection. And therefore we ought not to listen to this sophistical argument about the impossibility of enquiry: for it will make us idle, and is sweet only to the sluggard; but the other saying will make us active and inquisitive. In that confiding, I will gladly enquire with you into the nature of virtue....

Socrates now addresses Meno's uneducated slave.

SOCRATES: Tell me, boy, do you know that a figure like this is a square?

BOY: I do.

SOCRATES: And you know that a square figure has these four lines equal?

BOY: Certainly.

SOCRATES: And these lines which I have drawn through the middle of the square are also equal?

BOY: Yes.

SOCRATES: A square may be of any size?

BOY: Certainly.

SOCRATES: And if one side of the figure be of two feet, and the other side be of two feet, how much will the whole be? Let me explain: if in one direction the space was of two feet, and in the other direction of one foot, the whole would be of two feet taken once?

BOY: Yes.

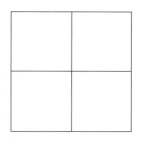

SOCRATES: But since this side is also of two feet, there are twice two feet?

BOY: There are.

SOCRATES: Then the square is of twice two feet?

BOY: Yes.

SOCRATES: And how many are twice two feet? Count and tell me.

BOY: Four, Socrates.

SOCRATES: And might there not be another square twice as large as this, and having like this the lines equal?

BOY: Yes.

SOCRATES: And of how many feet will that be?

BOY: Of eight feet.

SOCRATES: And now try and tell me the length of the line which forms the side of that double square: this is two feet—what will that be?

BOY: Clearly, Socrates, it will be double.

SOCRATES: Do you observe, Meno, that I am not teaching the boy anything, but only asking him questions; and now he fancies that he knows how long a line is necessary in order to produce a figure of eight square feet; does he not?

MENO: Yes.

SOCRATES: And does he really know?

MENO: Certainly not.

SOCRATES: He only guesses that because the square is double, the line is double.

MENO: True.

SOCRATES: Observe him while he recalls the steps in regular order. [*To the Boy.*] Tell me, boy, do you assert that a double space comes from a double line? Remember that I am not speaking of an oblong, but of a figure equal every way, and twice the size of this— that is to say of eight feet; and I want to know whether you still say that a double square comes from a double line?

BOY: Yes.

SOCRATES: But does not this line becomes doubled if we add another such line here?

BOY: Certainly.

SOCRATES: And four such lines will make a space containing eight feet?

BOY: Yes.

SOCRATES: Let us describe such a figure: Would you not say that this is the figure of eight feet?

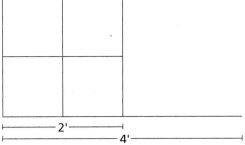

BOY: Yes.

SOCRATES: And are there not these four divisions in the figure, each of which is equal to the figure of four feet?

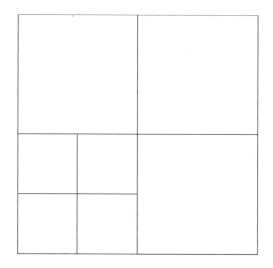

BOY: True.

SOCRATES: And is not that four times four?

BOY: Certainly.

SOCRATES: And four times is not double?

BOY: No, indeed.

SOCRATES: But how much?

BOY: Four times as much.

SOCRATES: Therefore the double line, boy, has given a space, not twice, but four times as much.

BOY: True.

SOCRATES: Four times four are sixteen—are they not?

BOY: Yes.

SOCRATES: What line would give you a space of eight feet, as this gives one of sixteen feet;—do you see?

BOY: Yes.

SOCRATES: And the space of four feet is made from this half line?

BOY: Yes.

SOCRATES: Good; and is not a space of eight feet twice the size of this, and half the size of the other?

BOY: Certainly.

SOCRATES: Such a space, then, will be made out of a line greater than this one, and less than that one?

BOY: Yes; I think so.

SOCRATES: Very good; I like to hear you say what you think. And now tell me, is not this a line of two feet and that of four?

BOY: Yes.

SOCRATES: Then the line which forms the side of eight feet ought to be more than this line of two feet, and less than the other of four feet?

BOY: It ought.

SOCRATES: Try and see if you can tell me how much it will be.

BOY: Three feet.

SOCRATES: Then if we add a half to this line of two, that will be the line of three. Here are two and there is one; and on the other side, here are two also and there is one: and that makes the figure of which you speak?

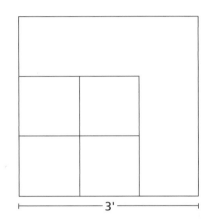

BOY: Yes.

SOCRATES: But if there are three feet this way and three feet that way, the whole space will be three times three feet?

BOY: That is evident.

SOCRATES: And how much are three times three feet?

BOY: Nine.

SOCRATES: And how much is the double of four?

BOY: Eight.

SOCRATES: Then the figure of eight is not made out of a line of three?

BOY: No.

SOCRATES: But from what line?—tell me exactly; and if you would rather not reckon, try and show me the line.

BOY: Indeed, Socrates, I do not know.

SOCRATES: Do you see, Meno, what advances he has made in his power of recollection? He did not know at first, and he does not know now, what is the side of a figure of eight

feet: but then he thought that he knew, and answered confidently as if he knew, and had no difficulty; now he has a difficulty, and neither know nor fancies that he knows.

MENO: True.

SOCRATES: Is he not better off in knowing his ignorance?

MENO: I think that he is.

SOCRATES: If we have made him doubt, and given him the 'torpedo's shock,' have we done him any harm?

MENO: I think not.

SOCRATES: We have certainly, as would seem, assisted him in some degree to the discovery of the truth; and now he will wish to remedy his ignorance, but then he would have been ready to tell all the world again and again that the double space should have a double side.

MENO: True.

SOCRATES: But do you suppose that he would ever have enquired into or learned what he fancied that he knew, though he was really ignorant of it, until he had fallen into perplexity under the idea that he did not know, and had desired to know?

MENO: I think not, Socrates.

SOCRATES: Then he was the better for the torpedo's touch?

MENO: I think so.

Although the slave boy has never been educated, he possesses innate knowledge of geometry. Socrates claims that all he is doing is helping the slave bring to consciousness that which he already knows. That is, education is recollection of innate ideas.

SOCRATES: Mark now the farther development. I shall only ask him, and not teach him, and he shall share the enquiry with me: and do you watch and see if you find me telling or explaining anything to him, instead of eliciting his opinion. Tell me, boy, is not this a square of four feet which I have drawn?

BOY: Yes.

SOCRATES: And now I add another square equal to the former one?

BOY: Yes.

SOCRATES: And a third, which is equal to either of them?

BOY: Yes.

SOCRATES: Suppose that we fill up the vacant corner?

BOY: Very good.

SOCRATES: Here, then, there are four equal spaces?

BOY: Yes.

SOCRATES: And how many times larger is this space than this other?

BOY: Four times.

SOCRATES: But it ought to have been twice only, as you will remember.

BOY: True.

SOCRATES: And does not this line, reaching from corner to corner, bisect each of these spaces? [BDEF]

BOY: Yes.

SOCRATES: And are there not here four equal lines which contain this space? [BD, DE, EF, and FB]

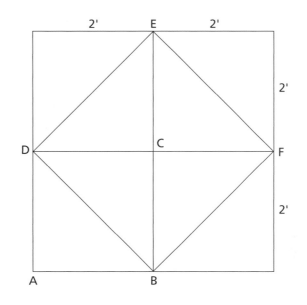

BOY: There are.

SOCRATES: Look and see how much this space is.

BOY: I do not understand.

SOCRATES: Has not each interior line cut off half of the four spaces? [BD, DE, EF, and FB]

BOY: Yes.

SOCRATES: And how many spaces are there in this section? [BDEF]

BOY: Four.

SOCRATES: And how many in this? [ABCD]

BOY: Two.

SOCRATES: And four is how many times two?

BOY: Twice.

SOCRATES: And this space is of how many feet? [BDEF]

BOY: Of eight feet.

SOCRATES: And from what line do you get this figure?

BOY: From this. [BDEF]

SOCRATES: That is, from the line which extends from corner to corner of the figure of four feet?

BOY: Yes.

SOCRATES: And that is the line which the learned call the diagonal. And if this is the proper name, then you, Meno's slave, are prepared to affirm that the double space is the square of the diagonal?

BOY: Certainly, Socrates.

SOCRATES: What do you say of him, Meno? Were not all these answers given out of his own head?

MENO: Yes, they were all his own.

SOCRATES: And yet, as we were just now saying, he did not know?

MENO: True.

SOCRATES: But still he had in him those notions of his—had he not?

MENO: Yes.

SOCRATES: Then he who does know may still have true notions of that which he does not know?

MENO: He has.

SOCRATES: And at present these notions have just been stirred up in him, as in a dream; but if he were frequently asked the same questions, in different forms, he would know as well as any one at last?

MENO: I dare say.

SOCRATES: Without any one teaching him he will recover his knowledge for himself, if he is only asked questions?

MENO: Yes.

SOCRATES: And this spontaneous recovery of knowledge in him is recollection?

MENO: True.

SOCRATES: And this knowledge which he now has must he not either have acquired or always possessed?

MENO: Yes.

SOCRATES: But if he always possessed this knowledge he would always have known; or if he has acquired the knowledge he could not have acquired it in this life, unless he has been taught geometry; for he may be made to do the same with all geometry and every other branch of knowledge. Now, has any one ever taught him all this? You must know about him, if, as you say, he was born and bred in your house.

MENO: And I am certain that no one ever did teach him.

SOCRATES: And yet he has the knowledge?

MENO: The fact, Socrates, is undeniable.

SOCRATES: But if he did not acquire the knowledge in this life, then he must have had and learned it at some other time?

MENO: Clearly he must.

SOCRATES: Which must have been the time when he was not a man?

MENO: Yes.

SOCRATES: And if there have been always true thoughts in him, both at the time when he was and was not a man, which only need to be awakened into knowledge by putting questions to him, his soul must have always possessed this knowledge, for he always either was or was not a man?

MENO: Obviously.

SOCRATES: And if the truth of all things always existed in the soul, then the soul is immortal. Wherefore be of good cheer, and try to recollect what you do not know, or rather what you do not remember.

MENO: I feel, somehow, that I like what you are saying.

SOCRATES: And I, Meno, like what I am saying. Some things I have said of which I am not altogether confident. But that we shall be better and braver and less helpless if we think that we ought to enquire, than we should have been if we indulged in the idle fancy that there was no knowing and no use in seeking to know what we do not know;—that is a theme upon which I am ready to fight, in word and deed, to the utmost of my power.

So what is Plato's answer to the question "How is learning possible?" set forth in the puzzle mentioned at the beginning of this reading? It is this: We possess innate knowledge of the Forms. Learning consists in having a suitable guide, a teacher, to bring out the best in us, to question and stimulate us like a midwife inducing labor, until at last we give birth to knowledge. The teacher has no truths of his own to impart but helps us recover knowledge that we must have learned in a previous existence.

Is Plato correct? How good is Socrates' argument in this dialogue? Has he proven his point? Has the slave recollected knowledge that he had learned in a previous existence but forgotten?

The Ascent to Knowledge

Next we examine Plato's ascent to knowledge of the highest forms. In *The Republic,* he distinguishes two possible approaches to knowledge: sense perception and reason. We may call these the *empirical* way and the *rational* way. Sense perception has as its object the fleeting world of particular objects, which appear differently at different times. Hence, it is an unstable relationship, yielding only fallible opinion, but not knowledge, not ultimate Truth. Reason, however, grasps that which is absolute, unchanging, and universal—the Forms (or Ideas, as they are called in this translation). Sense perception causes us to see specific triangles, horses, chairs, and people, but reason gives us understanding of the universal triangle, horse, chair, and person.

Sense perception may be the starting point for knowledge, but it can never itself bring us to the realm of reality, the world of being. By itself it leaves us in the realm of appearances, in the world of becoming:

> As for the man who believes in beautiful things, but does not believe in Beauty itself nor is able to follow if one leads him to the understanding of it—do you think his life is real or a dream? Is it not a dream? For whether a man be asleep or awake, is it not dream-like to mistake the image for the real thing?

The role of the philosopher is to use the world of sense perception in order to lead the soul out of the dreamlike state of becoming and into the real world of being.

In this selection, Plato describes a dialogue between his teacher, Socrates, and his (Plato's) brother, Glaucon, in which Socrates describes the nature of the Forms and the four levels of cognition, which each person must ascend if he or she is to attain knowledge and the liberation of the soul.

THE ASCENT TO KNOWLEDGE

Knowledge Versus Opinion

[Socrates has been arguing that unless philosophers become rulers or rulers become philosophers there will never be a truly good State. Glaucon now asks who the true philosophers are? Socrates, to whom the "I" refers, gives his answer in terms of possession of knowledge as opposed to mere opinion.]

GLAUCON: Who then are the true philosophers?

SOCRATES: Those who are lovers of the vision of truth.

GLAUCON: That is also good; but I should like to know what you mean?

SOCRATES: To another I might have a difficulty in explaining; but I am sure that you will admit a proposition which I am about to make.

GLAUCON: What is the proposition?

SOCRATES: That since beauty is the opposite of ugliness, they are two?

GLAUCON: Certainly.

SOCRATES: And inasmuch as they are two, each of them is one?

GLAUCON: True again.

SOCRATES: And of just and unjust, good and evil, and of every other class, the same remark holds; taken singly, each of them is one; but from the various combinations of them with actions and things and with one another, they are seen in all sorts of lights and appear many?

GLAUCON: Very true.

SOCRATES: And this is the distinction which I draw between the sight-loving, art-loving, practical class and those of whom I am speaking, and who are alone worthy of the name of philosophers.

GLAUCON: How do you distinguish them?

SOCRATES: The lovers of sounds and sights are, as I conceive, fond of tones and colors and forms and all the artificial products that are made out of them, but their mind is incapable of seeing or loving absolute beauty.

GLAUCON: True.

SOCRATES: Few are they who are able to attain to the sight of this. And the man who believes in beautiful things but does not believe in absolute beauty, nor is able to follow if one lead him to an understanding of it—do you think that his life is real or a dream? Is it not a dream? For whether a man be asleep or awake is it not dream-like to mistake the image for the real thing?

GLAUCON: I should certainly say that such an one was dreaming.

SOCRATES: But take the case of the other, who recognizes the existence of absolute beauty and is able to distinguish the idea from the objects which participate in the idea, neither putting the objects in the place of the idea nor the idea in the place of the objects—is he a dreamer, or is he awake?

GLAUCON: He is wide awake.

SOCRATES: And may we not say that the mind of the one who knows has knowledge and that the mind of the other, who opines only, has opinion?

GLAUCON: Certainly.

SOCRATES: But suppose that the latter should quarrel with us and dispute our statement, can we administer any soothing cordial or advice to him, without revealing to him that there is sad disorder in his wit?

From: Plato, *The Republic*, trans. Benjamin Jowett (Oxford, UK: Oxford University Press, 1896). I have edited the dialogue for pedagogical purposes.

GLAUCON: We must certainly offer him some good advice.

SOCRATES: Come, then, and let us think of something to say to him. Shall we begin by assuring him that he is welcome to any knowledge which he may have, and that we rejoice at his having it? But we should like to ask him a question? Does he who has knowledge know something or nothing?

GLAUCON: I answer that he knows something.

SOCRATES: Something that is or is not?*

GLAUCON: Something that is; for how can that which is not ever be known?

SOCRATES: And are we assured, after looking at the matter from many points of view, that absolute being is or may be absolutely known, but that the utterly non-existent is utterly unknown?

GLAUCON: Nothing can be more certain.

SOCRATES: Good. But if there be anything which is of such a nature as to be and not to be, that will have a place intermediate between pure being and the absolute negation of being?

GLAUCON: Yes, between them.

SOCRATES: And, as knowledge corresponds to being and ignorance of necessity to not-being, we must find something intermediate between ignorance and knowledge for that which lies between them, if there is such a thing.

GLAUCON: Yes.

SOCRATES: Would you admit the existence of opinion?

GLAUCON: No question.

SOCRATES: Is opinion the same faculty as knowledge or is it a different faculty?

GLAUCON: A different faculty?

SOCRATES: Then opinion and knowledge have to do with different kinds of matter corresponding to this difference of faculties?

GLAUCON: Yes.

SOCRATES: And knowledge is relative to being and knows being. But before I proceed further I will make a division. I will begin by placing faculties in a class by themselves: they are powers in us, and in all other things, by which we do as we do. Sight and hearing, for example, I should call faculties. Have I clearly explained the class which I mean?

GLAUCON: Yes, I quite understand.

SOCRATES: Then let me tell you my view about them. I do not see the faculties, and therefore the distinctions of shape, color, and the like, which enable me to discern the differences of some things, do not apply to them. In speaking of a faculty I think only of its sphere and its result; and that which has the same sphere and the same result I call the same faculty, but that which has another sphere and another result I call different. Would that be your way of speaking?

GLAUCON: Yes.

[*Note that Plato is referring to the Ideas, which have a true existence, as opposed to the objects of sense perception, which have only appearance and dwell in the zone of becoming, between being and nothingness.—Ed.]

SOCRATES: Would you say that knowledge is a faculty, or in what class would you place it?

GLAUCON: Certainly knowledge is a faculty, and the mightiest of all faculties.

SOCRATES: And is opinion also a faculty?

GLAUCON: Certainly; for opinion is that with which we are able to form an opinion.

SOCRATES: And yet you were acknowledging a little while ago that knowledge is not the same as opinion?

GLAUCON: Why, yes; how can any reasonable being ever identify that which is infallible with that which errs?

SOCRATES: An excellent answer, proving that we are quite conscious of a distinction between them.

GLAUCON: Yes.

SOCRATES: Then knowledge and opinion having distinct powers have also distinct spheres or subject-matters?

GLAUCON: That is certain.

SOCRATES: Being is the sphere or subject-matter of knowledge, and knowledge is to know the nature of being?

GLAUCON: Yes.

SOCRATES: And opinion is to have an opinion?

GLAUCON: Yes.

SOCRATES: And do we know what we opine? or is the subject-matter of opinion the same as the subject-matter of knowledge?

GLAUCON: Nay, that has been already disproven; if difference in faculty implies difference in the sphere or subject-matter, and if, as we were saying, opinion and knowledge are distinct faculties, then the sphere of knowledge and of opinion can not be the same.

SOCRATES: Then if being is the subject-matter of knowledge, something else must be the subject-matter of opinion?

GLAUCON: Yes, something else.

SOCRATES: Well then, is not-being the subject-matter of opinion? or, rather, how can there be an opinion at all about not-being? Reflect: when a man has an opinion, has he not an opinion about something? Can he have an opinion which is an opinion about nothing?

GLAUCON: Impossible.

SOCRATES: He who has an opinion has an opinion about some one thing?

GLAUCON: Yes.

SOCRATES: And not-being is not one thing but, properly speaking, nothing.

GLAUCON: True.

SOCRATES: Of not-being, ignorance was assumed to be the necessary correlative; of being, knowledge?

GLAUCON: True.

SOCRATES: Then opinion is not concerned either with being or with not-being?

GLAUCON: Not with either.

SOCRATES: And can therefore neither be ignorance nor knowledge?

GLAUCON: That seems to be true.

SOCRATES: But is opinion to be sought without and beyond either of them, in a greater clearness than knowledge, or in a greater darkness than ignorance?

GLAUCON: In neither.

SOCRATES: Then I suppose that opinion appears to you to be darker than knowledge, but lighter than ignorance?

GLAUCON: Both; and in no small degree.

SOCRATES: And also to be within and between them?

GLAUCON: Yes.

SOCRATES: Then you would infer that opinion is intermediate.

GLAUCON: No question.

SOCRATES: But were we not saying before, that if anything appeared to be of a sort which is and is not at the same time, that sort of thing would appear also to lie in the interval between pure being and absolute not-being; and that the corresponding faculty is neither knowledge nor ignorance, but will be found in the interval between them?

GLAUCON: True.

SOCRATES: And in that interval there has now been discovered something which we call opinion?

GLAUCON: There has.

SOCRATES: Then what remains to be discovered is the object which partakes equally of the nature of being and not-being, and can not rightly be termed either, pure and simple; this unknown term, when discovered, we may truly call the subject of opinion, and assign each to their proper faculty,—the extremes to the faculties of the extremes and the mean to the faculty of the mean.

GLAUCON: True.

SOCRATES: This being premised, I would ask the gentleman who is of opinion that there is no absolute or unchangeable idea of beauty—in whose opinion the beautiful is the manifold—he, I say, your lover of beautiful sights, who can not bear to be told that the beautiful is one, and the just is one, or that anything is one—to him I would appeal, saying, Will you be so very kind, sir, as to tell us whether, of all these beautiful things, there is one which will not be found ugly; or of the just, which will not be found unjust; or of the holy, which will not also be unholy?

GLAUCON: No; the beautiful will in some point of view be found ugly; and the same is true of the rest.

SOCRATES: And may not the many which are doubles be also halves?—doubles, that is, of one thing, and halves of another?

GLAUCON: Quite true.

SOCRATES: And things great and small, heavy and light, as they are termed, will not be denoted by these any more than by the opposite names?

GLAUCON: True; both these and the opposite names will always attach to all of them.

SOCRATES: And can any one of those many things which are called by particular names be said to be this rather than not to be this?

GLAUCON: They are like the punning riddles which are asked at feasts or the children's puzzle about the eunuch aiming at the bat, with what he hit him, as they say in the puzzle, and upon what the bat was sitting. The individual objects of which I am speaking are also a riddle, and have a double sense: nor can you fix them in your mind, either as being or not-being, or both, or neither.

SOCRATES: Then what will you do with them? Can they have a better place than between being and not-being? For they are clearly not in greater darkness or negation than not-being, or more full of light and existence than being.

GLAUCON: That is quite true.

SOCRATES: Thus then we seem to have discovered that the many ideas which the multitude entertain about the beautiful and about all other things are tossing about in some region which is half-way between pure being and pure not-being?

GLAUCON: We have.

SOCRATES: Yes; and we had before agreed that anything of this kind which we might find was to be described as matter of opinion, and not as matter of knowledge; being the intermediate flux which is caught and detained by the intermediate faculty.

GLAUCON: Quite true.

SOCRATES: Then those who see the many beautiful, and who yet neither see absolute beauty, nor can follow any guide who points the way thither; who see the many just, and not absolute justice, and the like,—such persons may be said to have opinion but not knowledge?

GLAUCON: That is certain.

SOCRATES: But those who see the absolute and eternal and immutable may be said to know, and not to have opinion only?

GLAUCON: Neither can that be denied.

SOCRATES: The one love and embrace the subjects of knowledge, the other those of opinion? The latter are the same, as I dare say you will remember, who listened to sweet sounds and gazed upon fair colors, but would not tolerate the existence of absolute beauty.

GLAUCON: Yes, I remember.

SOCRATES: Shall we then be guilty of any impropriety in calling them lovers of opinion rather than lovers of wisdom, and will they be very angry for thus describing them?

GLAUCON: I shall tell them not to be angry; no man should be angry at what is true.

SOCRATES: But those who love the truth in each thing are to be called lovers of wisdom and not lovers of opinion.

GLAUCON: Assuredly....

The Objects of Knowledge

SOCRATES: ... I must first come to an understanding with you, and remind you of what I have mentioned in the course of this discussion, and at many other times.

GLAUCON: What?

SOCRATES: The old story, that there is a many beautiful and a many good, and so of other things which we describe and define; to all of them the term "many" is applied.

GLAUCON: True.

SOCRATES: And there is an absolute beauty and an absolute good, and of other things to which the term "many" is applied there is an absolute; for they may be brought under a single idea, which is called the essence of each.

GLAUCON: Very true.

SOCRATES: The many, as we say, are seen but not known, and the ideas are known but not seen.

GLAUCON: Exactly.

SOCRATES: And what is the organ with which we see the visible things?

GLAUCON: The sight.

SOCRATES: And with the hearing, we hear, and with the other senses perceive the other objects of sense?

GLAUCON: True.

SOCRATES: But have you remarked that sight is by far the most costly and complex piece of workmanship which the artificer of the senses ever contrived?

GLAUCON: No, I never have.

SOCRATES: Then reflect: has the ear or voice need of any third or additional nature in order that the one may be able to hear and the other to be heard?

GLAUCON: Nothing of the sort.

SOCRATES: No, indeed; and the same is true of most, if not all, the other senses—you would not say that any of them requires such an addition?

GLAUCON: Certainly not.

SOCRATES: But you see that without the addition of some other nature there is no seeing or being seen?

GLAUCON: How do you mean?

SOCRATES: Sight being, as I conceive, in the eyes, and he who has eyes wanting to see; color being also present in them, still unless there be a third nature specially adapted to the purpose, the owner of the eyes will see nothing and the colors will be invisible.

GLAUCON: Of what nature are you speaking?

SOCRATES: Of that which you term "light."

GLAUCON: True.

SOCRATES: Noble, then, is the bond which links together sight and visibility, and great beyond other bonds by no small difference of nature; for light is their bond, and light is no ignoble thing?

GLAUCON: Nay, the reverse of ignoble.

SOCRATES: And which of the gods in heaven would you say was the lord of this element? Whose is that light which makes the eye to see perfectly and the visible to appear?

GLAUCON: You mean the sun, as you and all mankind say.

SOCRATES: May not the relation of sight to this deity be described as follows?

GLAUCON: How?

SOCRATES: Neither sight nor the eye in which sight resides is the sun?

GLAUCON: No.

SOCRATES: Yet of all the organs of sense the eye is the most like the sun?

GLAUCON: By far the most like.

SOCRATES: And the power which the eye possesses is a sort of effluence which is dispensed from the sun?

GLAUCON: Exactly.

SOCRATES: Then the sun is not sight, but the author of sight who is recognized by sight?

GLAUCON: True.

SOCRATES: And this is he whom I call the child of the good, whom the good begat in his own likeness, to be in the visible world, in relation to sight and the things of sight, what the good is in the intellectual world in relation to mind and the things of mind:

GLAUCON: Will you be a little more explicit?

SOCRATES: Why, you know, that the eyes, when a person directs them towards objects on which the light of day is no longer shining, but the moon and stars only, see dimly, and are nearly blind; they seem to have no clearness of vision in them?

GLAUCON: Very true.

SOCRATES: But when they are directed towards objects on which the sun shines, they see clearly and there is sight in them?

GLAUCON: Certainly.

SOCRATES: And the soul is like the eye: when resting upon that on which truth and being shine, the soul perceives and understands, and is radiant with intelligence; but when turned towards the twilight of becoming and perishing, then she has opinion only, and goes blinking about, and is first of one opinion and then of another, and seems to have no intelligence?

GLAUCON: Just so.

SOCRATES: Now, that which imparts truth to the known and the power of knowing to the knower is what I would have you term the idea of good, and this you will deem to be the cause of science, and of truth in so far as the latter becomes the subject of knowledge; beautiful too, as are both truth and knowledge, you will be right in esteeming this other nature as more beautiful than either; and, as in the previous instance, light and sight may be truly said to be like the sun, and yet not to be the sun, so in this other sphere, science and truth may be deemed to be like the good, but not the good; the good has a place of honor yet higher.

GLAUCON: What a wonder of beauty that must be, which is the author of science and truth, and yet surpasses them in beauty; for you surely can not mean to say that pleasure is the good?

SOCRATES: God forbid; but may I ask you to consider the image in another point of view?

GLAUCON: In what point of view?

SOCRATES: You would say, would you not, that the sun is not only the author of visibility in all visible things, but of generation and nourishment and growth, though he himself is not generation?

GLAUCON: Certainly.

SOCRATES: In like manner the good may be said to be not only the author of knowledge to all things known, but of their being and essence, and yet the good is not essence, but far exceeds essence in dignity and power.

GLAUCON: (With a ludicrous earnestness) By the light of heaven, how amazing!

The Four Levels of Knowledge: The Line

The Line

D
Ideas: *Reason*
(Forms)

C
Mathematics:
Intelligence

B

Physical
Phenomena:
Beliefs

A

Images:
Imagination

SOCRATES: You have to imagine that there are two ruling powers, and that one of them, the good, is set over the intellectual world, the other, the Sun, over the visible world. May I suppose that you have this distinction of the visible and intelligible fixed in your mind?

GLAUCON: I have.

SOCRATES: Now take a line which has been cut into two unequal parts, and divide each of them again in the same proportion, and suppose the two main divisions to answer, one to the visible and the other to the intelligible, and then compare the subdivisions in respect to their clearness and want of clearness, and you will find that the first section (A) in the sphere of the visible consists of images. And by images I mean, in the first place, shadows, and in the second place, reflections in water and in solid, smooth and polished bodies and the like. Do you understand?

GLAUCON: Yes, I understand?

SOCRATES: Imagine now, the other section (B), of which this is only the resemblance, to include the animals which we see, and everything that grows or is made. Would you not admit that both the sections of this division have different degrees of truth, and that the copy is to the original as the sphere of opinion is to the sphere of knowledge?

GLAUCON: Most undoubtedly.

SOCRATES: Next we proceed to consider the manner in which the sphere of the intellectual is to be divided. There are two subdivisions, in the lower (C) of which the soul uses the figures given by the former division as images; the inquiry can only be hypothetical, and instead of going upwards to a principle descends to the other end; in the higher of the two (D), the soul passes out of hypotheses, and goes up to a principle which is above hypotheses, making no use of images as in the former case, but proceeding only in and through the ideas themselves.

GLAUCON: I do not quite understand your meaning.

SOCRATES: Then I will try again; you will understand me better when I have made some preliminary remarks. [Regarding C], you are aware that students of geometry, arithmetic, and the kindred sciences assume the odd and the even and the figures and three kinds of angles and the like in their several branches of science; these are their hypotheses, which they and everybody are supposed to know, and therefore they do not deign to give any account of them either to themselves or others; but they begin with them, and go on until they arrive at last, and in a consistent manner, at their conclusion.

GLAUCON: Yes, I know.

SOCRATES: And do you not know also that although they make use of the visible forms and reason about them, they are thinking not of these, but of the ideals which they resemble; not of the figures which they draw, but of the absolute square and the absolute diameter, and so on. The forms which they draw or make are actual things, which have shadows and reflections in water of their own, but now they serve in turn as images, but the soul is really seeking to behold the things themselves, which can only be seen with the eye of the mind.

GLAUCON: That is true.

SOCRATES: And of this I spoke as the intelligible (C), although in the search after it the soul is compelled to use hypotheses; not ascending to a first principle, because she is unable to rise above the region of hypothesis, but employing the objects of which the shadows below are resemblances in their turn as images, they having in relation to the shadows and reflections of them a greater distinctness, and therefore a higher value.

GLAUCON: I understand, that you are speaking of the province of geometry and the sister arts.

SOCRATES: When I speak of the other division of the intelligible (D), you will understand me to speak of that other sort of knowledge which reason herself attains by the power of dialectic, using the hypotheses not as first principles, but only as hypotheses—that is to say, as steps and points of departure into a world which is above hypotheses, in order that she may soar beyond them to the first principle of the whole; and clinging to this and then to that which depends on this, by successive steps she descends again without the aid of any sensible object, from ideas, through ideas, and in ideas she ends.

GLAUCON: I understand you. Not perfectly, for you seem to me to be describing a task which is really tremendous; but at any rate, I understand you to say that knowledge and being, which the science of dialectic contemplates, are clearer than the notions of the arts, as they are termed, which proceed from hypotheses only. These are also contemplated by the understanding, and not by the senses: yet, because they start from hypotheses and do not ascend to a principle, those who contemplate them appear to you not to exercise the higher reason upon them, although when a first principle is added to them they are cognizable by the higher reason. And the habit which is concerned with geometry and the cognate sciences I suppose that you would term understanding and not reason, as being intermediate between opinion and reason.

SOCRATES: You have quite conceived my meaning; and now, corresponding to these four divisions, let there be four faculties in the soul—Reason answering to the highest (D), Understanding to the second (C), Belief (or conviction) to the third (B), and Imaging (or perception of shadows) to the last (A). And let us suppose that the several faculties have clearness in the same degree that their objects have truth.

GLAUCON: I understand and give my assent, and accept this arrangement of the matter.

Socrates illustrates his doctrine through one of the most famous of all parables, "The Allegory of the Cave."

THE ALLEGORY OF THE CAVE

SOCRATES: And now, let me show in a figure how far our nature is enlightened or unenlightened:—Behold! human beings living in an underground den, which has a mouth open towards the light and reaching all along the den; here they have been from their childhood, and have their legs and necks chained so that they can not move, and can only see before them, being prevented by the chains from turning round their

From: Plato, *The Republic*, trans. Benjamin Jowett (Oxford, UK: Oxford University Press, 1896). I have edited the dialogue for pedagogical purposes.

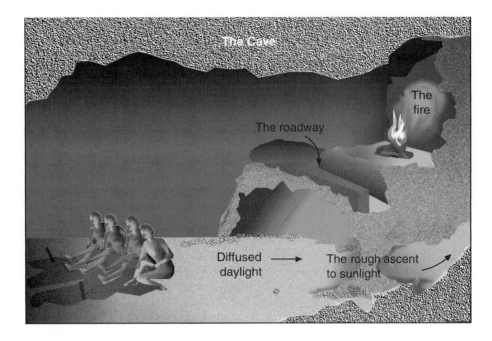

heads. Above and behind them a fire is blazing at a distance, and between the fire and the prisoners there is a raised way; and you will see, if you look, a low wall built along the way, like the screen which marionette players have in front of them, over which they show the puppets.

GLAUCON: I see.

SOCRATES: And do you see men passing along the wall carrying all sorts of vessels, and statues and figures of animals made of wood and stone and various materials, which appear over the wall? Some of them are talking, others silent.

GLAUCON: You have shown me a strange image, and they are strange prisoners.

SOCRATES: Like ourselves; and they see only their own shadows, or the shadows of one another, which the fire throws on the opposite wall of the cave?

GLAUCON: True; how could they see anything but the shadows if they were never allowed to move their heads?

SOCRATES: And of the objects which are being carried in like manner they would only see the shadows?

GLAUCON: Yes.

SOCRATES: And if they were able to converse with one another, would they not suppose that they were naming what was actually before them?

GLAUCON: Very true.

SOCRATES: And suppose further that the prison had an echo which came from the other side, would they not be sure to fancy when one of the passers-by spoke that the voice which they heard came from the passing shadow?

GLAUCON: No question.

SOCRATES: To them, the truth would be literally nothing but the shadows of the images.

GLAUCON: That is certain.

SOCRATES: And now look again, and see what will naturally follow if the prisoners are released and disabused of their error. At first, when any of them is liberated and compelled suddenly to stand up and turn his neck round and walk and look towards the light, he will suffer sharp pains; the glare will distress him, and he will be unable to see the realities of which in his former state he had seen the shadows; and then conceive some one saying to him, that what he saw before was an illusion, but that now, when he is approaching nearer to being and his eye is turned towards more real existence, he has a clearer vision,—what will be his reply? And you may further imagine that his instructor is pointing to the objects as they pass and requiring him to name them,—will he not be perplexed? Will he not fancy that the shadows which he formerly saw are truer than the objects which are now shown to him?

GLAUCON: Far truer.

SOCRATES: And if he is compelled to look straight at the light, will he not have a pain in his eyes which will make him turn away to take refuge in the objects of vision which he can see, and which he will conceive to be in reality clearer than the things which are now being shown to him?

GLAUCON: True.

SOCRATES: And suppose once more, that he is reluctantly dragged up a steep and rugged ascent, and held fast until he is forced into the presence of the sun himself, is he not likely to be pained and irritated? When he approaches the light his eyes will be dazzled, and he will not be able to see anything at all of what are now called realities.

GLAUCON: Not all in a moment.

SOCRATES: He will require to grow accustomed to the sight of the upper world. And first he will see the shadows best, next the reflections of men and other objects in the water, and then the objects themselves; then he will gaze upon the light of the moon and the stars and the spangled heaven; and he will see the sky and the stars by night better than the sun or the light of the sun by day?

GLAUCON: Certainly.

SOCRATES: Last of all he will be able to see the sun, and not mere reflections of him in the water, but he will see him in his own proper place, and not in another; and he will contemplate him as he is.

GLAUCON: Certainly.

SOCRATES: He will then proceed to argue that this is he who gives the season and the years, and is the guardian of all that is in the visible world, and in a certain way the cause of all things which he and his fellows have been accustomed to behold?

GLAUCON: Clearly, he would first see the sun and then reason about him.

SOCRATES: And when he remembered his old habitation, and the wisdom of the den and his fellow-prisoners, do you not suppose that he would felicitate himself on the change, and pity them?

GLAUCON: Certainly, he would.

SOCRATES: And if they were in the habit of conferring honors among themselves on those who were quickest to observe the passing shadows and to remark which of them went before, and which followed after, and which were together; and who were therefore best able to draw conclusions as to the future, do you think that he would care for such honors and glories, or envy the possessors of them? Would he not say with Homer,

> *[Better to be the poor servant of a poor master.]*

and to endure anything, rather than think as they do and live after their manner?

GLAUCON: Yes, I think that he would rather suffer anything than entertain these false notions and live in this miserable manner.

SOCRATES: Imagine once more, such an one coming suddenly out of the sun to be replaced in his old situation; would he not be certain to have his eyes full of darkness?

GLAUCON: To be sure.

SOCRATES: And if there were a contest, and he had to compete in measuring the shadows with the prisoners who had never moved out of the den, while his sight was still weak, and before his eyes had become steady (and the time which would be needed to acquire this new habit of sight might be very considerable), would he not be ridiculous? Men would say of him that up he went and down he came without his eyes; and that it was better not even to think of ascending; and if any one tried to loose another and lead him up to the light, let them only catch the offender, and they would put him to death.

What is the point of this parable? You might pause to ask yourself that question before continuing with Plato's explanation.

SOCRATES: This allegory is connected to the previous argument about the ascent of knowledge. The prison-house-cave is the world of sight; the light of the fire is the sun; and the journey upwards is the ascent of the soul into the intellectual world. My view is that in the world of knowledge the idea of the Good appears last of all, and is seen only with great effort; and when seen, is also inferred to be the universal author of all things beautiful and right, parent of light and of the lord of light in this visible world [the sun], and the immediate source of reason and truth in the intellectual; and that this is the power upon which he who would act rationally either in public or private life must have his eye fixed.

GLAUCON: I agree, as far as I am able to understand you.

SOCRATES: Moreover, you must not wonder that those who attain to this beatific vision are unwilling to descend to human affairs; for their souls are ever hastening into the upper world where they desire to dwell; which desire of theirs is very natural, if our allegory is to be trusted.

GLAUCON: Yes, very natural.

Socrates argues that enlightened people are very bad at mundane affairs like the casuistries of legal systems—activities he compares to the shadows in the cave:

SOCRATES: Will you be surprised if one who passes from divine contemplation to the evil state of man, if, while his eyes are blinking and before he has become accustomed to the surrounding darkness of the cave, he is compelled to fight in law courts or in other places, about the images or shadows of the images of justice, and is trying to meet the demands of those who have never seen absolute justice?

GLAUCON: I will not be surprised at all.

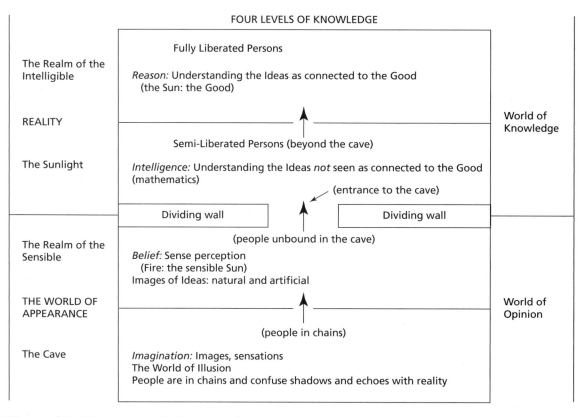

Figure 5.1 The relationship between the ascent to knowledge and the allegory of the cave

Figure 5.1 illustrates the relationship between the ascent of knowledge and the allegory of the cave. Salvation of the soul is found in recapturing a vision of the Forms, especially the Form of the Good, the highest Form. In the *Phaedrus* (247c), Plato writes of salvation consisting in the growth of spiritual wings, which takes place through mystic contemplation of the Forms:

> But of the place beyond heaven no one of our poets has yet sung nor will ever sing in a manner worthy. It is as follows, for one must dare to speak the truth, especially when talking of the true: in that place truly existent reality dwells colorless, shapeless, and intangible. As the object of true knowledge it is perceived only by that capacity for wisdom which is the pilot of the soul. The thought of the gods, matured by pure knowledge and wisdom, and that of every soul concerned to receive what is akin to it, seeing Being at last, rejoices, is nurtured by the contemplation of the true and is happy until it is brought back by the revolving circle to the same place. While thus going round it beholds justice itself, moderation itself and knowledge—not the knowledge that comes to be or that exists in another thing of those we

call real, but that which is truly knowledge in that which truly is. And feasting on the contemplation of the other things that likewise truly are, diving back into the inner heaven, the soul goes homeward.[4]

The theory of the Forms is the first great speculative metaphysical theory in Western philosophy. It explains the world and all our experience by reference to a transcendent realm. Together with Plato's idea of the ascent of the soul, it constitutes an exciting idealist way of salvation, salvation through knowledge, not faith. It makes reason the highest capacity in human nature, and it reduces the physical, the body, to a very low state—of appearance rather than reality. It has inspired many to a more spiritual way of life. But, the question is, Is it true?

Critique of the Forms

There are problems, of course, with the theory of Forms. One problem is simply that the theory seems to presuppose that every noun and adjective must have something it names. But the critic asks, why can't words simply be functional, helping us to communicate? Recall Lewis Carroll's *Through the Looking Glass:*

> "Just look along the road, and tell me if you can see either of the messengers," said the King.
> "I can see nobody on the road," said Alice
> "I only wish I had such eyes," the King remarked in a fretful tone. "To be able to see Nobody! and at that distance too! Why, it's as much as I can do to see real people, by this light."
> [The messenger arrives.]
> "Who did you pass on the road?" the King went on, holding out his hand to the Messenger for some more hay.
> "Nobody," said the Messenger.
> "Quite right," said the King; "the young lady saw him too. So of course Nobody walks slower than you."
> "I do my best," the Messenger said in a sullen tone. "I'm sure nobody walks much faster than I do!"
> "He can't do that," said the King, "or else he's have been here first."[5]

The king treats an indefinite, functional pronoun as a proper noun. In like manner, Plato and his followers have been accused of treating common nouns and adjectives as proper nouns. They seem to treat words like "good," "love," and "beautiful" like "Abraham Lincoln" and "Mary Jones."

There are three more problems with the theory of Forms; Plato himself noted these. The first problem has to do with "vile" things like dirt and mud. Do they have special forms too? The second problem has to do with whether the Forms can be divided into parts and so are not simple wholes after all. The third problem is called the *third-man argument*. Plato himself, being the honest philosopher he was, uses these criticisms against his own theory. The argument is contained in his dialogue *Parmenides* where the young Socrates is confronted with Parmenides' criticisms of the Forms.

PARMENIDES

PARMENIDES: What an admirable passion for argument you have, Socrates. Did you invent this distinction between the Forms themselves, on the one hand, and the things which partake of these, on the other? And do you believe that there is such an entity as Likeness itself apart from the likeness which we possess, and One, and all the lot of which you heard Zeno speaking just now?

SOCRATES: Yes, I do.

PARMENIDES: And such entities as an abstract Form of the Just, and of the Beautiful, and of the Good, and of all things of this sort too?

SOCRATES: Yes.

PARMENIDES: And what about a Form of Man apart from us and all like us, is there an abstract Form of Man, or of Fire, or even of Water?

SOCRATES: I have often been perplexed, Parmenides, about these, wondering whether I had to say the same about them or to say something else.

PARMENIDES: And are you perplexed too, Socrates, about the ones which would seem ridiculous, like Hair and Mud and Dirt or anything else which is very beastly and worthless—whether you have to say that there is a separate Form for each of these which is again different from what we have to do with?

SOCRATES: No, these things at any rate are as we see them and it would be quite absurd to believe that there is a Form for any of them. And yet I am sometimes troubled by the thought that the same thing may apply to all cases. Then whenever I find myself in this position, I run away from it, being afraid lest I should ruin myself by falling into some abyss of nonsense.

PARMENIDES: Because you are still young, Socrates, and philosophy has not yet got that grip on you which I believe it will get one day. Then you will not despise them, but now because of your youth you still take notice of what people think. Now tell me this. Do you believe as you say, that there are Forms, and that these other things which partake of them are named after them—for instance, that those which partake of Likeness become like, of Greatness great, of Beauty and Justice, beautiful and just?

SOCRATES: Absolutely.

PARMENIDES: Well then, does each individual which partakes partake of the whole Form or part of it? Or could there be some other kind of participation over and above these?

SOCRATES: How could there be?

PARMENIDES: So do you believe that the whole Form, being one, is in each of the many, or what?

SOCRATES: Yes it is, for what is to stop it being in them, Parmenides?

PARMENIDES: Then notwithstanding that it is one and the same it is simultaneously and as a whole in many separate entities, and so it would itself be separate from itself.

From: Plato, *Parmenides*, trans. Benjamin Jowett (Oxford, UK: Oxford University Press, 1896). I have edited the translation.

SOCRATES: No it would not, not if it were like day which is one and the same everywhere, is in many places at once, and is none the less not separate from itself. If it were like this with Forms each one though one and the same might be in the lot simultaneously.

PARMENIDES: Wonderful, Socrates. You make one and the same thing to be in many places simultaneously, just as if after spreading a sail over many people you were to say that one whole was over many. Or is this not what you are saying?

SOCRATES: Perhaps it is.

PARMENIDES: Would the whole sail be over each person or one part over one and one over another?

SOCRATES: Part over each.

PARMENIDES: Then, Socrates, the Forms themselves must be divisible into parts and what partakes of them would partake of a part; and so in each of these it would no longer be the whole Form but only part.

SOCRATES: So it appears.

PARMENIDES: Are you willing, Socrates, to say that the single Form is for us truly divided into parts and yet that it will still be one?

SOCRATES: No, I'm not.

PARMENIDES: No, for suppose you divide Largeness itself, then each of the many large things will be large by a smaller part of Largeness than Largeness itself, and will not appear unreasonable?

SOCRATES: Yes, of course.

PARMENIDES: And will anything, by acquiring a small part of the Equal, possess something by which—while it is less than the Equal itself—what has it will be equal to something else?

SOCRATES: That is impossible.

PARMENIDES: And suppose one of us has part of the Small, then the Small will be larger than this since this is a part of it, and so the Small itself will surely be larger. Yet that to which the subtracted part is added will be smaller, and not greater, than before.

SOCRATES: That can never be.

PARMENIDES: In what way will other things partake in these Forms of yours, Socrates, if they cannot partake either through parts or through wholes?

SOCRATES: Really, it seems difficult to decide what to say here.

PARMENIDES: How do you feel about this? I imagine your reason for believing in a single form in each case is this. When it seems to you that a number of things are large, there seems to be a certain single character which is the same when you look at them all. Hence, you think that largeness is a single thing.

SOCRATES: That's true.

PARMENIDES: But now take Largeness itself and the other things which are large. Suppose you look at all these in the same way in your mind's eye, will not yet another unity make its appearance—a Largeness by virtue of which they all appear large?

SOCRATES: So it would seem.

PARMENIDES: If so, a second Form of largeness will present itself, over and above Largeness itself and the things that share in it, and again, covering all these, yet another, which will make all of them large. So each of your forms will no longer be one, but an indefinite number.

Can you follow Parmenides' arguments? Regarding the first objection, Socrates has trouble accepting that hair, mud, and dirty things have special Forms. We may add manufactured goods such as computers and atom bombs—are there Forms of these objects? And what about negative ideas, such as injustice, error, and nonbeing? The second objection is, How can the whole Form be present in different objects and still remain one? If it doesn't retain its unity, we have a plurality once more, and the difficulty of accounting for plurality will be transferred to the world of Forms (the truly real world). Socrates suggests that the Forms may be like the day that is one yet everywhere present. Parmenides dismisses this. You might as well spread a sail over many people and say that one whole was over many. The sail obviously has parts. So by this analogy, the Forms must have parts too (which of course defeats their purpose).

The third objection is the most important, called, as we noted above, the third-man argument. Suppose we accept that *one* form of man accounts itself as well as for any particular man. But now, by the same one–many argument, there must be a third man (a second Form of man) to account for the fact that both the particular man and the original Form of man are accurately described as men. But then we need another Form (a third Form of man) to account for the fact that this second form accurately describes both the original Form and the particular man. A vicious regress follows. Something seems to have gone wrong.

We don't know whether the third-man argument or any other of these arguments convinced Plato, but they are never answered in his writings. Perhaps he thought the idea of the Forms sufficiently plausible that he held on to it despite the problems—much as a religious believer may concede problems with his or her beliefs about the existence of God but still maintain them. It is the mark of philosophical integrity to be able to admit that there are severe problems with your favorite theories. Can you think of solutions to the problems raised by Parmenides? If we reject the Forms, what are the implications? Must we become empiricists? We will continue the discussion of these metaphysical problems, especially that of dualism versus monism, in Part 5 (the body–mind problem), and we will examine rationalism versus empiricism in Part 4 (the theory of knowledge).

Summary

Plato sought to find the One in the Many, a unifying idea (the Form) that existed independently of objects in the world of appearances (the world of space and time) and in which those objects participated. All beautiful things are beautiful through the Form of the Beautiful. All equal things become equal through participating in the Form of the Equal. The Forms are divine, eternal, simple, immutable, and self-subsisting. The highest Form is the Good. Plato held that we had innate ideas of the Forms, and through suitable education we could find our way back to them. The way of the philosopher was to make his or her way out of the world of appearances (the cave) to the world of reality (the world of sunlight), wherein one participates in the Good. The theory of Forms has severe problems. Nevertheless, many philosophers have seen something cogent therein. Some have likened the Form of the Good to God, an idea we will entertain in Chapter 7.

FOR FURTHER REFLECTION

1. Discuss the nature of the Forms. Why was Plato led to devise this theory?

2. Discuss the four stages of the ascent to knowledge. Does Plato's scheme seem plausible? Why or why not?

3. Analyze "The Allegory of the Cave." What does Plato mean by it? Is the allegory a suggestive commentary on human existence?

4. What are the religious implications of Plato's thought? Can you see a mystic element in the passages included in this chapter? Look particularly at the quotation from the *Phaedrus.*

5. What is the puzzle about learning that Meno points out? Why does it seem impossible to learn anything? What is Socrates' response to the puzzle? How do we learn, and why is learning possible?

6. Describe the process by which the slave boy reaches the correct answer. Does he truly have innate knowledge of geometry? Has Socrates proved his point? Is there another way to explain this phenomenon?

7. Examine and critically discuss Parmenides' objections to the theory of the Forms.

8. Evaluate Plato's overall philosophy. How has it developed from its Socratic origins?

NOTES

1. Alfred North Whitehead, *Process and Reality* (1929; New York: Harper Torchbooks, 1960, reprint), 63. Thelma Z. Lavine elaborates on this:

Plato is the most celebrated, honored and revered of all the philosophers of the Western world. He lived in Athens twenty-four centuries ago, in the fourth century before Christ, and throughout history since then the praise of Plato has been expressed in figures of speech which compare with one another in their eloquence. He is said to be the greatest of the philosophers which Western civilization has produced; he is said to be the father of Western philosophy; the son of the god Apollo; a sublime dramatist and poet with a vision of beauty which enhances all human life; and mystic who, before Christ or St. Paul, beheld a transcendent realm of goodness, love, and beauty; he is said to be the greatest of the moralists and social philosophers of all time. The British philosopher and mathematician Alfred North Whitehead said of him that the history of Western philosophy is only a series of footnotes to Plato. And the American poet and philosopher Ralph Waldo Emerson said of him, "Plato is Philosophy, and Philosophy is Plato," and also, "Out of Plato comes all things that are still written and debated among men of thought" (T. Z. Lavine, *From Socrates to Sartre* [New York: Bantam Books, 1984], 9).

2. Aristotle *Metaphysics* 1078.

3. Plato *Phaedrus* 247 (Grube translation).

4. Ibid.

5. Lewis Carroll, *Through the Looking Glass* (Pan Books, 1947), 232f.

FOR FURTHER READING

By Plato

The Dialogues of Plato, 4th ed. Revised by D. J. Allan and H. E. Dale. Oxford, UK: Oxford University Press, 1953. Jowetts's translation is still among the best—literary and accurate.

Plato: The Collected Dialogues. Edited by Edith Hamilton and Huntington Cairns. Princeton, NJ: Princeton University Press, 1982. This complete set of Plato's dialogues is the best single-volume collection of his works. The translations are typically excellent.

Plato's Republic. Translated by G. M. A. Grube. Indianapolis: Hackett, 1980. This is the most accessible accurate translation available.

About Plato

Grube, G. M. A. *Plato's Thought.* London: Methuen, 1935. An insightful discussion of Plato's thought, especially of the Forms.

Ross, W. D. *Plato's Theory of Ideas.* Oxford, UK: Oxford University Press, 1951. This book traces the theory of the Forms from the early dialogues to the Laws. A brilliant analysis.

Taylor, A. E. *Plato: The Man and His Work.* London: Methuen, 1950. A splendid exposition of the entire Platonic corpus.

About the Period

Jones, W. T. *The Classical Mind.* New York: Harcourt, Brace. 1952. A helpful overview of the ancient Greeks and their culture.

Renault, Mary. *The Last of the Wine.* New York: Pantheon Books, 1956. A novel depicting Athens in the days of Socrates.

6 ✤ The Philosophy of Aristotle: Philosophical Realism

Reason is the true self of every person, since it is the supreme and better part. It will be strange, then, if he should choose not his own life, but some other's. . . . What is naturally proper to every creature is the highest and pleasantest for him. And so, to man, this will be the life of Reason, since Reason is, in the highest sense, a man's self.

(Nicomachean Ethics 1.7)[1]

It is evident that the state is a creation of nature, and that man is by nature a political animal.

(Politics 1.2)

Aristotle (384–322 BCE), Greek physician, biologist, tutor to Alexander the Great, and one of the most important philosophers who ever lived, wrote important treatises on every major subject in philosophy. He is the founder of formal logic. He founded the second university in Athens, the Lyceum. Plato was Aristotle's teacher in the Academy, where Aristotle studied and taught for 20 years. He wrote brilliantly on virtually every philosophical topic. Unfortunately, most of his works are lost, including his dialogues, which were said to be eloquent. What we have are his very technical works. They are a bit dry, highly qualified, and intricately argued, but a careful reading usually pays high dividends. I will discuss his general orientation in comparison to Plato and examine his views of human nature, especially as they appear in his major work, *Nicomachean Ethics* (hereafter abbreviated *NE*). In addition to his ethics, I will consider his ideas on the Good Life and the Ideal Human Being.

Plato and Aristotle

In Leonardo da Vinci's great painting *The School of Athens,* Plato and Aristotle stand together in the center of a group of philosophers, conversing, presumably about philosophy. Plato is pointing upwards to the heaven, as if to say, "That's where reality is." Aristotle has his hand flattened out before him, as if to counter his teacher, "No, reality is down here." Simply put, Plato was an idealist who took mathematics as his model and believed in a transcendent reality, the Forms, governed by the Form of the Good, whereas Aristotle was a realist who took biology as his working model for philosophy and produced a functionalist account of human nature and all reality. Let's look at the similarities and differences between these two great philosophers.

The relationship between Plato and Aristotle is complex. Antiochus of Ascalon, president of Plato's Academy two centuries after Plato's death, claimed that Plato and Aristotle held similar positions on ethics; Henry Sidgwick, the greatest ethical theorist of the 19th century agrees.[2]

There are similarities in their positions. Both Plato and Aristotle sought knowledge as a good in its own right. Both were *teleologists* in that they believed in a universal goal for all things, the Good or the *final cause.* In this they differ from modern science (nature knows no purposes), especially Darwinian evolution where chance or random selection and survival of the fittest replace rational order. Aristotle believed in teleology because of the regularity displayed in generation, astronomy, and physical behavior. Nature has unconscious purposes.

Both accept a functionalist account of ethics as linked with politics and whose purpose is to produce good citizens in a flourishing society. Both see reason as the essence of human nature (see the quotation at the head of this chapter), and both hold to a transcendent absolute. Plato's Form of the Good plays a roughly similar role as Aristotle's unmoved mover, who moves the world but is not itself moved. Both are rationalists who see reason at the heart of the human essence. However, both assume that moral insight is not simply a function of logical reasoning but depends on a proper relationship between reason and deeper aspects of the soul.

But the differences between Plato and Aristotle are enormous. Aristotle rejects Plato's notion of the Forms as divine patterns of all the types of things and relationships on Earth as well as the ontological dualism that underlies Plato's philosophy.

1. Aristotle's main disagreement with Plato is over the theory of the Forms. Aristotle criticizes it from various points of view: As a logician, he offers a different analysis of predication; as an ontologist and epistemologist, Aristotle argues that it is the concrete particular, not the universal or form that is substance in the primary sense and that provide the starting point in our investigation of form.

The Theory of Forms occurred to Plato because he was persuaded of the truth of Heraclitus' doctrine that all things accessible to the senses are always in a state of flux, so that if knowledge or thought is to have an object there must besides things accessible to the senses be certain other entities which persist; for there is no knowledge of things which are in a state of flux. Socrates occupied himself with the moral virtues, and was the first to look for general definitions in this area. There are two things which may fairly be ascribed to Socrates, arguments by analogy and general definitions, both of which are concerned with the starting point of knowledge. But whereas Socrates made neither the universal nor the definition exist separately, others gave them a separate existence and this was the sort of thing to which they gave the name of Forms. So for them it followed by almost the same argument that there are Forms for everything to which general words apply.[3]

2. As a physicist, Aristotle points out that the separate and transcendent forms are useless in accounting for change and coming into existence. Plato's Forms belong to the world of unchanging being, but the study of change involves the investigator of forms in the changing objects of the world of becoming. Aristotle shifted the focus from the study of pure, immutable being to physics, the study of nature (and natural change).

3. Whereas Plato viewed matter as evil and the mental as good and believed that humans had a soul that inhabited a material body, which in turn would be liberated from the body at death, Aristotle had no such metaphysical notions. The soul (*psyche*) is not a separate entity but the form of the person whose matter is the body. It is a function of the whole physical person. Reason is not a jewel in a corpse, as Plato held, but a distinguishing feature in a special kind of animal.

4. Aristotle also rejected Plato's theory of recollection and innate ideas and seems uninterested, if not skeptical, about life after death. Whereas for Plato, the Good is One, for Aristotle goodness is a functional concept, having to do with satisfying the *telos*, or purpose, of some natural or artificial being. Whereas, for the Socratic-Plato, virtue is knowledge, for Aristotle one can know the good but fail to do it. For Socrates and Plato, all evil is ignorance, but Aristotle accepts a notion of weakness of will, much like the theory found in St. Paul's account in Romans Chapter 7 ("The evil that I would not, that I do and the good that I would do, that I do not."). Evil can be committed through being in the grip of an emotion even though you know you ought not do what you are about to do.

5. Finally, the two philosophers differed on the nature of the relation of virtue to happiness. Socrates and Plato viewed moral virtue as a necessary and a sufficient condition for happiness so that even Socrates on the rack (a medieval torture device) is happy. The good person may be rejected, despised, tortured, ugly, sick, and poor but still be happy. Aristotle rejects such an idea as naive (*NE* 7.13). Morality is a necessary but not a sufficient condition for happiness. One also needs other external and internal goods for a completely good life. Externally, one needs moderate wealth, leisure, health, friends, a family, a well-managed state, good looks, and good luck. Internally, one must have a good upbringing, practical wisdom, and self-control. Given his emphasis on external goods, Socrates could not be considered happy on Aristotle's account.

Yet for all their differences, the similarities still remain equally impressive. Plato and Aristotle both believed that it is the universal Form that is knowable and that the world as a whole (and natural change in particular) exhibits order and purpose. Aristotle demythologizes Plato's otherworldly idealist metaphysics, but his purposefulness is still present in the Universe—in the nature of things.

This following represents the main comparison between the two great Greek philosophers:

Plato

An idealist who believed in the Forms and innate ideas. He was a dualist who believed in a soul within the body. He believed that reason was our primary guide to the Truth. He was mystical, loved ideas, and scorned the physical, empirical, and sensual. He had no gift or interest in material change. He loved myth and poetry despite his wanting to banish the poets. He was a supreme stylist: flowing, poetic, and elegant.

Aristotle

A realist who disbelieved in the Forms and innate ideas. He believed that the soul was only the Form of the human being. He believed that humans were rational animals and Forms were in objects. He was commonsensical and loved facts, physics, and scientific observation. He wanted to extract myth and symbol from philosophy (it angered him to see poetic metaphor substituted for rational explanation). He had a difficult style and wrote with terminological exactness.

Aristotle's Metaphysics

As we mentioned, Aristotle rejected Plato's idea of the forms and his radical dualism. The fundamental reality is the collection of things or substances that we experience daily. He never doubted the real world or that our common-sense knowledge was a good beginning for scientific investigation. Forms are not transcendent categories but the shape of a thing, one of its four causes. There were four causes in all: the material cause, the formal cause, the efficient cause, and the final cause (*telos*). To understand something, one needs to understand all four causes. Consider Donatello's statue of David, which is in Florence, Italy. The material cause is the bronze from which it is made. The formal cause is the shape of a nude young man, David. The efficient cause was Donatello and his sculpturing that produced the statue. The final cause was the purpose that the statue would serve—to function as a beautiful work of art. Or consider a natural object, an acorn. The material cause is the substance it's made of, the formal cause is its form, the efficient cause is the oak tree that produced it, and the final cause is the oak tree it will become under a process of natural growth. Aristotle applied this fourfold causal analysis to everything, but he also used it to infer to a higher transcendent reality.

There is, then, something which is always moved with an unceasing motion, which is motion in a circle; and this is plain not in theory only but in fact. Therefore the first heaven must be eternal. There is therefore also something which moves it. And since that which moves and is moved is intermediate, there is something which moves without being moved, being eternal, substance, and actuality. And the object of desire and the object of thought move in this way; they move without being moved. The primary objects of desire and of thought are the same. For the apparent good is the object of appetite, and the real good is the primary object of rational wish. But desire is consequent on opinion rather than opinion on desire; for the thinking is the starting-point. And thought is moved by the object of thought, and one of the two columns of opposites is in itself the object of thought; and in this, substance is first, and in substance, that which is simple and exists actually. (The one and the simple are not the same; for "one" means a measure, but "simple" means that the thing itself has a certain nature.) But the beautiful, also, and that which is in itself desirable are in the same column; and the first in any class is always best, or analogous to the best.

That a final cause may exist among unchangeable entities is shown by the distinction of its meanings. For the final cause is (a) some being for whose good an action is done, and (b) something at which the action aims; and of these the latter exists among unchangeable entities though the former does not. The final cause, then, produces motion as being loved, but all other things move by being moved. Now if something is moved it is capable of being otherwise than as it is. Therefore if its actuality is the primary form of spatial motion, then in so far as it is subject to change, in this respect it is capable of being otherwise, in place, even if not in substance. But since there is something which moves while itself unmoved, existing actually, this can in no way be otherwise than as it is. For motion in space is the first of the kinds of change, and motion in a circle the first kind of spatial motion; and this the first mover produces. The first mover, then, exists of necessity; and in so far as it exists by necessity, its mode of being is good, and it is in this sense a first principle. For the necessary has all these senses—that which is necessary perforce because it is contrary to the natural impulse, that without which the good is impossible, and that which cannot be otherwise but can exist only in a single way.

On such a principle, then, depend the heavens and the world of nature. And it is a life such as the best which we enjoy, and enjoy for but a short time (for it is ever in this state, which we cannot be), since its actuality is also pleasure. (And for this reason are waking, perception, and thinking most pleasant, and hopes and memories are so on account of these.) And thinking in itself deals with that which is best in itself, and that which is thinking in the fullest sense with that which is best in the fullest sense. And thought thinks on itself because it shares the nature of the object of thought; for it becomes an object of thought in coming into contact with and thinking its objects, so that thought and object of thought are the same. For that which is capable of receiving the object of thought, i.e. the essence, is thought. But it is active when it possesses this object. Therefore the possession rather than the receptivity is the divine element which thought seems to contain, and the act of contemplation is what is most pleasant and best. If, then, God is always in that good state in which we sometimes are, this compels our wonder; and if in a better this compels it yet more. And God is in a better state. And life also belongs to God; for the actuality of thought is life, and God is that actuality; and God's self-dependent actuality is life most good and eternal. We say therefore that God is a living being, eternal, most good, so that life and duration continuous and eternal belong to God; for this is God.

Those who suppose, as the Pythagoreans and Speusippus do, that supreme beauty and goodness are not present in the beginning, because the beginnings both of plants and of animals are causes, but beauty and completeness are in the effects of these, are wrong in their opinion. For the seed comes from other individuals which are prior and complete, and the first thing is not seed but the complete being; e.g. we must say that before the seed there is a man,—not the man produced from the seed, but another from whom the seed comes.

It is clear then from what has been said that there is a substance which is eternal and unmovable and separate from sensible things. It has been shown also that this substance cannot have any magnitude, but is without parts and indivisible (for it produces movement through infinite time, but nothing finite has infinite power; and, while every magnitude is either infinite or finite, it cannot, for the above reason, have finite magnitude, and it cannot have infinite magnitude because there is no infinite magnitude at all). But it has also been shown that it is impassive and unalterable; for all the other changes are posterior to change of place.[4]

Ethics as a Branch of Politics

"Man is a political animal."

The main work where Aristotle's ethical theory is found is the *Nicomachean Ethics,* written to his son Nicomachus, who was still a small boy when Aristotle died in 322 BCE at the age of 62. It has the format of a series of lectures, intended for the educated male minority of Athens.

1. Every art and every inquiry, and similarly every action and choice, is thought to aim at some good; and for this reason the good has rightly been declared to be that at which all things aim. But a certain difference is found among ends; some are activities, others are products apart from the activities that produce them. Where there are ends apart from the actions, it is the nature of the products to be better than the activities. Now, as there are many actions, arts, and sciences, their ends also are many;

the end of the medical art is health, that of shipbuilding a vessel, that of strategy victory, that of economics wealth. But where such arts fall under a single capacity—as bridle-making and the other arts concerned with the equipment of horses fall under the art of riding, and this and every military action under strategy, in the same way other arts fall under yet others—in all of these the ends of the master arts are to be preferred to all the subordinate ends; for it is for the sake of the former that the latter are pursued. It makes no difference whether the activities themselves are the ends of the actions, or something else apart from the activities, as in the case of the sciences just mentioned.

2. If, then, there is some end of the things we do, which we desire for its own sake (everything else being desired for the sake of this), and if we do not choose everything for the sake of something else (for at that rate the process would go on to infinity, so that our desire would be empty and vain), clearly this must be the good and the chief good. Will not the knowledge of it, then, have a great influence on life? Shall we not, like archers who have a mark to aim at, be more likely to hit upon what we should? If so, we must try, in outline at least, to determine what it is, and of which of the sciences or capacities it is the object. It would seem to belong to the most authoritative art and that which is most truly the master art. And politics appears to be of this nature; for it is this that ordains which of the sciences should be studied in a state, and which each class of citizens should learn and up to what point they should learn them; and we see even the most highly esteemed of capacities to fall under this, e.g. strategy, economics, rhetoric; now, since politics uses the rest of the sciences, and since, again, it legislates as to what we are to do and what we are to abstain from, the end of this science must include those of the others, so that this end must be the good for man. For even if the end is the same for a single man and for a state, that of the state seems at all events something greater and more complete both to attain and to preserve; for though it is worth while to attain the end merely for one man, it is finer and more godlike to attain it for a nation or for city-states. These, then, are the ends at which our inquiry, being concerned with politics, aims. (*NE* 1.1–2)

Like Plato before him, Aristotle sees ethics as a branch of political science, whose task is to produce good citizens. The virtues are simply those characteristics that enable individuals to live well in communities. To live well (that is, achieve a state of happiness, *eudaimonia*), proper social institutions are necessary.

In view of the fact that all knowledge and choice aims at some good, what it is that we say political science aims at and what is the highest of all goods achievable by action. Verbally there is very general agreement; for both the general run of men and people of superior refinement say that it is *happiness* [emphasis added], and identify living well and faring well with being happy; but with regard to what happiness is they differ, and the many do not give the same account as the wise. For the former think it is some plain and obvious thing, like pleasure, wealth, or honour; they differ, however, from one another—and often even the same man identifies it with different things, with health when he is ill, with wealth when he is poor; but, conscious of their ignorance, they admire those who proclaim some great thing that is above their comprehension. Now some thought that apart from these many goods there is another which is good in itself and causes the goodness of all these as well. To examine all the opinions that have been held would no doubt be somewhat fruitless: it is enough to examine those that are most prevalent or that seem to have some reason in their favour.

Let us not fail to notice, however, that there is a difference between arguments from and those to the first principles. For Plato, too, was right in raising this question and asking, as he used to do, "are we on the way from or to the first principles?" There is a difference, as there is in a race-course between the course from the judges to the turning-point and the way back. For, while we must begin with what is familiar, things are so in two ways—some to us, some without qualification. Presumably, then, we must begin with things familiar to us. Hence any one who is to listen intelligently to lectures about what is noble and just and, generally, about the subjects of political science must have been brought up in good habits. For the facts are the starting-point, and if they are sufficiently plain to him, he will not need the reason as well; and the man who has been well brought up has or can easily get starting-points. And as for him who neither has nor can get them, let him hear the words of Hesiod:

Far best is he who knows all things himself;
Good, he that hearkens when men counsel right;
But he who neither knows, nor lays to heart
Another's wisdom, is a useless wight.

Thus, the moral person is both the end and a necessary means to a flourishing political arrangement. Only the good state can produce good and happy people, and good people along with good laws are necessary for a well-governed state. Furthermore, the state must be actively engaged in moral education" "Legislators make the citizens good by forming habits in them" (*NE* 2.1). The legislator who fails to accomplish this task has failed in his task as a legislator.

Humans by nature are political animals. They are suited to develop their personalities, ranging from families and friendship to loose confederacies. So citizens must be actively engaged in social legislation. Good institutions and laws are necessary for personal happiness. The apolitical citizen is irresponsible. In fact, the Greek word *idiot* means "not interested in politics." Exceptions to this degrading designation are philosophers who, taking advantage of the well-governed state, devote all their time to contemplation (*theoria*), but these are rare beings.

The Functionalist Account of Human Nature

For both Plato and Aristotle, to know what something is is to know what it is used for, what it is meant to become—that is, what its function is. Like everything else, human beings have a distinct function and some humans fulfill this function better than others. Since one's value is determined by his or her capacity to fulfill this function, some people are more valuable than others.

Presumably, however, to say that happiness is the chief good seems a platitude, and a clearer account of what it is is still desired. This might perhaps be given, if we could first ascertain the function of man. For just as for a flute-player, a sculptor, or any artist, and, in general, for all things that have a function or activity, the good and the "well" is thought to reside in the function, so would it seem to be for man, if he has a function. Have the carpenter, then, and the tanner certain functions or activities, and has man none? Is he naturally functionless? Or as eye, hand, foot, and in general each of the parts evidently has a function, may one lay it down that man similarly has a function apart from all these? What then can this be? Life seems to be common even to plants, but we are seeking what is peculiar to man. Let us exclude, therefore, the life of nutrition and growth. Next there would be a life of perception, but it also seems to be common even to the horse, the ox, and every animal. There remains, then, an active life of the element that has a rational principle (of this, one part has such a principle in the sense of being obedient to one, the other in the sense of possessing one and exercising thought); and as this too can be taken in two ways, we must state that life in the sense of activity is what we mean; for this seems to be the more proper sense of the term. Now if the function of man is an activity of soul in accordance with, or not without, rational principle, and if we say a so-and-so and a good so-and-so have a function which is the same in kind, e.g. a lyre-player and a good lyre-player, and so without qualification in all cases, eminence in respect of excellence being added to the function (for the function of a lyre-player is to play the lyre, and that of a good lyre-player is to do so well): if this is the case, [and we state the function of man to be a certain kind of life, and this to be an activity or actions of the soul implying a rational principle, and the function of a good man to be the good and noble performance of these, and if any action is well performed when it is performed in accordance with the appropriate excellence: if this is the case,] human good turns out to be activity of soul in conformity with excellence, and if there are more than one excellence, in conformity with the best and most complete. But we must add "in a complete life." For one swallow does not make a summer, nor does one day; and so too one day, or a short time, does not make a man blessed and happy. (*NE* 1.7, 1097b–1098a)

All nature is teleological, purposive. Its function is to reach some definite pre-designed *telos*. An acorn's function is to become an oak tree, and a fetus's function is to become an adult member of the species. All elements have proper functions: fire is to rise, earth is to settle, water is to rest on earth, and air to hover over earth. The knife's function is to cut, and a good knife is one that does this well. All social roles have functions; the carpenter is to build, the shoemaker is to create shoes, the teacher is to teach, the mother is to bear and raise children.

If we suppose that all humans have a function or essence, we must distinguish what it is that our proper function is. For Aristotle, it was via the *differentia* that species distinguished themselves. We need nutrition in order to grow, but that is not what distinguishes us from plants and animals. We have sensory capacity, but that is not our function, for lower animals have that also. Only the ability to deliberate, to use reason in a practical and theoretical manner, makes us different from other animals: We are rational animals. "Reason is the true self of every man, since it is the supreme and better part. It will be strange, then, if he should choose not his own life, but some other's. . . . For man, this will be the life of reason, since reason is in the highest sense, man's true self" (*NE* 1.7).

Reason contributes to the human good on two levels: the practical and the theoretical. Practically, reason informs us as to the correct means to achieve our goals and steers us away from inappropriate means. Practical reason (*phronesis*) includes a judicial, legislative, and executive aspect. The judicial (deliberative) aspect enables us to discern our ends and evaluate the necessary means to reach them. The legislative aspects result from the judicial aspect and sets forth rules of action. The executive capacity enables us to carry out our plans and avoid succumbing to emotions or weakness of will. For example, in pursuing a valuable college degree, the judicial first determines the worthiness of the goal (*telos*), the legislative function sets about determining the best way to reach that goal, and the executive function acts to reach it, rejecting detours and sidetracks.

Theoretically, reason is used to think logically about scientific and philosophical problems and to contemplate on the nature of reality. Reason culminates in philosophical contemplation, which is the kind of life engaged in by the gods. The gods have rational form but not bodies (or emotions) and do nothing but contemplate. Humans have both material bodies and rational essences, so they can go in ether direction, toward animal life or toward the life of the gods. When they are engaged in philosophical reflection, they become like gods.

> But such a life [of complete contemplation] would be too high for man; for it is not in so far as he is man that he will live so, but in so far as something divine is present in him; and by so much as this is superior to our composite nature is its activity superior to that which is the exercise of the other kind of virtue. If reason is divine, then, in comparison with man, the life according to it is divine in comparison with human life. But we must not follow those who advise us, being men, to think of human things, and, being mortal, of mortal things, but must, so far as we can, make ourselves immortal, and strain every nerve to live in accordance with the best thing in us; for even if it be small in bulk, much more does it in power and worth surpass everything. This

would seem, too, to be each man himself, since it is the authoritative and better part of him. It would be strange, then, if he were to choose not the life of his self but that of something else. And what we said before will apply now; that which is proper to each thing is by nature best and most pleasant for each thing; for man, therefore, the life according to reason is best and pleasantest, since reason more than anything else is man. This life therefore is also the happiest. (*NE* 10.7)

What Is the Good Life?

Next, we want to ask what kind of life is most worth living. Aristotle wrote long ago that what all people seek is happiness.

> There is very general agreement; for both the common person and people of superior refinement say that it is happiness, and identify living well and doing well with being happy; but with regard to what happiness is they differ, and the many do not give the same account as the wise. For the former think it is some plain and obvious thing, like pleasure, wealth or honor. (*NE* 1.4)

What is happiness? The field divides up among objectivists, subjectivists, and combination theorists. The objectivists, following Plato and Aristotle, distinguish happiness from pleasure and speak of a single ideal form of human nature; if we do not reach that ideal, then we have failed. Happiness (Greek, ***eudaimonia;*** literally "good demon") is not merely a subjective state of pleasure or contentment but the kind of life we would all want to live if we understood our essential nature. Just as knives and forks and wheels have functions, so do species, including the human species. Our function (sometimes called our "essence") is to live according to reason and thereby to become a certain sort of highly rational, disciplined being. When we fulfill the ideal of living the virtuous life, we are truly happy.

The objectivist view fell out of favor with the rise of the evolutionary account of human nature, which undermined the sense of a preordained essence or function. Science cannot discover any innate *telos,* or goal, to which all people must strive. The contemporary bias is in favor of value pluralism—that is, the view that there are many ways of finding happiness: "Let a thousand flowers bloom." This leads to subjectivism.

The subjectivist version of happiness states that happiness is in the eyes of the beholder. You are just as happy as you think you are—no more, no less. The concept is not a descriptive one but a first-person evaluation. I am the only one who decides or knows whether I am happy. If I feel happy, I am happy, even though everyone else despises my lifestyle. Logically, happiness has nothing to do with virtue, though—due to our social nature—it usually turns out that we will feel better about ourselves if we are virtuous.

The combination view tries to incorporate aspects of both the objectivist and the subjectivist views. One version is John Rawls's "plan-of-life" conception of happiness: There is a plurality of life plans open to each person, and what is important is that the plan be an integrated whole, freely chosen by the person, and that the person be successful in realizing his or her goals. This view is predominantly subjective in that it recognizes the person as the autonomous chooser of goals and a plan. Even if a person should choose a life plan "whose only pleasure is to count blades of grass in various geometrically shaped areas such as park squares and well-trimmed lawns, . . . our definition of the good forces us to admit that the good for this man is indeed counting blades of grass."[5]

However, Rawls recognizes an objective element in an otherwise subjective schema. There are primary goods that are necessary to any worthwhile life plan: "rights and liberties, powers and opportunities, income and wealth, . . . self-respect, . . . health and vigor, intelligence and imagination."[6]

The primary goods function as the core (or the hub of the wheel) from which may be derived any number of possible life plans (the spokes). But unless these primary goods (or most of them) are present, the life plan is not an authentic manifestation of an individual's autonomous choice of his or her own selfhood. So it is perfectly possible that people believe themselves to be happy when they really are not.

Although subjectivist and plan-of-life views dominate the literature today, there is some movement back to an essentialist, or Aristotelian, view of happiness as a life directed toward worthwhile goals. Some lifestyles are more worthy than others, and some may be worthless. Philosopher Richard Kraut asks us to imagine a man who has as his idea of happiness the state of affairs of being loved, admired, or respected by his friends and who would hate to have his "friends" only pretend to care for him. Suppose his "friends" really do hate him but "orchestrate an elaborate deception, giving him every reason to believe that they love and admire him, though in fact they don't. And he is taken in by the illusion."[7] Can we really call this man happy?

Suppose a woman centers her entire life around an imaginary Prince Charming. She refuses to date—let alone marry—perfectly eligible young men; she turns down educational travel opportunities lest they distract her from this wonderful future event; for 95 years she bores all her patient friends with tales of the prince's imminent appearance. As death approaches at age 96, after a lifetime of disappointment, she discovers that she's been duped; she suddenly realizes that what appeared to be a happy life was a stupid, self-deceived, miserable existence. Would we say that our heroine was happy up until her deathbed revelation? Do these thought experiments not indicate that our happiness depends, at least to some extent, on reality and not simply on our own evaluation?

Suppose it were possible to create a Happiness Machine. This machine is a large tub that is filled with a chemical solution. Electrodes are attached to many parts of your brain. You work with the technician to program all the "happy experiences" that you have ever wanted. Suppose that includes wanting to be a football star, a halfback who breaks tackles like a dog shakes off fleas and who has a penchant for scoring last-minute game-winning touchdowns. Or perhaps you've always wanted to be a movie star and to bask in the public's love and admiration. Or maybe you've wanted to be the world's richest person, living in the splendor of a magnificent castle, with servants faithfully at your beck and call. In fact, with the Happiness Machine you can have all of these, plus passionate romance and the love of the most beautiful (or handsome) persons in the world. All of these marvelous adventures would be simulated, and you would truly believe you were experiencing them. Would you enter the Happiness Machine?

Plato and Aristotle would argue that the Happiness Machine is an illusion, a modern analog to his allegory of the cave. For in both the Happiness Machine and the cave, we are living in an illusion, not in reality. We don't know who we are or the nature of reality. We're not free and have no character, for we are not acting but only passive pleasure blobs reacting to sensory stimuli and imagining this is the real world.

The Happiness Machine, like Plato's cave, is a myth, all *appearance* and no *reality*—a bliss bought at too high a price, a deception! If this is so and if reality is a necessary condition for the truly worthwhile life, then we cannot be happy in the Happiness Machine. But neither can we be happy outside of the Happiness Machine when the same necessary ingredients are missing: activity, freedom, moral character, loving relationships, and a strong sense of reality.

The Aristotelian objective and the modern subjective views of happiness assess life from different perspectives, with the objectivist assuming that there is some kind of independent standard of assessment and the subjectivist denying it. Even though there seems to be an immense variety of lifestyles that could be considered intrinsically worthwhile or happy, and even though some subjective approval or satisfaction seems necessary before we are willing to attribute the adjective "happy" to a life, there do seem to be limiting conditions on what may count as happy. We have a notion of *fittingness* for the good life, which would normally *exclude* being severely retarded, being a slave, or being a drug addict (no matter how satisfied) and which would *include* being a deeply fulfilled, autonomous, healthy person. As John Stuart Mill said, "It is better to be Socrates dissatisfied than to be the pig satisfied, but only the satisfied Socrates is happy."

J. S. Mill gave a definition which is a combination of the Aristotelian and subjective views. According to Mill,

> Happiness is not a life of rapture; but moments of such, in an existence made up of few and transitory pains, many and various pleasures, with a decided predominance of the active over the passive, and having as the foundation of the whole, not to expect more from life than it is capable of bestowing.[8]

This conception of happiness is worth pondering. It includes "activity," "freedom," and "reality" components, which exclude being satisfied by the passive experiences in the Happiness Machine, and it supposes (the context tells us this) that some pleasing experiences are better than others. We might supplement

Mill's definition with the addition of the ingredients of moral character and loving relations. An approximation might go like this:

> Happiness is a life in which exist free action (including meaningful work), loving relations, and good moral character and in which the individual is not plagued by guilt and anxiety but is blessed with peace and satisfaction.

For Aristotle, happiness, or the good life, is rooted in the virtues. Virtue ethicists often cite Kant's deontic theory (see Chapter 9) as a paradigm of an antivirtue deontic ethics. They point out that an examination of Kant's extreme action-centered approach highlights the need for a virtue alternative. For Kant, natural goodness is morally irrelevant. The fact that you actually want to help someone (because you like them or just like doing good deeds) is of no moral importance. In fact, because of the emphasis he puts on the good will (doing duty for duty's sake), it seems that Kant's logic would force him to conclude that you are actually moral in proportion to the amount of temptation that you have to resist in performing your duty: For little temptation, you receive little moral credit; if you experience great temptation, you receive great moral credit for overcoming it.

To virtue ethicists, this is preposterous. Taken to its logical conclusion, the homicidal maniac who always just barely succeeds in resisting his perpetual temptation to kill is actually the most glorious saint, surpassing the "natural saint" who does good just because of a good character. True goodness is to spontaneously, cheerfully, and enjoyably do what is good. As Aristotle said,

> We may even go so far as to state that the man who does not enjoy performing noble actions is not a good man at all. Nobody would call a man just who does not enjoy acting justly, nor generous who does not enjoy generous actions, and so on. (*NE* 1099a)

It is not the hounded neurotic who barely manages to control himself before each passing temptation, but the natural saint—the one who does good out of habit and from the inner resources of good character—who is the morally superior person.

A criticism of Kantian deontic ethics, set forth by the Aristotelian scholar Alasdair MacIntyre in *After Virtue* (1981), claims that ordinary rule-governed ethics is a symptom of the European Enlightenment movement of the 17th and 18th centuries, which exaggerated the principle of autonomy—that is, the ability of each person to arrive at a moral code by reason alone. In fact, all moral codes are rooted in practices that themselves are rooted in traditions or forms of life. We do not make moral decisions as rational atoms in a vacuum, and it is sheer ideological blindness that allows this distorted perception. MacIntyre does not want to embrace relativism. We can discover better ways of living, but they will probably be founded on an account of what the good life is and what a good community is.

It is in communities that such virtues as loyalty, natural affection, spontaneous sympathy, and shared concerns arise and sustain the group. It is out of this primary loyalty (to family, friends, and community) that the proper dispositions arise that flow out to the rest of humanity. Hence, moral psychology is more important than traditional ethics has usually recognized. Seeing how people actually learn to be moral and how they are inspired to act morally is vital to moral theory itself, and this, it seems, has everything to do with the virtues.

In sum, rule-governed systems are uninspiring and unmotivating, negative, improperly legalistic, neglectful of the spiritual dimension, overly rationalistic, and atomistic. Against this background of dissatisfaction with traditional moral theory, virtue ethics has reasserted itself as offering something that captures the essence of the moral point of view.

As we saw in the last chapter, Plato speaks of happiness as "harmony of the soul." Just as the body is healthy when it is in harmony with itself and the political state is a good state when it is functioning harmoniously, so the soul is happy when all its features are functioning in harmonious accord, with the rational faculty ruling over the spirited and emotional elements. Though we no doubt know when we are happy and feel good about ourselves, the subjective feeling does not itself define happiness, for people who fail to attain human excellence can also feel happy, via self-deception or ignorance.

The Ideal Type of Human

We have seen that for Aristotle the virtues are those characteristics that enable individuals to live well in communities. To achieve a state of well-being (*eudaimonia*, meaning "happiness" or "human flourishing"), proper social institutions are necessary. Thus, the moral person cannot really exist apart from a flourishing political setting that enables him or her to develop the requisite virtues for the good life. For this reason, ethics is considered a branch of politics. The State is not neutral toward the good life, but should actively encourage citizens to inculcate the virtues, which in turn are the best guarantee of a flourishing political order.

For Aristotle, humanity has an essence, or *function*. Just as it is the function of a doctor to cure the sick and restore health, the function of a ruler to govern society well, and the function of a knife to cut well, so it is the function of humans to use reason in pursuit of the good life (*eudaimonia*). The virtues indicate the kind of moral–political characteristics necessary for people to attain happiness.

After locating ethics as a part of politics, Aristotle explains that the moral virtues are different from the intellectual ones. Whereas the intellectual virtues may be taught directly, we must live the moral ones to learn them. By living well, we acquire the right habits. These habits are in fact the virtues. The virtues are to be sought as the best guarantee to the happy life. But, again, happiness requires that we be lucky enough to live in a flourishing state. The morally virtuous life consists in living in moderation, according to the "Golden Mean." By the Golden Mean, Aristotle means that the virtues are a mean between excess and deficiency (for example, courage is the mean between cowardice and foolhardiness; liberality is the mean between stinginess and unrestrained giving):

> We can experience fear, confidence, desire, anger, pity, and generally any kind of pleasure and pain either too much or too little, and in either case not properly. But to experience all this at the right time, toward the right objects, toward the right people, for the right reason, and in the right manner—that is the mean and the best course, the course that is the mark of virtue. (*NE* 1099a)

Aristotle himself was an elitist who believed that people have unequal abilities to be virtuous: Some are endowed with great ability while others lack it altogether; some people are worthless, natural slaves. In addition, external circumstances could prevent even those capable of developing moral dispositions from reaching the goal of happiness. The moral virtues are a necessary but not a sufficient condition for happiness. One must, in addition to being virtuous, be healthy, wealthy, wise, and have good fortune.

What seems so remarkable to contemporary ethicists is that Aristotle hardly mentions principles. It wasn't that he thought them unnecessary; they are implied in what he says. For example, his condemnation of adultery may be read as a principle ("Thou shalt not commit adultery"). Aristotle seems to think that such activities are inherently and obviously bad, so it is laboring the point to speak of a rule against adultery or against killing innocent persons. What is emphasized in place of principles is the importance of a good upbringing, of good habits, of self-control, of courage and character, without which the ethical life is impossible. A person of moral excellence cannot help doing good—it is as natural as the change of seasons or the rotation of the planets.

Let me elaborate on the idea of the Golden Mean. We spoke above about the moral life being a life of virtue, living habitually. Like becoming healthy or strong, the moral life is lived by avoiding the extremes of excess or deficiency, hitting instead the middle, or mean. In maintaining health, one must not eat too little or too much but just the right amount; in building up strength, one must avoid too much or too little exercise, getting the right balance. So in becoming virtuous, one must avoid the Scalla and Charybdis of opposite vices and hit the intermediate, the Golden Mean. Greek society already had as one of the famous sayings of the sacred Oracle of Delphi "Nothing in excess." Aristotle was reaffirming that wise saying in a philosophical manner.

> Moral Virtue: for it is this that is concerned with passions and actions, and in these there is excess, defect, and the intermediate. For instance, both fear and confidence and appetite and anger and pity and in general pleasure and pain may be felt both too much and too little, and in both cases not well; but to feel them at the right times, with reference to the right objects, towards the right people, with the right motive, and in the right way, is what is both intermediate and best, and this is characteristic of virtue. Similarly with regard to actions also there is

excess, defect, and the intermediate. Now virtue is concerned with passions and actions, in which excess is a form of failure, and so is defect, while the intermediate. (*NE* 2.6)

Some examples may help. The mean between the vices of rashness and cowardice is courage, knowing what to fear and what not to fear and acting accordingly. The mean between irascibility and insensitivity is an even temper, getting appropriately angry for the right reason and in the right amount. The mean between prodigality and stinginess is liberality, giving away the right moderate amount in the right situation. Aristotle warns us that this kind of reasoning doesn't apply to every kind of act. There is no Golden Mean between too much and too little adultery or murder or injustice. These kinds of acts are simply wrong (*NE* 2.6).

The following chart, from the *Eudemian Ethics,* shows the kinds of intermediate relationships the virtues have to vices:

Vice	*Virtue*	*Vice*
Irascibility	Even temper	Impassivity
Foolhardiness	Bravery	Cowardice
Shamelessness	Modesty	Over-sensitiveness
Intemperance	Temperance	Insensibility
Envy	Fair-mindedness	[no name]
Unfair advantage	Justice	Disadvantage
Prodigality	Liberality	Meanness
Boastfulness	Truthfulness	False modesty
Flattery	Friendliness	Churlishness

Applying the idea to the moral virtues, concerned with emotions and actions, Aristotle says that finding the mean is an act of discernment. In every life situation, the wise person (*phronimos*) discerns the right act from an indefinite number of possible actions, most of which are wrong. "Bad men have many ways, good men but one." There are many ways to miss the bull's-eye, but only one way to hit it. There is no set of rules telling you exactly how to do the right thing, for each situation is different, but the skilled moral craftsperson, an expert in human virtue, knows just what the right thing to do is in every situation. "The judgment lies in perception"(*NE* 2.9).

Summary

The background of Aristotle's philosophy of human nature is his response to the idealism of his teacher, Plato. Rejecting the otherworldly dualism of Plato, Aristotle developed a more naturalist and realist account of human nature and the moral life.

Being a biologist, as well as a philosopher, Aristotle's theory of human nature is a functional account of all living beings. Believing that everything in nature had a purpose (*telos*), he held that the *telos* of human beings is to live as worthy, moral-political citizens, to live using practical reason to solve our problems and resolve our conflicts of interest. The highest form of life for the best humans was that of the philosopher, who engaged in contemplation, the life of the gods.

Aristotle's ethics is connected to his politics and is centered on the virtues. Virtues are inculcated by a good upbringing in a good society, and they lead to happiness (*eudaimonia*). Happiness is an objective state of affairs, which requires health, friends, and family, as well as good character. The wise person (*phronimo*s) uses reason to navigate through life, living in moderation, by the Golden Mean, avoiding excesses.

FOR FURTHER REFLECTION

1. Compare Aristotle's philosophy with that of Plato, noting the similarities and differences.

2. Describe Aristotle's theory of ethics.

3. Describe the ideal human being according to Aristotle.

4. Describe Aristotle's functional account of human nature.

5. According to Aristotle, how is ethics related to politics and politics to the heart of human nature?

6. What is Aristotle's view of happiness? Compare it with the thought experiment of the Happiness Machine.

7. What is the Golden Mean?

NOTES

1. All translations from Aristotle's works are by W. D. Ross.
2. Henry Sidgwick, *Outlines of the History of Ethics* (Macmillan, 1886), 51.
3. *Metaphysics* 1078.
4. *Metaphysics* Book 12.7
5. John Rawls, *A Theory of Justice* (Cambridge, MA: Harvard University Press, 1971), 432.
6. Ibid., 62.
7. Richard Kraut, "Two Concepts of Happiness," *Philosophical Review* (1979).
8. John Stuart Mill, *Utilitarianism* (1863), Chapter 2.

FOR FURTHER READING

Ackrill, J. L. *Aristotle, the Philosopher.* Oxford, UK: Oxford University Press, 1981.

Aristotle. *The Complete Works,* 2 vol. Edited by J. Barnes. Princeton, NJ: Princeton University Press, 1984.

Barnes, J. *Aristotle.* Oxford, UK: Oxford University Press, 1982.

Irwin, Terrance. *Aristotle's First Principles.* Oxford, UK: Oxford University Press, 1988.

Lloyd, G. E. R. *Aristotle, the Growth and Structure of His Thought.* Oxford, UK: Cambridge University Press, 1968.

Taylor, A. E. *Aristotle.* New York: Dover, 1955.

Urmson, J. O. *Aristotle's Ethics.* London: Basil Blackwell, 1988.

PART III
Philosophy of Religion: An Introduction

No other subject has so profoundly influenced human history as religion. Offering a comprehensive explanation of the universe and of our place in it, it offers us a cosmic map and shows us our place on the map; through its sacred books, it provides lessons in cosmic map reading, enabling us to find our way through what would otherwise be a labyrinth of chaos and confusion. It tells where we came from, where we are, where we are going, and how to get there. In this regard, religion legitimizes social mores, rituals, and morals. All have a coherent place on reality's map.

Moreover, religion is value laden. It typically gives us a sense of dignity and self-worth. "We hold these truths to be self-evident," wrote Thomas Jefferson in the Declaration of Independence, "that all men are created equal, that they are endowed by their Creator with certain unalienable rights, that among these are life, liberty and the pursuit of happiness." The notion of equal worth and dignity are originally religious notions, derived from the idea of a benevolent Creator creating humans in his own image, and becomes problematic apart from a religious framework.

Religion offers comfort in sorrow, hope in death, courage in danger, spiritual joy in the midst of despair. It tells us that this world is not a mere impersonal materialist conundrum but a friendly home, provided for us by our heavenly Father. As William James says, if religion is true, "The universe is no longer a mere *It* to us, but a *Thou*, and any relation that may be possible from person to person might be possible here."

The sacred tomes of the religions of the world—The Vedas, the Bhagavad Gita, the Bible, the Koran, the Dhammapada—are literary classics in their own right. In the Western tradition, who has not marveled at the elegance of the creation story in Genesis 1, the story of Joseph's brothers selling him into slavery, the story of Moses leading the children of Israel out of bondage in Egypt, or the story of the birth of Jesus, the Sermon on the Mount, and the parable of the Good Samaritan?

Religion has inspired millions in every age. Its architecture—from the pyramids to the Parthenon, from the Hindu Juggernaut and the Sikh Golden Temple at Amritsar to the cathedrals at Chartres and Notre Dame—rises high above ordinary human commerce and mercenary transactions as a testimony to faith in the transcendent; its art from the Muslim mosaics in Grenada to Raphael's *Transfiguration* and Michelangelo's Sistine Chapel is without peer; its music from Hindu chants through Bach's cantatas and Handel's *Messiah* to thousands of hymns and spirituals has lit the hearts in weal and in woe of people in all times and almost all places. The Hindu Divali, the Muslim Ramadan, the Jewish Yom Kippur, the Christian Easter and Christmas, and a thousand other holidays—rituals marking the journey from birth through rites of passage and marriage to death—punctuate the lives of human beings in almost every time and place. Every time we date a letter, a check, or a contract, we pay homage to the founder of Christianity, dividing the calendar into BC (before Christ) and AD (anno Domini, the year of our Lord). (In this text, I use the modern designation: BCE [before the Common Era] and CE [Common Era].)

Religion holds a power over humanity like nothing else. Saints and martyrs have been created in its crucible, reformations and revolutions ignited by its flame, outcasts and criminals have been catapulted to a higher level of existence by its propulsion. Auschwitz survivor Olga Lengyel writes that almost the only people to keep their dignity in the Nazi concentration camp were people animated by faith: "priests and nuns in the camp [who] proved that they had real strength of character."[1] When I worked with the poor in Bedford-Stuyvesant, Brooklyn, the work of the Pentecostal Christian David Wilkerson astounded the civil authorities, for drug addicts who were considered incorrigible, upon being converted through his ministry, suddenly would "kick the habit cold-turkey." Such is the power of religion.

Nonetheless, despite its enormous dynamics, its power and influence are no guarantees of Truth. It could be that the impact of religion in human affairs only shows that humans are myth-making and myth-craving animals. We need a Big Myth to help us make it through the darkness of existence, whether it be a religion, Nazism, Marxism, or astrology. And it could be that humanity will someday "come of age," outgrow religion and stand on its own as an autonomous adult. There is also a dark side to religion—its bigotry, fanaticism, inquisitions, "holy wars," and intolerance—which should give us pause in evaluating its merits.

All of this, however, is speculation. From a philosophical point of view, we want to know if religion is true. We want to assess the evidence and arguments for and against its claims in an impartial, judicious, open-minded manner. And this is what we will endeavor to do in this part of our work.

The key notion of most religions is the idea of a God, an all-powerful, benevolent, and providential being, who created the universe and all therein. Questions connected with the existence of God may be the most important that we can ask and try to answer. If God exists, then it is of the utmost importance that we come to know that fact and as much as possible about God and his plan.

Implications follow that affect our understanding of the world and ourselves. If God exists, the world is not accidental, a product of mere chance and necessity but a home that has been designed for rational and sentient beings, a place of personal purposefulness. We are not alone in our struggle for justice but are working together with One whose plan is to redeem the world from Evil. Most importantly, there is someone to whom we are responsible and to whom we owe absolute devotion and worship. Other implications follow for our self-understanding, the way we ought to live our lives and prospects for continued life after death. In short, if there is a God, we ought to do everything possible to discover this fact, including using our reason in the discovery itself or as a means to test the validity of claims of such a discovery.

On the other hand, it may be that a supreme, benevolent being does not exist. If there is no God, we want to know this too. Whether we believe in God or not will make a difference in the way we view the universe and in the way we live.

Many people have lived well without believing in God. Pierre-Simon Laplace (1749–1827), when asked about his faith, is reported to have replied, "I have no need of that hypothesis." But the testimony of humanity is against him. Millions have needed and been inspired by this notion. So great is the inspiration issuing from the idea of God that we could say that if God doesn't exist, the idea is the greatest invention of the human mind. What are all the world's works of literature, art, music, drama, architecture, science, and philosophy compared to this simple concept? To quote Anthony Kenny,

> If there is no God, then God is incalculably the greatest single creation of the human imagination. No other creation of the imagination has been so fertile of ideas, so great an inspiration to philosophy, to literature, to painting, sculpture, architecture, and drama. Set beside the idea of God, the most original inventions of mathematicians and the most unforgettable characters in drama are minor products of the imagination: Hamlet and the square root of minus one pale into insignificance by comparison.[2]

The field of philosophy of religion documents the history of humanity's quest for a supreme being. Even if God does not exist, the arguments centering on this quest are interesting in their own right, for their ingenuity and subtlety, even apart from their possible soundness. It may be argued that the Judeo-Christian tradition has informed our self-understanding to such a degree that it is imperative for every person who would be well informed to come to grips with the arguments and counterarguments surrounding its claims. Hence, even if one rejects the assertions of religion, understanding what is being rejected and why is important.

Arguments for the Existence of God

Can the existence of God be demonstrated or made probable by argument? The debate between those who believe that reason can demonstrate that God exists and those who do not has an ancient lineage, going back to Protagoras (circa 450 BCE) and Plato (427–347 BCE) but made famous by the work of the greatest Catholic philosopher of all time, St. Thomas Aquinas (1225–1274), who set forth five different arguments for the existence of God. The Roman Catholic Church has traditionally held that the existence of God is demonstrable by human reason. The strong statement of the First Vatican Council (1870) indicates that human reason is adequate to arrive at a state of—knowledge: "If anyone says that the one and true God, our creator and Lord, cannot be known with certainty with the natural light of human reason by means of the things that have been made: let him be anathema."

Many others, including theists of various denominations, including Catholics, have denied that human reason is adequate to arrive at knowledge or demonstrate the existence of God.

Arguments for the existence of God divide into two main groups: a priori and a posteriori arguments. An *a posteriori argument* is based on premises that can be known only by means of experience of the world (for example, that there is a world, and events have causes), whereas an *a priori argument* depends on no such premises. It rests on premises that can be known to be true independently of experience of the world. One need only clearly conceive of the proposition in order to see that it is true.

In this part of our book, we consider three types of a posteriori arguments for the existence of God and one a priori argument. The a posteriori arguments are the cosmological argument, the teleological argument, and the argument from religious experience. The a priori argument is the ontological argument. We then look at the main argument against the existence of God, the argument from Evil. Finally, we examine the relationship of faith to reason.

The question before us in this part of our work is, What do the arguments for the existence of God establish? Do any of them demonstrate beyond reasonable doubt the existence of a Supreme Being or deity? Do any of them make it probable (given the evidence at hand) that such a being exists? Can reason bring us to faith, or is faith contrary to reason?

NOTES

1. Olga Lengyel, *Five Chimneys* (New York: Grenada, 1972), 120.
2. Anthony Kenny, *Faith and Reason* (New York: Columbia University Press, 1983), 59.

7 ❧ The Cosmological Argument for the Existence of God

The First Cause Argument

Asking people why they believe in God is likely to evoke something like the following response: "Well, things just didn't pop up out of nothing. Someone, a pretty powerful Someone, had to cause the universe to come into existence. You just can't have causes going back forever. God must have made the world. Nothing else makes sense."

All the versions of the cosmological argument begin with the a posteriori **assumptions** that the universe exists and that something outside the universe is required to explain its existence. That is, it is **contingent,** depending on something outside of itself for its existence. That "something else" is logically prior to the universe. It constitutes the reason for the existence of the universe. Such a being is God.

One version of the cosmological argument is called the *First Cause argument.* From the fact that some things are caused, we may reason to the existence of a First Cause. The Catholic Dominican monk Thomas Aquinas (1225–1274), considered by many to be the greatest theologian in Western religion, gave a version of this argument. His "second way" is based on the idea of causation.

> We find that there is among material things a regular order of causes. But we do not find, nor indeed is it possible, that anything is the cause of itself, for in that case it would be prior to itself, which is impossible. Now it is not possible to proceed to infinity in causes. For if we

arrange in order all causes, the first is the cause of the intermediate, and the intermediate the cause of the last, whether the intermediate be many or only one. But if we remove a cause, the effect is removed; therefore, if there is no *first* among causes, neither will there be a last or an intermediate. But if we proceed to infinity in causes there will be no first cause, and thus there will be no ultimate effect, nor any intermediate cause, which is clearly false. Therefore it is necessary to suppose the existence of some first cause, and this men call God.[1]

The general outline, focusing on the second argument, goes something like this:

1. There exist things that are caused.
2. Nothing can be the cause of itself.
3. There cannot be an infinite regress of causes.
4. Therefore, there exists an uncaused first cause.
5. The word *God* means uncaused first cause.
6. Therefore, God exists.

What can we say of this argument? The first premise is certainly true—some things have causes. Indeed, we generally believe that every event has a cause that explains why the event happened. The second premise seems correct, for how could something that didn't exist cause anything, let alone its own existence? Note that premises 2 and 4 are not contradictions. There is nothing obviously incoherent about the idea that something or someone existed from eternity and so is uncaused, whereas there is something incoherent about the idea that something nonexistent caused itself to come into being.

One difficulty with the argument is premise 3: "There cannot be an infinite regress of causes." Why can't there be such a regress? You might object that there are an infinite regress of numbers, so why can't there be an infinite regress of causes? One response to this objection is that there is a significant difference between numbers and events and persons. Numbers are just abstract entities, whereas events and persons are concrete, temporal entities, the sort of things that need to be brought into existence. Numbers exist in all possible worlds. They are eternal, but Napoleon, Mt. Everest, and you are not eternal but need a causal explanation. The child asks, "Mommy, who made me?" and the mother responds, "You came from my womb." The child persists, "Mommy, who made you and your womb?" The mother responds that she came from a fertilized egg in her mother's womb, but the child persists in the query until the mother is forced to admit that she doesn't know the answer or perhaps says, "God made the world and all that is in it."

God may be one explanatory hypothesis, answering the question why the world came to be, but the question is, Does the argument from First Cause, even if it is valid, give us a full-blown proof of the existence of God?

Consider, does it rule out the possibility that this uncaused cause is matter itself? Does it prove that the First Cause is still around? There is a joke that God isn't dead, she's just moved to a better neighborhood. Could the Creator of this universe have moved off in a different, more satisfying neighborhood? Does the argument prove that just one Creator caused everything to come into being? Could there be many uncaused causes? Finally, does the First Cause argument give any indication that the First Cause is benevolent, let alone omnibenevolent? Furthermore, why couldn't the world simply be eternal, a *brute fact*, itself an uncaused entity?

The Argument from Contingency

Some philosophers believe that the English theologian and philosopher Samuel Clarke (1675–1729) has a superior version of the cosmological argument, called the *argument from contingency* (it may be helpful to read this passage out loud).

A DEMONSTRATION OF THE BEING AND ATTRIBUTES OF GOD

There has existed from eternity some one unchangeable and independent being. For since something must needs have been from eternity; as hath been already proved, and is granted on all hands: either there has always existed one unchangeable and *independent* Being, from which all other beings that are or ever were in the universe, have received their origin; or else there has been an infinite succession of changeable and *dependent* beings, produced one from another in an endless progression, without any original cause at all: which latter supposition is so very absurd, that tho' all atheism must in its account of most things terminate in it, yet I think very few atheists ever were so weak as openly and directly to defend it. For it is plainly impossible and contradictory to itself. I shall not argue against it from the supposed impossibility of infinite succession, *barely and absolutely considered in itself;* for a reason which shall be mentioned hereafter: but if we consider such an infinite progression, as *one* entire *series of dependent* beings; it is plain that this whole *series* of beings can have no cause *from without,* of its existence: because in it are supposed to be included *all things* that are or ever were in the universe: and it is plain it can have no reason *within itself,* of its existence; because no one being in this infinite succession is supposed to be self-existent or *necessary* (which is the only ground or reason of existence of any thing, that can be imagined *within the thing itself*), but every one *dependent* on the foregoing: and where *no part* is necessary; it is manifest *the whole* cannot be necessary; absolute necessity of existence, not being an outward, relative, and accidental determination; but an inward and essential property of the nature of the thing which so exists. An infinite succession therefore of merely *dependent* beings, without any original independent cause; is a *series* of beings, that has neither necessity nor cause, nor any reason *at all* of its existence, neither *within itself* nor *from without:* that is, it is an express contradiction and impossibility; it is a supposing *something* to be *caused;* and yet that in the whole it is caused *absolutely by nothing:* Which everyone knows is a contradiction to be done

From: Samuel Clarke, *A Demonstration of the Being and Attributes of God* (1705), Part 2.

in time; and because duration in this case makes no difference, it is equally a contradiction to suppose it done from eternity: And consequently there must *on the contrary,* of necessity have existed from eternity, *some one* immutable and *independent* Being.

Clarke, like Aquinas before him, identifies this independent and necessary Being with God. We are dependent, or contingent, beings. Reducing the argument to the bare bones, the argument from contingency goes like this:

1. Every being that exists is either contingent or necessary.
2. Not every being can be a contingent.
3. Therefore, there exists a necessary Being upon which the contingent beings depend.
4. A necessary Being on which all contingent beings exist is what we mean by "God."
5. Therefore, God exists.

A necessary Being is self-existing and independent and has the explanation of its existence in itself, whereas contingent beings do not have the reason for their existence in themselves but depend on other beings and, ultimately, depend on a necessary Being.

The argument from contingency has one advantage over the First Cause argument: The necessary Being must still exist as that which supports all else that is. It cannot have ceased to be or "moved to a better neighborhood." The world is like a set of chains that are supported in midair. You can trace the links of the chain backwards, but somewhere there has to be a being sufficient to sustain the whole chain of dependent beings; and that is a necessary or independent Being, God.

The argument is not without problems, however. The weak link occurs between premises 2 and 3. From the fact that not every being is contingent or dependent, it does not follow that there must be one necessarily existing, independent Being. The mistake in this inference is called the *fallacy of composition,* the form of which is the following:

1. Every member of the collection of dependent beings is accounted for by some explanation.
2. Therefore, the collection of dependent beings is accounted for by one explanation.

Premise 2 does not follow from premise 1 because every member of the collection can be explained by some other member of the collection (just in case the collection is infinitely large) or by several different explanations rather than just one.

Consider these illustrations of the fallacy. First,

1. Every human being has a mother.
2. Therefore, every human being has the same mother.

That is, one woman and only one woman has had all the children who have ever been born. Second,

1. Every sailor loves a girl.
2. Therefore, some girl—say, Sally—is loved by every sailor.

It is absurd to believe that there is just one mother in the world or that every sailor loves the same girl, Sally. But just as it is absurd to infer from the fact that every sailor loves someone, that there is just one girl that is loved, so it is illicit to infer from the fact that every contingent fact needs to be grounded in a non-contingent fact that there is just *one noncontingent* or *necessary* Being who explains all the contingent ones. Why couldn't there be many necessary beings? Or, recurring to the chain metaphor mentioned above, why couldn't there be many individual chains held by various necessary beings?

The American philosopher Richard Taylor has sought to revive the argument from contingency. He invites us to consider a fascinating thought experiment.

METAPHYSICS

Suppose you were strolling in the woods and, in addition to the sticks, stones, and other accustomed litter of the forest floor, you one day came upon some quite unaccustomed object, something not quite like what you had ever seen before and would never expect to find in such a place. Suppose, for example, that it is a large ball, about your own height, perfectly smooth and translucent. You would deem this puzzling and mysterious, certainly, but if one considers the matter, it is no more inherently mysterious that such a thing should exist than that anything else should exist. If you were quite accustomed to finding such objects of various sizes around you most of the time, but had never seen an ordinary rock, then upon finding a large rock in the woods one day you would be just as puzzled and mystified. This illustrates the fact that something that is mysterious ceases to seem so simply by its accustomed presence. It is strange indeed, for example, that a world such as ours should exist; yet few men are very often struck by this strangeness, but simply take it for granted.

Suppose, then, that you have found this translucent ball and are mystified by it. Now whatever else you might wonder about it, there is one thing you would hardly question; namely, that it did not appear there all by itself, that it owes its existence to something. You might not have the remotest idea whence and how it came to be there, but you would hardly doubt that there was an explanation. The idea that it might have come from nothing at all, that it might exist without there being any explanation of its existence, is one that few people would consider worthy of entertaining.

If we look at the starry skies, contemplate the vast expanse of the heavens, and then consider the mystery of the subatomic world of neutrons, electrons, protons, positrons, mesons, and so forth, do we not have a mystery more wonderful than a twenty-foot glowing, translucent sphere? Shouldn't the universe, life and, especially, consciousness cause a sense of deep wonder within? Do we

From: Richard Taylor, *Metaphysics,* 3rd ed. (Englewood Cliffs, NJ: Prentice Hall, 1983), 91–92. Reprinted by permission of Pearson Education.

take this mystery for granted simply because we are used to it? Should we not sit like little children before the wonder of the universe and ask fundamental questions? Taylor continues:

> This illustrates a metaphysical belief that seems to be almost a part of reason itself, even though few men ever think upon it; the belief, namely, that there is some explanation for the existence of anything whatever, some reason why it should exist rather than not. The sheer nonexistence of anything, which is not to be confused with the passing out of existence of something, never requires a reason; but existence does. That there should never have been any such ball in the forest does not require any explanation or reason, but that there should ever be such a ball does. If one were to look upon a barren plain and ask why there is not and never has been any large translucent ball there, the natural response would be to ask why there should be; but if one finds such a ball, and wonders why it is there, it is not quite so natural to ask why it should *not* be, as though existence should simply be taken for granted. That anything should not exist, then, and that, for instance, no such ball should exist in the forest, or that there should be no forest for it to occupy, or no continent containing a forest, or no earth, nor any world at all, do not seem to be things for which there needs to be any explanation or reason; but that such things should be, does seem to require a reason.
>
> The principle involved here has been called the principle of sufficient reason. Actually, it is a very general principle, and is best expressed by saying that, in the case of any positive truth, there is some sufficient reason for it, something which, in this sense, makes it true—in short, that there is some sort of explanation, known or unknown, for everything.[2]

The *principle of sufficient reason*, named by G. W. Leibniz (1646–1716), holds that nothing takes place without a reason sufficient to determine why it is as it is and not otherwise. A universe exists. Why? There must be a reason that explains this fact. Taylor continues with a rendition of the argument from contingency:

> Now some truths depend on something else, and are accordingly called *contingent*, while others depend only upon themselves, that is, are true by their very nature and are accordingly called *necessary*. There is, for example, a reason why the stone on my window sill is warm; namely, that the sun is shining upon it. This happens to be true, but not by its very nature. Hence it is contingent, and depends upon something other than itself. It is also true that all the points of a circle are equidistant from the center, but this truth depends upon nothing but itself. No matter what happens, nothing can make it false. Similarly, it is a truth, and a necessary one, that if the stone on my window sill is a body, as it is, then it has a form, because this fact depends upon nothing but itself for its confirmation. Untruths are also, of course, either contingent or necessary, it being contingently false, for example, that the stone on my window sill is cold, and necessarily false that it is both a body and formless, because this is by its very nature impossible.

Taylor concedes that the principle of sufficient reason cannot be proved, but it seems a natural presupposition for all thinking about reality. It's hard to argue for it, for in doing so we would have to appeal to the principle itself:

> For this reason it might be properly called a presupposition of reason itself. One can deny that it is true, without embarrassment or fear of refutation, but one is then apt to find that what he is denying is not really what the principle asserts. We shall, then, treat it here as a datum—not something that is provably true, but as something which all men, whether they ever reflect upon it or not, seem more or less to presuppose.

But the fact is. There is a world. Something exists. But why? Why is there something and not just nothing at all?

> Although no one ever seriously supposes that this might not be so, that there might exist nothing at all, there still seems to be nothing the least necessary in this, considering it just by itself. That no world should ever exist at all is perfectly comprehensible and seems to express not the slightest absurdity. Considering any particular item in the world it seems not at all necessary in itself that it should ever have existed, nor does it appear any more necessary that the totality of these things, or any totality of things, should ever exist.
>
> From the principle of sufficient reason it follows, of course, that there must be a reason, not only for the existence of everything in the world but for the world itself, meaning by "the world" simply everything that ever does exist, except God, in case there is a god. This principle does not imply that there must be some purpose or goal for everything, or for the totality of all things; for explanations need not, and in fact seldom are, teleological or purposeful. All the principle requires is that there be some sort of reason for everything. And it would certainly be odd to maintain that everything in the world owes its existence to something, that nothing in the world is either purely accidental, or such that it just bestows its own being upon itself, and then to deny this of the world itself. One can indeed *say* that the world is in some sense a pure accident, that there simply is no reason at all why this or any world should exist, and one can equally say that the world exists by its very nature, or is an inherently necessary being. But it is at least very odd and arbitrary to deny of this existing world the need for any sufficient reason, whether independent of itself or not, while presupposing that there is a reason for every other thing that ever exists.
>
> Consider again the strange ball that we imagine has been found in the forest. Now we can hardly doubt that there must be an explanation for the existence of such a thing, though we may have no notion what that explanation is. It is not, moreover, the fact of its having been found in the forest rather than elsewhere that renders an explanation necessary. It matters not in the least where it happens to be, for our question is not how it happens to be *there* but how it happens to exist at all. If we in our imagination annihilate the forest, leaving only this ball in an open field, our conviction that it is a contingent thing and owes its existence to something other than itself is not reduced in the least. If we now imagine the field to be annihilated, and in fact everything else as well to vanish into nothingness, leaving only this ball to constitute the entire physical

universe, then we cannot for a moment suppose that its existence has thereby been explained, or the need of any explanation eliminated, or that its existence is suddenly rendered self-explanatory. If we now carry this thought one step further and suppose that no other reality ever has existed or ever will exist, that this ball forever constitutes the entire physical universe, then we must still insist on there being some reason independent of itself why it should exist rather than not. If there must be a reason for the existence of any particular thing, then the necessity of such a reason is not eliminated by the mere supposition that certain other things do *not* exist. And again, it matters not at all what the thing in question is, whether it be large and complex, such as the world we actually find ourselves in, or whether it be something small, simple and insignificant, such as a ball, a bacterium, or the merest grain of sand. We do not avoid the necessity of a reason for the existence of something merely by describing it in this way or that. And it would, in any event, seem quite plainly absurd to say that if the world were comprised entirely of a single ball about six feet in diameter, or of a single grain of sand, then it would be contingent and there would have to be some explanation other than itself why such a thing exists, but that, since the actual world is vastly more complex than this, there is no need for an explanation of its existence, independent of itself.

Creation

This brings out an important point with respect to the concept of creation that is often misunderstood, particularly by those whose thinking has been influenced by Christian ideas. People tend to think that creation—for example, the creation of the world by God—*means* creation *in time,* from which it of course logically follows that if the world had no beginning in time, then it cannot be the creation of God. This, however, is erroneous, for creation means essentially *dependence,* even in Christian theology. If one thing is the creation of another, then it depends for its existence on that other, and this is perfectly consistent with saying that both are eternal, that neither ever came into being, and hence, that neither was ever created at any point of time. Perhaps an analogy will help convey this point. Consider, then, a flame that is casting beams of light. Now there seems to be a clear sense in which the beams of light are dependent for their existence upon the flame, which is their source, while the flame, on the other hand, is not similarly dependent for its existence upon them. The beams of light arise from the flame, but the flame does not arise from them. In this sense, they are the creation of the flame; they derive their existence from it. And none of this has any reference to time; the relationship of dependence in such a case would not be altered in the slightest if we supposed that the flame, and with it the beams of light, had always existed, that neither had ever *come* into being.

Now if the world is the creation of God, its relationship to God should be thought of in this fashion; namely, that the world depends for its existence upon God, and could not exist independently of God. If God is eternal, as those who believe in God generally assume, then the world may (though it need not) be eternal too, without that altering in the least its dependence upon God for its existence, and hence without altering its being the creation of God. The supposition of God's eternality, on the other hand, does not by itself imply that the world is eternal too; for there is not the least reason why something of finite duration might not depend for its existence upon something of infinite duration—though the reverse is, of course, impossible.

God

If we think of God as "the creator of heaven and earth," and if we consider heaven and earth to include everything that exists except God, then we appear to have, in the foregoing considerations, fairly strong reasons for asserting that God, as so conceived, exists. Now of course most people have much more in mind than this when they think of God, for religions have ascribed to God ever so many attributes that are not at all implied by describing him merely as the creator of the world; but that is not relevant here. Most religious persons do, in any case, think of God as being at least the creator, as that being upon which everything ultimately depends, no matter what else they may say about him in addition. It is, in fact, the first item in the creeds of Christianity that God is the "creator of heaven and earth." And, it seems, there are good metaphysical reasons, as distinguished from the persuasions of faith, for thinking that such a creative being exists.

Does Taylor's version escape the objections leveled against Clarke's version of the argument from contingency? I must leave it to your judgment to wrestle with this question. But even if the answer to these questions is affirmative, we may still ask whether God is the only answer to the perplexing mysteries of existence. Does God constitute a good explanation? Could we go on to ask "Who caused God?" Does the answer that God is eternal and uncaused satisfy us any better than saying that the world just is eternal or that matter is uncaused and eternal?

Summary

The cosmological arguments seek to answer the questions "Why is there a universe at all?" "Why is there something and not just nothing?" "Why are we here?" Some philosophers believe that these are inappropriate questions to ask because we have no basis for answering them. Others agree that they are valid questions, but the proper answer is "I don't know, and I don't know anyone else who does." But the religious person offers the existence of a personal, completely good Creator as the answer to that question. But unless he or she has more evidence than simply the cosmological argument, that answer will be an extraordinary leap in logic. The cosmological argument *may* offer some evidence for a divine creation, but more needs to be added before we can have the God of **theism**.

FOR FURTHER REFLECTION

1. What are the primary functions of religion in society? Why do you think religion has played such an important role in human affairs? Discuss your answer.

2. Sigmund Freud said that religion is a projection of the father image. Little children grow up thinking their parents, often their fathers, are godlike and very powerful. They stand in reverent awe of his grandeur and look to him for providential support. When they become teens, they realize that their fathers are also mortal and not especially powerful, but they still have this inclination to worship the kind of being that they revered as small children—hence the projection on the empty skies of the father image.

What do you think of Freud's account as an explanation of religious belief? How might a theist respond to it?

3. The current view of physicists and astronomers is that the universe came into being about 15 or 16 billion years ago when an incredibly tiny compact bit of matter exploded in the big bang. From this explosion, the universe swiftly expanded and is still doing so. Does the big bang theory offer an alternate account of the origin of the universe to the religious account? Can the big bang itself be viewed as a contingent event? Can we ask what caused the big bang? What is the explanation of the big bang?

4. Sometimes it is argued that the cosmological argument unwarrantedly assumes that an infinite regress is impossible and that we need a First Cause. Does science accept the possibility of an infinite regress of causes? Or is the idea of a big bang itself an attempt to stop the regress?

5. Is the theist's answer that God is the explanation for the universe really a better one than the nontheist's claim that the universe itself just is eternal or that matter is uncaused and eternal?

NOTES

1. Thomas Aquinas, *Summa Theologica,* trans. Laurence Shapcote (London: Benziger, 1911).
2. All remaining passages are from Richard Taylor, *Metaphysics,* 3rd ed. (Englewood Cliffs, NJ: Prentice Hall, 1983). Reprinted by permission.

FOR FURTHER READING

Philosophy of Religion in General

Hick, John. *Arguments for the Existence of God.* London: Macmillan, 1971. A clearly written, insightful examination of the central arguments.

Mackie, J. L. *The Miracle of Theism.* Oxford, UK: Oxford University Press, 1982. A lively discussion of the proofs for the existence of God and other issues by one of the ablest atheist philosophers of our time.

Martin, Michael. *Atheism.* Philadelphia: Temple University Press, 1990. The most comprehensive attack on theism in the English language. Clearly set forth.

Peterson, Michael, William Hasker, Bruce Reichenbach, and David Basinger. *Reason and Religious Belief.* New York: Oxford University Press, 1991. A clearly written, helpful book from a theist point of view.

Pojman, Louis, ed. *Philosophy of Religion: An Anthology,* 4th ed. Belmont, CA: Wadsworth, 2002. A comprehensive anthology, setting forth both sides of every issue.

Rowe, William. *Philosophy of Religion: An Introduction*. Belmont, CA: Wadsworth, 1978. A readable, reliable introductory work by a first-rate scholar.

Swinburne, Richard. *The Existence of God*. Oxford, UK: Oxford University Press, 1979. Perhaps the most sustained and cogent defense of theism in the literature.

Wainwright, William J. *Philosophy of Religion*. Belmont, CA: Wadsworth, 1988. A careful, well-argued text from a theistic perspective.

The Cosmological Argument

(All the books listed above have important chapters on the cosmological argument.)

Craig, William. *The Cosmological Argument from Plato to Leibniz*. New York: Barnes & Noble, 1980. A good survey of the history of the argument.

Gale, Richard. *On the Nature and Existence of God*. Cambridge, UK: Cambridge University Press, 1992. Chapter 7 is an excellent discussion of the argument.

Rowe, William. *The Cosmological Argument*. Princeton, NJ: Princeton University Press, 1971. A thorough and penetrating study.

8 ⚘ The Teleological Argument for the Existence of God

A Designer

The teleological argument for the existence of God begins with the premise that the world exhibits intelligent purpose or order and proceeds to the conclusion that there must be or probably is a divine intelligence, a supreme designer to account for the observed or perceived intelligent purpose or order. Although the argument has been cited in Plato and in Cicero, we find expressions of the argument in the Bible, both the Hebrew Bible (Old Testament) and in the New Testament:

> The heavens declare the glory of God; and the firmament showeth his handiwork. Day unto day uttereth speech, and night unto night showeth knowledge. There is no speech nor language where their voice is not heard. Their line is gone out through all the earth. (Psalms 19, King James Version)

> For the wrath of God is revealed from heaven against all ungodliness and wickedness of men who by their wickedness suppress the truth. For what can be known about God is plain to them, because God has shown it to them. Ever since the creation of the world his invisible nature, namely, his eternal power and deity, has been clearly perceived in the things that have been made. So they are without excuse. (Romans 1, Revised Standard Version)

The clearest sustained treatment is found in William Paley's *Natural Theology,* where he offers his famous "watch" argument.

NATURAL THEOLOGY

In crossing a heath, suppose I pitched my foot against a stone, and were asked how the stone came to be there: I might possibly answer, that for any thing I knew to the contrary, it had lain there for ever: nor would it perhaps be very easy to shew the absurdity of this answer. But suppose I had found a watch upon the ground, and it should be inquired how the watch happened to be in that place. I should hardly think of the answer which I had before given, that, for any thing I knew, the watch might have always been there. Yet why should not this answer serve for the watch as well as for the stone? Why is it not as admissible in the second case, as in the first?

For this reason, and for no other, namely, that when we come to inspect the watch, we perceive (what we could not discover in the stone) that its several parts are framed and put together for a purpose, e.g., that they are so formed and adjusted as to produce motion, and that motion so regulated as to point out the hour of the day; that, if the different parts had been differently shaped from what they are, of a different size from what they are, or placed after any other manner, or in any other order, than that in which they are placed, either no motion at all would have been carried on in the machine, or none that would have answered the use that is now served by it. This mechanism being observed, the inference is inevitable, that the watch must have had a maker. That there must have existed, at some time, and at some place or other, an artificer or artificers, who formed it for the purpose which we find it actually to answer; who comprehended its construction, and designed its use.

Every indication of contrivance, every manifestation of design, which existed in the watch, exists in the works of nature; with the difference, on the side of nature, of being greater and more, and that in a degree which exceeds all computation.

Paley argues that just as we infer an intelligent designer to account for the purpose-revealing watch, we must analogously infer to an intelligent grand designer to account for the purpose-revealing world: "Every indication of contrivance, every manifestation of design, which existed in the watch, exists in the works of nature; with the difference, on the side of nature, of being greater and more, and that in a degree which exceeds all computation." The skeleton of the argument looks like this:

1. Human artifacts are products of intelligent design. (Purpose)
2. The universe resembles these human artifacts.
3. Therefore, the universe is (probably) a product of intelligent design. (Purpose)
4. But the universe is vastly more complex and gigantic than a human artifact.
5. Therefore, there probably is a powerful and vastly intelligent designer who designed the universe.

From: William Paley, *Natural Theology* (1802).

Hume's Critique

Ironically, Paley's argument was attacked even before Paley had set it down, for the great Scottish skeptic David Hume (1711–1776) had long before written his famous *Dialogues Concerning Natural Religion* (published posthumously in 1779), which constitutes the classic critique of the teleological argument. Paley seems to have been aware of it. In it, the natural theologian Cleanthes debates the orthodox believer Demea and the skeptic or critic Philo who does most of the serious arguing.

First, Hume allows Cleanthes to set forth with argument from design with greater force.

DIALOGUES CONCERNING NATURAL RELIGION

The chief argument for divine existence is derived from the order of nature. Where there appear marks of intelligence and design, you think it extravagant to assign for its cause either chance or the blind unguided force of matter. This is an argument from effects to causes. From the order of the work, you infer there must have been project and forethought in the workman.

Look around the world. Contemplate the whole and every part of it. You will find it to be nothing but one great machine, subdivided into an infinite number of lesser machines, which again admit of subdivisions to a degree beyond what human senses can trace and explain.

All these various machines, and even their most minute parts, are adjusted to each other with an accuracy which ravishes into admiration all men who have ever contemplated them. The curious adapting of means to ends, throughout all nature, resembles exactly, though it much exceeds, the productions of human contrivance, human design, human thought, wisdom, and intelligence.

Anatomize the eye. Survey its structure and contrivance. Does not the idea of contriver immediately flow in upon you with the force like that of a sensation? Behold the male and female of each species, their instincts, their passions, the whole course of their life before and after generation. Millions of such instances present themselves through every part of the universe. Can language convey a more intelligible, more irresistible meaning than the curious adjustment of means to ends in nature?

Since the effects (natural productions and human productions) resemble each other, you led to infer, by analogy, that the causes also resemble; that the author of nature is somewhat similar to the mind of man, though possessed of larger powers, proportioned to the grandeur of the work He has created.

You compare the universe to productions of human intelligence, to houses, ships, furniture, machines, and so forth. Since both terms to the comparison exhibit adaptation and design, you argue that the cause of the one must resemble the cause of the other.

From: David Hume, *Dialogues Concerning Natural Religion* (1779).

Hume, through Philo, attacks the argument from different angles. He first argues that the universe is not sufficiently like the productions of human design to support the argument.

> But can you think, Cleanthes, that your usual phlegm and philosophy have been pre-served in so wide a step as you have taken, when you compare to the universe, houses, ships, furniture, machines; and from their similarity in some circumstances infer a simi-larity in their causes? But can a conclusion, with any propriety, be transferred from the parts to the whole? Does not the great disproportion bar all comparison and infer-ences? From observing the growth of a hair, can we learn anything concerning the generation of a man?[1]

Hume claims that we cannot argue from the parts to the whole, but is he cor-rect? If I test the waters of the Atlantic Ocean off the coast of North Carolina and find them to be salt water, and then test the waters off the coast of New Jersey with the same result, and then off the coast of Wales, can't I make an inductive inference about the rest of the Atlantic Ocean, that it is probably filled with salt water?

When is it and when is it not legitimate to reason from the parts to the whole? If all we have are a few instances that point to a common conclusion (like our ocean-water case), we have a *weak* inductive argument, though one that grows stronger each time new confirming evidence is forthcoming. But until it is well confirmed, as it is in the case of ocean water being salty, we should not base too much weight on our slight experience.

Hume (through Philo) continues to question the argument from design.

> When two things (human intelligence and human products) have always been observed to be conjoined together, I can infer, by custom, the existence of one wher-ever I see the existence of the other; and this I call an *argument from experience*, but how this argument can have place where the objects are, as in the present case, single, individual, without parallel or specific resemblance, may be difficult to explain. And will any man tell me with a serious countenance that an orderly universe must arise from some thought and art like the human because we have experience of it? To justify such reasoning it would be necessary that we had experience of the origin of worlds; and it is not sufficient, surely, that we have seen ships and cities arise from human art and contrivance.

So the analogy from artifact to divine designer fails because we have no other universe to compare this one with, which would be necessary in order to decide if it were the kind of universe designed or simply the kind that developed on its own. As C. S. Peirce put it, "Universes are not plentiful as blackberries." Since there is only one of them, we have no standard of com-parison by which to judge it. Paley's answer to this would be that if we can find one clear instance of purposiveness in nature (for example, the eye), we have a sufficient instance enabling us to conclude that there is probably an intelligent designer.

The theist may object, however, that Hume misses the point of the argument from analogy. If the analogy comes close enough to what it is compared with, it makes its conclusion probable. Note how the argument from analogy works:

1. We have an object O_1 and want to determine whether it has a property P_1. We note that it has other properties in common with objects O_2, O_3, and so on.
2. O_1, O_2, O_3, . . . all have P_2, P_3, and P_4.
3. Then we discover that O_2, O_3, . . . all have P_1, the property in question. So we infer that *probably* O_1 also has P_1.

Suppose I am interested in buying a certain kind of Ford. I reason that other Fords of this kind that I or my acquaintances have owned have served us very well, so I reason that this Ford will probably serve me well.

Suppose I want to determine whether a mushroom (O_1), which I have just pulled up from the ground, is edible (P_1). I note that it is similar in shape, color, and constituency (P_2, P_3, P_4) with other mushrooms (O_2, O_3, . . .) that turned out to be edible (P_1). So I infer that probably this mushroom (O_1) is edible (P_1).

Similarly, this world resembles manufactured machines (O_2, O_3, . . .), so it probably has the property (P_1) of having an intelligent designer.

Hume, however, points out a fundamental problem with such reasoning from analogy. Let's return to the text.

> Now *Cleanthes,* said *Philo,* with an air of alacrity and triumph, mark the consequences. *First,* by this method of reasoning you renounce all claim to infinity in any of the attributes of the Deity. For, as the cause ought only to be proportioned to the effect, and the effect, so far as it falls under our cognizance, is not infinite: What pretensions have we, upon your suppositions, to ascribe that attribute to the Divine Being? You will still insist that, by removing him so much from all similarity to human creatures, we give in to the most arbitrary hypothesis, and at the same time weaken all proofs of his existence.
>
> *Secondly,* you have no reason, on your theory, for ascribing perfection to the Deity, even in his finite capacity; or for supposing him free from every error, mistake, or incoherence, in his undertakings. There are many inexplicable difficulties in the works of Nature which, if we allow a perfect author to be proved *a priori,* are easily solved, and become only seeming difficulties from the narrow capacity of man, who cannot trace infinite relations. But according to your method of reasoning, these difficulties become all real; and, perhaps, will be insisted on as new instances of likeness to human art and contrivance. At least, you must acknowledge that it is impossible for us to tell, from our limited views, whether this system contains any great faults or deserves any considerable praise if compared to other possible and even real systems. Could a peasant if the *Aeneid* were read to him, pronounce that poem to be absolutely faultless, or even assign to it its proper rank among the productions of human wit, he who had never seen any other production?

> But were this world ever so perfect a production, it must still remain uncertain whether all the excellences of the work can justly be ascribed to the workman. If we survey a ship, what an exalted idea must we form of the ingenuity of the carpenter who framed so complicated, useful, and beautiful a machine? And what surprise must we feel when we find him a stupid mechanic who imitated others, and copied an art which, through a long succession of ages, after multiplied trials, mistakes, corrections, deliberation, and controversies, had been gradually improving? Many worlds might have been botched and bungled, throughout an eternity, ere this system was struck out; much labor lost; many fruitless trials made; and a slow but continued improvement carried on during infinite ages in the art of world-making. In such subjects, who can determine where the truth, nay, who can conjecture where the probability lies, amidst a great number of hypotheses which may be proposed, and a still greater which may be imagined?

What is Hume saying in this passage? To the extent that the universe resembles a man-made artifact, to that extent God becomes finitized or limited (that is, we are guilty of **anthropomorphism**—the tendency to humanize God), but if we go the other way and say that the universe is much vaster and different than anything (in order to save the infinity of God), the analogy breaks down, for then the necessary likeness becomes attenuated:

Anthropomorphism ◄─────────────────────────── Infinity
(Analogy works, but God is limited.)   *(Analogy breaks down.)*

Following up on this last point, Hume offers a third criticism of the analogy argument. The analogy leads us to infer the existence of a grand anthropomorphic designer, a human writ large, who has all the properties that we have: "Why not become a perfect anthropomorphite? Why not assert the Deity or Deities to be corporeal, and to have eyes, a nose, mouth, ears, etc.?"

Hume's fourth objection is that the so-called design of the universe seems to be flawed with evil and inexactness, so that we should consistently infer that the designer is imperfect or not terribly intelligent or no longer interested in his work of bygone years. Perhaps there is a plurality of designers. (We will deal with the problem of evil in Chapter 11.)

Hume makes several other points against the design argument. The universe resembles in some ways an animal and in other ways a plant, in which case argument fails since it depends on our seeing the world as a grand machine rather than as an animal or plant. Do you agree with Hume here?

Hume also points out that the universe might well be the result of mere chance. Here is Hume's conclusion.

> In a word, *Cleanthes,* a man who follows your hypothesis is able, perhaps, to assert or conjecture that the universe sometimes arose from something like design: But beyond that position he cannot ascertain one single circumstance, and is left afterwards to fix every point of his theology by the utmost license of fancy and hypothesis. This world, for aught he knows, is very faulty and imperfect, compared to a superior standard; and was only the first rude essay of some infant deity who afterwards abandoned it,

ashamed of his lame performance: It is the work only of some dependent, inferior deity, and is the object of derision to his superiors: It is the production of old age and dotage in some superannuated deity; and ever since his death has run on at adventures, from the first impulse and active force which it received from him.... You justly give signs of horror, *Demea*, at these strange suppositions; but these, and a thousand more of the same kind, are *Cleanthes'* suppositions, not mine. From the moment the attributes of the Deity are supposed finite, all these have place. And I cannot, for my part, think that so wild and unsettled a system of theology is, in any respect, preferable to none at all.

The Darwinian Objection

A modern objection to the argument, one that was anticipated by Hume, is that based on Darwinian evolution, which has cast doubt upon the notion of the teleological explanation all together. Charles Darwin, in his *Origin of the Species* (1859), observed that the process from simpler organisms to more complex ones took place gradually over many centuries through an apparently nonpurposive process of trial and error, of natural selection and survival of the fittest. As Julian Huxley put it,

> The evolutionary process results immediately and automatically from the basic property of living matter—that of self-copying, but with occasional errors. Self-copying leads to multiplication and competition; the errors in self-copying are what we call mutations, and mutations will inevitably confer different degrees of biological advantage or disadvantage on their possessors. The consequence will be differential reproduction down the generations—in other words, natural selection.[2]

As important as Darwin's contribution is in offering us an alternative model with respect to biological development, it doesn't altogether destroy the argument from design, for the theist can still argue that the process of natural selection is the *way* an ultimate designer is working out his purpose for the world. The argument from design could still be used as an argument to the best explanation, as an abductive argument.

Oxford University philosopher Richard Swinburne, a modern Cleanthes, rejects Hume's skepticism with regard to the design argument. We cannot simply take the orderliness of the universe for granted. It calls out for an explanation.

THE EXISTENCE OF GOD

Suppose that a madman kidnaps a victim and shuts him in a room with a card-shuffling machine. The machine shuffles ten packs of cards simultaneously and then draws a card from each pack and exhibits simultaneously ten cards. The kidnapper tells the victim that he will shortly set the machine to work and it will exhibit its first draw, but that unless the draw consists of an ace of hearts from each pack, the machine will simultaneously set off an explosion which will kill the victim, in consequence of which he will not see which cards the machine drew. The machine is then set to work, and to the amazement and relief of the victim the machine exhibits an ace of hearts drawn from each pack. The victim thinks that this extraordinary fact needs an explanation in terms of the machine having been rigged in some way. But the kidnapper, who now reappears, casts doubt on this suggestion. "It is hardly surprising," he says, "that the machine draws only aces of hearts. You could not possibly see anything else. For you would not be here to see anything at all, if any other cards had been drawn." But of course the victim was right and the kidnapper is wrong. There is indeed something extraordinary in need of explanation in ten aces of hearts being drawn. The fact that this peculiar order is a necessary condition of the draw being perceived at all makes what is perceived no less extraordinary and in need of explanation. The teleologist's starting-point is not that we perceive order rather than disorder, but that order rather than disorder is there.

Evaluate this argument. Does it lend credence to the teleological argument?

Swinburne rejects all deductive forms of arguments for the existence of God and in their place sets a series of inductive arguments: versions of the cosmological argument, the teleological argument, the argument from religious experience and others. Though none of these alone proves the existence of God or shows it to be more probable than not, each adds to the probability of God's existence. Together they constitute a cumulative case in favor of theism. There is something crying for an explanation: Why does this grand universe exist? Together the arguments for God's existence provide a plausible explanation of the existence of the universe, of why we are here, of why there is anything at all and not just nothing.

Swinburne's arguments are set in terms of confirmation theory. He distinguishes arguments that are *P*-inductive (where the premises make the conclusion probable) from those that are *C*-inductive (where the premises confirm the probability of the conclusion or make it more probable than it otherwise would be—although not showing the conclusion to be more probable than not). The cosmological and teleological arguments are, according to Swinburne, good *C*-inductive arguments. Since there is no counterargument to theism and religious experience offers "considerable evidential force" in favor of theism, the cumulative effect is "sufficient to make theism all over probable."

Whether and how the cumulative case for theism can be made is a task I must leave for you to decide, but a common objection to it is the "ten leaky buckets" argument. The objector claims that theist is using several bad arguments to make a cumulative case, much as one would try to carry water by putting it into ten leaky buckets. Ten leaky buckets won't hold water any more than one leaky bucket will.

The counterobjection to this objection is to argue that the ten leaky buckets will hold water better than one leaky one just in case the buckets are put inside

From: Richard Swinburne, *The Existence of God* (Oxford, UK: Oxford University Press, 1979).

one another and the leaks of one bucket are covered by the base of the one below it. In the end, the answer may depend on what turns out to be the best explanation of the world and conscious life.

Summary

The teleological argument proceeds from the perceived orderly process in the world and argues to the conclusion that such orderly processes must have an orderer or designer. It is unreasonable to suppose that the incredible intricacy and lawlikeness of the world is just a product of chance. Nevertheless, there are several problems with the argument, among these being the tendency toward anthropomorphism and our inability to make intercosmic comparisons.

FOR FURTHER REFLECTION

1. Evaluate the teleological argument for yourself. What does it indicate about the origins of the universe? Is the hypothesis of a designer plausible? Or can the processes of chance and necessity account for the orderliness we perceive?

2. Assess Swinburne's idea of a cumulative case for the existence of God. Is this a good use of abductive argument, discussed in Chapter 2? Is the case for the existence of God like a case in civil law where both sides try to assemble the evidence in a way that best supports their side of the issue?

3. It is sometimes objected that the "ten leaky buckets" argument begs the question for theism because the metaphor suggests that a composite arrangement of the buckets (and so the arguments) very likely can be made to hold water (demonstrate the existence of God). Evaluate this criticism.

NOTES

1. All remaining passages in this section are from David Hume, *Dialogues Concerning Natural Religion* (1779).
2. Julian Huxley, *Evolution as Process* (New York: Harper & Row, 1953), 4.

FOR FURTHER READING

Hume, David. *Dialogues Concerning Natural Religion,* 1779. A classic critique of the teleological argument.

Swinburne, Richard. "The Argument from Design." *Philosophy* 43 (1968). A response to Hume.

Swinburne, Richard. *The Existence of God*. Oxford, UK: Oxford University Press, 1979.

9 ✢ The Ontological Argument for the Existence of God

The ontological argument for the existence of God is the most intriguing of all the arguments for theism. It is one of the most remarkable arguments ever devised. First set forth by Anselm (1033–1109), Archbishop of Canterbury in the eleventh century, the argument has continued to puzzle and fascinate philosophers ever since. Let the testimony of the agnostic philosopher Bertrand Russell serve as a typical example here.

> I remember the precise moment, one day in 1894, as I was walking along Trinity Lane [at Cambridge University where Russell was a student], when I saw in a flash (or thought I saw) that the ontological argument is valid. I had gone out to buy a tin of tobacco; on my way back, I suddenly threw it up in the air, and exclaimed as I caught it: "Great Scott, the ontological argument is sound!"[1]

The argument is not only important because it claims to be an a priori proof for the existence of God, but it also is the primary locus of such philosophical problems as whether existence is a property and whether the notion of necessary existence is intelligible. Furthermore, it has special religious significance because it is the only one of the traditional arguments that clearly concludes to the necessary properties of God, that is, his omnipotence, omniscience, omnibenevolence, and other great-making properties.

Anselm's Argument

Although there are many versions of the ontological argument and many interpretations of some of these, most philosophers agree on the essential form of Anselm's version in the second chapter of his *Proslogium*. Anselm believes that God's existence is absolutely certain so that only a fool would doubt or deny it. Yet he desires understanding to fulfill his faith.

PROSLOGIUM

And so, Lord, do thou, who dost give understanding to faith, give me, so far as thou knowest it to be profitable, to understand that thou art as we believe; and that thou art that which we believe. And indeed, we believe that thou art a being than which nothing greater can be conceived. Or is there no such nature, since the fool hath said in his heart, there is no God? (Psalms 14:1). But at any rate, this very fool, when he hears of this being of which I speak—a being than which nothing greater can be conceived—understands what he hears, and what he understands is in his understanding; although he does not understand it to exist.

For, it is one thing for an object to be in the understanding, and another to understand that the object exists. When a painter first conceives of what he will afterwards paint, he has it in his understanding, but he does not yet understand it to be, because he has not yet painted it. But after he has made the painting, he both has it in his understanding and he understands that it exists, because he has made it.

Hence, even the fool is convinced that something exists in the understanding, at least, than which nothing greater can be conceived. For, when he hears of this, he understands it. And whatever is understood, exists in the understanding. And assuredly that, than which nothing greater can be conceived, cannot exist in the understanding alone. For, suppose it exists in the understanding alone: then it can be conceived to exist in reality; which is greater.

Therefore, if that, than which nothing greater can be conceived, exists in the understanding alone, the very being, than which nothing greater can be conceived, is one, than which a greater can be conceived. But obviously this is impossible. Hence, there is no doubt that there exists a being, than which nothing greater can be conceived, and it exists both in the understanding and in reality.

Anselm's reasoning may be treated as a reductio ad absurdum argument. That is, it begins with a supposition (S: suppose the greatest conceivable being exists in the mind alone) that is contradictory to what one desires to prove. One then goes about showing that (S) together with other certain or self-evident assumptions (A_1 and A_2) yields a **contradiction,** which in turn demonstrates that the contradictory of (S) must be true.

Anselm's argument goes like this:

From: Anselm, *Proslogium,* trans. S. W. Deane, slightly edited (La Salle, IL: Open Court, 1903).

1. Suppose that the greatest conceivable being (GCB) exists in the mind alone (and not in reality). (S)
2. Existence in reality is greater than existence in the mind alone. (A_1)
3. We can conceive of a GCB that exists in reality as well as the mind. (A_2)
4. Therefore, there is a being that is greater than the GCB. (From premises 1, 2, and 3)
5. But this is impossible, for it is a contradiction.
6. Therefore, it is false that a GCB exists in the mind alone and not in reality (from premises 1 and 5). So a GCB must exist in reality as well as in the mind. This being is, *per definition*, God.

Criticism of Anselm's Argument

Questions immediately arise. Is existence a perfection so that we can say that it is better to exist than not to exist? Or is such a locution nonsense, since you can't compare existing things with nonexisting ones? Does some possible entity become greater by becoming actual?

Gaunilo, Anselm's contemporary, sets forth the first objection to Anselm's argument. Accusing Anselm of "pulling rabbits out of hats," he tells the story of a delectable lost island, one that is more excellent than all lands. Since it is better that such a perfect island exists in reality than simply in the mind alone, this Isle of the Blest must necessarily exist. Anselm's reply is that the analogy fails, for unlike the greatest possible being, the greatest possible island can be conceived as not existing.

Is Gaunilo correct? Some philosophers say no because, simply, some properties do and some properties don't have intrinsic maximums. No matter how wonderful you make the Isle of the Blest, we can conceive of a more wonderful island. The greatness of islands is like the greatness of numbers in this respect. There is no greatest natural number, for no matter how large the number is that you choose, we can always conceive of one twice as large. On the other hand, the properties of God have intrinsic maximums. For example, we can define perfect knowledge this way. For any proposition, an omniscient being knows whether it is true or false.

A second criticism of the ontological argument was lodged by Immanuel Kant (1724–1804), who accused the proponent of the argument of defining God into existence. "Being" is not a real predicate like "red" or "six feet tall" or "rational." The following is the relevant passage.

CRITIQUE OF PURE REASON

"Being" is obviously not a real predicate; that is, it is not a concept of something which could be added to the concept of a thing. It is merely the positing of a thing, or of certain determinations, as existing in themselves. Logically, it is merely the copula of a judgment. The proposition, "God is omnipotent," contains two concepts, each of which

has its object—God and omnipotence. The small word "is" adds no new predicate, but only serves to posit the predicate *in its relation* to the subject. If, now, we take the subject (God) with all its predicates (among which is omnipotence), and say "God is," or "There is a God," we attach no new predicate to the concept of God, but only posit the subject in itself with all its predicates, and indeed posit it as being an *object* that stands in relation to my *concept*. The content of both must be one and the same; nothing can have been added to the concept, which expresses merely what is possible, by my thinking its object (through the expression "it is") as given absolutely. Otherwise stated, the real contains no more than the merely possible. A hundred real thalers do not contain the least coin more than a hundred possible thalers. For as the latter signify the concept, and the former the object and the positing of the object, should the former contain more than the latter, my concept would not, in that case, express the whole object, and would not therefore be an adequate concept of it. My financial position is, however, affected very differently by a hundred real thalers than it is by the mere concept of them (that is, of their possibility). For the object, as it actually exists, is not analytically contained in my concept, but is added to my concept (which is a determination of my state) synthetically; and yet the conceived hundred thalers are not themselves in the least increased through thus acquiring existence outside my concept.

By whatever and by however many predicates we may think a thing—even if we completely determine it—we do not make the least addition to the thing which we further declare that this thing *is*. Otherwise, it would not be exactly the same thing that exists, but something more than we had thought in the concept; and we could not, therefore, say that the exact object of my concept exists. If we think in a thing every feature of reality except one, the missing reality is not added by my saying that this defective thing exists.

Kant claims that Anselm makes the mistake of treating "existence" or "being" as a first-order predicate like "blue" or "great." When you say that the castle is blue, you are adding a property (namely, blueness) to the idea of a castle; but when you say that the castle *exists*, you are not adding anything to the concept of a castle, only saying that the concept is exemplified or instantiated. You are taking a possible property (B) and affirming that it is exemplified (A), claiming that it is actual.

(A) First-order property (actual)

(B) Nonexisting property (possible)

We might say that "real" predicates or properties are first-order properties, but the idea of existence is a second-order property, which asserts something about the status of possible properties. In Anselm's argument, "existence" is treated as a first-order predicate that adds something to the concept of an entity, making it *greater*. This, according to Kant and those who follow him is the fatal flaw in the argument.

Here is another way to make this point. Consider the table on which you are writing and abstract from it all its properties except *existence*. That is, imagine that you could leave it existing without all the other properties: color, shape, substance, function, and so forth. What would be left? Existence alone. But what is the difference between existence alone and nothing at all?

Existence is a funny kind of property that can't *exist* without first-order properties. This is why we label it a second-order property; it tells us whether the other properties are exemplified.

If existence is not a property, it is not a perfection either. Suppose Lisa and Jane each write down the qualities of a perfect husband. Here are their two lists:

Lisa's List	*Jane's List*
Intelligence	Intelligence
Kindness	Kindness
Sense of humor	Sense of humor
Attractive	Attractive
Moral integrity	Moral integrity
	Existence

Lisa and Jane's lists are identical except for the quality of existence on Jane's list. But is Jane's list really better? I don't think so. Jane has misunderstood the purpose of the list, which is to set forth the qualities a perfect husband would have. It's another matter whether these qualities are exemplified in an actual man.

If existence were a perfection, we could define things into existence simply by building the concept of existence into the definition. Suppose we define a "Unicorn" as a horse with horns. No unicorns exist. But suppose we defined a "lunicorn" as a unicorn that exists. So unicorns must exist, since lunicorns exist by definition. Of course, this is just a verbal trick; we cannot define things into existence. This is the point of Kant's criticism.

The Second Version of Anselm's Argument

Although Kant's criticism may work against the standard version of the ontological argument, some philosophers—namely, Charles Hartshorne, Norman Malcolm, and William Lawhead—argue that Anselm had a second version of the argument, based on *necessary* existence. They contend that while existence itself may not be a property or a perfection, necessary existence is. The second version of the ontological argument, as set forth by Lawhead, goes like this:

1. It is possible that God exists.

2. God must be conceived as being the greatest possible being.

3. The greatest possible being must be a necessary being.

From: Immanuel Kant, *Critique of Pure Reason,* trans. J. Meiklejohn (New York: Colonial Press, 1900), 335–336.

4. The existence of a necessary being must be either (a) impossible, (b) merely possible (contingent), or (c) necessary.

5. We can exclude (a), for it cannot be impossible for a necessary being to exist. There is no contradiction in the concept of a necessary being.

6. Nor can it be (b), a mere possibility that God exists, for such existence would be (i) dependent and (ii) happenstance, and such a being could not be God.

7. Therefore, a necessary being necessarily exists. That is, God exists.

Has this new improved version of the ontological argument proved that God exists? Consider the premises. Are they all true? Premise 1 seems all right. Even most atheists acknowledge that it is logically possible that God exists. Premise 2 seems right. God must be thought to be unsurpassably great: omnipotent, omniscient, omnibenevolent, and so forth. Premise 3 also seems all right. It cannot just be an accident that God exists, otherwise his existence needs an explanation. What caused it? A greatest possible being is not contingent or a mere outcome of luck but must necessarily exist, as premises 4 and 5 argue. So it would seem that a necessary being must necessarily exist. God exists! This, if it is true, is a momentous discovery.

Have we really proved that God exists? Well, there are two objections you might consider. The first is that the same argument can be used to prove the existence of an all-powerful devil, defined as the worst possible being. The argument goes like this:

1. It is possible that the devil exists.

2. The devil must be thought as the worst possible being.

3. The worst possible being must be a necessary being.

4. The existence of a necessary being must be either (a) impossible, (b) merely possible (contingent), or (c) necessary.

5. We can exclude (a), for it cannot be impossible for a necessary being to exist. There is no contradiction in the concept of a necessary being.

6. Nor can it be (b), a mere possibility that the devil exists, for such existence would be (i) dependent and (ii) happenstance, and such a being could not be the devil.

7. Therefore, a worst possible being must necessarily exist. That is, the devil exists.

Since it seems contradictory to suppose a best possible being and a worst possible being both exist, for they could not both be all powerful, something must be wrong with this form of the argument.

Some argue that we can only argue for the greatest possible being and not for a worst possible one, since all the other qualities of the devil would be good ones (for example, knowledge, power, and presence). But proponents of the devil argument would argue, following Kant, that the only intrinsically good quality is the goodwill so that all other virtues turn out to be vice-enhancing. If this is correct, the devil argument seems valid.

There is a second objection to Anselm's second argument. The argument still defines things into existence, only this time it defines things into necessary existence. Suppose we list all the triangles ever drawn and someone argues that it is necessary that a greatest possible triangle exists:

1. It is possible that the perfect triangle exists.
2. The perfect triangle must be thought as the best possible triangle.
3. The best possible triangle must be a necessary being.
4. Something that necessarily exists must exist.
5. Therefore, the greatest possible triangle must exist.

But something seems absurd about this argument. There is no reason to believe that such a thing really does exist. Furthermore, couldn't we use the concept of necessary existence to define other things into existence? Consider Lisa and Jane's idea of an ideal husband. When Jane argues that her ideal is better than Lisa's because hers (Jane's) contains the concept of existence, Lisa can shoot back, "But mine contains the property of necessary existence, so my notion of a husband is better." Of course, some would argue that the idea of necessary existence does not apply to such innately contingent beings as husbands, but the question for you to consider is, Why?

Suppose these two criticisms fail to dislodge Anselm's second version of the ontological argument; have we then proved that God exists? I don't think so. What we have done is something interesting but less than a proof. An opponent could still attack the first premise and say that, although it may not be obvious at first sight, it really is not possible that God exists. This is because the argument really gives us only two choices: Either God necessarily exists or necessarily does not exist. Since we do not know which to choose on the basis of the concept of necessary being alone, we may suppose that, given the lack of other evidence, God's existence is impossible.

So the ontological argument, at best, does not prove that God exists. At best, it shows that it is reasonable to believe that he exists, but even that may be too generous. Perhaps it is simply that it is not altogether foolish to believe that a necessary being exists. It is a difficult question.

Summary

The ontological argument is an a priori argument for the existence of God, which attempts to establish the necessity of the existence of God through an understanding of the concept of existence or necessary being. Its strength is that it gives one an idea of an adequate God, one who is maximally powerful and benevolent (a greatest possible being). Though it is difficult to assess in all its multifarious ramifications, no version has been completely successful in proving the existence of God. On the other hand, it may lend a measure of plausibility to the idea of the existence of a maximally powerful and benevolent being. The issue is controversial.

FOR FURTHER REFLECTION

1. Go over the two versions of the ontological argument discussed in this chapter. How telling are Gaunilo's and Kant's criticisms? Does Anselm misunderstand the concept of being, as the critics claim?

2. Is it greater to exist than not to exist, as Anselm argues? Or is the term *greater* used ambiguously or wrongly here?

3. Could a similar argument as Anselm's be used to prove that a perfectly powerful devil exists as the supreme being and creator of the universe?

NOTE

1. Bertrand Russell, *Autobiography of Bertrand Russell* (New York: Little, Brown, 1967).

FOR FURTHER READING

Gale, Richard. *On the Nature and Existence of God.* Cambridge, UK: Cambridge University Press, 1991. Chapter 6 contains an excellent discussion of this argument.

Plantinga, Alvin, ed. *The Ontological Argument from St. Anselm to Contemporary Philosophers.* Garden City, NY: Doubleday, 1965. A good anthology on the subject.

Plantinga, Alvin. *God, Freedom, and Evil.* New York: Harper & Row, 1974. Part 2 contains a brilliant contemporary defense of the argument.

See also the sections in Mackie, Martin, and Pojman listed in the general bibliography in Chapter 7.

10 ✢ The Argument from Religious Experience

There was not a mere consciousness of something there, but fused in the central happiness of it, a startling awareness of some ineffable good. Not vague either, not like the emotional effect of some poem, or scene, or blossom, or music, but the sure knowledge of the close presence of a sort of mighty person, and after it went, the memory persisted as the one perception of reality. Everything else might be a dream, but not that.

William James[1]

The Ego has disappeared. I have realized my identity with Brahman and so all my desires have melted away. I have arisen above my ignorance and my knowledge of this seeming universe. What is this joy I feel? Who shall measure it? I know nothing but joy, limitless, unbounded! The treasure I have found there cannot be described in words. The mind cannot conceive of it. My mind fell like a hailstone into that vast expanse of Brahman's ocean. Touching one drop of it, I melted away and became one with Brahman. Where is this universe? Who took it away? Has it merged into something else? A while ago, I beheld it—now it exists no longer. Is there anything apart or distinct from Brahman? Now, finally and clearly, I know that I am the Atman [the soul identified with Brahman], whose nature is eternal joy. I see nothing, I hear nothing, I know nothing that is separate from me.

Hindu mysticism[2]

Of one who has entered the first trance the voice has ceased; of one who has entered the second trance reasoning and reflection have ceased; of one who has entered the third trance joy has ceased; of one who has entered the fourth trance the inspiration and expiration have ceased; of one who has entered the realm of the infinity of space the perception of form has ceased; of one who has entered the realm of the infinity of consciousness the perception of the realm of the infinity of space has ceased; of one who has entered the realm of nothingness the perception of the realm of the infinity of consciousness has ceased.

Buddhist testimony[3]

Encounters with God

The heart of religion is and always has been experiential. Encounters with the supernatural, a transcendent dimension, the Wholly Other are at the base of every great religion. Abraham hears a Voice that calls him to leave his family in Haran and venture out into a broad unknown, thus becoming the father of Israel. Abraham's grandson, Jacob, wrestles all night with an angel and is transformed, gaining the name "Israel, prince of God." While tending his father-in-law's flock, Moses is appeared to by "I am that I am" (Yahweh) in the burning bush and ordered to deliver Israel out of slavery into a land flowing with milk and honey. Isaiah has a vision of the Lord "high and exalted, and the train of his robe filled the temple" of heaven. In the New Testament, John, James, and Peter behold Jesus gloriously transformed on the Mount of Transfiguration and are themselves transformed by the experience. After the death of Jesus, Saul is traveling to Damascus to persecute Christians, when he is met by a blazing light and hears a Voice, asking him why he is persecuting the Lord.[4] Changing his name to Paul, he becomes the leader of the Christian missionary movement. The Hindu experiences the Atman (soul) as the Brahman (God), "Om sat tat" ("That art Thou") or Arjuna conversing with the glorious Krishna on the battlefield of Kuruksetra. The Advaitian Hindu merges with the One, as a drop of water merges with the vast ocean. The Buddhist merges with Nirvana or beholds a vision of the Buddha. Allah reveals his holy word, the Koran, to Mohammed. Joan of Arc hears voices calling her to save her people, and Joseph Smith has a vision of the angel Moroni calling him to do a new work of God.

Saints, mystics, prophets, ascetics, and common believers—of every creed, of every race, in every land, throughout recorded history—have undergone esoteric experiences that are hard to explain but difficult to dismiss as mere nonsense. Common features appear to link these otherwise disparate experiences to one another, resulting in a common testimony to this Otherness, *a consensus mysticum*. Rudolf Otto characterizes the religious (or "numinal" spiritual) dimension in all of these experiences as the "mysterium tremendum et fascinans." Religion is an unfathomable mystery, *tremendum* ("to be trembled at"), awe inspiring, *fascinans* ("fascinating"), and magnetic. To use a description from Søren Kierkegaard, religious experience is a "sympathetic antipathy and an antipathetic sympathy" before a deep unknown. Like looking into an abyss, it both repulses and strangely attracts.

An Analysis of Religious Experience

What, then, is the problem with religious experience? If I say that I hear a pleasant tune, and you listen and say, "Yes, I hear it now too," we have no problem; but if you listen carefully and don't hear it, you might well wonder whether I am really hearing sounds or only imagine that I am. Perhaps we could bring in others to check the matter out. If they agree with me, well and good; but if they agree with you and don't hear the sounds, then we have a problem. Perhaps we could bring in an audiometer to measure the decibels in the room. If the meter confirms my report, then it is simply a case of my having better hearing than you and the rest of the witnesses; but if the meter doesn't register at all, assuming that it is in working order, we would then have good evidence that I am only imagining the sounds. Perhaps I need to change my claim and say, "Well, I seem to be hearing a pleasant tune."

One problem is that religious experience is typically private. You have the sense of God forgiving you or an angel speaking to you, but I, who am in the same room with you, neither hear, nor see, nor feel anything unusual. You are praying and suddenly feel transported by grace and sense the unity of all reality. I, who am sitting next to you, wonder at the strange expression on your face and ask you if something is wrong. Perhaps you are having an epileptic seizure?

Yet, numerous people, from dairymaids like Joan of Arc to mystics like St. Theresa of Avila and St. John of the Cross, have reported various types of religious experiences. They cannot be simply dismissed without serious analysis.

There are two levels of problem here: (1) To what degree, if any, is the subject of a religious experience justified in inferring from the psychological experience (the subjective aspect) to the reality of that which is the object of the experience (the objective aspect)? (2) To what degree, if any, does the cumulative witness of those undergoing religious experience justify the claim that there is a God or transcendent reality?

Traditionally, the argument from religious experience has not been one of the "proofs" for God's existence. At best it has confirmed and made existential what the proofs conveyed with icy logic. Some philosophers, such as C. D. Broad (1887–1971), as well as contemporary philosophers, such as Richard Swinburne and Gary Gutting, believe that the common experience of mystics is *strong justification* or evidence for all of us for the existence of God.[5] Others, such as William James (1842–1910), believe that religious experience is sufficient evidence for the subject himself or herself for the existence of a divine reality, but only constitutes a possibility for the nonexperiencer. That is, religious experience grants us only *weak justification*. Religious skeptics, like Walter Stace (1886–1967) and Bertrand Russell (1872–1970), doubt this and argue that a subjective experience by itself is never warranted for making an existential claim (of an object existing outside oneself). It is a fallacy to go from the psychological experience of X to the reality of X.

There are two main traditions regarding religious experience. One, which we may call *mystical,* posits the unity of all reality or the unity of the subject with its object (the mystic is absorbed in God, becomes one with God, and so on). The second type of religious experience may be called simply *religious experience* in order to distinguish it from the mystical. It does not conflate the subject with the object but is a numinal experience wherein the believer (or subject) experiences the presence of God or an angel or Christ or the Holy Spirit, either speaking to or appearing to the experient or forgiving him or her. While in prayer believers often experience a sense of the presence of God or the Holy Spirit.

Could religious experiences be delusions? Many psychological explanations cast doubt on its validity. One of the most famous is the Freudian interpretation. In his *The Future of an Illusion,* Freud said that it was the result of the projection of the father image within oneself.

THE FUTURE OF AN ILLUSION

[W]e turn our attention to the psychical origin of religious ideas. These, which are given out as teachings, are not precipitates of experience or end results of thinking: they are illusions, fulfillments of the oldest, strongest and most urgent wishes of mankind. The secret of their strength lies in the strength of those wishes. As we already know, the terrifying impression of helplessness in childhood aroused the need for protection—for protection through love—which was provided by the father; and the recognition that this helplessness lasts throughout life made it necessary to cling to the existence of a father, but this time a more powerful one. Thus the benevolent rule of a divine Providence allays our fear of the dangers of life; the establishment of a moral world-order ensures the fulfillment of the demands of justice, which have so often remained unfulfilled in human civilization; and the prolongation of earthly existence in a future life provides the local and temporal framework in which these wish-fulfillments shall take place. Answers to the riddles that tempt the curiosity of man, such as how the universe began or what the relation is between body and mind, are developed in conformity with the underlying assumptions of this system. It is an enormous relief to the individual psyche if the conflicts of its childhood arising from the father-complex—conflicts which it has never wholly overcome—are removed from it and brought to a solution which is universally accepted.

When I say that these things are all illusions, I must define the meaning of the word. An illusion is not the same thing as an error; nor is it necessarily an error. Aristotle's belief that vermin are developed out of dung (a belief to which ignorant people still cling) was an error; so was the belief of a former generation of doctors that *tabes dorsalis* is the result of sexual excess. It would be incorrect to call these errors illusions. On the other hand, it was an illusion of Columbus's that he had discovered a new searoute to the Indies. The part played by his wish in this error is very clear. One may describe as an illusion the assertion made by certain nationalists that the

---

From: Sigmund Freud, *The Future of an Illusion,* trans. James Starchey (New York: Norton, 1961).

Indo-Germanic race is the only one capable of civilization; or the belief, which was only destroyed by psycho-analysis, that children are creatures without sexuality. What is characteristic of illusions is that they are derived from human wishes. In this respect they come near to psychiatric delusions. But they differ from them, too, apart from the more complicated structure of delusions. In the case of delusions, we emphasize as essential their being in contradiction with reality. Illusions need not necessarily be false—that is to say, unrealizable or in contradiction of reality....Thus we call a belief an illusion when a wish-fulfillment is a prominent factor in its motivation, and in doing so we disregard its relations to reality, just as the illusion itself sets no store by verification.

Although an illusion is not necessarily false, according to Freud, it might just as well be, for wishful thinking is no evidence for a belief. His argument seems to go like this: When you were a child, you looked upon your father as a powerful hero who could do everything, meet all your needs, and overcome the normal obstacles that hindered your way at every step. When you grew older, you sadly realized that your father was fallible and very finite, indeed. But you still had the need of the benevolent, all-powerful father. So, subconsciously you projected your need for that long lost parent onto the empty heavens and invented a god for yourself. Since this is a common phenomenon, all of us who have successfully projected daddy onto the big sky go to church or synagogue or mosque or whatever and worship the illusion on our favorite holy day. But it is a myth. The sky is empty and the sooner we realize it, the better for everyone.

Has Freud disproved the validity of religious experience? No, he has only offered a fascinating hypothesis. Even if it is psychologically true that we tend to think of God like a powerful and loving parent, it could still be the case that the parental relationship is God's way of teaching us about himself—by analogy.

In his classic on the subject, *The Varieties of Religious Experience* (1902), William James describes what he considers the deepest kind of religious experience, mystical experience, a type of experience that transcends our ordinary, sensory experience and that cannot be described in terms of our normal concepts and language. It is *ineffable experience.*

THE VARIETIES OF RELIGIOUS EXPERIENCE

Ineffability—the handiest of the marks by which I classify a state of mind as mystical is negative. The subject of it immediately says that it defies expression, that no adequate report of its contents can be given in words. It follows from this that its quality must be directly experienced; it cannot be imparted or transferred to others. In this peculiarity mystical states are more like states of feelings than like states of intellect. No one can make clear to another who has never had a certain feeling, in what the quality or worth

From: William James, *The Varieties of Religious Experience* (New York: Modern Library, 1902).

of it consists. One must have musical ears to know the value of a symphony; one must have been in love for one's self to understand a lover's state of mind. Lacking the heart or ear, we cannot interpret the musician or the lover justly, and are even likely to consider him weak-minded or absurd. The mystic finds that most of us accord to his experience an equally incompetent treatment.

The experient realizes that the experience "defies expression, that no adequate report of its content can be given in words. It follows from this that its quality must be directly experienced; it cannot be imparted or transferred to others." And yet it contains a *noetic quality*, a content.

Noetic quality—Although so similar to states of feeling, mystical states seem to those who experience them to be also states of knowledge. They are states of insight into depths of truth unplumbed by the discursive intellect. They are illuminations, revelations, full of significance and importance, all inarticulate though they remain; and as a rule they carry with them a curious sense of authority for aftertime.[6]

It purports to convey truth about the nature of reality, namely, that there is a unity of all things and that unity is spiritual, not material. It is antinaturalistic, pantheistic, and optimistic. Ineffability and the noetic aspect are the two main characteristics of mystical experience, but James mentions two others that are usually found in the experience:

Transiency—Mystical states cannot be sustained for long. Except in rare instances, half an hour, or at most an hour or two, seems to be the limit beyond which they fade into the light of common day. Often, when faded, their quality can but imperfectly be reproduced in memory; but when they recur it is recognized; and from one recurrence to another it is susceptible of continuous development in what is felt as inner richness and importance.

Passivity—Although the oncoming of mystical states may be facilitated by preliminary voluntary operations, as by fixing the attention, or going through certain bodily performances, or in other ways which manuals of mysticism prescribe; yet when the characteristic sort of consciousness once has set in, the mystic feels as if his own will were in abeyance, and indeed sometimes as if he were grasped and held by a superior power.[7]

Next, James gives several examples of mystic states, ranging from deep new insight through feeling born again to being in direct contact with the God or the Transcendent. Here is an example of the latter:

I remember the night, and almost the very spot on the hilltop, where my soul opened out, as it were, into the Infinite, and there was a rushing together of the two worlds, the inner and the outer. I stood alone with Him who had made me, and all the beauty of the world, and love, and sorrow, and even temptation. I did not seek Him, but felt the perfect unison of my spirit with His. The darkness held a presence that was all the more felt because it was not seen. I could not any more have doubted that He was there than that I was. I felt myself to be, if possible, the less real of the two.[8]

James is cautious about what can be deduced from mystic experience. While mystic states are and ought to be absolutely authoritative over the individuals to whom they come, "no authority emanates from them which should make it a duty for those who stand outside of them to accept their revelations uncritically."[9] However, their value is that they provide us a valid alternative to the "non-mystical rationalistic consciousness, based on understanding and the senses alone. They open out the possibility of other orders of truth, in which, so far as anything in us vitally responds to them, we may freely continue to have faith."[10]

C. D. Broad goes even further than James. In his article "The Argument from Religious Experience," he likens the religious sense to an ear for music.

THE ARGUMENT FROM RELIGIOUS EXPERIENCE

There are a few people who are unable to recognize and distinguish the simplest tune. But they are in the minority, like people who have no kind of religious experience. Most people have some light appreciation of music. But the differences of degree in this respect are enormous, and those who have not much gift for music have to take the statement of accomplished musicians very largely on trust. Let us, then, compare tone-deaf persons to those who have no recognizable religious experience at all; the ordinary followers of a religion to men who have some taste for music but can neither appreciate the more difficult kinds nor compose; highly religious men and saints to persons with an exceptionally fine ear for music who may yet be unable to compose it; and the founders of religions to great musical composers, such as Bach and Beethoven.

Broad indicates that the analogy with music is incomplete and that three problems are connected with religious experience:

1. What is the *psychological analysis* of religious experience? Does it contain factors that are also present in nonreligious experiences?
2. What are the *genetic and causal conditions* of religious experience? Can we trace the origins of the experiences in (a) the human race and (b) the individual?
3. Is religious experience veridical? Are its claims to knowledge of the nature of reality true or probable? Broad calls this the *epistemological problem*.

The analogy with musical experience works with regard to the psychological problem and to the causal problem, but not the epistemological one: "So far as I am aware, no part of the content of musical experience is alleged

From: C. D. Broad, "The Argument from Religious Experience," in *Philosophy and Psychical Research* (London: Routledge & Kegan Paul, 1930).

knowledge about the nature of reality; and therefore no question of its being veridical or delusive can arise." But despite this difference, an important point must be recognized.

> If a man who had no ear for music were to give himself airs on that account, and were to talk boastfully about those who can appreciate music and think it highly important, we should regard him, not as an advanced thinker, but as a self-satisfied Philistine. And if, then he did not do this but only propounded theories about the nature and causation of musical experience, we might think it reasonable to feel very doubtful whether his theories would be adequate or correct. In the same way, when persons without religious experience regard themselves as being on *that ground* superior to those who have it, their attitude must be treated as merely silly and offensive. Similarly, any theories about religious experience constructed by persons who have little or none of their own should be regarded with grave suspicion.[11]

Broad argues that what makes testimony of religious experience especially interesting, if not persuasive, is the common agreement between mystics. They exhibit the sort of features described by William James, a feeling of unity with the rest of the universe, a sense of transcendence at the core of reality, and so forth. There are differences in detail, to be sure, but so are there in perceptual experience. The relation between the religious experiences and the mystic's traditional beliefs is complex and may point to a double causation—both the transcendent unity and the specific tradition may be causing the experience. Here is Broad's comment on this hypothesis.

> Much the same double process of causation takes place in sense-perception. On the one hand, the beliefs and expectations which we have at any moment largely determine what *interpretation* we shall put on a certain sensation which we should in any case have had then. On the other hand, our beliefs and expectations do to some extent determine and modify some of the sensible characteristics of the *sensa themselves*. When I am thinking only of diagrams a certain visual stimulus may produce a sensation of a sensibly flat sensum; but a precisely similar stimulus may produce a sensation of a sensible solid sensum when I am thinking of solid objects.
>
> Such explanations, however, plainly do not account for the first origin of religious beliefs, or for the features which are common to the religious experiences of persons of widely different times, races, and traditions.
>
> Now, when we find that there are certain experiences which, though never very frequent in a high degree of intensity, have happened in a high degree among a few men at all times and places; and when we find that, in spite of differences in detail which we can explain, they involve certain fundamental conditions which are common and peculiar to them; two alternatives are open to us. (i) We may suppose that these men are in contact with an aspect of reality which is not revealed to ordinary persons in their everyday experience. And we may suppose that the characteristics which they agree in ascribing to reality on the basis of these experiences probably do belong to it. Or (ii) we may suppose that they are all subject to a delusion from which other men are free.

Are those who have religious experience deluded or in touch with a higher reality? To examine this question, Broad considers three partly analogous cases, two of them real and one imaginary:

(*a*) Most of the detailed facts which biologists tell us about the minute structure and changes in cells can be perceived only by persons who have had a long training in the use of the microscope. In this case we believe that the agreement among trained microscopists really does correspond to facts which untrained persons cannot perceive. (*b*) Persons of all races who habitually drink alcohol to excess eventually have perceptual experiences in which they seem to themselves to see snakes or rats crawling about their rooms or beds. In this case we believe that this agreement among drunkards is merely a uniform hallucination. (*c*) Let us now imagine a race of beings who can walk about and touch things but cannot see. Suppose that eventually a few of them developed the power of sight. All that they might tell their still blind friends about colour would be wholly unintelligible to and unverifiable by the latter. But they would also be able to tell their blind friends a great deal about what the latter would feel if they were to walk in certain directions. These statements would be verified. This would not, of course, *prove* to the blind ones that the unintelligible statements about colour correspond to certain aspects of the world which they cannot perceive. But it would show that the seeing persons had a source of additional information about matters which the blind ones could understand and test for themselves. It would not be unreasonable then for the blind ones to believe that probably the seeing ones are also able to perceive other aspects of reality which they are describing correctly when they make their unintelligible statements containing colour-names. The question then is whether it is reasonable to regard the agreement between the experiences of religious mystics as more like the agreement among trained microscopists about the minute structure of cells, or as more like the agreement among habitual drunkards about the infestation of their rooms by pink rats or snakes, or as more like the agreement about colours which the seeing men would express in their statements to the blind men.

Why do we commonly believe that habitual excess of alcohol is a cause of a uniform delusion and not a source of additional information? The main reason is as follows. The things which drunkards claim to perceive are not fundamentally different in kind from the things that other people perceive. We have all seen rats and snakes, thought the rats have generally been grey or brown and not pink. Moreover the drunkard claims that the rats and snakes which he sees are literally present in his room and on his bed, in the same sense in which his bed is in his room and his quilt is on his bed. Now we may fairly argue as follows. Since these are the sort of things which we could see if they were there, the fact that we cannot see them makes it highly probable that they are not there. Again, we know what kinds of perceptible effect would generally follow from the presence in a room of such things as rats or snakes. We should expect fox-terriers or mongooses to show traces of excitement, cheese to be nibbled, corn to disappear from bins, and so on. We find that no such effects are observed in the bedrooms of persons suffering from *delirium tremens*. It therefore seems reasonable to conclude that the agreement among drunkards is a sign, not of a revelation, but of a delusion.

Now the assertions in which religious mystics agree are not such that they conflict with what we can perceive with our senses. They are about the structure and organization of the world as a whole and about the relations of men to the rest of it. And they have so little in common with the facts of daily life that there is not much chance of direct collision. I think that there is only one important point on which there is conflict. Nearly all mystics seem to be agreed that time and change and unchanging duration are unreal or extremely superficial, whilst these seem to plain men to be the most fundamental features of the world. But we must admit, on the one hand, that these temporal characteristics present very great philosophical difficulties and puzzles when we reflect upon them. On the other hand, we may well suppose that the mystic finds it impossible to state clearly in ordinary language what it is that he experiences about the facts which underlie the appearance of time and change and duration. Therefore it is not difficult to allow that what we experience as the temporal aspect of reality corresponds in some sense to certain facts, and yet that these facts appear to us in so distorted a form in our ordinary experience that a person who sees them more accurately and directly might refuse to apply temporal names to them.

Let us next consider why we feel fairly certain that the agreement among trained microscopists about the minute structure of cells expresses an objective fact, although we cannot get similar experiences. One reason is that we have learned enough, from simpler cases of visual perception, about the laws of optics to know that the arrangement of lenses in a microscope is such that it will reveal minute structure, which is otherwise invisible, and will not simply create optical delusions. Another reason is that we know of other cases in which trained persons can detect things which untrained people will overlook, and that in many cases the existence of these things can be verified by indirect methods. Probably most of us have experienced such results of training in our own lives.

Now religious experience is not in nearly such a strong position as this. We do not know much about the laws which govern its occurrence and determine its variations. No doubt there are certain standard methods of training and meditation which tend to produce mystical experiences. These have been elaborated to some extent by certain Western mystics and to a very much greater extent by Eastern Yogis. But I do not think that we can see here, as we can in the case of microscopes and the training which is required to make the best use of them, any conclusive reason why these methods should produce veridical rather than delusive experiences. Uniform methods of training and meditation would be likely to produce more or less similar experiences, whether these experiences were largely veridical or wholly delusive.

Is there any analogy between the facts about religious experience and the fable about the blind men some of whom gained the power of sight? It might be said that many ideals of conduct and ways of life, which we can all recognize now to be good and useful, have been introduced into human history by the founders of religions. These persons have made actual ethical discoveries which others can afterwards recognize to be true. It might be said that this is at least roughly analogous to the case of the seeing men telling the still blind men of facts which the latter could and did verify for themselves. And it might be said that this makes it reasonable for us to attach some weight to what founders of religions tell us about things which we cannot understand or verify for ourselves; just as it would have been reasonable for the blind men to attach some weight to the unintelligible statements which the seeing men made to them about colours.

Broad thinks this argument deserves a certain amount of respect, but he is unsure just how much:

> I should be inclined to sum up as follows. When there is a nucleus of agreement between the experiences of men in different places, times, and traditions, and when they all tend to put much the same kind of interpretation on the cognitive content of these experiences, it is reasonable to ascribe this agreement to their all being in contact with a certain objective aspect of reality *unless there be some positive reason to think otherwise.* The practical postulate which we go upon everywhere else is to treat cognitive claims as veridical unless there be some positive reason to think them delusive. This, after all, is our only guarantee for believing that ordinary sense-perception is veridical. We cannot *prove* that what people agree in perceiving really exists independently of them; but we do always assume that ordinary waking sense-perception is veridical unless we can produce some positive grounds for thinking that it is delusive in any given case. I think it is inconsistent to treat the experiences of religious mystics on different principles. So far as they agree they should be provisionally accepted as veridical unless there be some positive ground for thinking that they are not.

The argument can be outlined this way:

1. There is an enormous unanimity among the mystics concerning the spiritual nature of reality.
2. When there is such unanimity among observers as to what they take themselves to be experiencing, it is reasonable to conclude that their experiences are veridical (unless we have good reason to believe that they are deluded).
3. There are no positive reasons for thinking that mystical experiences are delusive.
4. Therefore, it is reasonable to believe that mystical experiences are veridical.

Premise 3 is weak, for there is evidence that mystics are neuropathic or sexually repressed. Broad considers these charges, admits some plausibility in them, but suggests that they are not conclusive. Regarding the charge of neuropathology, he urges that "one might need to be slightly 'cracked' in order to have some peep-holes into the super-sensible world"; and with regard to sexual abnormality, it could simply be the case that no one who was "incapable of strong sexual desires and emotions could have anything worth calling religious experience."

His own guarded judgment is that, given what we know about the origins of religious belief and emotions, there is no reason to think that religious experience is "specially likely to be delusive or misdirected," so that religious experience can be said to offer us strong justification for a transcendent reality.

Is Broad correct? Does the evidence for religious experience support the conclusion that there is a transcendent reality, a God? One could question whether the agreement between mystics is really all that significant—that this agreement centers around broad ideas of transcendence and little more and that the doctrinal or interpretative nuances are more significant than he admits. You may consider this objection. However, there is a more important objection to his comparison between mystical experience and perceptual experience: *When taken seriously as candidates of veridical experience, religious experience fails in not being confirmed in the same way that perceptual experience is.* This objection is the Achilles' heel (if anything is) of those who would place a lot of weight on religious experience as *evidence* for the content of religion. This is the complex criterion of *checkability-predictability* (I link them purposefully). The chemist who says that Avogadro's law holds (that is, equal volumes of different gases at the same temperature and pressure contain an equal number of molecules) predicts exactly to what degree the inclusion of certain gases will increase the overall weight of a gaseous compound. Similarly, if, under normal circumstances, we heat water to 100°C, we can predict ahead of time that it will boil. If you doubt my observation, check it out yourself. After suitable experiment, we see these propositions confirmed in such a way as to leave little room for doubt in our minds about their truth. After studying some chemistry, we see that they play a role in a wider network of beliefs that are mutually supportive. The perceptual beliefs force themselves upon us.

This notion of predictability may be applied to social hypotheses as well as physical. For instance, an orthodox Marxist states that if his theory is true, capitalism will begin to collapse in industrialized countries. If it doesn't, we begin to doubt it. Of course, the Marxist may begin to revise his theory and bring in **ad hoc** hypotheses to explain why the expected didn't occur; however, the more ad hoc hypotheses he has to bring to bear in order to salvage the unconfirmed thesis, the weaker the hypothesis itself becomes. It is a fact of human experience that we come to believe many important propositions through experiments, either our own or those of others (whom we take as authoritative—for the moment at least). The presumption is, with regard to authority, that we could check out the propositions in question if we had time or need to do so.

How do we confirm the truth of religious experience? Does it make any predictions that we could test now in order to say, "Look and see, the fact that X occurs shows that the content of the religious experience is veridical"? How do we check on other people's religious experiences, especially if they purport to be nonsensory perceptions?

The checkability factor is weak in the account of Gary Gutting, who claims that we have a duty to believe simply on the report of others, not on the basis of our own experience or any special predictions that the experient would be able to make. But, if the Bible is to be believed, this wasn't always the case, nor should it be today. We read in 1 Kings 18 that in order to convince the Israelites that Yahweh, not Baal, was worthy of being worshiped, Elijah challenged the priests of Baal to a contest. He proposed that they prepare a bullock and call on

Baal to set fire to it. Then he would do the same with Yahweh. The priests failed, but Elijah succeeded. Convincing evidence! Similarly, at the end of Mark, we read of Jesus telling his disciples that "signs shall follow them that believe; in my name they shall cast out devils; they shall speak with new tongues; they shall take up serpents; and if they drink any deadly thing, it shall not hurt them; they shall lay hands on the sick, and they shall recover" (Mark 16:17, 18). Some believers doubt whether this text is authentic, and others seek to explain it away (for example, "Jesus only meant his apostles and was referring to the apostolic age"), but if a religion is true, we might well expect some outward confirmation of it, such as we find in Elijah's actions at Mt. Carmel or in Jesus' miracles. The fact that religious experience isn't testable and doesn't yield any nontrivial predictions surely makes it less reliable than perceptual experience.

Not only doesn't religious experience usually generate predictions that are confirmed, but also it sometimes yields false predictions. Witness an incident that happened to me as a student in an evangelical Christian college. A group of students believed that the Bible is the inerrant Word of God and cannot contain an untruth. Now the Gospel of Matthew 18:19 records Jesus as saying that "if two of you shall agree on earth as touching anything that they shall ask, it shall be done for them of my Father which is in heaven" and Matthew 17:20 tells of faith being able to move mountains, "Nothing shall be impossible for you." Verses in Mark confirm this, adding that God will answer our prayer if we pray in faith and do not doubt. So, one night several believers prayed through the entire night for the healing of a student who was dying of cancer. They prayed for her in childlike faith believing that God would heal her. As morning broke, they felt the presence of God among them, telling them that their prayer had been answered. As they left rejoicing and were walking out of the room, they received the news that the woman had just died.

It is interesting to note that none of the participants lost faith in God over this incident. Some merely dismissed it as one of the mysteries of God's ways, others concluded that the Bible wasn't to be taken literally, and still others concluded that they hadn't prayed hard enough or with enough faith. But as far as the argument for the veridicality of the content of religion is concerned, this has to be taken as part of the total data. How it weighs against the empirically successful prayers or times when the content of the experience was confirmed, I have no idea and I don't think Gutting has either. But unless we do, it is hard to see how the argument from religious experience could be used as strong evidence for the existence of God *to anyone else except those who had the experiences.* As James concludes about mystical states (one form of religious experience), while those having the experience have a right to believe in their content, "no authority emanates from them which should make it a duty for those who stand outside of them to accept their revelations uncritically."

Finally, let me close with an illustration of what might be a publicly verifiable experience of God, one that would be analogous to the kind of perceptual experience by which we check scientific hypotheses. What if tomorrow morning (8 a.m. CST) there was a loud trumpet call, and all over North America people heard a voice speak out, saying, "I am the Lord, your God, speaking. I have a message for you all. I am deeply saddened by the violence and lack of concern you have for each other. I am calling upon all nations to put aside your nuclear weapons. This same message is being delivered to all the other nations of Earth at different times today. I want you all to know that I shall take all means necessary to prevent a nuclear war and punish those nations who persist on the mad course on which they are now embarked. I love each one of you. A few signs will confirm this message. Later today, while speaking to Israel and the Arab states, I will cause an island to appear west of Lebanon in the Mediterranean, which is intended as a homeland for the Palestinians. I will also cause the Sahara desert to become fruitful in order to provide food for the starving people in that area. But I will have you know that I shall not intervene often in your affairs. I'm making this exception simply because it is an emergency situation."

Imagine that all over the world the same message is conveyed during the next twenty-four hours. The predictions are fulfilled. Would your religious faith be strengthened by such an event? The question is, Why don't religious experiences like this happen? If there is a God, why does he seem to hide from us? Why doesn't God give us more evidence? I leave this question for you to reflect on.

Summary

Religious experience is at the core of the religious life. Throughout the ages, in virtually every culture, people have reported deeply religious, even mystical experiences that have confirmed their religious beliefs and added meaning to their lives. Yet problems surround the phenomena: There are discrepancies between accounts, they tend to be amorphous and varied, and they seldom are verified.

FOR FURTHER RLECTION

1. To what degree, if any, is a person who has a religious experience (of God) justified in inferring the existence of God? Should he or she seriously consider that the experience might be delusionary? How can he or she tell the difference between veridical and delusionary experiences?

2. Suppose that we agree with James that the subject of a deep religious experience is justified in believing it to be veridical. How much should this influence the rest of us who have not had such an experience to accept the content of his or her experience?

3. What do you make of the criticism that religious experiences are too amorphous and varied to yield conclusions with regard to the existence of God?

4. What do you make of the criticism that belief in religious experience tends to be circular so that the belief in it will rest upon premises that are not self-evident to everyone?

5. What do you make of the criticism that religious experience is not a good candidate for veridical experience like perceptual experience, because it cannot be verified?

NOTES

1. William James, *The Varieties of Religious Experience* (New York: Modern Library, 1902), 63.

2. *Shankara's Crest Jewel of Discrimination,* trans. Swami Prabhavandanda (New York: Mentor Books, 1970), 103–104.

3. Samyutta-Nikaya 36:115, in *Buddhism in Translation,* ed. Henry C. Warren (New York: Atheneum, 1973), 384.

4. "Now as he journeyed, Saul approached Damascus, and suddenly a light from heaven flashed about him. And he fell to the ground and heard a voice saying to him, 'Saul, Saul, why do you persecute me?' And he said, 'Who are you, Lord?' And he said, 'I am Jesus whom you are persecuting; but rise and enter the city, and you will be told what you are to do.' The men traveling with him stood speechless, hearing the voice but seeing no one. Saul arose from the ground; and when his eyes were opened, he could see nothing; so they led him into Damascus" (Acts 9).

5. C. D. Broad, *Religion, Philosophy, and Psychical Research* (London: Routledge & Kegan Paul, 1930); Richard Swinburne, *The Existence of God* (Oxford, UK: Clarendon Press, 1979); and Gary Gutting, *Religious Belief and Religious Skepticism* (Notre Dame, IN: University of Notre Dame Press, 1982).

6. William James, *The Varieties of Religious Experience* (New York: Modern Library, 1902), 371.

7. Ibid.

8. Ibid.

9. Ibid.

10. Ibid.

11. All remaining passages are from C. D. Broad, "The Argument from Religious Experience," in *Philosophy and Psychical Research.*

FOR FURTHER READING

Gale, Richard. *On the Nature and Existence of God.* Cambridge, UK: Cambridge University Press, 1991. Chapter 8 contains a penetrating critique.

Gutting, Gary. *Religious Belief and Religious Skepticism.* Notre Dame, IN: University of Notre Dame Press, 1982. A well-argued contemporary discussion. A significant portion of the section on religious experience is reprinted in Pojman (see below).

James, William. *Varieties of Religious Experience.* New York: Modern Library, 1902. This marvelous treatise is the definitive work on the subject.

Otto, Rudolf. *The Idea of the Holy.* Translated by J. Harvey. Oxford, UK: Oxford University Press, 1923. A classic study on religious experience.

Pojman, Louis, ed. *Philosophy of Religion: An Anthology,* 2nd ed. Belmont, CA: Wadsworth, 1994. Part 2 contains several important articles.

Swinburne, Richard. *The Existence of God.* Oxford, UK: Oxford University Press, 1979. Contains an important discussion of religious experience.

Wainwright, William. *Mysticism.* Madison: University of Wisconsin Press, 1981. A comprehensive and sympathetic study of mysticism.

11 ⚘ The Problem of Evil

Is he willing to prevent evil, but not able? Then he is impotent. Is he able, but not willing? Then he is malevolent. Is he both able and willing? Whence then is evil?

Epicurus 341–270 BCE

The Mystery of Evil

Why is there evil in the world? Why do bad things happen to good people? "The whole earth is cursed and polluted," says Philo in Hume's famous dialogue on natural religion. He continues:

> A perpetual war is kindled among all living creatures. Necessity, hunger, want stimulate the strong and courageous; fear, anxiety, terror agitate the weak and infirm. The first entrance into life gives anguish to the new-born infant and to its wretched parent; weakness, impotence, distress attend each stage of that life, and it is, at last, finished in agony and horror. Man is the greatest enemy of man. Oppression, injustice, contempt, contumely, violence, sedition, war, calumny, treachery, fraud—by these they mutually torment each other, and they would soon dissolve that society which they had formed were it not for the dread of still greater ills which must attend their separation.[1]

The Russian novelist-philosopher Fyodor Dostoyevsky (1821–1881), although a devout Christian, was haunted by the mystery of evil. He repeatedly asks, why do bad things happen to innocent and good people? In his novel *The Brothers Karamazov,* he describes a conversation between two Karamazov brothers, Ivan the cynic and Alyosha the committed Christian who has recently joined a monastery. To begin this reading, Ivan is speaking.

THE BROTHERS KARAMAZOV

"Adults have something to compensate them for their suffering. They have eaten their apple of knowledge. They know about good and evil and are like gods themselves. And they keep eating the apple. But little children haven't eaten it. They're not yet guilty of anything. Do you like small children, Alyosha? I know you do and that you'll understand why I have chosen to speak exclusively of them. Well then, if they suffer here in this world, it's because they're paying for the sins of their fathers who ate the apple. But that is the reasoning of another world and it's incomprehensible to the human heart here on earth. No innocent should be made to suffer for another man's sins, especially innocents such as these!

"...Do you understand why this infamy must be and is permitted? Without it, I am told, man could not have known good and evil. Why should he know that diabolical good and evil when it costs so much? Why, the whole world of knowledge is not worth that child's prayer to 'dear, Kind God'! I say nothing of the sufferings of grown-up people, they have eaten the apple, damn them, and the devil take them all! But these little ones! I am making you suffer, Alyosha, you are not yourself. I'll leave off if you like."

"Never mind, I want to suffer too," muttered Alyosha.

"One picture, only one more, because it's so curious, so characteristic, and I have only just read it in some collection of Russian antiquities. I've forgotten the name. I must look it up. It was in the darkest days of serfdom at the beginning of the century, and long live the Liberator of the People! There was in those days a general of aristocratic connections, the owner of great estates, one of these men—somewhat exceptional, I believe, even then—who, retiring from the service into a life of leisure, are convinced that they've earned absolute power over the lives of their subjects. There were such men then. So our general, settled on his property of two thousand souls, lives in pomp and domineers over his poor neighbors as though they were dependents and buffoons. He has kennels of hundreds of hounds and nearly a hundred dog-boys—all mounted, and in uniform. One day a serf boy, a little child of eight, threw a stone in play and hurt the paw of the general's favorite hound. 'Why is my favorite dog lame?' He is told that the boy threw a stone that hurt the dog's paw. 'So you did it.' The general looked the child up and down. 'Take him.' He was taken—taken from his mother and kept shut up all night. Early that morning the general comes out on horseback, with the hounds, his dependents, dog-boys, and huntsmen, all mounted around him in full hunting parade. The servants are summoned for their edification, and in front of them all stands the mother of the child. The child is brought from the lockup. It's a gloomy, cold, foggy autumn day, a capital day for hunting. The general orders the child to be undressed; the child is stripped naked. He shivers, numb with terror not daring to cry.... 'Make him run,' commands the general. 'Run! run!' shout the dog-boys. The boy runs.... 'At him!' yells

From: Fyodor Dostoyevsky, *The Brothers Karamazov*, trans. Constance Garrett (London: Heinemann, 1912).

the general, and he sets the whole pack of hounds on the child. The hounds catch him, and tear him to pieces before his mother's eyes! . . . I believe the general was afterwards declared incapable of administering his estates. Well—what did he deserve? To be shot? To be shot for the satisfaction of our moral feelings? Speak, Alyosha!"

"To be shot," murmured Alyosha, lifting his eyes to Ivan with a pale twisted smile.

"Bravo!" cried Ivan delighted. "If even you say so . . . You're a pretty monk! So there is a little devil sitting in your heart, Alyosha Karamazov!"

"What I said was absurd, but—"

"That's just the point that 'but'!" cried Ivan. "Let me tell you, novice, that the absurd is only too necessary on earth. The world stands on absurdities, and perhaps nothing would have come to pass in it without them. We know what we know!"

"What do you know?"

"I understand nothing," Ivan went on, as though in delirium. "I don't want to understand anything now. I want to stick to the fact. I made up my mind long ago not to understand. If I try to understand anything, I shall be false to the fact and I have determined to stick to the fact."

"Why are you trying me?" Alyosha cried, with sudden distress. "Will you say what you mean at last?"

"Of course, I will; that's what I've been leading up to. You are dear to me. I don't want to let you go, and I won't give you up to your Zossima."

Ivan for a minute was silent, his face became all at once very sad.

"Listen! I took the case of the children only to make my case clearer. Of the other tears of humanity with which the earth is soaked from its crust to its center, I will say nothing. I have narrowed my subject on purpose. I am a bug, and I recognize in all humility that I cannot understand why the world is arranged as it is. Men are themselves to blame, I suppose; they were given paradise, they wanted freedom, and stole fire from heaven, though they knew they would become unhappy, so there is no need to pity them. With my pitiful, earthly, Euclidian understanding, all I know is that there is suffering and that there are none guilty; that cause follows effect, simply and directly; that everything flows and finds its level—but that's only Euclidian nonsense, I know that, and I can't consent to live by it! What comfort is it to me that there are none guilty and that cause follows effect simply and directly, and that I know it—I must have justice, or I will destroy myself. And not justice in some remote infinite time and space, but here on earth, and that I could see myself. I have believed in it. I want to see it, and if I am dead by then, let me rise again, for if it all happens without me, it will be too unfair. Surely I haven't suffered, simply that I, my crimes and my sufferings, may manure the soil of the future harmony for somebody else. I want to see with my own eyes the hind lie down with the lion and the victim rise up and embrace his murderer. I want to be there when everyone suddenly understands what it has all been for. All the religions of the world are built on this longing, and I am a believer. But then there are the children, and what am I to do about them? That's a question I can't answer. For the hundredth time I repeat, there are numbers of questions, but I've only taken the children, because in their case what I mean is so unanswerably clear. Listen! If all must suffer to pay for the eternal harmony, what have children to do with it, tell me please? It's beyond all comprehension why they should suffer, and why they should pay for the harmony. Why should they, too, furnish material to enrich the soil for the harmony of the future? I understand solidarity in sin among men. I understand solidarity in retribution, too; but there can be no such solidarity with children. And if it is really true that they must share responsibility for all their fathers' crimes, such a truth is not of this world and is beyond my comprehension. Some jester will say, perhaps, that the child would have grown up and have sinned, but you see he didn't grow up, he was torn to pieces by the dogs, at eight years old. Oh, Alyosha, I am not blaspheming! I understand, of course, what an upheaval of the universe it will be, when everything in heaven and earth blends in one hymn of praise and everything that lives and has lived cries aloud: 'Thou art just, O Lord, for Thy ways are revealed,' when the mother embraces the fiend who threw her child to the dogs, and all three cry aloud with tears. 'Thou are just, O Lord!' then, of course, the crown of knowledge will be reached and all will be made clear. But what pulls me up here is that I can't accept that harmony. And while I am on earth, I make haste to take my own measures. You see, Alyosha, perhaps it really may happen that if I live to that moment, or rise again to see it, I, too, perhaps, may cry aloud with the rest, looking at the mother embracing the child's torturer, 'Thou art just, O Lord!' but I don't want to cry aloud then. While there is still time, I hasten to protect myself and so I renounce the higher harmony altogether. It's not worth the tears of that one tortured child who beat itself on the breast with its little fist and prayed in its stinking outhouse, with its unexpiated tears to 'dear, kind God'! It's not worth it, because those tears are unatoned for. They must be atoned for, or there can be no harmony. But how? How are you going to atone for them? Is it possible? By their being avenged? But what do I care for avenging them? What do I care for a hell for oppressors? What good can hell do, since those children have already been tortured? And what becomes of harmony, if there is hell? I want to forgive. I want to embrace. I don't want more suffering. And if the sufferings of children go to swell the sum of sufferings which was necessary to pay for truth, then I protest that the truth is not worth such a price. I don't want the mother to embrace the oppressor who threw her son to the dogs! She dare not forgive him! Let her forgive him for herself, if she will, let her forgive the torturer for the immeasurable suffering of her mother's heart. But the sufferings of her tortured child she has no right to forgive; she dare not forgive the torturer, even if the child were to forgive him!"

There can be no justified forgiveness for such a crime. Ivan cannot accept a world where children are tortured for any reason, even for cosmic harmony. He cannot accept God's entrance ticket.

"And so I hasten to give back my entrance ticket, and if I am an honest man I am bound to give it back as soon as possible.... Tell me yourself, I challenge you. Imagine that you are creating a fabric of human destiny with the object of making men happy in the end, giving them peace and rest at last, but that it was essential and inevitable to torture to death only one tiny creature—that baby beating its breast with its fist, for instance—and to found that edifice on its unavenged tears, would you consent to be the architect on those conditions? Tell me, and tell me the truth."

"No, I wouldn't consent," said Alyosha softly.[2]

The Argument from Evil

The problem of evil arises because of the paradox of an omnibenevolent, omnipotent deity allowing the existence of evil. The Judeo-Christian tradition has affirmed these three propositions:

1. God is all-powerful (including omniscience).
2. God is perfectly good.
3. Evil exists.

But if God is perfectly good, why does he allow evil to exist? Why didn't he create a better world, if not with no evil at least with substantially less evil than in this world? Many have contended that this paradox, first schematized by Epicurus, is worse than a paradox. It is an implicit contradiction for it contains premises that are inconsistent with one another. They argue something like the following:

4. If God (an all-powerful, omniscient, omnibenevolent being) exists, there would be no (or no unnecessary) evil in the world.
5. There is evil (or unnecessary evil) in the world.
6. Therefore, God does not exist.

To see whether they are right, let's review each of the basic propositions that generate the paradox.

Proposition 1: "God is all-powerful" has been a cornerstone of Christian theology since the early centuries of the Church. Though it is debatable whether one can show that the biblical writers had such a strong concept (or whether the exact formulation is derived from Platonic and Aristotelian metaphysics), most Judeo-Christian theologians have seen it as entailed by any adequate view of deity. Some philosophers and theologians—such as John Stuart Mill, William James, Alfred North Whitehead, and Charles Hartshorne—have relinquished this property to get God "off the hook" with regard to evil. Many more believe that it either doesn't get God off the hook or it tends to denude God's essence. That is, even if God is not all powerful, he certainly must be exceedingly powerful (and knowledgeable), and if so, he should have been able to prevent evil (or most of the evil) in the world. On the other hand, if he is not so powerful, why do we call him "God" and not a demiurge and worship instead the ideal of moral goodness? This is not to say that such theologians and philosophers (usually in a tradition called *process theology*) do not have a case, but it may not be any better than some of the alternative solutions. Many will find it too radical altogether.

Finally, when theists speak of God being omnipotent, they usually mean that God can do anything that is *logically possible*. God cannot make a stone heavier than he can lift, will that he never existed, or make 2 + 2 = 5. This will be important with regard to the defense of theism from the charge of the atheologian (that is, one who argues against the existence of God).

Proposition 2: God is perfectly good. The Judeo-Christian, Muslim, and Hindu traditions all subscribe to the doctrine of complete divine benevolence.

Take the property of benevolence from God, and what is the difference between God and a supreme devil? God somehow has moral obligations and cannot do evil. There is a tradition (very Greek in origin) that contends that God's immutability prevents his having obligations, for he cannot change, so he cannot *do* anything. But this surely is unbiblical, for the God of the Bible is one who *creates* the heavens and Earth, as well as humanity, and *redeems* people from sin and despair. It is a God who acts and who acts well.

Proposition 3: Evil exists. Some Eastern religions deny the reality of evil, viewing it as an illusion, but the Judeo-Christian tradition has always taken it as a fundamental datum to be overcome, if not explained. Suffering and pain, disease and death, cruelty and violence, rape and murder, poverty and natural havoc—all have been viewed as the enemy of the good. The millions of humans who have starved to death or died victims of bloody battle and brutal wars, the myriads who have been abandoned, abused, and aborted—all testify to the tragedy of the human condition: Evil exists in abundance.

Generally, Western thought has distinguished between two types of evil: moral and natural. *Moral evil* covers all those bad things for which humans are morally responsible. *Natural evil,* or *surd evil,* stands for all those terrible events that nature does of its own accord (for example, hurricanes, tornadoes, earthquakes, volcanic eruptions, natural diseases), which bring suffering to humans and animals. However, some defenses of theism affirm that all evil is essentially moral evil. Here the devil is brought in as the cause of natural evil.

The Free-Will Defense

The main defense of theism in the light of evil is the free-will defense, going back as far as St. Augustine (354–430) and receiving modern treatment in the work of John Hick, Alvin Plantinga, and Richard Swinburne. The free-will defense adds a fourth premise to Epicurus's paradox in order to show that premises 1–3 are consistent and not contradictory. This premise is:

7. It is logically impossible for God to create free creatures and guarantee that they will never do evil.

Because it is a good thing to create free creatures who are morally responsible agents, there is no assurance that they will not also do evil. Imagine that God viewed an infinite set of possible worlds. In some of them, he saw humans as not sinning, but in those they were not free. In others, he saw humans as free and doing less evil than in this world, but he chose to create this world with its enormous amount of good and evil. Perhaps he could have created other worlds with more good or less evil, but he would not create a world with a worse proportion of good over evil than this one has, and no world he could have created could have a better proportion of good over evil. This is the best an omnipotent, omnibenevolent God could do.

This defense assumes a libertarian view of freedom of the will. That is, humans are free to choose between good and evil acts. They are not caused (though they may be influenced) to do one deed rather than the other, but they are causally underdetermined. Given two identically similar situations, with identical causal antecedents, an agent could do act A at one time and act B at the other. This view is opposed to **determinism,** as well as **compatibilism** (a view that tries to reconcile freedom of action with determinism). If you are committed to compatibilism or determinism, the free-will defense will not be effective against the argument from evil. (We will examine this issue in Part 6 of this book.)

To return to the main issue, the proponent of the free-will defense claims that all moral evil derives from creature freedom of the will. But what about natural evil? How does the theist account for it? There are two different ways. The first one, favored by Plantinga and Stephen Davis, is to attribute natural evil to the work of the devil and his angels. Disease and tornadoes are caused by the devil and his minion. The second way, favored by Swinburne and Hick, argues that natural evil is part and parcel of the nature of things: a result of the combination of deterministic physical laws, which are necessary for consistent action, and the responsibility given to humans to exercise their freedom.

Hick's thesis is particularly interesting, since he endeavors to put forth a **theodicy,** a justification for God's permitting the evil in the world. Why does God allow natural evil, and why does he not normally intervene in either natural or moral evil? Hick answers: so that human beings, as free responsible agents, may use this world as a place of "soul making."

First, Hick distinguishes two positions on why God allowed sin. The first is the Augustinian (named after the great theologian St. Augustine [354–430]) position, which holds that God created humans without sin and set them in a sinless, paradisiacal world. However, humanity fell into sin through misuse of its free will. God's grace will save some of us, but others will perish everlastingly. This is the position that won out in mainline Christianity. But there is a second ("minority") position, stemming from an earlier Christian theologian, Irenaeus (120–202) of the Greek Orthodox Church. The Irenaean tradition views Adam not as a free agent rebelling against God but as a child. The Fall is humanity's first faulty step in the direction of freedom. Let's see how Hick develops his argument.

Evil and the God of Love

Instead of regarding man as having been created by God in a finished state, as a finitely perfect being fulfilling the divine intention for our human level of existence, and then falling disastrously away from this, the minority report sees man as still in process of creation. Irenaeus himself expressed the point in terms of the (exegetically dubious) distinction between the "image" and the "likeness" of God referred to in Genesis i.26:

"Then God said, Let us make man in our image, after our likeness." His view was that man as a personal and moral being already exists in the image, but has not yet been formed into the finite likeness of God. By this "likeness" Irenaeus means something more than personal existence as such; he means a certain valuable quality of personal life which reflects finitely the divine life. This represents the perfecting of man, the fulfillment of God's purpose for humanity, the "bringing of many sons of glory," the creating of "children of God" who are "fellow heirs with Christ" of his glory.

And so man, created as a personal being in the image of God, is only the raw material for a further and more difficult stage of God's creative work. This is the leading of men as relatively free and autonomous persons, through their own dealings with life in the world in which He has placed them, towards that quality of personal existence that is the finite likeness of God. The features of this likeness are revealed in the person of Christ, and the process of man's creation into it is the work of the Holy Spirit. In St. Paul's words, "And we all, with unveiled faces, beholding the glory of the Lord, are being changed into his likeness (εἰκών) from one degree of glory to another; for this comes from the Lord who is the Spirit"; or again, "For God knew his own before ever they were, and also ordained that they should be shaped to the likeness (εἰκών) of his Son." In Johannine terms, the movement from the image to the likeness is a transition from one level of existence, that of animal life (*Bios*), to another and higher level, that of eternal life (*Zoe*), which includes but transcends the first. And the fall of man was seen by Irenaeus as a failure within the second phase of this creative process, a failure that has multiplied the perils and complicated the route of the journey in which God is seeking to lead mankind.

In the light of modern anthropological knowledge some form of two-stage conception of the creation of man has become an almost unavoidable Christian tenet. At the very least we must acknowledge as two distinguishable stages the fashioning of *homo sapiens* as a product of the long evolutionary process, and his sudden or gradual spiritualization as a child of God. But we may well extend the first stage to include the development of man as a rational and responsible person capable of personal relationship with the personal Infinite who has created him. This first stage of the creative process was, to our anthropomorphic imaginations, easy for divine omnipotence. By an exercise of creative power God caused the physical universe to exist, and in the course of countless ages to bring forth within it organic life, and finally to produce out of organic life personal life; and when man had thus emerged out of the evolution of the forms of organic life, a creature had been made who has the possibility of existing in conscious fellowship with God. But the second stage of the creative process is of a different kind altogether. It cannot be performed by omnipotent power as such. For personal life is essentially free and self-directing. It cannot be perfected by divine fiat, but only through the uncompelled responses and willing co-operation of human individuals in their actions and reactions in the world in which God has placed them. Men may eventually become the perfected persons whom the New Testament calls "children of God," but they cannot be created ready-made as this.

The value-judgement that is implicitly being invoked here is that one who has attained to goodness by meeting and eventually mastering temptations, and thus by rightly making responsible choices in concrete situations, is good in a richer and more valuable sense than would be one created *ab initio* in a state either of innocence or of virtue. In the former case, which is that of the actual moral achievements of mankind, the individual's goodness has within it the strength of temptations overcome, a stability based upon an accumulation of right choices, and a positive and responsible character that comes from the investment of costly personal effort. I suggest, then, that it is an ethically reasonable judgement, even though in the nature of the case not one that is capable of demonstrative proof, that human goodness slowly built up through personal histories of moral effort has a value in the eyes of the Creator which justifies even the long travail of the soul-making process.

The picture with which we are working is thus developmental and teleological. Man is in process of becoming the perfected being whom God is seeking to create. However, this is not taking place—it is important to add—by a natural and inevitable evolution, but through a hazardous adventure in individual freedom. Because this is a pilgrimage within the life of each individual, rather than a racial evolution, the progressive fulfillment of God's purpose does not entail any corresponding progressive improvement in the moral state of the world. There is no doubt a development in man's ethical situation from generation to generation through the building of individual choices into public institutions, but his involves an accumulation of evil as well as of good. It is thus probable that human life was lived on much the same moral plane two thousands years ago or four thousand years ago as it is today. But nevertheless during this period uncounted millions of souls have been through the experience of earthly life, and God's purpose has gradually moved towards its fulfillment within each one of them, rather than within a human aggregate composed of different units in different generations.

The skeptic errs in complaining about the structure of the world because he or she makes the assumption that God created humanity as a completed creation. The skeptic mistakenly thinks

that God's purpose in making the world was to provide a suitable dwelling-place for this fully-formed creature. Since God is good and loving, the environment which he has created for human life to inhabit is naturally as pleasant and comfortable as possible. The problem is essentially similar to that of a man who builds a cage for some pet animal. Since our world, in fact, contains sources of hardship, inconvenience, and danger of innumerable kinds, the conclusion follows that this world cannot have been created by a perfectly benevolent and all-powerful deity.[3]

Suppose the world were a paradise without the possibility of suffering and pain and death. In that case, we would not be seriously accountable for our deeds.

No one could ever injure anyone else; the murderer's knife would turn to paper or his bullets to thin air; the bank safe, robbed of a million dollars, would miraculously become filled with another million dollars; fraud, deceit, conspiracy, and treason would somehow always leave the fabric of society undamaged.... The reckless driver would never meet with disaster. There would be no need to work, since no harm could result from avoiding work; there would be no call to be concerned for others in time of need or danger, for in such a world there could be no real needs or dangers.

Our present ethical concepts would not apply in such a safe "playpen paradise"; courage, honesty, love, benevolence, and kindness would make no sense, since no one could do any harm and there would be no need for heroism or saintliness. Such a world would certainly promote pleasure, but it would be wholly inadequate for character development. But our world is not such a hedonistic romper room. It is a place where we must take full responsibility for our actions, for they have serious consequences. It is a place where we can and should develop our characters and develop ourselves into the full likeness of God.

But if we are right in supposing that God's purpose for man is to lead him from human *Bios,* or the biological life of man, to that quality of *Zoe,* or the personal life of eternal worth, which we see in Christ, then the question that we have to ask is not, Is this the kind of world that an all-powerful and infinitely loving being would create as an environment for his human pets? or, Is the architecture of the world the most pleasant and convenient possible? The question that we have to ask is rather, Is this the kind of world that God might make as an environment in which moral beings may be fashioned, through their own free insights and responses, into "children of God"?

Such critics as Hume are confusing what heaven ought to be, as an environment for perfected finite beings, with what this world ought to be, as an environment for beings who are in process of becoming perfected. For if our general conception of God's purpose is correct the world is not intended to be a paradise, but rather the scene of a history in which human personality may be formed towards the pattern of Christ. Men are not to be thought of on the analogy of animal pets, whose life is to be made as agreeable as possible, but rather on the analogy of human children, who are to grow to adulthood in an environment whose primary and overriding purpose is not immediate pleasure but the realizing of the most valuable potentialities of human personality.

Needless to say, this characterization of God as the heavenly Father is not a merely random illustration but an analogy that lies at the heart of the Christian faith. Jesus treated the likeness between the attitude of God to man, and the attitude of human parents at their best towards their children, as providing the most adequate way for us to think about God. And so it is altogether relevant to a Christian understanding of this world to ask, How does the best parental love express itself in its influence upon the environment in which children are to grow up? I think it is clear that a parent who loves his children, and wants them to become the best human beings that they are capable of becoming, does not treat pleasure as the sole and supreme value. Certainly we seek pleasure for our children, and take great delight in obtaining it for them; but we do not desire for them unalloyed pleasure at the expense of their growth in such even greater values as moral integrity, unselfishness, compassion, courage, humour, reverence for the truth, and perhaps above all the capacity for love. We do not act on the premise that pleasure is the supreme end of life; and if the development of these other values sometimes clashes with the provision of pleasure, then we are willing to have our children miss a certain amount of this, rather than fail to come to possess and to be possessed by the finer and more precious qualities that are possible to the human personality. A child brought up on the principle that the only or the supreme value is pleasure would not be likely to become an ethically mature adult or an attractive or happy personality. And to most parents it seems more important to try to foster quality and strength of character in their children than to fill their lives at all times with the utmost possible degree of pleasure. If, then, there is any true analogy between God's purpose for his human creatures, and the purpose of loving and wise parents for their children, we have to recognize that the presence of pleasure and the absence of pain cannot be the supreme and overriding end for which the world exists. Rather, this world must be a place of soul-making. And its value is to be judged, not primarily by the quantity of pleasure and pain occurring in it at any particular moment, but by its fitness for its primary purpose, the purpose of soul-making.

Problems with the Free-Will Defense

I must leave it to you to analyze Hick's argument fully, but a few questions are in order. First, if this world with all its "heartaches and the thousand natural shocks that flesh is heir to" is useful for suffering, couldn't a world with less suffering and evil than this be adequate for the task? Were Auschwitz and Buchenwald and the torture chamber really necessary for soul building? When astronauts train, they are allowed to make mistakes, but built-in feedback mechanisms are present to correct mistakes before disaster sets in. Couldn't God have given us free will, allowed us to learn from our mistakes, and still constructed a world in which feedback mechanisms prevented the kind of monstrous disasters that occur every day in every place in the world?

With or without the free-will defense, many philosophers maintain that the problem of evil still persists. Some contend that the burden of proof is on the theist to explain why God does not intervene in the suffering of the world. If by the mere pressing of a button I could have caused Hitler to have had a fatal heart attack before starting World War II, I would have been obliged to do so. Why did God not intervene in 1939? Why didn't God intervene in the event described by Dostoyevsky, where the mad general set his hounds on the 8-year-old boy? Why does he not intervene in the sufferings of millions all over the world? Perhaps some evil is impossible to prevent, but why is there so much of it? Couldn't an all-knowing God have foreseen the evil in this world and created one in which people do not commit the amount of evil that occurs in our world? Couldn't he have seen another possible world in which humans are free but do a lot better than we do? Is this the best that an all-powerful, all-knowing deity could do?

The skeptic continues: If God does not intervene in human suffering, don't we have grounds to suspect that he doesn't exist or doesn't care or is severely limited? Or perhaps God is not omnibenevolent, but only partly good and partly bad?

Of course, theists counter each of these objections. Some, we have noted, maintain that God is not all powerful but limited in what he can do. Others argue that, while all powerful, it is simply a mystery why God doesn't intervene to prevent more evil than he does. How do we know that he hasn't prevented a lot more evil than there is? Or perhaps in heaven there will be due recompense for the suffering here on Earth. Perhaps the lesson of evil is to show us just how serious our moral responsibilities are. Why blame God for evil, when it is we humans who are producing it?

With regard to natural evil (for example, genetic deformities, diseases, earthquakes, and volcanic eruptions, which kill innocent people), the theist argues that it is simply part of an orderly process of nature. The laws of nature are necessarily such that the good is interconnected with the bad. The same rain that causes one farmer's field to germinate ruinously floods another farmer's field. Although there are no doubt limits to the amount of evil God will allow, he cannot constantly intervene without eroding human responsibility or the laws of nature. Where those limits of evil are, no one of us finite humans can know. And yet we wonder. Couldn't an all-powerful God have created a better world than this, a world with a significantly greater proportion of good over evil?

Evolutionary Theory and Evil

As we saw in Chapter 8 when discussing the argument from design, theists may have good reason to fear evolutionary theory and support creationist accounts of the origin of life and human beings, for evolution proposes a radical alternative paradigm to a theistic, purposive creation. This point can now be employed to undermine theism with regard to evil. Evolution holds that evil is not the result of Satan's sin or Adam's fall or human misuse of free will, but rather the consequence of the species developing adaptive strategies that tend to be accompanied by pain, suffering, unhappiness, and conflicts of interest, the major categories of evil. It is our evolution first from nonsentient to sentient beings that enables us to experience pain. Pain serves as a warning mechanism, but extreme contingencies can utilize the capacity for no protective reason. The sensation of pain may cause us to withdraw our hand from a fire, but being immolated in a burning building or funeral pyre serves no warning purpose at all and seems entirely gratuitous. Much of our physical suffering is simply the failure of evolution's adaptive strategies. For example, bipedalism, the ability to walk upright on two limbs, enables "higher" primates—including humans—to free up their forelimbs for other purposes, like grasping and thrusting; however, it incurs several liabilities: the loss of speed of its quadripedal ancestors; an imbalanced vertebral column, which increases the likelihood of lower-back pain; troublesome birth pangs; and even stomach problems and herniation, as the center of balance shifts and more pressure is placed on the abdominal region. On a more local scale, sickle-shaped red blood cells are adaptive in areas where malaria is rampant, but where it is not, they are lethal: Children born with sickle-cell anemia have only one fifth the chance of other children of surviving to maturity. Similarly, human aggressivity may be adaptive in hunting and defending one's self against predators, but in social groups, in the face of conflicts of interest, it tends to be maladaptive, causing suffering, injury, and death. Use of reason is necessary for social cooperation and coexistence, but the instincts of our ancestor species are more reliable and efficient. Reason leads to institutions like morality and law, necessary for civilization, but creates their own liabilities in terms of guilt, shame, litigation, and frustration. No lion deliberates as to whether he should kill an antelope or copulate with an available lioness, nor are his forays followed by guilt or remorse. He enjoys his conquests without worrying about whether he has violated antelope rights. He simply follows his instincts, and usually gets away with it. No police officer arrests him for violating the antelope's right to life.

The point is not that we should go back to the state of the Noble Savage. We can't—even if we tried. The point I'm trying to make is that each evolutionary adaptive strategy tends to incur a loss of some other virtue or capability, and this is what accounts for evil. What we call *moral evil* is simply part of the natural evolutionary process, which, as Tennyson pointed out, "is red in tooth and claw." Much, if not most of moral or human-made evil is the "unintended" result of nature's making us creatures with insatiable wants but limited resources and sympathies.

This evolutionary account of the origins of evil fits within the broader framework of human biology and animal ethology. To that extent, it is confirmable by scientific research, whereas the religious accounts of the origin of evil have less impressive credentials. How do we re-create or confirm the record of the Fall of Adam and Eve? The naturalistic account holds that we don't need myths or dogmas about the Fall or original sin. Simply investigating evolutionary processes of adaptation is sufficient as an explanation for our greatest problems. Evil has a biological basis, being simply the inextricable concomitant of characteristics that served (and still serves) an adaptive function.

The theist has responses to this account of evil. She may either reject evolution in favor of a creationist account or absorb the evolutionary account within a theistic framework. The first strategy seems a lost cause since all we know about animal biology and genetics is supported by evolution. The second strategy is more promising but is haunted by problems of explaining why God wasn't more efficient and benevolent in developing the species. Couldn't he have avoided the waste (sacrificing the millions of less fit individuals and species) and done things more benevolently—for example, made carnivorous animals herbivores and so avoided the predator–prey cycle of death and destruction?

So the problem of evil persists in haunting theism, and theists continue to devise strategies to ward off the attacks. On which side do the best reasons lie?

Summary

The problem of evil has to do with three propositions that, at first glance, seem incompatible: God's benevolence, God's omnipotence, and evil in the world. Why did an all-powerful and omnibenevolent God permit evil in the first place, and once established, why did he not eliminate it? The theist generally replies that it is better that God creates free beings who sin but who can be redeemed than for God to create a paradise where only automatons mechanically do good. John Hick provides a second argument in terms of evil being necessary for soul building, so that humans may perfect themselves by developing into full spiritual beings, into the likeness of God. The skeptic objects to both of these proposals, arguing that it is implausible to suppose that an all-powerful, omnibenevolent God couldn't do better than make a world with this much evil in it.

Finally, we noted how an evolutionary explanation of the origins of evil competes with a theological account. Not Adam's Fall but the evolution of the species is the best explanation of evil in the world.

FOR FURTHER REFLECTION

1. Go over the argument from evil against the existence of God. How cogent is it? Does the fact of evil or the amount of evil in the world count against the hypothesis that God exists? Explain your answer.

2. Does John Hick's account of soul making successfully answer the skeptic on why there is so much natural and moral evil? How would Hick meet the objection that God is "overdoing it" with Auschwitz and torture chambers?

3. What do you make of the suggestion that God is limited and is either not all knowing or all powerful and thus is not ultimately responsible for the amount of evil in the world? Does this view solve the problem of evil? Or does it merely extinguish the notion of a sovereign deity?

4. Some Christians, like Marilyn McCord Adams, argue that part of the solution to the problem of evil is the incarnation (of God in Christ) and crucifixion, wherein God himself suffers horrendous evil, thus identifying with us in our suffering. How comforting is this thought?

5. Examine the evolutionary account of the origins and present reality of evil. Does it make more sense than theistic accounts? How should theists respond? By denial, accommodation, or surrender? Explain your answer.

NOTES

1. David Hume, *Dialogues Concerning Natural Religion* (1779).
2. Fyodor Dostoyevsky, *The Brothers Karamazov,* trans. Constance Garrett (London: Heinemann, 1912).
3. All remaining passages are from John Hick, *Evil and the God of Love,* rev. ed. (New York: Harper & Row, 1977). Reprinted by permission.

FOR FURTHER READING

Adams, Marilyn McCord. *Horrendous Evils and the Goodness of God* (Ithaca, NY: Cornell University Press, 1999). A comprehensive and illuminating contemporary treatment of the problem of horrendous evil.

Anders, Timothy. *The Evolution of Evil.* LaSalle, IL: Open Court Books, 1994. A good account of the thesis set forth at the end of this chapter, defending an evolutionary explanation of evil.

Hick, John. *Evil and the God of Love*. New York: Harper & Row, 1977. Contains the account of a theodicy discussed in this chapter.

Lewis, C. S. *The Problem of Pain*. London: Geoffrey Bles, 1940. A clear and cogent defense of theism.

Mackie, J. L. *The Miracle of Theism*. Oxford, UK: Oxford University Press, 1982. Chapter 9 is an insightful, well-argued essay from an atheist's perspective.

Martin, Michael. *Atheism*. Philadelphia: Temple University Press, 1990. A comprehensive critique of theist arguments regarding the problem of evil. See especially Chapters 14–17.

Plantinga, Alvin. *God, Freedom, and Evil*. New York: Harper & Row, 1974. A clear, cogent account of the free-will defense from a theist perspective.

Swinburne, Richard. *The Existence of God*. Oxford, UK: Oxford University Press, 1978. Chapter 11 contains a careful defense of theism against the charges of the skeptic.

12 ⚜ Faith and Reason

The Challenge to Faith: An Outline of the Central Issues

One of the most important areas of philosophy of religion is that of the relationship of faith to reason. Is religious belief rational? Or is faith essentially an irrational or, at least, an arational activity? If we cannot prove the claims of religious belief, is it nevertheless reasonable to believe these claims? For example, even if we do not have a deductive proof for the existence of God, is it nevertheless reasonable to believe that God exists? In the debate over faith and reason, two opposing positions have dominated the field. The first position asserts that faith and reason are compatible (that is, it is rational to believe in God). The second position denies this assertion. Those holding to the first position differ among themselves about the extent of the compatibility between faith and reason; most adherents follow Thomas Aquinas in relegating the compatibility to the "preambles of faith" (for example, the existence of God and his nature) over against the "articles of faith" (for example, the doctrine of the Incarnation). Few have gone as far as Immanuel Kant who maintained complete harmony between reason and faith—that is, a religious belief within the realm of reason alone.

The second position divides into two subpositions: (1) Faith is opposed to reason (which includes such unlikely bedfellows as David Hume and Søren Kierkegaard), placing faith in the area of irrationality; (2) faith, being transrational, is higher than reason. John Calvin (1509–1564) and Karl Barth (1886–1968) assert that a **natural theology** is inappropriate because it seeks to meet unbelief on its own ground (ordinary, finite reason). Revelation, however, is "self-authenticating," "carrying with it its own evidence." We can call this position the *transrational* view of faith. Faith is not against reason so much as above and beyond it. Actually, Kierkegaard shows that the two subpositions are compatible, for he holds both that faith is above reason (superior to it) and against reason (because human reason has been affected by sin). The irrationalist and transrationalist positions are sometimes hard to separate as nonrationalist views. At least, it seems that faith gets such a high value that reason comes off looking not simply inadequate but culpable. To use reason where faith claims the field is not only inappropriate but also irreverent and faithless.

Can faith be rationally justified? Is it rationally acceptable to believe in God? This is the challenge that rationalists put to religion. Can it be met? Should it be met?

Pragmatic Justification of Religious Belief

Sometimes religious philosophers concede that religion cannot be justified through rational argument. However, they continue, it can be justified by its practical results. Religious belief has a *practical* reasonableness. That is, even if we cannot find good evidence for religious beliefs, would it perhaps be in our interest to get ourselves to believe in these propositions anyway? And would such believing be morally permissible? In his classic work *Pensées* (*Thoughts*), Blaise Pascal (1623–1662), a renowned French physicist and mathematician, sets forth the "wager" argument, contending that if we do a cost–benefit analysis of the matter, it turns out that it is eminently reasonable to get ourselves to believe that God exists regardless of whether we have good evidence for that belief. The heart of the argument is contained in the following passage.

THOUGHTS

Either God exists or He does not. But to which side shall we incline? Reason can decide nothing here. A game is being played where heads or tails will turn up. What will you wager? According to reason, you can do neither the one thing nor the other; according to reason, you can defend neither proposition. But you must wager. It is not optional. You are embarked. Which will you choose then? Your reason is no more shocked in choosing one rather than the other, since you must of necessity choose. This is one point settled. But which course will affect your happiness? Let us weigh the gain and the loss in wagering that God is. Let us estimate these two chances. If you gain, you gain all; if you lose, you lose nothing. Wager, then, without hesitation that He is.

"That is very fine," you say. "Yes, I must wager; but I may perhaps wager too much."

Let us see. Since there is an equal risk of gain and of loss, if you had only to gain two lives, instead of one, you might still wager. But if there were three lives to gain, you would have to play, and you would be imprudent, when you are forced to play, not to chance your life to gain three at a game where there is an equal risk of loss and gain. But there is an eternity of life and happiness....

You may object, "My hands are tied, my mouth is gagged. I am forced to wager, so I am not free. But, despite this, I am so made that I cannot believe. What then should I do?"

From: Blaise Pascal, *Thoughts,* trans. W. F. Trotter (New York: Collier, 1910).

> I would have you understand your incapacity to believe. Labor to convince yourself, not by more "proofs" of God's existence, but by disciplining your passions and wayward emotions. You would arrive at faith, but know not the way. You would heal yourself of unbelief, yet know not the remedies. I answer you: Learn of those who have been bound as you are. These are they who know the way you would follow, who have been cured of a disease you would be cured of. Follow the way by which they began, by acting as if you believe, taking holy water, having masses said, and so forth. Even this will naturally make you believe.

The argument goes something like this. Regarding the proposition "God exists," reason is neutral. It can neither prove nor disprove it. But we must make a choice on this matter, for not to choose for God is in effect to choose against him and lose the possible benefits that belief would bring. Since these benefits promise to be infinite and the loss equally infinite, we might set forth the possibilities like this:

	God Exists	*God Does Not Exist*
I Believe in God	A. Infinite gain with minimal finite loss	B. Overall finite loss in terms of sacrifice of earthly goods
I Do Not Believe in God	C. Infinite loss with finite gain	D. Overall finite gain

There is some sacrifice of earthly pleasures involved in belief in God, but by multiplying the various combinations, we find that there is an incommensurability between A and C on the one hand and B and D on the other. For no matter how enormous the *finite* gain, the mere possibility of *infinite* gain will always make the latter infinitely preferable to the former. Thus, the only relevant considerations are A and C. Since A (believing in God) promises infinite happiness and C (not believing in God) infinite unhappiness, a rational cost–benefit analysis leaves no doubt about what we should do. We have a clear self-interested reason for believing in God.

Go over this argument closely. Are there any weaknesses in it? Does it demonstrate that we all should do whatever necessary to come to believe that God exists? Is such a belief necessary and sufficient for eternal happiness?

In a famous rejoinder to such gambling with God, the British philosopher W. K. Clifford (1845–1879) argued that believing has moral ramifications so that believing without sufficient evidence is immoral. Pragmatic justifications are not justifications at all but counterfeits of genuine justifications, which must always be based on evidence. Clifford illustrates his thesis with the example of a shipowner who sends an emigrant ship to sea.

THE ETHICS OF BELIEF

> A shipowner was about to send to sea an emigrant ship. He knew that she was old, and not over-well built at the first; that she had seen many seas and climes, and often had

---

From: W. K. Clifford, "The Ethics of Belief," in *Lectures and Essays* (London: Macmillan, 1879).

needed repairs. Doubts had been suggested to him that possibly she was not seaworthy. These doubts preyed upon his mind and made him unhappy; he thought that perhaps he ought to have her thoroughly overhauled and refitted, even though this should put him to great expense. Before the ship sailed, however, he succeeded in overcoming these melancholy reflections. He said to himself that she had gone safely through so many voyages and weathered so many storms that it was idle to suppose she would not come safely home from this trip also. He would put his trust in Providence, which could hardly fail to protect all these unhappy families that were leaving their fatherland to seek for better times elsewhere. He would dismiss from his mind all ungenerous suspicions about the honesty of builders and contractors. In such ways he acquired a sincere and comfortable conviction that his vessel was thoroughly safe and seaworthy; he watched her departure with a light heart, and benevolent wishes for the success of the exiles in their strange new home that was to be; and he got his insurance money when she went down in midocean and told no tales.

What shall we say of him? Surely this, that he was verily guilty of the death of those men. It is admitted that he did sincerely believe in the soundness of his ship; but the sincerity of his conviction can in no wise help him, because he had no right to believe on such evidence as was before him. He had acquired his belief not by honestly earning it in patient investigation, but by stifling his doubts. And although in the end he may have felt so sure about it that he could not think otherwise, yet inasmuch as he had knowingly and willingly worked himself into that frame of mind, he must be held responsible for it.

Let us alter the case a little, and suppose that the ship was not unsound after all; that she made her voyage safely, and many others after it. Will that diminish the guilt of her owner? Not one jot. When an action is once done, it is right or wrong forever; no accidental failure of its good or evil fruits can possibly alter that. The man would not have been innocent, he would only have been not found out. The question of right or wrong has to do with the origin of his belief, not the matter of it; not what it was, but how he got it; not whether it turned out to be true or false, but whether he had a right to believe on such evidence as was before him.

Clifford comments that although the shipowner sincerely believed that all was well with the ship, his sincerity in no way exculpates him because "he had no right to believe on such evidence as was before him." One has an obligation to get oneself in a position where one will only believe propositions on sufficient evidence. Furthermore, it is not a valid objection to say that what the shipowner had an obligation to do was *act* in a certain way (namely, inspect the ship), not *believe* in a certain way. Although he does have an obligation to inspect the ship, the objection overlooks the function of believing as action guiding. "No man holding a strong belief on one side of a question, or even wishing to hold a belief on one side, can investigate it with such fairness and completeness as if he were really in doubt and unbiased, so that the existence of a belief not founded on fair inquiry unfits a man for the performance of this necessary duty."

And no one man's belief is in any case a private matter which concerns himself alone. Our lives are guided by that general conception of the course of things which has been created by society for social purposes. Our words, our phrases, our forms and processes and modes of thought, are common property, fashioned and perfected from age to age; an heirloom which every succeeding generation inherits as a precious deposit and a sacred trust to be handed on to the next one, not unchanged but enlarged and purified, with some clear marks of its proper handiwork. Into this, for good or ill, is woven every belief of every man who has speech of his fellows. An awful privilege, and an awful responsibility, that we should help to create the world in which posterity will live.[1]

Who has this duty to believe strictly in accord with the evidence, to doubt all in order to preserve him- or herself from the self-deception of false belief? Everyone.

Whoso would deserve well of his fellows in this matter will guard the purity of his belief with a very fanaticism of jealous care, lest at any time it should rest on an unworthy object, and catch a stain which can never be wiped away.[2]

It is true that the duty to believe only in accordance with the evidence is a hard one, for we want the power that attaches to a sense of knowledge and we want the security of belief, not the insecurity of doubt.

This sense of power is the highest and best of pleasures when the belief on which it is founded is a true belief, and has been fairly earned by investigation. For then we may justly feel that it is common property, and holds good for others as well as for ourselves. Then we may be glad, not that *I* have learned secrets by which I am safer and stronger, but that *we men* have got mastery over more of the world; and we shall be strong, not for ourselves, but in the name of Man and in his strength. But if the belief has been accepted on insufficient evidence, the pleasure is a stolen one. Not only does it deceive ourselves by giving us a sense of power which we do not really possess, but it is sinful, because it is stolen in defiance of our duty to mankind. That duty is to guard ourselves from such beliefs as from a pestilence, which may shortly master our own body and then spread to the rest of the town. What would be thought of one who, for the sake of a sweet fruit, should deliberately run the risk of bringing a plague upon his family and his neighbors?

And, as in other such cases, it is not the risk only which has to be considered; for a bad action is always bad at the time when it is done, no matter what happens afterwards. Every time we let ourselves believe for unworthy reasons, we weaken our powers of self-control, of doubting, of judicially and fairly weighing evidence. We all suffer severely enough from the maintenance and support of false beliefs and the fatally wrong actions which they lead to, and the evil born when one such belief is entertained is great and wide. But a greater and wider evil arises when the credulous character is maintained and supported, when a habit of believing for unworthy reasons is fostered and made permanent. If I steal money from any person, there may be no harm done by the mere transfer of possession; he may not feel the loss, or it may prevent him from using the money badly. But I cannot help doing this great wrong towards Man, that I make myself dishonest. What hurts society is not that it should lose its property, but that it should become a den of thieves; for then it must cease to be society. This is why we ought not to do evil that good may come; for at any rate this great evil has come, that we have done evil and are made wicked thereby. In like manner, if I let myself believe anything on insufficient evidence, there may be no great harm done by the mere belief; it may be true after all, or I may never have occasion to exhibit it in outward acts. But I cannot help doing this great wrong toward Man, that I make myself credulous. The danger to society is not merely that it should believe wrong things, though that is great enough; but that it should become credulous, and lose the habit of testing things and inquiring into them; for then it must sink back into savagery.

The harm which is done by credulity in a man is not confined to the fostering of a credulous character in others, and consequent support of false beliefs. Habitual want of care about what I believe leads to habitual want of care in others about the truth of what is told to me. Men speak the truth to one another when each reveres the truth in his own mind and in the other's mind; but how shall my friend revere the truth in my mind when I myself am careless about it, when I believe things because I want to believe them, and because they are comforting and pleasant? Will he not learn to cry, "Peace," to me, when there is no peace? By such a course I shall surround myself with a thick atmosphere of falsehood and fraud, and in that I must live. It may matter little to me, in my cloud-castle of sweet illusions and darling lies; but it matters much to Man that I have made my neighbors ready to deceive. The credulous man is father to the liar and the cheat; he lives in the bosom of this his family, and it is no marvel if he should become even as they are. So closely are our duties knit together, that whoso shall keep the whole law, and yet offend in one point, he is guilty of all.[3]

Clifford ends with a *summary* of his argument: "It is wrong always and for anyone to believe anything on insufficient evidence."[4]

Before you read on, pause to consider Clifford's case. Do duties attach to beliefs? All beliefs? Has Clifford answered Pascal's wager? Do you see any problem with Clifford's *summary* formulation? Do we have sufficient evidence for it?

The classic response to Clifford's ethics of belief is William James's "The Will to Believe," in which he argues that life would be greatly impoverished if we confined our beliefs to such a Scrooge-like epistemology as Clifford proposes. Here James comments on Clifford's summary statement.

THE WILL TO BELIEVE

All this strikes one as healthy, even when expressed, as by Clifford, with somewhat too much of robustious pathos in the voice. Free will and simple wishing do seem, in the matter of our credences, to be only fifth wheels to the coach. Yet if any one should thereupon assume that intellectual insight is what remains after wish and will and sentimental preference have taken wing, or that pure reason is what then settles our opinions, he would fly quite as directly in the teeth of the facts.

It is only our already dead hypotheses that our willing nature is unable to bring to life again. But what has made them dead for us is for the most part a previous action of our willing nature of an antagonistic kind. When I say "willing nature," I do not mean only such deliberate volitions as may have set up habits of belief that we cannot now escape from—I mean all such factors of belief as fear and hope, prejudice and passion, imitation and partisanship, the circumpressure of our caste and set. As a matter of fact we find ourselves believing, we hardly know how or why. Mr. Balfour gives the name of "authority" to all those influences, born of the intellectual climate, that make hypotheses possible or impossible for us, alive or dead. Here in this room, we all of us believe in molecules and the conservation of energy, in democracy and necessary progress, in Protestant Christianity and the duty of fighting for "the doctrine of the immortal Monroe," all for no reasons worthy of the name. We see into these matters with no more inner clearness, and probably with much less, than any disbeliever in them might possess. His unconventionality would probably have some grounds to show for its conclusions; but for us, not insight, but the *prestige* of the opinions, is what makes the spark shoot from them and light up our sleeping magazines of faith. Our reason is quite satisfied, in nine hundred and ninety-nine cases out of every thousand of us, if it can find a few arguments that will do to recite in case our credulity is criticized by some one else. Our faith is faith in some one else's faith, and in the greatest matters this is the most the case....

Evidently, then, our non-intellectual nature does influence our convictions. There are passional tendencies and volitions which run before and others which come after belief, and it is only the latter that are too late for the fair; and they are not too late when the previous passional work has been already in their own direction. Pascal's argument, instead of being powerless, then seems a regular clincher, and is the last stroke needed to make our faith in masses and holy water complete. The state of things is evidently far from simple; and pure insight and logic, whatever they might do ideally, are not the only things that really do produce our creeds.

In everyday life, where the evidence for important propositions is often unclear, we must live by faith or cease to act at all. Although we may not make leaps of faith just anywhere, sometimes practical considerations force us to make a decision regarding propositions that do not have their truth-value written on their faces. Logical scrutiny is not the only part of our human nature that matters, for there is an important nonrational dimension too.

Our next duty, having recognized this mixedup state of affairs, is to ask whether it be simply reprehensible and pathological, or whether, on the contrary, we must treat it as a normal element in making up our minds. The thesis I defend is, briefly stated, this: *Our passional nature not only lawfully may, but must, decide an option between propositions, whenever it is a genuine option that cannot by its nature be decided on intellectual grounds; for to say, under such circumstances, "Do not decide, but leave the question open," is itself a passional decision—just like deciding yes or no—and is attended with the same risk of losing the truth....*[5]

In "The Sentiment of Rationality" (1879), James defines *faith* as "a belief in something concerning which doubt is still theoretically possible; and as the test of belief is willingness to act, one may say that faith is the readiness to act in a cause the prosperous issue of which is not certified to us in advance." In "The Will to Believe," he speaks of belief as a live, momentous optional hypothesis, on which we cannot avoid a decision, for not to choose is in effect to choose against the hypothesis. There is a good illustration of this notion of faith in "The Sentiment of Rationality." A mountain climber in the Alps finds himself in a position from which he can only escape by means of an enormous leap. If he tries to calculate the evidence, only believing on sufficient evidence, he will be paralyzed by emotions of fear and mistrust and, hence be lost. Without evidence of being able to perform this feat successfully, the climber would be better off getting himself to believe that he can and will make the leap.

> In this case…the part of wisdom clearly is to believe what one desires; for the belief is one of the indispensable preliminary conditions of the realization of its object. *There are then cases where faith creates its own verification.*[6]

James claims that religion may be such an optional hypothesis for many people, and where it is, the individual has the right to believe the better story rather than the worse. To do so, one must will to believe what the evidence alone is inadequate to support.

You should keep two questions in mind at this point: One is descriptive, and the other is normative. The first is whether it is possible to believe propositions at will. In what sense can we get ourselves to believe propositions that the evidence doesn't force on us. Surely, we can't believe that the world is flat or that $2 + 2 = 5$ simply by willing to do so, but which propositions (if any) are subject to volitional influences? Is it psychologically impossible to make the kinds of moves that Pascal and James advise? Does it involve self-deception? If we know that the only cause for our belief in a religious proposition is our desire to believe, can we, if rational, continue to believe that proposition? Is there something self-defeating about volitional projects?

The second question deals with the ethics of belief, stressed by Clifford. Supposing we can get ourselves to believe or disbelieve propositions, is this morally permissible? What are the arguments for and against integrity of belief?

Note that Pascal's volitionalism is indirect, whereas James's might be interpreted as direct. In Pascal's case, one must will to believe the proposition *p*, discover the best means to get into that state (for example, going to church, saying mass, taking holy water) and act in such a way as to make the acquisition of the belief likely. In direct volitionalism, one supposes that one can obtain some beliefs simply by fiat of the will.

Finally, note that there is a difference between getting oneself to believe propositions where one has no control over the truth of the proposition and where the truth has still not been decided on but where belief might help bring about the desired state of affairs (for example, the mountain-climbing case). Should we have a different attitude about each of these types of cases?

Fideism: Faith Without/Against Reason

Fideism is the position that holds that objective reason is simply inappropriate for religious belief. Faith does not need reason for its justification, and the attempt to apply rational categories to religion is completely inappropriate. Faith creates its own justification, its own criteria of internal assessment. Perhaps there are two versions of fideism. The first states that religion is bound to appear **absurd** when judged by the standards of theoretical reason. The second merely says that religion is an activity in which reason is properly inoperative. It is not so much against reason as above reason. The two positions are compatible. The third-century theologian Tertullian seemed to hold that religious faith was both against and beyond human reason (and perhaps St. Paul holds the same in 1 Corinthians 1), but many fideists (for example, Calvin) would only subscribe to the latter position.

Søren Kierkegaard (1813–1855), the Danish philosopher and father of **existentialism,** seems to hold to both versions of fideism. For him, faith—not reason—is the highest virtue a human can reach, a trait that is necessary for the deepest human fulfillment. If Kant, the rationalist, adhered to a "religion within the limits of reason alone," Kierkegaard adhered to "reason within the limits of religion alone." He unashamedly proclaimed faith as being higher than reason in the development of essential humanness, that alone which promised eternal happiness. In a more everyday sense, Kierkegaard thought that we all lived by simple faith in plans, purposes, and people. It is rarely the case in ordinary life that reason is our basic guide. Paraphrasing Hume, he might have said that "reason is and ought to be a slave to faith," for we all have an essential faith in something, and reason comes in largely as an afterthought in order to rationalize our intuitions and commitments.

No one writes more passionately about faith nor values it more highly than Kierkegaard. Whereas his predecessors had largely viewed it as a necessary evil, a distant cousin to the princely knowledge, Kierkegaard reversed the order. Knowledge about metaphysical issues is really not a good thing, for it prevents the kind of human striving that is essential for our fullest development. Faith is the highest virtue precisely because it is objectively uncertain, for it is risk and uncertainty that are crucial for personal growth into selfhood. Spiritual self-realization needs to venture forth, to swim over 700,000 fathoms of ocean water. Faith is the lover's loyalty to the beloved when all the evidence is against her. Faith is the soul's deepest yearnings and hopes, which the rational part of us cannot fathom. Even if we had direct proof for theism or Christianity, we would not want it, for such objective certainty would take the venture out of the religious pilgrimage, reducing it to a set of dull mathematical certainties.

Genuine theistic faith appears when reason reaches the end of its tether, when the individual sees that without God there is no purpose to life.

CONCLUDING UNSCIENTIFIC POSTSCRIPT

In this manner God becomes a postulate, but not in the otiose manner in which this word is commonly understood. It becomes clear rather that the only way in which an existing individual comes into relation with God, is when the dialectical contradiction brings his passion to the point of despair, and helps him to embrace God with the

From: Søren Kierkegaard, *Concluding Unscientific Postscript* (1846); my translation.

"category of despair" (faith). Then the postulate is so far from being arbitrary that it is precisely a life-necessity. It is then not so much that God is a postulate, as that the existing individual's postulation of God is necessary.

Kierkegaard, often writing through pseudonyms like Johannes Climacus (John the Climber—presumably, to heaven), argues that there is something fundamentally misguided in trying to base one's religious faith on objective evidence or reason. It is both useless (it won't work) and a bad thing (it distracts one from the essential task of growing in faith). Then he goes on to develop a theory of subjectivity wherein faith finds an authentic home. One version of his argument is called the *approximation argument,* for it claims that reason and scholarship only give us approximate results, whereas faith demands infinite passion and subjective certainty. Here is a key passage.

If a naked dialectical analysis reveals that *no approximation to faith is possible,* that an attempt to construct a quantitative approach to faith is a misunderstanding, and that any appearance of success in this endeavor is an illusion; if it is seen to be a *temptation* for the believer to concern himself with such considerations, a temptation to be resisted with all his strength, lest he succeed in transforming faith into something else, into a certainty of an entirely different order, *replacing its passionate conviction by those probabilities and guarantees* which he rejected in the beginning when he made the leap of faith, the qualitative transition from non-belief to belief—if this be true, then everyone who so understands the problem, insofar as he is not wholly unfamiliar with scientific scholarship or bereft of willingness to learn, must feel the difficulty of his position, when his admiration for the scholars teaches him to think humbly of his own significance in comparison with their distinguished learning and acumen and well-merited fame, so that he returns to them repeatedly, seeking the fault in himself, until he is finally compelled to acknowledge dejectedly that he is in the right.[7]

Kierkegaard is here examining the need for biblical scholarship to establish the credibility of the Bible and Christian claims of revelation, but in other places he discusses attempts to prove the existence of God through rational demonstrations. All they give us is approximate objective results. For example, years ago most biblical scholars believed in the literal narrative of the Creation and Fall from Grace of Adam and Eve (in Genesis 2 and 3). Today most biblical scholars do not believe in the literal interpretation of that narrative, so it cannot serve as the basis for a believer's faith. But suppose tomorrow new evidence comes up against the authenticity of the New Testament Gospels or a plausible theory arises explaining how the disciples were deluded into believing that Jesus of Nazareth rose from the dead. If the believer's faith is hostage to the fortunes of scholarship, one week the faith may be strong, but the next week it may be very weak. Indeed, some weeks, there may be no faith at all, since the evidence is insufficient.

But this just is silly, argues Kierkegaard. Our eternal happiness can't rest on the luck of what scholars find or on intellectual hypotheses. Faith is not simply for scholars and intellectuals—perhaps it is least of all for them, for they are preoccupied with reason and miss the glory of faith; faith is something even peasants and uneducated people can possess. It is certain, something absolute, that demands one's whole heart and soul. The leap of faith transcends all scholarly pretensions. It's more like falling in love than figuring out a crossword puzzle, to which the scholars would have us liken it.

What do you make of this argument? Is faith wholly cut off from reasons? Or is it simply a fact of life that most of us, at least, have no rational basis for religious certainty?

A question may be asked: Why do we value reason so highly? In most areas of life, it seems to give us good results. In science, as well as in our daily lives, following reason is generally the best guarantee for success. Even the recognition of the limits of reason seems to be a function of reason at a higher reflective level—exactly what you might be doing right now—using reason to recognize the limits of reason.

This is a deep question, for which a lifetime of experience may be necessary. You must decide for yourself the answer. However, the rationalist has one advantage over the fideist. The rationalist can bring his or her evidence into the discussion so that we may all evaluate it and decide how credible it is, but the fideist has no such justification. In most other important areas of life, we trust the person with good reasons over the person with no reasons. Why should things be different with regard to religious belief?

Summary

There are three main positions regarding the relationship of faith to reason: (1) Faith and reason are compatible; they work in harmony. (2) Faith transcends reason so that there are limits to reason, but faith never contradicts reason rightly used. (3) Faith is against reason. Human reason is fallible and should not be given much weight in religious affairs. The weakness of positions 2 and 3 is that, if we give up reason, how do we distinguish nonsense, which claims to be transcendent from the veridical message of God?

Pascal's wager offers a pragmatic justification for believing in God without sufficient evidence. We examined Clifford's critique and other problems with Pascal's position, as well as James's defense.

FOR FURTHER REFLECTION

1. Examine the three major positions regarding faith and reason. What are the strengths and weaknesses of each one? Which seems the most plausible to you, and why?

2. Examine Pascal's wager. What are its strengths and weaknesses?

3. Do you think that you can get yourself to believe propositions (for example, that God exists or that Hinduism is the true religion) just by willing to do so? Or do beliefs force themselves upon people, depending on how the evidence or testimony of others affects them? Discuss your answer.

4. Is it immoral to believe a proposition against the evidence? Why or why not?

NOTES

1. W. K. Clifford, "The Ethics of Belief," in *Lectures and Essay* (London: Macmillan, 1879).
2. Ibid.
3. Ibid.
4. Ibid.
5. William James, "The Will to Believe," in *The Will to Believe* (New York: Longmans, Green, 1897).
6. Ibid.
7. Søren Kierkegaard, *Concluding Unscientific Postscript* (1846), my translation.

FOR FURTHER READING

Mackie, J. L. *The Miracle of Theism*. Oxford, UK: Clarendon Press, 1982. An atheist's defense of rationality and against religious belief.

Penelhum, Terrence, ed. *Faith*. New York: Macmillan, 1989. A good collection of classical and contemporary articles on the nature of faith.

Plantinga, Alvin, and Nicholas Wolterstorff, eds. *Faith and Rationality*. Notre Dame, IN: University of Notre Dame Press, 1983. Contains a set of articles defending the rationality of theism from the perspective of reformed epistemology.

Pojman, Louis. *Religious Belief and the Will*. London: Routledge & Kegan Paul, 1986. An examination of the relationship between faith and reason, arguing for a compatibilist position.

Swinburne, Richard. *Faith and Reason*. Oxford, UK: Clarendon Press, 1981. A strong defense of the rationality of religious belief.

PART IV
The Theory of Knowledge

13 ✦ What Can We Know?
An Introduction

There was once a young man who was troubled because he discovered that many of the things he believed, many of which he had been taught by his elders and in school, were false or, at least, were unsupported by the evidence. Despite having the best education available, he found it filled with error. For some years, he resolved that were he to obtain leisure time, he would use it not for entertainment or professional purposes but to rework his entire system of knowledge.

DISCOURSE ON METHOD

I had been nourished on the humanities since childhood, and since I was given to believe that by their means a clear and certain knowledge could be obtained of all that is useful in life, I was extremely eager to learn them. But as soon as I had finished my course of study at the end of which one is normally admitted among the ranks of the learned, I completely altered my view on the matter. For I found myself embarrassed by so many doubts and errors, that it seemed to me that the only profit I had had from my efforts to acquire knowledge was the progressive discovery of my own ignorance. And yet I was in one of the most prestigious schools in Europe, and if knowledge existed anywhere, it must be in the scholars there. I had learned everything that the others were learning there, and, not content with the studies in which we were instructed, I had even perused all the books that came into my hands, treating of subjects considered advanced and esoteric. At the same time I knew that others regarded me with respect, even though some of these were as brilliant as any age has produced.

From: René Descartes, *Discourse on Method*, in *The Philosophical Works of Descartes*, vol. 1, trans. Elizabeth Haldane and G. R. T. Ross (New York: Dover, 1911).

Having studied with the best, and learned from them, I was confident that I should seek knowledge in myself, or at least in the great books of the world. I employed the rest of my youth in travel, in seeing courts and armies, in conversation with men of diverse temperaments and conditions, in collecting varied experiences, in testing myself in the various predicaments in which I was placed by fortune. In all circumstances I sought to bring my mind to bear on the things that came before it so that I might derive some profit from my experience. I had a passion to learn to distinguish truth from falsehood in order to have clear insight into my actions and how to live my life.

So for nine years I did nothing but roam hither and thither, trying to be a spectator rather than an actor in all the comedies which the world displays. I considered the manners and customs of other men, and found nothing to give me settled convictions. I noticed in people's beliefs and customs as much diversity as I had earlier noticed in the views of philosophers. So much was this so, that I learned not to believe too firmly anything that I had been convinced of only by example and custom. I thus gradually freed myself from many errors that may obscure the light of nature in us and make us less capable of hearing reason. But after spending these years in the study of the books of the world and in trying to gain experience, the day came when I resolved to make my studies within myself, and use all of my power to choose the path that I must follow.

These are the words of the man considered to be the father of modern philosophy, René Descartes. Descartes was born in France in 1596 and educated by the Jesuits, an intellectually elite order in the Roman Catholic Church, in La Fleche. At age 17, he left school for Paris where he plunged into a fast-moving social life. After a few years of high society, he withdrew to a more contemplative life. In 1618, he became a soldier, serving in three different European armies. After 4 years, he was sufficiently well-off, so he retired from the army and resumed his travels to Switzerland, Italy, and, finally, Holland, where he settled and became a writer of philosophy. He reputedly did most of his research and writing, especially in winter, sitting up in bed. He became famous, and even the rulers of Europe wrote to him for advice. One of the rulers who admired him was Queen Christina of Sweden. She invited Descartes to visit her in Stockholm and teach her philosophy. Against the advice of friends, he moved to Stockholm. The Queen insisted that the lessons be given three times a week at 5 a.m., despite his being a late-night owl. He was not happy in Sweden and hated the cold weather, and a few months later caught he pneumonia from which he died on February 11, 1650.

Descartes's classic work in the theory of knowledge is his *Meditations on First Philosophy* written in Holland in November 1640. It is a short but tightly written set of six philosophical meditations, one for each day of the week (even philosophers should rest on the Sabbath). Each meditation is to occupy the mind in reflection for an entire day. Let's begin with the first meditation.

MEDITATIONS ON FIRST PHILOSOPHY

It is now some years since I detected how many were the false beliefs that I had from my earliest youth admitted as true, and how doubtful was everything I had since constructed on this basis; and from that time I was convinced that I must once for all

> seriously undertake to rid myself of all the opinions which I had formerly accepted, and commence to build anew from the foundation, if I wanted to establish any firm and permanent structure in the sciences.

His project is to doubt all his previous knowledge in order to build a secure house of knowledge. He begins the destruction by showing that sensory experience is unstable.

> All that up to the present time I have accepted as most true and certain I have learned either from the senses or through the senses; but it is sometimes proved to me that these senses are deceptive, and it is wiser not to trust entirely to any thing by which we have once been deceived. Reason persuades me that I ought to withhold my assent from matters which are not entirely certain and indubitable.[1]

Certainty demands reliable sources, but the senses are fickle and fallible, unreliable witnesses, and wisdom teaches that unreliable witnesses are not to be completely trusted, so that I should withhold assent from them. The *unreliable witness argument* can be formulated this way:

1. Whatever has been found to be an unreliable witness should (prudentially) never again be entirely trusted, since I can never be sure that it is not presently deceiving me.
2. The senses have sometimes been found to be unreliable witnesses.
3. Therefore, the senses should not be entirely trusted.

In itself this argument doesn't tell us to withhold belief, but if we want to be assured of complete certainty in our belief system, then we may add:

4. If one wants complete certainty in one's belief system, one should never trust what has sometimes been an unreliable witness.

And joining this with premise 2, we obtain:

5. Therefore, since I want complete certainty in my belief system, I should not trust my senses. I should withhold judgment regarding all sense experience.

There are problems with this, two of which are worth mentioning. The first, not mentioned by Descartes, is the observation that it is only by trusting or observing your senses that you discover that your senses sometimes deceive you. The second problem is one Descartes makes. That is, only a lunatic would doubt some experiences, such as this body is mine and I have two hands and feet. On deeper reflection, however, these beliefs too should be called into question. For I sometimes sleep and therein dream.

> How often has it happened to me that in the night I dreamt that I found myself in this particular place, that I was dressed and seated near the fire, whilst in reality I was lying undressed in bed! At this moment it does indeed seem to me that it is with eyes awake

---

From: René Descartes, *Meditations on First Philosophy*, in *The Philosophical Works of Descartes*, vol. 1, trans. Elizabeth Haldane and G. R. T. Ross (Dover, 1911).

that I am looking at this paper; that this head which I move is not asleep, that it is deliberately and of set purpose that I extend my hand and perceive it; what happens in sleep does not appear so clear nor so distinct as does all this. But in thinking over this I remind myself that on many occasions I have in sleep been deceived by similar illusions, and in dwelling carefully on this reflection I see so manifestly that there are no certain indications by which we may clearly distinguish wakefulness from sleep that I am lost in astonishment. And my astonishment is such that it is almost capable of persuading me that I now dream.

Or I could be hallucinating or a demon could be deceiving me about my experiences. The essential point is that we do not have a criterion to distinguish illusory experience from veridical perception. The argument may be formulated in this way:

1. To have knowledge we must be able to tell the difference between a hallucination (deception) and a perception. (Where there is no relevant difference, no epistemological distinction can be made.)

2. It is impossible to distinguish between an hallucination (or deception) and a normal perception.

3. Therefore, we do not know whether any of our perceptual beliefs are true.

If this is so, then we do not have any knowledge of the external world. All our experiences could be illusory. Not only Descartes but all of us have lost the whole world of experience.

Descartes goes on to doubt even our mathematical judgments. He imagines that an ingenious demon is deceiving him about everything, even about the most secure mathematical sums, so that it is possible that he is mistaken about adding 2 + 3.

Nevertheless, I have long believed that there is a God who can do anything, by whom I have been created and made what I am. But how do I know that He has not brought it about that there is no earth, no sky, no extended bodies, no shape, no size, no place and that nevertheless I have the impressions of all these things and cannot imagine that things might be other than as I now see them? Likewise could it not be that God has brought it about that I am always mistaken when I add two and three or count the sides of a square? But perhaps God would not so deceive me, since He is supremely good.

There may be those who would prefer to deny the existence of a God, so powerful, rather than to believe that everything else is uncertain. Let us not oppose them. Let us, instead, suppose that some evil genius or demon not less powerful than deceitful, has employed his whole energies in deceiving me.

I shall suppose, then, that some evil demon not less powerful than deceitful is employing his whole energies to deceive me. I shall consider that the heavens, the earth, colors, shapes, sounds, and all other external things, are nothing but illusions and dreams by which this demon has laid traps for my credulity. I shall consider myself as having no hands, no eyes, no flesh, no blood, nor any senses; yet falsely believing myself to possess all these things. I shall remain obstinately attached to this idea. If, by this means, it is not in my power to arrive at the knowledge of any truth, I may at least do what is in my power, namely, suspend judgment, and thus avoid belief in anything false and avoid being imposed upon by this arch deceiver, however powerful and deceptive he may be.

Having reduced all his previous knowledge to doubt, having withheld judgment on perceptual beliefs, including beliefs about Earth, his own body, his memories, even extending to mathematical and logical beliefs, Descartes is left without any knowledge at all, in complete skepticism, or so it may seem—for, actually, it is just from this state of doubting all that he reconstructs the world.

We turn to his second meditation that occurs on the second day of his deliberations:

The Meditation of yesterday filled my mind with so many doubts that it is no longer in my power to forget them. And yet I do not see in what manner I can resolve them; and, just as if I had all of a sudden fallen into very deep water, I am so disconcerted that I can neither make certain of setting my feet on the bottom, nor can I swim and so support myself on the surface. I shall nevertheless make an effort and follow anew the same path as that on which I yesterday entered, i.e. I shall proceed by setting aside all that in which the least doubt could be supposed to exist, just as if I had discovered that it was absolutely false; and I shall ever follow in this road until I have met with something which is certain, or at least, if I can do nothing else, until I have learned for certain that there is nothing in the world that is certain. Archimedes, in order that he might draw the terrestrial globe out of its place, and transport it elsewhere, demanded only that one point should be fixed and immovable; in the same way I shall have the right to conceive high hopes if I am happy enough to discover one thing only which is certain and indubitable.

I suppose, then, that all the things that I see are false; I persuade myself that nothing has ever existed of all that my fallacious memory represents to me. I consider that I possess no senses; I imagine that body, figure, extension, movement and place are but the fictions of my mind. What, then, can be esteemed as true? Perhaps nothing at all, unless that there is nothing in the world that is certain.

But how can I know there is not something different from those things that I have just considered, of which one cannot have the slightest doubt? Is there not some God, or some other being by whatever name we call it, who puts these reflections into my mind? That is not necessary, for is it not possible that I am capable of producing them myself, I myself, am I not at least something? But I have already denied that I had senses and body. Yet I hesitate, for what follows from that? Am I so dependent on body and senses that I cannot exist without these? But I was persuaded that there was nothing in all the world, that there was no heaven, no earth, that there were no minds, nor any bodies: was I not then likewise persuaded that I did not exist? Not at all; of surety I myself did exist since I persuaded myself of something [or merely because I thought of something]. But there is some deceiver or other, very powerful and very cunning, who ever employs his ingenuity in deceiving me. Then without doubt I exist also if he deceives me, and let him deceive me as much as he will, he can never cause me to be nothing so long as I think that I am something. So that after having reflected well and carefully examined all things, we must come to the definite conclusion that this proposition: I am, I exist, is necessarily true each time that I pronounce it, or that I mentally conceive it.

Descartes succeeds at discovering certain knowledge: *cogito ergo sum,* as he puts it in his earlier *Discourse on Method:* "I think, therefore I am." We will refer to this statement as the "Cogito." Even an evil demon, as powerful as he is evil, could not deceive me into believing falsely that I exist. If I am doubting, I must exist in order to be doubting. Doubting is one form of thinking, so I can conclude that I am thinking. So every time I am thinking, there must be an "I" who is doing the thinking. Hence, I must exist—at least I must exist whenever I am conscious of thinking. My existence is a self-evident truth to myself.

Descartes proceeds to reason from these discoveries to the conclusions that he must be a mental substance (since he still has not proved he has a body—but only has mental experiences). From these self-evident truths, he generalizes that whatever is "a clear and distinct idea" must be true. We need not follow Descartes further into these troubled waters since it seems that the idea of exactly what is a "clear and distinct idea" is neither clear nor distinct. We should only point out the peculiar *circular reasoning* that he engages in. When inquiring how I know that clear and distinct ideas are necessarily true, he appeals to the existence of God. God is not a deceiver and so would not allow us to be deceived about self-evident truths. When asked to justify his belief in God, he argues that the idea of God is a clear and distinct idea. Attempts have been made to save Descartes from such apparently fallacious reasoning, but most philosophers agree that the argument breaks down after the discovery of the Cogito.

For our purposes, however, we have all that we need to grasp the significance of Descartes's project. We want to understand exactly what we can know, what we can be certain of. What can we really know? How can we be certain that we have the truth about anything at all, besides our own existence? Indeed, we need to go back even further and ask, What is knowledge? Are there different kinds of knowledge? How is knowledge different from belief? If we know something, must we know that we know it? Or can we be ignorant of the fact that we really do *know* something? Can we have genuine knowledge of the external world, or must we be content with mere appearances? Can we know metaphysical truths? Whether God exists? Whether we have souls? Whether we will live again after death? Whether we have free will? Exactly what is the nature and scope of knowledge? These are the kinds of questions we examine in this part of our work, both through the readings of leading philosophers and through expositing the main elements of a theory of knowledge. But first we need to examine the basic ideas surrounding the theory of knowledge.

The Theory of Knowledge

The theory of knowledge—**epistemology** (Greek, "the science of knowing")—inquires into the nature of knowledge and justification of belief. Many philosophers, I among them, believe that it is the central area of philosophy, for if philosophy is the quest for truth and wisdom, then we need to know how we are to obtain the truth and justify our beliefs. We need to know how to distinguish the true from the false and justified beliefs from unwarranted beliefs.

If we consult the *Oxford English Dictionary,* we will find the following definition of the verb *know:* "to recognize, to identify, to distinguish, to be acquainted with, to apprehend or comprehend as a fact or truth." This sort of definition puts us in the ballpark of an understanding of the term, but it is too broad for philosophical purposes. So let's note some typical uses of the verb *know:*

- I know my friend John very well.
- I know how to speak English.
- I know that Washington, DC, is the capital of the United States.

These three sentences illustrate three different types of knowledge: knowledge by acquaintance, competence knowledge, and descriptive or propositional knowledge. We can characterize each of them this way:

1. *Knowledge by acquaintance:* A person S knows something or someone *X* (where *X* is the direct object of the sentence). In this way, we are familiar with the objects in the world and our thoughts and sensations. We have acquaintance knowledge of our pains and sensations, our friends, and the house and town in which we grew up. We also have acquaintance knowledge of our introspective reports, our loves and hates, beliefs, desires, and memory reports.

2. *Competence knowledge* (sometimes called *skill knowledge*): A person S knows how to *D* (where *D* stands for an infinitive). This is *know-how.* You know how to speak English and get around campus or at least your room, when it isn't too cluttered. You may know how to ride a bicycle, drive a car, use a computer, speak a foreign language as well as your native one, play the piano, or swim. Competence knowledge involves an ability to perform a skill and may be done consciously or unconsciously.

3. *Propositional knowledge* (or *descriptive knowledge*): A person S knows *that p* (where *p* is some statement or proposition). Propositions have truth-value; that is, they are true or false. They are the objects of propositional knowledge. When we claim to know *that p* is the case, we are claiming that *p* is true. Examples of the use of propositional knowledge are: "I know that the Sun will rise tomorrow," and "I know that Sacramento is the capital of California," "I know that I have a mind," and "I know that Columbus discovered America in 1492."

Epistemology is primarily interested in propositional knowledge, and it is the kind of knowledge we will examine in the following chapters. However, this only scratches the surface of what we are concerned with in the theory of knowledge.

The field of epistemology seeks to throw light upon the following kinds of questions:

- What is knowledge? That is, what are its essential characteristics, its necessary and sufficient conditions?

- Can we know anything at all? Or are we doomed to ignorance about the most important subjects in life?
- How do we obtain knowledge? Is it through the use of our senses, our intellect, or both?

Let's briefly examine each of these questions.

What is knowledge? First, knowledge entails truth. As mentioned above, propositional knowledge is knowledge of true propositions. To claim to know something is to claim to possess a *truth*. If you claim to know that $10 \times 10 = 100$, you implicitly claim that the statement "$10 \times 10 = 100$" is true. It would be a misuse of language to make statements like "I know that $10 \times 10 = 13$, but it is false," for knowledge claims are claims about grasping the truth. Of course, we may be wrong about our knowledge claims. The drunk claims to know that pink elephants are in the room with him, the child claims to know that Santa Claus exists, and two witnesses may make contradictory knowledge claims in reporting an accident. We often believe falsely that we know. Sometimes the evidence on which our knowledge claim is based is inadequate or misleading, or we misremember or misperceive. Sometimes our knowledge claims are contradicted by those of others, as when two people of different religious faiths each claims that his or hers is the only true religion or when one person claims with certainty that abortion is morally wrong and the other person claims with equal certainty that it is morally permissible.

Knowledge involves possessing the truth but includes more than having a true belief. Imagine that I am holding up four cards so that I can see their faces but you can only see their backs. I ask you to guess what types of cards I am holding. You feel a hunch or a weak belief that I am holding up four aces and correctly announce, "You are holding four aces in your hands." Although we both possess the truth, I have something you don't—an adequate justification for my belief that four aces are in my hand. Thus, knowledge differs from mere true belief in that the knower has an adequate justification for claiming truth.

Now the question shifts to the nature of justification. Hunches, guesses, conjectures, and wishful thinking are not cases of knowledge even if they are true, for they are not the kind of things that justify beliefs. But what kinds of things do justify beliefs? Must the evidence be undeniable, such as when we believe that $2 + 2 = 4$ or when we feel pain and cannot help believe that we are in pain? Can we have sufficient evidence to justify belief in physical objects? Our belief in other minds? Beliefs about metaphysical propositions such as the existence of God or freedom of the will? How much evidence must one have before claiming to know a belief is true? (We will examine the problem of justification in Chapter 15.)

Let's turn to our second question: Can we know anything at all? Or are we doomed to ignorance about the most important subjects in life? Could it be that our most treasured beliefs are merely unjustified biases, that even our sense of being a self is an illusion? Could it be that we really know nothing at all? **Skepticism** is the theory that we do not have any knowledge or at least that we do not know most of the things we claim to know. Moderate skepticism claims that we cannot be completely justified regarding any of our beliefs.

Weak skepticism holds that we can know some a priori truths, such as mathematical and logical truths, but not metaphysical or empirical truths. Radical skepticism goes even further and claims that we cannot even be certain of the belief that we cannot be completely certain that any of our beliefs are true. We cannot even know that we cannot have knowledge.

Can you defeat the skeptic? We already examined skepticism in Descartes's *Meditations.* We will continue that examination in Chapter 14.

Rationalism and Empiricism

We turn to our third question: How do we obtain knowledge? Is it through use of our senses, our intellect, or both? Rationalism and empiricism are the two classic theories on the acquisition of knowledge. **Rationalism,** which may be a misleading name for the first theory since both theories use reason in acquiring knowledge, simply states that reason is sufficient to discover truth, whereas **empiricism** holds that all knowledge originates through sense perception (that is, through seeing, hearing, touching, tasting and smelling).

The first comprehensive rationalist theory was put forth by Plato (circa 427–347 BCE), who distinguishes two approaches to knowledge: sense perception and reason. Sense perception cannot be adequate for possessing the truth because its objects are subject to change and decay. All one gets in this way of apprehending things is beliefs about particular objects. Knowledge, on the other hand, goes beyond the particular and grasps universal *Ideas,* or *Forms.* Plato argues that all knowing is the knowing of objects, so that these Ideas must exist in the really real world, the world of Being. The philosopher is a person who works his way through the world of Becoming, the empirical world, to this higher reality. Plato uses "The Allegory of the Cave" (see Chapter 5) to illustrate his doctrine:

> Imagine a group of prisoners who from infancy have had their necks and legs chained to posts within a dark cave. Behind them is a raised walkway on which people and animals travel to and fro, bearing diverse objects. Behind the walkway is a large fire that projects the shadows of the people, animals and objects onto the wall in front of the prisoners. The shadows on the wall grow and diminish, move up and down and around as the fire behind the objects wafts and wanes. But the prisoners do not know that the shadows are merely appearances of real objects. They take the shadows for reality, talk about them as though they were real, name them, reidentify them, incorporate their knowledge of the various forms into their social life. Their lives are centered on the shadows.
>
> Now imagine that someone tries to liberate one of the prisoners from the cave. At first, the prisoner kicks and screams as he is forcibly moved from the only home and social milieu he has ever known. Being dragged through the cave against his will, he is, at last taken outside, where the dazzling bright sunlight blinds him. Our prisoner cries to be

allowed to be returned to his safe shelter in the cave, but the way is closed. Gradually, his eyes adjust to the sunlight, and he can see the beautifully colored flowers and wide-spreading branches of oak trees, hear the songs of birds, and watch the play of animals. Delighted, his powers of sight increase until, at last, he can look at the bright sun itself and not be harmed.

But now his liberator, who has become his friend and teacher, instructs him to return to the cave to teach the other prisoners of the real world and to get them to give up their chains and journey upward to the sunlight. But our hero quakes with fear at such an ordeal, for he wants no part of that dark, dismal existence, preferring to enjoy the light of day to the dark of the abyss.

He is told that it is his duty to go, and so he makes his way into the cave again, returns to his chained mates, tells them that the shadows are merely illusions and that a real world of sunlight and beauty exists above outside the cave. As he is proclaiming this gospel, his former mates grab him, beat him for impugning their belief and value system, and put him to death.

But every now and then, the liberator comes back, drags one or two prisoners out of the cave against their will, and teaches them to enjoy the light. Such is the process of educating the soul to perceive the Truth, the form of the Good.

The bridge between the world of Being and the world of Becoming is **innate ideas.** Plato held that learning is really a recollecting of what we learned in a previous existence. He believed in reincarnation, that in a previous existence we saw all essential truths but have lost awareness of them through birth. The educator should be a spiritual midwife who stimulates the labors of the soul so that a person recalls what he or she really possesses but has forgotten. In the *Meno,* Socrates (Plato's mouthpiece) claims to demonstrate this doctrine of recollection of innate ideas by teaching an uneducated slave geometry. Drawing a square in the sand, Socrates asks the boy to try to double the area of the figure. Through a process of questions and answers in which the boy consults his own unschooled understanding, he eventually performs this feat. He seems to have "brought up knowledge from within." Similarly, Socrates argues, we can teach virtue only by causing our auditors to recollect what they have forgotten about the Good.

Plato thought that all knowledge was **a priori** (that which is prior) knowledge, knowledge one has independently of sense experience—as opposed to **a posteriori** (that which is posterior) knowledge, contingent, empirical knowledge, which comes to us from experience through the five senses. Ordinary empirical beliefs, according to Plato, unless they are related to the forms, are not knowledge but simply unstable appearances. An example of a priori knowledge is the mathematical equation $5 + 7 = 12$. To see that this equation is true, you don't have to appeal to experience.

Gottfried Leibniz (1646–1716) used a posteriori knowledge to signify contingent truths of fact, truths about what is discoverable by experience, and a priori knowledge to signify truths of reason, truths that depend on the principle of identity ($A = A$), which the mind could discover without the aid of the senses.

Immanuel Kant (1724–1804) further refined these notions, making a posteriori knowledge refer to judgments depending on empirical experience and a priori knowledge refer to judgments *not* depending on empirical experience. But he went further; he took the linguistic, or semantic, notions of analytic and synthetic statements and combined them with a priori and a posteriori knowledge. *Analytic statements* are those in which the predicate is already contained in the subject (for example, "All mothers are women," in which the subject term *mother* already contains the idea of "woman" so that we learn nothing new in our statement). *Synthetic statements* are just the opposite. The predicate term adds something new about the subject. For example, "Mary is now a mother" is a sentence in which we learn something new about Mary.

The empiricists John Locke (1632–1704) and David Hume (1711–1776) had argued that at birth our minds were an empty slate, a *tabula rasa,* on which the world via our sense organs made impressions, which in turn produced ideas. All knowledge of the world is a posteriori knowledge, and knowledge of logic and mathematics is purely analytic and a priori.

A classification of the relevant concepts is as follows:

Epistemologic Categories

- A priori knowledge does *not* depend on evidence from sense experience (Plato's innate ideas and Leibniz's truths of reason)—for example, mathematics and logic.

- A posteriori knowledge depends on evidence from sense experience (Plato's appearance and Leibniz's "truths of fact")—empirical knowledge.

Semantic Categories

- *Analytic:* The predicate is contained in the subject, and is explicative, not ampliative (for example, "All mothers are women").

- *Synthetic:* The predicate is *not* contained in the subject but adds something to the subject and is ampliative, not explicative (for example, "Mary is a mother").

Kant rejected the theory that there were only two kinds of knowledge: a priori and a posteriori knowledge. Combining a priori knowledge with synthetic propositions, he argued that we had a third kind of knowledge, *synthetic a priori knowledge,* knowledge that may begin with experience but did not arise from experience but was nevertheless known directly.

CRITIQUE OF PURE REASON

There can be no doubt that all our knowledge begins with experience. For how should our faculty of knowledge be awakened into action if objects affecting our senses did not produce representations and arouse the activity of our understanding to compare these representations, and, by combining or separating them, work up the raw material of the sensible impressions into that knowledge of objects that is entitled experience? In the order of time, therefore, we have no knowledge before experience, and with experience all our knowledge begins.

But though all our knowledge begins with experience, it does not follow that it all arises out of experience. For it may well be that even our empirical knowledge is made up of what we receive through impressions and of what our own faculty of knowledge supplies from itself.

Kant rejected the idea of *analytic a posteriori knowledge* because the very idea of an analytic judgment depends solely on the relations of the concepts involved and is discoverable by determining whether its denial entails a contradiction. That is, the analytic makes no reference to experience, whereas the a posteriori depends on experience.

The essential claim of those who hold to *synthetic a priori* knowledge is that the mind can grasp connections between ideas (concepts) that are not strictly analytically related. For example, we simply know upon reflection that all events have causes or that space is real without having an empirical proof or logical argument. Kant thought that our knowledge of mathematical truths and the laws of logic was really synthetic a priori, rather than analytic. Similarly, the moral law—that we ought to act in such a way that we could will that the maxims of our actions would be universal laws—is known without appeal to experience.

We can imagine a world with different physical laws, where Einstein's laws do not govern, where water is not wet nor fire hot, where mice are smarter than men and human babies are born from elephants, but we cannot imagine a world without time. Yet we have no argument that establishes time's reality. It is a given in all our experiences, a lens through which we see the world. It may not be real, but we cannot live without assuming its reality.

Like time, all synthetic a priori judgments are presupposed in all our experiences. They are the conditions through which all experience gets filtered down to us as *appearances* of the world. That is, we are so constructed that we can have no knowledge of the world as it really is (the "thing-in-itself"), but only as it comes in spatiotemporal–causal categories. As red-tinted glasses cause us to see the world in shades of red, so the constraints of synthetic a priori categories cause us to experience the world causally, temporally, and spatially.

Other synthetic a priori propositions referred to by the rationalists typically are metaphysical propositions such as "God exists," "I have a free will," "Every event has a cause," and "All things have sufficient reasons to explain them." If we combine these categories, we arrive at the information shown in Table 13.1.

─────────────

From: Immanuel Kant, *Critique of Pure Reason,* my translation.

Table 13.1

	Analytic	**Synthetic**
A Priori	Entailments Identity statements Tautologies Definitions EXAMPLES: "All bachelors are unmarried." "All bodies are extended."	*Mathematics* $5 + 7 = 12$ *Exclusionary* EXAMPLE: "Nothing red is green." *Presuppositions of experience* Space, time, and causality *Moral judgments* The categorical imperative EXAMPLE: "It's always wrong to torture for the fun of it." *The laws of logic* The principle of non-contradiction *Metaphysical* God's existence Freedom of the will
A Posteriori	[None]	All empirical statements EXAMPLES: "All bodies are heavy." "All copper conducts electricity." "John is a bachelor."

As mentioned above, all a priori knowledge is necessary and has universal application. It is true in all possible worlds, whereas statements known a posteriori are contingent. They could have turned out to be false rather than true.

Empiricists, such as A. J. Ayer (1910–1989), deny that there are any synthetic a priori truths and argue that all such supposed knowledge can be reduced to analytic truths. For example, mathematical statements are really analytic, the idea of "5" and "7" is "contained" in the idea of "12." Similarly, moral judgments, such as "killing innocent people is wrong," are not truths at all but emotings—for example, "Boo on the killing of innocent people!"

The rationalist responds to this reductionist attempt by claiming that a transcendental argument is in its favor: Ayer's very statement that "there can be no synthetic a priori truths" is itself a synthetic a priori statement, so that if it's true, it's false. Even if all other cases are doubtful, the laws of logic seem to function as synthetic a priori truths. The principle of noncontradiction is necessary for the very possibility of thought, including the thought of the principle itself. Its denial is self-refuting since to deny the principle depends on the very principle it is denying. For if the principle of noncontradiction is not true, then the denial of its denial is just as valid as the denial itself.

Let's turn to empiricism. Empiricism, the classic rival of rationalism, is the doctrine that all knowledge originates in the senses. Locke systematically attacked the notions of innate ideas and a priori knowledge, arguing that if our claims to knowledge are to make sense they must be derived from the world of sense experience:

> Let us then suppose the mind to be, as we say, white paper, void of all characters, without any ideas; how comes it by that vast store, which the busy and boundless fancy of man has painted on it with an almost endless variety? Whence has it all the materials of reason and knowledge? To this I answer, in one word, from experience: in that all our knowledge is founded.[2]

Locke goes on to set forth a representational theory of knowledge: The core of what we know is caused by the world itself, though some qualities are the products of the way our perceptual mechanisms are affected by the world. The former qualities, called *primary qualities* (for example, motion, size, shape, number), are the true building blocks of knowledge because these qualities are accurate representatives of the objective features of the world. On the other hand, *secondary qualities* are modes of apprehending the primary qualities. Examples of these qualities are taste, color, odor, and sound. Because the color or taste of the same object can appear differently to different people or to the same person at different times, secondary qualities are subjective, even though they are caused by the objective primary qualities. (We will examine these concepts further in Chapter 15 when we treat the problem of perception.)

The difference between a rationalist and an empiricist can be illustrated by the way they would answer two important questions:

- Question 1: How do we acquire ideas?
  The rationalist: Some nonanalytic propositions are innate or known a priori (independent of experience).
  The empiricist: All nonanalytic propositions are acquired from experience. No nonanalytic propositions are known a priori.

- Question 2: How is knowledge organized in the mind?
  The rationalist: The mind brings to experience principles of order from the mind's own nature.
  The empiricist: The mind arranges and stores materials that are given in experience.

Which theory is closer to the truth? On the basis of what we have discussed, you may at least be able to understand the significance of the issue and begin to formulate your own ideas.

Summary

The theory of knowledge centers on the nature of knowledge and justification of belief. Propositions are the basic unit of epistemology. Only propositions can be said to be true or false. A necessary condition for having knowledge is that the proposition in question be true. Classically, two schools of knowledge distinguish themselves from one another: Rationalists hold that knowledge is centered in reason and innate ideas. We have synthetic a priori knowledge. Empiricists deny that there are any innate ideas or synthetic a priori knowledge and hold that all knowledge begins with sense perception. All knowledge that is not merely analytic is a posteriori (after experience).

FOR FURTHER REFLECTION

1. Distinguish three ways we use the verb *know*. Which way is most important from the view of the theory of knowledge? Are the other ways important for philosophy? Explain your answer.

2. Can there be false knowledge? Why or why not? Can there be false beliefs? Can you name any of your false beliefs? Why or why not? Try to define a belief.

3. Distinguish between a priori and a posteriori knowledge. Then go over Kant's notion of synthetic a priori knowledge. Do you agree with his view that we cannot think about the world apart from such concepts? Do you agree that time, space, causality, and arithmetic are examples of such knowledge?

4. Why do empiricists reject the notion of synthetic a priori knowledge? Do you agree with their assessment?

NOTES

1. All remaining passages in this section are from René Descartes, *Meditations on First Philosophy* in *The Philosophical Works of Descartes,* vol. I, trans. Elizabeth Haldane and G. Ross (New York: Dover, 1911).

2. John Locke, *An Essay Concerning Human Understanding* (Oxford, UK: Oxford University Press, 1924), Book 2, Chapter 1, 121.

FOR FURTHER READING

Audi, Robert. *Belief, Justification, and Knowledge.* Belmont, CA: Wadsworth, 1988. An excellent short introduction to the subject.

BonJour, Laurence. *The Structure of Empirical Knowledge.* Cambridge, MA: Harvard University Press, 1985. A comprehensive treatment, advanced but well written.

Capaldi, Nicholas. *Human Knowledge.* New York: Pegasus, 1969. A helpful, accessible introduction to the subject.

Chisholm, Roderick. *Theory of Knowledge,* 3rd ed. Englewood Cliffs, NJ: Prentice-Hall, 1988. A rich exposition of the major problems.

Lehrer, Keith. *Theory of Knowledge*. Boulder, CO: Westview, 1990. A thorough and thoughtful survey of the subject.

Pojman, Louis. *The Theory of Knowledge: Classical and Contemporary Readings*. Belmont, CA: Wadsworth, 1993. A comprehensive anthology containing many of the authors referred to and works used in this part of our book.

Pojman, Louis. *What Can We Know?* Belmont, CA: Wadsworth, 1994. *An Introduction to the Theory of Knowledge*.

Russell, Bertrand. *The Problems of Philosophy*. Oxford, UK: Oxford University Press, 1912. A classic—pithy, succinct, and engaging.

14 ⚚ Skepticism

The Meaning of Skepticism

Can we ever be certain that we have the truth? How can we be certain that we know anything at all? If we know something, must we know that we know it? Is the skeptic right in claiming that we know almost nothing at all?

Can we know anything at all? Or are we doomed to ignorance about the most important subjects in life? Could it be that we really know nothing at all? Could it be that either none of our beliefs are completely true or that none of our true beliefs are sufficiently justified to constitute knowledge? How can we show that we really do know anything at all?

The term *skeptic* (Greek, "to inquire or investigate") got its impetus from Socrates who frequently stated, "We ought to investigate this," regarding numerous philosophical problems. To him, no subject was too sacred for rational inquiry. The greater the system, the greater the challenge of the inquiring mind and the greater the fall. **Skepticism** as a theory holds that we do not have any knowledge. We cannot be completely certain that any of our beliefs are true. There are two classic types of skepticism, both originating in ancient Greek philosophy: academic skepticism and Pyrrhonian skepticism. *Academic skepticism*—first formulated by Arcesilaus (circa 315—240 BCE), a philosopher in Plato's Academy—builds on Socrates' confession in the *Apology*, "All that I know is that I know nothing," and argues that the only thing we can know is that we know nothing. The academics argued that there is no criterion by which we can distinguish veridical perceptions from illusions and that at best we have only probable true belief.

Pyrrhonian skepticism, named after Pyrrho of Elis (circa 360–270 BCE), flourished in Alexandria in the first century BCE. Pyrrho must have been an extraordinary figure. Stories of his impracticality abound, but so do stories of his wisdom. In one story, Pyrrho was a passenger on a ship caught up in a violent storm. The passengers were panic stricken, wailing and crying with horror. Pyrrho calmly observed the storm and the panic of the passengers. When the storm grew even worse and the cries of the passengers crescendoed, Pyrrho pointed to a little pig standing before them on the deck calmly munching its food. He told them that the unperturbedness of that pig was the mark of wisdom. Imitate the pig by living calmly in the midst of madness all around!

The Pyrrhonians seem to have been influenced by the pre-Socratic philosopher Heraclitus who taught that everything is in flux and that we cannot even step into the same river twice, signifying human inability to discover any stable, immutable truths about reality. They rejected academic skepticism and dogmatism, the view that we could have knowledge, and set forth "tropes," skeptical arguments leading to *equipollence,* the balancing of reasons on both sides of an issue, which led to *epoche,* the suspension of judgment. Whereas the academics claimed to know one thing (that they didn't have any other knowledge), the Pyrrhonians denied that we could know even that. The Greek Pyrrhonist Sextus Empiricus (second century CE) said that Pyrrhonism was like a purge that eliminates everything, including itself.

One other distinction regarding skepticism needs to be made: that between global and local skepticism. *Global skepticism* maintains universal doubt. Global skeptics deny that we know that there is an external world, that there are other minds, or that we can have knowledge of metaphysical truths, such as whether we have free will, whether God exists, whether we have souls, and so forth. Some superglobal skeptics, such as Keith Lehrer and Peter Unger, even deny that we can know simple mathematical truths or that the laws of logic are valid (an evil genius could be deceiving us). The other type of skepticism is *local skepticism,* of which the British philosophers Anthony Flew and A. J. Ayer (1910–1989) are adherents, admits that we can have mathematical and empirical knowledge but denies that we can have metaphysical knowledge (God's existence, the nature of matter, whether all events have antecedent causes, whether there are other minds, and so on).

Skeptics like David Hume (1711–1776) do not deny that we should act from the best evidence available, but they insist that we can never be sure that we are correct in our truth claims. For all we know, the universe and everything in it could have been created 10 minutes ago with all our apparent memories created with it. Or the universe and everything in it may have doubled in size last night while we were sleeping. How could we check on this? It wouldn't help to use a ruler to measure our height to see if we doubled in size, would it?

How do you know that you are not the only person who exists and that everyone else is a robot who is programmed to speak and smile and write exams? Can you prove that other people have consciousness? Have you ever felt their consciousness, their pain, or their sense of the color green? In fact, come to think of it, how do you know that you are not just dreaming right now?

That all you are experiencing is part of a dream? Soon you will awake and be surprised to discover that what you thought were dreams were really minidreams within your maxidream. How can you prove that you are not dreaming? Or perhaps you are simply a brain suspended in a tub full of a chemical solution in a scientist's laboratory and wired to a computer that is causing you to have the simulated experiences of what you now seem to be experiencing? If you are under the control of an ingenious scientist, you would never discover it, for she has arranged that you will only be able to compare your beliefs to experiences that she simulates. Your tub is your destiny!

In Chapter 13, we examined the global skepticism of René Descartes's *Meditations,* in which Descartes places all his previous knowledge in doubt in order to build a secure house of knowledge. Recall the key ideas:

> All that up to the present time I have accepted as most true and certain
> I have learned either from the senses or through the senses; but it is
> sometimes proved to me that these senses are deceptive, and it is wiser
> not to trust entirely to any thing by which we have once been
> deceived.

Certainty demands reliable sources, but the senses are fickle and fallible, unreliable witnesses, and wisdom teaches that unreliable witnesses are not to be completely trusted. But then, again, only a lunatic would doubt some experiences, such as this body is mine and I have two hands and feet. On deeper reflection, however, these beliefs too should be called into question, for I sometimes sleep and therein dream:

> How often has it happened to me that in the night I dreamt that
> I found myself in this particular place, that I was dressed and seated
> near the fire, whilst in reality I was lying undressed in bed! At this
> moment it does indeed seem to me that it is with eyes awake that
> I am looking at this paper; that this head which I move is not asleep,
> that it is deliberately and of set purpose that I extend my hand and
> perceive it; what happens in sleep does not appear so clear nor so dis-
> tinct as does all this. But in thinking over this I remind myself that on
> many occasions I have in sleep been deceived by similar illusions, and
> in dwelling carefully on this reflection I see so manifestly that there
> are no certain indications by which we may clearly distinguish wake-
> fulness from sleep that I am lost in astonishment. And my astonish-
> ment is such that it is almost capable of persuading me that I now
> dream.

Recall that the essential point is that we do not have a criterion to distinguish illusory experience from veridical perception. The argument was formulated this way:

1. To have knowledge, we need to be able to tell the difference between a hallucination (deception) and a perception. (Where there is no relevant difference, no epistemological distinction can be made.)

2. It is impossible to distinguish between an hallucination (or deception) and a normal perception.

3. Therefore, we do not know whether any of our perceptual beliefs are true.

Stop for a moment to analyze Descartes's arguments. How strong are they? Do we have a criterion by which to distinguish between dreaming and being awake? Between hallucinations and veridical perceptions?

Descartes goes on to doubt even our mathematical judgments. He imagines that an ingenious demon is deceiving him about everything, even about the most secure mathematical sums, so that it is possible that he is mistaken about adding 2 + 3. Finally, he arrives at the self as the one thing he can know with certainty. He also thought he proved the existence of God and the mental nature of the self, but whether he did is more controversial.

Hume's Empirical Skepticism

David Hume was born in Edinburgh in 1711 into a Presbyterian family. He was taught at home until the age of 12, when he entered the University of Edinburgh, where he was to pursue a legal career. Instead, he fell in love with philosophy. He lost his religious faith and tended toward skepticism. Still in his early twenties, he tried a career in business, which soon bored him. In 1734, he traveled to France and eventually found lodging at La Fleche, Descartes's alma mater, where he argued with the Jesuits about miracles. There he completed his *Treatise of Human Nature*. The book, published in England in January 1739, sold few copies and received very little attention. Hume complained bitterly that it "fell dead-born from the press." Today this work of the youthful Hume is considered one of the classics of philosophy. Hume was disappointed in love, having been rejected by the woman he proposed to marry—apparently she found him obese and clumsy. He was nevertheless a charming man with a good sense of humor, popular at social occasions, modest, mild and moral, a generous friend. He died of colon cancer on August 25, 1776, the year of the signing of the American Declaration of Independence.

Whereas Descartes was a rationalist, who believed that reason could discover all truth, especially metaphysical truth, Hume was an empiricist, who believed that we must start with our perceptions and reason from there. Whereas Descartes was a global skeptic, doubting even mathematical truth, Hume was a local skeptic. He did not doubt truths of mathematical or logic as well as commonsense truth (for example, memory reports and sensory impressions), but he did doubt all metaphysical propositions: the existence of God, miracles, the idea of a self, material substance, free will, cause and effect, and induction.

Hume divides perceptions into two kinds: impressions and ideas. Impressions (both internal and external, the emotions and sense experiences) are more forceful and lively when they strike the mind, whereas ideas are the faint copies of impressions that we have when we remember past experiences or reason. All sensations, feelings, and passions are impressions. All thinking consists of ideas.

A TREATISE OF HUMAN NATURE

Of the Origin of Our Ideas

All the perceptions of the human mind resolve themselves into two distinct kinds, which I shall call Impressions and Ideas. The difference betwixt these consists in the degrees of force and liveliness with which they strike upon the mind, and make their way into our thought or consciousness. Those perceptions, which enter with most force and violence, we may name *impressions;* and under this name I comprehend all our sensations, passions and emotions, as they make their first appearance in the soul. By *ideas* I mean the faint images of these in thinking and reasoning; such as, for instance, are all the perceptions excited by the present discourse, excepting only, those which arise from the sight and touch, and excepting the immediate pleasure or uneasiness it may occasion. I believe it will not be very necessary to employ many words in explaining this distinction. Every one of himself will readily perceive the difference betwixt feeling and thinking. The common degrees of these are easily distinguished; tho' it is not impossible but in particular instances they may very nearly approach to each other. Thus, in sleep, in a fever, in madness, or in any very violent emotions of soul, our ideas may approach to our impressions: As on the other hand it sometimes happens, that our impressions are so faint and low, that we cannot distinguish them from our ideas. But notwithstanding this near resemblance in a few instances, they are in general so very different, that no-one can make a scruple to rank them under distinct heads, and assign to each a peculiar name to mark the difference.

There is another division of our perceptions, which it will be convenient to observe, and which extends itself both to our impressions and ideas. This division is into Simple and Complex. Simple perceptions or impressions and ideas are such as admit of no distinction nor separation. The complex are the contrary to these, and may be distinguished into parts. Tho' a particular colour, taste, and smell are qualities all united together in this apple, 'tis easy to perceive they are not the same, but are at least distinguishable from each other.

Hume next notes that complex ideas may never have been experienced as whole perceptions and that complex impressions may never have been made into ideas:

> I observe, that many of our complex ideas never had impressions that correspond to them, and that many of our complex impressions never are exactly copied in ideas. I can imagine to myself such a city as the *New Jerusalem,* whose pavement is gold and walls are rubies, though I never saw any such. I have seen Paris, but shall I affirm I can form such an idea of that city, as will perfectly represent all its streets and houses in their real and just proportions?[1]

From: David Hume, *A Treatise of Human Nature,* ed. L. A. Selby-Bigge (Oxford, UK: Oxford University Press, 1888).

His conclusion is that simple ideas and impressions resemble each other and *"that all our simple ideas in their first appearance are derived from simple impressions which are correspondent to them, and which they exactly represent."*[2]

All knowledge must be reduced to its foundational impressions. If I am to justify my belief in horses, houses, trees, or unicorns, I must identify the simple ideas and trace them back to simple impressions. This works fine for observable entities, but what about such ideas as causality, induction, substance, miracles, or God? They are ideas beyond immediate experience and don't seem to lend themselves to such empirical reduction. Let's examine his discussion of causality and induction in his *Enquiry Concerning Human Understanding* (1748). He begins by distinguishing *relations of ideas* from *matters of fact*.

ENQUIRY CONCERNING HUMAN UNDERSTANDING

All the objects of human reason or inquiry may naturally be divided into two kinds, namely, *Relations of Ideas* and *Matters of Fact*. Of the first kind are the sciences of Geometry, Algebra, and Arithmetic; and in short, every affirmation which is either intuitively or demonstratively certain. *That the square of the hypotenuse is equal to the squares of the two sides,* is a proposition which expresses a relation between these figures. *That three times five is equal to the half of thirty* expresses a relation between these numbers. Propositions of this kind are discoverable by the mere operation of thought, without dependence on what is anywhere existent in the universe. Though there were never a circle or triangle in nature, the truths demonstrated by Euclid would for ever retain their certainty and evidence.

Matters of fact, which are the second objects of human reason, are not ascertained in the same manner; nor is our evidence of their truth, however great, of a like nature with the foregoing. The contrary of every matter of fact is still possible; because it can never imply a contradiction, and is conceived by the mind with the same facility and distinctness, as if ever so conformable to reality. *That the sun will not rise tomorrow* is no less intelligible a proposition, and implies no more contradiction than the affirmation, *that it will rise*. We should in vain, therefore, attempt to demonstrate its falsehood. Were it demonstratively false, it would imply a contradiction, and could never be distinctly conceived by the mind.

Hume next turns to the doctrine of causality. Before Hume, the idea of universal causality in nature was believed to be a **necessary truth.** Every event must have a cause, and the connection between cause and effect is a necessary one, like the relationship between triangularity and three-sidedness. Hume first shows how crucial the idea of causality is for our daily lives.

All reasonings concerning matter of fact seem to be founded on the relation of Cause and Effect. By means of that relation alone we can go beyond the evidence of our memory and senses. If you were to ask a man, why he believes any matter of fact,

From: David Hume, *Enquiry Concerning Human Understanding* (Oxford, UK: Clarendon Press, 1748).

which is absent; for instance, that his friend is in the country, or in France; he would give you a reason; and this reason would be some other fact; as a letter received from him, or the knowledge of his former resolutions and promises. A man finding a watch or any other machine in a desert island, would conclude that there had once been men in that island. All our reasonings concerning fact are of the same nature. And here it is constantly supposed that there is a connection between the present fact and that which is inferred from it. Were there nothing to bind them together, the inference would be entirely precarious. The hearing of an articulate voice and rational discourse in the dark assures us of the presence of some person: Why? because these are the effects of the human make and fabric, and closely connected with it. If we anatomize all the other reasonings of this nature, we shall find that they are founded on the relation of cause and effect, and that this relation is either near or remote, direct or collateral. Heat and light are collateral effects of fire, and the one effect may justly be inferred from the other.[3]

Now he turns to an examination of the justification for our belief in causality. He begins with the example of a magnet ("two smooth pieces of marble").

This proposition, *that causes and effects are discoverable, not by reason but by experience,* will readily be admitted with regard to such objects, as we remember to have once been altogether unknown to us; since we must be conscious of the utter inability, which we then lay under, of foretelling what would arise from them. Present two smooth pieces of marble to a man who has no tincture of natural philosophy [that is, science]; he will never discover that they will adhere together in such a manner as to require great force to separate them in a direct line, while they make so small a resistance to a lateral pressure. Such events, as bear little analogy to the common course of nature, are also readily confessed to be known only by experience; nor does any man imagine that the explosion of gunpowder, or the attraction of a loadstone, could ever be discovered by argument *a priori*. In like manner, when an effect is supposed to depend upon an intricate machinery or secret structure of parts, we have no difficulty in attributing all our knowledge of it to experience. Who will assert that he can give the ultimate reason why milk or bread is proper nourishment for a man, not for a lion or a tiger?

But the same truth may not appear, at first sight, to have the same evidence with regard to events, which have become familiar to us from our first appearance in the world, which bear a close analogy to the whole course of nature, and which are supposed to depend on the simple qualities of objects, without any secret structure of parts. We are apt to imagine that we could discover these effects by the mere operation of our reason, without experience. We fancy, that were we brought on a sudden into this world, we could at first have inferred that one Billiard-ball would communicate motion to another upon impulse; and that we needed not to have waited for the event, in order to pronounce with certainty concerning it. Such is the influence of custom, that, where it is strongest, it not only covers our natural ignorance, but even conceals itself, and seems not to take place, merely because it is found in the highest degree.

But to convince us that all the laws of nature, and all the operations of bodies without exception, are known only by experience, the following reflections may, perhaps, suffice. Were any object presented to us, and were we required to pronounce concerning the effect, which will result from it, without consulting past observation; after what manner, I beseech you, must the mind proceed in this operation? It must invent or imagine some event, which it ascribes to the object as its effect; and it is plain that this invention must be entirely arbitrary. The mind can never possibly find the effect in the supposed cause, by the most accurate scrutiny and examination. For the effect is totally different from the cause, and consequently can never be discovered in it. Motion in the second Billiard-ball is a quite distinct event from motion in the first; nor is there anything in the one to suggest the smallest hint of the other. A stone or piece of metal raised into the air, and left without any support, immediately falls: but to consider the matter *a priori,* is there anything we discover in this situation which can beget the idea of a downward, rather than an upward, or any other motion, in the stone or metal?

And as the first imagination or invention of a particular effect, in all natural operations, is arbitrary, where we consult not experience; so must we also esteem the supposed tie or connection between the cause and effect, which binds them together, and renders it impossible that any other effect could result from the operation of that cause. When I see, for instance, a Billiard-ball moving in a straight line towards another; even suppose motion in the second ball should by accident be suggested to me, as the result of their contact or impulse; may I not conceive, that a hundred different events might as well follow from that cause? May not both these balls remain at absolute rest? May not the first ball return in a straight line, or leap off from the second in any line or direction? All these suppositions are consistent and conceivable. Why then should we give the preference to one, which is no more consistent or conceivable than the rest? All our reasonings *a priori* will never be able to show us any foundation for this preference.

In a word, then, every effect is a distinct event from its cause. It could not, therefore, be discovered in the cause, and the first invention or conception of it, *a priori,* must be entirely arbitrary. And even after it is suggested, the conjunction of it with the cause must appear equally arbitrary; since there are always many other effects, which to reason, must seem fully as consistent and natural. In vain, therefore, should we pretend to determine any single event, or infer any cause of effect, without the assistance of observation and experience....[4]

Hume argues that the inferences we make about causality are not logical ones (truths of reason) but arise solely out of experience. He attributes our belief in causality to the observation of regular conjunctions of events: "When many uniform instances appear, and the same object is always followed by the same event, we then begin to entertain the notion of cause and connection." We see two events in constant conjunction and *unjustifiably* infer a necessary connection. But there is nothing *necessary* about this connection. Our belief is merely a psychologically habitual inference derived from experience.

Next Hume applies this reasoning to the problem of induction.

But we have not yet attained any tolerable satisfaction with regard to the question first proposed. Each solution still gives rise to a new question as difficult as the foregoing, and leads us on to farther inquiries. When it is asked, *What is the nature of all our reasonings concerning matter of fact?* the proper answer seems to be, that they are founded on the relation of cause and effect. When again it is asked, *What is the foundation of all our reasonings and conclusions concerning that relation?* it may be replied in one word, Experience. But if we still carry on our sifting process and ask, *What is the foundation of all conclusions from experience?* this implies a new question, which may be of more difficult solution and explication. Philosophers, that give themselves airs of superior wisdom and sufficiency, have a hard task when they encounter persons of inquisitive dispositions, who push them from every corner to which they retreat, and who are sure at last to bring them to some dangerous dilemma. The best expedient to prevent this confusion, is to be modest in our pretensions; and even to discover the difficulty ourselves before it is objected to us. By this means we may make a kind of merit of our very ignorance.

I shall content myself with an easy task, and shall offer only a negative answer to the question proposed here [What is the foundation of all conclusions from experience?]. I say, then, that even after we have experience of the operations of cause and effect, our conclusions from that experience are *not* founded on reasoning, or any process of the understanding. This answer we must endeavor both to explain and defend.

In reality, all arguments from experience are founded on the similarity which we discover among natural objects, and by which we are induced to expect effects similar to those which we have found to follow from such objects. And though none but a fool or madman will ever pretend to dispute the authority of experience, or to reject that great guide of human life, it may surely be allowed a philosopher to have so much curiosity at least as to examine the principle of human nature, which gives this mighty authority to experience, and makes us draw advantage from that similarity which nature has placed among different objects. From causes which appear *similar* we expect similar effects. This is the sum of all our experimental conclusions. Now it seems evident that, if this conclusion were formed by reason, it would be as perfect at first, and upon one instance, as after ever so long a course of experience. But the case is far otherwise. Nothing [is] so like as eggs; yet no one, on account of this appearing similarity, expects the same taste and relish in all of them. It is only after a long course of uniform experiments in any kind, that we attain a firm reliance and security with regard to a particular event. Now where is that process of reasoning which, from one instance, draws a conclusion, so different from that which it infers from a hundred instances that are nowise different from that single one? This question I propose as much for the sake of information, as with an intention of raising difficulties. I cannot find, I cannot imagine any such reasoning. But I keep my mind still open to instruction, if any one will vouchsafe to bestow it on me.

Should it be said that, from a number of uniform experiments, we *infer* a connection between the sensible qualities and the secret powers; this, I must confess, seems the same difficulty, couched in different terms. The question still recurs, on what process of argument this *inference* is founded? Where is the medium, the interposing ideas, which join propositions so very wide of each other? It is confessed that the color, consistency, and other sensible qualities of bread appear not, of themselves, to have any connection with the secret powers of nourishment and support. For otherwise we could infer these secret powers from the first appearance of these sensible qualities, without the aid of experience; contrary to the sentiment of all philosophers, and contrary to plain matter of fact. Here, then, is our natural state of ignorance with regard to the powers and influence of all objects. How is this remedied by experience? It only shows us a number of uniform effects, resulting from certain objects, and teaches us that those particular objects, at that particular time, were endowed with such powers and forces. When a new object, endowed with similar sensible qualities, is produced, we expect similar powers and forces, and look for a like effect. From a body of like color and consistency with bread we expect like nourishment and support. But this surely is a step or progress of the mind, which wants to be explained. When a man says, *I have found, in all past instances, such sensible qualities conjoined with such secret powers.* And when he says, *Similar sensible qualities will always be conjoined with similar secret powers,* he is not guilty of a tautology, nor are these propositions in any respect the same. You say that the one proposition is an inference from the other. But you must confess that the inference is not intuitive; neither is it demonstrative: Of what nature is it, then? To say it is experimental, is begging the question. For all inferences from experience suppose, as their foundation, that the future will resemble the past, and that similar powers will be conjoined with similar sensible qualities. If there be any suspicion that the course of nature may change, and that the past may be no rule for the future, all experience becomes useless, and can give rise to no inference or conclusion.

It is impossible, therefore, that any arguments from experience can prove this resemblance of the past to the future; since all these arguments are founded on the supposition of that resemblance. Let the course of things be allowed hitherto ever so regular; that alone, without some new argument or inference, proves not that, for the future, it will continue so. In vain do you pretend to have learned the nature of bodies from your past experience. Their secret nature, and consequently all their effects and influence, may change, without any change in their sensible qualities. This happens sometimes, and with regard to some objects: Why may it not happen always, and with regard to all objects? What logic, what process of argument secures you against this supposition? My practice, you say refutes my doubts. But you mistake the purpose of my question. As an agent, I am quite satisfied in the point; but as a philosopher, who has some share of curiosity, I will not say skepticism, I want to learn the foundation of this inference. No reading, no inquiry has yet been able to remove my difficulty, or give me satisfaction in a matter of such importance. Can I do better than propose the difficulty to the public, even though, perhaps, I have small hopes of obtaining a solution? We shall, at least, by this means, be sensible of our ignorance, even if we do not increase our knowledge.[5]

Hume has argued that our belief that the future will be like the past is founded on the idea of the uniformity of nature, which in turn depends on the idea that the future will be like the past, thus reasoning in a circle. There is no contradiction in denying induction or the uniformity of nature. We cannot reason that the Sun will rise tomorrow because it has always done so in the past, for that assumes that the future will be like the past, which in turn assumes the uniformity of nature. In fact, the future is not always like the past. As Bertrand

Russell once pointed out, the chicken who comes to the farmer each day to be fed one day finds herself the object of a feeding.

Hume continues his attack on the received opinion of his day. Applying his doctrine of "locate the original impression" to the idea of substance or matter, Hume writes:

> Some philosophers base much of their reasonings on the distinction of *substance* and *quality*. I would ask them whether the idea of *substance* be derived from the impression of a sensation or reflection? If it be conveyed to us by our senses, I ask, which of them; and after what manner? If it be perceived by the eyes, it must be a color; if by the ears, a sound; if by the palate, a taste; and so on of the other senses. But I believe none will assert that substance is either a color or a sound or a taste. The idea of substance must therefore be derived from an impression or reflection, if it really exists.
>
> But impressions of reflection resolve themselves into our feelings, passions, and emotions, none of which can possibly resemble a substance. We have, therefore, no idea of substance, apart from that of a collection of qualities.
>
> The idea of substance is nothing but a collection of ideas of qualities, united by the imagination and given a particular name by which we are able to recall that collection. The particular qualities which form a substance are commonly referred to an unknown something in which they are supposed to "inhere." This is a fiction.[6]

Having set the ideas of causality and induction in doubt and having disposed of the notion of substance, Hume now questions the most basic idea of all, the idea of a self:

> There are some philosophers (e.g., Berkeley) who imagine we are every moment intimately conscious of what we call our *self;* that we feel its existence and its continuance in existence, and are certain of its identity and simplicity.
>
> Unluckily all these positive assertions are contrary to that very experience which is pleaded for them. Have we any idea of a self?[7]

Hume goes on to apply his "find the original impression" criterion to belief in free will and the existence of God, both of which are found wanting (see Chapter 8 for his criticisms of belief in God). Since all these metaphysical beliefs lack proper foundational credentials, they are completely unjustified and not fit for rational belief. Here is his conclusion of the matter.

> When we run over libraries, persuaded of these principles [of empiricism], what havoc must we make? If we take in our hands any volume of divinity or school metaphysics, for instance, let us ask, Does it contain any abstract reasoning concerning quantity or number? No. Does it contain any experimental reasoning concerning matter of fact and existence? No. Commit it to the flames, for it can contain nothing but sophistry and illusion.[8]

Can you defeat the skeptic? Can you find fault with any of Hume's reasoning?

Do We Have Knowledge of the External World?

In the *Treatise,* Hume also argues that we lack knowledge of the external world; that is, we have no justification for believing in the individual and continued existence of physical objects. Our senses only give us impressions, not knowledge, of the existence of the physical objects, and our ideas are derived from impressions, which are inadequate for justification. Our belief in external objects most likely is derived from our imagination, but this is no justification for the reality of external objects, since imagination is free to invent any fiction it likes.

Let's examine the problem of knowledge of objects in the external world. Suppose we are looking at a lush, red McIntosh apple. We take it into our hands, feel its firmness, bring it to our mouths, bite into it, and experience its luscious taste. Our senses work in harmony, it seems, conveying powerful experiences about the apple. But could we not be deceived about all of this? Could not the taste be due to our taste buds—lusciousness not being a property in the world but an effect manufactured in our minds; firmness being likewise a property in us, not the apple (which physics tells us is made up of mostly space and microphysical particles)? Or could we not be hallucinating or be brains in a vat?

We might set forth the argument in this way:

1. If I know that I have a McIntosh apple in my hand, then I know that I am not hallucinating or dreaming this.

2. But I do not *know* that I am not hallucinating or dreaming this, since knowledge entails a complete justification for what is known and I have no complete justification that I am not hallucinating (or dreaming).

3. Therefore, I do not know that I have a McIntosh apple in my hand.

What can we make of this argument? It seems valid. Premise 1 seems true. If I really do have an apple in my hand, then I am not simply hallucinating (or dreaming) that I do. Premise 2 seems true also. I can't prove that I am not hallucinating or dreaming, for even if I am not hallucinating or dreaming, I wouldn't know the difference if I were. My experience would be relevantly similar. Thus, the argument seems sound. If I don't know that I'm not hallucinating or dreaming all this, how can I know that I really do have an apple in my hand? If I can't prove or don't know that I am not hallucinating at any particular moment of my life, how can I know anything about the external world—even if I'm not hallucinating?

The force of the argument is not that we don't have *justified* beliefs or even true, justified beliefs. We're doing the best we can, and perhaps that's enough to give us truth. But it's not enough, claims the skeptic, to give us knowledge or justified certainty about the truth of our experiences. We could be wrong about any of our appearances. So we don't have knowledge.

Hume himself despaired of solving these problems. Here is his conclusion to the matter.

As long as our attention is bent upon the subject, the philosophical and studied principle may prevail; but the moment we relax our thoughts, nature will display herself, and draw us back to our former opinion....The skeptical doubt, both with respect to reason and the senses, is a malady, which can never be radically cured, but must return upon us every moment, however we may chance it away....As the skeptical doubt arises naturally from a profound and intense reflection on those subjects, it always increases, the farther we carry our reflections, when in opposition or conformity to it. *Carelessness and inattention alone can afford us any remedy.*[9]

Fortunately, Hume concludes,

It happens that since reason is incapable of dispelling these clouds, nature herself suffices to that purpose, and cures me of this philosophical melancholy and delirium, either by relaxing this bent of mind, or by some avocation, and lively impression of my senses, which obliterate all these chimeras. I dine, I play a game of backgammon, I converse, and am merry with my friends; and when after three or four hours' amusement, I would return to these speculations, they appear so cold, and strained, and ridiculous, that I cannot find in my heart to enter into them any farther.[10]

A natural propensity prohibits perseverance in skepticism and forces us to act as though the deliberations of reason were chimeras. But when we come back to philosophical reflection, we must suspect, if not profoundly conclude, that we know very little indeed.

Arguments Against Skepticism: Moore's and Malcolm's Defense of Common Sense

Two related attempts to defeat skepticism have been offered. The first is G. E. Moore's (1873–1959) claims that we can know that there is an external world, for we can know we have bodies, that my body was born at a certain time in the past, and has existed continuously ever since.

PROOF OF THE EXTERNAL WORLD

It was much smaller when it was born, and for some time afterwards, than it is now. Ever since it was born, it has been either in contact with or not far from the surface from the earth; and, at every moment since it was born, there have also existed many other things, having shape and size in three dimensions, from which it has been at various distances.

From: G. E. Moore, "Proof of the External World," in *Philosophical Papers* (London: Allen & Unwin, 1959).

In a famous lecture, Moore claimed that he would then and there prove two things, that he has two hands. How? Here is Moore's proof.

> I can prove now ... that two human hands exist. How? By holding up my two hands, and saying, as I make a certain gesture with the right hand, "Here is one hand," and adding, as I made a certain gesture with the left, "and here is another." But now I am perfectly well aware that, in spite of all I have said, many philosophers will still feel that I have not given any satisfactory proof of the point in question.... If I had proved the proposition which I used as *premises* in my two proofs, then they would perhaps admit that I had proved the existence of external things.... They want a proof of what I assert *now* when I hold up my hands and say "Here's one hand and here's another." ... They think that, if I cannot give such extra proofs, then the proofs that I have given are not conclusive proofs at all.... Such a view, though it has been very common among philosophers, can, I think, be shown to be wrong.... I can know things which I cannot prove; and among things which I certainly did know were the premises of my two proofs. I should say, therefore, that those, if any, who are dissatisfied with these proofs merely on the grounds that I did not know their premises, have no good reasons for their dissatisfaction.[11]

Moore claimed that we do not need to be able to prove all the premises of our argument in order to end up with a sound argument. If our premises are self-evident, we may consider them innocent until proven guilty. Accordingly, Moore claimed to have thereby given a rigorous proof that there was an external world because the premises are known to be true (even though we can't prove them), and the conclusion follows by valid inference from these premises. The general form of Moore's strategy is the following:

1. If skepticism is true, we do not have knowledge of the external world.
2. But we do have knowledge of the external world (the examples given).
3. Therefore, skepticism is false.

Skeptics have not taken kindly to Moore's refutation, claiming that it has all the virtues of theft over honest labor. Moore, they claim, is begging the question against the skeptic, for the question of whether Moore—or those "watching" him—is dreaming or hallucinating cannot be so easily ruled out.

In the second type of attempt, related to the first and set forth by the American philosopher Norman Malcolm (1911–1990), two types of knowledge are distinguished: weak and strong. Many philosophers, including the British philosopher H. A. Prichard, believe that we can discover in ourselves whether we *know* some proposition or whether we merely believe it. Malcolm rejects the idea that knowledge lights up a different mental state than belief, but he seeks to establish that some experiences are so strong that we cannot admit to the skeptic that we do not possess knowledge. But other experiences of knowing are not as certain. He characterizes these two types of knowledge as *strong* and *weak*. We begin with Malcolm's discussion of knowing the answer to a multiplication problem.

KNOWLEDGE AND CERTAINTY

Consider [an] example from mathematics of the difference between the strong and weak senses of "know." I have just now rapidly calculated that 92 times 16 is 1472. If I had done this in the commerce of daily life where a practical problem was at stake, and if someone had asked, "Are you sure that $92 \times 16 = 1472$?" I might have answered "I *know* that it is; I have just now calculated it." But also I might have answered, "I know that it is; but I will calculate it again to *make sure*." And here my language points to a distinction. I say that I *know* that $92 \times 16 = 1472$. Yet I am willing to *confirm* it—that is, there is something that I should *call* "making sure"; and, likewise there is something that I should *call* "finding out that it is false." If I were to do this calculation again and obtain the result that $92 \times 16 = 1372$, and if I were to carefully check this latter calculation without finding any error, I should be disposed to say that I was previously mistaken when I declared that $92 \times 16 = 1472$. Thus when I say that I know that $92 \times 16 = 1472$, I allow for the possibility of a *refutation,* and so I am using "know" in a *weak* sense.

Now consider propositions like $2 + 2 = 4$ and $7 + 5 = 12$. It is hard to think of circumstances in which it would be natural for me to say that I know that $2 + 2 = 4$, because no one ever questions it. Let us try to suppose, however, that someone whose intelligence I respect argues that certain developments in arithmetic have shown that $2 + 2$ does not equal 4. He writes out a proof of this in which I can find no flaw. Suppose that his demeanor showed me that he was in earnest. Suppose that several persons of normal intelligence became persuaded that his proof was correct and that $2 + 2$ does not equal 4. What would be my reaction? I should say "I can't see what is wrong with your proof; but it *is* wrong, because I *know* that $2 + 2 = 4$." Here I should be using "know" in its *strong* sense. I should not admit that any argument or any future development in mathematics could show that it is false that $2 + 2 = 4$.

The propositions $2 + 2 = 4$ and $92 \times 16 = 1472$ do not have the same status. There *can* be a demonstration that $2 + 2 = 4$. But a demonstration would be for me (and for any average person) only a curious exercise, a sort of *game.* We have no serious interest in proving that proposition. It does not *need* a proof. It stands without one, and would not fall if a proof went against it. The case is different with the proposition that $92 \times 16 = 1472$. We take an interest in the demonstration (calculation) because that proposition *depends* upon its demonstration. A calculation may lead me to reject it as false. But $2 + 2 = 4$ does *not* depend on its demonstration. It does not depend on anything! And in the calculation that proves that $92 \times 16 = 1472$, there are steps that do not depend on any calculation (e.g., $2 \times 6 = 12$; $5 + 2 = 7$; $5 + 9 = 14$).

There is a correspondence between this dualism in the logical status of mathematical propositions and the two senses of "know." When I use "know" in the weak sense I am prepared to let an investigation (demonstration, calculation) determine whether the something that I claim to know is true or false. When I use "know" in the strong sense I am not prepared to look upon anything as an *investigation;* I do not concede that anything whatsoever could prove me mistaken; I do not regard the matter as

From: Norman Malcolm, *Knowledge and Certainty* (Englewood Cliffs, NJ: Prentice Hall, 1963).

open to any *question;* I do not admit that my proposition could turn out to be false, that any future investigation *could* refute it or cast doubt on it.

There are some knowledge claims that, on being challenged, I would be wise to admit I could be wrong. For example, I believe that the Sun is about 90 million miles from Earth, but if someone were to challenge me on this, I might well admit that I'm not certain about it. Here is Malcolm's discussion of three cases of knowledge.

Consider the following propositions:

 (i) The sun is about ninety million miles from the earth.

(ii) There is a heart in my body.

(iii) Here is an ink-bottle.

In various circumstances I should be willing to assert of each of these propositions that I know it to be true. Yet they differ strikingly. This I see when, with each, I try to imagine the possibility that it is false.

(i) If in ordinary conversation someone said to me "The sun is about twenty million miles from the earth, isn't it?" I should reply "No, it is about ninety million miles from us." If he said "I think that you are confusing the sun with Polaris," I should reply "I *know* that ninety million miles is roughly the sun's distance from the earth." I might invite him to verify the figure in an encyclopedia. A third person who overheard our conversation could quite correctly report that I knew the distance to the sun, whereas the other man did not. But this knowledge of mine is little better than hearsay. I have seen that figure mentioned in a few books. I know nothing about the observations and calculations that led astronomers to accept it. If tomorrow a group of eminent astronomers announced that a great error had been made and that the correct figure is twenty million miles, I should not insist that they were wrong. It would surprise me that such an enormous mistake could have been made. But I should no longer be willing to say that I *know* that ninety million is the correct figure. Although I should *now* claim that I know the distance to be about ninety million miles, it is easy for me to envisage the possibility that some future investigation will prove this to be false.

(ii) Suppose that after a routine medical examination the excited doctor reports to me that the X-ray photographs show that I have no heart. I should tell him to get a new machine. I should be inclined to say that the fact that I have a heart is one of the few things that I can count on as absolutely certain. I can feel it beat. I know it's there. Furthermore, how could my blood circulate if I didn't have one? Suppose that later on I suffer a chest injury and undergo a surgical operation. Afterwards the astonished surgeons solemnly declare that they searched my chest cavity and found no heart, and that they made incisions and looked about in other likely places but found it not. They are convinced that I am without a heart. They are unable to understand how circulation can occur or what accounts for the thumping in my chest. But they are in agreement and obviously sincere, and they have clear photographs of my interior spaces. What would be my attitude? Would it be to insist that they were all mistaken? I think not. I believe that I should eventually accept their testimony and the evidence of the photographs. I should consider to be false what I now regard as an absolute certainty.

(iii) Suppose that as I write this paper someone in the next room were to call out to me "I can't find an ink-bottle; is there one in the house?" I should reply "Here is an ink-bottle." If he said in a doubtful tone "Are you sure? I looked there before," I should reply "Yes, I know there is; come and get it."

Now could it turn out to be false that there is an ink-bottle directly in front of me on this desk? Many philosophers have thought so. They would say that many things could happen of such a nature that if they did happen it would be proved that I am deceived. I agree that many extraordinary things could happen, in the sense that there is no logical absurdity in the supposition. It could happen that when I next reach for this ink-bottle my hand should seem to pass *through* it and I should not feel the contact of any object. It could happen that in the next moment the ink-bottle will suddenly vanish from sight; or that I should find myself under a tree in the garden with no ink-bottle about; or that one or more persons should enter this room and declare with apparent sincerity that they see no ink-bottle on this desk; or that a photograph taken now of the top of the desk should clearly show all of the objects on it except the ink-bottle. Having admitted that these things *could happen,* am I compelled to admit that if they did happen then it would be proved that there is no ink-bottle here *now*? Not at all! I could say that when my hand seemed to pass through the ink-bottle I should *then* be suffering from hallucination; that if the ink-bottle suddenly vanished it would have miraculously ceased to exist; that the other persons were conspiring to drive me mad, or were themselves victims of remarkable concurrent hallucinations; that the camera possessed some strange flaw or that there was trickery in developing the negative. I admit that in the next moment I could find myself under a tree or in the bathtub. But this is not to admit that it could be revealed in the next moment that I am now dreaming. For what I admit is that I might be instantaneously transported to the garden, but not that in the next moment I might *wake up* in the garden. There is nothing that could happen to me in the next moment that I should call "waking up"; and therefore nothing that could happen to me in the next moment would be accepted by me now as proof that I now dream.

Not only do I not *have* to admit that those extraordinary occurrences would be evidence that there is no ink-bottle here; the fact is that I *do not* admit it. There is nothing whatever that could happen in the next moment or the next year that would by me be called *evidence* that there is not an ink-bottle here now. No future experience or investigation could prove to me that I am mistaken. Therefore, if I were to say "I know that there is an ink-bottle here," I should be using "know" in the strong sense.

It will appear to some that I have adopted an *unreasonable* attitude towards that statement. There is, however, nothing unreasonable about it. It seems so because one thinks that the statement that here is an ink-bottle *must* have the same status as the statements that the sun is ninety million miles away and that I have a heart and that there will be water in the gorge this afternoon. But this is a *prejudice*.

In saying that I should regard nothing as evidence that there is no ink-bottle here now, I am not *predicting* what I should do if various astonishing things happened. If other members of my family entered this room and, while looking at the top of this desk, declared with apparent sincerity that they see no ink-bottle, I might fall into a swoon or become mad. I *might* even come to believe that there is not and has not been an ink-bottle here. I cannot foretell with certainty how I should react. But if it is *not* a prediction, what is the meaning of my assertion that I should regard nothing as evidence that there is no ink-bottle here?

That assertion describes my *present* attitude towards the statement that here is an ink-bottle. It does not prophesy what my attitude *would* be if various things happened. My present attitude towards that statement is radically different from my present attitude towards those other statements (e.g., that I have a heart). I do *now* admit that certain future occurrences would disprove the latter. Whereas no imaginable future occurrence would be considered by me *now* as proving that there is not an ink-bottle here.[12]

Some kinds of knowledge claims, however, are so certain that no conceivable challenges could cause me to give them up, and these are the kind that Moore was so adamant about: that I have a body, that I am now reading a philosophy book, that I am now sitting on a chair, that I am not sleeping. So while we are willing to let further investigation determine whether we really have knowledge in the instances of weak knowledge, we do not concede that anything whatsoever could prove us mistaken in the cases of strong knowledge.

Malcolm's argument is really an elaboration of Moore's, but the distinction is important. There are experiences about which we cannot imagine being wrong. We want to say that the burden of proof is on the skeptic to tell us why we should doubt these things. Of course, the skeptic is not going to be convinced about this sort of claim to knowledge. The skeptic's point is that we are not completely justified in our knowledge claims. Since we could be wrong, we should hold back claims to knowledge.

Whatever the truth of the matter is on making knowledge claims, at least one value of skepticism is to make us correctly modest about our pretensions to knowledge. It is harder than most of us imagine to justify our claims to knowledge, and much of what we claim to know turns out to be mistaken. Such lessons in humility are steps toward wisdom.

Summary

Skepticism is the theory that we do not have any knowledge at all. Academic skepticism holds that we can know one higher-level truth: We can know nothing else but that we cannot have any other knowledge (except for knowing this fact). Pyrrhonian skepticism holds that we cannot even know that we can't have knowledge. Global skepticism denies that we can know anything at all—except *perhaps* mathematical and simple logical truths. Local skepticism admits that we can have empirical knowledge but denies that we can have metaphysical knowledge. Descartes represents the global skeptic, arguing that a demon could be deceiving us about even simple mathematical statements. Hume, while denying that we can have empirical knowledge, admits that we are justified in our empirical beliefs but denies metaphysical knowledge. Moore and Malcolm have each tried to undermine the skeptic's arguments.

FOR FURTHER REFLECTION

1. Go over the various types of skepticism. Which are the strongest types? Can you defeat the skeptic? Which arguments seem most plausible?

2. Examine Hume's thesis that all ideas are based on impression. Do you find this unduly restrictive? How would he handle abductive reasoning (discussed in Chapter 2)? Could proponents of causality, free will, the self, substance, and the existence of God appeal to such a procedure to get around Hume's criticisms?

3. Do you think that Moore's strategy is convincing? Why can't the skeptic accuse Moore of begging the question against skepticism? Can the skeptic simply argue that Moore has not provided a justification for why he believes he has two hands?

4. Are you convinced by Malcolm's argument for the distinction between strong and weak knowledge? Does it answer the skeptic?

NOTES

1. David Hume, *A Treatise of Human Nature,* ed. L. A. Selby-Bigge (Oxford, UK: Oxford University Press, 1888), 1–2.
2. Ibid.
3. David Hume, *Enquiry Concerning Human Understanding* (Oxford, UK: Clarendon Press, 1748).
4. Ibid.
5. David Hume, *Enquiries Concerning the Human Understanding,* ed. L. A. Selby-Bigge. (Oxford, UK: Clarendon Press, 1902). I have slightly edited the text.
6. Hume, *Treatise,* 252.
7. Hume, *Treatise.*
8. Ibid.
9. Ibid., 218.
10. Ibid., 219.
11. G. E. Moore, "Proof of the External World," in *Philosophical Papers* (London: Allen & Unwin, 1959), 144f.
12. Norman Malcolm, *Knowledge and Certainty* (Englewood Cliffs, NJ: Prentice Hall, 1963).

FOR FURTHER READING

Burnyeat, Myles, ed. *The Skeptical Tradition.* Berkeley: University of California Press, 1983. A set of scholarly essays on the skeptical tradition from the Greeks to Kant.

Descartes, René. *The Philosophical Works of Descartes.* Translated by Elizabeth Haldane and G. Ross. Cambridge, UK: Cambridge University Press, 1931. Especially Descartes's classic *Meditations.*

Klein, Peter. *Certainty: A Refutation of Skepticism*. Minneapolis: University of Minnesota Press, 1981. A clear and cogent argument against skepticism.

Pojman, Louis, ed. *The Theory of Knowledge: Classical and Contemporary Readings*. Belmont, CA: Wadsworth, 1993. Part 3 contains several relevant essays.

Pojman, Louis. *What Can We Know? An Introduction to the Theory of Knowledge*. Belmont, CA: Wadsworth, 2001. A basic introduction, with two chapters on skepticism.

Sextus Empiricus. *Selections from the Major Writings on Skepticism, Man, and God*. Edited by Philip Hallie and translated by Sanford G. Etheridge. Indianapolis: Hackett, 1985.

Stroud, Barry. *The Significance of Philosophical Skepticism*. Oxford, UK: Oxford University Press, 1984. A sympathetic exposition of the major skeptical arguments.

Unger, Peter. *Ignorance: A Case for Skepticism*. Oxford, UK: Clarendon Press, 1975. A radical, superglobal skeptical view.

Williams, Michael. *Unnatural Doubts*. Oxford, UK: Blackwells, 1991. An advanced discussion, arguing that skeptical doubts are not natural or intuitive but founded on a false theory of "epistemological realism."

15 ✦ Perception: Our Knowledge of the External World

In daily life, we assume as certain many things which, on a closer scrutiny, are found to be so full of apparent contradictions that only a great amount of thought enables us to know what it is that we really may believe. In the search for certainty, it is natural to begin with our present experiences, and in some sense, no doubt, knowledge is to be derived from them. But any statement as to what it is that our immediate experience makes us know is very likely to be wrong. It seems to me that I am now sitting in a chair, at a table of a certain shape, on which I see sheets of paper with writing or print. . . . I believe that, if any other normal person comes into my room, he will see the same chairs and tables and books as I see, and that the table which I see is the same as the table which I feel pressing against my arm. All this seems to be so evident as to be hardly worth stating, except in answer to a man who doubts whether I know anything. Yet all this may be reasonably doubted, and all of it requires much careful discussion before we can be sure that we have stated it in a form that is wholly true.

Bertrand Russell[1]

Appearance is different from reality. An object may look, sound, feel, taste, or smell differently from the way it actually is. We see two parallel railroad tracks as if they converge in the distance. We hear the sound of an ambulance gradually increase in loudness as it approaches us and gradually diminish as it recedes into the distance, though the sound remains constant to those in the ambulance. Place one hand on a warm stove and the other in a bowl of ice cubes and then place both hands in a bowl of lukewarm water. What happens? The hand that was in the warm place feels as though the water is cold, while the other hand feels as though the water is hot, yet the temperature of the water remains constant. Mirages of oases appear in the desert or on a road during a sunny summer day. A coin looks elliptical when viewed from a certain angle, and stars that are several times larger than our Sun appear as tiny sparks in the heavens. We never see these gigantic objects as they really are. (What size would that be? How close would we have to be to see a star its actual size?) A straight stick placed halfway in water looks bent. White shirts, walls, and paper appear red in red lighting and blue in blue lighting. When we put on sunglasses, the colors around us appear differently than they are. Pineapples and yogurt taste different before and after we have brushed our teeth with a pungent toothpaste or when we have a fever. In more serious cases, in hallucinations, we see ghosts and people who are not present. Remember Shakespeare's Macbeth:

Is this a dagger which I see before me,
The handle toward my hand? Come, let me clutch thee:
I have thee not, and yet I see thee still.
Art thou not, fatal vision, sensible
To feeling as to sight? or art thou but
A dagger of the mind, a false creation,
Proceeding from the heat-oppressed brain?

We want to distinguish these appearances from veridical perceptions; it is clear that these illusory appearances are not the way the world really is. They are images in our mind, caused by the world but not in the world. Philosophers call these images or appearances *sense data*, or *sense impressions*.

So far, so good, but now the real problem arises. How do we know that we ever do have veridical appearances of the world? How do we know that what we take for nonillusory appearances really are such? There doesn't seem to be any intrinsic difference between illusions and veridical appearances. We see a white table as blue in blue lighting and red in red lighting, but the only reason we see it as white is because of the way light waves reflect off the surfaces of the table onto our retinas, which send information to the visual center at the back of our brain. The table is not really colored at all. Here is how the British physicist Arthur Eddington describes our experience of the table—or rather the two tables.

THE NATURE OF THE PHYSICAL WORLD

The Two Tables

I have settled down to the task of writing these lectures and have drawn up my chairs to my two tables. Two tables! Yes; there are duplicates of every object about me—two tables, two chairs, two pens.

This is not a very profound beginning to a course which ought to reach transcendent levels of scientific philosophy. But we cannot touch bedrock immediately; we must

From: Arthur Eddington, *The Nature of the Physical World* (London: Macmillan, 1929).

scratch a bit at the surface of things first. And whenever I begin to scratch the first thing I strike is—my two tables.

One of them has been familiar to me from earliest years. It is a commonplace object of that environment which I call the world. How shall I describe it? It has extension; it is comparatively permanent; it is colored; above all it is *substantial*. By substantial I do not merely mean that it does not collapse when I lean upon it; I mean that it is constituted of "substance" and by that word I am trying to convey to you some conception of its intrinsic nature. It is a *thing*; not like space, which is a mere negation; nor like time, which is—Heaven knows what! But that will not help you to my meaning because it is the distinctive characteristic of a "thing" to have this substantiality, and I do not think substantiality can be described better than by saying that it is the kind of nature exemplified by an ordinary table. And so we go round in circles. After all if you are a plain commonsense man, not too much worried with scientific scruples, you will be confident that you understand the nature of an ordinary table. I have even heard of plain men who had the idea that they could better understand the mystery of their own nature if scientists would discover a way of explaining it in terms of the easily comprehensible nature of a table.

Table No. 2 is my scientific table. It is a more recent acquaintance and I do not feel so familiar with it. It does not belong to the world previously mentioned—that world which spontaneously appears around me when I open my eyes, though how much of it is objective and how much subjective I do not here consider. It is part of a world which in more devious ways has forced itself on my attention. My scientific table is mostly emptiness. Sparsely scattered in that emptiness are numerous electric charges rushing about with great speed; but their combined bulk amounts to less than a billionth of the bulk of the table itself. Notwithstanding its strange construction it turns out to be an entirely efficient table. It supports my writing paper as satisfactorily as table No. 1; for when I lay the paper on it the little electric particles with their headlong speed keep on hitting the underside, so that the paper is maintained in shuttlecock fashion at a nearly steady level. If I lean upon this table I shall not go through; or, to be strictly accurate, the chance of my scientific elbow going through my scientific table is so excessively small that it can be neglected in practical life. Reviewing their properties one by one, there seems to be nothing to choose between the two tables for ordinary purposes; but when abnormal circumstances befall, then my scientific shows to advantage. If the house catches fire my scientific table will dissolve quite naturally into scientific smoke, whereas my familiar table undergoes a metamorphosis of its substantial nature which I can only regard as miraculous.

There is nothing *substantial* about my second table. It is nearly all empty space—space pervaded, it is true, by fields of force, but these are assigned to the category of "influences," not of "things." Even in the minute part which is not empty we must not transfer the old notion of substance. In dissecting matter into electric charges we have travelled far from that picture of it which first gave rise to the conception of substance, and the meaning of that conception—if it ever had any—has been lost by the way. The whole trend of modern scientific views is to break down the separate categories of "things," "influences," "forms" etc., and to substitute a common background of all experience. Whether we are studying a material object, a magnetic field, a geometrical figure, or a duration of time, our scientific information is summed up in measures; neither the apparatus of measurement nor the mode of using it suggests that there is anything essentially different in these problems. The measures themselves afford no ground for a classification by categories. We feel it necessary to concede some background to the measures—an external world; but the attributes of this world, except in so far as they are reflected in the measures, are outside scientific scrutiny. Science has at last revolted against attaching the exact knowledge contained in these measurements to a traditional picture-gallery of conceptions which convey no authentic information of the background and obtrude irrelevancies into the scheme of knowledge....

I need not tell you that modern physics has by delicate test and remorseless logic assured me that my second table is the only one which is really there—wherever "there" may be. On the other hand I need not tell you that modern physics will never succeed in exorcising that first table—strange compound of external nature, mental imagery and inherited prejudice—which lies visible to my eyes and tangible to my grasp.

So the question is forced upon us. What exactly do we know of the external world? What is the direct object of awareness when we perceive? Traditionally, three answers have been given to that question: (1) direct realism (sometimes referred to as naive realism or commonsense realism), (2) representationalism, and (3) phenomenalism. *Direct realism* claims that the immediate object of perception is a physical object existing independently of our awareness of it. *Representationalism* and *phenomenalism* answer that the immediate object of perception is a sense datum (or sense impression), an object that cannot exist apart from our awareness of it. Sense data, according to these two theories, are internal presentations—for example, the colors, shapes, and sizes of appearances in our minds. But representationalism and phenomenalism divide over the relationship of sense data to the physical world. For the representationalist, the physical world exists independently of and is the cause of our perceptions. Physical objects give rise to sense data that we perceive, so we only have mediate knowledge of the external world. For the phenomenalist, on the other hand, physical objects are simply constructions of sense data; they do not exist independently of sense impressions. Although both theories agree that all our experience is confined to sense data, only representationalism says that there really is something outside us that they represent, whereas phenomenalism says that there is nothing besides sense data in the world.

Common sense rejects both representationalism and phenomenalism and tells us that we, through our five senses (sight, hearing, touch, taste, and smell), do directly perceive the *real* world. It tells us that the physical world exists independently of our awareness of it and that the things we perceive are pretty much the way we perceive them. They exist here and now. Common sense supports naive, or direct, realism.

Unfortunately for common sense, science casts doubt on this simple picture of our relationship to the world. As Bertrand Russell succinctly said, "Naive realism leads to physics, and physics, if true, shows that naive realism is false. Therefore, naive realism, if true, is false; therefore it is false."[2] Science tells us that the physical objects we perceive are not what they seem to be, nor do we ever see things in the present. Colors are not in the objects but are the way objects appear as they reflect light. Since light travels at 186,000 miles per second, it takes time to reach our eyes; all that we see really existed in the past. It takes 8 minutes for the light from the Sun to reach us, over 8 years for light to reach us from the distant and brightest star Sirius, and 650 years for the light from the distant star Rigel to reach us. So when we look up into the heavens at the stars, we do not see one of them as they now are but as they existed in the near or distant past. Indeed, some of these stars may no longer exist. In fact, since it takes light time to reach us, we *never* see anything as it is in the present. Even our vision of near objects is seen as they presently existed. All sight is of the past.

Similarly, science tells us that the sounds we hear, the flavors we taste, the sensations of touch, and the odors we smell are not what they seem to be. They are mediated through our ways of perceiving so that we seldom or never experience them as they really are in themselves.

Thus, representationalism seems to succeed in giving an explanation of perception that is more faithful to science than direct realism. Representationalism holds that the real world causes our appearances or perceptions by representing the physical world through sense data, mental entities that are private to individual perceivers.

The English physician, diplomat, and philosopher John Locke (1632–1704) set forth the classic expression of this view in his *Essay Concerning Human Understanding* (1689). Attacking the notion that we have innate knowledge of metaphysical truths, Locke argued that all our knowledge derives ultimately from sense experience:

> Let us then suppose the mind to be, as we say, a blank tablet (*tabula rasa*) of white paper, void of all characters, without any ideas; how comes it by that vast store, which the busy and boundless fancy of man has painted on it with an almost endless variety? Whence has it all the materials of reason and knowledge? To this I answer, in one word, From *experience*: in that all our knowledge is founded, and from that it ultimately derives itself.[3]

Locke held a causal theory of perception in which processes in the external world impinge on the perceiver's sense organs, which in turn send messages to the brain where they are transformed into mental events. Here is how he describes the process.

AN ESSAY CONCERNING HUMAN UNDERSTANDING

1. Concerning the simple ideas of Sensation, it is to be considered—that whatsoever is so constituted in nature as to be able, by affecting our senses, to cause any perception in the mind, doth thereby produce in the understanding a simple idea; which, whatever be the external cause of it, when it comes to be taken notice of by our discerning faculty, it is by the mind looked on and considered there to be a real positive idea in the understanding, as much as any other whatsoever; though, perhaps, the cause of it be but a privation of the subject.

From: John Locke, *An Essay Concerning Human Understanding* (London, 1689), Book 2, viii.

2. Thus the ideas of heat and cold, light and darkness, white and black, motion and rest, are equally clear and positive ideas in the mind; though perhaps, some of the causes which produce them are barely privations, in those subjects from whence our senses derive those ideas. These the understanding, in its view of them, considers all as distinct positive ideas, without taking notice of the causes that produce them: which is an inquiry not belonging to the idea, as it is in the understanding, but to the nature of the things, and carefully to be distinguished; it being one thing to perceive and know the idea of white or black, and quite another to examine what kind of particles they must be, and how ranged on the surfaces, to make any object appear white or black.

.

.

.

.

7. To discover the nature of our *ideas* the better, and to discourse of them intelligibly, it will be convenient to distinguish them *as they are ideas or perceptions in our minds:* and *as they are modifications of matter in the bodies that cause such perceptions in us:* that so we may not think (as perhaps is usually done) that they are exactly the images and resemblances of something inherent in the subject; most of those of sensation being in the mind no more the likeness of something existing without us, than the names that stand for them are the likeness of our ideas, which yet upon hearing they are apt to excite in us.

8. Whatsoever the mind perceives *in itself,* or is the immediate object of perception, thought, or understanding, that I call idea; and the power to produce any idea in our mind, I call quality of the subject wherein that power is. Thus a snowball having the power to produce in us the ideas of white, cold, and round—the power to produce those ideas in us, as they are in the snowball, I call qualities; and as they are sensations or perceptions in our understanding, I call them ideas; which ideas, if I speak of something as in the things themselves, I should be understood to mean those qualities in the objects which produce them in us.

Locke thinks of this as a commonsense view of perception. Objects in the world with all of their powers (or qualities) impinge on our perceptual mechanisms and cause ideas in the mind. We can diagram Locke's causal theory of perception this way:

Objects and Events in the Real World
　(Energy coming to sense organs: insensible particles reflected from the object onto the sense organ or coming into contact with the sense organ)

↓

Sense Organs
　(Signals to brain)

↓

Brain Event

(Transformation from physical to mental event)

↓

Perceptual Experience

(The mechanical input yields the nonmechanical idea in the mind)

Although the process is physical and mechanistic, it yields a nonphysical result, a mental event, the perceptual experience, which subsequent philosophers will describe as a *percept, sense datum,* or *sense impression.*

We are aware of not the thing in itself, the object that is perceived and that causes the idea to arise in our mind, but only the idea or *representation* of the object. We are directly aware of the idea, but inasmuch as the object is the *cause* of the idea, we may be indirectly aware of the object.

Now a problem arises. Do these ideas, which occur in the mind faithfully, accurately represent the external world that is taken to be their cause? Locke said yes and no. His answer has to do with two types of qualities of physical objects. Locke divides the qualities of physical objects into two basic classes: primary qualities and secondary qualities. Here is Locke's classic passage.

> Qualities thus considered in bodies are, First, such as are utterly inseparable from bodies, in what estate soever it be; such as, in all the alterations and changes it suffers, all the force can be used upon it, it constantly keeps; and such as sense constantly finds in every particle of matter which has bulk enough to be perceived, and the mind finds inseparable from every particle of matter, though less than to make itself singly be perceived by our senses; e.g., take a grain of wheat, divide it into two parts, each part has still solidity, extension, figure, and mobility; divide it again, and it retains still the same qualities: and so divide it on till the parts become insensible, they must retain still each of them all those qualities. For, division ... can never take away either solidity, extension, figure, or mobility from any body, but only makes two or more distinct separate masses of matter of that which was but one before; all which distinct masses, reckoned as so many distinct bodies, after division, make a certain number. These I call *original* or *primary* qualities of body, ... solidity, extension, figure, motion, or rest, and number.
>
> Secondly, such qualities which in truth are nothing in the objects themselves but powers to produce various sensations in us by their primary qualities, i.e., by bulk, figure, texture, and motion of their insensible parts, as colors, sounds, tastes, etc. These I call *secondary qualities.* To these might be added a *third* sort, which are allowed to be barely powers; though they are as much real qualities in the subject as those which I, to comply with the common way of speaking, call qualities, but for distinction, secondary qualities. For the power in fire to produce a new color, or consistency, in *wax* or *clay*—by its primary qualities, is as much a quality in fire, as the power it has to produce in *me* a new idea or sensation of warmth or burning, which I felt not before—by the same primary qualities, namely, the bulk, texture, and motion of its insensible parts.[4]

Primary qualities are inseparable from their objects and so truly represent them. Such qualities are solidity (or bulk), extension, figure, movement (and rest), and number. These are the true building blocks of knowledge because they accurately represent features in the world. Ultimately, the world is made up of indivisible, minute atoms, which underlie physical objects. *Secondary qualities* are not in the things themselves but are caused by the primary qualities. These qualities include color, sound, smell, taste, touch, and sensation. These secondary qualities are types of *powers*, potentialities, or dispositions that reside in a physical object. Fire has the power to change liquids into gases, sugar is soluble in warm water, and glass is fragile. Solubility, flammability, and fragility are dispositional qualities in bodies. Dispositional qualities cause changes in the external world.

Secondary qualities are powers that produce sensations (that is, perceptions) in the perceiver. The primary qualities (motion or whatever) cause the secondary qualities, which we perceive. When we look at an object under normal circumstances, it looks a certain color, say, red. The redness that we are acquainted with is not in the object itself but in the way the light reflects off the object into our eyes and is communicated to our brain. Secondary qualities are the ways things have of appearing to us.

There is a problem with Locke's theory of representationalism, for it is difficult to see how we could justify any knowledge claim regarding the external world if we are never directly aware of anything except the ideas in our mind. Locke, aware of this problem, said that we have as much certainty as our condition needs, but in reality we can't know very much. Our senses only represent large objects and not their smaller particles, so the mysteries of the natural world are forever hidden from our view.

The critic can press the point, however, making a criticism that has been labeled the "permanent-picture-gallery" objection. Ordinarily, we check a picture of a landscape against the scene pictured; but in perception, if Locke is right, we never get a look at the scene itself. How can we know if the picture faithfully represents it? No comparison seems possible, so we pause to wonder whether Locke's theory doesn't really lead to skepticism? Or, if not skepticism, immaterialism?

Locke thought that it was incoherent to speak of qualities existing in their own right, so he relied on the Aristotelian notion of substance as that which underlies all other properties, the foundation of matter itself. Substance is an unknown "something I know not what."

Being a devout Christian, Locke inferred that this mechanistic materialism could not be the last word on the subject of substance, so he posited a second, spiritual substance with nonmaterial properties, including the soul, consciousness, and sensations. Locke was aware that he had no philosophical grounds for this distinction. Faith dictated **dualism.**

Locke thought that he had done justice to both science and faith with this dualism, but his theory soon came under attack as being dangerous, repugnant, and absurd. The philosopher who led the attack was the Irish bishop George Berkeley (1685–1753), who in his *Treatise Concerning the Principles of*

Human Knowledge (1710) was unsparing in his zeal to demolish the damned doctrine of mechanistic materialism. In its place, Berkeley erected an ingenious idealism called *immaterialism*. First, let's note Berkeley's criticisms of Locke's representationalism.

1. Locke's ideas were *dangerous,* for they made religion (and God) unnecessary, reducing all to a Newtonian mechanistic model of the universe, under physical causation—matter in motion, with bodies interacting in accordance with rigorously formulated mechanical laws. If this is true, where does God fit in?

Locke's God, reduced to a prime mover (or the Big Push), is largely superfluous for daily purposes. Furthermore, Locke's notion of atomism and his vague concept of substance really was a thinly disguised materialism (not that he thought Locke realized this), for Locke made it possible that the world was exclusively material, that there were no souls or spirits, but that consciousness was merely a property of matter. Thus, the mind would cease to exist at death.

Berkeley, being a devout Christian and a bishop, felt it his duty to combat this incipient materialism, secularism, and atheism. Locke, though a Christian himself, had played right into the enemy's hands: yielding either skepticism or materialism.

2. Locke's ideas were *loathsome* because they took away the beauty of the physical world. Common sense was outraged in supposing, as Locke's theory did, that the visible beauty of creation was no more than "a false imaginary glare" that—for example, the flowers in our garden are not really colored and have no fragrant aroma.

3. Locke's ideas yielded *absurd consequences.* First, Berkeley noted that Locke's distinction of primary/secondary qualities was very weak. The primary qualities are no more "in" the objects of perception than the secondary ones. Both types or qualities are relative to the perceiving mind.

> It is said that heat and cold are affections only in the mind, and not at all patterns of real beings existing in the corporeal substances which excite them, for that the same body which appears cold to one hand seems warm to another. Now, why may we not as well argue that figure and extension are not patterns or resemblances of qualities existing in matter, because to the same eye at different stations, or eyes of a different texture at the same station, they appear various and cannot, therefore, be the images of anything settled and determined without the mind.[5]

Second, he argued that logical problems plagued the theory that our perceptions resembled physical objects ("an idea can be like nothing but an idea"). Locke's theory led to skepticism because it offered no basis for comparing representations with their objects. Recall our permanent-picture-gallery objection. Third, Berkeley undermined the whole notion of substance, which Locke needed to maintain his theory. What is the difference, Berkeley rhetorically asked, between a "something I know not what" (Locke's notion of substance) and nothing at all? Ultimately, Locke's causal theory really supports materialism.

4. Finally, Berkeley charged that Locke's system was an *explanatory failure*. Locke asserted that ideas in the mind were caused by mechanical actions on our sense organs and brains. Berkeley pointed out, however, that this fails to explain mental events both in detail and principle: in *detail* because it was impossible to explain why a certain physical event should produce certain but quite different (in character) mental states (for example, light waves producing the color red); in *principle* because the whole notion of **dualistic interactionism** was incoherent, misusing the notion of "cause." A cause makes something happen, but for this you need a notion of a *will*, an agency—all causation is agent causation, but events in nature do not make other events happen. One only sees two events in temporal succession—with regularity. But this only signals the reality of a cause, it is not the cause, for it is not an agent and exerts no will. If Locke's model for the world was a clock, Berkeley's was an agent with radical free will.

What was Berkeley's own solution to the problem of how we know the external world? It was incredibly simple, but read for yourself and draw your own conclusion. Berkeley is a clear writer.

THE PRINCIPLES OF HUMAN KNOWLEDGE

Part I

1. It is evident to any one who takes a survey of the objects of human knowledge, that they are either ideas actually imprinted on the senses, or else such as are perceived by attending to the passions and operations of the mind, or lastly, ideas formed by help of memory and imagination, either compounding, dividing, or barely representing those originally perceived in the aforesaid ways. By sight I have the ideas of light and colours with their several degrees and variations. By touch I perceive, for example, hard and soft, heat and cold, motion and resistance, and of all these more and less either as to quantity or degree. Smelling furnishes me with odours; the palate with tastes; and hearing conveys sounds to the mind in all their variety of tone and composition. And as several of these are observed to accompany each other, they come to be marked by one name, and so to be reputed as one thing. Thus, for example, a certain colour, taste, smell, figure, and consistence having been observed to go together, are accounted one distinct thing, signified by the name apple. Other collections of ideas constitute a stone, a tree, a book, and the like sensible things; which, as they are pleasing or disagreeable, excite the passions of love, hatred, joy, grief, and so forth.

2. But besides all that endless variety of ideas or objects of knowledge, there is likewise something which knows or perceives them, and exercises divers operations,

From: George Berkeley, *A Treatise Concerning the Principles of Human Knowledge* (1710).

as willing, imagining, remembering about them. This perceiving, active being is what I call mind, spirit, soul, or myself. By which words I do not denote any one of my ideas, but a thing entirely distinct from them, wherein they exist, or, which is the same thing, whereby they are perceived; for *the existence of an idea consists in being perceived*.

3. That neither our thoughts, nor passions, nor ideas formed by the imagination, exist without the mind, is what every body will allow. And (to me) it seems no less evident that the various sensations or ideas imprinted on the sense, however blended or combined together (that is, whatever objects they compose), cannot exist otherwise than in a mind perceiving them. I think an intuitive knowledge may be obtained of this, by any one that shall attend to what is meant by the term exist, when applied to sensible things. The table I write on, I say, exists, that is, I see and feel it; and if I were out of my study I should say it existed, meaning thereby that if I was in my study I might perceive it, or that some other spirit actually does perceive it. There was an odour, that is, it was smelled; there was a sound, that is to say, it was heard; a colour or figure, and it was perceived by sight or touch. This is all that I can understand by these and the like expressions. For as to what is said of the absolute existence of unthinking things without any relation to their being perceived, that seems perfectly unintelligible. Their *esse est percipi,* nor is it possible they should have any existence, out of the minds or thinking things which perceive them.

Berkeley is describing the relationship of the world to us; he enumerates the objects of human knowledge as *ideas* that are perceived or produced from the mind by the help of memory and imagination. But notice something seems missing—a material world that causes these ideas to arise in us. Can you now answer the question: What is Berkeley's solution to the problem of our knowledge of the external world? If you said it was "to deny matter," you are right. In one fell swoop, the intractable problems of substance, dualist interactionism, causation, and knowledge of the external world are swept away in the supposition that material substance doesn't exist.*

Berkeley held that there were only two realities: minds and mental events—ideas exist in the mind alone. All qualities are essentially secondary and have their reality by being perceived (*esse est percipi*—"to be is to be perceived"). There is no material world. Physical objects are simply mental events. "The table I write on exists, that is, I see and feel it; and if I were out of my study I should say it existed—meaning thereby that if I was in my study I might perceive it, or that some other spirit actually perceives it." What would happen to a so-called physical object if it were not perceived?

6. Some truths there are so near and obvious to the mind, that a man need only open his eyes to see them. Such I take this important one to be, to wit, that all the

---

*Berkeley wrote in his notebook: "I wonder not at my sagacity in discovering the obvious though amazing truth. I rather wonder at my stupid, inadvertency in not finding it out before." He was astonished at the strong reaction against his position.

choir of heaven and furniture of the earth, in a word all those bodies which compose the mighty frame of the world, have not any subsistence without a mind, that their being (esse) is to be perceived or known; that consequently so long as they are not actually perceived by me, or do not exist in my mind or that of any other created spirit, they must either have no existence at all, or else subsist in the mind of some eternal spirit: it being perfectly unintelligible and involving all the absurdity of abstraction, to attribute to any single part of them an existence independent of a spirit. To be convinced of which, the reader need only reflect and try to separate in his own thoughts the being of a sensible thing from its being perceived.

7.   From what has been said, it follows, there is not any other substance than spirits, or that which perceives. But for the fuller proof of this point, let it be considered, the sensible qualities are colour, figure, motion, smell, taste, and such like, that is, the ideas perceived by sense. Now for an idea to exist in an unperceiving thing, is a manifest contradiction; for to have an idea is all one as to perceive: that therefore wherein colour, figure, and the like qualities exist, must perceive them; hence it is clear there can be no unthinking substance or substratum of those ideas.

8.   But say you, though the ideas themselves do not exist without the mind, yet there may be things like them whereof they are copies or resemblances, which things exist without the mind, in an unthinking substance. I answer, an idea can be like nothing but an idea; a colour or figure can be like nothing but another colour or figure. If we look but ever so little into our thoughts, we shall find it impossible for us to conceive a likeness except only between our ideas. Again, I ask whether those supposed originals or external things, of which our ideas are the pictures or representations, be themselves perceivable or no? if they are, then they are ideas, and we have gained our point; but if you say they are not, I appeal to any one whether it be sense, to assert a colour is like something which is invisible; hard or soft, like something which is intangible; and so of the rest.[6]

As noted previously, this point is leveled against Locke's representative theory of perception. Ideas can't resemble physical objects since they are wholly distinct—"an idea can be like nothing but an idea."

Now Berkeley shows why Locke's theory of primary/secondary qualities fails.

9.   Some there are who make a distinction betwixt primary and secondary qualities: by the former, they mean extension, figure, motion, rest, solidity or impenetrability, and number: by the latter they denote all other sensible qualities, as colours, sounds, tastes, and so forth. The ideas we have of these they acknowledge not to be the resemblances of any thing existing without the mind or unperceived; but they will have our ideas of the primary qualities to be patterns or images of things which exist without the mind, in an unthinking substance which they call matter. By matter therefore we are to understand an inert, senseless substance, in which extension, figure and motion, do actually subsist. But it is evident from what we have already shown, that extension, figure, and motion, are only ideas

existing in the mind, and that an idea can be like nothing but another idea, and that consequently neither they nor their archetypes can exist in an unperceiving substance. Hence it is plain, that the very notion of what is called matter, or corporeal substance, involves a contradiction in it.

10. They who assert that figure, motion, and the rest of the primary or original qualities, do exist without the mind, in unthinking substances, do at the same time acknowledge that colours, sounds, heat, cold, and such like secondary qualities, do not, which they tell us are sensations existing in the mind alone, that depend on and are occasioned by the different size, texture, and motion of the minute particles of matter. This they take for an undoubted truth, which they can demonstrate beyond all exception. Now if it be certain, that those original qualities are inseparably united with the other sensible qualities, and not, even in thought, capable of being abstracted from them, it plainly follows that they exist only in the mind. But I desire any one to reflect and try, whether he can, by any abstraction of thought, conceive the extension and motion of a body, without all other sensible qualities. For my own part, I see evidently that it is not in my power to frame an idea of a body extended and moved, but I must withal give it some colour or other sensible quality which is acknowledged to exist only in the mind. In short, extension, figure, and motion, abstracted from all other qualities, and inconceivable. Where therefore the other sensible qualities are, there must these be also, to wit, in the mind and nowhere else.[7]

Berkeley next turns to these questions: What is matter (or extension as the mode of matter), and does it exist?

16. But let us examine a little the received opinion. It is said extension is a mode or accident of matter, and that matter is the substratum that supports it. Now I desire that you would explain what is meant by matter's supporting extension: say you, I have no idea of matter, and therefore cannot explain it. I answer, though you have no positive, yet if you have any meaning at all, you must at least have a relative idea of matter; though you know not what it is, yet you must be supposed to know what relation it bears to accidents, and what is meant by its supporting them. It is evident support cannot here be taken in its usual or literal sense, as when we say that pillars support a building: in what sense therefore must it be taken?

17. If we inquire into what the most accurate philosophers declare themselves to mean by material substance, we shall find them acknowledge, they have no other meaning annexed to those sounds, but the idea of being in general, together with the relative notion of its supporting accidents. The general idea of being appeareth to me the most abstract and incomprehensible of all other; and as for its supporting accidents, this, as we have just now observed, cannot be understood in the common sense of those words; it must therefore be taken in some other sense, but what that is they do not explain. So that when I consider the two parts or branches which make the signification of the words material substance, I am convinced there is no distinct meaning annexed to them. But why should we

trouble ourselves any further, in discussing this material substratum or support of figure and motion, and other sensible qualities? does it not suppose they have an existence without the mind? and is not this a direct repugnancy, and altogether inconceivable?

18. But though it were possible that solid, figured, moveable substances may exist without the mind, corresponding to the ideas we have of bodies, yet how is it possible for us to know this? either we must know it by sense, or by reason. As for our senses, by them we have the knowledge only of our sensations, ideas, or those things that are immediately perceived by sense, call them what you will: but they do not inform us that things exist without the mind, or unperceived, like to those which are perceived. This the materialists themselves acknowledge. It remains therefore that if we have any knowledge at all of external things, it must be by reason, inferring their existence from what is immediately perceived by sense. But (I do not see) what reason can induce us to believe the existence of bodies without the mind, from what we perceive, since the very patrons of matter themselves do not pretend, there is any necessary connexion betwixt them and our ideas. I say, it is granted on all hands (and what happens in dreams, frenzies, and the like, puts it beyond dispute) that it is possible we might be affected with all the ideas we have now, though no bodies existed without, resembling them. Hence it is evident the supposition of external bodies is not necessary for producing our ideas: since it is granted they are produced sometimes, and might possibly be produced always, in the same order we see them in at present, without their concurrence.[8]

All physical objects are mental phenomena that would cease to exist if they were not perceived. Why do physical objects continue to exist when no one perceives them? What happens to trees or mountains when we are not looking at them? Do they cease to be? Here is Berkeley's reply as stated by his mouthpiece, Philonous, who has been accused of being a skeptic and is concerned to deny that charge.

THREE DIALOGUES BETWEEN HYLAS AND PHILONOUS

HYLAS: My comfort is you are as much a skeptic [regarding the existence of an external world] as I am.

PHILONOUS: There, Hylas, I must beg leave to differ with you.

HYLAS: What! have you all along agreed to the premises, and do you now deny the conclusion and leave me to maintain those paradoxes by myself which led me into? This is not fair.

PHILONOUS: I deny that I agreed with you in those notions that led to skepticism. You indeed said the *reality* of sensible things consisted in an *absolute existence* out of the minds or spirits, or distinct from their being perceived. And, pursuant to this notion of reality, you are obliged to deny sensible things any real existence; that is, according to your own definition, you profess yourself a skeptic. But I neither said nor thought the

From: George Berkeley, *Three Dialogues Between Hylas and Philonous* (London: 1713).

reality of sensible things was to be defined after that manner. To me it is evident, for the reasons you allow of, that sensible things cannot exist other than in a mind or spirit. Whence I conclude, not that they have no real existence, but that, seeing they depend not on my thought and have an existence distinct from being perceived by me, *there must be some other mind wherein they exist.* As sure, therefore, as the sensible world really exists, so sure is there an infinite omnipresent Spirit, who contains and supports it.

HYLAS: What! This is no more than I and all Christians hold; nay, and all others too, who believe there is a God and that He knows and comprehends all things.

PHILONOUS: Aye, but here lies the difference. Men commonly believe that all things are known or perceived by God, because they believe the being of a God; whereas I, on the other side, immediately and necessarily conclude the being of a god, because all sensible things must be perceived by him.

HYLAS: But so long as we all believe the same things, what matter is it how we come by that belief?

PHILONOUS: But neither do we agree in the same opinion. For philosophers, though they acknowledge all corporeal beings to be perceived by God, yet they attribute to them an absolute subsistence distinct from their being perceived by any mind whatever, which I do not. Besides, is there no difference between saying, *there is a God, therefore He perceives all things,* and saying, *sensible things do really exist; and if they really exist, they are necessarily perceived by an infinite mind: therefore there is an infinite mind, or God?* This furnishes you with a direct and immediate demonstration, from a most evident principle, of the *being of a God.* Divines and philosophers had proved beyond all controversy, from the beauty and usefulness of the several parts of the creation, that it was the workmanship of God. But that—setting aside all help of astronomy and natural philosophy, all contemplation of the contrivance, order and adjustment of things—an infinite mind should be necessarily inferred from the bare *existence* of the sensible world is an advantage peculiar to them only who have made this easy reflection, that the sensible world is that which we perceive by our several senses; and that nothing is perceived by the senses besides ideas; and that no idea or archetype of an idea can exist otherwise than in a mind.

The question: Do objects in the world cease to exist when we are not perceiving them? Berkeley answers, no, someone is always perceiving them; God's eye keeps the world from dissolving. A limerick was composed to summarize Berkeley's position:

There was a young man who said, "God
Must think it exceedingly odd
If he finds that this tree
Continues to be
When there's no one about in the quad."
Dear Sir, your astonishment's odd
I'm always about in the quad,
And that's why the tree
Will continue to be
Since observed by,
Yours faithfully, God

CHAPTER 15

Hence, we bring God back into philosophy and science (indeed, Berkeley claims to have offered a new proof of God's existence) as the necessary being who keeps our world intact. This thought frees us from mechanism, skepticism, and atheism all at once and offers us dignity—for we are not mere machines but infinitely valuable souls: finite and infinite spirits.

God communicates directly with our finite minds by the mediation of ideas—the orderly, regular, and admirable connection of which form the rational discourse of the infinite Creator with finite spirits.

Berkeley sought to stave off the charge that his theory eliminated the need for scientific investigation. He argued that his theory reduces science to general rules (instrumentalism). The atomistic theory is a useful myth (serviceable fiction).

Contemporary phenomenalism differs with Berkeley only in his theological moorings. It doesn't posit God as necessary to hold the physical world in existence. Instead, it views the physical world as a construct of ideas. In John Stuart Mill's words, objects are "permanent possibilities of sensation," meaning that if one were to get into the appropriate condition, one would experience the sense data. Philosophers like W. T. Stace argue that the realist's view of the world as containing material objects behind the perceived world is an unjustified faith. The world of scientific discourse (for example, atoms, gravity, and conservation of energy) is not to be taken literally but instrumentally, as providing useful fictions that help us predict experiences. Consider his argument:

> So far as I know scientists still talk about electrons, protons, neutrons, and so on. We never directly perceive these, hence, if we ask how we know of their existence the only possible answer seems to be that they are an inference from what we do directly perceive. What sort of an inference? Apparently a causal inference. The atomic entities in some way impinge upon the sense of the animal organism and cause [it] to perceive the familiar world of tables, chairs, and the rest.
>
> But is it not clear that such a concept of causation, however interpreted, is invalid? The only reason we have for believing in the law of causation is that we *observe* certain regularities or sequences. We observe that, in certain conditions, A is always followed by B. We call A the cause, B the effect. And the sequence A–B becomes a causal law. It follows that all *observed* causal sequences are between sensed objects in the familiar world of perception, and that all known causal laws apply solely to the world of sense and not to anything beyond or behind it. And this in turn means that we have not got, and never could have, one jot of evidence for believing that the law of causation can be applied *outside* the realm of perception, or that the realm can have any causes (such as the supposed physical objects) which are not themselves perceived.[9]

Strictly speaking, "*Nothing exists except sensations* (and the minds that perceive them). The rest is mental construction or fiction." All that the so-called laws of science do is help us organize our experiences in order to predict future sensations.

Bertrand Russell has defended representational realism, developing Locke's causal theory of perception in the light of contemporary science. According to Russell, our knowledge of physical objects is inferred from percepts in our brain. One may ask why Russell does not simply accept phenomenalism since he makes percepts primary to our knowledge. Russell concedes that phenomenalism is not impossible, but there are deeper reasons for rejecting it. Let me mention three of them, together with the phenomenalist response.[10]

1. *Appearance and reality.* The stick in water appears bent, and we all agree that this is an illusion, but the phenomenalist can find no essential difference between our visual perception of the stick out of water (or our tactile perception of the straightness of the stick even while in water) and the way it is really shaped, for the phenomenalist can admit no difference between appearance and reality. The real/unreal and genuine/counterfeit distinctions vanish. Material things consist of sense data and nothing else.

The phenomenalist responds that the everyday distinctions between reality and appearance are not metaphysical ones but practical, enabling us to deal with the experiences we encounter:

> What causes us to condemn an experience as an "illusion" is that it leads us astray. A mirage is an illusion because it causes us to make a mistake. But what kind of mistake? Surely, not the mistake of thinking that we now see trees and water, but the mistake of expecting that we shall soon be able to have a drink and sit down in the shade. The mistake consists in the false expectation of certain other sense data. Thus the illusoriness is not in the sense data itself, but in the expectation which we form when we sense it.[11]

The bent-stick-in-the-water is an illusion too because sticks that "look bent" usually "feel bent" as well, and so we are surprised to find that it feels straight.

2. *The permanency of material things.* Sensations are flighty and intermittent, depending on our sense organs, but material objects (we intuitively suppose) are permanent things, enduring uninterruptedly for long periods of time (and are not mind-dependent).

I don't annihilate this room and all of you every time I close my eyes. On a phenomenalist account, it would seem that we could not say this stone has existed 10 years or a million years without it having a rotation shift of nurse watchers to keep it in existence.

The phenomenalist replies with Mill that sense data are "permanent possibilities of sensation" so that we can distinguish between an actual/possible sense datum. To say that there is a table in my office now is to say that if there were anyone in the room, he would be having the kind of experience that we call seeing a table. "There is a table" means "go and look and you will see a table."

3. *Causal activity.* Causal interaction in nature seems undermined by phenomenalism. As C. H. Whiteley says, "Surely, the room cannot be warmed by my visual sense-datum of a fire! Still less can it be warmed by the possibility of a visual sense datum of a fire during my absence, when I am not looking at the fire, but the room gets warmed all the same." Ideas are inert and can do nothing.

The phenomenalist responds, as Stace has argued: We should reinterpret the concept of causality. We never see "causes" but only regular succession of events. I think this response is inadequate, for we generally believe that (1) a cause is something actually existing and (2) something *not* actually existing or occurring can have no effects. Phenomenalism implausibly makes causality a relation between something and nothing, since most of the causes are unperceived.

Representationalism, we saw, leads to phenomenalism, and phenomenalism seems to take the world away from us, landing us, if not completely back into skepticism, then into solipsism—the view that no one else exists. For if I can only have sense experiences of my own, then how can I take other people's experiences into account?

So where does that leave us? Perhaps you will choose between phenomenalism and representationalism, but some philosophers—like D. M. Armstrong, John Searle, and William Alston—have returned to direct realism, though not a "naive" variety but one chastened by the long history of the problem. Armstrong defines perception as the acquiring of beliefs (true or false) about the current state of our bodies or environment. In perceiving, we do encounter the world directly, though always through the interpretive powers of our mind.

One reason Armstrong rejects representationalism and phenomenalism is due to the problematic notion of sense data. These intermediary things seem unnecessary and even paradoxical. They are unnecessary because we can give an account of our perceptions as taking in objects in the world directly. They are paradoxical in two ways:

- Paradox 1: *The nontransitivity of perception.* Consider three pieces of red colored paper. Suppose we cannot distinguish between sample A and B; they seem exactly the same color. Similarly, samples B and C are indistinguishable, but we can distinguish between A and C! On the sense-data account, this is puzzling, since we should be able to distinguish our sense data from one another.

- Paradox 2: *Indeterminateness.* Suppose we see a speckled hen. How many speckles does our sense datum hold? If we say that it is indeterminate, we seem to have a paradox between the indeterminate sense datum and the determinate objects that are supposed to be represented.[12]

Many philosophers have sought to avoid taking a strong stand on the philosophy of perception by simply using adverbial language. For example, when seeing a red book, I state my perception in appearance language: "I am appeared to redly and bookishly"; or when seeing a red ball: "I am appeared to redly and ballishly." This strikes me as humorously desperate. It seems wiser to admit how little we know, choose the least objectionable theory, and interpret ordinary language accordingly.

Summary

The problem of perception has to do with our knowledge of the external world. Three theories have been advanced to solve that problem: (1) direct realism, which holds that we know the world directly and pretty much as it is; (2) representationalism, which holds that we know the world indirectly pretty much as it is—at least regarding the primary qualities; and (3) idealism, or phenomenalism, which holds that all we really know are sense data. Locke set forth the classical rendition of representationalism, distinguishing between primary and secondary qualities. Berkeley—criticizing Locke's theory as dangerous, loathsome, absurd, and an explanatory failure—put forth the classic version of idealism, whose motto was "to be is to be perceived." The fact that God always perceives us and the world ensures our continued existence. Modern phenomenalists follow Berkeley but subtract the notion of God from the epistemic domain. There has been a move by contemporary epistemologists like Armstrong and Searle back to direct realism, but the issue is one of lively debate.

FOR FURTHER REFLECTION

1. Why is the subject of perception a philosophical problem? Do you think that science has decided on the answer? Explain.

2. Explain the theory of direct realism. What are the objections to it? Can you defend a version of direct realism against criticisms?

3. Examine Locke's theory of indirect realism (representationalism). What are its strengths and weaknesses? Do you agree with Berkeley's criticisms?

4. What are sense data? What are the objections to their existence?

5. Examine phenomenalism. What are its strengths and weaknesses?

6. Having worked through the problem of perception, which theory makes the most sense?

NOTES

1. Bertrand Russell, *Problems of Philosophy* (Oxford, UK: Oxford University Press, 1912), 7 and 8.

2. Bertrand Russell, *Inquiry into Meaning and Truth* (London: Allen & Unwin, 1940), 15.

3. John Locke, *An Essay Concerning the Principles of Human Understanding* (London: Awsham Y John Churchill, 1689), 104.

4 John Locke, *An Essay Concerning Human Understanding* (London, 1689), Book 2, viii. 9.

5. George Berkeley, *A Treatise Concerning the Principles of Human Knowledge* (1710) par. 14.

6. Ibid.

7. Ibid.

8. Ibid.

9. W. T. Stace, "Science and the Physical World," in *Man Against Darkness and Other Essays* (Pittsburgh: University of Pittsburgh Press, 1967).

10. I am indebted to C. H. Whiteley, *An Introduction to Metaphysics* (London: Methuen, 1950), who points out three advantages of phenomenalism. It removes doubt and skepticism. We can't really doubt that there is a table before us, but the representationalist program would lead us to doubt it. The sense data are all there is, so there is no cause to doubt—unless we suspect that there are pseudosense data. It answers the problem of deception, but does it solve the problem of Descartes's demon or dream hypothesis? It saves us from worrying about involvement with unobservable matter. We can preserve our empiricism. Science becomes "the recording, ordering, and forecasting of human experience."

11. Ibid. See also A. J. Ayer, *Central Questions of Philosophy* (New York: Holt, Rinehart & Winston, 1973), 106.

12. D. M. Armstrong, *Perception and the Physical World* (London: Routledge & Kegan Paul, 1961). See also John Searle, *Intentionality* (Oxford, UK: Oxford University Press, 1983), and William Alston, *Epistemic Justification* (Ithaca, NY: Cornell University Press, 1989).

FOR FURTHER READING

Armstrong, D. M. *Perception and the Physical World*. London: Routledge & Kegan Paul, 1961. A thorough defense of direct realism; advanced.

Berkeley, George. *Three Dialogues Between Hylas and Philonous*. London, 1713. The classic defense of idealism.

Heil, John. *Perception and Cognition*. Berkeley: University of California Press, 1983. A clear, thoughtful presentation.

Landesman, Charles. *Color and Consciousness*. Philadelphia: Temple University Press, 1989. A provocative defense of representationalism.

Locke, John. *An Essay Concerning Human Understanding*. London, 1689. The classic defense of representationalism.

Pojman, Louis, ed. *The Theory of Knowledge: Classical and Contemporary Readings*. Belmont, CA: Wadsworth, 1993. Contains several relevant essays on the topics discussed in this chapter.

16 ❧ Kant's Copernican Revolution

The Kantian Epistemic Revolution

Immanuel Kant (1724–1804), who was born into a deeply pietistic Lutheran family in Königsberg, Germany, lived in that town his entire life and taught at the University of Königsberg. He lived a duty-bound, methodical life, so regular that citizens were said to have set their clocks by his walks. Kant is one of the premier philosophers in the Western tradition, the last philosopher over whose greatness there is virtually universal consensus. In his monumental work *The Critique of Pure Reason* (1781; henceforth *CPR*), he inaugurated a revolution in the theory of knowledge, a revolution that completely reversed our orientation to reality in a manner analogous to the great Copernican revolution in 1543, when the Polish priest-scientist Nicolaus Copernicus (1473–1543) undermined the traditional view that the Sun revolved around Earth and replaced it with the radical view that Earth and other planets revolved around the Sun. And like Copernicus's theory in astronomy, Kant's ideas have had a revolutionary influence in the history of Western philosophy ever since.

Kant began as a rationalist in the Leibnizian tradition, but on reading Hume he was struck with the cogency of his skeptical arguments on the nature of perception and causality. Hume "woke me from my dogmatic slumbers," Kant wrote, and henceforth accepted the empiricist doctrine that all our knowledge begins with experience.

THE CRITIQUE OF PURE REASON

That all our knowledge begins with experience there can be no doubt. For how is it possible that the faculty of cognition should be awakened into exercise otherwise than by means of objects which affect our senses, and partly of themselves produce representations, partly rouse our powers of understanding into activity, to compare to connect, or to separate these, and so to convert the raw material of our sensuous impressions into a knowledge of objects, which is called experience? In respect of time, therefore, no knowledge of ours is antecedent to experience, but begins with it.

But, though all our knowledge begins with experience, it by no means follows that all arises out of experience. For, on the contrary, it is quite possible that our empirical knowledge is a compound of that which we receive through impressions, and that which the faculty of cognition supplies from itself (sensuous impressions giving merely the occasion), an addition which we cannot distinguish from the original element given by sense, till long practice has made us attentive to, and skilful in separating it. It is, therefore, a question which requires close investigation, and not to be answered at first sight, whether there exists a knowledge altogether independent of experience, and even of all sensuous impressions. Knowledge of this kind is called *a priori*, in contradistinction to empirical knowledge, which has its sources *a posteriori*, that is, in experience.

Kant thought, however, that Hume had made an invalid inference in concluding that all our knowledge arises from experience. Kant sought to demonstrate that the rationalists had an invaluable insight, which had been lost in their flamboyant speculation, that something determinate in the mind causes us to know what we know.

Kant argued that the mind is so structured and empowered that it imposes interpretive categories onto our experience, so we do not simply experience the world, as the empiricists alleged, but interpret it through the constitutive mechanisms of the mind. This is sometimes called Kant's Copernican revolution. Until now we have assumed that all our knowledge must conform to objects.

But every attempt to extend our knowledge of objects by establishing something in regard to them *a priori*, by means of concepts, has, on this assumption, ended in failure. Therefore, we must see whether we may have better success in our metaphysical task if we begin with the assumption that objects must conform to our knowledge. In this way we would have knowledge of objects *a priori*. We should then be proceeding in the same way as Copernicus in his revolutionary hypothesis. After he failed to make progress in explaining the movements of the heavenly bodies on the supposition that they all revolved around the observer, he decided to reverse the relationship and made the observer revolve around the heavenly body, the sun, which was at rest. A similar experiment can be done in metaphysics with regard to the intuition of objects. If our intuition must conform to the constitution of the object, I do not see how we could

---

From: Immanuel Kant, *The Critique of Pure Reason*, trans. Norman Kemp Smith (New York: St. Martin's Press, 1969; originally published in 1781), 41.

know anything of the object *a priori*, but if the object of sense must conform to the constitution of our faculty of intuition, then *a priori* knowledge is possible.[1]

Our fundamental categories of thinking, space, time and causality, do not exist in the world but are part of the necessary interpretive structure of our minds, analogous to wearing red tinted glasses, which imposes spatiotemporal and causal order onto the *manifold of experience*.* Behind the phenomena which we perceive, lies the numinal world, the *ding an sich* (things in themselves) which we cannot know in any pure form but only as mediated through the categories of the mind.

In the paragraph just quoted, Kant makes his famous distinction between a priori and a posteriori knowledge. A priori knowledge is what we know *prior* to experience. It is opposed to a posteriori knowledge, which is based *on* experience. For Hume, all knowledge of matters of fact is a posteriori and only analytic statements (such as mathematical truths or statements such as "All mothers are women") are known a priori. Kant rejects this formula. For him it is possible to have a priori knowledge of matters of fact. "But though all our knowledge begins with experience, it does not follow that it all arises out of experience." Indeed, he thinks that mathematical truth is not analytic but synthetic (the predicate adds something to the subject) and that there is other synthetic a priori knowledge, such as our knowledge of time, space, causality, and the moral law. The schema looks like this:

	Priori	*A Posteriori*
Analytic	Tautologies and entailments ("All bachelors are unmarried.")	None
Synthetic	Causality, space, and time ($5 + 7 = 12$, the moral law)	Empirical judgments (There are people in this room.")

We now turn to Kant's account of his theory in his *Prolegomena to Any Future Metaphysics* (1783), a book written as a succinct summary of his larger and more difficult *The Critique of Pure Reason*.

Preamble on the Peculiarities of All Metaphysical Knowledge

PROLEGOMENA TO ANY FUTURE METAPHYSICS

Of the Sources of Metaphysics

If it becomes desirable to organize any knowledge as science, it will be necessary first to determine accurately those peculiar features which no other science has in

---

* The New Shorter Oxford English Dictionary defines *manifold* as follows: "That which is manifold; *specific in Kantian philosophy*, the sum of the particulars furnished by sense before they have been unified by the synthesis of the understanding."

common with it, constituting its peculiarity; otherwise the boundaries of all sciences become confused, and none of them can be treated thoroughly according to its nature.

The peculiar characteristic of a science may consist of a simple difference of object, or of the sources of knowledge, or of the kind of knowledge, or perhaps of all three conjointly. On these, therefore, depends the idea of a possible science and its territory.

First, as concerns the sources of metaphysical knowledge, its very concept implies that they cannot be empirical. Its principles (including not only its maxims but its basic *notions*) must never be derived from experience. It must not be physical but metaphysical knowledge, namely, knowledge lying beyond experience. It can therefore have for its basis neither external experience, which is the source of physics proper, nor internal, which is the basis of empirical psychology. It is therefore *a priori* knowledge, coming from pure understanding and pure reason....

Kant now analyzes the kinds of knowledge which could qualify as Metaphysical, distinguishing first between analytic and synthetic judgments.

a. On the Distinction between Analytical and Synthetical Judgments in General.—The peculiarity of its sources demands that metaphysical knowledge must consist of nothing but *a priori* judgments. But whatever be their origin or their logical form, there is a distinction in judgments, as to their content, according to which they are either merely *explicative,* adding nothing to the content of knowledge, or *expansive,* increasing the given knowledge. The former may be called *analytical,* the latter *synthetical,* judgments.

Analytical judgments express nothing in the predicate but what has been already actually thought in the concept of the subject, though not so distinctly or with the same (full) consciousness. When I say: "All bodies are extended," I have not amplified in the least my concept of body, but have only analyzed it, as extension was really thought to belong to that concept before the judgment was made, though it was not expressed. This judgment is therefore analytical. On the contrary, this judgment, "All bodies have weight," contains in its predicate something not actually thought in the universal concept of body; it amplifies my knowledge by adding something to my concept, and must therefore be called synthetical.

b. The Common Principle of All Analytical Judgments Is the Law of Contradiction.—All analytical judgments depend wholly on the law of contradiction, and are in their nature *a priori* cognitions, whether the concepts that supply them with matter be empirical or not. For the predicate of an affirmative analytical judgment is already contained in the concept of the subject, of which it cannot be denied without contradiction. In the same way its opposite is necessarily denied of the subject in an analytical, but negative, judgment, by the same law of contradiction. Such is the

Immanuel Kant, *Prolegomena to Any Future Metaphysics,* trans. Paul Carus (Chicago: University of Chicago Press, 1902; originally published in 1783).

nature of the judgments: "All bodies are extended," and "No bodies are unextended (that is, simple)."

For this very reason all analytical judgments are *a priori* even when the concepts are empirical, as, for example, "Gold is a yellow metal"; for to know this I require no experience beyond my concept of gold as a yellow metal. It is, in fact, the very concept, and I need only analyze it without looking beyond it.

c. Synthetical Judgments Require a Different Principle from the Law of Contradiction.—There are synthetical *a posteriori* judgments of empirical origin; but there are also others which are certain *a priori,* and which spring from pure understanding and reason. Yet they both agree in this, that they cannot possibly spring from the principle of analysis, namely, the law of contradiction, alone. They require a quite different principle from which they may be deduced, subject, of course, always to the law of contradiction, which must never be violated, even though everything cannot be deduced from it. I shall first classify synthetical judgments.

Judgments of Experience are always synthetical. For it would be absurd to base an analytical judgment on experience, as our concept suffices for the purpose without requiring any testimony from experience. That body is extended is a judgment established *a priori,* and not an empirical judgment. For before appealing to experience, we already have all the conditions of the judgment in the concept, from which we have but to elicit the predicate according to the law of contradiction, and thereby to become conscious of the necessity of the judgment, which experience could not in the least teach us.

2. *Mathematical Judgments* are all synthetical. This fact seems hitherto to have altogether escaped the observation of those who have analyzed human reason; it even seems directly opposed to all their conjectures, though it is incontestably certain and most important in its consequences. For as it was found that the conclusions of mathematicians all proceed according to the law of contradiction (as is demanded by all apodictic certainty), men persuaded themselves that the fundamental principles were known from the same law. This was a great mistake, for a synthetical proposition can indeed be established by the law of contradiction, but only by presupposing another synthetical proposition from which it follows, but never by that law alone.

First of all, we must observe that all strictly mathematical judgments are *a priori,* and not empirical, because they carry with them necessity, which cannot be obtained from experience. But if this be not conceded to me, very good; I shall confine my assertion to *pure mathematics,* the very notion of which implies that it contains pure *a priori* and not empirical knowledge.

It must at first be thought that the proposition $7 + 5 = 12$ is a mere analytical judgment, following from the concept of the sum of seven and five, according to the law of contradiction. But on closer examination it appears that the concept of the sum of $7 + 5$ contains merely their union in a single number, without its being at all thought what the particular number is that unites them. The concept of twelve is by no means thought by merely thinking of the combination of seven and five; and, analyze this possible sum as we may, we shall not discover twelve in the concept. We must go beyond these concepts, by calling to our aid some intuition which corresponds to one of the concepts—that is, either our five fingers or five points …—and we must add successively the units of the five given in the intuition to the concept of seven. Hence our concept is really amplified by the proposition $7 + 5 = 12$, and we add to the first concept a second concept not thought in it. Arithmetical judgments are therefore synthetical, and the more plainly according as we take larger numbers; for in such cases it is clear that, however closely we analyze our concepts without calling intuition to our aid, we can never find the sum by such mere dissection.

Just as little is any principle of geometry analytical. That a straight line is the shortest path between two points is a synthetical proposition. For my concept of straight contains nothing of quantity, but only a quality. The concept "shortest" is therefore altogether additional and cannot be obtained by any analysis of the concept "straight line." Here, too, intuition must come to aid us. It alone makes the synthesis possible. What usually makes us believe that the predicate of such apodictic judgments is already contained in our concept, and that the judgment is therefore analytical, is the duplicity of the expression. We must think a certain predicate as attached to a given concept, and necessity indeed belongs to the concepts. But the question is not what we must join in thought *to* the given concept, but what we actually think together with and in it, though obscurely; and so it appears that the predicate belongs to this concept necessarily indeed, yet not directly but indirectly by means of an intuition which must be present.

Some other principles, assumed by geometers, are indeed actually analytical, and depend on the law of contradiction; but they only serve, as identical propositions, as a method of concatenation, and not as principles—for example $a = a$, the whole is equal to itself, or $a + b > a$, the whole is greater than its part. And yet even these, though they are recognized as valid from mere concepts, are admitted in mathematics only because they can be represented in some intuition.

The essential and distinguishing feature of pure mathematical knowledge among all other *a priori* knowledge is that it cannot at all proceed from concepts, but only by means of the construction of concepts. As therefore in its propositions it must proceed beyond the concept to that which its corresponding intuition contains, these propositions neither can, nor ought to, arise analytically, by dissection of the concept, but are all synthetical.

I cannot refrain from pointing out the disadvantage resulting to philosophy from the neglect of this easy and apparently insignificant observation. Hume being prompted to cast his eye over the whole field of *a priori* cognitions in which human understanding claims such mighty possessions (a calling he felt worthy of a philosopher) heedlessly severed from it a whole, and indeed its most valuable, province, namely, pure mathematics; for he imagined its nature or, so to speak, the state constitution of this empire depended on totally different principles, namely, on the law of contradiction alone; and although he did not divide judgments in this manner formally and universally as I have done here, what he said was equivalent to this: that mathematics contains only analytical, but metaphysics synthetical, *a priori* propositions. In this, however, he was greatly mistaken, and the mistake had a decidedly injurious effect upon his whole conception. But for this, he would have extended his question concerning the origin of our synthetical judgments far beyond the metaphysical concept of causality and included in it the possibility of mathematics *a priori* also, for this latter he must have assumed to be equally synthetical. And then he could not have based his metaphysical propositions on mere experience without subjecting the axioms of mathematics equally to experience, a thing which he was far too acute to do. The good company into which metaphysics would thus have been brought would have saved it from the danger of a contemptuous ill-treatment, for the thrust intended for it must have reached mathematics, which was not and could not have been Hume's intention. Thus that acute man would have been led into considerations which must needs be similar to those that now occupy us, but which would have gained inestimably by his inimitably elegant style.

   3. *Metaphysical Judgments,* properly so called, are all synthetical. We must distinguish judgments pertaining to metaphysics from metaphysical judgments properly so called. Many of the former are analytical, but they only afford the means for metaphysical judgments, which are the whole end of the science and which are always synthetical. For if there be concepts pertaining to metaphysics (as, for example, that of substance), the judgments springing from simple analysis of them also pertain to metaphysics, as, for example, substance is that which only exists as subject, etc.; and by means of several such analytical judgments we seek to approach the definition of the concepts. But as the analysis of a pure concept of the understanding (the kind of concept pertaining to metaphysics) does not proceed in any different manner from the dissection of any other, even empirical, concepts, not belonging to metaphysics (such as, air is an elastic fluid, the elasticity of which is not destroyed by any known degree of cold), it follows that the concept indeed, but not the analytical judgment, is properly metaphysical. This science has something peculiar in the production of its *a priori* cognitions, which must therefore be distinguished from the features it has in common with other rational knowledge. Thus the judgment that all the substance in things is permanent is a synthetical and properly metaphysical judgment.

   If the *a priori* concepts which constitute the materials and tools of metaphysics have first been collected according to fixed principles, then their analysis will be of great value; it might be taught as a particular part (as a *philosophia definitiva*), containing nothing but analytical judgments pertaining to metaphysics, and could be treated separately from the synthetical which constitute metaphysics proper. For indeed these analyses are not of much value except in metaphysics, that is, as regards the synthetical judgments which are to be generated by these previously analyzed concepts.

   The conclusion drawn in this section then is that metaphysics is properly concerned with synthetical propositions *a priori,* and these alone constitute its end, for which it indeed requires various dissections of its concepts, namely, analytical judgments, but wherein the procedure is not different from that in every other kind of knowledge, in which we merely seek to render our concepts distinct by analysis. But the generation of *a priori* knowledge by intuition as well as by concepts, in fine, of synthetical propositions *a priori*, especially in philosophical knowledge, constitutes the essential subject of metaphysics....[2]

Kant concludes this investigation on the possibility of metaphysics with the question: Is metaphysics at all possible?

Were a metaphysics which could maintain its place as a science really in existence, could we say: "Here is metaphysics; learn it and it will convince you irresistibly and irrevocably of its truth"? This question would then be useless, and there would only remain that other question (which would rather be a test of our acuteness than a proof of the existence of the thing itself): "How is the science possible, and how does reason come to attain it?" But human reason has not been so fortunate in this case. There is no single book to which you can point as you do to Euclid, and say: "This is metaphysics; here you may find the noblest objects of this science, the knowledge of a highest being and of a future existence, proved from principles of pure reason." We can be shown indeed many propositions, demonstrably certain and never questioned; but these are all analytical, and rather concern the materials and the scaffolding for metaphysics than the extension of knowledge, which is our proper object in studying it. Even supposing you produce synthetical judgments (such as the law of sufficient reason, which you have never proved, as you ought to, from pure reason *a priori*, though we gladly concede its truth), you lapse, when you try to employ them for your principal purpose, into such doubtful assertions that in all ages one metaphysics has contradicted another, either in its assertions or their proofs, and thus has itself destroyed its own claim to lasting assent. Nay, the very attempts to set up such a science are the main cause of the early appearance of skepticism, a mental attitude in which reason treats itself with such violence that it could never have arisen save from complete despair of ever satisfying its most important aspirations. For long before men began to inquire into nature methodically, they consulted abstract reason, which had to some extent been exercised by means of ordinary experience; for reason is ever present, while laws of nature must usually be discovered with labor. So metaphysics floated to the surface, like foam, which dissolved the moment it was scooped off. But immediately there appeared a new supply on the surface, to be ever eagerly gathered up by some; while others, instead of seeking in the depths the cause of the phenomenon, thought they showed their wisdom by ridiculing the idle labor of their neighbors.

Weary therefore of dogmatism, which teaches us nothing, and of skepticism, which does not even promise us anything—even the quiet state of a contented ignorance—disquieted by the importance of knowledge so much needed, and rendered suspicious by long experience of all knowledge which we believe we possess or which offers itself in the name of pure reason, there remains but one critical question on the answer to which our future procedure depends, namely, "Is metaphysics at all possible?" But this question must be answered, not by skeptical objections to the asseverations of some actual system of metaphysics (for we do not as yet admit such a thing to exist), but from the conception, as yet only problematical, of a science of this sort....

But it happens, fortunately, that though we cannot assume metaphysics to be an actual science, we can say with confidence that there is actually given certain pure *a priori* synthetical cognitions, pure mathematics and pure physics; for both contain propositions which are unanimously recognized, partly apodictically certain by mere reason, partly by general consent arising from experience and yet as independent of experience. We have therefore at least some uncontested synthetical knowledge *a priori* and need not ask *whether* it be possible, for it is actual, but *how* it is possible, in order that we may deduce from the principle which makes the given knowledge possible the possibility of all the rest.[3]

The answer to this question is as indispensable as it is difficult. Kant thought that philosophers simply neglected the possibility of the question. There is yet another reason, namely, that a satisfactory answer to this one question requires a much more persistent, profound, and painstaking reflection than the most diffuse work on metaphysics, which on its first appearance promised immortal fame to its author. And every intelligent reader, when he or she carefully reflects what this problem requires, must at first be struck with its difficulty and would regard it as insoluble and even impossible did there not actually exist pure synthetic cognitions a priori. This actually happened to David Hume, though he did not conceive the question in its entire universality as is done here and as must be done if the answer is to be decisive for all metaphysics. For how is it possible, says that acute person, that when a concept is given me I can go beyond it and connect with it another that is not contained in it, in such a manner as if the latter *necessarily* belonged to the former? Nothing but experience can furnish us with such connections (thus he/she concluded from the difficulty that he/she took to be impossibility), and all that vaunted necessity or, what is the same thing, knowledge assumed to be a priori is nothing but a long habit of accepting something as true and hence mistaking subjective necessity for objective.

Should my reader complain of the difficulty and the trouble which I shall occasion him in the solution of this problem, he is at liberty to solve it himself in an easier way. Perhaps he will then feel under obligation to the person who has undertaken for him a labor of so profound research and will rather feel some surprise at the facility with which, considering the nature of the subject, the solution has been attained. Yet it has cost years of work to solve the problem in its whole universality (using the term in the mathematical sense, namely, for that which is sufficient for all cases), and finally to exhibit it in the analytical form, as the reader will find it here.

All metaphysicians are therefore solemnly and legally suspended from their occupations till they shall have adequately answered the question, "How are synthetical cognitions *a priori* possible?" For the answer contains the only credentials which they must show when they have anything to offer us in the name of pure reason. But if they do not possess these credentials, they can expect nothing else of reasonable people, who have been deceived so often, than to be dismissed without further inquiry.

If they, on the other hand, desire to carry on their business, not as a science, but as an art of wholesome persuasion suitable to the common sense of man, this calling cannot in justice be denied them. They will then speak the modest language of a rational belief; they will grant that they are not allowed even to conjecture, far less to know, anything which lies beyond the bounds of all possible experience, but only to assume (not for speculative use, which they must abandon, but for practical use only) the existence of something possible and even indispensable for the guidance of the understanding and of the will in life. In this manner alone can they be called useful and wise men, and the more so as they renounce the title of metaphysicians. For the latter profess to be speculative philosophers; and since, when judgments *a priori* are under discussion, poor probabilities cannot be admitted (for what is declared to be known *a priori* is thereby announced as necessary), such men cannot be permitted to play with conjectures, but their assertion must be either science or nothing at all.

It may be said that the entire transcendental philosophy, which necessarily precedes all metaphysics, is nothing but the complete solution of the problem here propounded, in systematic order and completeness, and hence we have hitherto never had any transcendental philosophy. For what goes by its name is properly a part of metaphysics, whereas the former science is intended only to constitute the possibility of the latter and must therefore precede all metaphysics. And it is not surprising that when a whole science, deprived of all help from other sciences and consequently in itself quite new, is required to answer a single question satisfactorily, we should find the answer troublesome and difficult, nay, even shrouded in obscurity.[4]

Kant gives two criteria for a priori judgments: necessity and universality. These two criteria seem to coalesce into the concept of "necessity," in that by universality he simply means that a universal proposition has no conceivable exception. After all, an empirical judgment could be universally true but not true by necessity. As examples of synthetic a priori judgments, he offers "$7 + 5 = 12$" and "everything occurs in time."

Although the idea of analytic a posteriori knowledge is not discussed in Kant's work, it seems clear that he rejected the idea because it was contradictory. That is, the idea of an analytic judgment—which depends solely on the relations of the concepts involved—makes no essential reference to experience, whereas a posteriori knowledge depends on experience.

The essential claim of those who recognize synthetic a priori knowledge is that the mind is able to grasp connections between concepts that are not analytically related. For example, we simply know upon reflection that all events have causes: "For every change there is an antecedent event which is necessarily connected with it." Similarly, we need not consult our senses to tell us that space is something that exists independently of matter. "If we remove from our empirical concept of a body, one by one, every feature in it which is [merely] empirical, the color, the hardness or softness, the weight, even the impenetrability, there still remains the space which the body (now entirely vanished) occupied, and this cannot be removed."[5] Kant, as we have noted, also thought our knowledge of mathematical truths was really synthetic a priori, rather than analytic. The moral law—the judgment that we ought to act in such a way that we could will that the maxims of our actions would be universal laws—is known without appeal to experience. Finally, he argues that the existence of substantial time is a synthetic a priori concept. To give you a sense of Kant's argument, let's quote him at length.

1. Time is not an empirical concept that has been derived from any experience. For neither coexistence nor succession would ever come within our perception, if the representation of time were not presupposed as underlying them *a priori*.

2. Time is a necessary representation that underlies all intuitions. We cannot, in respect of appearances in general, remove time itself, though we can quite well think time as void of appearances. Time is, therefore, given *a priori*. In it alone is the actuality of appearances possible at all. Appearances may, one and all, vanish; but time (as the universal condition of their possibility) cannot itself be removed.

3. Time has only one dimension; different times are not simultaneous but successive (just as different spaces are not successive but simultaneous). These principles cannot be derived from experience, for experience would give neither strict universality nor necessary certainty. We should only be able to say that common experience teaches us that it is so; not that it must be so. These principles are valid as rules under which alone experiences are possible; and they instruct us in regard to the experiences, not by means of them.

4. Time is not a discursive, or what is called a general concept, but a pure form of sensible intuition. Different times are but parts of one and the same time. Moreover, the proposition that different times cannot be simultaneous is not to be derived from a general concept.

Time is not something which exists of itself, or which inheres in things as an objective determination. . . . Time is nothing but the form of our inner sense, that is, of the intuition of ourselves and of our inner state. . . . Time is the formal a priori condition of all appearances whatsoever. . . . Time is therefore a purely subjective condition of our human intuition, and in itself, apart from the subject, is nothing.[6]

We can imagine a world with different physical laws—where Einstein's laws do not govern, where water is not wet nor fire hot, where mice are smarter than men, and human babies are born from elephants—but we cannot imagine a world without time. And yet we have no argument that establishes time's reality. It is a given in all our experience, a lens through which we see the world. It may not be real, but we cannot live without assuming its reality.

Time, space, and causality are categories of the mind that we impose on phenomena, on the world as we perceive it. But we can never get behind the phenomena and synthetic a priori knowledge to the *ding an sich*, to the world as it really is. Similarly, we only know our empirical self, not our true essence, our numinal self, the *transcendent ego*. But we can infer that we have such a self, for it is the only satisfying explanation of why we have perceptions at all.

Kant's Transcendental Apperception

Hume had reduced the self to a series of perceptions, a succession of awareness, thus eliminating any basis for an essential self behind appearances. Kant thinks he can go beyond Hume. He argues that "the manifold of the representation would never form a [coherent] whole," if there were no unifying self behind the appearances.

If, in counting, I forget that the units, which now hover before me, have been added to one another in succession, I should never know that a total is being produced through this successive addition of unit to unit, and so would remain ignorant of the number. For the concept of the number is nothing but the consciousness of this unity of synthesis. The word "concept" might of itself suggest this remark. For this unitary consciousness is what combines the manifold, successively intuited, and thereupon also reproduced, into one representation. This consciousness may often be only faint, so that we do not connect it with the act itself, that is, not in any direct manner with the *generation* of the representation, but only with the outcome [that which is thereby represented]. But notwithstanding these variations, such consciousness, however indistinct, must always be present; without it, concepts, and therewith knowledge of objects, are altogether impossible.

At this point we must make clear to ourselves what we mean by the expression "an object of representations." We have stated above that appearances are themselves nothing but sensible representations, which, as such and in themselves, must not be taken as objects capable of existing outside our power of representation. What, then, is to be understood when we speak of an object corresponding to, and consequently also distinct from, our knowledge? It is easily seen that this object must be thought only as something in general $= x$, since outside our knowledge we have nothing which we could set over against this knowledge as corresponding to it.

Now we find that our thought of the relation of all knowledge to its object carries with it an element of necessity; the object is viewed as that which prevents our modes of knowledge from being haphazard or arbitrary, and which determines them *a priori* in some definite fashion. For in so far as they are to relate to an object, they must necessarily agree with one another, that is, must possess that unity which constitutes the concept of an object....

But this unity is impossible if the intuition cannot be generated in accordance with a rule by means of such a function of synthesis as makes the reproduction of the manifold *a priori* necessary, and renders possible a concept in which it is united. Thus we think a triangle as an object, in that we are conscious of the combination of three straight lines according to a rule by which such an intuition can always be represented. This *unity of rule* determines all the manifold, and limits it to conditions which make unity of apperception possible. The concept of this unity is the representation of the object $= x$, which I think through the predicates, above mentioned, of a triangle.

All knowledge demands a concept, though that concept may, indeed, be quite imperfect or obscure. But a concept is always, as regards its form, something universal which serves as a rule. The concept of body, for instance, as the unity of the manifold which is thought through it, serves as a rule in our knowledge of outer appearances. But it can be a rule for intuitions only in so far as it represents in any given appearances the necessary reproduction of their manifold, and thereby the synthetic unity in our consciousness of them. The concept of body, in the perception of something outside us, necessitates the representation of extension, and therewith representations of impenetrability, shape, etc.

All necessity, without exception, is grounded in a transcendental condition. There must, therefore, be a transcendental ground of the unity of consciousness in the synthesis of the manifold of all our intuitions, and consequently also of the concepts of objects in general, and so of all objects of experience, a ground without which it would be impossible to think any object for our intuitions; for this object is no more than that something, the concept of which expresses such a necessity of synthesis.

This original and transcendental condition is no other than *transcendental apperception*. Consciousness of self according to the determinations of our state in inner perception is merely empirical, and always changing. No fixed and abiding self can present itself in this flux of inner appearances. Such consciousness is usually named *inner sense,* or *empirical apperception*. What has *necessarily* to be represented as numerically identical cannot be thought as such through empirical data. To render such a transcendental presupposition valid, there must be a condition which precedes all experience, and which makes experience itself possible. There can be in us no modes of knowledge, no connection or unity of one mode of knowledge with another, without that unity of consciousness which precedes all data of intuitions, and by relation to which representation of objects is alone possible. This pure original unchangeable consciousness I shall name *transcendental apperception*. That it deserves this name is clear from the fact that even the purest objective unity, namely, that of the *a priori* concepts (space and time), is only possible through relation of the intuitions to such unity of consciousness. The numerical unity of this apperception is thus the *a priori* ground of all concepts, just as the manifoldness of space and time is the *a priori* ground of the intuitions of sensibility. This transcendental unity of apperception forms out of all possible appearances, which can stand alongside one another in one experience, a connection of all these representations according to laws. For this unity of consciousness would be impossible if the mind in knowledge of the manifold could not become conscious of the identity of function whereby it synthetically combines it in one knowledge. The original and necessary consciousness of the identity of the self is thus at the same time a consciousness of an equally necessary unity of the synthesis of all appearances according to concepts, that is, according to rules, which not only make them necessarily reproducible but also in so doing determine an object for their intuition, that is, the concept of something wherein they are necessarily interconnected. For the mind could never think its identity in the manifoldness of its representations, and indeed think this identity *a priori*, if it did not have before its eyes the identity of its act, whereby it subordinates all synthesis of apprehension (which is empirical) to a transcendental unity, thereby rendering possible their interconnection according to *a priori* rules.

Now, also, we are in a position to determine more adequately our concept of an *object* in general. All representations have, as representations, their object, and can themselves in turn become objects of other representations. Appearances are the sole objects which can be given to us immediately, and that in them which relates immediately to the object is called intuition. But these appearances are not things in themselves; they are only representations, which in turn have their object—an object which cannot itself be intuited by us, and which may, therefore, be named the non-empirical, that is, transcendental object = x. The pure concept of this transcendental object, which in reality throughout all our knowledge is always one and the same, is what can alone confer upon all our empirical concepts in general relation to an object, that is, objective reality. This concept cannot contain any determinate intuition, and therefore refers only to that unity which must be met with in any manifold of knowledge which stands in relation to an object. This relation is nothing but the necessary unity of consciousness, and therefore also of the synthesis of the manifold, through a common function of the mind, which combines it in one representation. Since this unity must be regarded as necessary *a priori*—otherwise knowledge would be without an object—the relation to a transcendental object, that is, the objective reality of our empirical knowledge, rests on the transcendental law, that all appearances, in so far as through them objects are to be given to us, must stand under those *a priori* rules of synthetical unity whereby the interrelating of these appearances in empirical intuition is alone possible. In other words, appearances in experience must stand under the conditions of the necessary unity of apperception, just as in mere intuition they must be subject to the formal conditions of space and of time. Only thus can any knowledge become possible at all.[7]

So although we can never reach our essential self directly, we can know we have a transcendental self, a nominal essence beyond appearances. Otherwise we could not hold the manifold of perceptions together. Instead of Hume's succession of awarenesses, we have an awareness of succession, a unifying transcendent self behind the empirical self.

Freedom of the Will

In the section on the Antimonies of Reason (a section in *The Critique of Pure Reason* showing how reason sets forth opposite conclusions on metaphysical matters), Kant applies his doctrine of pure apperception to freedom of the will:

Man is one of the appearances of the sensible world, and in so far one of the natural causes the causality of which must stand under empirical laws. Like all other things in nature, he must have an empirical character. This character we come to know through the powers and faculties which he reveals in his actions. In lifeless, or merely animal, nature we find no ground for thinking that any faculty is conditioned otherwise than in a merely sensible manner. Man, however, who knows all the rest of nature solely through the senses, knows himself also through *pure apperception;* and this, indeed, in acts and inner determinations which he cannot regard as impressions of the senses. He is thus to himself, on the one hand *phenomenon,* and on the other hand, in respect of certain faculties the action of which cannot be ascribed to the receptivity of sensibility, a *purely intelligible object.* We entitle these faculties understanding and reason. The latter, in particular, we distinguish in a quite peculiar and especial way from all empirically conditioned powers. For it views its objects exclusively in the light of ideas, and in accordance with them determines the understanding, which then proceeds to make an empirical use of its own similarly pure concepts. That our reason has causality, or that we at least represent it to ourselves as having causality, is evident from the *imperatives* which in all matters of conduct we impose as rules upon our active powers. "*Ought*" expresses a kind of necessity and of connection with grounds which is found nowhere else in the whole of nature. The understanding can know in nature only what is, what has been, or what will be. We cannot say that anything in nature *ought to be* other than what in all these time-relations it actually is. When we have the course of nature alone in view, "*ought*" has no meaning whatsoever. It is just as absurd to ask what ought to happen in the natural world as to ask what properties a circle ought to have. All that we are justified in asking is: what happens in nature? what are the properties of the circle?

This "*ought*" expresses a possible action the ground of which cannot be anything but a mere concept; whereas in the case of a merely natural action the ground must always be an appearance. The action to which the "*ought*" applies must indeed be possible under natural conditions. These conditions, however, do not play any part in determining the will itself, but only in determining the effect and its consequences in the [field of] appearance. No matter how many natural grounds or how many sensuous impulses may impel me to *will*, they can never give rise to the "*ought*," but only to a willing which, while very far from being necessary, is always conditioned; and the "*ought*" pronounced by reason confronts such willing with a limit and an end—nay more, forbids or authorises it. Whether what is willed be an object of mere sensibility (the pleasant) or of pure reason (the good), reason will not give way to any ground which is empirically given. Reason does not here follow the order of things as they present themselves in appearance, but frames to itself with perfect spontaneity an order of its own according to ideas, to which it adapts the empirical conditions, and according to which it declares actions to be necessary, even although they have never taken place, and perhaps never will take place. And at the same time reason also presupposes that it can have causality in regard to all these actions, since otherwise no empirical effects could be expected from its ideas.[8]

On the one hand, a person, as an appearance, our empirical self, comes under the ordinary laws of nature—that is, under the domain of causality. On the other hand, we can introspect and know that we are free, that we have an inner pure apperception of our self-determination. To be morally responsible, one must be free to do either the right or wrong act, so it follows for Kant, that since morality is true, we must be free to do otherwise.

On God and Immortality

Kant argues that all so-called *proofs* for the existence of God and immortality are "altogether fruitless and by their nature null and void."[9] But proofs against the existence of God and immortality are equally unsound. We simply cannot be dogmatic either way. What does Kant's theory advise in such a predicament?

The positive value of the critical principles of pure reason in relation to the conception of God and of the simple nature of the soul, admits of a similar exemplification; but on

> this point I shall not dwell. I cannot even make the assumption—as the practical interests of morality require—of God, freedom, and immortality, if I do not deprive speculative reason of its pretensions to transcendent insight. For to arrive at these, it must make use of principles which, in fact, extend only to the objects of possible experience, and which cannot be applied to objects beyond this sphere without converting them into phenomena, and thus rendering the practical extension of pure reason impossible. *I must, therefore, deny knowledge, to make room for faith.* The dogmatism of metaphysics, that is, the presumption that it is possible to advance in metaphysics without previous criticism, is the true source of the unbelief (always dogmatic) which militates against morality.[10]

Kant was a Christian who believed that there were practical, moral reasons for believing in God and immortality. God and immortality are necessary postulates of ethics. Immortality is necessary in this way: According to Kant, the moral law commands us to be morally perfect. Since *ought* implies *can*, we must be *able* to reach moral perfection. But we cannot attain perfection in this life, for the task is infinite. So there must be an afterlife in which we continue progressing toward this ideal.

God is a necessary postulate in that morality requires someone to enforce the moral law; that is, for the moral law to be completely justified, there must finally be a just recompense of happiness in accordance with virtue. We must get what we deserve. The good must be rewarded by happiness in proportion to their virtue, and the evil must be punished in proportion to their vice. This harmonious correlation of virtue and happiness does not happen in this life, so it must happen in the next life. Thus, there must be a God, acting as judge and enforcer of the moral law, without which the moral law would be unjustified.

Kant is not saying that we can *prove* that God exists or that we ought to be moral *in order* to be happy. Rather, the idea of God serves as a completion of our ordinary ideas of ethics.

Summary

Kant's view of human nature centers around three deep philosophical questions:

1. *What can I know?* Our knowledge is structured by synthetic a priori categories of space, time, and causality so that we only know appearances, never the numinal world, the thing-in-itself. However, we are not confined to complete skepticism. Through transcendental reasoning, we can know that we have an essential self that exists beyond appearances, and we can know or have good reason to believe that the self is free to act morally or immorally.

2. *What ought I do?* Kant thought the practical side of reason was decisive, entailing that the most important thing in life was morality, acting out of a purely good will ("the only thing good in itself"). We ought to act morally simply because it is right to do so, and we deserve to be treated

on the basis of our moral character and actions. Immoral people forfeit their rights, so murderers ought to be executed for their crimes.

3. *What may I hope?* I may hope in God and immortality. Although we can neither prove the existence or nonexistence of God and immortality, we may hope in them. *"I must, therefore, deny knowledge, to make room for faith."* Faith in God for Kant was a keystone to morality and meaning in life, without which neither morality nor a meaningful life was truly complete or fully justified.

Although Kant's theory of human nature is epistemically pessimistic (we can never reach the real world, the thing-in-itself), he is basically an optimist: Humans, as rational beings, have inherent dignity through reason and thereby can know the moral law. We can reject Hume's skepticism about the self and via transcendental reason, apperceive both an essential self and freedom of the will. Moreover, we ought to postulate the existence of God as the assumption necessary to justify the moral law. We can hope in God and immortality despite a paucity of rational evidence. This is the high watermark of philosophical optimism. We will see how the Kantian revolution, in the hands of the children of the revolution, resulted in a more pessimistic view of human nature.

FOR FURTHER REFLECTION

1. What is Kant's Copernican revolution? How does it relate to earlier epistemologies?

2. What is synthetic a priori knowledge? Explain.

3. What is the phenomena/numina distinction in Kant? Can we know the world as it really is?

4. What, according to Kant, are our notions of time, space, and causality?

5. What is Kant's notion of the transcendental apperception?

6. Examine Kant's theory of free will. How cogent is his reasoning?

7. Kant claims that God is a necessary postulate in that morality requires someone to enforce the moral law. Is Kant right about this?

8. Kant's philosophy of human nature strives to combine the most rigorous rational analysis with the most hopeful moral conclusions. The question is, Is he successful?

NOTES

1. From the preface of *CPR* (1781), my translation.
2. *Prolegomena to Any Future Metaphysic,* trans. Paul Carus (Chicago: University of Chicago Press, 1902; originally published in 1783).
3. Ibid.
4. Ibid.
5. *CPR* Introduction B14.
6. *CPR,* 74–75.
7. *CPR* (A104–109), 134–38.

8. *CPR* (A546–548/B574–576), 472–473.
9. *CPR* (A636).
10. *CPR* Preface B, xxx.

FOR FURTHER READING

Allison, Henry. *Kant's Transcendental Idealism*. New Haven, CT: Yale University Press, 1983.

Beck, Lewis White. *A Commentary on Kant's Critique of Practical Reason*. Chicago: University of Chicago Press, 1960.

Beck, Lewis White, ed. *Studies in the Philosophy of Kant*. Indianapolis: Bobbs-Merrill, 1965.

Ewing, A. C. *A Short Commentary on Kant's Critique of Pure Reason*. London: Methuen, 1950.

Guyer, Paul. *Kant and the Claims of Knowledge*. Cambridge, UK: Cambridge University Press, 1987.

Kant, Immanuel. *The Critique of Pure Reason*. Translated by Norman Kemp Smith. New York: St. Martin's Press, 1969.

Kemp, John. *The Philosophy of Kant*. Oxford, UK: Oxford University Press, 1968.

Kemp Smith, Norman. *A Commentary to Kant's "Critique of Pure Reason."* London: Macmillan, 1918.

Louden, Robert. *Morality and Moral Theory*. Oxford University Press, 1991.

O'Neill, Onora. *Acting on Principle: An Essay on Kantian Ethics*. New York: Columbia University Press, 1975.

Ross, W. D. *Kant's Ethical Theory*. Oxford, UK: Clarendon Press, 1954.

Strawson, P. F. *The Bounds of Sense: An Essay on Kant's Critique of Pure Reason*. London: Methuen, 1966.

Walker, Ralph C. S. *Kant: The Arguments of the Philosophers*. London: Routledge & Kegan Paul, 1978.

Walker, Ralph C. S., ed. *Kant on Pure Reason*. Oxford University Press, 1982.

Werkmeister, W. H. *Kant*. LaSalle, IL: Open Court, 1980.

Wolff, Robert Paul, ed. *Kant*. Garden City, NY: Doubleday, 1967.

17 ❧ Arthur Schopenhauer and Transcendental Idealism

Will to power is to the mind like a strong blind man who carries on his shoulders a lame man who can see.
I teach that the inner nature of everything is will.

Arthur Schopenhauer

Arthur Schopenhauer (1788–1860) saw himself as the philosopher who alone developed Kant's Copernican revolution to its correct conclusion. A genius who wrote his major work, *The World as Will and Representation,* while still in his mid-20s, a pessimist who thought that life was meaningless, and the first Western philosopher to be deeply influenced by Eastern religion, Schopenhauer believed that all individual wills are mere manifestations of a cosmic Will. He was ferociously contentious, cantankerous,[1] cynical, irascible, obstinate, pessimistic, and egotistic but also generous, kind, witty, charming, and prodigiously energetic. He was depressed by the suffering in the world as well as by his own disappointments in life. He was a renaissance man, a polymath, mastering several intellectual subjects. He studied all morning and played the flute every afternoon. His mental energy was phenomenal, as was his philosophical acumen. Modeling his style on that of the Scottish philosopher, David Hume, he more than any other philosopher proved that German philosophy could be written in a clear and interesting manner. No German philosopher has ever exceeded his clear and scintillating style.

Schopenhauer was born to a wealthy cosmopolitan business family in the free city of Danzig in 1788. He was educated in Germany, France, and England and was fluent in each of these country's languages. Although prepared by his father for a career in international business, young Arthur detested that vocation and, after his father's death in 1805, was allowed by his mother to pursue a career in philosophy. Studying under the eminent German philosophers Johann Fichte (1762–1814) and Friedrich Schleiermacher (1768–1834), Schopenhauer was soon recognized as a brilliant student. He wrote his doctoral dissertation *On the Fourfold Root of the Principle of Sufficient Reason,* a development of the idea, set forth by Leibniz and developed by Kant, that every object and event in the world has an explanation, a sufficient reason for why it exists or happened. After his father's death, he moved to Weimar with his novelist mother who opened a literary salon wherein Schopenhauer would meet some of the most famous people of the age, among them the greatest poet of his time, Johann Goethe (1749–1832), with whom he became friends. However, Schopenhauer and his mother quarreled, and he moved into his own apartment. In 1813, he was introduced to Hinduism and began reading the Upanishads. From that day for the rest of his life, he derived comfort and spiritual sustenance from these ancient scriptures. From 1814 to 1818, he wrote his *magnum opus, The World as Will and Representation* (henceforth *WWR*), a work ingeniously combining Kant's transcendental idealism with Hindu monism. His hopes for the book were soon dashed to the ground, as the intellectual and literary world ignored it. Undaunted by this poor reception, Schopenhauer obtained permission to lecture at the University of Berlin where he unwisely scheduled his lectures at the same hour as the most renown philosopher of his day, G. W. F. Hegel (1770–1831), whose work Schopenhauer despised as a fraud and betrayer of Kant, was lecturing.[2] No one attended Schopenhauer's lectures, and his academic career abruptly ended.

For the next two decades, Schopenhauer traveled and wrote singularly lucid essays on ethics and freedom of the will. In 1844, he wrote a second volume to his *WWR*, developing the earlier work in a coherent manner. Finally, in 1853, an English literary journal, *The Westminster Review,* published an anonymous critical review of Schopenhauer's work that began to stir up interest in his unconventional work. Seeing fame finally in the offing, Schopenhauer published a new edition of his major treatise. His final work was a set of short essays and aphorisms, written in 1851 and entitled *Parega and Paralipomena.* He died of a heart attack in Frankfurt on September 21, 1860.

The World as Representation

Schopenhauer sees himself as a child of the revolution, Kant's Copernican revolution, who alone is carrying out his master's project to its logical conclusion. Kant had argued that there is an epistemic distinction between the world we experience, the world of appearances, and the real world, the *ding an sich.* We do not experience the world as it is but only as we impose the categories of the mind onto it, the categories of space, time, and causality. But whereas Kant thought he had denied reason to make way for faith, Schopenhauer remained an atheist, deeming Kant's departure from his own logic an unknowable flight into "Cloud-Cuckooland." The idea of a First Cause, which is what God would be, simply violates the Kantian principle of causality, that everything must have a cause, so even a God must have one. All we have are ideas or representations (*Vorstellung*). "The world is my representation," Schopenhauer writes.

WWR (Book 1) is divided into four books with an appendix on Kant's philosophy. The first book presents the world as representation, as the manner in which we experience it. The second book deals with the world as will, how we must understand our wills as parts of a universal will. This doctrine is the answer to Kant's *ding an sich*. The thing in itself is the universal will. The third book shows that aesthetic contemplation is a means of making sense of the world. The fourth book, exemplifying Schopenhauer's pessimism, advocates resignation as the means of overcoming the perennial suffering in the world and the meaninglessness of life. We begin our reading with the first few sections of Book 1.

THE WORLD AS WILL AND REPRESENTATION

"The world is my representation": this is a truth valid with reference to every living and knowing being, although man alone can bring it into reflective, abstract consciousness. If he really does so, philosophical discernment has dawned on him. It then becomes clear and certain to him that he does not know a sun and an earth, but only an eye that sees a sun, a hand that feels an earth; that the world around him is there only as representation, in other words, only in reference to another thing, namely that which represents, and this is himself. If any truth can be expressed *a priori,* it is this; for it is the statement of the form of all possible and conceivable experience, a form that is more general than all others, than time, space, and causality, for all these presuppose it. While each of these forms, which we have recognized as so many particular modes of the principle of sufficient reason, is valid only for a particular class of representations, the division into object and subject, on the other hand, is the common form of all those classes; it is that form under which alone any representation, of whatever kind it be, abstract or intuitive, pure or empirical, is generally possible and conceivable. Therefore no truth is more certain, more independent of all others, and less in need of proof than this, namely that everything that exists for knowledge, and hence the whole of this world, is only object in relation to the subject, perception of the perceiver, in a word, representation. Naturally this holds good of the present as well as of the past and future, of what is remotest as well as of what is nearest; for it holds good of time and space themselves, in which alone all these distinctions arise. Everything that in any way belongs and can belong to the world is inevitably associated with this being-conditioned by the subject, and it exists only for the subject. The world is representation.

This truth is by no means new. It was to be found already in the sceptical reflections from which Descartes started. But Berkeley was the first to enunciate it positively, and he has thus rendered an immortal service to philosophy, although the remainder of his doctrines cannot endure. Kant's first mistake was the neglect of this principle....On the other hand, how early this basic truth was recognized by the sages of India, since it appears as the fundamental tenet of the Vedânta philosophy ascribed to Vyasa,

---

From: Arthur Schopenhauer, *The World as Will and Representation,* trans. E. F. J. Payne (New York: Dover, 1969; originally published in 1819, republished in 1851). Reprinted by permission of Dover Publications.

is proved by Sir William Jones in the last of his essays: "On the Philosophy of the Asiatics" (*Asiatic Researches,* vol. IV, p. 164): "The fundamental tenet of the Vedânta school consisted not in denying the existence of matter, that is, of solidity, impenetrability, and extended figure (to deny which would be lunacy), but in correcting the popular notion of it, and in contending that it has no essence independent of mental perception; that existence and perceptibility are convertible terms." These words adequately express the compatibility of empirical reality with transcendental ideality.

As this passage shows, Schopenhauer finds antecedents of his representational view of reality in the Vedânta school of Hinduism, especially in the doctrine of Maya, or illusion (all our perceptions and immediate experiences are illusory). He also notes that Berkeley was the first modern philosopher to clearly set forth this view in his theory that *esse est percipi* (to be is to be perceived). Later he will acknowledge Plato's doctrine of the Forms as the real world, which is similar to his own view. But the nearest antecedent, one that deeply and critically influenced Schopenhauer, is Kant's *transcendental idealism* and, in particular, Kant's Copernican revolution (the categories of time, space, and causality are not in the world but part of our understanding). All these philosophies are versions of transcendentalism, meaning that reality transcends our comprehension, but Schopenhauer's version rejects Kant's and Berkeley's theism. With Kant, Schopenhauer holds that space, time, and causality are categories of the understanding, not part of reality. We never experience the world as it is in itself, but only as it appears to us through the categories of the mind.

This phenomenon of representations constitutes one of two essential aspects of the world. The other, to be dealt with below, is what Kant called *ding an sich*, which Schopenhauer will identify as the cosmic will-to-live. All other supposed philosophical realisms holding that we have direct (for example, Aristotle) or indirect (for example, Galileo, Descartes, and Locke) access to "reality" are "the phantom of a dream, and its acceptance is an *ignis fatuus* [that is, a lot of hot air] in philosophy."

We move on to Section 2 of Book 2.

That which knows all things and is known by none is the *subject.* It is accordingly the supporter of the world, the universal condition of all that appears, of all, objects, and it is always presupposed; for whatever exists, exists only for the subject. Everyone finds himself as this subject, yet only in so far as he knows, not in so far as he is object of knowledge. But his body is already object, and therefore from this point of view we call it representation. For the body is object among objects and is subordinated to the laws of objects, although it is immediate object.* Like all objects of perception, it lies within the forms of all knowledge, in time and space through which there is plurality. But the subject, the knower never the known, does not lie within these forms; on the contrary, it is always presupposed by those forms themselves, and hence neither plurality nor its opposite, namely unity, belongs to it. We never know it, but it is precisely that which knows wherever there is knowledge.

---

*On the Principle of Sufficient Reason, 2nd ed., § 22.

Therefore the world as representation, in which aspect alone we are here considering it, has two essential, necessary, and inseparable halves. The one half is *object,* whose forms are space and time, and through these plurality. But the other half, the subject, does not lie in space and time, for it is whole and undivided in every representing being. Hence a single one of these beings with the object completes the world as representation just as fully as do the millions that exist. And if that single one were to disappear, then the world as representation would no longer exist. Therefore these halves are inseparable even in thought, for each of the two has meaning and existence only through and for the other; each exists with the other and vanishes with it. They limit each other immediately; where the object begins, the subject ceases. The common or reciprocal nature of this limitation is seen in the very fact that the essential, and hence universal, forms of every object, namely space, time, and causality, can be found and fully known, starting from the subject, even without the knowledge of the object itself, that is to say, in Kant's language, they reside a priori in our consciousness....[3]

So far, we have mainly a review of the idealist tradition from Plato and Hinduism to Berkeley and Kant. Schopenhauer has argued along Kantian lines that space, time, and causality are inherently unstable concepts. We cannot formulate a clear idea of time having a beginning, nor can we grasp the idea of beginningless time. We cannot formulate the notion of space having boundaries, but neither can we imagine boundless space. We cannot form the notion of an infinite set of causes, but neither can we conceive of a first cause. The theological doctrine of God as the eternal, nonspatial, first cause, which Berkeley and others resort to as the solution of these problems, must be rejected for it violates the principle of causality (*every object and event must have a cause*) and so raises the question, What caused God? He chides Kant for the inconsistency of both denying causality as part of the numinal world and then implying that the numinal world causes us to have the perceptions we have. So far, Schopenhauer is simply correcting the idealist tradition. Now in Book 2, Schopenhauer makes an advance on *transcendental idealism.*

The Will to Live

Schopenhauer believes he has solved the riddle of the ***ding an sich,*** Kant's numinal world that is behind appearance. He had criticized Kant for making the numinon an unperceptible but ultimately real substratum of everything there is, but now he seems to do so himself, only it is now named as *Will.* He begins by showing that we can never get at ultimate reality simply by examining representations.

Here we already see that we can never get at the inner nature of things *from without.* However much we may investigate, we obtain nothing but images and names. We are like a man who goes round a castle, looking in vain for an entrance, and sometimes sketching the facades. Yet this is the path that all philosophers before me have followed.[4]

Schopenhauer will perform his own revolution by locating the *ding an sich* within the world, within our consciousness. We don't have to find a door into the castle, for we are already within it.

The meaning that I am looking for of the world that stands before me simply as my representation, or the transition from it as mere representation of the knowing subject to whatever it may be besides this, could never be found if the investigator himself were nothing more than the purely knowing subject (a winged cherub without a body). But he himself is rooted in that world; and thus he finds himself in it as an *individual,* in other words, his knowledge, which is the conditional supporter of the whole world as representation, is nevertheless given entirely through the medium of a body, and the affections of this body are, as we have shown, the starting-point for the understanding in its perception of this world. For the purely knowing subject as such, this body is a representation like any other, an object among objects. Its movements and actions are so far known to him in just the same way as the changes of all other objects of perception; and they would be equally strange and incomprehensible to him, if their meaning were not unravelled for him in an entirely different way. Otherwise, he would see his conduct follow on presented motives with the constancy of a law of nature, just as the changes of other objects follow upon causes, stimuli, and motives. But he would be no nearer to understanding the influence of the motives than he is to understanding the connexion with its cause of any other effect that appears before him. He would then also call the inner, to him incomprehensible, nature of those manifestations and actions of his body a force, a quality, or a character, just as he pleased, but he would have no further insight into it.

All this, however, is not the case; on the contrary, the answer to the riddle is given to the subject of knowledge appearing as individual, and this answer is given in the word *Will.* This and this alone gives him the key to his own phenomenon, reveals to him the significance and shows him the inner mechanism of his being, his actions, his movements. To the subject of knowing, who appears as an individual only through his identity with the body, this body is given in two entirely different ways. It is given in intelligent perception as representation, as an object among objects, liable to the laws of these objects. But it is also given in quite a different way, namely as what is known immediately to everyone, and is denoted by the word *will.* Every true act of his will is also at once and inevitably a movement of his body; he cannot actually will the act without at the same time being aware that it appears as a movement of the body. The act of will and the action of the body are not two different states objectively known connected by the bond of causality; they do not stand in the relation of cause and effect, but are one and the same thing, though given in two entirely different ways, first quite directly, and then in perception for the understanding. The action of the body is nothing but the act of will objectified, i.e., translated into perception. Later on we shall see that this applies to every movement of the body, not merely to movement following on motives, but also to involuntary movement following on mere stimuli; indeed, that the whole body is nothing but the objectified will, i.e., will that has become representation. All this will follow and become clear in the course of our discussion. Therefore the body, which in the previous book and in the essay *On the Principle of*

Sufficient Reason I called the *immediate* object, according to the one-sided viewpoint deliberately taken there (namely that of the representation), will here from another point of view be called the *objectivity of the will*.

Therefore, in a certain sense, it can also be said that the will is knowledge *a priori* of the body, and that the body is knowledge *a posteriori* of the will. Resolutions of the will relating to the future are mere deliberations of reason about what will be willed at some time, not real acts of will. Only the carrying out stamps the resolve; till then, it is always a mere intention that can be altered; it exists only in reason, in the abstract. Only in reflection are willing and acting different; in reality they are one. Every true, genuine, immediate act of the will is also at once and directly a manifest act of the body; and correspondingly, on the other hand, every impression on the body is also at once and directly an impression on the will. As such, it is called pain when it is contrary to the will, and gratification or pleasure when in accordance with the will. The gradations of the two are very different. However, we are quite wrong in calling pain and pleasure representations, for they are not these at all, but immediate affections of the will in its phenomenon, the body; an enforced, instantaneous willing or not-willing of the impression undergone by the body. There are only a certain few impressions on the body which do not rouse the will, and through these alone is the body an immediate object of knowledge; for, as perception in the understanding, the body is an indirect object like all other objects. These impressions are therefore to be regarded directly as mere representations, and hence to be excepted from what has just been said. Here are meant the affections of the purely objective senses of sight, hearing, and touch, although only in so far as their organs are affected in the specific natural way that is specially characteristic of them. This is such an exceedingly feeble stimulation of the enhanced and specifically modified sensibility of these parts that it does not affect the will, but, undisturbed by any excitement of the will, only furnishes for the understanding data from which perception arises. But every stronger or heterogeneous affection of these sense-organs is painful, in other words, is against the will; hence they too belong to its objectivity. Weakness of the nerves shows itself in the fact that the impressions which should have merely that degree of intensity that is sufficient to make them data for the understanding, reach the higher degree at which they stir the will, that is to say, excite pain or pleasure, though more often pain. This pain, however, is in part dull and inarticulate; thus it not merely causes us to feel painfully particular tones and intense light, but also gives rise generally to a morbid and hypochondriacal disposition without being distinctly recognised. The identity of the body and the will further shows itself, among other things, in the fact that every vehement and excessive movement of the will, in other words, every emotion, agitates the body and its inner workings directly and immediately, and disturbs the course of its vital functions.

Finally, the knowledge I have of my will, although an immediate knowledge, cannot be separated from that of my body. I know my will not as a whole, not as a unity, not completely according to its nature, but only in its individual acts, and hence in time, which is the form of my body's appearing, as it is of every body. Therefore, the body is the condition of knowledge of my will. Accordingly, I cannot really imagine this will without my body. In the essay *On the Principle of Sufficient Reason* the will, or rather the subject of willing, is treated as a special class of representations or objects. But even there we saw this object coinciding with the subject, in other words, ceasing to be object. We then called this coincidence the miracle *par excellence*. To a certain extent the whole of the present work is an explanation of this. In so far as I know my will really as object, I know it as body; but then I am again at the first class of representations laid down in that essay, that is, again at real objects. As we go on, we shall see more and more that the first class of representations finds its explanation, its solution, only in the fourth class enumerated in that essay, which could no longer be properly opposed to the subject as object; and that, accordingly, we must learn to understand the inner nature of the law of causality valid in the first class, and of what happens according to this law, from the law of motivation governing the fourth class.

The identity of the will and of the body, provisionally explained, can be demonstrated only as is done here, and that for the first time, and as will be done more and more in the further course of our discussion. In other words, it can be raised from immediate consciousness, from knowledge in the concrete, to rational knowledge of reason, or be carried over into knowledge in the abstract. On the other hand, by its nature it can never be demonstrated, that is to say, deduced as indirect knowledge from some other more direct knowledge, for the very reason that it is itself the most direct knowledge. If we do not apprehend it and stick to it as such, in vain shall we expect to obtain it again in some indirect way as derived knowledge. It is a knowledge of quite a peculiar nature, whose truth cannot therefore really be brought under one of the four headings by which I have divided all truth in the essay *On the Principle of Sufficient Reason*, § 29, namely, logical, empirical, transcendental, and metalogical. For it is not, like all these, the reference of an abstract representation to another representation, or to the necessary form of intuitive or of abstract representing, but it is the reference of a judgement to the relation that a representation of perception, namely the body, has to that which is not a representation at all, but is *toto genere* different therefrom, namely will. I should therefore like to distinguish this truth from every other, and call it *philosophical truth par excellence*. We can turn the expression of this truth in different ways and say: My body and my will are one; or, What as representation of perception I call my body, I call my will in so far as I am conscious of it in an entirely different way comparable with no other; or, My body is the objectivity of my will; or, Apart from the fact that my body is my representation, it is still my will, and so on.[5]

We have immediate knowledge of our bodies, which are the incarnations of will, our intentional stances. We do not infer our volitions from our bodily movements but intuit that the two are aspects of one another. Schopenhauer now brings the two aspects of our knowledge together.

The double knowledge which we have of the nature and action of our own body, and which is given in two completely different ways, has now been clearly brought out. Accordingly, we shall use it further as a key to the inner being of every phenomenon in nature. We shall judge all objects which are not our own body, and therefore are given to our consciousness not in the double way, but only as representations, according to the analogy of this body. We shall therefore assume that as, on the one hand, they are representation, just like our body, and are in this respect homogeneous with it, so on the other hand, if we set aside their existence as the subject's representation, what still remains over must be, according to its inner nature, the same as what in ourselves we call *will*. For what other kind of existence or reality could we attribute to the rest of the material world? From what source could we take the elements out of which we construct such a world? Besides the will and the representation, there is absolutely nothing known or conceivable for us. If we wish to attribute the greatest known reality to the material world, which immediately exists only in our representation, then we give it that reality which our own body has for each of us, for to each of us this is the most real of things. But if now we analyse the reality of this body and its actions, then, beyond the fact that it is our representation, we find nothing in it but the will; with this even its reality is exhausted. Therefore we can nowhere find another kind of reality to attribute to the material world. If, therefore, the material world is to be something more than our mere representation, we must say that, besides being the representation, and hence in itself and of its *inmost nature*, it is what we find immediately in ourselves as will....Therefore, if I say that the force which attracts a stone to the earth is of its nature, in itself, and apart from all representation, will, then no one will attach to this proposition the absurd meaning that the stone moves itself according to a known motive, because it is thus that the will appears in man.[6]

For Schopenhauer, the will encompasses all intentional activity, including desiring, wanting, fearing, hating, and mere wishing. It includes a general will-to-live, found in plants, as well as in the subconscious and the conscious desires of animals and humans. It is the inner force of nature, in stones and sand and water and air. Schopenhauer writes, "I teach that the inner nature of everything is will."

The will considered purely in itself is devoid of knowledge, and is only a blind irresistible cure, as we see it appear in inorganic and vegetable nature and in their laws, and also in the vegetative part of our own life. Through the addition of the world as representation, developed for its service, the will obtains knowledge of its own willing and what it wills, namely that this is nothing but this world, life, precisely as it exists. We have heretofore called the phenomenal world the mirror, the objectivity of the will; and as what the will wills is always life, just because this is nothing but the presentation of that willing for the representation, it is immaterial and a mere pleonasm if, instead of simply saying "the will" we say "the will-to-live."[7]

Will is the force behind all nature, the energy of existence, of which my body is a manifestation.

As the will is the thing-in-itself, the inner content, the essence of the world, but life, the visible world, the phenomenon, is only the mirror of the will, this world will accompany the will as inseparably as a body is accompanied by its shadow; and if will exists, then life, the world, will exist. Therefore life is certain to the will-to-live, and as long as we are filled with the will-to-live, we need not be apprehensive for our existence, even at the sight of death. It is true that we see the individual come into being and pass away; but the individual is only phenomenon, exists only for knowledge involved in the principle of sufficient reason, in the *principium individuationis*. Naturally, for this knowledge, the individual receives his life as a gift, rises out of nothing, and then suffers the loss of this gift through death, and returns to nothing.[8]

The representations of our spatiotemporal selves, our egoistic identities, which Schopenhauer, borrowing a medieval formula, labels *principium individuationis* (individuating principle), are illusory and the loci of suffering. The idea that existence is one of suffering is Eastern more than Western, which is centered more in sin, seeing suffering as a symptom of sin.

Salvation from the Sufferings of Existence

For Schopenhauer, reality is will—spiritual, not material. But the will is the cause of suffering. Because our wills are insatiable, because we continuously desire, moving from one desire to another, we are doomed to suffering. Deep suffering is the common lot of human beings—the more sensitive, the more painful.

Unless suffering is the direct and immediate object of life, our existence must entirely fail of its aim. It is absurd to look upon the enormous amount of pain that abounds everywhere in the world, originating in needs and necessities inseparable from life, as serving no purpose, as being the result of mere chance.

Let us consider the human race. Here life presents itself as a task to be performed. Here we see, in great and small, universal need, ceaseless wars, compulsory activity, extreme exertion of mind and body. Millions united into nations, striving for a common good, each individual on account of his own. But thousands are sacrificed. Now silly delusions, now intriguing politics, excite them to wars. Then sweat and blood must flow to carry out someone's ideas or expiate someone's folly. In peace time it is industry and trade. Inventions work miracles, seas are navigated, delicacies are brought from the ends of the earth, waves engulf thousands. The tumult passes description. And all to what end? To sustain life through a brief span, and then to reproduce and begin again.

From whence did Dante take the materials for his hell but from our actual world? And a very proper hell he was able to make of it. When, on the other hand, he came to describe heaven and its delights, he was confronted with difficulty, for our world affords no material for this.[9]

All of creation, as containing the cosmic will, suffers, but especially human beings, and among humans, the most intelligent and sensitive, for they are able to feel joys and disappointments more keenly than the dull and stupid.

What can be done to liberate us? Schopenhauer offers two ways of salvation, a *lesser* and a *greater* means of salvation. In Book 3 of his *WWR*, he describes the lesser, incidental mode, aesthetic contemplation. Aesthetic pleasure or beauty takes us beyond our banal existence for the moment and delights us. This transcendent moment is the highest state we can attain in life. Aesthetic contemplation raises the individual to a will-less, painless, atemporal mode of being, beyond the chains of egoism and illusion. But few of us can maintain this level of aesthetic consciousness for more than a very short time, so it is not a means of salvation open to most of us or a complete means of salvation for anyone.

The greater, more permanent, mode is described in Book 4.

We, however, wish to consider life philosophically, that is to say, according to its Ideas, and then we shall find that neither the will, the thing-in-itself in all phenomena, nor the subject of knowing, the spectator of all phenomena, is in any way affected by birth and death. Birth and death belong only to the phenomenon of the will, and hence to life; and it is essential to this that it manifest itself in individuals that come into being and pass away, as fleeting phenomena, appearing in the form of time, of that which in itself knows no time, but must be manifested precisely in the way aforesaid in order to objectify its real nature. Birth and death belong equally to life, and hold the balance as mutual conditions of each other, or, if the expression be preferred, as poles of the whole phenomenon of life. The wisest of all mythologies, the Indian, expresses this by giving to the very god who symbolizes destruction and death, . . . i.e., to Shiva as an attribute not only the necklace of skulls, but also the lingam,* that symbol of generation which appears as the counterpart of death. In this way it is intimated that generation and death are essential correlatives which reciprocally neutralize and eliminate each other. It was precisely the same sentiment that prompted the Greeks and Romans to adorn the costly sarcophags, just as we still see them, with feasts, dances, marriages, hunts, fights between wild beasts, bacchanalia, that is, with presentations of life's most powerful urge. This they present to us not only through such diversions and merriments, but even in sensual groups, to the point of showing us the sexual intercourse between satyrs and goats. The object was obviously to indicate with the greatest emphasis from the death of the mourned individual the immortal life of nature, and thus to intimate, although without abstract knowledge, that the whole of nature is the phenomenon, and also the fulfillment, of the will-to-live. The form of this phenomenon is time, space, and causality, and through these, individuation, which requires that the individual must come into being and pass away. But this no more disturbs the will-to-live—the individual being only a particular example or specimen, so to speak, of the phenomenon of the will— than does the death of an individual injure the whole of nature. For it is not the individual that nature cares for, but only the species; and in all seriousness she urges the preservation of the species, since she provides for this so lavishly through the immense surplus of the seed and the great strength of the fructifying impulse. The individual, on the contrary, has no value for nature, and can have none for infinite time, infinite space, and the infinite number of possible individuals therein are her kingdom. Therefore nature is always ready to let the individual fall, and the individual is accordingly not only exposed to destruction in a thousand ways from the most insignificant accidents, but is even destined for this and is led toward it by nature herself, from the moment that individual has served the maintenance of the species. In this way, nature united openly expresses the great truth that only Ideas, not individuals, have the highest reality proper, in other words are a complete objectivity of the will. Now man is nature herself, and indeed nature at the highest grade of her self-consciousness, but nature is only the objectified will-to-live; the person who has

> grasped and retained this point of view may certainly and justly console himself for
> his own death and for that of his friends by looking back on the immortal life of
> nature, which he himself is.[10]

The way of salvation is Hindu-Stoical resignation, of surrendering one's individual will with all its desires, thus freeing oneself from illusion and suffering. In ascetic self-denial, one renounces one's particular will and merges the reality of the *ding an sich,* the ultimately real cosmic will to live. "What remains after the complete abolition of the will is, for all who are still full of the will, assuredly nothing. But also conversely, to those in whom the will has turned and denied itself, this very real world of ours with all its suns and galaxies, is — nothing."[11] That is, the solution of the problem of the suffering will is to give up your egoistic will and surrender to the cosmic will-to-live. Perhaps the following illustration will help make this idea clearer.

An incident reported by the religious scholar Joseph Campbell illustrates Schopenhauer's theory. One day, two policemen were driving up a road in Hawaii when they noticed, just beyond the railing that keeps the cars from rolling over, a young man preparing to jump. The police car stopped, and the policeman on the right jumped out to grab the man but caught him just as he jumped, and he was himself being pulled over when the second cop arrived in time and pulled the two of them back. Campbell writes,

> Do you realize what had suddenly happened to that policeman who
> had given himself to death with that unknown youth? Everything else
> in his life had dropped off—his duty to his family, his duty to his job,
> his duty to his own life—all of his wishes and hopes for his lifetime had
> just disappeared. He was about to die. Later, a newspaper reporter
> asked him, "Why didn't you let go? You would have been killed." And
> his reported answer was "I couldn't let go. If I had let that young man
> go, I couldn't have lived another day of my life." How come?[12]

Schopenhauer's answer is that such a psychological crisis represents the breakthrough of a metaphysical realization: You and the other are one, you are two aspects of the one life, and your apparent separateness is but an effect of the way we experience the eternal forms under the conditions of space and time. "Our true reality is in our identity and unity with all life. This is a metaphysical truth which may become spontaneously realized under circumstances of crisis. For it is, according to Schopenhauer, the truth of your life."[13] Joseph Campbell comments on this:

> The hero is the one who has given his physical life to some order of
> realization of that truth. The concept of love your neighbor is to put
> you in tune with this fact. But whether you love your neighbor or not,
> when the realization grabs you, you may risk your life. That Hawaiian
> policeman didn't know who the young man was to whom he had
> given himself. Schopenhauer declares that in small ways you can see
> this happening every day, all the time, moving life in the world, people
> doing selfless things to and for each other.[14]

Summary

Schopenhauer thought of his philosophy as continuing the Kantian epistemic revolution to its logical conclusion. He answers Kant's riddle on the *ding an sich,* arguing that we have knowledge of the numinal world. He combines the Kantian Copernican revolution in epistemology with Berkeley's theory of perception, with Plato's metaphysical doctrine of the Forms, or Ideas, and with Eastern (Hindu) metaphysical teachings about Maya and the sufferings of humanity. Representations and will-to-live or power are the two aspects of our world. They are the objective and subjective aspects of the world, combined in a harmonious synthesis. "Will to power is to the mind like a strong blind man who carries on his shoulders a lame man who can see."

But our individual wills lead us inevitably to disappointment and frustration, for they can never be satisfied and are continuously replaced by fresh desires. Our lot in life is suffering, pervasive, penetrating, and painful. Aesthetic contemplation can enable us temporarily to transcend suffering. But the deepest and only abiding salvation comes in resigning one's self in the oceanic body of the World Soul.

Many find Schopenhauer's transcendental idealism implausible. The criticism goes like this: At least Plato had a larger metaphysical theory of the Forms, and Berkeley had God to keep the college quad in existence when no conscious animal or human was present to perceive it. But what accounts for the world when no Cosmic Mind is present? Science tells us that the universe existed for billions of years before we had any representation of it. How can Schopenhauer's theory account for that fact? And what is this cosmic will-to-live except the physical force of energy? Isn't it an instance of what Alfred North Whitehead called the fallacy of misplaced concreteness: to subsume our individual conscious identities under the metaphor of physical energy? Even if our consciousness is an emergent property of energy states, it seems more than a mere energy state These are the kinds of challenges Schopenhauer's transcendental idealism faces. I leave them for your consideration.

FOR FURTHER REFLECTION

1. How does Schopenhauer carry on Kant's Copernican revolution?

2. According to Schopenhauer, what are the two aspects of the world that we experience?

3. Explain Schopenhauer's doctrine of the will-to-live.

4. What is the relationship between our body and the will?

5. According to Schopenhauer, what is the human condition? Do you agree with him?

6. How may we find liberation from the suffering and meaninglessness of existence?

7. According to Schopenhauer, what should be our attitude toward our death?

8. Examine Schopenhauer's closing statement (of his book): "What remains after the complete abolition of the will is, for all who are still full of the will, assuredly nothing. But also conversely, to those in whom the will has turned and

denied itself, this very real world of ours with all its suns and galaxies, is noth-ing." What does he mean?

What is the meaning of Joseph Campbell's illustration of the policeman risking his life or the man who attempted suicide?

9. Assess Schopenhauer's philosophy. How plausible is it? Discuss the prob-lems with his system. What are its strengths and weaknesses?

NOTES

1. Once when he quarreled with his landlady, he threw her down the stairs, seriously injuring her. She sued and won a settlement. When she died, Schopenhauer wrote, "Obit anus, abit onus." ("The old woman dies, the burden departs.")

2. Schopenhauer referred to Hegel as an "intellectual Caliban," a "philosophical creature of ministries . . . manufactured from above with a political but miscalculated purpose; a flat, commonplace, repulsive, ignorant charlatan, who, with unparalleled presumption, conceit, and absurdity, pasted together a system which was trumpeted by his venal adherents as immortal wisdom" [*The Wisdom of Life and Other Essays,* trans. T Bailey Saunders and E. B. Bax (New York: Walter Dunne, 1901)].

3. Schopenhauer, *WWR.*

4. Ibid., 99.

5. Ibid., 100–103.

6. Ibid., 104–105.

7. Ibid.

8. Ibid., 275.

9. Schopenhauer, *Parega and Paralipomena.*

10. Schopenhauer, *WWR,* 275f.

11. Ibid., 412. This is the conclusion of the book: It all comes down to nothing.

12. Joseph Campbell, *The Power of Myth* (New York: Anchor Books, 1988), 138.

13. Cited in Campbell, *The Power of Myth,* 138–139

14. Campbell, *The Power of Myth.*

FOR FURTHER READING

Atwell, J. *Schopenhauer: The Human Character.* Philadelphia: Temple University Press, 1990.

Atwell, J. *Schopenhauer on the Character of the World.* Berkeley: University of California Press, 1995.

Copleston, F. *Arthur Schopenhauer: Philosopher of Pessimism.* London: Barnes and Noble, 1975.

Gardiner, P. *Schopenhauer.* Middlesex, UK: Penguin Books, 1967.

Hamlyn, D. W. *Schopenhauer.* London: Routledge & Kegan Paul, 1980.

Jacquette, D., ed. *Schopenhauer, Philosophy and the Arts.* Cambridge, UK: Cambridge University Press, 1996.

Janaway, C., ed. *The Cambridge Companion to Schopenhauer.* Cambridge, UK: Cambridge University Press, 1999.

Janaway, Christopher. *Schopenhauer*. Oxford, UK: Oxford University Press, 1994.

Magee, Bryan. *The Philosophy of Schopenhauer*. Oxford, UK: Oxford University Press, 1997.

Schopenhauer, Arthur. *The World as Will and Representation*. Translated by E. F. J. Payne. New York: Dover, 1969; originally published in 1819, republished in 1851.

Schopenhauer, Arthur. *Essays and Aphorisms*. Translated by R. J. Holingdale. London: Penguin Books, 1970.

18 ✢ Truth, Rationality, and Cognitive Relativism

To say that what is, is not, or that what is not is, is false; but to say that what is, is, and what is not, is not, is true.

Aristotle (384–322 BCE)

Man is the measure of all things
Both of things that are,
Man is the measure that they are,
And of the things that are not,
Man is the measure that they are not.

Protagoras the Sophist (fifth century BCE)

A professor, call him D, from the English Department at a major university recently gave a talk on political biases in university curriculum, arguing that the curricula was oppressive to women and minorities. After the speech, a philosopher came up to D and pointed out that he, D, had contradicted himself in his speech. The English professor responded, saying, "So, what's wrong with that? Look young man, I'm sure you know more logic than I do, but I know more about logic than you do! I know that it's a phallologocentric instrument for the oppression of minorities." He explained that all our so-called truths were simply cultural inventions. Another professor, holding a similar position, once told me that there was no such thing as impartial truth; all truth is relative to some interest. As Nietzsche said, "There are no facts, only interpretations."

The Correspondence Theory of Truth

Two diametrically opposed views on truth exist in contemporary culture, especially among intellectuals in academia. One position, call it *cognitive realism*, accepts one or another version of the **correspondence theory of truth** and holds the classical view that some things exist independently of whether anyone thinks about them. Some propositions are true whether or not anyone believes them. Mind-independent facts exist whether or not anyone believes them. Examples of this are the propositions "2 + 2 = 4," "a contradiction cannot be true," "the solar system has more than one planet," and "pigs can't fly." The other position, which is called *cognitive relativism*, or *anti-realism*, holds that there are no mind-independent facts or truths. Cognitive relativists generally combine anti-realism with a pragmatic notion of truth. A pragmatic theory of truth defines truth in terms of usefulness or workability. The proposition "2 + 2 = 4" is part of a human mathematical invention, and the proposition "the solar system has more than one planet" can be analyzed into specific concepts, which are human inventions. The same is true for the idea of a "planet," a "sun," a "system," and "more." Similarly, "pigs can't fly" depends on the way we divide up reality. A culture might not have a concept of "pig" or "fly," or they might have several "pig-concepts" or "fly-concepts." We invent reality via our conceptual–linguistic systems. Many cognitive relativists would not go as far as our English professor (D) who believes even the laws of logic are inventions, but they may agree that formal constraints are on what can be intelligibly said to be within a system of thought and that contradictions are formal criteria of exclusion. But other intellectuals would bite the bullet, as it were, and deny that contradictions need be false.

The realists trace their lineage back to Plato, who distinguished reality from appearance, and Aristotle, who defined truth as a *correspondence* between statements and facts (see the quotation at the chapter's start). In our readings, Bertrand Russell explains and defends the correspondence theory of truth.

The new cognitive relativists can trace their roots back to Protagoras, who said "Man is the measure of all things"—that is, what we think is true is so. They are also reminiscent of Berkeley's idealism (see Chapter 15), with the important difference that they reject idealism, as well as Berkeley's God. They agree with Berkeley against Locke that we cannot build a bridge from our conceptual schemes to the world itself, but they reject a God's-eye perspective wherein reality is unified ideally. Instead, we have many worlds, many realities, many perspectives. In the words of Nietzsche (see Chapter 34), who is quoted approvingly,

> Truth is a mobile army of metaphors, metonyms, and anthropomorphisms—in short a sum of human relations, which have been enhanced, transposed, and embellished poetically and rhetorically and which after long use seem firm, canonical, and obligatory to a people.

Richard Rorty (our third selection) identifies his version of this anti-realism with the pragmatism of the American philosophers William James (1842–1910;

our second selection) and John Dewey (1859–1952) and characterizes it as a civilized ethnocentricism, one that chooses social solidarity over objectivity and rejects the notion that truth is the correspondence between our ideas and an independent reality. Since there is no privileged perspective and no unifying reality, there is no absolute knowledge, no Truth (with a capital T). These ideas must be deconstructed. What is left is our ways of justifying our beliefs, "warranted assertability," as Dewey would say. So the division between truth and opinion collapses, and truth becomes what our peers will let us get away with. In our reading, Rorty first defends his *epistemological pragmatism* (sometimes called *epistemological behaviorism*), the thesis that truth, rather than being a correspondence between our ideas and the world, is what we agree on, what it is better to believe. In the second selection, "Science and Solidarity," Rorty applies his thesis to the idea that science seeks to secure objectivity, arguing that science, objectivity, and truth need to be replaced or reinterpreted by more pragmatic, ethnocentric notions.

Bertrand Russell, who was born in England in 1872 and studied and taught at Cambridge University, was one of the great philosophers in the 20th century. His work covers virtually all areas of philosophical inquiry, from logic through philosophy of language and philosophy of mind to ethics. He died in 1970 at the age of 97. In this defense of the correspondence theory of truth, Russell first distinguishes knowledge by acquaintance (for example, knowledge by experience or from appearances, such as "I seem to see a red book" or "I am in pain") from knowledge by description (knowledge of propositional truths—e.g., your knowing that you are seeing a red book or that you're in pain). Knowledge by acquaintance (knowledge of things), according to Russell, is infallible, for believing makes the proposition true. But descriptive beliefs have no such guarantee. They could be wrong. Thus, descriptive knowledge is *dualist* or *bipolar*—it has the properties of Truth and Falsity (or "Error") as opposites.

THE PROBLEMS OF PHILOSOPHY

Our knowledge of truths, unlike our knowledge of things, has an opposite, namely *error*. So far as things are concerned, we may know them or not know them, but there is no positive state of mind which can be described as erroneous knowledge of things, so long, at any rate, as we confine ourselves to knowledge by acquaintance. Whatever we are acquainted with must be something: we may draw wrong inference from our acquaintance, but the acquaintance itself cannot be deceptive. Thus there is no dualism as regards acquaintance. But as regards knowledge of truths, there is a dualism. We may believe what is false as well as what is true. We know that on very many subjects different people hold different and incompatible opinions: hence some beliefs must be erroneous. Since erroneous beliefs are often held just as strongly as true beliefs, it becomes a difficult question how they are to be distinguished from true beliefs. How are we to know, in a given case, that our belief is not erroneous? That is a question of

From: Bertrand Russell, *The Problems of Philosophy* (Oxford, UK: Oxford University Press, 1912). Reprinted by permission of Oxford University Press.

the very greatest difficulty, to which no completely satisfactory answer is possible. There is however, a preliminary question which is rather less difficult, and that is: What do we *mean* by truth and falsehood?

Seeking to develop a theory of the truth, Russell now turns to this question: What is truth? He begins by stating three conditions an adequate theory of truth must meet.[1]

There are three points to observe in the attempt to discover the nature of truth, three requisites which any theory must fulfill.

(1) Our theory of truth must be such as to admit of its opposite, falsehood. A good many philosophers have failed adequately to satisfy this condition: they have constructed theories according to which all our thinking ought to have been true, and have then had the greatest difficulty in finding a place for falsehood. In this respect our theory of belief must differ from our theory of acquaintance, since in the case of acquaintance it was not necessary to take account of any opposite.

(2) It seems fairly evident that if there were no beliefs there could be no falsehood, and no truth either, in the sense in which truth is correlative to falsehood. If we imagine a world of mere matter, there would be no room for falsehood in such a world, and although it would contain what may be called "facts," it would not contain any truths, in the sense in which truths are things of the same kind as falsehoods. In fact, truth and falsehood are properties of beliefs and statements: hence a world of mere matter, since it would contain no beliefs or statements, would also contain no truth or falsehood.

(3) But, as against what we have just said, it is to be observed that the truth or falsehood of a belief always depends upon something which lies outside the belief itself. If I believe that Charles I died on the scaffold, I believe truly, not because of any intrinsic quality of my belief, which could be discovered by merely examining the belief, but because of an historical event which happened two and a half centuries ago. If I believe that Charles I died in his bed, I believe falsely: no degree of vividness in my belief, or of care in arriving at it, prevents it from being false, again because of what happened long ago, and not because of any intrinsic property of my belief. Hence, although truth and falsehood are properties of beliefs, they are properties dependent upon the relations of the beliefs to other things, not upon any internal quality of the beliefs.

We may call these three conditions (1) the *bipolarity condition* (every proposition is either true or false), (2) the *belief condition*, and (3) the *realism condition* (the truth or falsity of belief depends on something that lies outside the belief itself). Russell next shows how this third feature distinguishes the correspondence theory of truth from one of its rivals, the **coherence theory of truth.**

The third of the above requisites leads us to adopt the view—which has on the whole been commonest among philosophers—that truth consists in some form of correspondence between belief and fact. It is, however, by no means an easy matter to discover a form of correspondence to which there are no irrefutable objections. By this partly—and partly by the feeling that, if truth consists in a correspondence of thought with something outside thought, thought can never know when truth has been attained—many philosophers have been led to try to find some definition of truth which shall not consist in relation to something wholly outside belief. The most important attempt at a definition of this sort is the theory that truth consists in *coherence*. It is said that the mark of falsehood is failure to cohere in the body of our beliefs, and that it is the essence of a truth to form part of the completely rounded system which is The Truth.

There is, however, a great difficulty in this view, or rather two great difficulties. The first is that there is no reason to suppose that only one coherent body of beliefs is possible. It may be that, with sufficient imagination, a novelist might invent a past for the world that would perfectly fit on to what we know, and yet be quite different from the real past. In more scientific matters, it is certain that there are often two or more hypotheses which account for all the known facts on some subject, and although, in such cases, men of science endeavor to find facts which will rule out all the hypotheses except one, there is no reason why they should always succeed.

In philosophy, again, it seems not uncommon for two rival hypotheses to be both able to account for all the facts. Thus, for example, it is possible that life is one long dream, and that the outer world has only that degree of reality that the objects of dreams have; but although such a view does not seem inconsistent with known facts, there is no reason to prefer it to the common-sense view, according to which other people and things do really exist. Thus coherence as the definition of truth fails because there is no proof that there can be only one coherent system.

The other objection to this definition of truth is that it assumes the meaning of "coherence" known, whereas, in fact, "coherence" presupposes the truth of the laws of logic. Two propositions are coherent when both may be true, and are incoherent when one at least must be false. Now in order to know whether two propositions can both be true, we must know such truths as the law of contradiction. For example, the two propositions "this tree is a beech" and "this tree is not a beech," are not coherent, because of the law of contradiction. But if the law of contradiction itself were subjected to the test of coherence, we should find that, if we choose to suppose it false, nothing will any longer be incoherent with anything else. Thus the laws of logic supply the skeleton or framework within which the test of coherence applies, and they themselves cannot be established by this test.

For the above reasons, coherence cannot be accepted as giving the *meaning* of truth, though it is often a most important *test* of truth after a certain amount of truth has become known.

Hence we are driven back to *correspondence with fact* as constituting the nature of truth. It remains to define precisely what we mean by "fact," and what is the nature of the correspondence which must subsist between belief and fact, in order that belief may be true.

In accordance with our three requisites, we have to seek a theory of truth which (1) allows truth to have an opposite, namely falsehood, (2) makes truth a property of beliefs, but (3) makes it a property wholly dependent upon the relation of the beliefs to outside things.

Russell now returns to his discussion of the correspondence theory, focusing on the example from Shakespeare's *Othello*, of Othello believing falsely that Desdemona loves Cassio.

The necessity of allowing for falsehood makes it impossible to regard belief as a relation of the mind to a single object, which could be said to be what is believed. If belief were so regarded, we should find that, like acquaintance, it would not admit of the opposition of truth and falsehood, but would have to be always true. This may be made clear by examples. Othello believes falsely that Desdemona loves Cassio. We cannot say that this belief consists in a relation to a single object, "Desdemona's love for Cassio," for if there were such an object, the belief would be true. There is in fact no such object, and therefore Othello cannot have any relation to such an object. Hence his belief cannot possibly consist in a relation to this object.

It might be said that his belief is a relation to a different object, namely "that Desdemona loves Cassio"; but it is almost as difficult to suppose that there is such an object as this, when Desdemona does not love Cassio, as it was to suppose that there is "Desdemona's love for Cassio." Hence it will be better to seek for a theory of belief which does not make it consist in a relation of the mind to a single object.

It is common to think of relations as though they always held between *two* terms, but in fact this is not always the case. Some relations demand three terms, some four, and so on. Take, for instance, the relation "between." So long as only two terms come in, the relation "between" is impossible: three terms are the smallest number that render it possible. York is between London and Edinburgh; but if London and Edinburgh were the only places in the world, there could be nothing which was between one place and another. Similarly *jealousy* requires three people: there can be no such relation that does not involve three at least. Such a proposition as "A wishes B to promote C's marriage with D" involves a relation of four terms: that is to say, A and B and C and D all come in, and the relation involved cannot be expressed otherwise than in a form involving all four. Instances might be multiplied indefinitely, but enough has been said to show that there are relations which require more than two terms before they can occur.

The relation involved in *judging* or *believing* must, if falsehood is to be duly allowed for, be taken to be a relation between several terms, not between two. When Othello believes that Desdemona loves Cassio, he must not have before his mind a single object, "Desdemona's love for Cassio," or "that Desdemona loves Cassio," for that would require that there should be objective falsehoods, which subsist independently of any minds; and this, though not logically refutable, is a theory to be avoided if possible. Thus it is easier to account for falsehood if we take judgment to be a relation in which the mind and the various objects concerned all occur severally; that is to say, Desdemona and loving and Cassio must all be terms in the relation which subsists when Othello believes that Desdemona loves Cassio. This relation, therefore, is a relation of four terms, since Othello also is one of the terms of the relation. When we say that it is a relation of four terms, we do not mean that Othello has a certain relation to Desdemona, and has the same relation to loving and also to Cassio. This may be true of some other relation than believing; but believing, plainly, is not a relation which Othello has to *each* of the three terms concerned, but to *all* of them together: there is only one example of the relation of believing involved, but this one example knits together four terms. Thus the actual occurrence, at the moment when Othello is entertaining his belief, is that the relation called "believing" is knitting together into one complex whole the four terms Othello, Desdemona, loving, and Cassio. What is called belief or judgment is nothing but this relation of believing or judging, which relates a mind to several things other than itself. An *act* of belief or of judgment is the occurrence between certain terms at some particular time, of the relation of believing or judging.

We are now in a position to understand what it is that distinguishes a true judgment from a false one. For this purpose we will adopt certain definitions. In every act of judgment there is a mind which judges, and there are terms concerning which it judges. We will call the mind the *subject* in the judgment, and the remaining terms the *objects*. Thus, when Othello judges that Desdemona loves Cassio, Othello is the subject, while the objects are Desdemona and loving and Cassio. The subject and the objects together are called the *constituents* of the judgment. It will be observed that the relation of judging has what is called a "sense" or "direction." We may say, metaphorically, that it puts its objects in a certain *order,* which we may indicate by means of the order of the words in the sentence.... Othello's judgment that Cassio loves Desdemona differs from his judgment that Desdemona loves Cassio, in spite of the fact that it consists of the same constituents, because the relation of judging places the constituents in a different order in the two cases. Similarly, if Cassio judges that Desdemona loves Othello, the constituents of the judgment are still the same, but their order is different. This property of having a "sense" or "direction" is one which the relation of judging shares with all other relations....

We spoke of the relation called "judging" or "believing" as knitting together into one complex whole the subject and the objects. In this respect, judging is exactly like every other relation. Whenever a relation holds between two or more terms, it unites the terms into a complex whole. If Othello loves Desdemona, there is such a complex whole as "Othello's love for Desdemona." The terms united by the relation may be themselves complex, or may be simple, but the whole which results from their being united must be complex. Wherever there is a relation which relates certain terms, there is a complex object formed of the union of those terms; and conversely, wherever there is a complex object, there is a relation which relates its constituents. When an act of believing occurs, there is a complex, in which "believing" is the uniting relation, and subject and objects are arranged in a certain order by the "sense" of the relation of believing. Among the objects, as we saw in considering "Othello believes that Desdemona loves Cassio," one must be a relation—in this instance, the relation "loving." But this relation, as it occurs in the act of believing, is not the relation which creates the unity of the complex whole consisting of the subject and the objects. The relation "loving," as it occurs in the act of believing, is one of the objects—it is a brick in the structure, not the cement. The cement is the relation "believing." When the belief is *true,* there is another complex unity, in which the relation which was one of the objects of the belief relates the other objects. Thus, e.g., if Othello believes *truly* that Desdemona loves Cassio, then there is a complex unity, "Desdemona's love for Cassio," which is composed exclusively of the *objects* of the belief, in the same order as they had in the belief, with the relation which was one of the objects occurring now as the cement that binds together the other objects of the belief. On the other hand, when a belief is *false,* there is no such complex unity composed only of the objects of the belief. If Othello believes *falsely* that Desdemona loves Cassio, then there is no such complex unity as "Desdemona's love for Cassio."

Thus a belief is *true* when it *corresponds* to a certain associated complex, and *false* when it does not. Assuming, for the sake of definiteness, that the objects of the belief are two terms and a relation, the terms being put in a certain order by the "sense" of the believing, then if the two terms in that order are united by the relation into a complex, the belief is true; if not, it is false. This constitutes the definition of truth and falsehood that we were in search of. Judging or believing is a certain complex unity of which a mind is a constituent; if the remaining constituents, taken in the order which they have in the belief, form a complex unity, then the belief is true; if not, it is false.

Thus although truth and falsehood are properties of beliefs, yet they are in a sense extrinsic properties, for the condition of the truth of a belief is something not involving beliefs, or (in general) any mind at all, but only the *objects* of the belief. A mind, which believes, believes truly when there is a *corresponding* complex not involving the mind, but only its objects. This correspondence ensures truth, and its absence entails falsehood. Hence we account simultaneously for the two facts that beliefs (*a*) depend on minds for their *existence,* (*b*) do not depend on minds for their *truth.*

We may restate our theory as follows: If we take such a belief as "Othello believes that Desdemona loves Cassio," we will call Desdemona and Cassio the *object-terms,* and loving the *object-relation.* If there is a complex unity "Desdemona's love for Cassio," consisting of the object-terms related by the object-relation in the same order as they have in the belief, then this complex unity is called the *fact corresponding to the belief.* Thus a belief is true when there is a corresponding fact, and is false when there is no corresponding fact....

...Minds do not *create* truth or falsehood. They create beliefs, but when once the beliefs are created, the mind cannot make them true or false, except in the special case where they concern future things which are within the power of the person believing, such as catching trains. What makes a belief true is a *fact,* and this fact does not (except in exceptional cases) in any way involve the mind of the person who has the belief.

The key idea is that beliefs are true when they *correspond* to the facts and false when they do not. Thus, we cannot say that "facts are true (or false)." Facts just are; they are what make beliefs true or false, depending on whether the beliefs are related to them in the right way.

What do you thing of Russell's logic? Do you agree that the correspondence metaphor captures our intuitive idea of truth better than the idea of coherence? Does it seem commonsensical? But there is another way to look at truth.

The Pragmatic Theory of Truth

This other way is called the **pragmatic theory of truth.** First, we turn to a defense of it in the form of William James's classical statement and, second, in Richard Rorty's discussion of Truth in *Philosophy and the Mirror of Nature* (1979) and his essay "Science and Solidarity." Here is the classical passage from James.

PRAGMATISM: A NEW NAME FOR SOME OLD WAYS OF THINKING

Pragmatism's Conception of Truth

I fully expect to see the pragmatist view of truth run through the classic stages of a theory's career. First, you know, a new theory is attacked as absurd; then it is admitted to be true, but obvious and insignificant; finally it is seen to be so important that its adversaries claim that they themselves discovered it. Our doctrine of truth is at present in the first of these three stages, with symptoms of the second stage having begun in certain quarters. I wish that this lecture might help it beyond the first stage in the eyes of many of you.

Truth, as any dictionary will tell you, is a property of certain of our ideas. It means their "agreement," as falsity means their "disagreement," with "reality." Pragmatists and intellectualists both accept this definition as a matter of course. They begin to quarrel only after the question is raised as to what may precisely be meant by the term "agreement," and what by the term "reality," when reality is taken as something for our ideas to agree with.

In answering these questions the pragmatists are more analytic and painstaking, the intellectualists more offhand and irreflective. The popular notion is that a true idea must copy its reality. Like other popular views, this one follows the analogy of the most usual experience. Our true ideas of sensible things do indeed copy them. Shut your eyes and think of yonder clock on the wall, and you get just such a true picture or copy of its dial. But your idea of its "works" (unless you are a clockmaker) is much less of a copy, yet it passes muster, for it in no way clashes with the reality. Even though it should shrink to the mere word "works," that word still serves you truly; and when you speak of the "time-keeping function" of the clock, or of its spring's "elasticity," it is hard to see exactly what your ideas can copy.

You perceive that there is a problem here. Where our ideas cannot copy definitely their object, what does agreement with that object mean? Some idealists seem to say that they are true whenever they are what God means that we ought to think about that subject. Others hold the copy-view all through, and speak as if our ideas possessed truth just in proportion as they approach to being copies of the Absolute's eternal way of thinking.

These views, you see, invite pragmatistic discussion. But the great assumption of the intellectualists is that truth means essentially an inert static relation. When you've got your true idea of anything, there's an end of the matter. You're in possession; you *know;* you have fulfilled your thinking destiny. You are where you ought to be mentally; you have obeyed your categorical imperative; and nothing more need follow on that climax of your rational destiny. Epistemologically you are in stable equilibrium.

Pragmatism, on the other hand, asks its usual question. "Grant an idea or belief to be true," it says, "what concrete difference will its being true make in any one's actual life? How will the truth be realized? What experiences will be different from those which

From: William James, *Pragmatism: A New Name for Some Old Ways of Thinking* (New York: Haefner, 1907).

would obtain if the belief were false? What, in short, is the truth's cash-value in experiential terms?

The moment pragmatism asks this question, it sees the answer: *True ideas are those that we can assimilate, validate, corroborate and verify. False ideas are those that we cannot.* That is the practical difference it makes to us to have true ideas; that, therefore, is the meaning of truth, for it is all that truth is known-as.

This thesis is what I have to defend. The truth of an idea is not a stagnant property inherent in it. Truth *happens* to an idea. It *becomes* true, is *made* true by events. Its verity *is* in fact an event, a process: the process namely of its verifying itself, its veri-*fication*. Its validity is the process of its valid-*ation*.

But what do the words verification and validation themselves pragmatically mean? They again signify certain practical consequences of the verified and validated idea. It is hard to find any one phrase that characterizes these consequences better than the ordinary agreement-formula—just such consequences being what we have in mind whenever we say that our ideas "agree" with reality. They lead us, namely, through the acts and other ideas which they instigate, into or up to, or towards, other parts of experience with which we feel all the while—such feeling being among our potentialities—that the original ideas remain in agreement. The connexions and transitions come to us from point to point as being progressive, harmonious, satisfactory. This function of agreeable leading is what we mean by an idea's verification.

Rather than see truth as a correspondence between fact and a statement about the fact, James thinks truth is a practical concept: "True ideas are those that we can assimilate, validate, corroborate and verify. False ideas are those that we cannot. That is the practical difference it makes to us to have true ideas."

Next we turn to the successor of James, Richard Rorty, a professor at Stanford University. Rorty is the author of several works, including *Philosophy and the Mirror of Nature* (1979), and he argues that truth means, not what corresponds to the facts, but what it is *better* for us to believe. Later in the book, he describes truth as "what you can defend against all comers, . . . what our peers will [all things considered] let us get away with saying." In this passage, he defends the thesis that we should give up metaphysical and epistemological notions of reality and truth in favor of those built on ethnocentric solidarity.

PHILOSOPHY AND THE MIRROR OF NATURE

Epistemological Pragmatism

Quine asks how an anthropologist is to discriminate the sentences to which natives invariably and wholeheartedly assent into contingent empirical platitudes on the one hand and necessary conceptual truths on the other. Sellars asks how the authority of first-person reports of, for example, how things appear to us, the pains from which we suffer, and the thoughts that drift before our minds differ from the authority of expert reports on, for example, metal stress, the mating behavior of birds, or the colors of physical objects. We can lump both questions together and simply ask, "How do our peers know which of our assertions to take our word for and which to look for further confirmation of?" It would seem enough for our peers to believe there to be no better way of finding out our inner states than from our reports, without their knowing what "lies behind" our making them. It would also seen enough for *us* to know that our peers have this acquiescent attitude. That alone seems sufficient for that inner certainty about our inner states which the tradition has explained by "immediate presence to consciousness," "sense of evidence," and other expressions of the assumption that reflections in the Mirror of Nature are intrinsically better known than nature itself. For Sellars, the certainty of "I have a pain" is a reflection of the fact that nobody cares to question it, not conversely. Just so, for Quine, the certainty of "All men are animals," and of "There have been some black dogs." Quine thinks that the "meanings" drop out as wheels that are not part of the mechanisms, and Sellars thinks the same of "self-authenticating non-verbal episodes." More broadly, if assertions are justified by society rather than by the character of the inner representations they express, then there is no point in attempting to isolate *privileged* representation.

Explaining rationality and epistemic authority by reference to what society lets us say, rather than the latter by the former, is the essence of what I call "epistemic behaviorism," an attitude common to Dewey and Wittgenstein. This sort of behaviorism can best be seen as a species of holism—but one which requires no idealist metaphysical underpinnings. It claims that if we understand the rules of a language-game, we understand all that there is to understand about why moves in that language-game are made ... If we are behaviorists in this sense, then it will not occur to us to invoke either of the traditional Kantian distinctions. But can we just go ahead and be behaviorists? Or, as Quine and Sellar's critics suggest, doesn't behaviorism simply beg the question? Is there any reason to think that fundamental epistemic notions *should* be explicated in behavioral terms?

The last question comes down to: Can we treat the study of "the nature of human knowledge" just as the study of certain ways in which human beings interact, or does it require an ontological foundation (involving some specific philosophical way of describing human beings)? Shall we take "S knows that p" (or "S knows noninferentially that p," or "S believes incorrigibly that p," or "S's knowledge that p is certain") as a remark about the status of S's reports among his peers, or shall we take it as a remark about the relation between subject and object, between nature and its mirror? The first alternative leads to a pragmatic view of truth and a therapeutic approach to ontology (in which philosophy can straighten out pointless quarrels between common sense and science, but not contribute any arguments of its own for the existence or [non]existence of something). Thus for Quine, a necessary truth is just a statement such that nobody has given us any interesting alternatives which would lead us to question it. For Sellars, to say that a report of a passing thought is incorrigible is to say that nobody has yet suggested a good way of predicting and controlling human behavior which does not take sincere first-person contemporary reports of thoughts at face-value. The second alternative leads to "ontological" explanations of the relations between minds and meanings, minds and immediate data of awareness, universals and particulars, thought and language, consciousness and brains, and so on. For philosophers like Chisholm and Bergmann, such explanations *must* be attempted if the realism of common sense is to be preserved. The aim of all such explanations is to make truth something more than what Dewey called "warranted assertability": more than what our peers will, *ceteris paribus,* let us get away with saying. Such explanations, when ontological, usually take the form of a redescription of the object of knowledge so as to "bridge the gap" between it and the knowing subject. To choose between these approaches is to choose between truth as "what it is good for us to believe" and truth as "contact with reality."

Do you see what Rorty is getting at? There is a lot going on here, but two points stand out. First, even if we accept the idea of objective truth, we can never be certain that we have the final truth on any interesting issue. When we accept a statement or theory as "true," we are simply indicating that our culture has decided not to question that statement or theory any further for the moment. But we can always revise our beliefs in the light of new evidence or interests. Second, since interpretation is a product of our culture and our interests, there is no "God's eye," an impartial perspective from which to judge the world. All perception is interest relative. The farmer, real estate dealer, and artist looking at the "the same field" see radically different things.

Rorty continues his attack on the correspondence theory of truth and begins to argue against the subject–object distinction. He sides with the philosopher of science Thomas Kuhn in arguing that we can have no theory-independent notion of reality and proposes to erase the essential difference between science and the humanities and arts. Embracing the title of "the new fuzzies," Rorty proposes that a notion of social solidarity replace the enlightenment notion of objective truth. He begins by pointing out that the idea of rationality is bound up with science. He wants to reject this equation or privileged role of science, allowing for equal status to the humanities and arts.

SCIENCE AND SOLIDARITY

In our culture, the notions of "science," "rationality," "objectivity" and "truth" are bound up with one another. Science is thought of as offering "hard," "objective" truth—truth as correspondence to reality, the only sort of truth worthy of the name. Humanists—philosophers, theologians, historians, literary critics—have to worry about whether they are being "scientific"—whether they are entitled to think of their conclusions, no matter how carefully argued, as worthy of the term "true." We tend to identify seeking "objective truth" with "using reason," and so we think of the natural sciences as paradigms of rationality. We also think of rationality as a matter of following procedures laid down in advance, of being "methodical." So we tend to use "methodical," "rational," "scientific" and "objective" as synonyms.

Worries about "cognitive status" and "objectivity" are characteristic of a secularized culture in which the scientist replaces the priest. The scientist is now seen as the person who keeps humanity in touch with something beyond itself. As the universe was depersonalized, beauty (and, in time, even moral goodness) came to be thought of as "subjective." So truth is now thought of as the only point at which human beings are responsible to something nonhuman. A commitment to "rationality" and to "method" is thought to be a recognition of this responsibility. The scientist becomes a moral exemplar, one who selflessly exposes himself again and again to the hardness of facts.

One result of this way of thinking is that any academic discipline which wants a place at the trough, but is unable to offer the predictions and the technology provided by the natural sciences, must either pretend to imitate science or find some way of obtaining "cognitive status" without the necessity of discovering facts. Practitioners of these disciplines must either affiliate themselves with this quasi-priestly order by using terms like "behavioral sciences" or else find something other than "fact" to be concerned with. People in the humanities typically choose the latter strategy. They describe themselves either as concerned with "values" as opposed to facts, or as developing and inculcating habits of "critical reflection."

Rorty suggests that this kind of rhetoric, the opposing hard facts to soft values, is misleading and that it is better to make a different kind of distinction: between two senses of "rationality."[2]

To get to such a way of thinking we can start by distinguishing two senses of the term "rationality." In one sense, the one I have already discussed, to be rational is to be methodical: that is, to have criteria for success laid down in advance. We think of poets and painters as using some other faculty than "reason" in their work because, by their own confession, they are not sure of what they want to do before they have done it. They make up new standards of achievement as they go along. By contrast, we think of judges as knowing in advance what criteria a brief will have to satisfy in order to invoke a favorable decision, and of businessmen as setting well-defined goals and being judged by their success in achieving them. Law and business are good examples of rationality, but the scientist, knowing in advance what would count as disconfirming his hypothesis and prepared to abandon that hypothesis as a result of the unfavorable outcome of a single experiment, seems a truly heroic example. Further, we seem to have a clear criterion of the success of a scientific theory—namely, its ability to predict, and thereby to enable us to control some portion of the world. If to be rational means to be able to lay down criteria in advance, then it is plausible to take natural science as the paradigm of rationality.

The trouble is that in this sense of "rational" the humanities are never going to qualify as rational activities. If the humanities are concerned with ends rather than means, then there is no way to evaluate their success in terms of antecedently specified criteria. If we already knew what criteria we wanted to satisfy, we would not worry about whether we were pursuing the right ends. If we thought we knew the goals of culture and society in advance, we would have no use for the humanities—as totalitarian societies in fact do not. It is characteristic of democracies and pluralistic societies to redefine their goals continually. But if to be rational means to satisfy criteria, then this process of redefinition will be bound to be non-rational. So if the humanities are to be viewed as rational activities, rationality will have to be thought of as something other than the satisfaction of criteria which are statable in advance.

[The second] meaning of "rational" is, in fact, available. In this sense, the word means something like "sane" or "reasonable" rather than "methodical." It names a set of moral virtues: tolerance, respect for the opinion of those around one, willingness to listen, reliance on persuasion rather than force. These are the virtues which members of a civilized society must possess if the society is to endure. In this sense of "rational," the word means something more like "civilized" than like "methodical." When so construed, the distinction between the rational and the irrational has nothing in particular to do with the difference between the arts and the sciences. On this construction, to be rational is simply to discuss any topic—religious, literary, or scientific—in a way which eschews dogmatism, defensiveness, and righteous indignation.

There is no problem about whether, in this latter, weaker sense the humanities are "rational disciplines." Usually humanists display the moral virtues in question. Sometimes they do not, but then sometimes scientists don't either. Yet these moral virtues are felt to be not enough. Both humanists and the public hanker after rationality in the first, stronger sense of the term: a sense which is associated with objective truth, correspondence to reality, method and criteria.

We should not try to satisfy this hankering, but rather try to eradicate it. No matter what one's opinion of the secularization of culture, it was a mistake to try to make the natural scientist into a new sort of priest, a link between the human and the non-human. So was the idea that some sorts of truths are "objective" whereas others are merely "subjective" or "relative"—the attempt to divide up the set of true sentences into "genuine knowledge" and "mere opinion," or into the "factual" and the "judgmental." So was the idea that the scientist has a special method which, if only the humanists would apply it to ultimate values, would give us the same kind of self-confidence about moral ends as we now have about technological means. I think that we should content ourselves with the second, "weaker" conception of rationality and avoid the first, "stronger" conception. We should avoid the idea that there is some special virtue in knowing in advance what criteria you are going to satisfy, in having standards by which to measure progress.

Having rejected the correspondence theory of truth and the idea of methodological rationality for the weaker notion of reasonableness, Rorty applies these points to the question of rationality in science. He refers to Kuhn's monumental *The Structure of Scientific Revolutions* in which Kuhn argues that scientists change their theories because of nonrational paradigm shifts (somewhat like religious conversions), rather than because of purely methodological reason.

What I am calling "pragmatism" might also be called "left-wing Kuhnianism." It has also been rather endearingly called (by one of its critics, Clark Glymour) "the new fuzziness," because it is an attempt to blur just those distinctions between the objective and the subjective and between fact and value which the criterial conception of rationality has developed. We fuzzies would like to substitute the idea of "unforced agreement" for that of "objectivity." We should like to put all culture on an epistemological level (or get rid of the idea of "epistemological level") . . . On our view, "truth" is a univocal term. It applies equally to the judgments of lawyers, anthropologists, physicists, philologists and literary critics. There is point in assigning degrees of "objectivity" or "hardness" to such disciplines. For the presence of unforced agreement in all of them gives us everything in the way of "objective truth" which one could possibly want: namely, intersubjective agreement.

Having set forth his pragmatic notion of truth as unforced intersubjective agreement, Rorty defends himself against the objection that he is a relativist and clarifies his thesis as based on solidarity, not objectivity.

As soon as one says that all there is to objectivity is intersubjectivity, one is likely to be accused of being a relativist. That is the epithet traditionally applied to pragmatists. But this epithet is ambiguous. It can name any of three different views. [1] the silly and self-refuting view that every belief is as good as every other. [2] the wrong-headed view that "true" is an equivocal term, having as many meanings as there are contexts of justification. [3] the ethnocentric view that there is nothing to be said about either truth or rationality apart from descriptions of the familiar procedures of justification which a given society—*ours*—uses in one or another area of inquiry. The pragmatist does hold this third, ethnocentric view. But he does not hold the first or the second view of relativism.

But "relativism" is not an appropriate term to describe this sort of ethnocentricism. For we pragmatists are not holding a positive theory which says that something is relative to something else. Instead, we are making the purely *negative* point that we would be better off without the traditional distinctions between knowledge and opinion, construed as the distinction between truth as correspondence to reality and truth as a commendatory term for well-justified beliefs. Our opponents call this negative claim "relativistic" because they cannot imagine that anybody would seriously deny that truth has an intrinsic nature. So when we say that there is nothing to be said about truth save that each of us will commend as true those beliefs which he finds good to believe, the realist is inclined to interpret this as one more positive theory about the nature of truth: a theory according to which truth is simply the contemporary opinion of a chosen individual or group. Such a theory would, of course, be self-refuting. But we pragmatists do not have a theory of truth, much less a relativistic one. As partisans of solidarity, our account of the value of cooperative human enquiry has only an *ethical base,* not an epistemological or metaphysical one.

To say that we must be ethnocentric may sound suspicious, but this will only happen if we identify ethnocentricism with pig-headed refusal to talk to representatives of other communities. In my sense of ethnocentrism, to be ethnocentric is simply to work by our own lights. The defense of ethnocentrism is simply that there are no other lights to work by. Beliefs suggested by another individual or another culture must be tested by trying to weave them together with beliefs which we already have . . .

This way of thinking runs counter to the attempts, familiar since the eighteenth century, to think of political liberalism as based on a conception of the nature of man. To most thinkers of the Enlightenment, it seemed clear that the access to Nature which physical science had provided should now be followed by the establishment of social, political and economic institutions which were "in accordance with Nature." Ever since, liberal social thought has centered around social reform as made possible by objective knowledge of what human beings are like—not knowledge of what Greeks or Frenchmen or Chinese are like, but of humanity as such. This tradition dreams of a universal human community which will exhibit a non-parochial solidarity because it is the expression of an ahistorical human nature.

Philosophers who belong to this tradition, who wish to ground solidarity in objectivity, have to construe truth as correspondence to reality. So they must construct an epistemology which has room for a kind of justification which is not merely social but natural, springing from human nature itself, and made possible by a link between that part of nature and the rest of nature. By contrast we pragmatists, who wish to reduce objectivity to solidarity, do not require either a metaphysics or an epistemology ... We see the gap between truth and justification not as something to be bridged by isolating a natural and trans-cultural sort of rationality which can be used to criticize certain cultures and praise others, but simply as the gap between the actual good and the possible better. From a pragmatist point of view, to say that what is rational for us now to believe may not be *true,* is simply to say that somebody may come up with a better idea....

To drop the criterial conception of rationality in favor of the pragmatist conception would be to give up the idea of Truth as something to which we were responsible. Instead we should think of "true" as a word which applies to those beliefs upon which we are able to agree, as roughly synonymous with "justified" ...

Pragmatists would like to replace the desire for objectivity—the desire to be in touch with a reality which is more than some community with which we identify ourselves—with the desire for solidarity with that community. They think that the habits of relying on persuasion rather than force, of respect for opinions of colleagues, of curiosity and eagerness for new data and ideas, are the *only* virtues which scientists have. They do not think that there is an intellectual virtue called "rationality" over and above these moral virtues....

Finally, Rorty defends his pragmatism against objectivists by appealing to a thought experiment.

Imagine that a few years from now you open your copy of the *New York Times* and read that the philosophers, in convention assembled, have unanimously agreed that values are objective, science rational, truth a matter of correspondence to reality, etc. Recent breakthroughs in semantics and meta-ethics, the report goes on, have caused the last remaining non-cognitivists in ethics to recant. Similarly breakthroughs in the philosophy of science have led Kuhn formally to abjure his claim that there is no theory-independent way to reconstruct statements about what is "really there." All the new fuzzies have repudiated all their former views. By way of making amends for the intellectual confusion which the philosophical profession has recently caused, the philosophers have adopted a short, crisp set of standards of rationality and morality. Next year the convention is expected to adopt the report of the committee charged with formulating a standard of aesthetic taste.

Surely the public reaction to this would not be "Saved!" but rather "Who on earth do these philosophers think they *are*?" It is one of the best things about the form of intellectual life we Western liberals lead that this *would* be our reaction. No matter how much we moan about the disorder and confusion of the current philosophical scene, about the treason of the clerks, we do not really want things any other way. What prevents us from relaxing and enjoying the new fuzziness is perhaps no more than cultural lag, the fact that the rhetoric of the Enlightenment praised the emerging natural sciences in a vocabulary which was left over from a less liberal and tolerant era. This rhetoric enshrined all the old philosophical opposition between mind and world, appearance and reality, subject and object, truth and pleasure. Dewey thought that it was the continued prevalence of such opposition which prevented us from seeing that modern science was a new and promising invention, a way of life which had not existed before and which ought to be encouraged and imitated, something which required a new rhetoric rather than justification by an old one.

On the other hand, suppose that his "new fuzzy" position is the right one (true?), what would "the rhetoric of the culture, and in particular, the humanities, sound like"? It would be more like the way Kuhn describes science as involving paradigm shifts and concrete agreement in interpretation and less like methodological rhetoric.

There would be less talk about rigor and more about originality. The image of the great scientist would not be of somebody who got it right but of somebody who made it new. The new rhetoric would draw more on the vocabulary of Romantic poetry and socialist politics, and less on that of Greek metaphysics, religious morality or Enlightenment scientism. A scientist would rely on a sense of solidarity with the rest of her profession, rather than a picture of herself as battling through the veils of illusion, guided by the light of reason.

If all this happened, the term "science," and thus the opposition between the humanities, the arts and the sciences might gradually fade away. Once "science" was deprived of an honorific sense, we might not need it for taxonomy. . . . The people now called "scientists" would no longer think of themselves as members of a quasi-priestly order, nor would the public think of themselves as in the care of such an order.

In this situation, the "humanities" would no longer think of themselves as such, nor would they share a common rhetoric. Each of the disciplines which now fall under that rubric would worry as little about its method, cognitive status or "philosophical foundations" as do mathematics, civil engineering or sculpture. For terms which denoted disciplines would not be thought to divide "subject matter," chunks of the world which had "interfaces" with each other. Rather, they would be thought to denote communities whose boundaries were as fluid as the interests of their members. In this heyday of the fuzzies, there would be as little reason to be self-conscious about the nature and status of one's discipline as, in the ideal democratic community, about the nature and status of one's race or sex. For one's ultimate loyalty would be to the larger community which permitted and encouraged this kind of freedom and insouciance. This community would serve no higher end than its own preservation and self-improvement, the preservation and enhancement of civilization. It would identify rationality with that effort, rather than with the desire for objectivity. So it would feel no need for a foundation more solid than reciprocal loyalty.

Rorty has rejected the correspondence theory of truth because it implies a subject–object distinction, which he rejects. He claims his pragmatic considerations do not constitute a theory. What does this mean? Several questions arise: Isn't his discussion a defense of a different kind of theory? Isn't the idea that there is no objective truth or foundations of knowledge a theory in its own right? Suppose an opponent, say Bertrand Russell, asks Rorty and other pragmatists regarding their claim that "there are no objective truths." "Is that statement itself true? If it is true, then it is false, so it is false." How would pragmatists respond? Rorty wants to reject the fact–value distinction, but you may ask whether this is a sound maneuver. Can we ask, Is it true (objectively so) that there is no fact–value distinction? It seems like there is such a distinction: The statements "John took the money from the drawer" and "John's taking the money from the drawer was wrong" are very different kinds of sentences. Similarly, Rorty denies he is a relativist, but he surely seems to be a moral relativist—since morality resides in the ethnocentric community. My ethnocentric community may differ from yours. Some African tribal ethnocentric communities prescribe clitoridectomies, whereas mine condemns them. Are clitoridectomies bad things in my culture but good things in the African cultures? Likewise, he seems to be a cognitive relativist. If my community reaches a reasonable intersubjective agreement that the world is flat and yours that it is round, according to Rorty do both have truth? That surely seems like relativism. But does the shape of Earth depend on what either of our communities believe? Rorty says that "truth is what our peers . . . will let us get away with saying." As his peers, should we let him get away with that definition?

There are many challenging issues in Rorty's article, and perhaps he has answers to all of these questions. Perhaps he can accuse his opponent of presupposing the very idea that he is rejecting, namely, the subject–object distinction and the notion of objective truth. Perhaps, but unless he is supposing it, what sense does it make to argue about reality at all? Don't we need an idea that something independent of us exists even to bother to argue with another person? Finally, we must ask, Doesn't abolishing the subject–object distinction lead to solipsism—that the other and I are one? What could this mean? At this point, I must let you consider the pragmatist's challenge to objective thinking, to the idea of the correspondence notion of truth. You must consider "which is true?"

Summary

Two theories of truth compete in contemporary philosophy: the correspondence theory and the pragmatic theory. The correspondence theory, defended by Aristotle and Russell, holds that statements and beliefs are true if and only if they correspond to the facts. Statements and beliefs are false if they fail to correspond to the facts in question. This theory supposes a strong subject–object distinction: The knower is separate from what is known. The pragmatic theory of truth, defended by James and Rorty, defines truth as that which works, that which is defensible within a cultural context. All "truth" is interpretive rather than objective. Thus, a strong distinction between the subject and object is rejected. We cannot separate the knower from what is known.

FOR FURTHER REFLECTION

The Selections from Bertrand Russell and William James

1. What are the three conditions a theory of truth must meet? Do you agree with Russell here?

2. Explain Russell's critique of the coherence theory of truth.

3. What does Russell mean by saying "Minds do not create truth or falsehood"?

4. Is the correspondence theory of truth plausible? Do you think that it adequately conveys what we mean by "truth," or is something important left out? Explain your answer.

5. Some opponents of the correspondence theory say that it has a certain usefulness for trivial statements like "the cat is on the mat," where correspondence between words and things is plausible, but it loses its appeal when applied to more complex matters such as "there is no such thing as natural motion" or "the universe is infinite" (Rorty's examples). How would a defender of the correspondence theory respond to this criticism?

6. How does James define *true* and *false,* and how does his definition differ from the intellectualist (correspondence) definition? Does his dynamic idea of truth appeal to you? What are its strengths and weaknesses?

7. Suppose the Nazis had been successful in winning World War II. Would their theories be "true"? Is success or usefulness the correct criterion of the true?

8. James elsewhere (see Chapter 12) applied his ideas to religion and maintained that since religious beliefs were inspiring, we ought (or at least should be permitted) to believe them and make them true for ourselves. Do you agree with this? What if it turned out that the truth was bad news rather than good news ("badspel" instead of "gospel"). Would you still rather know it than believe an expedient and inspiring falsehood?

The Selections from Richard Rorty

1. What are Rorty's major motivations in rejecting the correspondence theory of truth and the subject–object distinction? Why does he think that the notion of intersubjective agreement (or unforced agreement) is a better idea? What are the strengths and weaknesses of Rorty's proposal?

2. Rorty distinguishes three types of relativism. What are they and which does he choose? Do you agree with his argument here? Explain your answer.

3. What does Rorty mean when he says that pragmatic truth has only an ethical base, not an epistemological or metaphysical one? What is his argument for this? Is it sound?

4. Has Rorty successfully eliminated metaphysical and epistemological notions? Has he argued successfully against the distinction between the ideas of objectivity and subjectivity and against the correspondence theory of truth? Critically discuss his argument.

5. Do you detect any hidden assumptions in this article? Who is the community that Rorty identifies with? What are its values? Does it include religious people? Conservatives? Socialists? Explain your answer.

6. Elsewhere Rorty describes "truth" as "what you can defend against all comers, . . . what our peers will, *ceteris paribus,* let us get away with saying."[3] Analyze this characterization of truth.

NOTES

1. All remaining passages in this section are from Bertrand Russell, *The Problem of Philosophy* (Oxford, UK: Oxford University Press, 1912). Reprinted by permission of Oxford University Press.

2. All remaining passages in this section are from Richard Rorty, "Science and Solidarity," in *Rhetoric of the Human Sciences: Language and Arguments in Scholarship and Public Affairs,* . . . , ed. J. Nelson et al. (Madison: University of Wisconsin Press, 1987). Reprinted by permission of University of Wisconsin Press.

3. Richard Rorty, *Philosophy and the Mirror of Nature* (Princeton, NJ: Princeton University Press, 1979), 176.

FOR FURTHER READING

Horwich, Paul. *Truth*. Oxford, UK: Basil Blackwell, 1990.

Johnson, Lawrence E. *Focusing on Truth*. London: Routledge, 1992.

Lawson, Hilary, and Lisa Appignanesi, eds. *Dismantling Truth*. London: Weidenfeld and Nicolson, 1989.

Newton-Smith, W. H. "Rationality, Truth, and the New Fuzzies: A Critique of Rorty's Dismantling of Truth." In *Philosophy: The Quest for Truth*, 3rd ed. Edited by Louis Pojman. Belmont, CA: Wadsworth, 1996.

Rorty, Richard. *Philosophy and the Mirror of Nature*. Princeton, NJ: Princeton University Press, 1979.

PART V

Metaphysics: Philosophy of Mind

19 ✻ What Am I? A Mind or a Body?

The curiosity of Man and the cunning of his Reason have revealed much of what Nature held hidden. The structure of spacetime, the constitution of matter, the many forms of energy, the nature of life itself; all of these mysteries have become open books to us. To be sure, deep questions remain unanswered and revolutions await us still, but it is difficult to exaggerate the explosion in scientific understanding we humans have fashioned over the past 500 years.

Despite this general advance, a central mystery remains largely a mystery: the nature of conscious intelligence.

Paul Churchland[1]

Intuitively, there seem to be two different types of reality: *material* and *mental.* There are bodies and minds. *Bodies* are solid, material entities, extended in three-dimensional space, publicly observable, measurable, and capable of causing things to happen in accordance with invariant laws of mechanics.

A *mind,* on the other hand, has none of these properties. Consciousness is not solid or material, is not extended in three-dimensional space, does not occupy space at all, is directly observable only by the person who owns it, cannot be measured, and seems incapable of causing things to happen in accordance with invariant laws of mechanics. Only the person himself can think his thoughts, feel his emotions, and suffer his pain. Although a neurosurgeon can open the skull and observe the brain, she cannot observe a person's mind or its beliefs, sensations, emotions, or desires.

Unlike physical bodies, mental entities have no shape, weight, length, width, height, color, mass, velocity, or temperature. It would sound odd, indeed, to speak of a belief weighing 10 pounds like a sack of potatoes, a feeling of love measuring 8-by-12 feet like a piece of carpet, a pain being as heavy as a cement bag, or a desire that was green and had a temperature of 103 degrees.

Yet common sense tells us that these two entities somehow interact. You step on a nail, and it pierces your skin, sending a message through your nervous system that results in something altogether different from the shape or size of the nail or skin, something that does not possess size or shape and that cannot be seen, smelled, tasted, or heard—a feeling of distress or pain. Whereas the nail is public, the pain is private.

On the other hand, your mind informs you that it would be a good thing to get a bandage to put over the cut that has resulted from stepping on the nail (maybe a tetanus shot, too); thus, the mind causes you to move your body. Your legs carry you to the medicine cabinet, where you stop, raise your arms and with your hands take hold of the cabinet door, open it and take the bandage out, and then apply it dexterously to the wound.

Here we have an instance where the body affects the mind and the mind in turn affects the body. Thus, common sense shows that a close interactive relationship exists between these two radically different entities. This position is called **dualistic interactionism:** The theory that the body, including the brain, and the mind are different substances that causally interact on each other.

We can represent it pictorially in the following manner: Let BS represent "brain state," MS represent "mental state," and ($\rightarrow$ represent "causation." The dualistic interactive process looks like this:

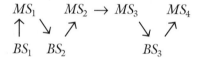

For example, stepping on the nail causes the first brain state (BS_1) that in turn causes the first mental state (MS_1—the feeling of pain in one's foot) that in turn causes us (via a brain state) to decide to move our foot (BS_2) that brings relief from the pain (MS_2) as well as the intention to get a bandage for our wound (MS_3) that leads to the brain state (BS_3) that causes us to move toward the first-aid kit in the bathroom. We are conscious of moving toward the bathroom (MS_4) that in turn leads to new brain states and bodily motions.

But the questions arise: Exactly how does this transaction between the mind and brain occur? *Where* does it occur? Or could it be, as materialists contend, that the mind is really simply a function of the body, not a separate substance at all? Or could the idealist monists be correct in asserting that the body is really an illusion and that there is only one substance, the mind alone? The following schema (Table 19.1) represents the three main positions discussed in this chapter. (We considered Berkeley's idealism in Part 4, so we need not deal with it here.) Both idealism and materialism are **monisms,** reducing all reality to one underlying substance. Dualism opposes both types of monism.

There are several types of dualism besides interactionism. The most notable is **epiphenomenalism,** which posits a one-way causal relationship: The body affects the mind, causing mental events, but the mind does not affect the body. Mental events are like the babbling of brooks, the exhaust from a car's engine, or the smoke from a train's chimneys. They are effects of physical processes but do not themselves cause motion in the water, the car, or the train. Epiphenomenalism is represented in the following schema:

Table 19.1

Theory	Nature of Substance	Philosophers	Religion
Dualistic interactionism	Mental and physical	Plato René Descartes John Locke John Eccles J. P. Moreland	Most Christian denominations
Idealist monism	Mental	George Berkeley	Hinduism Christian Science
Materialist monism	Physical	Thomas Hobbes Julien La Mettrie Bertrand Russell Paul Churchland Daniel Dennett Modern science	

$$MS_1 \qquad MS_2 \qquad MS_3$$
$$\uparrow \qquad\quad \uparrow \qquad\quad \uparrow$$
$$BS_1 \rightarrow BS_2 \rightarrow BS_3$$

There is also a view known as **parallelism,** which holds that there are two parallel realities: one mental and one physical, connected with human action. Gottfried Wilhelm Leibniz (1646–1716) held that God established two separate causal series that were set to run side by side, like two clocks, in a preestablished harmony so that it appears that they are related to each other:

$$MS_1 \rightarrow MS_2 \rightarrow MS_3 \rightarrow MS_4$$
$$BS_1 \rightarrow BS_2 \rightarrow BS_3 \rightarrow BS_4$$

Finally, there is a view called **panpsychism,** which holds that everything in nature has mind or a soul. Panpsychism is a correlate to **pantheism,** which holds that everything is God or contains God. According to panpsychism, there is soul or mind in the ultimate particles of physics and only because there is can we experience consciousness.

Materialism, the theory that matter and the laws of physics constitute ultimate reality, has several versions. The simplest is *metaphysical behaviorism,* which either denies the existence of mental events or denies their importance in understanding behavior. Metaphysical behaviorism should be distinguished from simple **behaviorism** (or *psychological behaviorism*), the psychological–scientific theory stating that science cannot and need not take introspective reports into consideration because they are too subjective for measurement. It need not deny the reality of mental events. Psychological behaviorism is not so much a theory about the mind–body problem as a theory about how to understand the language we use in describing mental events. All talk about beliefs, desires, and emotions should be set in terms of dispositions to behave.

Metaphysical behaviorism, however, goes beyond mere psychological behaviorism. It denies that there are any mental events. The American behaviorist John Watson (1878–1958) claimed that belief in consciousness is a product of superstition and magic: "No one has ever touched a soul, or seen one in a test tube, or has in any other way come into relationship with it as he has with the other objects of his daily experience."[2] Our belief in mental events is illusory. Metaphysical behaviorism and psychological behaviorism were prominent in the first half of the 20th century, but two strong objections have caused both positions to be virtually abandoned in philosophy of mind. First, a person is concerned not just with his outward behavior but with inner events. Patients undergoing operations who are given a paralyzing drug such as curare manifest no outward behavior yet feel pain. A traditional behaviorist model does not take such "nonbehavioral" states seriously. Second, the idea of "dispositions to behave" cannot easily be spelled out, for an infinite number of different conditions may be potential factors in a dispositional account.

The second version of materialism is **reductive materialism,** which attempts to find a one-to-one correlation between mental states and brain states and identifies the former with the latter. Beliefs, pains, and desires will turn out, on this account, to be simply brain states.

The third version is **functionalism,** which denies that any one type of brain state or event will always be correlated with a type of mental event. For example, I may feel pain in my hand on two *different* occasions but may have two different areas of the brain activated. Actually, functionalism need not be materialist at all. It could be agnostic on the mind–body problem, confining itself to outputs of human activity.

The final version is **eliminative materialism,** which contends that our ordinary conceptual framework in which we talk about mental events is mistaken. Our commonsense conceptual scheme is labeled **Folk Psychology** and includes our concepts of belief, desire, intentions, emotions, perceptions, and sensations. Eliminativists hold that all reality can be explained in and through scientific laws. Since Folk Psychology is prescientific, it can have no ultimate validity. When we learn more about our brains and the way they work, we will be able to replace this subjectivist speech with a more scientific discourse. For example, instead of talking about a headache in my forehead, we might talk about certain C-fibers firing in my brain.

One other theory should be noted: **neutral monism,** the view that one common but unknown substance underlies all reality, matter, and mind. Baruch Spinoza (1632–1677) first put forth this position, though it was developed by William James (1842–1910) at the end of the 19th century. The advantage of neutral monism is that it relieves us of the difficulty of choosing between materialism and mentalism as the basic stuff of the universe, affirming that a deeper reality contains both as aspects of the same substance. Although this may seem a suitable compromise between those who are attracted to monism and those who are inclined to dualism, neutral monism actually compounds the problem: Now not only do we not understand matter and mind, but we also have a third mystery to worry about. If it is true, there seems little evidence for it. Yet, given the difficulties with the other positions, you may finally select it as the least offensive of the lot.

The main historical debate has been between interactive dualism and two forms of materialism: reductive and eliminative. We will spend most of our time in this chapter examining these three theories.

First we turn to René Descartes's (1596–1650) classic rendition of interactive dualism (sometimes called *substance dualism*). Recall our discussion of Descartes's global skepticism in Part 4. Descartes, after doubting everything that it is possible to doubt, including that he has a body, discovers that he cannot doubt that he exists, for insofar as he is doubting, he must exist in order to think (*"cogito ergo sum"*). But he asks, what exactly is this thinking self? "What am I?" We turn to his *Meditations.*

MEDITATIONS ON FIRST PHILOSOPHY

Meditation II

I discover that thought is an attribute that really belongs to me. This alone cannot be detached from me. I am. I exist. This is certain. But for how long? For as long as I think. Because perhaps it could also come to pass that if I should cease from thinking I would then utterly cease to exist. I now admit nothing that is not necessarily true. I am therefore precisely only a thing that thinks; that is, a mind or soul or intellect or reason—words the meaning of which I was ignorant before. Now I am a true thing, and truly existing; but what kind of thing? I have said it already: a thing that thinks.

I will set my imagination going to see if I am not something more. I am not a collection of members which we call the human body: I am not a subtle air infused into these members, not a wind, not a fire, not a vapor, not a breath, nor anything at all which I can imagine or conceive; because I have assumed that all these were nothing. This supposition holds: I find that I only leave myself certain of the fact that I am something.

Descartes has ruled out certain possibilities. He knows what he is not, and he knows that he is a thing that thinks (*res cogitans*), "doubts, understands, affirms, denies wills, refuses, which also imagines and feels." He next takes up the question, What is a body? He wants to know what is the nature of bodies in general, as well as the nature of his own body (assuming he has one).[3]

Let us begin by considering the commonest matters, those which we believe to be the most distinctly comprehended, to wit, the bodies which we touch and see; not indeed bodies in general, for these general ideas are usually a little more confused, but let us consider one body in particular. Let us take, for example, this piece of wax: it has been taken quite freshly from the hive, and it has not yet lost the sweetness of the honey which it contains; it still retains somewhat of the odour of the flowers from which it has been culled; its colour, its figure, its size are apparent; it is hard, cold, easily handled, and

From: *The Philosophical Works of Descartes,* vol. 1, trans. E. Haldane and G. Ross (Cambridge, UK: Cambridge University Press, 1911).

if you strike it with the finger, it will emit a sound. Finally all the things which are requisite to cause us distinctly to recognise a body, are met with in it. But notice that while I speak and approach the fire what remained of the taste is exhaled, the smell evaporates, the colour alters, the figure is destroyed, the size increases, it becomes liquid, it heats, scarcely can one handle it, and when one strikes it, no sound is emitted. Does the same wax remain after this change? We must confess that it remains; none would judge otherwise. What then did I know so distinctly in this piece of wax? It could certainly be nothing of all that the senses brought to my notice, since all these things which fall under taste, smell, sight, touch, and hearing, are found to be changed, and yet the same wax remains.

Perhaps it was what I now think, viz. that this wax was not that sweetness of honey, nor that agreeable scent of flowers, nor that particular whiteness, nor that figure, nor that sound, but simply a body which a little while before appeared to me as perceptible under these forms, and which is now perceptible under others. But what, precisely, is it that I imagine when I form such conceptions? Let us attentively consider this, and, abstracting from all that does not belong to the wax, let us see what remains. Certainly nothing remains excepting a certain extended thing which is flexible and movable. But what is the meaning of flexible and movable? Is it not that I imagine that this piece of wax being round is capable of becoming square and of passing from a square to a triangular figure? No, certainly it is not that, since I imagine it admits of an infinitude of similar changes, and I nevertheless do not know how to compass the infinitude by my imagination, and consequently this conception which I have of the wax is not brought about by the faculty of imagination. What now is this extension? Is it not also unknown? For it becomes greater when the wax is melted, greater when it is boiled, and greater still when the heat increases; and I should not conceive [clearly] according to truth what wax is, if I did not think that even this piece that we are considering is capable of receiving more variations in extension than I have ever imagined. We must then grant that I could not even understand through the imagination what this piece of wax is, and that it is my mind alone which perceives it. I say this piece of wax in particular, for as to wax in general it is yet clearer. But what is this piece of wax which cannot be understood excepting by the [understanding or] mind? It is certainly the same that I see, touch, imagine, and finally it is the same which I have always believed it to be from the beginning. But what must particularly be observed is that its perception is neither an act of vision, nor of touch, nor of imagination, and has never been such although it may have appeared formerly to be so, but only an intuition of the mind, which may be imperfect and confused as it was formerly, or clear and distinct as it is at present, according as my attention is more or less directed to the elements which are found in it, and of which it is composed.

Yet in the meantime I am greatly astonished when I consider [the great feebleness of mind] and its proneness to fall [insensibly] into error; for although without giving expression to my thoughts I consider all this in my own mind, words often impede me and I am almost deceived by the terms of ordinary language. For we say that we see the same wax, if it is present, and not that we simply judge that it is the same from its having the same colour and figure. From this I should conclude that I knew the wax by means of vision and not simply by the intuition of the mind; unless by chance I remember that, when looking from a window and saying I see men who pass in the street, I really do not see them, but infer that what I see is men, just as I say that I see wax. And yet what do I see from the window but hats and coats which may cover automatic machines? Yet I judge these to be men. And similarly solely by the faculty of judgment which rests in my mind, I comprehend that which I believed I saw with my eyes.

A man who makes it his aim to raise his knowledge above the common should be ashamed to derive the occasion for doubting from the forms of speech invented by the vulgar; I prefer to pass on and consider whether I had a more evident and perfect conception of what the wax was when I first perceived it, and when I believed I knew it by means of the external senses or at least by the common sense as it is called, that is to say by the imaginative faculty, or whether my present conception is clearer now that I have most carefully examined what it is, and in what way it can be known. It would certainly be absurd to doubt as to this. For what was there in this first perception which was distinct? What was there which might not as well have been perceived by any of the animals? But when I distinguish the wax from its external forms, and when, just as if I had taken from it its vestments, I consider it quite naked, it is certain that although some error may still be found in my judgment, I can nevertheless not perceive it thus without a human mind.

But finally what shall I say of this mind, that is, of myself, for up to this point I do not admit in myself anything but mind? What then, I who seem to perceive this piece of wax so distinctly, do I not know myself, not only with much more truth and certainty, but also with much more distinctness and clearness? For if I judge that the wax is or exists from the fact that I see it, it certainly follows much more clearly that I am or that I exist myself from the fact that I see it. For it may be that what I see is not really wax, it may also be that I do not possess eyes with which to see anything; but it cannot be that when I see, or (for I no longer take account of the distinction) when I think I see, that I myself who think am nought. So if I judge that the wax exists from the fact that I touch it, the same thing will follow, to wit, that I am; and if I judge that my imagination, or some other cause, whatever it is, persuades me that the wax exists, I shall still conclude the same. And what I have here remarked of wax may be applied to all other things which are external to me [and which are met with outside of me]. And further, if the [notion or] perception of wax has seemed to me clearer and more distinct, not only after the sight or the touch, but also after many other causes have rendered it quite manifest to me, with how much more [evidence] and distinctness must it be said that I now know myself, since all the reasons which contribute to the knowledge of wax, or any other body whatever, are yet better proofs of the nature of my mind! And there are so many other things in the mind itself which may contribute to the elucidation of its nature, that those which depend on body such as these just mentioned, hardly merit being taken into account.

But finally here I am, having insensibly reverted to the point I desired, for, since it is now manifest to me that even bodies are not properly speaking known by the senses or by the faculty of imagination, but by the understanding only, and since they are not known from the fact that they are seen or touched, but only because they are understood, I see clearly that there is nothing which is easier for me to know than my mind. But because it is difficult to rid oneself so promptly of an opinion to which one was accustomed for so long, it will be well that I should halt a little at this point, so that by the length of my meditation I may more deeply imprint on my memory this new knowledge.

So far all we know about bodies is that they are extended things (*res extensa*). Our conception of bodies is as abstract as our idea of mind. Both are known only by the understanding. The mind is not extended. It is a thinking thing (*res cogitans*) or substance. The body is an extended thing. The mind is more certain than the body, for Descartes can doubt that he has a body, but he cannot doubt that he has a mind. We turn to *Meditation III*.

Meditation III: Of God: That He Exists

I shall now close my eyes, I shall stop my ears, I shall call away all my senses, I shall efface even from my thoughts all the images of corporeal things, or at least (for that is hardly possible) I shall esteem them as vain and false; and thus holding converse only with myself and considering my own nature, I shall try little by little to reach a better knowledge of and a more familiar acquaintanceship with myself. I am a thing that thinks, that is to say, that doubts, affirms, denies, that knows a few things, that is ignorant of many [that loves, that hates], that wills, that desires, that also imagines and perceives; for as I remarked before, although the things which I perceive and imagine are perhaps nothing at all apart from me and in themselves, I am nevertheless assured that these modes of though that I call perceptions and imaginations, inasmuch only as they are modes of thought, certainly reside [and are met with] in me....

On the Separation of the Mind from the Body

But now that I begin to know myself better, and to discover more clearly the author of my being, I do not in truth think that I should rashly admit all the matters which the senses seem to teach us, but, on the other hand, I do not think that I should doubt them all universally.

And first of all, because I know that all things which I apprehend clearly and distinctly can be created by God as I apprehend them, it suffices that I am able to apprehend one thing apart from another clearly and distinctly in order to be certain that the one is different from the other, since they may be made to exist in separation at least by the omnipotence of God; and it does not signify by what power this separation is made in order to compel me to judge them to be different: and, therefore, just because I know certainly that I exist, and that meanwhile I do not notice that any other thing necessarily pertains to my nature or essence, excepting that I am a thinking thing, I rightly conclude that my essence consists solely in the fact that I am a thinking thing [or a substance whose whole essence or nature is to think]. And although possibly (or rather certainly, as I shall say in a moment) I possess a body with which I am very intimately conjoined, yet because, on the one side, I have a clear and distinct idea of myself inasmuch as I am only a thinking and unextended thing, and as, on the other, I possess a distinct idea of body, inasmuch as it is only an extended and unthinking thing, it is certain that this I [that is to say, my soul by which I am what I am], is entirely and absolutely distinct from my body, and can exist without it.

I further find in myself faculties employing modes of thinking peculiar to themselves, to wit, the faculties of imagination and feeling, without which I can easily conceive myself clearly and distinctly as a complete being; while, on the other hand, they cannot be so conceived apart from me, that is without an intelligent substance in which they reside, for [in the notion we have of these faculties, or, to use the language of the Schools] in their formal concept, some kind of intellection is comprised, from which I infer that they are distinct from me as its modes are from a thing. I observe also in me some other faculties such as that of change of position, the assumption of different figures and such like, which cannot be conceived, any more than can the preceding, apart from some substance to which they are attached, and consequently cannot exist without it; but it is very clear that these faculties, if it be true that they exist, must be attached to some corporeal or extended substance, and not to an intelligent substance, since in the clear and distinct conception of these there is some sort of extension found to be present, but no intellection at all. There is certainly further in me a certain passive faculty of perception, that is, of receiving and recognising the ideas of sensible things, but this would be useless to me [and I could in no way avail myself of it], if there were not either in me or in some other thing another active faculty capable of forming and producing these ideas. But this active faculty cannot exist in me [inasmuch as I am a thing that thinks] seeing that it does not presuppose thought, and also that those ideas are often produced in me without my contributing in any way to the same, and often even against my will; it is thus necessarily the case that the faculty resides in some substance different from me in which all the reality which is objectively in the ideas that are produced by this faculty is formally or eminently contained, as I remarked before. And this substance is either a body, that is, a corporeal nature in which there is contained formally [and really] all that which is objectively [and by representation] in those ideas, or it is God Himself, or some other creature more noble than body in which that same is contained eminently. But, since God is no deceiver, it is very manifest that He does not communicate to me these ideas immediately and by Himself, nor yet by the intervention of some creature in which their reality is not formally, but only eminently, contained. For since He has given me no faculty to recognise that this is the case, but, on the other hand, a very great inclination to believe [that they are sent to me or] that they are conveyed to me by corporeal objects, I do not see how He could be defended from the accusation of deceit if these ideas were produced by causes other than corporeal objects. Hence we must allow that corporeal things exist. However, they are perhaps not exactly what we perceive by the senses, since this comprehension by the senses is in many instances very obscure and confused; but we must at least admit that all things which I conceive in them clearly and distinctly, that is to say, all things which, speaking generally, are comprehended in the object of pure mathematics, are truly to be recognised as external objects.

As to other things, however, which are either particular only, as, for example, that the sun is of such and such a figure, etc., or which are less clearly and distinctly conceived, such as light, sound, pain and the like, it is certain that although they are very dubious and uncertain, yet on the sole ground that God is not a deceiver, and that consequently He has not permitted any falsity to exist in my opinion which He has not likewise given me the faculty of correcting, I may assuredly hope to conclude that I have within me the means of arriving at the truth even here. And first of all there is no doubt that in all things which nature teaches me there is some truth constrained; for by nature, considered in general, I now understand no other thing than either God Himself or else the order and disposition which God has established in created things; and by my nature in particular I understand no other thing than the complexus of all the things which God has given me.

But there is nothing which this nature teaches me more expressly [nor more sensibly] than that I have a body which is adversely affected when I feel pain, which has need of food or drink when I experience the feelings of hunger and thirst, and so on; nor can I doubt there being some truth in all this.

Nature also teaches me by these sensations of pain, hunger, thirst, etc., that I am not only lodged in my body as a pilot in a vessel, but that I am very closely united to it, and so to speak so intermingled with it that I seem to compose with it one whole. For if that were not the case, when my body is hurt, I, who am merely a thinking thing, should not feel pain, for I should perceive this wound by the understanding only, just as the sailor perceives by sight when something is damaged in his vessel; and when my body has need of drink or food, I should clearly understand the fact without being warned of it by confused feelings of hunger and thirst. For all these sensations of hunger, thirst, pain, etc. are in truth none other than certain confused modes of thought which are produced by the union and apparent intermingling of mind and body....

...It still remains to inquire how the goodness of God does not prevent the nature of man so regarded from being fallacious.

In order to begin this examination, then, I here say, in the first place, that there is a great difference between mind and body, inasmuch as body is by nature always divisible, and the mind is entirely indivisible. For, as a matter of fact, when I consider the mind, that is to say, myself inasmuch as I am only a thinking thing, I cannot distinguish in myself any parts, but apprehend myself to be clearly one and entire; and although the whole mind seems to be united to the whole body, yet if a foot, or an arm, or some other part, is separated from my body, I am aware that nothing has been taken away from my mind. And the faculties of willing, feeling, conceiving, etc., cannot be properly speaking said to be its parts, for it is one and the same mind which employs itself in willing and in feeling and understanding. But it is quite otherwise with corporeal or extended objects, for there is not one of these imaginable by me which my mind cannot easily divide into parts, and which consequently I do not recognise as being divisible; this would be sufficient to teach me that the mind or soul of man is entirely different from the body, if I had not already learned it from other sources.

I further notice that the mind does not receive the impressions from all parts of the body immediately, but only from the brain, or perhaps even from one of its smallest parts, to wit, from that in which the common sense is said to reside, which, whenever it is disposed in the same particular way, conveys the same thing to the mind, although meanwhile the other portions of the body may be differently disposed, as is testified by innumerable experiments which it is unnecessary here to recount....

Descartes holds that all and only those things known as clear and distinct (like the self as mind) qualify as knowledge. He thinks that the reality of God is similarly clear and distinct. (I have omitted his elaborate discussion of this point.) It is a version of the ontological argument, which goes something like this:

1. God by definition has all perfections.
2. Existence is a perfection (it is better to exist than not to exist).
3. Therefore, God exists.

Whether some version of the ontological argument is sound, this version isn't, since it crudely defines God into existence. It is not clear that existence is a perfection. One may also inquire: Why should we believe that everything clear and distinct is true? To which Descartes answers: Because God is not a deceiver and would not cause us to be deluded about self-evident truths. But when we ask, How do you know that God exists? Descartes answers: Because it is a clear and distinct idea. Such reasoning is circular, but this doesn't invalidate his argument that the mind and body are separate substances.

According to Descartes, three kinds of objects or substances exist in the universe: (1) the eternal substance, God, (2) his creation in terms of mind, and (3) his creation in terms of matter. Humans are made up of the latter two types of substance: "We may thus easily have two clear and distinct notions or ideas, the one of created substance which thinks, and the other of corporeal substances, provided we carefully separate all the attributes of thought from those of extension." That is, mind and matter have different properties, so they must be different substances:

We are thinking substances or embodied minds, for I am not only lodged in my body as a pilot in a ship, but I am very closely united to it, and so to speak so intermingle with it that I seem to compose with it one whole. For if that were not the case, when my body is hurt, I, who am merely a thinking thing, should perceive this wound by the understanding only, just as the sailor perceives by sight when something is damaged in his vessel.

The two kinds of substances that make us each a person intermingle in such a way that they causally act upon each other. Although it might be that a mind interacts with each part of its body separately, Descartes's view is that mind interacts only with the brain. The material event that causally stimulates one of our five senses (light hitting the retina of the eye) results in a chain of physical causation that leads to a certain brain process that results in a certain sensation. Then, being affected by the brain, the mind through mental events in turn acts on the brain, which affects the body. Descartes thought he could pinpoint the place in the brain where the interaction between mind and brain took place:

> The part of the body in which the soul exercises its function immediately is in nowise the heart, nor the whole of the brain, but merely the most inward of all its parts, to wit, a certain very small gland which is situated in the middle of its substance.
>
> The small gland which is the main seat of the soul is so suspended between the cavities which contain the spirits that it can be moved by them in as many ways as there are sensible diversities in the object but that it may also be moved in diverse ways by the soul, whose nature is such that it receives in itself as many diverse impressions, that is to say, that it possesses as many diverse perceptions, as there are diverse movements in this gland. Reciprocally, likewise, the machine of the body is so formed that from the simple fact that this gland is diversely moved by the soul, it thrusts the spirits which surround it towards the pores of the brain, which conducts them by the nerves into the muscles, by which means it causes them to move the limbs.

This gland, the seat of the mind, is the pineal gland. It functions as the intermediary that transmits the effects of the mind to the brain and the effects of the brain to the mind. We will disregard his mistake about the pineal gland and accept the essential structure of Descartes's theory as the classic expression of dualistic interactionism.

Descartes's view seems close to what we arrive at through common sense. We seem to be aware of two different kinds of events: physical and mental, as was described earlier. Mental events cause physical events, and physical events cause mental events. At this point, the interactionist argues against epiphenomenalism. Epiphenomenalism seems mistaken in making the causal direction only one way. What evolutionary use is the mind if it does no work? It seems to violate Newton's dictum that "Nature does nothing in vain." It is a useless, fifth wheel. On the contrary, the dualist avers, our intuitions tell us that the reasons (grasped by the mind) set forth causal chains resulting in physical actions and other mental events. For example, I may decide (a mental event) to imagine all the friends I have ever had and call them up to consciousness. The epiphenomenalist account glosses over the introspective process and states that all these decisions and imaginings are simply the by-products of mysterious physical processes. With friends like that, the interactionist reasons, who needs materialist enemies?

Our mental states seem private and incorrigible, at least most of them. Only I can know whether I am really in pain, whether I really believe that God exists, whether I really desire to stay celibate or to be a moral person. True, perhaps I can misremember, be mistaken about a borderline feeling (is it a slight pain or a sharp tickle? lemon-flavored ice cream or a variety of orange-flavored ice cream?), but for a whole host of experiences, introspection is reliable. Folk Psychology works.

Nonetheless, there are severe problems with interactive dualism. Here are the four most prominent problems:

- Where does the interaction of the soul and body take place?
- How does the interaction take place?

- The idea of the mental causing the physical seems to violate the principle of the conservation of energy.
- The idea of two realities, body and mind, seems to violate Occam's Razor, the principle of simplicity.

Let's consider each criticism in turn. First, where does the interaction take place? Descartes thought it took place in the pineal gland, but experiments have shown that this gland has nothing to do with consciousness. The problem is that, whereas physical states have spatial location, mental states do not. Mental substance is not subject to the laws of physics (otherwise, we would conclude it was material). However, if we cannot speak of mental states having location, it seems odd to speak of a *where* in which they "touch," or "meet," or "interact" with physical objects.

This certainly raises an interesting puzzle. The dualist responds that we do not have to understand where the mind is located (that may be a nonsensical question) to be able to say that it affects the brain *in* the brain. That is, we posit that there are metaphysical laws in addition to physical laws. God, mind, and the realm of the spirit operate within the realm of the former kind of laws.

The second objection—how does the interaction take place?—is very similar to the first. How can physical states result in something wholly other, something mental? To move a stalled car, several people must push it. Force must be exerted in every physical change, and force is a product of mass and acceleration, so whatever exerts force must be capable of physical movement. However, nothing mental has mass or acceleration (mental objects do not travel through space from your hometown to the university), so nothing mental can exert physical force or be affected by force. Thus, nothing physical can be causally affected by anything mental, nor can anything mental be causally influenced by anything physical.

Once again, this seems like a difficult problem for dualists. How might they reply? One way might be to respond like Hamlet: "There are more things under the heavens, Horatio, than are written in your philosophies." Why should we suppose that substances must be qualitatively similar before they can influence each other? Doesn't the very thought that someone is out to harm you cause a state of psychological and physical depression or fear? Isn't my decision to raise my hand an example of the mind causing the body to move? Isn't agency itself testimony to the truth of interactionism?

Perhaps free agency is a myth or an illusion, but it cannot be dismissed out of hand. An argument is needed to exclude introspective reports for free will as evidence for dualistic interactionism. (We will turn to the problem of freedom of the will in Part 6.)

The third problem involves the principle of the conservation of energy. This principle states that the amount of energy in a closed physical system remains constant; so if there is causal interaction between mental events and physical events, the conservation-of-energy principle is violated. Energy is a function of matter, not mind. But the dualist believes that my decision to pick up the book in front of me somehow creates the necessary energy to cause the book to rise.

So it would seem, on dualist premises, that the conservation-of-energy principle is violated.

Once again, dualists are faced with a formidable challenge. At least three options are open for them:

1. The principle of the conservation of energy applies only to closed systems, but the universe may be an open system. Energy may come and go at different points. The trouble with this answer is that contemporary physics operates on the assumption that the universe is a closed system. This has ramifications for the notion of divine intervention.

2. There may be a replacement of energy within the closed system so that when 10 ergons appear via my decision to lift the book, 10 ergons disappear in another place. This is possible, but it is just an ad hoc hypothesis necessary to save the theory.

3. It may not be necessary that mental causation involves a transfer of energy but only a harnessing or redirection of energies. The problem with the redirection hypothesis is that one would like to know how the mind can affect the direction of energy flow without itself being a form of energy. This brings us back to problem 2 (how does the interaction take place?).

We turn to the fourth objection to dualism, which gets us into the arguments for materialist monism. The idea of two realities, body and mind, seems to violate **Occam's Razor,** the principle of simplicity. All things being equal, isn't it better to have one all-embracing explanation of several different events rather than two? Instead of the puzzle of substance interaction, wouldn't the posit of a single substance with a single set of laws have the advantage of giving us a unified picture of reality?

Imagine that two murders have been committed in a large nearby city, one in the southern part of town on Monday afternoon during rush hour and one in the northern part a half hour later. In both cases, a woman has been killed by an assailant who sucks blood from her neck and leaves a picture of Dracula on the corpse. One the one hand, the evidence points to two murderers committing the crimes independently, for no one could possibly get from the southern part of town to the northern part of town in a half hour, especially during rush hour. However, it would greatly simplify the investigation if police could assume some way of traveling between the two places and so be on the lookout for one murderer instead of two. The quest for economy and reduction to simpler basic units seems to be of great importance in explaining phenomena.

This is the commonsense motivation that informs the tendency toward monism. Unless there is a compelling reason not to do so, simplicity and economy of explanation, reducing differences to an underlying unity is desirable for problem solving. The question is whether there is a compelling reason for not making a move to simplicity. Since the dualist's response at this point is global, having to do with the entire product of materialist monism, we might well postpone it until we see the case for materialism.

Summary

The mind–body problem arises because we have at least two separate types of strong beliefs. On the one hand, it seems obvious that consciousness and mental states like pains and feelings are not physical entities; they are mental, not material. On the other hand, neuroscience seems to indicate that our mental states are reducible to brain states, where there is no place for a separate mental faculty. Interactive dualism seems intuitively obvious until we notice the philosophical objections to it. Epiphenomenalism, the one-way causal traffic from matter to mind, seems to make mind a useless fifth wheel. Neutral monism, panpsychism, idealism, and eliminativism were also discussed in this chapter as possible options; all seem to have deep difficulties. Hence, the problem perdures. We turn now to the main rival of dualism, materialism.

FOR FURTHER REFLECTION

1. What are the primary issues involved in the mind–body problem? How do the various theories discussed in this chapter answer those concerns?

2. Examine the arguments for and against dualistic interactionism. How strong are the criticisms against this position? Can these criticisms be answered?

3. What is epiphenomenalism? What are its strengths and weaknesses?

4. What is the principle of simplicity (Occam's Razor), and how does it affect the discussion of dualism?

NOTES

1. Paul Churchland, *Matter and Consciousness* (Cambridge, MA: MIT Press, 1990), 1.
2. John Watson, *Behaviorism* (New York: Norton, 1930).
3. All remaining passages in this chapter are taken from *The Philosophical Works of Descartes*, vol. 1, trans. E. Haldane and G. Ross (Cambridge, UK: Cambridge University Press, 1911). Reprinted in Louis Pojman, ed. *Philosophy: The Quest for Truth*, 3rd ed. (Belmont, CA: Wadsworth, 1996), 208–214.

FOR FURTHER READING

Beakley, Brian, and Peter Ludlow, eds. *The Philosophy of Mind: Classical Problems and Contemporary Issues*. Cambridge, MA: MIT Press, 1992. An excellent anthology.

Churchland, Paul. *Matter and Consciousness*. Cambridge, MA: MIT Press, 1990. A superb introductory text from a materialist perspective.

Dennett, Daniel. *The Intentional Stance*. Cambridge, MA: MIT Press, 1989. A brilliant discussion of the mental states.

Levin, Michael E. *Metaphysics and the Mind–Body Problem*. Oxford, UK: Clarendon Press, 1979. An excellent defense of materialism. My illustration of the principle of simplicity was taken from this work.

Lycan, William, ed. *Mind and Cognition*. Oxford, UK: Blackwell, 1991. An excellent anthology.

McGinn, Colin. *The Character of Mind*. Oxford, UK: Oxford University Press, 1982. A rich, compact exposition of the major issues.

Moreland, J. P. *Scaling the Secular City*. Grand Rapids, MI: Baker Books, 1987. Contains a defense of dualistic interactionism from a Christian perspective.

Rosenthal, David M., ed. *The Nature of Mind*. Oxford, UK: Oxford University Press, 1992. The best anthology of contemporary work available.

Searle, John. *Mind, Brains and Science*. Cambridge, MA: Harvard University Press, 1984). A perceptive work, setting forth puzzles and providing a brilliant analysis of the issues.

Stich, Stephen. *From Folk Psychology to Cognitive Science: The Case Against Belief*. Cambridge, MA: MIT Press, 1983.

20 ⚶ Materialist Monism

In the afternoon of September 13, 1848, in the Vermont countryside, an affable 25-year-old foreman, Phineas P. Gage, was leading a group of men in laying a new line of the Rutland and Burlington Railroad. They needed to blast a huge rock blocking their way, and so Phineas poured gunpowder into the narrow hole that had been drilled in the rock. Powder in place, the next step was to tamp down the charge, which Phineas proceeded to do. But the iron tamping rod rubbed against the side of the shaft and a spark ignited the powder, causing an explosion. The iron rod—$3\frac{1}{2}$ feet in length and $1\frac{1}{4}$ inch in diameter—burst from the hole, struck Phineas just beneath his left eye, tore through his skull, and landed 50 feet away.

Phineas was thrown to the ground, his limbs twitching convulsively, but soon he was able to speak. He was taken to a hotel where doctors were able to stop the bleeding. Amazingly, Phineas lived, but he was transformed from a friendly intelligent leader into an intemperate, unreliable, childish ox with the evil temper to match it.

Materialism says that what we call mind is really a function of the brain; that when the brain is injured, as was the case with Phineas P. Gage, or diseased, the effect is seen in behavior and impaired mental functioning. In Alzheimer's disease, for example, the cerebral cortex and the hippocampus contain abnormal twisted tangles and filaments as well as abnormal neurites. The loss of neurons in the nucleus basalis results in a reduction of choline acetyltransferase, an enzyme needed for normal brain life. The result is the slow death of the brain. Without the brain (or some physical equivalent), no mental states are possible.

Cutting the corpus callosum, the thick band of nerves linking the two hemispheres of the cerebral cortex, can result in two separate centers of consciousness. Different parts of the brain are responsible for different mental operations. Over 30 years ago, the Canadian neurosurgeon Wilder Penfield conducted a set of famous experiments in which he used electrodes to stimulate the cerebral cortex of patients. They began to recall memories from the past and even sang lullabies learned in early childhood, which they had forgotten, lending support for the thesis that memories are stored in the neurons of the cerebral cortex.

Furthermore, a systematic correspondence seems to exist between the structure of different animals' brains and the sort of behavior they exhibit. Why do we need such a complex brain with billions of cells and trillions of connections if the mind is located in its own separate substance? If dualism is correct, this intricately constructed, complex brain is unnecessary baggage, superfluous machinery. All that the mind should require is some channel for linking the mental with the physical worlds.

Metaphysical **materialism,** the doctrine that matter and the laws of physics make up and govern the entire universe, has a long history. It was held by the first Greek Cosmologists (discussed in Chapter 4), expounded in greater detail by the Greek philosopher Democritus (circa 460–370 BCE) and the Roman Atomist Lucretius (circa 99–55 BCE), and given still deeper expression in the work of Thomas Hobbes (1588–1679). Hobbes, a *theist* materialist, believed that all reality except God is material. God alone is spirit. We are entirely material beings:

> The world (the universe, that is the whole mass of all things that are) is corporeal, that is to say, body; and hath the dimensions of magnitude, namely, length, breadth, and depth; also every part of body, is likewise body, and hath the like dimensions; and consequently every part of the universe is body; and that which is not body, is no part of the universe. And because the universe is all, that which is no part of it, is nothing; and consequently no where. Nor does it follow from this that spirits are nothing; for they have dimensions, and are therefore really bodies; though that name in common speech is only given to visible bodies. Spirit, that which is incorporeal, is a term that rightly belongs to God himself, in whom we consider not what attribute expresses best his nature, which is incomprehensible, but that which best expresses our desire to honor him.[1]

Bringing the discussion into the present, the British philosopher Colin McGinn puts it this way:

> What we call mind is in fact made up of a great number of sub-capacities, and each of these depends upon the functioning of the brain. [Neurology] compellingly demonstrates . . . that everything about the mind, from the sensory-motor periphery to the inner sense, is minutely controlled by the brain: if your brain lacks certain chemicals or gets locally damaged, your mind is apt to fall apart at the seams. If parts of the mind depend for their existence upon parts of the brain, then the whole of the mind must so depend too. Hence the soul dies with the brain, which is to say it is mortal.[2]

By materialism, neither Hobbes nor contemporary materialists, like McGinn, mean *value materialism,* the thesis that only money and the things money can buy have any value, nor do they necessarily mean that religion or the spiritual aspects of life are ruled out. Indeed, some scholars interpret the biblical view of humanity as materialist rather than dualist (see Chapter 22). The materialists mean simply that the physical system of the brain and the physical events that take place within it are the entirety of our conscious lives. There is no separate mental substance, and mental events are really physical events.

There are two central varieties of materialist monism: reductivism and eliminativism. Both distinguish themselves from metaphysical **behaviorism,** the view that denies or ignores mental events and describes the human condition in terms of dispositions to act. Reductivism acknowledges that there are mental events, and eliminativism acknowledges that there are events to which mental terms refer. In this chapter, we examine both forms of materialism.

Reductive materialism, sometimes known as the *identity theory,* admits mental events (but not a separate mental substance) but claims that each mental event is really a brain state or event. Our center of consciousness resides in the brain, probably about 2 inches behind the forehead. We are conscious of happenings in our cerebral cortex even though they appear to be different from measurable brain states. Thus, a pain in my foot can be identified with a brain event—say, a C-fiber firing—and a belief can be identified with certain sentences symbolically stored in some area of the cerebral cortex. J. J. C. Smart states this position well.

SENSATIONS AND BRAIN PROCESSES

It seems to me that science is increasingly giving us a viewpoint whereby organisms are able to be seen as physico-chemical mechanisms: it seems that even the behavior of man himself will one day be explicable in mechanistic terms. There does seem to be, so far as science is concerned, nothing in the world but increasingly complex arrangements of physical constituents. All except for one place: in consciousness. That is, for a full description of what is going on in a man you would have to mention not only the physical processes in his tissue, glands, nervous system, and so forth, but also his states of consciousness: his visual, auditory, and tactual sensations, his aches and pains. That these should be *correlated* is to say that they are something "over and above." You cannot correlate something with itself. You correlate footprints with burglars, but not Bill Sikes the burglar with Bill Sikes the burglar. So sensations, states of consciousness, do seem to be the one sort of thing left outside the physicalist picture, and for various reasons I just cannot believe that this can be so. That everything should be explicable in terms of physics (together of course with descriptions of the ways in which the parts are put together—roughly, biology is to physics as radio-engineering is to electromagnetism) except the occurrence of sensations seems to me to be frankly unbelievable. Such sensations would be "nomological danglers," to use Feigl's expression. It is not often realized how odd would be the laws whereby these nomological danglers would dangle. It is sometimes asked, "Why can't there be psycho-physical laws which are of a novel sort, just as the laws of electricity and magnetism were novelties from

From: J. J. C. Smart, "Sensations and Brain Processes," *Philosophical Review* 68 (1959): 141–156.

the standpoint of Newtonian mechanics?" Certainly we are pretty sure in the future to come across new ultimate laws of a novel type, but I expect them to relate simple constituents: for example, whatever ultimate particles are then in vogue. I cannot believe that ultimate laws of nature could relate simple constituents to configurations consisting of perhaps billions of neurons (and goodness knows how many billion billions of ultimate particles) all put together for all the world as though their main purpose in life was to be a negative feedback mechanism of a complicated sort. Such ultimate laws would be like nothing so far known in science. They have a queer "smell" to them. I am just unable to believe in the nomological danglers themselves, or in the laws whereby they would dangle. If any philosophical arguments seemed to compel us to believe in such things, I would suspect a catch in the argument. In any case it is the object of this paper to show that there are no philosophical arguments which compel us to be dualists.

Smart's argument is a version of the argument from simplicity (Occam's Razor) mentioned in Chapter 19. He is committed to the unity of science, to the idea that a single set of laws exists whereby everything that exists and happens can be explained. But the last sentence in the paragraph (above) is much weaker. It contends only that reductive materialism is consistent.

Smart now considers the identity of brain processes with mental states (sensations).

Why should sensations just be brain processes of a certain sort? There are, of course, well-known (as well as lesser-known) philosophical objections to the view that reports of sensations are reports of brain processes, but I shall try to argue that these arguments are by no means as cogent as is commonly thought to be the case.

Let me first try to state more accurately the thesis that sensations are brain processes. It is not the thesis that, for example, "after-image" or "ache" means the same as "brain process of sort X" (where "X" is replaced by a description of a certain sort of brain process). It is that, in so far as "after-image" or "ache" is a report of a process, it is a report of a process that *happens to be* a brain process. It follows that the thesis does not claim that sensation statements can be *translated* into statements about brain processes. Nor does it claim that the logic of a sensation statement is the same as that of a brain-process statement. All it claims is that in so far as a sensation statement is a report of something, that something is in fact a brain process. Sensations are nothing over and above brain processes. Nations are nothing "over and above" citizens, but this does not prevent the logic of nation statements being very different from the logic of citizen statements, nor does it insure the translatability of nation statements into citizen statements.[3]

Smart is stating a negative point. Two statements can refer to the same entity while having different logical relations. For example, Bill Clinton happened to be the forty-second President of the United States, but we may know many things about Clinton without knowing that he was the president and we may describe the office of the president without referring to Bill Clinton. We may say it is necessary for Bill Clinton, being who he is, that he was born of his two parents, but it is not necessary that to be the forty-second president of the United States that one be born of those two parents.

> *Remarks on Identity.* When I say that a sensation is a brain process or that lightning is an electric discharge, I am using "is" in the sense of strict identity (just as in the proposition "7 is identical with the smallest prime number greater than 5"). When I say that a sensation is a brain process or that lightning is an electric discharge I do not mean just that the sensation is somehow spatially or temporally continuous with the discharge. When on the other hand I say that the successful general is the same person as the small boy who stole the apples I mean only that the successful general I see before me is a time slice of the same four-dimensional object of which the small boy stealing apples is an earlier time slice. However, the four-dimensional object which has the general-I-see-before-me for its late time slice is identical in the strict sense with the four-dimensional object which has the small-boy-stealing-apples for an early time slice. I distinguish these two senses of "is identical with" because I wish to make it clear that the brain-process doctrine asserts identity in the *strict* sense.[4]

Jeffrey Olen offers the following analogy on the relation of interactive dualism, epiphenomenalism, and the identity theory.

PERSONS AND THEIR WORLDS

Some people who have never seen a watch find one alongside a road. They pick it up and examine it, noticing that the second hand makes a regular sweep around the watch's face. After some discussion, they conclude that the watch is run by a gremlin inside. They remove the back of the watch but cannot find the gremlin. After further discussion, they decide that it must be invisible. They also decide that it makes the hands go by running along the gears inside the watch. They replace the watch's back and take it home.

The next day the watch stops. Someone suggests that the gremlin is dead. Someone else suggests that it's probably sleeping. They shake the watch to awaken the gremlin, but the watch remains stopped. Someone finally turns the stem. The second hand begins to move. The person who said that the gremlin was asleep smiles triumphantly. The winding has awakened it.

For a long time the people hold the gremlin hypothesis, but finally an innovative citizen puts forth the hypothesis that the watch can work without a gremlin. He dismantles the watch and explains the movements of the inner parts. His fellows complain that he has left out the really important aspect, the gremlin. "Of course," they agree, "the winding contributes to the turning of the gears. But only because it wakes up the gremlin, which then resumes its running." But gradually the suggestion of the innovative citizen converts a number of others to his position. The gremlin is not vital to run the watch. Nevertheless, they are reluctant to reject the gremlin altogether. So they compromise and conclude that there is a gremlin inside, but he is not needed to run the watch.

From: Jeffrey Olen, *Persons and Their Worlds* (New York: Random House, 1983), 223.

> But the man who figured out that the watch worked without the intervention of a gremlin is dissatisfied. If we do not need the gremlin to explain how the watch works, why continue to believe that it exists? Isn't it simpler to say that it does not?

Applied to the mind–body problem, the watch is the human body, and the gremlin is the mind. Olen suggests that the people who believed that the gremlin operated the watch are equivalent to dualistic interactionists, and the people who believed that the gremlin was inside the watch but inactive were like epiphenomenalists, and the man who held that the watch was self-operating was like the materialist.

> A nonphysical mind is just as suspect as the gremlin. The only difference between the two cases is this: whereas there is no gremlin at all, there is a mind. The mistake is in thinking that it is anything over and above the brain.[5]

Eliminative materialism, which goes even further than reductivism in rejecting dualism, calls on us to reject as false the whole **Folk Psychology** language that makes reference to pains, beliefs, and desires (see Chapter 19). Such language supposes that our introspective states are incorrigible or infallible reporters of our inner life. Psychological experiments seem to show that we can be mistaken about our introspective reports, so we should reject Folk Psychology for a richer scientific theory. Here is how Richard Rorty, one of the earliest proponents puts it.

MIND–BODY IDENTITY, PRIVACY, AND CATEGORIES

A certain primitive tribe holds the view that illnesses are caused by demons—a different demon for each sort of illness. When asked what more is known about these demons than that they cause illness, they reply that certain members of the tribe—the witch-doctors—can see, after a meal of sacred mushrooms, various (intangible) humanoid forms on or near the bodies of patients. The witch-doctors have noted, for example, that a blue demon with a long nose accompanies epileptics, a fat red one accompanies sufferers from pneumonia, etc. They know such further facts as that the fat red demon dislikes a certain sort of mold which the witch-doctors give people who have pneumonia. If we encountered such a tribe, we would be inclined to tell them that there are no demons. We would tell them that diseases were caused by germs, viruses, and the like. We would add that the witch-doctors were not seeing demons, but merely having hallucinations.

Rorty goes on to argue that this belief in demons is analogous to our belief that we have pains.

> The absurdity of saying "Nobody has ever felt a pain" is no greater than that of saying "Nobody has ever seen a demon," if we have a suitable answer to the question, "what

From: Richard Rorty, "Mind–Body Identity, Privacy, and Categories," *Review of Metaphysics* (1965): 28–29.

was I reporting when I said I felt a pain?" To this question, the science of the future may reply, "You were reporting the occurrence of a certain brain-process, and it would make life simpler for us if you would in the future, say 'My C-fibers are firing' instead of saying 'I'm in pain.'" In so saying, he has as good a *prima facie* case as the scientist who answers the witch-doctors' question, "What was I reporting when I reported a demon?" by saying, "You were reporting the content of your hallucination, and it would make life simpler if, in the future, you would describe your experience in those terms."[6]

If philosophers like Rorty are right, our Folk Psychology language is as superstitious and misleading as the witch doctors' belief that demons cause illness. Mental events like pains should not merely be identified with brain states (like C-fibers firing) but should be *replaced* by neurological language, Neurospeak. Instead of saying, "I've a pain in my foot," Neurospeak will say something like "a C-fiber is firing in quadrant A2 of brain LP" (it's unclear whether "persons" will survive Neurospeak). Instead of saying "I believe that so and so will win the presidential election," Neurospeak will tell us to say, "the sentence S17 is manifesting itself in quadrant C56 of cerebral cortex LP."

Whatever the future prospects of eliminativism, at present it seems like science fiction or, at best, a research project to excite neuroscientists and their philosopher kin. But we need not choose between reductivism and eliminativism for our purposes. They both suppose a materialist monism and the question is whether materialist monism is true.

The main criticism of such monism is that it is obvious to introspection that we have mental events, and any theory that would deny them has a strong presumption of self-evidence to overcome. Reductivism, under the guise of reinterpreting mental events, claims it is not doing away with the events, only showing their true identity as physical events lodged in the brain.

The dualist's criticism of this identification rests on an appeal to *Leibniz's law* (the identity of indiscernibles): Two things are numerically identical if and only if they have all the same properties in common. That is, for any two things x and y, if they really are the same, then it must be the case that if x has property P, y also has it (and vice versa—if y has the property, x must also). For example, if Superman is really Clark Kent, then it could not be the case that if Superman was 6 feet tall, Clark Kent was 5 feet 9 inches tall. You certainly couldn't have Superman not being located in space!

The dualist points out that the mind has different properties from the body. The body occupies space and is subject to the laws of physics, whereas the mind doesn't occupy space and doesn't appear to be subject to the same laws. We might set forth the argument like this. Let M stand for "mind," B for "body," and P for property. Then,

1. B has property P (for example, extension in space).
2. M lacks property P.
3. If B has P and M lacks P, then M is not identical with B.
4. Therefore, the mind is not identical with the brain.

As we noted in Chapter 19, bodies are solid, material entities, extended in three-dimensional space, publicly observable, and measurable, while minds have none of these properties. Consciousness is not solid or material, is not extended in three-dimensional space, does not occupy space at all, is directly observable only by the person who owns it, cannot be measured, and seems incapable of causing things to happen in accordance with invariant laws of physics. Only the person herself can think her thoughts, feel her emotions, and suffer her pain.

How might the materialist respond to this? Materialists point out that what seems to be different is not always so. In times past, lightning was deemed a mysterious and spiritual force. The ancient Greeks thought that lightning was a thunderbolt of Zeus. Now we know that it is a luminous electrical discharge in the atmosphere, produced by the separation of electrical charges in thunderstorm clouds. Although it may not *appear* to us as electrical charges, physics assures us of that identity.

For eons, the nature of life was held to be a mysterious *élan vital,* a spiritual substance that animated whatever was living. In this century, however, such vitalism was undermined by discoveries in molecular biology. Life is made up of the same basic elements as other material, nonliving things. The difference between living and nonliving things, biology tells us, is not in the *kind* of substance that underlies the two types of things but in the *arrangement* of those substances.

Similarly, water has different properties than hydrogen and oxygen (such as wetness) but is nevertheless nothing but H_2O. So it could turn out that mental events are really physical events and states and nothing more. Materialists believe we are especially likely to be misled by thinking that consciousness has certain "phenomenological" properties it really does not have. For instance, when we imagine a green apple, we are inclined to say that our memory image is green. But nothing in our brain is green, so the critic of materialism triumphantly concludes that the mental image is not in our brain. The materialist replies that the image is not literally green and that, indeed, we do not literally have an image before our mind's eye, as we might literally have a picture of an apple before our physical eye in an art gallery. What is happening when you imagine an apple, according to the materialist, is that something is going on in your brain like what goes on when you see a real green apple. You are imagining seeing something green, and in that sense your imagination may be said to be green, but there is nothing literally green in your mind. Thus, nothing impedes the identification of mental with physical processes. Smart refers to this kind of mistake as the phenomenological fallacy:

> The phenomenological fallacy: to say that an image or sense datum is green is not to say that the conscious experience of having the image or sense datum is green. It is to say that it is the sort of experience we have when in normal conditions we look at a green apple, for example. Apples and unripe bananas can be green, but not the experiences of seeing them. An image or a sense datum can be green in a derivative sense, but this need not cause any worry, because, on the view I am

defending, images and sense data are not constituents of the world, though the processes of having an image or a sense datum are actual processes in the world. The experience of having a green sense datum is not itself green; it is a process occurring in grey matter. The world contains plumbers, but does not contain the average plumber; it also contains the having of a sense datum, but does not contain the sense datum.[7]

The materialist points out that our increased understanding of brain behavior makes it a plausible hypothesis that conscious thought and feeling are simply phenomenological descriptions of that which neuroscience describes from an externalist point of view.

The goal is to have a unified explanatory theory of the mind–brain interaction in which both science and common sense can take satisfaction.

Where does this leave us? The materialist has a certain amount of empirical success to his credit, which should give the dualist pause. The more that neuroscience can explain, the more impressive the credentials of materialism become. But can it really explain the self? Consciousness? Free will? Or is there an element of hubris at the very core of the materialist project?

The dualist agrees with the materialist monist that a unified explanation would be a good thing if we could get it. The questions, however, arise: Does something get left out in the shuffle? What is the price of such unity? Free will? Human dignity based on the idea of mental substance? God? The spiritual order? If there is independent evidence for these things, then unity of explanation is not worth the price.

Tom Nagel expresses nagging doubts about the attempt to capture the essence of humanness via a detached, scientific approach to the subject:

> There are things about the world and life and ourselves that cannot be adequately understood from a maximally objective standpoint, however much it may extend our understanding beyond the point from which we started. A great deal is essentially connected to a particular point of view. . . , and the attempt to give a complete account of the world in objective terms detached from these perspectives inevitably leads to false reductions or to outright denials that certain patently real phenomena exist at all. . . . To the extent that such no-nonsense theories have an effect, they merely threaten to impoverish the intellectual landscape for a while by inhibiting the serious expression of certain questions. In the name of liberation, these movements have offered us intellectual repression.[8]

Is Nagel right? The dualist fears that he is, while the materialist is "exhilarated by the prospect . . . by the [prospect of developing] an evolutionary explanation of the human intellect."[9] Why should we fear honest inquiry? Isn't the search for truth at the heart of science?

Perhaps the mind–body problem cannot be viewed in isolation from the rest of philosophy. What you decide regarding the theory of knowledge generally, philosophy of religion, and the problem of free will and determinism will influence your conclusion on the mind–body problem.

Summary

Reductive materialism and eliminative materialism seem to satisfy the principle of simplicity and conform to a scientific view of the world. Eliminativism seems a promissory note that science will eventually reinterpret our experience in a new framework and language. As such, we probably should admit it is a possibility, but not one for which there is presently much evidence. Reductivism is less radical but still faces problems, especially that of seeming to leave out of its account the phenomenology of conscious experience, of consciousness itself.

FOR FURTHER REFLECTION

1. What do you make of the story of Phineas Gage? Do such examples provide evidence that we are mistaken in supposing that the mind or consciousness is a separate reality?

2. If someone accepts materialism, is he or she thereby committed to determinism? Determinism will be discussed in Part 6, but you should be thinking about the relationship between the mind–body problem and free will/determinism.

3. If someone opts for materialism, which version (reductive or eliminitive) is more plausible?

4. Do you agree with Olen's analogy of the gremlins in the watch? Is it a caricature of dualism, or do you think it is an accurate analogy?

NOTES

1. Thomas Hobbes, *Leviathan* (New York: Dutton, 1950), Chapter 46.
2. Colin McGinn, *The London Review of Books* (January 23, 1986): 24–25.
3. J. J. C. Smart, "Sensations and Brain Processes," *Philosophical Review* 68 (1959).
4. Ibid.
5. Jeffrey Olen, *Persons and Their Worlds* (New York: Random House, 1983).
6. Richard Rorty, "Mind–Body Identity, Privacy, and Categories," *Review of Metaphysics* (1965): 30–31.
7. J. J. C. Smart, "Materialism," *Journal of Philosophy* 22 (1963).
8. Tom Nagel, *A View from Nowhere* (Oxford, UK: Oxford University Press, 1986), 7, 11.
9. Daniel Dennett, *The Intentional Stance* (Cambridge, MA: MIT Press, 1987), 5.

FOR FURTHER READING

Beakley, Brian, and Peter Ludlow, eds. *The Philosophy of Mind: Classical Problems and Contemporary Issues.* Cambridge, MA: MIT Press, 1992. An excellent anthology.

Churchland, Paul. *Matter and Consciousness.* Cambridge, MA: MIT Press, 1990. A superb introductory text from a materialist perspective.

Dennett, Daniel. *The Intentional Stance.* Cambridge, MA: MIT Press, 1989. A brilliant discussion of the mental states.

Levin, Michael E. *Metaphysics and the Mind–Body Problem.* Oxford, UK: Clarendon Press, 1979. An excellent defense of materialism.

Lycan, William, ed. *Mind and Cognition.* Oxford, UK: Blackwell, 1991. An excellent anthology.

McGinn, Colin. *The Character of Mind.* Oxford, UK: Oxford University Press, 1982. A rich, compact exposition of the major issues.

Moreland, J. P. *Scaling the Secular City.* Grand Rapids, MI: Baker Books, 1987. Contains a defense of dualistic interactionism from a Christian perspective.

Rosenthal, David M., ed. *The Nature of Mind.* Oxford, UK: Oxford University Press, 1992. The best anthology of contemporary work available.

Searle, John. *Mind, Brains and Science.* Cambridge, MA: Harvard University Press, 1984. A perceptive work, setting forth puzzles and providing a brilliant analysis of the issues.

Stich, Stephen. *From Folk Psychology to Cognitive Science: The Case Against Belief.* Cambridge, MA: MIT Press, 1983.

21 ⚶ Functionalism

At this point, you may be frustrated by the problems surrounding each theory that we have examined so far. The debates over whether we are made of one or two different substances, whether mental events can be reduced to brain events, and whether mental events exist at all seem fraught with insurmountable problems. "A plague on all your houses," we are tempted to shout, after working through these theories. A group of philosophers of like mind feels exactly the same way. In the 1960s and early 1970s, philosophers like Jerry Fodor of MIT and Hilary Putnam of Harvard criticized the current versions of materialist monism, the identity theory (roughly, what we have examined in Chapter 20 as reductive materialism), and in its place they offered a new theory, **functionalism.**[1] In this chapter, we examine both the functionalist's critique of the identity theory and functionalism itself as a replacement of other theories. Then we look at criticisms of functionalism.

Functionalists take issue with aspects of the identity theory, the form of reductivism that identifies types of mental events with types of brain events and with metaphysical behaviorism, which denies the reality of mental events. First, they argue—against the behaviorists and identity theorists—that mental states and events must be accounted for. The behaviorist, we noted in Chapter 19, is interested in input and output states. Functionalism, which is the heir to behaviorism, argues that this formula leaves out the uniqueness of mental states. Not only must environmental input and behavioral output be accounted for, but a third factor, types of mental states, must be recognized (see Figure 21.1).

A similar first criticism is leveled by the functionalist against the reductivists (or identity theory). First, functionalists argue that, although it may or may not be the case that physical matter is the only substance of which we partake, mental events exist and must be accounted for. Second, they accuse reductivists of chauvinism, in thinking that material brains like those found in humans and mammals are the *only* things that can account for mental events. Just as racism

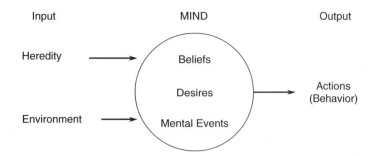

Figure 21.1

is chauvinism about race, as sexism is a prejudice about gender, and as speciesism is an unjustified view about one's own species, so reductivism is a chauvinism that unwarrantedly excludes all other forms of realization of mental events. "Just because Martians don't have brains like ours doesn't mean that they don't suffer or use reason!" the functionalist is apt to insist. Here functionalism sets forth the doctrine of *multiple realizability*, the view that mental events could be realized in many different forms and structures.

Note that the identity theorists hold that mental events are reducible to types of brain events, that consciousness is really nothing but a brain state or event. It is this doctrine of type identity at which the functionalist aims her attack.

Functionalists draw their inspiration from Aristotle who distinguished between form and matter, arguing that a form could be realized in many different ways, in different substances. For example, a statue of Abraham Lincoln could be made of marble, wood, clay, steel, aluminum, or papier-mâché. That is, for Aristotle there is no single *type* of matter that defines an entity. The form of the substance, not the substance itself, is the defining feature.

The doctrine of multiple realizability applies this insight to mental events, interpreting them as functions. Let's illustrate the doctrine itself by applying it to artifacts. Consider five different examples of mousetraps:

- A standard spring trap, where cheese is placed on a trigger. The mouse is attracted to the cheese, trips the trigger that in turn releases a spring, causing a metal bar to come crashing down on the head or neck of the mouse.

- Like the standard trap, only instead of a bar coming down, the trigger releases a rope. It surrounds the neck of the mouse, tightens and at the same time pulls the mouse off the ground, hanging him.

- A trapdoor mousetrap. When the mouse touches the cheese, a trapdoor opens and the mouse falls into a shoot, leading directly to an incinerator.

- A scented model of a mouse of the opposite sex is poisoned with a lethal perfume and left for the mouse to embrace. When he or she does so, the mouse imbibes the poison and soon expires.

- An awesome model of a ferocious cat, which when seen by mice causes them to die of fright.

All these instruments qualify as mousetraps. They all have the same purpose or function. We could invent other ways of trapping mice, but enumerating the different types of mousetraps is not the way of accounting for the idea of a mousetrap. There is no single material feature that all and only mousetraps have in common. All that they have in common is the *abstract* idea that their purpose or function is to catch mice. They can realize that function in multiple ways—hence the name, the doctrine of multiple realizability.

Similarly, the functionalist hypothesizes, there is no reason to rule out the possibility that mental events are realized in different ways in different structures. They could be realized in brain tissue like ours or a different kind of tissue in other animals, in the silicon chips of computers, in some other structure of Galacticans, or in an unknown substance that makes up angels. From artificial intelligence to angels, all that counts is that mental events be the result and that these mental events be part of the causal process mediating environmental input and behavioral output.

Similarly, in different humans there may be different ways in which the same function is realized. The cerebral cortex may have more than one type of structural mechanism that produces mental events. And two different people may function identically though they have different types of inward processes taking place.

At the core of the functionalist position is the idea that what makes a mental state like pain what it is is its functional role: Pain simply is whatever causes the rapid withdrawal of hands from the fire and whatever results from putting one's hand in the fire. So if a creature with entirely different wiring than we have was behaviorally isomorphic to us, the inner states that mediated its behavior would be our inner states because the essence of an inner state is the causes and effects it has.

This is where functionalism runs into problems. If the processes that produce the same function are too different, couldn't functionalism be missing an important feature of mental events? The *inverted-spectrum argument* is offered to illustrate this point: You have a particular type of sensation when you look at a red object and a different kind of sensation when you look at a green object. But isn't it possible for someone else to have the reverse sensations? When he looks at the green apple, he has a red sensation, and when he looks at the red apple, he has a green sensation. His behavior—his use of the words *red* and *green* would be *functionally* identical with yours—and his sensations of seeing a red and green apple would be functionally identical with yours. However, despite the functional equivalence, inner states are really different. Would this show that functionalism has missed an essential feature in accounting for mental events? That it is not just the function that counts but the reality of what is going on inside of one's mind or brain?

Functionalism concentrates on the input–output relations. I step on a nail (the input), and that action sends a message to my brain that in turn *causes* me to cry "Ouch" (the output). Other people simply withdraw their feet. Some grimace, others cry out, and still others weep. Concentrating on the functional analysis of cause and effect, however, seems to have the defects of behaviorism (which is what functionalism was in part meant to answer). The functionalist account leaves out precisely what is important, the *quality* of the inner state. That is, it is not enough to say that there are functionally equivalent types of mental events in conscious beings; we must also pay attention to the conscious experience itself that could be of a different type despite functional identity.

The functionalist generally meets this objection by denying the possibility or likelihood of the inverted-spectrum case or radically different qualitative states given the same biological state, but they seem conceivable.

A related objection by John Searle, called "The Chinese Room Objection," aims specifically at the claim that artificial intelligence thinks but is applicable to functionalism as a whole. Functionalism, on Searle's account, lacks sensitivity to our concepts of understanding and intentionality. Searle describes *understanding* as implying "both the possession of mental (intentional) states and the truth (validity, success) of these states" and *intentionality* as "that feature of certain mental states by which they are directed at or about objects and states of affairs in the world. Thus, beliefs, desires, and intentions are intentional states; undirected forms of anxiety and depression are not." Searle first distinguishes between strong and weak artificial intelligence (AI). Here is Searle's discussion.

MINDS, BRAINS AND PROGRAMS

What psychological and philosophical significance should we attach to recent efforts at computer simulations of human cognitive capacities? In answering this question, I find it useful to distinguish what I will call "strong" AI from "weak" or "cautious" AI (artificial intelligence). According to weak AI, the principal value of the computer in the study of the mind is that it gives us a very powerful tool. For example, it enables us to formulate and test hypotheses in a more rigorous and precise fashion. But according to strong AI, the computer is not merely a tool in the study of the mind; rather, the appropriately programmed computer really *is* a mind, in the sense that computers given the right programs can be literally said to *understand* and have other cognitive states. In strong AI, because the programmed computer has cognitive states, the programs are not mere tools that enable us to test psychological explanations; rather, the programs are themselves the explanations.

I have no objection to the claims of weak AI, at least as far as this article is concerned. My discussion here will be directed at the claims I have defined as those of strong AI, specifically the claim that the appropriately programmed computer literally has cognitive states and that the programs thereby explain human cognition. When I hereafter refer to AI, I have in mind the strong version, as expressed by these two claims.

I will consider the work of Roger Schank and his colleagues at Yale (Schank and Abelson 1977), because I am more familiar with it than I am with any other similar claims, and because it provides a very clear example of the sort of work I wish to examine. But nothing that follows depends upon the details of Schank's programs. The same

From: John Searle, "Minds, Brains and Programs," *Behavioral and Brain Sciences* 3 (1980). Reprinted by permission.

arguments would apply to Winograd's SHRDLU (Winograd 1973), Weizenbaum's ELIZA (Weizenbaum 1965), and indeed any Turing machine simulation of human mental phenomena....

Very briefly, and leaving out the various details, one can describe Schank's program as follows: The aim of the program is to simulate the human ability to understand stories. It is characteristic of human beings' story-understanding capacity that they can answer questions about the story even though the information that they give was never explicitly stated in the story. Thus, for example, suppose you are given the following story: "A man went into a restaurant and ordered a hamburger. When the hamburger arrived it was burned to a crisp, and the man stormed out of the restaurant angrily, without paying for the hamburger or leaving a tip." Now, if you are asked "Did the man eat the hamburger?" you will presumably answer, "No, he did not." Similarly, if you are given the following story: "A man went into a restaurant and ordered a hamburger; when the hamburger came he was very pleased with it; and as he left the restaurant he gave the waitress a large tip before paying his bill," and you are asked the question, "Did the man eat the hamburger?" you will presumably answer, "Yes, he ate the hamburger." Now Schank's machines can similarly answer questions about restaurants in this fashion. To do this, they have a "representation" of the sort of information that human beings have about restaurants, which enables them to answer such questions as those above, given these sorts of stories. When the machine is given the story and then asked the question, the machine will print out answers of the sort that we would expect human beings to give if told similar stories. Partisans of strong AI claim that in this question and answer sequence the machine is not only simulating a human ability but also (1) that the machine can literally be said to *understand* the story and provide the answers to questions, and (2) that what the machine and its programs do *explains* the human ability to understand the story and answer questions about it.

Both claims seem to me to be totally unsupported by Schank's work, as I will attempt to show in what follows. I am not, of course, saying that Schank himself is committed to these claims.

One way to test any theory of the mind is to ask oneself what it would be like if my mind actually worked on the principles that the theory says all minds work on. Let us apply this test to the Schank program with the following *Gedankenexperiment*.* Suppose that I'm locked in a room and given a large batch of Chinese writing. Suppose furthermore (as is indeed the case) that I know no Chinese, either written or spoken, and that I'm not even confident that I could recognize Chinese writing as Chinese writing distinct from, say, Japanese writing or meaningless squiggles. To me, Chinese writing is just so many meaningless squiggles. Now suppose further that after this first batch of Chinese writing I am given a second batch of Chinese script together with a set of rules for correlating the second batch with the first batch. The rules are in English, and I understand these rules as well as any other native speaker of English. They enable me to correlate one set of formal symbols with another set of formal symbols, and all

---

[*Experiment in the imagination.—Ed.]

that "formal" means here is that I can identify the symbols entirely by their shapes. Now suppose also that I am given a third batch of Chinese symbols together with some instructions, again in English, that enable me to correlate elements of this third batch with the first two batches, and these rules instruct me how to give back certain Chinese symbols with certain sorts of shapes in response to certain sorts of shapes given me in the third batch. Unknown to me, the people who are giving me all of these symbols call the first batch a "script," they call the second batch a "story," and they call the third batch "questions." Furthermore, they call the symbols I give them back in response to the third batch "answers to the questions," and the set of rules in English that they gave me, they call the "program." Now just to complicate the story a little, imagine that these people also give me stories in English, which I understand, and they then ask me questions in English about these stories, and I give them back answers in English. Suppose also that after a while I get so good at following the instructions for manipulating the Chinese symbols and the programmers get so good at writing the programs that from the external point of view—that is, from the point of view of somebody outside the room in which I am locked—my answers to the questions are absolutely indistinguishable from those of native Chinese speakers. Nobody just looking at my answers can tell that I don't speak a word of Chinese. Let us also suppose that my answers to the English questions are, as they no doubt would be, indistinguishable from those of other native English speakers, for the simple reason that I am a native English speaker. From the external point of view—from the point of view of someone reading my "answers"—the answers to the Chinese questions and the English questions are equally good. But in the Chinese case, unlike the English case, I produce the answers by manipulating uninterpreted formal symbols. As far as the Chinese is concerned, I simply behave like a computer; I perform computational operations on formally specified elements. For the purposes of the Chinese, I am simply an instantiation of the computer program.

Now the claims made by strong AI are that the programmed computer understands the stories and that the program in some sense explains human understanding. But we are now in a position to examine these claims in light of our thought experiment.

1. As regards the first claim, it seems to me quite obvious in the example that I do not understand a word of the Chinese stories. I have inputs and outputs that are indistinguishable from those of the native Chinese speaker, and I can have any formal program you like, but I still understand nothing. For the same reasons, Schank's computer understands nothing of any stories, whether in Chinese, English, or whatever, since in the Chinese case the computer is me, and in cases where the computer is not me, the computer has nothing more than I have in the case where I understand nothing.

2. As regards the second claim, that the program explains human understanding, we can see that the computer and its program do not provide sufficient conditions of understanding since the computer and the program are functioning, and there is no understanding. But does it even provide a necessary condition or a significant contribution to understanding? One of the claims made by the supporters of strong AI is that when I understand a story in English, what I am doing is exactly the same—or

perhaps more of the same—as what I was doing in manipulating the Chinese symbols. It is simply more formal symbol manipulation that distinguishes the case in English, where I do understand, from the case in Chinese, where I don't. I have not demonstrated that this claim is false, but it would certainly appear an incredible claim in the example. Such plausibility as the claim has derives from the supposition that we can construct a program that will have the same inputs and outputs as native speakers, and in addition we assume that speakers have some level of description where they are also instantiations of a program. On the basis of these two assumptions we assume that even if Schank's program isn't the whole story about understanding, it may be part of the story. Well, I suppose that is an empirical possibility, but not the slightest reason has so far been given to believe that it is true, since what is suggested—though certainly not demonstrated—by the example is that the computer program is simply irrelevant to my understanding of the story. In the Chinese case I have everything that artificial intelligence can put into me by way of a program, and I understand nothing; in the English case I understand everything, and there is so far no reason at all to suppose that my understanding has anything to do with computer programs, that is, with computational operations on purely formally specified elements. As long as the program is defined in terms of computational operations on purely formally defined elements, what the example suggests is that these by themselves have no interesting connection with understanding. They are certainly not sufficient conditions, and not the slightest reason has been given to suppose that they are necessary conditions or even that they make a significant contribution to understanding. Notice that the force of the argument is not simply that different machines can have the same input and output while operating on different formal principles—that is not the point at all. Rather, whatever purely formal principles you put into the computer, they will not be sufficient for understanding, since a human will be able to follow the formal principles without understanding anything. No reason whatever has been offered to suppose that such principles are necessary or even contributory, since no reason has been given to suppose that when I understand English I am operating with any formal program at all.

Well, then, what is it that I have in the case of the English sentences that I do not have in the case of the Chinese sentences? The obvious answer is that I know what the former mean, while I haven't the faintest idea what the latter mean. But in what does this consist and why couldn't we give it to a machine, whatever it is? ...

...My critics point out that there are many different degrees of understanding; that "understanding" is not a simple two-place predicate; that there are even different kinds and levels of understanding, and often the law of excluded middle doesn't even apply in a straightforward way to statements of the form "*x* understands *y*"; that in many cases it is a matter for decision and not a simple matter of fact whether *x* understand *y;* and so on. To all of these points I want to say: of course, of course. But they have nothing to do with the points at issue. There are clear cases in which "understanding" literally applies and clear cases in which it does not apply; and these two sorts of cases are all I need for this argument. I understand stories in English; to a lesser degree I can understand stories in French; to a still lesser degree, stories in German; and in Chinese, not at all. My car and my adding machine, on the other hand, understand nothing: they are not in that line of business.* We often attribute "understanding" and other cognitive predicates by metaphor and analogy to cars, adding machines, and other artifacts, but nothing is proved by such attributions. We say, "The door *knows* when to open because of its photoelectric cell," "The adding machine *knows how* (*understands how,* is *able*) to do addition and subtraction but not division," and "The thermostat *perceives* changes in the temperature." The reason we make these attributions is quite interesting, and it has to do with the fact that in artifacts we extend our own intentionality;[†] our tools are extensions of our purposes, and so we find it natural to make metaphorical attributions of intentionality to them; but I take it no philosophical ice is cut by such examples. The sense in which an automatic door "understands instructions" from its photoelcetric cell is not at all the sense in which I understand English. If the sense in which Schank's programmed computers understand stories is supposed to be the metaphorical sense in which the door understands, and not the sense in which I understand English, the issue would not be worth discussing....

From the viewpoint of an observer, the answers to the Chinese questions and the English questions are equally good. However, in the Chinese case, unlike the English case, you produce the answers by manipulating uninterpreted formal symbols. As far as the Chinese case is concerned, you simply behave like a computer; you perform computational operations on formally specified elements. For the purpose of the Chinese cases, you are "simply an instantiation of the computer program." You have inputs and outputs that are indistinguishable from a Chinese speaker, but you understand nothing.

Thus, according to Searle, there are no grounds to suppose that robots or artificial intelligence can understand, have intentions, or perform mental acts. Do you agree? Can you think of a response that the functionalist may make to Searle's Chinese Room Objection?

Searle concludes his critique of AI with his own view on the question "Can a machine think?"

"Could a machine think?" My own view is that *only* a machine could think, and indeed only very special kinds of machines, namely brains and machines that had the same causal powers as brains. And that is the main reason strong AI has had little to tell us about thinking, since it has nothing to tell us about machines. By its own definition, it is about programs, and programs are not machines. Whatever else intentionality is, it is a biological phenomenon, and it is as likely to be as causally dependent on the specific biochemistry of its origins as lactation, photosynthesis, or any other biological

---

*Also, "understanding" implies both the possession of mental (intentional) states and the truth (validity, success) of these states. For the purposes of this discussion we are concerned only with the possession of the states.

†Intentionality is by definition that feature of certain mental states by which they are directed at or about objects and states of affairs in the world. Thus, beliefs, desires, and intentions are intentional states; undirected forms of anxiety and depression are not.

phenomena. No one would suppose that we could produce milk and sugar by running a computer simulation of the formal sequences in lactation and photosynthesis, but where the mind is concerned many people are willing to believe in such a miracle because of a deep and abiding dualism: The mind they suppose is a matter of formal processes and is independent of quite specific material causes in the way that milk and sugar are not.

In defense of this dualism the hope is often expressed that the brain is a digital computer (early computers, by the way, were often called "electronic brains"). But that is no help. Of course the brain is a digital computer. Since everything is a digital computer, brains are too. The point is that the brain's causal capacity to produce intentionality cannot consist in its instantiating a computer program, since for any program you like it is possible for something to instantiate that program and still not have any mental states. Whatever it is that the brain does to produce intentionality, it cannot consist in instantiating a program since no program, by itself, is sufficient for intentionality.[2]

One may ask whether this form of emergentism is simply a version of epiphenomenalism (a one-directional causal relation from biology to mental events) or whether it is a kind of reductivism.

One can also raise a question of Searle's critique of artificial intelligence: If mental states can't arise from silicon computer chips, what reason is there to believe that they can arise from biological chips (cells)?

Whether functionalism is a significant advance over behaviorism and whether it is superior to reductive materialism is a highly controversial question in philosophy of mind. What seems correct is the idea of multiple realizability. No reason has been given against the possibility that same types of behavioral or mental events arise in different types of structures. The question is, Can some form of eliminative materialism or dualism account for this feature while giving a better account of how the various structures actually work? This is one of the exciting challenges of contemporary philosophy of mind, which I must leave you to ponder.

Summary

We have noted the strengths and weakness of functionalism, the theory that different structures could give rise to mental events and that we need not understand these processes in order to have a workable understanding of the workings of our mind. The strength is that it improves on behaviorism in that it recognizes the reality of mental states and events and keeps open the possibility of mental events in other types of structures (physical or nonphysical) from ours. Consciousness could be present in Galacticans made up of different types of molecules than ourselves or in human-made artificial intelligence. Strictly speaking, functionalists need not be materialists (though most are), which indicates the open endedness of this position.

You must ask yourself whether functionalism or any of its rivals, discussed in these three chapters, gives a satisfactory account of the central mystery of humanity, the conundrum of intelligent consciousness.

FOR FURTHER REFLECTION

1. What are the advantages of functionalism? How plausible a theory is it? What does it do that the other theories don't? What does it leave out that is important? Can eliminative materialism answer the problems raised by functionalism?

2. Review the major theories discussed in the last three chapters. Assess their strengths and weaknesses. What is your conclusion?

3. The functionalist claims that what makes a mental state like pain what it is is its functional role. Is this a plausible claim? Is what makes pain its causes and effects or rather what it is in itself?

4. Consider Searle's "Chinese Room Objection." Is Searle's concept of *understanding* clear? Could you argue that we really understand in degrees, so that robots and computers simply have low-level understanding whereas we have high levels?

5. Is Searle's own conclusions on the mind being a purely biological phenomenon satisfactory? How might a dualist object to it?

NOTES

1. See Jerry Fodor, *Psychological Explanations* (New York: Random House, 1968); and Hilary Putnam, "The Nature of Mental States" in his *Mind, Language and Reality* (London: Cambridge University Press, 1975). Both articles are found in Beakley and Ludlow's anthology and Rosenthal's anthology, both mentioned in For Further Reading below.

2. John Searle, "Minds, Brains and Programs," *Behavioral and Brain Sciences* 3 (1980). Reprinted by permission.

FOR FURTHER READING

Beakley, Brian, and Peter Ludlow, eds. *The Philosophy of Mind: Classical Problems and Contemporary Issues.* Cambridge, MA: MIT Press, 1992. An excellent anthology.

Churchland, Paul. *Matter and Consciousness.* Cambridge, MA: MIT Press, 1990. A superb introductory text from a materialist perspective.

Dennett, Daniel. *The Intentional Stance.* Cambridge, MA: MIT Press, 1989. A brilliant discussion of the mental states.

Levin, Michael E. *Metaphysics and the Mind–Body Problem.* Oxford, UK: Clarendon Press, 1979. An excellent defense of materialism. My illustration of the principle of simplicity was taken from this work.

Lycan, William, ed. *Mind and Cognition.* Oxford, UK: Blackwell, 1991. An excellent anthology.

McGinn, Colin. *The Character of Mind*. Oxford, UK: Oxford University Press, 1982. A rich, compact exposition of the major issues.

Moreland, J. P. *Scaling the Secular City*. Grand Rapids, MI: Baker Books, 1987. Contains a defense of dualistic interactionism from a Christian perspective.

Rosenthal, David M., ed. *The Nature of Mind*. Oxford, UK: Oxford University Press, 1992. The best anthology of contemporary work available.

Searle, John. *Mind, Brains and Science*. Cambridge, MA: Harvard University Press, 1984. A perceptive work, setting forth puzzles and providing a brilliant analysis of the issues.

Stich, Stephen. *From Folk Psychology to Cognitive Science: The Case Against Belief*. Cambridge, MA: MIT Press, 1983.

22 ✢ Who Am I? The Problem of Personal Identity

Suppose you wake up tomorrow in a strange room. There are pictures of unfamiliar people on the light blue walls. The furniture in the room is very odd. You wonder how you got here. You remember being in the hospital where you were dying of cancer. Your body was wasting away, and your death was thought to be a few days away. Your physician, Dr. Matthews, had kindly given you an extra dose of morphine to kill the pain. That's all you can remember. You notice a calendar on the wall in front of you. The date is April 1. "This can't be," you think, "for yesterday was January second." Not quite your normal, alert self, you try to take this all in. "Where have I been all this time?" Suddenly, you see a mirror. In horror you reel back, for it's not your body that you spy in the glass, but a large woman's body. Your color has altered, and, if you're male, so has your sex. You have more than doubled your previous normal weight and look 25 years older. You feel tired, confused, and frightened and can scarcely hold back tears of dismay. Soon a strange man, about 45 years of age, comes into your room. "I was wondering when you would waken, Maria. The doctor said that I should let you sleep as long as possible, but I didn't think that you would be asleep two whole days. Anyway, the operation was a success. We had feared that the accident had ended your life. The children and I are so grateful. Jean and John will be home in an hour and will be so happy to see you awake. How do you feel?"

"Can this be a bad joke, an April Fool's prank?" you wonder, noting the date on the calendar. "Who is this strange man, and who am I?" Unbeknown to you, Dr. Matthews needed a living brain to implant in the head of Mrs. Maria Martin, mother of four children, who had suffered a massive head injury in a car accident. After arriving at the hospital, her body was kept alive by technology, but her brain was dead. Your brain was in excellent shape but lacked a healthy body; Maria Martin's body was intact but needed a brain. Being an enterprising

331

brain surgeon, Dr. Matthews saw his chance of performing the first successful brain transplant. Later that day, Matthews breaks the news of your transformation to you. He congratulates you on being the first human to survive a brain transplant and reminds you, just in case you are not completely satisfied with the transformation, that you would have been dead had he not performed the operation. Still dazed by the news, you try to grasp the significance of what has happened to you. You wonder whether you'd be better off dead. The fact that the operation was a success is of little comfort to you, for you're not sure whether you are you!

Given the technological possibility of this imaginary take, would you still be you inside Maria's body? What are you anyway? What exactly defines your personal identity over time and place? The same body? The same brain? The same soul? Some psychological properties, such as the same desires and beliefs or the same memories? Or something else? Are you the same person you were at one day old? At 10 years of age? At 15? Last night? What does it mean to be the same person?

The problem of personal identity is one of the most fascinating in the history of philosophy. It is especially complicated since it involves not one but at least three, and possibly four, philosophical questions. What is it to be a person? What is identity? What is personal identity? How is survival possible given the problems of personal identity? We will briefly discuss the first three questions in this chapter. Chapter 23 discusses the fourth question.

What Is It to Be a Person?

What is it that sets off us human beings as having special value, as being entities with serious moral rights? What characteristics must one have to have high moral value? The Judeo-Christian tradition generally defines personhood in terms of our ability to reason and make moral choices. Writing within the Judeo-Christian tradition, the English philosopher John Locke (1632–1704)—himself a Cartesian dualist, believing that we possess a soul within a body—distinguishes being a *human being* from being a *person*. Being a human being just means being a *Homo sapiens,* an animal of a particular species. A person, however, is "a thinking, intelligent being which has reason and can consider itself as itself."[1] We may label this the *psychological states criterion* of personal identity. Although Locke believes we have souls, having a soul is not sufficient for personal identity.

AN ESSAY CONCERNING HUMAN UNDERSTANDING

If the *identity of the soul alone* makes the same *man,* and there be nothing in the nature of matter why the same individual spirit may not be united to different bodies, it will be possible that those men, living in distant ages, and of different tempers, may have

From: John Locke, *An Essay Concerning Human Understanding,* ed. A. C. Fraser (Oxford, UK: Clarendon Press, 1894; first published in 1688), Book II.27.9.

been the same man. This is a very strange way of using the word "man," applied as it is to an idea of which the body and shape are excluded....

An animal is a living organized body; and consequently the same animal, as we have observed, is the same continued *life* communicated to different particles of matter, as they happen successively to be united to that organized living body. And whatever is talked of other definitions, ingenious observation puts it past doubt, that the idea in our minds, of which the sound "man" in our mouths is a sign, is nothing else but of an animal of such a certain form.

A soul, or *essence of a person*, could take on different bodily forms and still preserve the same essential identity. But we are not simply souls. We are animals, having a living organized body. Locke goes on to define personal identity.

I presume it is not the idea of a thinking or rational being alone that makes the *idea of a man* in most people's sense: but of a body, so and so shaped, joined to it; and if that be the idea of a man, the same successive body not shifted all at once, must, as well as the same immaterial spirit, go to the making of the same man.

This being assumed, to find wherein personal identity consists, we must consider what *person* stands for;—which, I think, is a thinking intelligent being, that has reason and reflection, and can consider itself as itself, the same thinking thing, in different times and places; which it does only by that consciousness which is inseparable from thinking, and, as it seems to me, essential to it: it being impossible for any one to perceive without *perceiving* that he does perceive. When we see, hear, smell, taste, feel, meditate, or will anything, we know that we do so. Thus it is always as to our present sensation and perceptions: and by this every one is to himself that which he calls self:—it not being considered, in this case, whether the same self be continued in the same or diverse substances. For, since consciousness always accompanies thinking, and it is that which makes every one to be what he calls self, and thereby distinguishes himself from all other thinking things, in this alone consists personal identity, i.e., the sameness of a rational being: and as far as this consciousness can be extended backwards to any past action or thought, so far reaches the identity of that person; it is the same self now it was then; and it is by the same self with this present one that now reflects on it, that that action was done.[2]

It is our ability to reason, introspect, and survey our memories and intentions that sets us apart from other animals as being of greater value. A soul or spirit is "a thinking intelligent being, that has reason and reflection, and can consider itself as itself, the same thinking thing, in different times and places; which it does only by that consciousness which is inseparable from thinking, and as it seems to me, essential to it." Personal identity through time consists in having a continuity of consciousness since it is by consciousness that our various thoughts and sensations belong to the same person. It is via memories that the person possesses this connection of consciousness, for memories link past consciousness with the present. If you remember doing act A 10 years ago, you were the person who did that act—regardless whether you had this body or another—for after all, our cells are constantly replacing one another so that every 7 years we have essentially a new body.

Thus we may be able without difficulty to conceive the same person at the resurrection, though in a body not exactly in make or parts the same which he had here,—the same consciousness going along with the soul that inhabits it. But yet the soul alone, in the change of bodies, would scarce to any one but to him that makes the soul the man, be enough to make the same man. For should the soul of a prince, carrying with it the consciousness of the prince's past life, enter and inform the body of a cobbler, as soon as deserted by his own soul, every one sees he would be the same *person* with the prince, accountable only for the prince's actions: but who would say it was the same *man*? The body too goes to the making of the man, and would, I guess, to everybody determine the man in this case, wherein the soul, with all its princely thoughts about it, would not make another man: but he would be the same cobbler to every one besides himself. I know that, in the ordinary way of speaking, the same person, and the same man, stand for one and the same thing. And indeed every one will always have a liberty to speak as he pleases, and to apply what articulate sounds to what ideas he thinks fit, and change them as often as he pleases. But yet, when we will inquire what makes the same *spirit, man,* or *person,* we must fix the ideas of spirit, man, or person in our minds; and having resolved with ourselves what we mean by them, it will not be hard to determine in either of them, or the like, when it is the same, and when not.

But it will still be objected: Suppose I wholly lose my memory of some parts of my life, beyond a possibility of retrieving them, so that perhaps I shall never be conscious of them again; yet am I not the same person that did those actions, had those thoughts that I once was conscious of, though I have now forgot them? To which I answer, that we must here take notice what the word *I* is applied to; which, in this case, is the *man* only. And the same man being presumed to be the same person, I is easily here supposed to stand also for the same person. But if it be possible for the same man to have distinct incommunicable consciousness at different times, it is past doubt the same man would at different times make different persons; which, we see, is the sense of mankind in the solemnest declaration of their opinions, human laws not punishing the mad man for the sober man's actions, nor the sober man for what the mad man did,—thereby making them two persons: which is somewhat explained by our way of speaking in English when we say such an one is "not himself," or is "besides himself"; in which phrases it is insinuated, as if those who now, or at least first used them, thought the self was changed; the selfsame person was no longer in that man.

But yet it is hard to conceive that Socrates, the same individual man, should be two persons. To help us a little in this, we must consider what is meant by Socrates, or the same individual *man.*

First, it must be either the same individual, immaterial, thinking substance; in short, the same numerical soul, and nothing else.

Secondly, or the same animal, without any regard to the immaterial soul.

Thirdly, or the same immaterial spirit united to the same animal.

Now, take which of these suppositions you please, it is impossible to make personal identity to consist in anything but consciousness; or reach any further than that does.[3]

Thus, personal identity over time consists in the continuity of memories. The implications are that having the same soul is not sufficient for personal identity, for the same soul could transfer from Napoleon's body to yours, but if the soul lost Napoleon's memories, you would not be Napoleon. On the other hand, we could imagine the same consciousness occupying two different bodies so that the two were one person.

Do you see any problems with Locke's theory? What about memories that are not continuous? In partial amnesia, do we cease to be who we were? Thomas Reid suggested a problem with regard to Locke's theory. Suppose there is a military officer who at age 25 is a hero in battle and who remembers getting a flogging in his childhood, say, at age 10. Later, at age 65, he recalls the heroic deed done at 25 but cannot recall the flogging. Yet the memory of the flogging defined his personhood at 25, so if he (now at 65) is the same person who was a hero at 25 (as he must be on Locke's account), must he not also be the same person who was flogged at 10, even though he no longer recalls the flogging? Does Locke have a way out of this problem?

What would Locke say about people with split personalities? There is a famous case of a girl named Sybil, who allegedly expressed sixteen different personalities with sixteen different sets of memories. On a Lockean psychological states account, would we have to say that one body contains sixteen different persons? Are there different persons inside each of us, expressed by different "sides" of our personality?

Sometimes a person expresses apparent memories of events that occurred in distant times and to different "persons." Does another person possess the body of the contemporary? If your friend suddenly starts reminiscing about the Battle of Waterloo and the beautiful Empress Josephine, has Napoleon suddenly come alive in your friend's body? This would truly be a case of reincarnation! But what if two of your friends came to you with the same "foreign" memories? And what is to prohibit complete soul flow, a different person inside you each day? The consciousness might pass from body to body, as in the prince and cobbler tale, so that personal identity transferred itself from one body to the next in indefinite succession. How do you know that the soul that is remembering today is the same soul that remembered yesterday? You might object that this couldn't be the case because you have the same body, but that objection won't work since the body has nothing to do with the psychological states criterion. If you think that the body is important, this might be an indication that the memory criterion is inadequate on its own and depends on a physical body for continuity. One might also ask what are the implications of Locke's theory for moral and legal responsibility. If John Gacy committed several heinous murders 10 years ago but no longer remembers them, is the present John Gacy the same person who committed those atrocities and should *he* be held accountable for them?

Radical as Locke's theory is, an even more radical theory is that of David Hume (1711–1776), who denies that we even have a self. Recall from our discussion of Hume's views of knowledge (Part 4) that all learning comes from sensory impressions. Since there does not seem to be a separate impression of the self that we experience, there is no reason to believe that we have a self. The most we can identify ourselves with is our consciousness, and that constantly changes. There is no separate, permanent self that endures over time. Hence, personal identity is a fiction—albeit one we cannot help having.

A TREATISE OF HUMAN NATURE

There are some philosophers, who imagine we are every moment intimately conscious of what we call our Self; that we feel its existence and its continuance in existence; and are certain, beyond the evidence of a demonstration, both of its perfect identity and simplicity....

Unluckily all these positive assertions are contrary to that very experience, which is pleaded for them, nor have we any idea of *self,* after the manner it is here explained. For from what impression could this idea be derived? This question 'tis impossible to answer without a manifest contradiction and absurdity; and yet 'tis a question, which must necessarily be answered, if we would have the idea of self pass for clear and intelligible. It must be some one impression, that gives rise to every real idea. But self or person is not any one impression, but that to which our several impressions and ideas are supposed to have a reference. If any impression gives rise to the idea of self, that impression must continue invariably the same, through the whole course of our lives; since self is supposed to exist after that manner. But there is no impression constant and invariable. Pain and pleasure, grief and joy, passions and sensations succeed each other, and never all exist at the same time. It cannot, therefore, be from any of these impressions, or from any other, that the idea of self is derived; and consequently there is no such idea.

But farther, what must become of all our particular perceptions upon this hypothesis? All these are different, and distinguishable, and separable from each other, and may be separately considered, and may exist separately, and have no need of any thing to support their existence. After what manner, therefore, do they belong to self; and how are they connected with it? For my part, when I enter most intimately into what I call *myself,* I always stumble on some particular perception or other, of heat or cold, light or shade, love or hatred, pain or pleasure. I never can catch *myself* at any time without a perception, and never can observe any thing but the perception. When my perceptions are removed for any time, as by sound sleep; so long am I insensible of *myself,* and may truly be said not to exist. And were all my perceptions removed by death, and could I neither think, nor feel, nor see, nor love, nor hate after the dissolution of my body, I should be entirely annihilated, nor do I conceive what is farther requisite to make me a perfect nonentity. If any one upon serious and unprejudiced reflection, thinks he has a different notion of *himself,* I must confess I can reason no longer with him. All I can allow him is, that he may be in the right as well as I, and that we are essentially different in this particular. He may, perhaps, perceive something simple and continued, which he calls *himself;* though I am certain there is no such principle in me.

But setting aside some metaphysicians of this kind, I may venture to affirm of the rest of mankind, that they are nothing but a bundle or collection of different perceptions, which succeed each other with an inconceivable rapidity, and are in a perpetual flux and movement. Our eyes cannot turn in their sockets without varying our perceptions.

From: David Hume, *A Treatise of Human Nature.* First published in 1738.

Our thought is still more variable than our sight; and all our other senses and faculties contribute to this change; nor is there any single power of the soul, which remains unalterably the same, perhaps for one moment. The mind is a kind of theatre, where several perceptions successively make their appearance; pass, re-pass, glide away, and mingle in an infinite variety of postures and situations. There is properly no *simplicity* in it at one time, nor *identity* in different; whatever natural propension we may have to imagine that simplicity and identity. The comparison of the theatre must not mislead us. They are the successive perceptions only, that constitute the mind; nor have we the most distant notion of the place, where these scenes are represented, or of the materials, of which it is composed.

What then gives us so great a propension to ascribe an identity to these successive perceptions, and to suppose ourselves possessed of an invariable and uninterrupted existence through the whole course of our lives? …

We have a distinct idea of an object, that remains invariable and uninterrupted through a supposed variation of time; and this idea we call that of *identity* or *sameness*. We have also a distinct idea of several different objects existing in succession, and connected together by a close relation; and this to an accurate view affords as perfect a notion of *diversity,* as if there was no manner of relation among the objects. But though these two ideas of identity, and a succession of related objects be in themselves perfectly distinct, and even contrary, yet 'tis certain, that in our common way of thinking they are generally confounded with each other. That action of the imagination, by which we consider the uninterrupted and invariable object, and that by which we reflect on the succession of related objects, are almost the same to the feeling, nor is there much more effort of thought required in the latter case than in the former. The relation facilitates the transition of the mind from one object to another, and renders its passage as smooth as if it contemplated one continued object. This resemblance is the cause of the confusion and mistake, and makes us substitute the notion of identity, instead of that of related objects….

Thus we feign the continued existence of the perceptions of our senses, to remove the interruption; and run into the notion of a *soul,* and *self,* and *substance,* to disguise the variation. But we may farther observe, that where we do not give rise to such a fiction, our propension to confound identity with relation is so great, that we are apt to imagine something unknown and mysterious, connecting the parts, beside their relation; and this I take to be the case with regard to the identity we ascribe to plants and vegetables. And even when this does not take place, we still feel a propensity to confound these ideas, though we are not able fully to satisfy ourselves in that particular, nor find any thing invariable and uninterrupted to justify our notion of identity.

Thus, the controversy concerning identity is not merely a dispute of words. For when we attribute identity, in an improper sense, to variable or interrupted objects, our mistake is not confined to the expression, but is commonly attended with a fiction, either of something invariable and uninterrupted, or of something mysterious and inexplicable, or at least with a propensity to such fictions….

The notion of a self or soul is very likely a fiction. "I" am merely a bundle of perceptions. There is consciousness of a continuing succession of experiences but not of a continuing experiencer. This view is compatible with the physicalist view of personhood.

How do we decide what it is that makes us valuable? Perhaps self-consciousness is a necessary or minimal condition, but is it a sufficient one? Are primates and other mammals persons? The subject is a difficult philosophical problem whose solution will likely depend on wider metaphysical and theoretical considerations. But if the question of personhood is a difficult problem, the question of identity is no less so.

What Is Identity?

At first glance, this sounds like an absurdly simple question. Identity is the fact that everything is itself and not another. In logic, the law of identity (the formula $A = A$) formally states the definition. We are not interested, however, in a formal definition of mere identity but identity *over time* or reidentification (sometimes this is referred to as *numerical identity*). What is it to be the *same* thing over time? Suppose you go to an automobile dealership to buy a new car. You see several blue Fords parked side by side. They resemble each other so much that you cannot tell them apart. They are the same type of car and are *exactly similar* to each other. Now you pick out one at random and buy it. Your car is a different car than the other blue Fords even though you couldn't tell the difference between them. A year passes, and your blue Ford now has 20,000 miles on it and a few scratches. Is it the same car that you originally bought? Most of us would probably agree that it is. The changes have altered but not destroyed its identity as the blue car that you bought and have driven 20,000 miles.

What does your blue Ford have that causes it to be the same car over the period of one year? A common history, continuity over time. The car is linked together by a succession of spatiotemporal events from its origins in Detroit to its present place in your driveway. This distinguishes it from all the other Fords that were ever built, no matter how similar they appear. Thus, we might conclude that *continuity over time* is the criterion of identity.

But immediately we find problems with this criterion. The Rio Grande dries up in places in New Mexico every summer, only to reappear as a running river in the early spring. Is the Rio Grande the same river this year as it was the last? There isn't any continuity over time of water flowing over the riverbed. Perhaps we can escape the problem by saying that by "river" we really mean the riverbed, which must hold running water sometimes but need not always convey it. Does this solve the problem?

Consider another counterexample: The Chicago White Sox are playing the New York Yankees in Yankee Stadium in late April. The game is called in the fifth inning with the Yankees leading 3–2. Shortly afterward there is a baseball strike, and all players take to the picket lines while a new set of players come up from the minor leagues to fill their positions. The "game" is continued in Chicago in August with a whole new set of players on both sides. The White Sox win, and the game decides who wins the division. Suppose the Yankee

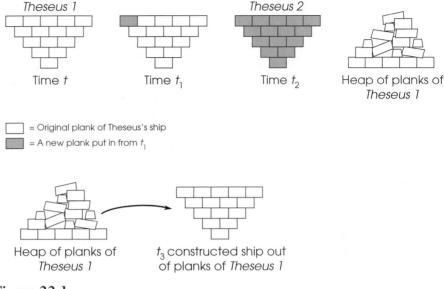

Figure 22.1

shortstop, who had been a philosophy major in college, protests that this hybrid game must not count, so a new game must be played in its stead. He argues that since there was no continuity between the two segments of the "game," that not even the same players played in both halves, the two segments cannot count as constituting one and the same baseball game. Does the shortstop have a point? Should the Yankee manager accept his argument and appeal the game to the commissioner of baseball? Should the commissioner call for a new game? Why or why not?

The most perplexing problem with regard to the notion of "sameness" or identity over time is illustrated by the ancient tale of Theseus's ship. Suppose you have a small ship (*Theseus 1*) that is in need of some repairs. You begin (at time t_1) to replace the old planks and material one by one with new planks and material until after 1 year (time t_2) the ship is completely made up of different material (see Figure 22.1). Do you have the same ship at t_2 as you had at t_1? If so, at what point did it (call it *Theseus 2*) become a different ship?

People disagree about whether Theseus's ship has changed its identity. Suppose you argue that it has not changed its identity, for it had a continuous history over time and therefore is the same ship. But now suppose your friend takes the material discarded from the original *Theseus* and reconstructs that ship (call it *Theseus 3*). Which ship is now Theseus's ship? There is the *continuity of the ship* between *Theseus 1* and *2* but *continuity of material* between *Theseus 1* and *3*. Which type of continuity should be decisive here? If it worries you that there was a time when the material of *Theseus 1* was not functioning as a ship, we could alter the example and suppose that as the planks were taken from *Theseus 1* they were transferred to another ship *Argos* where they replaced

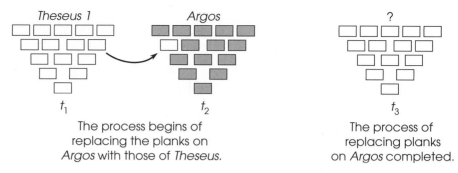

Figure 22.2

the *Argos*'s planks, ending up with a ship that contained every board and nail from the original *Theseus* (call this transformed *Argos Theseus 4*). Which is now the original *Theseus*? (See Figure 22.2.)

Does there not seem something puzzling about the notion of identity? Now we must take the two puzzling concepts, personhood and identity, and combine them.

What Is Personal Identity?

What is it to be the same person over time? Are you the same person that you were when you were 1 year old or even 16 years old? Recall Locke's idea of personhood, that mental characteristics (ability to reflect or introspect) constitute personhood. Personal identity is indicated by the successive memories that the person has had, the continuity over time of a set of experiences that were remembered. We called this the psychological states criterion of personal identity. The main competitor of this view is the *brain criterion* of personal identity, though some philosophers hold to a *body criterion*. Let's examine each of these briefly.

The psychological states criterion holds that our memories constitute our identity over time. You are the same person you were at 10 years of age because you have a continuous set of memories that contains all those that you had at age 10 plus others that continued after that year. We already noted problems with this view when considering Locke's theory.

But the body criterion has difficulties too, one of which is the fact that the body can undergo radical changes and we would still want to call the person the same person. Almost all cells in our body change every 7 years. Do we become a new person every 7 years? Or think of the story at the beginning of this chapter in which Dr. Matthews transplants your brain into Maria Martin's body. Despite these physical changes, wouldn't you still be you?

This suggests the third criterion, the brain criterion of personal identity. Our memories are contained within our brain, so we might want to say that having the same brain constitutes the same person. But this has difficulties, as brought out by Oxford University philosopher Derek Parfit. It is well known that if the corpus callosum, the great band of fibers that unites the two hemispheres of the brain, is cut, two different centers of consciousness can be created. When either side of the cerebral cortex of the brain is destroyed, the person can live on as a conscious being. It is also possible in principle to transplant brains. Suppose your body is destroyed and neurologists transplant each half of your brain into a different body. Dr. Matthews transplants one half of your brain into Maria Martin and the other half into the head of a 7-foot-tall basketball player. "You" wake up with two personalities. Do you survive the operation? There seems to be just three possible answers: (1) You do not survive; (2) you survive as one of the two; and (3) you survive as two people.

In the following dialogue between two British philosophers, Godfrey Vesey and Derek Parfit, these alternatives are applied to the possibility of split-brain transplants. Noting that a team from the Metropolitan Hospital in Cleveland has successfully transplanted the head of one monkey onto the body of another, Vesey asks us to imagine a successful human brain transplant—much like the story told at the beginning of this chapter of your brain being transplanted into the body of Maria Martin.

The next step is to imagine that your brain is not simply transplanted whole into someone else's brainless head, but is divided in two and half put into each of two other people's brainless heads. The same memories have been coded in many parts of the cortex; both people say they are Brown and can describe events in Brown's life as if they are their own. Parfit argues that there is nothing more to personal identity than psychological continuity.

BRAIN TRANSPLANTS AND PERSONAL IDENTITY

VESEY: Derek, can we begin with the belief that you claim most of us have about personal identity? It's this: whatever happens between now and some future time either I shall still exist or I shan't. And any future experience will either be my experience or it won't. In other words, personal identity is an all or nothing matter: either I survive or I don't. Now what do you want to say about that?

PARFIT: It seems to me just false. I think the true view is that we can easily describe and imagine large numbers of cases in which the question, "Will that future person be me—or someone else?", is a question which doesn't have any answer at all, and there's no puzzle that there's no answer.

VESEY: Will you describe one such case?

PARFIT: One of them is the case discussed in the correspondence material, the case of division in which we suppose that each half of my brain is to be transplanted into a new body and the two resulting people will both seem to remember the whole of my life, have my character and be psychologically continuous with me in every way. Now in this case of division there were only three possible answers to the question, "What's going to happen to *me*?" And all three of them seem to me open to very serious objections. So the conclusion to be drawn from the case is that the question of what's going

From: "Brain Transplants and Personal Identity" in *Philosophy in the Open*, ed. Godfrey Vesey (London: Open University Press, 1974).

to happen to me just doesn't have an answer. I think the case also shows that that's not mysterious at all.

VESEY: Right, let's deal with these three possibilities in turn.

PARFIT: Well, the first is that I'm going to be both of the resulting people. What's wrong with that answer is that it leads very quickly to a contradiction.

VESEY: How?

PARFIT: The two resulting people are going to be different people from each other. They're going to live completely different lives. They're going to be as different as any two people are. But if they're different people from each other it can't be the case that I'm going to be both of them. Because if I'm both of them, then one of the resulting people is going to be the same person as the other.

VESEY: Yes. They can't be different people and be the same person, namely me.

PARFIT: Exactly. So the first answer leads to a contradiction.

VESEY: Yes. And the second?

PARFIT: Well, the second possible answer is that I'm not going to be both of them but just one of them. This doesn't lead to a contradiction, it's just wildly implausible. It's implausible because my relation to each of the resulting people is exactly similar.

VESEY: Yes, so there's no reason to say that I'm one rather than the other?

PARFIT: It just seems absurd to suppose that, when you've got exactly the same relation, one of them is identity and the other is nothing at all.

VESEY: It does seem absurd, but there are philosophers who would say that sort of thing. Let's go on to the third.

PARFIT: Well, the only remaining answer, if I'm not going to be both of them or only one of them, is that I'm going to be neither of them. What's wrong with this answer is that it's grossly misleading.

VESEY: Why?

PARFIT: If I'm going to be neither of them, then there's not going to be anyone in the world after the operation who's going to be me. And that implies, given the way we now think, that the operation is as bad as death. Because if there's going to be no one who's going to be me, then I cease to exist. But it's obvious on reflection that the operation isn't as bad as death. It isn't bad in any way at all. That this is obvious can be shown by supposing that when they do the operation only one of the transplants succeeds and only one of the resulting people ever comes to consciousness again.

VESEY: Then I think we would say that this person is me. I mean we'd have no reason to say that he wasn't.

PARFIT: On reflection I'm sure we would all think that I would survive as that one person.

VESEY: Yes.

PARFIT: Yes. Well, if we now go back to the case where both operations succeed. . . .

VESEY: Where there's a double success . . .

PARFIT: It's clearly absurd to suppose that a double success is a failure.

VESEY: Yes.

PARFIT: So the conclusion that I would draw from this case is firstly, that to the question, "What's going to happen to me?" there's no true answer.

VESEY: Yes.

PARFIT: Secondly, that if we decide to say one of the three possible answers, what we say is going to obscure the true nature of the case.

VESEY: Yes.

PARFIT: And, thirdly, the case isn't in any way puzzling. And the reason for that is this. My relation to each of the resulting people is the relation of full psychological continuity. When I'm psychologically continuous with only one person, we call it identity. But if I'm psychologically continuous with two future people, we can't call it identity. It's not puzzling because we know exactly what's going to happen.

VESEY: Yes, could I see if I've got this straight? Where there is psychological continuity in a one-one case, this is the sort of case which we'd ordinarily talk of in terms of a person having survived the operation, or something like that.

PARFIT: Yes.

VESEY: Now what about when there is what you call psychological continuity—that's to say, where the people seem to remember having been me and so on—in a one-two case? Is this survival or not?

PARFIT: Well, I think it's just as good as survival, but the block we have to get over is that we can't say that anyone in the world after the operation is going to be me.

VESEY: No.

PARFIT: Well, we can say it but it's very implausible. And we're inclined to think that if there's not going to be anyone who is me tomorrow, then I don't survive. What we need to realize is that my relation to each of those two people is just as good as survival. Nothing is missing at all in my relation to both of them, as compared with my relation to myself tomorrow.

VESEY: Yes.

PARFIT: So here we've got survival without identity. And that only seems puzzling if we think that identity is a further fact over and above psychological continuity.

VESEY: It is very hard not to think of identity being a further fact, isn't it?

PARFIT: Yes, I think it is. I think that the only way to get rid of our temptation to believe this is to consider many more cases than this one case of division. Perhaps I should give you another one. Suppose that the following is going to happen to me. When I die in a normal way, scientists are going to map the states of all the cells in my brain and body and after a few months they will have constructed a perfect duplicate of me out of organic matter. And this duplicate will wake up fully psychologically continuous with me, seeming to remember my life with my character, etc.

VESEY: Yes.

PARFIT: Now in this case, which is a secular version of the Resurrection, we're very inclined to think that the following question arises and is very real and very important. The question is, "Will that person who wakes up in three months be me or will he be some quite other person who's merely artificially made to be exactly like me?"

VESEY: It does seem to be a real question. I mean in the one case, if it is going to be me, then I have expectations and so on, and in the other case, where it isn't me, I don't.

PARFIT: I agree, it seems as if there couldn't be a bigger difference between it being me and it being someone else.

VESEY: But you want to say that the two possibilities are in fact the same?

PARFIT: I want to say that those two descriptions, "It's going to be me" and "It's going to be someone who is merely exactly like me," don't describe different outcomes, different courses of events, only one of which can happen. They are two ways of describing one and the same course of events. What I mean by that perhaps could be shown if we take an exactly comparable case involving not a person but something about which I think we're not inclined to have a false view.

VESEY: Yes.

PARFIT: Something like a club. Suppose there's some club in the nineteenth century ...

VESEY: The Sherlock Holmes Club or something like that?

PARFIT: Yes, perhaps. And after several years of meeting it ceases to meet. The club dies.

VESEY: Right.

PARFIT: And then two of its members, let's say, have emigrated to America, and after about fifteen years they get together and they start up a club. It has exactly the same rules, completely new membership except for the first two people, and they give it the same name. Now suppose someone came along and said: "There's a real mystery here, because the following question is one that must have an answer. But how can we answer it?" The question is, "Have they started up the very same club—is it the same club as the one they belonged to in England—or is it a completely new club that's just exactly similar?"

VESEY: Yes.

PARFIT: Well, in that case we all think that this man's remark is absurd; there's no difference at all. Now that's my model for the true view about the case where they make a duplicate of me. It seems that there's all the difference in the world between its being me and its being this other person who's exactly like me. But if we think there's no difference at all in the case of the clubs, why do we think there's a difference in the case of personal identity, and how can we defend the view that there's a difference?

VESEY: I can see how some people would defend it. I mean, a dualist would defend it in terms of a soul being a simple thing, but ...

PARFIT: Let me try another case which I think helps to ease us out of this belief we're very strongly inclined to hold.

VESEY: Go on.

PARFIT: Well, this isn't a single case, this is a whole range of cases. A whole smooth spectrum of different cases which are all very similar to the next one in the range. At the start of this range of cases you suppose that the scientists are going to replace one per cent of the cells in your brain and body with exact duplicates.

VESEY: Yes.

PARFIT: Now if that were to be done, no one has any doubt that you'd survive. I think that's obvious because after all you can *lose* one per cent of the cells and survive. As we get further along the range they replace a larger and larger percentage of cells with exact duplicates, and of course at the far end of this range, where they replace a hundred per cent, then we've got my case where they just make a duplicate out of wholly fresh matter.

VESEY: Yes.

PARFIT: Now on the view that there's all the difference in the world between its being me and its being this other person who is exactly like me, we ought in consistency to think that in some case in the middle of that range, where, say, they're going to replace fifty per cent, the same question arises: is it going to be me or this completely different character? I think that even the most convinced dualist who believes in the soul is going to find this range of cases very embarrassing, because he seems committed to the view that there's some crucial percentage up to which it's going to be him and after which it suddenly ceases to be him. But I find that wholly unbelievable.

VESEY: Yes. He's going to have to invent some sort of theory about the relation of mind and body to get round this one. I'm not quite sure how he would do it. Derek, could we go on to a related question? Suppose that I accepted what you said, that is, that there isn't anything more to identity than what you call psychological continuity in a one-one case. Suppose I accept that, then I would want to go on and ask you, well, what's the philosophical importance of this?

PARFIT: The philosophical importance is, I think, that psychological continuity is obviously, when we think about it, a matter of degree. So long as we think that identity is a further fact, one of the things we're inclined to think is that it's all or nothing, as you said earlier. Well, if we give up that belief and if we realize that what matters in my continued existence is a matter of degree, then this does make a difference in actual cases. All the cases that I've considered so far are of course bizarre science fiction cases. But I think that in actual life it's obvious on reflection that, to give an example, the relations between me now and me next year are much closer in every way than the relations between me now and me in twenty years. And the sorts of relations that I'm thinking of are relations of memory, character, ambition, intention—all of those. Next year I shall remember much more of this year than I will in twenty years. I shall have a much more similar character. I shall be carrying out more of the same plans, ambitions and, if that is so, I think there are various plausible implications for our moral beliefs and various possible effects on our emotions.

VESEY: For our moral beliefs? What have you in mind?

PARFIT: Let's take one very simple example. On the view which I'm sketching it seems to me much more plausible to claim that people deserve much less punishment, or even perhaps no punishment, for what they did many years ago as compared with what they did very recently. Plausible because the relations between them now and them many years ago when they committed the crime are so much weaker.

VESEY: But they are still the people who are responsible for the crime.

PARFIT: I think you say that because even if they've changed in many ways, after all it was just as much they who committed the crime. I think that's true, but on the view for which I'm arguing, we would come to think that it's a completely trivial truth. It's like the following truth: it's like the truth that all of my relatives are just as much my relatives. Suppose I in my will left more money to my close relatives and less to my distant relatives; a mere pittance to my second cousin twenty-nine times removed. If you said, "But that's clearly unreasonable because all of your relatives are just as much your relatives," there's a sense in which that's true but it's obviously too trivial to make my will an unreasonable will. And that's because what's involved in kinship is a matter of degree.

VESEY: Yes.

PARFIT: Now, if we think that what's involved in its being the same person now as the person who committed the crime is a matter of degree, then the truth that it was just as much him who committed the crime, will seem to us trivial in the way in which the truth that all my relatives are equally my relatives is trivial.

VESEY: Yes. So you think that I should regard myself in twenty years' time as like a fairly distant relative of myself?

PARFIT: Well, I don't want to exaggerate; I think the connections are much closer.

VESEY: Suppose I said that this point about psychological continuity being a matter of degree—suppose I said that this isn't anything that anybody denies?

PARFIT: I don't think anybody does on reflection deny that psychological continuity is a matter of degree. But I think what they may deny, and I think what may make a difference to their view, if they come over to the view for which I'm arguing—what they may deny is that psychological continuity is all there is to identity. Because what I'm arguing against is this further belief which I think we're all inclined to hold even if we don't realize it. The belief that however much we change, there's a profound sense in which the changed us is going to be just as much us. That even if some magic wand turned me into a completely different sort of person—a prince with totally different character, mental powers—it would be just as much me. That's what I'm denying.

VESEY: Yes. This is the belief which I began by stating, and I think that if we did lose that belief that would be a change indeed.

Do I survive the split-brain operation? Consider Parfit's three possible answers: (1) You do not survive; (2) you survive as one of the two; and (3) you survive as two people.

Parfit argues that all these options seem unsatisfactory. It seems absurd to say (1) that you don't survive, for there is continuity of consciousness (in the Lockean sense) as though you had gone to sleep and awakened. If you had experienced the destruction of one half of your brain, we would still say you survived with half a brain, so why not say so now when each half is autonomous? The logic of this thesis would seem to say that double life equals death.

But (2) seems arbitrary. Why say that you only survive as one of the two, and which one is it? And (3)—that you survive as both—is not satisfactory either since it gives up the notion of identity. You cannot be numerically one with two centers of consciousness and two spatiotemporal bodies. Otherwise, we might say when we wreck our new Ford that the other one left in the automobile dealer's parking lot (the blue Ford that was exactly like yours) was indeed yours.

If this is an accurate analysis of the personal identity problem, what sense can we make of the concept? Not much, according to Parfit. We should speak of survival of the person, not the identity of the person. Persons, as psychological states, survive and gradually merge (like Theseus's rebuilt ship) into descendant persons. Your memories and personality gradually emerged from the 15-year-old who gradually developed from the 6-year-old and, before that, the 1-year-old who bore your name. These were your ancestor selves, but you too will merge with future or descendant selves as you have different experiences, take on new memories, and forget old ones. Suppose every year neurologists could transplant half of your brain into another body, in which a new half would duplicate the present state of the transferred half. In this way, a treelike operation would continue to spread successors of yourself as though by psychological parthenogenesis. You would survive in a sense, but it would make no sense to speak of personal identity, a concept that Parfit wants to get rid of. We could also imagine a neurological game of "musical hemispheres" as half of your brain was merged with half of someone else's brain in a third person's head. You could continue the hemisphere-moving game every 6 months so that you might even get remerged with your own other half at some future time—much like meeting your high school companion again after years of separation and interesting adventures. You'd have a lot to talk about through the medium of the corpus callosum!

Of course, Parfit's point is that we are going through significant changes all the time, so that as we have new experiences, we take on new selfhood. Something in us survives but with a difference. If Parfit is right about the relativity of identity in survival, then we might be less interested in our distant future than our immediate future. After all, that person 10 years down the line is less like us than the person we'll be tomorrow. This might encourage a sort of general **utilitarianism,** for since our distant interests really are not as closely related to us as the needs of our contemporaries, we could be free to work for the total greater good. On the other hand, it could have the deleterious effect of making us indifferent to the future of society. This notion of proximate identity also raises the question of whether we should be concerned about our distant death 50 years down the line, which one of our successor selves will have to face. Why should we fear death, when it won't touch us but only one of our successor selves in the distant future? Of course, one of our successor selves might be angry with us for not taking out an insurance policy or pension plan necessary for his or her well-being.

This notion of relative and proximate identity might also cause us to prohibit long-term prison sentences for criminal actions, for why punish a descendant for what one of his ancestors did? Finally, it could be used to argue against exorbitant awards in malpractice litigation. Often a jury is asked to award a sum of money (as high as $12 million) to a severely retarded child who has been injured through medical malpractice. The justification for the large sum is the expectation that the child would have become a highly talented professional (physician or lawyer) and made an enormous sum of money in her lifetime. But if we were to take the notion of proximate identity seriously, we could only sue the physician for the damages done to the immediate person, not to her descendant selves.

What is the truth about personal identity? What constitutes the essential you? Are you the same person that you were at age five or sixteen? Will you be still the same person at age sixty-five?

Summary

The problem of personal identity is a compound set of paradoxes and puzzles. It involves three difficult questions: What is a person? What is identity over time? What is it to be the same person through change and time? The first question relates to the mind–body problem in general and cannot be satisfactorily answered without a solution to that problem. The second question seems to be context-dependent; that is, the answer will depend on subtleties of meaning that depend on various contexts. The third question, which depends in part on the first two, has had two main answers: the psychological state criterion and the brain criterion. Far-reaching implications flow from how we decide this issue.

FOR FURTHER REFLECTION

1. How would you respond to the question raised by the brain operation? Do you survive the operation? Consider the three possible answers: (a) You do not survive; (b) you survive as one of the two; and (c) you survive as two people. Discuss the reasons for and against each answer.

2. How would you solve the puzzle about the identity of Theseus's ship? What happens to it at t_2? One of my students says, "It just disappears." Do you agree? Why or why not?

3. Explain the difference between the psychological states criterion for personal identity and the brain criterion. Which has the best case in its favor? Why?

4. What do you make of the phenomenon of split personalities and multiple personalities, such as the case of Sybil, who allegedly expressed sixteen different personalities with sixteen different sets of memories? On a psychological states account, would we have to say that one body contained sixteen persons? Are there different persons inside each of us, expressed by different "sides" of our personalities?

5. Some dualist philosophers (in the Cartesian sense), such as Thomas Reid and Richard Swinburne, hold that personal identity is a simple notion. It is unanalyzable and indefinable, not reducible to anything else. Reid wrote that "the conviction which every man has of his identity, as far back as his memory reaches, needs no aid of philosophy to strengthen it; and no philosophy can weaken it, without producing some degree of insanity."[4] Discuss this position in the light of Parfit's analysis.

6. In the last section of this chapter, we discussed the implications flowing from relative and proximate identity. Discuss these consequences. Can you think of other implications?

NOTES

1. John Locke, *An Essay Concerning Human Understanding,* ed. A. C. Fraser (Oxford, UK: Clarendon Press, 1894; first published in 1688), Book II. 27.9.

2. Ibid.

3. Ibid., Book II.27.
4. Thomas Reid, *Essays on the Intellectual Powers of Man*, ed. A. D. Woozley, (London: Macmillan, 1941), Essay III, Chapters 4 and 6.

FOR FURTHER READING

Perry, John, ed. *Personal Identity*. Berkeley: University of California Press, 1975. Contains the essential classical readings.

Perry, John. *A Dialogue on Personal Identity and Immortality*. Indianapolis: Hackett, 1978. A philosophically rich, entertaining discussion of the problem of personal identity.

Pojman, Louis, ed. *Philosophy: The Quest for Truth,* 3rd ed. Belmont, CA: Wadsworth, 1996. Contains Parfit's discussion as well as the first part of Perry's dialogue and other essays.

Rorty, Amelie, ed. *The Identities of Persons*. Berkeley: University of California Press, 1976. A good selection of essays on the nature of personhood.

Swinburne, Richard. "Personal Identity: The Dualist Theory." In *Personal Identity,* edited by S. Shoemaker and R. Swinburne. Oxford, UK: Basil Blackwell, 1984.

Unger, Peter. *Identity, Consciousness and Value*. New York: Oxford University Press, 1990. A highly imaginative, penetrating discussion of the issues discussed in this chapter.

23 ☙ Is There Life After Death? Personal Identity and Immortality

The soul, herself invisible, departs to the invisible world,—to the divine and immortal and rational: thither arriving, she lives in bliss and is released from the error and folly of men, their fears and wild passions and all other human ills, and forever dwells, as they say of the initiated, in the company of the gods.

Plato[1]

After death we rot.

From a student paper

Is There Life After Death?

Is there life after death? Few questions have troubled humans as deeply as this one. Is this finite, short existence of three score and ten years all that we have? Or is there reason to hope for a blessed postmortem existence where love, justice, and peace, which we now experience in fragmented forms, will unfold in all their fullness and enable human existence to find fulfillment? Are we merely mortal or blessedly immortal?

Anthropological studies reveal a widespread and ancient sense of immortality. Prehistoric societies buried their dead with food so that the deceased would not be hungry in the next life. Most cultures and religions have some version

350

of a belief in another life, whether it be in the form of a resurrected body, a transmigrated soul, reincarnation, or an ancestral spirit present with the tribe.

Let's begin by understanding what we mean by *immortality*. For our purposes, we will not mean living on through our works or in the memories of our loved ones but rather a conscious existence where the individual continues to exist. The definition given in *A Catholic Dictionary* is

> that attribute in virtue of which a being is free from death. A being is incorruptible if it does not contain within itself a principle of dissolution; it is indestructible if it can resist every external power tending to destroy or annihilate it. If the indestructible and incorruptible being is endowed with life it is called immortal. Annihilation is always possible to God by the mere withdrawal of his conserving act.[2]

Death for most humans is the ultimate tragedy. It is the paramount evil, for it deprives us of all that we know and love on Earth. Although there may be fates worse than death (living a completely evil life, being a heavy burden on others), our fear of death is profound. We want to live as long as possible (given a certain quality of life). We have a general craving for continued existence. The more life, the better.

Unfortunately, there is precious little direct evidence for life after death. After the brain ceases to function, a person cannot be resuscitated. We don't know of anyone personally who has come back from the dead to tell us about the next life.

So on the one hand, we have a passionate longing to live again and be with our loved ones, while on the other hand, there is little or no direct evidence that we will live again. The grave seems the last environment for humankind, and yet we search for indirect evidence for immortality. We welcome any news from this possible distant clime as good news indeed and cannot but regard the promise of eternal life as an incentive to meet whatever a credible guide states as the necessary conditions for entry. In the Western tradition, three views have dominated the scene: One denies life after death and two affirm it. The negative view, going back to the ancient Greek Atomist philosophers Democritus (circa 460–370 BCE) and Leucippus (circa 450 BCE), holds that we are identical with our bodies (including our brains) so that when the body dies, so does our self. There is nothing more. We can call this view materialist monism because it does not allow for the possibility of a soul or spiritual self that can live without the body.

Plato's Theory of Immortality

The positive views divide into dualist and monist theories of life after death. The dualist views separate the body from the soul or self of the agent and affirm that it is the soul or self that lives forever. This view was held by the pre-Socratic philosopher Pythagoras (580–496 BCE) and developed by Plato (427–347 BCE). In modern philosophy, it is represented by René Descartes (1596–1650). It is sometimes referred to as the Platonic–Cartesian view of immortality. These philosophers argue that we are essentially spiritual or mental beings and that our bodies are either unreal or not part of our essential selves, so death is merely the separation of our souls from our bodies, a sort of spiritual liberation. Although Plato has many arguments for this thesis, one of the most famous is found in the *Phaedo* where Socrates is speaking to his disciple Simmias.

PHAEDO

SOCRATES: What shall we say of the actual acquisition of knowledge? Is the body, if invited to share in the inquiry, a hinderer or a helper? I mean to say, have sight and hearing any truth in them? Are they not, as the poets are always telling us, inaccurate witnesses? and yet, if even they are inaccurate and indistinct, what is to be said of the other senses?—for you will allow that they are the best of them?

SIMMIAS: Certainly.

SOCRATES: Then when does the soul attain truth?—for in attempting to consider anything in company with the body, she is obviously deceived.

SIMMIAS: Yes, that's true.

SOCRATES: Then must not existence be revealed to her in thought, if at all?

SIMMIAS: Yes.

SOCRATES: When the soul employs the body in any inquiry, and makes use of sight, or hearing, or any other sense—for inquiry with the body must signify inquiry with the senses—she is dragged away by the body to the things which are impermanent, changing, and the soul wanders about blindly, and becomes confused and dizzy, like a drunken man, from dealing with things that are changing … [But] When the soul investigates any question by herself, she goes away to the pure and eternal, and immortal and unchangeable, to which she is intrinsically related, and so she comes to be ever with it, as soon as she is by herself, and can be so; and then she rests from her wandering and dwells with it unchangingly, for she is related to what is unchanging. And is not this state of the soul called wisdom?

The argument may be analyzed as follows:

1. If a person's soul while in the body is capable of any activity independently of the body, then it can perform that activity in separation from the body (that is, after death, surviving death).

2. In pure or metaphysical thinking (that is, in contemplating the forms and their interrelationships), a person's soul performs an activity independently of the body. No observation is necessary for this investigation.

3. Therefore, a person's soul can engage in pure or metaphysical thinking in separation from the body. That is, it can and must survive death.

From: Plato *Phaedo* 79.

This is a positive argument for the existence of the soul. It does seem that we can think about logic, mathematics, metaphysics, and other subjects without reference to bodies. Unfortunately, the second premise is dubious, for it could be the case that the mind's activity is epiphenomenal (that is, dependent on the brain). Thus, although Plato is right in saying that we need not make an empirical examination of the world in order to think analytically or metaphysically, he has not shown that analytic and metaphysical thinking can go on without a body or brain.

We have already examined the problem of dualism in general (Chapter 19), noting especially the problems of how and where the soul interacts with the body. Furthermore, as far as I know, no one has offered a sound argument to *prove* that we have a soul that succeeds our physical existence. However, this is not to say that no evidence exists for this point of view; we note some next.

The Christian View of a New and Glorified Body

The second positive view on immortality is associated with the Christian tradition, namely, St. Paul's statement in 1 Corinthians 15. It is interesting to note that very little mention is made in the Old Testament of life after death. It is at best a shadowy existence in Sheol, the place under Jerusalem where the dead lie dormant or vaguely aware, a place comparable to Hades in Greek mythology. The one exception is the celebrated passage in Handel's *Messiah* from the Book of Job (19:2–26):

> I know that my Redeemer liveth,
> And that He shall stand at the latter day upon the earth,
> And though after my skin worms destroy this body,
> Yet in my flesh shall I see God.

Note that it is *in the flesh,* not as a disembodied spirit, that Job expects to live again.

In the New Testament, though there are references to a spiritual existence, the soul (*psyche*) is not separated from the body (*soma*), but the person is a holistic unified being with the soul or self being the form of the material body (in an almost Aristotelian sense). In death, the soul is not liberated from the body as from a corpse, but rather a new, glorified *body* comes into being that is somehow related to our present earthly body. The classic passage is from Paul's first letter to the Corinthians.

THE FIRST EPISTLE TO THE CORINTHIANS

Now if Christ preached that he rose from the dead, how say some among you that there is no resurrection of the dead? But if there be no resurrection of the dead, then Christ is not risen: And if Christ be not risen, then our preaching is in vain, and your faith

---

From: 1 Corinthians 15: 12–53, King James Version, edited.

is also in vain . . . Ye are still in your sins. Then they which are fallen asleep in Christ are perished. If in this life only we have hope in Christ, we are of all men most miserable.

But now Christ is risen from the dead, and become the firstfruits of them that slept. For since by man came death by man came also the resurrection of the dead. . . . For Christ must reign until he hath put all enemies under his feet. The last enemy that shall be destroyed is death.

But some man will say, How are the dead raised up? and with what body do they come? Thou fool, that which thou sowest is not quickened, except it die: and that which thou sowest, thou sowest not that body that shall be, but bare grain, it may chance of wheat, or of some other grain. But God giveth it a body as it hath pleased him, and to every seed his own body. All flesh is not the same flesh; but there is one kind of flesh of men, another flesh of beasts, another of fishes, and another of birds. There are also celestial bodies, and bodies terrestrial: but the glory of the celestial is one, and the glory of the terrestrial is another. There is one glory of the sun, and another glory of the moon, and another glory of the stars: for one star differeth from another star in glory. So also is the resurrection of the dead. It is sown in corruption; it is raised in incorruption; it is sown in weakness; it is raised in power: It is sown a natural body; it is raised a spiritual body. And so it is written, The first man Adam was made a living soul; the last Adam was made a quickening spirit. Howbeit that was not first which is spiritual, but that which is natural; and afterward that which is spiritual. The first man is of the earth, earthly: the second man is the Lord from heaven. As is the earthly, such are they also that are earthly: and as is the heavenly, such are they also that are heavenly. And as we have borne the image of the earthly, we shall also bear the image of the heavenly. Now this I say, brethren, that flesh and blood cannot inherit the kingdom of God; neither doth corruption inherit incorruption. Behold, I show you a mystery; We shall not all sleep, but we shall all be changed. In a moment, in a twinkling of an eye, at the last trump: for the trumpet shall sound, and the dead shall be raised incorruptible, and we shall be changed. For this corruptible must put on incorruption, and this mortal must put on immortality.

When I approach the subject of immortality in an undergraduate philosophy class, I poll the students to ask them which is the Christian view of life after death, the view that in death the soul leaves the body and goes to heaven or the view that our bodies will be raised. Almost every student chooses the first view, which I then point out is basically Platonic and not Christian. This view is reflected in popular religion, not the least being the bedtime prayer taught to children: "Now I lay me down to sleep, I pray the Lord my soul to keep. If I should die before I wake, I pray the Lord my soul to take." Of course, one could have a view that while there is eventually a new body, there is an intermediate state where the soul dwells disembodied, waiting for the resurrection day, at which time it will receive its new form.

Are there good arguments for either of these versions of survival after death? Each raises the question of personal identity, discussed in the previous chapter. Given the fact that we all undergo physical and mental change, under what conditions can we be said to be the *same* person over time (that is, what gives us the right to say that some person P is the same person at t_2 as P was at some time earlier, t_1)?

Recall the two standard views on this matter: the psychological states criterion and the body (including the brain) criterion. The psychological states (or memory) criterion goes back to John Locke and states that a person is the same person if and only if he is psychologically continuous in character, desires, and memories. There are, at least, three problems with this view:

1. There is no way to distinguish *apparent* memories from *genuine* remembering, so it could be the case that someone came among us, detailing the events of Napoleon's life in such a way as to cause us to believe that he had somehow gotten hold of those memories. But we would probably be reluctant to say that this person was Napoleon, especially if we already knew him to be our uncle.

2. There is a problem with multiple remembers; that is, it could be the case that our memories (and characters and desires for that matter) could be duplicated in other people so that multiple subjects have the same "memories." We would not be able to tell which of the persons was the rememberer. As we noted in an earlier chapter, if Brendan and Maria both possess the same memories, they would be each other!

3. There is the problem of whether memory itself makes any sense apart from a body. What kind of existence would a purely mental existence be? Would it be in time and space? If it were in space, how does it, a nonsensory entity, perceive anything at all? It seems that memory and character predicates are tied to a physical existence. This leads us to consider the body criterion as the proper criterion for personal identity.

The body criterion (especially the brain) states that a person is the same person over time if she is continuous with her body (including the brain). The notion of resurrection (or reconstitution) states that I will continue to survive my death in a new, glorified body. God will reconstitute me. This is eloquently (if grandiosely) stated on Benjamin Franklin's tombstone:

> This body of B. Franklin in Christ Church cemetery,
> Printer, Like the Cover of an old Book,
> Its Contents torn out,
> And stript of its Lettering and Gilding,
> Lies here, Food for Worms.
> But the work shall not be lost;
> For it will, as he believed,
> Appear once more in a new and more elegant Edition,
> Corrected and Improved by its Author.

But the resurrection view supposes that God will create a new being like yourself. The problem with this view is that it does not seem all that comforting to learn that someday someone just like you will enjoy a blessed existence, for if there is no continuity between you and your future self, it is really not you but your successor (someone very similar, even exactly similar to you, a sort of twin) who will enjoy eternal life.

Taking this criterion literally, we would have to conclude that when a zygote divides into identical twins during the first weeks of its existence, the two resulting entities are identical to each other (rather than being exactly similar). Furthermore, we can imagine situations where the personality of one person is transferred to another, such as in Locke's story of the prince and the cobbler, where the body of the prince wakes up one day with all the memories, desires, and character of the cobbler. We might be inclined to say that although the prince's body was before us, we were really speaking with the cobbler. We could also imagine futurist split body–brain operations where our bodies and/or brains are divided and merged with prosthetic bodies or brains. The notions of continuity and uniqueness would conflict.

Suppose our ingenious neurologist Dr. Matthews designed a brain and a body just like yours in his laboratory, but the body was virtually indestructible (well, a nuclear bomb could destroy it, but failing that it would be impervious to alteration). The brain is now dormant, but at your death Dr. Matthews will activate it and bring it to life within the prosthetic body. Now Matthews tells you that he needs to kill you in order to allow your alter ego to exist. You complain, but Matthews assures you that one exactly similar to you will live again with all your memories (or copies of them but Alter Ego won't know the difference). Would you be comforted by that news? Would you take comfort in the fact that "you" will live again?

Where does all of this leave us with regard to survival after death? If there is no continuity of consciousness, is it the same person who would be resurrected or reconstituted by God at some future time? Or is the reconstituted person like Matthews's replica? A different token of the same generic type? Could God make several tokens of your type—say, five of you—that could be reconstituted and go on to live a new and eternal life? Quintuple resurrection!

Is the survival of the disembodied memories of a person sufficient to satisfy you with regard to your survival after death? The question is perplexing. On the one hand, it seems that our identity is somehow tied to our psychological states (for example, memories and personality traits), which don't seem to depend on a body. But then if this is so, would our survival occur if a computer stored much of the information about our personalities and memory states?

We seem to need both a body and brain to instantiate our consciousness and personalities. It is hard to imagine any learning, experiencing, or communication with others without a recognizable body. The brain seems to be the locus of conscious experience, but our bodies and brains die and disintegrate. What happens to our consciousness and our personal identity? Is the gap between the present conscious life and the next simply like a long sleep during which God prepares a new and glorified body for our personality? Or does the fact that there will have to be a new creation rule out the possibility of personal survival altogether? Or can it be that there is an intrinsically spiritual character to ourselves that both survives the death of the body and perdures in a life beyond this one?

Of course, many Christians believe that, although there must be a body for one's full existence, it could be the case that the personality is preserved in an interim state of disembodiment between the first corruptible bodily existence and the second incorruptible bodily existence. But this still has the problem of whether it makes sense to speak of a disembodied self.

Indirect Evidence for Life After Life?

However, there is indirect evidence for a soul or the disembodied survival of the self, that recorded by individuals who have been pronounced clinically dead but who have had out-of-body experiences. James Moody documents several cases of "clinically dead" persons who were revived and reported remarkably similar experiences. Moody sets down a composite of the reports in the following passage.

LIFE AFTER LIFE

A man is dying and, as he reaches the point of greatest physical distress, he hears himself pronounced dead by his doctor. He begins to hear an uncomfortable noise, a loud ringing or buzzing, and at the same time feels himself moving very rapidly through a long dark tunnel. After this, he suddenly finds himself outside of his own physical body, but still in the immediate physical environment, and he sees his own body from a distance, as though he is a spectator. He watches the resuscitation attempt from this unusual vantage point and is in a state of emotional upheaval.

After a while, he collects himself and becomes more accustomed to his odd condition. He notices that he still has a "body," but one of a very different nature and with very different powers from the physical body he has left behind. Soon other things begin to happen. Others come to meet and to help him. He glimpses the spirits of relatives and friends who have already died, and a loving, warm spirit of a kind he has never encountered before—a being of light—appears before him. This being asks him a question, nonverbally, to make him evaluate his life and helps him along by showing him a panoramic, instantaneous playback of the major events of his life. At some point he finds himself approaching some sort of barrier or border, apparently representing the limit between earthly life and the next life. Yet, he finds that he must go back to the earth, that the time for his death has not yet come. At this point he resists, for by now he is taken up with his experiences in the afterlife and does not want to return. He is overwhelmed by intense feelings of joy, love, and peace. Despite his attitude, though, he somehow reunites with his physical body and lives.

This passage is not meant to represent any one person's report but is the model or composite of the common elements found in many stories. Moody himself makes no claims for the interpretation that the patients really experienced what they claim to have experienced. There could be neurological causes for the experiences, or they could be attributed to wish fulfillment. The point is simply that these experiences should be considered as part of the evidence to be examined carefully, perhaps being followed up with further research.

But even if these reports survive close scrutiny, in themselves they do not constitute a strong case for immortality. It could be the case that we do survive our death for one or two more existences but then perish. But for those who

---

From: Raymond Moody, *Life After Life* (New York: Bantam Books, 1976), 21.

can find other arguments for life after death, the Moody reports may serve as a corroboration of this doctrine.

The Possibility of Reincarnation

Reincarnation, the view that after death human beings live again in other forms, was held by Plato and is a tenet in Hinduism and Buddhism. In the Hindu scripture Bhagavad Gita (circa 500 BCE), the Supreme God, Lord Krishna, comforts the unenlightened Arjuna, who is engaged in warfare with his evil cousins, by telling him that there is no reason to grieve over the death of someone we love, for the "eternal in man cannot die." "We have all been for all time: I, and thou, and those king of men. And we shall be for all time, we all for ever and ever." Here is a key selection. We enter the battlefield scene, wherein Arjuna is weeping over the prospects of killing his relatives in battle. Lord Krishna first reprimands Arjuna.

A DIALOGUE BETWEEN LORD KRISHNA AND ARJUNA

KRISHNA: My dear Arjuna, how have these impurities come upon you? They are not at all befitting a man who knows the value of life. They lead not to higher planets but to infamy. Do not yield to this degrading impotence. It does not become you. Give up such petty weaknesses of heart and arise, O chastiser of the enemy.

ARJUNA: How can I counterattack with arrows in battle men like Bhisma and Drona, who are worthy of my worship? It would be better to live in this world by begging than to live at the cost of the lives of great souls who are my teachers. If they are killed, everything we enjoy will be tainted with blood.

Now I am confused about my duty and have lost all composure because of miserly weakness. In this condition I am asking You to tell me for certain what is best for me. Krishna, I shall not fight.

KRISHNA: While speaking learned words, you are mourning for what is not worthy of grief. Those who are wise lament neither for the living nor for the dead. Never was there a time when I did not exist, nor you, nor all these kings; nor in the future shall any of us cease to be. As the embodied soul continuously passes, in this body, from boyhood to youth to old age, the soul similarly passes into another body at death. A sober person is not bewildered by such a change.

O son of Kunti, the nonpermanent appearance of happiness and distress, and their disappearance in due course, are like the appearance and disappearance of winter and summer seasons. They arise from sense perception, O scion of Bharata, and one must learn to tolerate them without being disturbed. The person who is not disturbed by happiness and distress and is steady in both is certainly eligible for liberation.

Those who are seers of truth have concluded that of the nonexistent [material body] there is no endurance and of the eternal [the soul] there is no change. This they

From: Bhagavad Gita, trans. A. C. Bhaktivedanta Swami Prabhupada in *Readings in the Vedic Literature*, ed. Satsvarupa dasa Goswami (Bhaktivedanta Book Trust, 1977).

have concluded by studying the nature of both. That which pervades the entire body you should know to be indestructible. No one is able to destroy that imperishable soul. The material body of the indestructible, immeasurable and eternal living entity is sure to come to an end; therefore, fight, O descendent of Bharata.

For the soul there is neither birth nor death at any time. He has not come into being, does not come into being, and will not come into being. He is unborn, eternal, ever-existing and primeval. He is not slain when the body is slain.

O [Arjuna], how can a person who knows that the soul is indestructible, eternal, unborn and immutable kill anyone or cause anyone to kill? As a person puts on new garments, giving up old ones, the soul similarly accepts new material bodies, giving up the old and useless ones. The soul can never be cut to pieces by any weapon, nor burned by fire, nor moistened by water, now withered by the wind. This individual soul is unbreakable and insoluble, and can be neither burned nor dried. He is everlasting, present everywhere, unchangeable, immovable and eternally the same . . . Knowing this, you should not grieve the body.

One who has taken his birth is sure to die, and after death one is sure to take birth again. Therefore, in the unavoidable discharge of your duty, you should not lament. All created beings are unmanifest in their beginning, manifest in their interim state, and unmanifest again when annihilated. So what need is there for lamentation?

Krishna informs Arjuna that it is his religious duty to fight and it is sinful to neglect one's duty. Arjuna then asks Krishna to explain the characteristics of a self-realized, or transcendental, person.

ARJUNA: What are the symptoms of one whose consciousness is thus merged in transcendence? How does he speak and what is his language? How does he sit, and how does he walk?

KRISHNA: When a man gives up all varieties of desire for sense gratification, which arise from mental concoction, and when his mind, thus purified, finds satisfaction in the self alone, then he is said to be in pure transcendental consciousness. One who is not disturbed in mind even amidst the threefold miseries or elated when there is happiness, and who is free from attachment, fear and anger, is called a sage of steady mind. . . . One who is able to withdraw his senses from sense objects, as the tortoise draws its limbs within the shell, is firmly fixed in perfect consciousness. The embodied soul may be restricted from sense enjoyment, though the taste for sense objects remains. But ceasing such engagements by experiencing a higher taste, he is fixed in consciousness.

As a boat on the water is swept away by a strong wind, even one of the roaming senses on which the mind focuses can carry away a man's intelligence. Therefore, one whose senses are restrained from their objects is certainly of steady intelligence . . . A person who is not disturbed by the incessant flow of desires—that enter like rivers into the ocean, which is ever being filled but is always still—can alone achieve peace, and not the man who strives to satisfy such desires. A person who has given up all desires for sense gratification, who lives free from desires, who has given up all sense of proprietorship and is devoid of false ego—he alone can attain real peace. That is the way of spiritual and godly life, after attaining which a man is not bewildered. If one is thus situated even at the hour of death, one can enter into the kingdom of God.

A person's body is different in every incarnation, but the same mind inhabits each body: "As a man leaves an old garment and puts on the one that is new, the Spirit leaves his mortal body and then puts on one that is new." There are two main interpretations of the Gita. They both say that the goal of existence is to end the cycle of rebirths, but the Advaitian (monist) interpretation holds that the goal is to be absorbed into God (or Nirvana), whereas the Vaisnavan (dualist) interpretation holds that the person retains his spiritual or personal identity in a relationship with God. Reincarnation is typically linked with *karma*, the doctrine that whatsoever a man sows, whether in action or thought, the fruits will eventually be reaped by him—if not in this life, then in the next. Thus, a person who led an evil existence might be reborn as a lower animal (for example, a reptile or insect). Evidence cited for reincarnation includes déjà vu experiences, the sense that you've been in this place before, seen this person some other time—in another existence—as well as reports of children and others of experiences that they couldn't have had in this life.

Objections to reincarnation include the problem of uniform age. When a 90-year-old man dies, one would expect him to be reborn as an old man or at least with the maturity and memories of an old man, but he is always born as a baby without wisdom, maturity, or apparent memories. Why is that?

If memories are a criterion of personal identity, can the baby be said to be the same person as the 90-year-old man? Or is it simply a successor self, or does this problem indicate that reincarnation is a myth? Furthermore, what happens to the soul in the interregnum between incarnations? Where do these souls rest while they are waiting rebirth?

Third, if one holds the view that consciousness is dependent on the brain, then the very idea of a disembodied soul will seem implausible. This brings us back to the question of dualism itself. If dualism is plausible, reincarnation may be too. If the idea of a separate soul is not plausible on the evidence, reincarnation will be rejected as a grossly mistaken notion.

But even if one remains open to dualism and the idea of a soul, there is one further objection: Will the person your soul becomes in the next life be you? Suppose I become someone of the opposite sex in a distant country (or even a different planet) with a different culture. The new YOU has no memories of the old YOU. So how is this different from merely being cloned (having a cell from your body nurtured to produce a similar but distinct person as yourself)? Why should you or I care what happens to someone who is the descendant of your or my "soul"? Should I care more about my descendant self than I do about my children?

Summary

The question whether there is life after death has haunted human beings from time immemorial. Virtually every religion addressed it and attempts to answer it. Plato and many through the ages have held that our essential self is spiritual, so it does not die with the body but endures, either in heaven or as reincarnated in another body. The Hebrew view, which is reflected in Paul's writings in the New Testament, holds that our personhood is a function of our bodies, so you cannot separate body from soul in any absolute manner. Paul taught that after death the redeemed will inherit a new and glorified body. We noted problems with both views. Recently, Moody has recorded evidence of out-of-body experiences, though these testimonies have been challenged.

FOR FURTHER REFLECTION

1. Analyze the Platonic and Judeo-Christian views on life after death. Which view is more plausible? Explain your answer.

2. What do you make of the evidence for out-of-body experiences described by Moody? What are the arguments for and against using this evidence for the thesis that we survive our deaths?

3. Analyze the selection from the Bhagavad Gita on reincarnation. What is *karma*? What are the arguments for reincarnation? What are the objections to it?

NOTES

1. Plato, *The Phaedo,* trans. Benjamin Jowett (Oxford, UK: Oxford University Press, 1896).
2. *A Catholic Dictionary,* ed. D. Attwater (New York: Macmillan, 1941), 261.

FOR FURTHER READING

Bhagavad Gita. There are many translations of this Hindu scripture. I prefer the translation by Swami Prabhupada in *Bhagavad Gita as It* (Bhaktivedanta Book Trust, 1985).

Ducasse, C. J. *Nature, Mind and Death.* La Salle, IL: Open Court, 1951. A defense of immortality.

Edwards, Paul, ed. *Immortality.* New York: Macmillan, 1992. The best collection of articles available. Edwards's own introductory article is valuable.

Flew, Anthony. "Immortality." In the *Encyclopedia of Philosophy,* vol. 4, 139–150. New York: Macmillan, 1967.

Geach, Peter. *God and Soul.* London: Routledge & Kegan Paul, 1969. A defense of the Judeo-Christian view of survival after death.

Johnson, Raynor. *The Imprisoned Splendor.* London: Hodder & Stoughton, 1953. A defense of reincarnation.

Moody, Raymond. *Life After Life.* New York: Bantam Books, 1976. A fascinating though controversial account of near-death experiences.

PART VI

Freedom of the Will and Determinism

There is the unmistakable intuition of virtually every human being that he is free to make the choices he does and that the deliberations leading to those choices are also free flowing. The normal [person] feels too, after he has made a decision, that he could have decided differently. That is why regret or remorse for a past choice can be so disturbing.

Corliss Lamont[1]

The actions of man are never free; they are always the necessary consequence of his temperament, of the received ideas, and of the notions, either true or false, which he has formed to himself of happiness.

Baron Henri d'Holbach[2]

The problem of freedom of the will and determinism is one of the most intriguing and difficult in the whole area of philosophy; it constitutes a paradox. If we look at ourselves, at our ability to deliberate and make choices, it seems obvious that we are free. On the other hand, if we look at what we believe about causality—namely, that every event and thing must have a cause—then it appears that we do not have free wills but are determined. So we seem to have inconsistent beliefs.

Let's look closer at the two theses involved in order to see how they work and what support there is for each of them:

1. *Determinism:* The theory that everything in the universe (or at least the macroscopic universe) is entirely determined by causal laws so that whatever

happens at any given moment, including human actions, is the effect of some antecedent cause.

2. *Libertarianism:* The theory that claims some actions are exempt from the causal laws, in which the individual is the sole (or decisive) cause of the act, the act originating *ex nihilo* (out of nothing), cut off from all other causes but the self's doing it.

A third position tries to combine the best of the two positions. Called *compatibilism,* it says that although everything is determined, we can still act voluntarily.

Chapter 24 presents the classical picture of determinism. Chapter 25 sets forth arguments for and against libertarianism, and Chapter 26 sets forth the case for and against compatibilism, concluding with some thoughts on the implications of the debate for moral responsibility.

NOTES

1. Corliss Lamont, *Freedom of Choice Affirmed* (New York: Horizon, 1967), 3.
2. Baron Henri d'Holbach, *The System of Nature* (1770).

24 ⚶ Determinism

Physical Determinism

Philosophers who have espoused determinism include Baruch Spinoza (1632–1677), Arthur Schopenhauer (1788–1860), and John Hospers (1918–), but no one has set forth the theory with more force than the German-born Enlightenment philosopher Baron Henri d'Holbach (1723–1789), who rejected Cartesian dualism (that reality consists of matter and mind) and argued that the whole universe is simply matter in motion. Since human beings are part of the universe, they too must be reducible to matter in motion. Here is the heart of his argument for the determinist thesis.

THE SYSTEM OF NATURE

In whatever manner man is considered, he is connected to universal nature, and submitted to the necessary and immutable laws that she imposes on all the beings she contains, according to their peculiar essences or to the respective properties with which, without consulting them, she endows particular species. Man's life is a line that nature commands him to outline upon the surface of the earth, without his ever being able to swerve from it, even for an instant. He is born without his own consent; his organization does in nowise depend upon himself; his ideas come to him involuntarily; his habits are in the power of those who cause him to contract them; he is unceasingly modified by causes, whether visible or concealed, over which he has no control, which necessarily regulate his mode of existence, give the hue to his way of thinking, and determine his

From: Baron Henri d'Holbach, *The System of Nature* (1770).

manner of acting. He is good or bad, happy or miserable, wise or foolish, reasonable or irrational, without his will counting for anything in these various states....

The will, as we have elsewhere said, is a modification of the brain, by which it is disposed to action, or prepared to give play to the organs. This will is necessarily determined by the qualities, good or bad, agreeable or painful, of the object or the motive that acts upon his senses, or of which the idea remains with him, and is resuscitated by his memory. In consequence, he acts necessarily, his action is the result of the impulse he receives either from the motive, from the object, or from the idea which has modified his brain, or disposed his will. When he does not act according to this impulse, it is because there comes some new cause, some new motive, some new idea, which modifies his brain in a different manner, gives him a new impulse, determines his will in another way, by which the action of the former impulse is suspended: thus, the sight of an agreeable object, or its idea, determines his will to set him in action to procure it; but if a new object or a new idea more powerfully attracts him, it gives a new direction to his will, annihilates the effect of the former, and prevents the action by which it was to be procured.... In all this he always acts according to necessary laws from which he has no means of emancipating himself.

The will (more precisely the brain) finds itself in the same situation as a ball, which although it receives an impulse that drives it forward in a straight line, is deranged in its course whenever a force superior to the first obliges it to change its direction. The man who drinks the poisoned water appears a madman; but the actions of fools are as *necessary* as those of the most prudent individuals. The motives that determine the voluptuary and the debauchee to risk their health, are as powerful and their actions are as necessary, as those which decide the wise man to manage his. "But," the critic will object, "the debauchee may be prevailed on to change his conduct," to which I would respond: This does not imply that he is a free agent, but that motives may be found sufficiently powerful to annihilate the effect of those that previously acted upon him, and if so, then these new motives determine his will to the new mode of conduct he may adopt as necessarily as the former did to the old mode.

Man, then, is not a free agent in any one instant of his life. He is necessarily guided in each step by those advantages, whether real or fictitious, that he attaches to the objects by which his passions are roused. These passions themselves are necessary in a being who unceasingly tends towards his own happiness.

There is, in fact, no difference between the man that is cast out of the window by another, and the man who throws himself out of it, except that the impulse in the first case comes immediately from without, whereas in the second case it springs from within his own peculiar machine, having its more remote cause also exterior to himself. When Mutius Scaevola held his hand in the fire, he was as much acting under the influence of necessity (caused by interior motives) that urged him to this strange action, as if his arm had been held by strong men: pride, despair, the desire of braving his enemy, a wish to astonish him, and anxiety to intimidate him, etc., were the invisible chains that held his hand bound to the fire.

He may be compared to a heavy body that finds itself arrested in its descent by any obstacle whatever: take away this obstacle, it will gravitate or continue to fall; but who shall say this dense body is free to fall or not? Is not its descent the necessary effect of

> its own specific gravity? The virtuous Socrates submitted to the laws of his country, although they were unjust; and though the doors of his jail were left open to him, he would not save himself; but in this he did not act as a free agent: the invisible chains of opinion, the secret love of propriety, the inward respect for the laws, even when they were unjust, the fear of tarnishing his glory, kept him in his prison: they were motives sufficiently powerful with this enthusiast for virtue, to induce him to accept death with tranquility.

Thus, we must distinguish external and internal causes. If you are pushed from the bridge into the river, an external cause is responsible for your fall into the river, but if you dive in voluntarily, inner processes are the *proximate* cause of the fall. But the proximate cause can be further traced to other *remote* causes, such as your being taught to dive, your finding pleasure in swimming, your body's ability to stay afloat in water, the peculiar structure of your brain that "anticipates" finding pleasure in diving, and so forth. Doubtless, it would be difficult, if not impossible, in practice to explain all the causal factors that go into any one of our actions. Determinists have insisted, however, such is in principle possible. T. E. Buckle, who published Holbach's work, sums up his position in this way:

> If I were capable of correct reasoning, and if, at the same time, I had a complete knowledge both of his disposition and of all the events by which he was surrounded, I should be able to foresee the line of conduct which, in consequence of those events, he would adopt.[1]

Extending this idea further, we may say that if we knew all the possible states of matter and motion in the universe, we could know all the events of the universe past, present, and future. We could predict every future event and postdict every past event.

Determinism is the theory that everything in the universe is governed by causal laws. That is, everything in the universe is entirely determined so that whatever happens at any given moment is the effect of some antecedent cause. If we were omniscient, we could predict exactly everything that would happen for the rest of this hour in this hour, for the rest of our lifetime, for the rest of time itself, simply because we know how everything hitherto is causally related. This theory—which, it is claimed, is the basic presupposition of science—implies that there is no such thing as an uncaused event (sometimes this is modified to include only the macrocosmic world, leaving the microcosmic world in doubt). Hence, since all human actions are events, human actions are not undetermined, are not *free* in a radical sense but are also the product of a causal process. Hence, while we may self-importantly imagine that we are autonomous and possess free will, in reality we are totally conditioned by heredity and environment.

The outline of the argument for determinism goes something like this:

1. Every event (or state of affairs) must have a cause.
2. Human actions (as well as the agent who gives rise to those actions) are events (or state of affairs).

3. Therefore, every human action (including the agent himself) is caused.

4. Hence, determinism is true.

Although the hypothesis of universal causality cannot be proved, it is something we all assume—either because of considerable inductive evidence or as an a priori truth that seems to make sense of the world. We cannot easily imagine an uncaused event taking place in ordinary life. For example, imagine how you would feel if, on visiting your dentist for relief of a toothache, he concluded his oral examination with the remark, "I certainly can see that you are in great pain because of your toothache, but I'm afraid that I can't help you, for there is no cause of this toothache." Perhaps he calls his partner over to confirm his judgment. "Sure enough," she says, "this is one of those interesting noncausal cases. Sorry, there's nothing we can do for you. Even medicine and pain relievers won't help these noncausal types."

Let's take another example. In Melbourne, Australia, weather forecasts for a 24-hour period are exceedingly reliable. The predictions based on the available atmospheric data and the known meteorological laws are almost always correct. On Star Island off the New Hampshire coast, on the other hand, the official forecasts for a 24-hour period are more often wrong than right. Suppose someone came along and said, "There is an easy explanation for the success of the Australian forecasts and the lack of success of the Star Island forecasts. In Melbourne, the weather is caused by preceding conditions, but on Star Island, more often than not, the weather has no cause. It's cut off from what happened before." Most of us would explain the failure of the meteorologists differently, believing that the weather on Star Island is just as much the outcome of preceding conditions as the weather in Melbourne. The forecasts are less reliable on Star Island because of the greater complexities of the factors that have to be taken into account and the greater difficulty of observing them, but *not* because sufficient causal factors do not exist.

It's an interesting question whether the belief in causality is universal in humans or simply a product of experience. When does it arise in children? When our children were about ages 4 and 6, respectively, I discovered a mess in the pantry. A package of cookies had been opened, and the cookies and cookie crumbs were strewn about on the floor, some having been eaten. We asked our children which one of them had pilfered the cookies. They both denied having anything to do with the matter. We pressed them, for there were no other people but ourselves who had access to the cookies. Finally, my exasperated 4-year-old son volunteered, "Why does someone have to have done it? Why couldn't it just have happened?" "Impossible," I remonstrated, "every event must have a sufficient cause!" My son looked at me with bewilderment. Two weeks later I went to the pantry and again saw a similar sight. Bags of cookies had been broken into, and cookies were scattered all over the floor. But in the midst of the cookies was a dead mouse caught in a mousetrap with a piece of cheese in his mouth but cookie crumbs lining his whiskers. Greed summoned his downfall. Exhilarated by the discovery and confirmation of my theory, I summoned my children to the scene of the crime and triumphantly exclaimed, "Behold, every event must have a cause!" And so the not-so-subtle indoctrination commences.

Why do we believe that everything has a cause? Most philosophers have echoed John Stuart Mill's (1806–1873) answer that the doctrine of universal causality is a conclusion of inductive reasoning. We have had an enormous range of experience wherein we have found causal explanations to individual events, which in turn seem to participate in a further causal chain. The problem with this answer, however, is that we have only experienced a very small part of the universe, not enough of it to warrant the conclusion that every event must have a cause.

It was David Hume (1711–1776) who pointed out that the idea of causality is not a logical truth (like the notion that all triangles have three sides). The hypothesis that every event has a cause arises from the observation of regular conjunctions: "When many uniform instances appear, and the same object is always followed by the same event; we then begin to entertain the notion of cause and connexion."[2] So after a number of successful tries at putting a pot of water to heat over a fire and seeing it disappear, we conclude that heat (or fire) causes water to disappear (or vaporize, turn into gas). We cannot prove causality, however, for we never see it. All we see are two events in constant spatiotemporal order and infer from this constant conjunction a binding relation between them. For example, we see billiard ball A hit ball B, we see B move away from A, and we conclude that A's hitting B at a certain velocity is the cause of B's moving away as it did. However, we cannot prove that it is the sufficient cause of the movement.

Immanuel Kant (1724–1804) first suggested that the principle of universal causality is a synthetic a priori—that is, an assumption that we cannot prove by experience but simply cannot conceive not to be the case. Our mental construction demands that we read all experience in the light of universal causation. We have no knowledge of what the world is in itself or whether there really is universal causation, but we cannot understand experience except by means of causal explanation. The necessary idea of causality is part and parcel of the framework of our noetic structure. We are programmed to read our experience in the causal script.

Kant saw that there was a powerful incentive to believe in determinism, but he also thought that the notion of morality provided a powerful incentive to believe in freedom of the will. Kant was faced with a dilemma: "How can I reconcile the free will necessary for morality and the causal determinism necessary for science?" (We will say more about his problem in Chapters 25 and 26.)

The man who used the idea of determinism more effectively for practical purposes than any one before him was the great American criminal lawyer Clarence Darrow. In the 1920s, in a sensational crime, two teenage geniuses, named Leopold and Loeb, students at the University of Chicago, committed what they regarded as the perfect murder. They grotesquely dismembered a child and buried the parts of his body in a prairie. Caught, they faced an outraged public who demanded the death penalty. The defense attorney was Clarence Darrow, champion of lost causes. He conceded that the boys committed the deed, but argued that they were nevertheless "innocent."

His argument was based on the theory of determinism. It is worth reading part of the plea.

ATTORNEY FOR THE DAMNED

We are all helpless . . . This weary world goes on, begetting, with birth and with living and with death; and all of it is blind from the beginning to the end. I do not know what it was that made these boys do this mad act, but I do know there is a reason for it. I know they did not beget themselves. I know that anyone of an infinite number of causes reaching back to the beginning might be working out in these boys' minds, whom you are asked to hang in malice and in hatred and injustice. . . .

Nature is strong and she is pitiless. She works in her own mysterious way, and we are her victims. We have not much to do with it ourselves. Nature takes this job in hand, and we play our part. In the words of old Omar Khayam, we are:

But helpless pieces in the game He plays
Upon the chess board of nights and days;
Hither and thither moves, and checks and slays,
And one by one back in the closet lays.

What had this boy to do with it? He was not his own father, he was not his own mother; he was not his own grandparents. All of this was handed to him. He did not surround himself with governesses and wealth. He did not make himself. And yet he is to be compelled to pay.

This was sufficient to convince the jury to go against public opinion and recommend a life sentence in lieu of the death penalty. If Leopold and Loeb were determined by antecedent causes to do the deed they did, we cannot blame them for what they did, any more than we can blame a cow for not being able to fly.

Determinism has received new attention and respect due to modern neurological studies that suggest this hypothesis: There is a one-to-one correlation between mental states and brain states so that every conscious action can be traced back to a causally sufficient brain state. In other words, the laws of physics deterministically produce mental states.[3]

Teleological Determinism

Let me immediately point out that determinism need not be crudely mechanistic but can take into account rational intentions and purposes. While it generally holds that mental events are dependent on neural events or brain states, sophisticated teleological determinism (as opposed to simple physical determinism) can recognize the conceptual connection between intention and action. That is, in analyzing why you raised your hand, I need to know whether

From: Clarence Darrow, *Attorney for the Damned* (New York: Simon & Schuster, 1957).

you were intending to wave to a friend, to vote, or to swat a fly. A purely physical description of your bodily motions is quite inadequate as a full account of what you are doing.

However, despite what some libertarians have argued, intentions are no great problem for determinism. Guided missiles, thermostats, and chess-playing computers are also purposive and self-regulating, having feedback mechanisms that enable them to reach their goals despite changing factors in the environment. Chess-playing computers, for example, can learn, devise new strategies, and decide between alternate moves. Although computers are not conscious, they have purposes. The determinist notes that the only advantage that human chess players have over the artifact is that humans are conscious while playing chess. But the question is, What exactly is so important about consciousness? How does consciousness—mere awareness—add to our ability to act freely? We could well imagine a chess-playing computer suddenly conscious of its strategies and moves. Would that awareness by itself make it free?

Summary

The determinist argues that all human action can be subsumed under scientific causal laws that govern the rest of physical behavior. Since every action is completely caused by heredity and environmental factors, there are no free actions. Since there are no free actions, we are not responsible for any of our actions.

FOR FURTHER REFLECTION

1. Analyze Hobach's argument. Do you see any weaknesses in his argument?

2. Go over the main arguments for determinism. How strong are they? What are the chief problems?

3. Assess Darrow's defense of Leopold and Loeb. Do you think that his argument is sound? How would an opponent challenge it?

NOTES

1. H. T. Buckle in his *History of Civilization in England* (1857), cited in Albury Castell and Donald Borchert, *An Introduction to Modern Philosophy* (New York: Macmillan, 1976), 76f.

2. David Hume, *Enquiry* (1748), 78.

3. See Donald M. MacKay, *Freedom of Action in a Mechanistic Universe* (Cambridge, UK: Cambridge University Press, 1967).

FOR FURTHER READING

See For Further Reading, Chapter 26.

25 ⚹ Libertarianism

Libertarianism is the theory stating that we do have free wills. It contends that given the same antecedent (prior) conditions at time t_1, an agent S could do either act A_1 or A_2. That is, it is up to S what the world will look like after t_1, and that his act is causally *underdetermined,* the self making the unexplained difference. Libertarians do not contend that all our actions are free, only some of them. Neither do they argue that our actions are indetermined. **Indeterminism,** the contradictory position to determinism, holds that some events in the universe are *not* caused. As we will see, libertarianism is not the same thing as indeterminism, for the free will presumes the self as a sufficient cause and indeterminism implies that actions are random, chaotic, and uncaused. But neither do they offer an explanatory theory of free will, for our concept of explanation is typically a causal account, which already concedes the field to determinism. Instead, libertarian arguments are indirect, appealing to the introspective experience of deliberation or deep intuitions of spontaneous actions or our sense of moral responsibility.

The Argument from Deliberation

One of the main arguments for the libertarian thesis is the *argument from deliberation*. Here is how one of the leading libertarians, Corliss Lamont, puts it:

> There is the unmistakable intuition of virtually every human being that he is free to make the choices he does and that the deliberations leading to those choices are also free flowing. The normal man feels too, after he has made a decision, that he could have decided differently. That is why regret or remorse for a past choice can be so disturbing.[1]

As an example, there is a difference between a knee jerk and purposefully kicking a football. In the first case, the behavior is involuntary, a reflex action. In the second case, we deliberate, notice that we have an alternative (namely, not kicking the ball), consciously choose to kick the ball, and, if successful, we find our body moving in the requisite manner so that the ball is kicked.

Deliberation may take a short or long time, be foolish or wise, but the process is a conscious one wherein we believe that we really can do either of the actions (or any of many possible actions). That is, in deliberating, we assume that we are free to choose between alternatives and that we are not determined to do simply one action. Otherwise, why deliberate? This should seem obvious to everyone who introspects on what it is to deliberate.

Furthermore, there seems to be something psychologically lethal about accepting determinism in human relations; it tends to curtail deliberation and paralyze actions. If people really believe themselves totally determined, the tendency is for them to excuse their behavior. Human effort seems pointless. As Arthur Eddington puts it,

> What significance is there to my mental struggle tonight whether I shall or shall not give up smoking, if the laws which govern the matter of the physical universe already preordain for the morrow a configuration of matter consisting of pipe, tobacco, and smoke connected to my lips.[2]

The Determinist's Objection to the Argument from Deliberation

The determinist responds to this by admitting that we often feel "free," and feel that we could do otherwise, but these feelings are illusory. The determinist may admit that at any given time t_1, while deliberating, she feels that she is free—at least on one level. But on a higher level or after the deliberation process is over, she acknowledges that even the deliberation is the product of antecedent causes. Ledger Wood suggests that the libertarian argument from deliberation can be reduced to this formula: "I feel myself free, *therefore,* I am free." He analyzes the deliberative decision into three constituents: (1) the recognition of two or more incompatible courses of action, (2) the weighing of considerations favorable and unfavorable to each of the conflicting possibilities of action, and (3) the choice among the alternative possibilities. "At the moment of making the actual decision, the mind experiences a *feeling* of self-assertion and of independence both external and internal." However, Wood insists that the determinist can give a satisfactory account of this feeling, regarding it as "nothing but a sense of relief following upon earlier tension and indecision."

> After conflict and uncertainty, the pent-up energies of the mind—or rather of the underlying neural processes—are released and this process

is accompanied by an inner sense of power. Thus the feeling of freedom or voluntary control over one's actions is a mere subjective illusion which cannot be considered evidence for psychological indeterminacy.[3]

Sometimes, the determinist will offer an account of action in terms of action being the result of the strongest motive. Adolf Grunbaum puts it this way:

> Let us carefully examine the content of the feeling that on a certain occasion we could have acted other than the way we did in fact act. What do we find? Does the feeling we have inform us that we could have acted otherwise under exactly the same external and internal motivational conditions? No, says the determinist, this feeling simply discloses that we were able to act in accord with our strongest desire at the time, and that we could indeed have acted otherwise if a different motive had prevailed at that time.[4]

We could break up the concept of motivation into two parts, that of belief and desire (or wants), resulting in the combination of a desire based on certain beliefs. If Mary strongly desires to fly to New York from Los Angeles at a certain time and believes that taking a certain American Air Lines flight is the best way to do this, she will, unless there are other intervening factors, take such a flight. There is no mystery about the decision. She may deliberate on whether she really wants to pay the $50 more on American than she would have to pay on a later economy flight, but once she realizes that she values getting to New York at a certain time more than saving $50, she will act accordingly. If Mary is rational, her wants and desires will function in a reliable pattern.

Since wants and beliefs are not under our direct control, are not products of free choice, and the act is a product of desires and beliefs, the act is not a product of free choice either. The argument goes something like this:

1. Actions are the results of (are caused by) beliefs and desires.
2. We do not freely choose our beliefs and desires.
3. Beliefs and desires are thrust upon us by our environment in conjunction with innate dispositions.
4. Therefore, we do not freely choose our actions, but our actions are caused by the causal processes that form our beliefs and desires.

If this is so, it is hard to see where free will comes into the picture. The controversial premise is probably item 2, whether we choose our beliefs and desires. The determinist would maintain that we do not choose our beliefs but that they, as truth-directed, are events in our lives, the way the world represents itself to us. That is, beliefs function as truth detectors—so as it is not up to us what the truth is, so it is not up to us to form beliefs about the world. You may check this in a small way by asking why it is you believe that the world is spherical and not flat. Because of evidence or because you choose to believe it? If the latter, could you give up the belief by simply deciding to do so? Neither do we choose our desires, but our desires simply formulate choices. We do not choose to be hungry or to love knowledge, though when we find ourselves in conflict between two conflicting desires (for example, the desire to eat chocolate chip cookies and the desire to lose weight), we have to adjudicate the difference. But this decision is simply a process of allowing the strongest desire (or deepest desire—a deep dispositional desire could win out over a sharply felt occurrent desire) to win out. But all this can be explained in a purely deterministic way, without resorting to a mysterious free act of the will.

The Libertarian Counterresponse: Agent Causation

Now the libertarian objects that this is too simplistic a notion of action. We cannot isolate the desires and beliefs in such a rigid manner. Intangibles are at work here and may be decisive in bringing all the factors of desire and belief together and formulating the final decision.

Some libertarians, such as Roderick Chisholm and Richard Taylor, respond to this view of motivation by putting forward an alternate picture of causation to account for actions. According to Chisholm and Taylor, it is sometimes the case that the agent himself is the cause of his own acts. That is, the agent causes actions without himself changing in any essential way. Richard Taylor argues for it this way.

METAPHYSICS

The only conception of action that accords with the data [of human experience] is one according to which men are sometimes, but of course not always, self-determining beings. That is, beings which are sometimes the causes of their own behavior. In the case of an action that is free, it must be such that it is caused by the agent who performs it, but such that no antecedent conditions were sufficient for his performing just that action. In the case of an action that is both free and rational, it must be such that the agent who performed it did so for some reason, but this reason cannot have been the cause of it.

Now this conception fits what men take themselves to be: namely, beings who act, or who are agents, rather than things that are merely acted upon, and whose behavior is simply the causal consequences of conditions which they have not wrought. When I believe that I have done something, I do believe that it was I who caused it to be done, I who made something happen, and not merely something within me, such as one of my own subjective states, which is not identical with myself. If I believe that something not identical with myself was the cause of my behavior—some event wholly external to myself, for instance, or even one internal to myself, such as a nerve impulse, volition, or whatnot—then I cannot regard that behavior as being an act of myself. I do not, accordingly, regard this activity of my body as my action, and would be no more tempted to do so if I became suddenly conscious within myself of those conditions or impulses that produce it. This is behavior with which I have nothing to do, behavior that is not within my immediate control, behavior that is not only not free activity, but

From: Richard Taylor, *Metaphysics*, 2nd ed. (Englewood Cliffs, NJ: Prentice Hall, 1974), 54–56.

not even the activity of an agent to begin with; it is nothing but a mechanical reflex. Had I never learned that my very life depends on this pulse beat, I would regard it with complete indifference, as something foreign to me, like the oscillations of a clock pendulum that I idly contemplate.

Now this conception of activity, and of an agent who is the cause of it, involves two rather strange metaphysical notions that are never applied elsewhere in nature. The first is that of a *self* or *person*—for example, a man—who is not merely a collection of things or events, but a substance and a self-moving being. For on this view it is a man himself, and not merely some part of him or something within him, that is the cause of his own activity. Now we certainly do not know that a man is anything more than an assemblage of physical things and processes, which act in accordance with those laws that describe the behavior of all other physical things and processes. Even though a man is a living being, of enormous complexity, there is nothing, apart from the requirements of this theory, to suggest that his behavior is so radically different in its origin from that of other physical objects, or that an understanding of it must be sought in some metaphysical realm wholly different from that appropriate to the understanding of non-living things.

Second, this conception of activity involves an extraordinary conception of causation, according to which an agent, which is a substance and not an event, can nevertheless be the cause of an event. Indeed, if he is a free agent then he can, on this conception, cause an event to occur—namely, some act of his own—without anything else causing him to do so. This means that an agent is sometimes a cause, without being an antecedent sufficient condition; for if I affirm that I am the cause of some act of mine, then I am plainly not saying that my very existence is sufficient for its occurrence, which would be absurd. If I say that my hand causes my pencil to move, then I am saying that the motion of my hand is, under the other conditions then prevailing, sufficient for the motion of the pencil. But if I then say that I cause my hand to move, I am not saying anything remotely like this, and surely not that the motion of my self is sufficient for the motion of my arm and hand, since these are the only things about me that are moving.

This conception of the causation of events by beings or substances that are not events is, in fact, so different from the usual philosophical conception of a cause that it should not even bear the same name, for "being a cause" ordinarily just means "being an antecedent sufficient condition or set of conditions." Instead, then, of speaking of agents as *causing* their own acts, it would perhaps be better to use another word entirely, and say, for instance, that they *originate* them, *initiate* them, or simply that they *perform* them.

The self is a unique phenomenon in the world. It is not merely a collection of material particles but has consciousness and is able to deliberate and intend. It can initiate action without itself being caused by antecedent sufficient conditions. Taylor next shows how this concept, which may at first glance seem "dubious," is consistent with our concept of deliberation and superior to both indeterminism and determinism. No account need be given on how this is possible since we cannot get behind the self in order to analyze it. It would be tantamount to gouging out your two eyes in order to examine them.

Now this is on the face of it a dubious conception of what a man is. Yet it is consistent with our data, reflecting the presuppositions of deliberation, and appears to be the only conception that is consistent with them, as determinism and simple indeterminism are not. The theory of agency avoids the absurdities of simple indeterminism by conceding that human behavior is caused, while at the same time avoiding the difficulties of determinism by denying that every chain of causes and effects is infinite. Some such causal chains, on this view, have beginnings, and they begin with agents themselves. Moreover, if we are to suppose that it is sometimes up to me what I do, and understand this in a sense which is not consistent with determinism, we must suppose that I am an agent or a being who initiates his own actions, sometimes under conditions which do not determine what action he shall perform. Deliberation becomes, on this view, something that is not only possible but quite rational, for it does make sense to deliberate about activity that is truly my own and that depends in its outcome upon me as its author, and not merely upon something more or less esoteric that is supposed to be intimately associated with me, such as my thoughts, volitions, choices, or whatnot.[5]

This notion of the self as agent differs radically from Hume's notion of the self as simply a bundle of perceptions, insisting instead that it is a substance and self-moving being.

[Persons] are sometimes, but of course not always, self-determining beings; that is, beings which are sometimes the causes of their own behavior. In the case of an action that is free, it must be such that it is caused by the agent who performs it, but such that no antecedent conditions were sufficient for his performing just that action. In the case of an action that is both free and rational, it must be that the agent who performed it did so for some reason, but this reason cannot have been the cause of it.[6]

Human beings are not simply assemblages of material processes but complex wholes, with a different metaphysical status than physical objects. Furthermore, this view of the self sees the self as a substance and not an event. It is a being that initiates action without being caused to act by antecedent causes. If I raise my hand, it is not the events leading up to the raising of my hand that cause this act, but I myself am the cause.

In a sense, the self becomes a "god," creating *ex nihilo*, in that reasons may influence but do not determine the acts. In the words of Chisholm,

If we are responsible, and if what I have been trying to say [about agent causality] is true, then we have a prerogative which some would attribute only to God: each of us, when we act, is a prime mover unmoved. In doing what we do, we cause certain events to happen and nothing—or no one—causes us to cause those events to happen.[7]

Perhaps the libertarian draws some support for this thesis from Genesis 1:26, where God says, "Let us make man in our image." The image of God may be our ability to make free, causally underdetermined decisions. When students tell me that they do not believe in miracles, I often ask them whether they believe in freedom of the will. Most say they do. I tell them that I think they really do believe in miracles, for in a sense every libertarian believes in at least one "godlike" being who in acting creates miracles.

This theory, though attractive in that it preserves the notion of free agency, suffers from the fact that it leaves agent causation unexplained. The self is a mystery that is unaccounted for. Actions are seen as miracles that are unrelated to antecedent causal chains, detached from the laws of nature. Nevertheless, something like the argument from free agency seems to be intuitively satisfying upon introspection. We do feel that we are free agents.

Along these lines, the libertarian dismisses the determinist's hypothesis of a complete causal explanation based on a correlation of brain events with mental events. Though memories may be stored in the brain, the self is not. Whether as an emergent property, a transcendent entity, or simply an unexplained mystery, the self must be regarded as primitive. In a Cartesian manner, it is to be accepted as more certain than anything else and the source of all other certainties.

An Objection to Arguments from Introspection

We said that the argument from deliberation, and hence of agent causation, depends on our introspective reports, but there is a problem with using introspection as evidence for freedom of the will. The problem with the argument from introspection is that our introspections and intuitions about our behavior are often misguided. Freudian psychology and common sense tell us that sometimes when we believe that we are acting from one motive, another hidden subconscious motive is really at play. The hypnotized person believes that she is free when she is uttering her preordained speech, while the audience looks on knowingly. Chris Frederickson, a neurophysiologist at the University of Texas at Dallas, has told of experiments with electrodes that illustrate this point nicely. Patients with electrodes attached to their neocortex are set before a button that sets off a bell. The patients are told that they may press the button whenever they like. The patients proceed to press the buttons and ring the bells. They report that they are entirely free in doing this. However, the monitoring of the brain shows that an impulse is started in the cerebral cortex before they become aware of their desire and decision to press the button, and when this impulse reaches a certain level, the patients feel the volition and press the button. Is it fair to suppose that all our behavior may follow this model? Do we only become conscious of the workings of our subconscious at discrete moments? Notice in this regard that often we seem to have unconsciously formulated our speech before we are conscious of what we are saying. The words flow naturally, as though some inner speechwriter were working them out beforehand.

It seems, then, that our introspective reports must be regarded as providing very little evidence in favor of free will in the libertarian sense. As Baruch Spinoza (1632–1677) said, if a stone hurled through the air were to become conscious, it would probably deem itself free.

The Argument from Quantum Mechanics (A Peephole of Free Will)

At this point, libertarians sometimes refer to an argument from quantum mechanics in order to defend themselves against the insistence of determinists that science is on their side in their espousal of universal causality. Quantum mechanics holds that the world is not deterministic, but *indeterministic,* not governed by complete causal laws. The argument from quantum mechanics is negative and indirectly in support of the libertarian thesis. According to quantum mechanics as developed by Neils Bohr (1885–1962) and Max Born (1882–1970), the behavior of subatomic particles does not follow causal processes but instead yields only statistically predictable behavior. That is, we can not predict the motions of individual particles, but we can successfully predict the percentage that will act in certain ways. A certain randomness seems to operate on this subatomic level. Hence, there is a case for indeterminacy.

This thesis of quantum mechanics is controversial. Albert Einstein (1879–1955) never accepted it. "God doesn't play dice!" he said. Quantum physics may only indicate the fact that we do not know the causes operative at subatomic levels. After all, we are only in the kindergarten of subatomic physics. Thus, the indeterminist may be committing the fallacy of ignorance in reading too much into the inability of quantum physicists to give causal explanations of subatomic behavior.

On the other hand, perhaps quantum physics should make impartial persons reconsider what they mean by *causality,* and whether it could be the case that it is an unclear concept in the first place. The fact that our notion of causality is vague and unanalyzed was pointed out long ago by David Hume (1711–1776) and reiterated in this century by William James (1842–1910):

> The principle of causality . . .—what is it but a postulate, an empty name covering simply a demand that the sequence of events shall some day manifest a deeper kind of belonging of one thing with another than the mere arbitrary juxtaposition which now phenomenally appears? It is as much an altar to an unknown god as the one that Saint Paul found at Athens. All our scientific and philosophic ideas are altars to unknown gods.[8]

Recent work by philosophers on the subject of causality hasn't substantially improved this state of affairs. The notion, while enjoying an intuitively privileged position in our noetic structure, is still an enigma.

Nevertheless, although the quantum theory and doubts about causality may cause us to loosen up our grip on the notion of universal causality, it doesn't help the libertarians in any positive way, for it only shows at best that there is randomness in the world, not that there is purposeful free agency. Uncaused behavior suggests erratic, impulsive reflex motion without any rhyme or reason, the behavior of the maniac, lacking all predictability and explanation, behavior out of our rational control. But free action must be under *my* control if it is to be counted as *my* behavior. That is, the thesis of libertarianism is that the agent is underdetermined when he makes a purposeful, rational decision. All that quantum mechanics entails is that there are random events in the brain (or wherever) that yield unpredictable behavior for which the agent is not responsible.

The Argument from Moral Responsibility

If we are determined by causal antecedents to do the things we do, are we morally responsible for our actions? It would seem not. Determinism entails that we could not do otherwise than we did, but moral responsibility entails that we could have done otherwise. Essentially, all human actions, according to determinism, are equivalent to events in nature. The greater force overrides lesser forces. Where there are different forces operating on an object, vectors determine the direction of the movement of that object. It is true that King Darius whipped the sea because it would not calm down for him to sail across to Greece, but we think that his behavior was absurd. But if human beings are wholly determined by antecedent events, then it makes no more sense to punish humans than to whip the sea. Neither do we deserve praise or rewards for our good deeds because we could not have done otherwise. The fact that we feel that we could do otherwise, that we were free, and hence responsible, is an illusion.

We are loathe to relinquish the idea that we are morally responsible for our deliberate actions. We are justified, we think, in punishing criminals who harm others with malice aforethought and in reprimanding those who insult or are insensitive to other people. It is hard to understand how society could survive, let alone flourish, without a deep notion of moral responsibility. We do have duties, we hold, so we must not be completely determined. The argument might be represented in this way:

1. If determinism is true and our actions are merely the product of the laws of nature and antecedent states of affairs, then it is not up to us to choose how we act.

2. But if it is not up to us how we act, we cannot be said to be responsible for our actions.

3. So if determinism is true, we are not responsible for our actions.

4. But we strongly believe that we do have moral responsibility. This belief is more certain than our belief that every act has a cause.

5. Therefore, if we hold more strongly to moral responsibilities than causal determinism, determinism must be rejected.

Thus, we must reject the notion of determinism even if we cannot give a full explanatory account of how agents choose.

Here the determinist usually bites the bullet and admits that we do not have moral responsibilities and that it is just an illusion that we do. However, we are determined to have such an illusion, so there is nothing we can do about it. We cannot consciously live as determinists, but why should we think that we could? We are finite and fallible creatures, driven by causal laws, but with self-consciousness that makes us aware of part (but only a part) of the process that governs our behavior.

However, there is another response to the problem of free will and determinism, which claims to save both the notion of determinism and the notion of moral responsibility. To this reconciling project, called compatibilism, we will turn to in Chapter 26.

Summary

Libertarianism is the theory that we have free will. In many cases, given the same prior conditions, an agent could do either one act or its alternative. The main arguments for free will are the argument from deliberation, the argument from agent causation, the argument from introspection, and the argument from moral responsibility. The libertarian contends that without free will we are not justified in holding people accountable for their actions. Each argument evokes a response from the determinist.

FOR FURTHER REFLECTION

1. Analyze Taylor's idea of agent causation. What are the two "rather strange metaphysical notions that are never applied elsewhere in nature"? What is their significance for his theory of agent causation?

2. It is often claimed that our moral intuitions—that we are responsible for our actions and have duties, that people should be praised or blamed and punished or rewarded for their actions—turn out to be illusory if the libertarian answer is not true. The argument goes as follows:

   1. If determinism is true and our actions are merely the product of the laws of nature and antecedent states of affairs, then it is not up to us to choose what we do.

   2. But if it is not up to us to choose what we do, we cannot be said to be responsible for what we do.

   3. So if determinism is true, we are not responsible for what we do.

   4. But our belief in moral responsibility is self-evident, at least as strong as our belief in universal causality.

   5. Therefore, if we believe that we have moral responsibilities, determinism cannot be accepted.

We must reject the notion of determinism even if we cannot give a full explanatory account of how agents choose. Of course, even if this is a sound argument, the determinist can bite the bullet and admit that we do not have moral responsibilities and that it is just an illusion that we do. We are determined to have such an illusion, so there is nothing we can do about it.

Evaluate this argument and the determinist response. How would the compatibilist respond to it? Discuss your answer.

NOTES

1. Corliss Lamont, *Freedom of Choice Affirmed* (New York: Horizon, 1967), 3.
2. Arthur Eddington, *The Nature of the Physical World* (New York: Macmillan, 1928).
3. Ledger Wood, "The Free Will Controversy," *Philosophy* 16 (1941): 386.
4. Adolf Grunbaum, "Causality and the Science of Human Behavior," reprinted in part in *Philosophical Problems,* ed. Maurice Mandelbaum (New York: Macmillan, 1957), 336.
5. Richard Taylor, *Metaphysics,* 2nd ed. (Englewood Cliffs, NJ: Prentice Hall, 1974) 54–56.
6. Ibid.
7. Roderick Chisholm, "Human Freedom and the Self," in *Free Will,* ed. Gary Watson (Oxford, UK: Clarendon Press, 1982), 32.
8. William James, "The Dilemma of Determinism," in his *Essays on Faith and Morals* (Cleveland: World, 1962).

FOR FURTHER READING

See For Further Reading, Chapter 26.

26 ⚘ Compatibilism: How to Have Your Cake and Eat It Too

A Reconciling Project

We have been struggling with the dilemma of free will and determinism. Causal determinism seems to account for all the events in the world. Even if we modify this to include the conclusions of quantum physics, this does not give us evidence for free will but only randomness that yields statistical probability. On the other hand, we have a deep conviction that we can do otherwise, act freely. What is more, morality seems to require that we choose freely and thus may be held accountable for our actions. Which theory is right? Are we free or determined? Or a little bit of each?

A third doctrine has been developed to make sense of our dilemma, one going back to David Hume (1711–1776) and Immanuel Kant (1724–1804) but receiving a more thorough defense in the works of John Stuart Mill (1806–1873) and the British-born Princeton University professor Walter Stace (1886–1967).[1] It may be called *reconciling determinism*, or *soft determinism*, or, my choice, **compatibilism.** It argues that although we are determined, we still have moral responsibilities, that the basis of the distinction is that between *voluntary* and *involuntary* behavior. Taking the soft-determinist perspective into account, what we called *determinism* in Chapter 24 we should rename *hard determinism*, the view that no reconciliation with free will is possible.

The language of freedom and the language of determinism are but two different ways of talking about certain human or rational events, both necessary for humankind (one is necessary for science, and the other is necessary for morality and personal relationships). The compatibilist argues that the fact that we are determined does not affect our interpersonal relations. We will still have feelings that we must deal with, using internalist insights. We will still feel resentment when someone hurts us "on purpose." We will still feel grateful for services rendered and hold people responsible for their actions. However, we will still acknowledge that from the external perspective the determinist's account of all of this is valid.

Along these lines, Stace has argued that the problem of freedom and determinism is really only a semantic one, a dispute about the meanings of words. Freedom has to do with acts done voluntarily and determinism with the causal processes that underlie all behavior and events. These need not be incompatible.

Stace begins by showing why it is important to secure the free-will thesis.

THE PROBLEM OF FREE WILL

I shall first discuss the problem of free will, for it is certain that if there is no free will there can be no morality. Morality is concerned with what men ought and ought not to do. But if a man has no freedom to choose what he will do, if whatever he does is done under compulsion, then it does not make sense to tell him that he ought not to have done what he did and that he ought to do something different. All moral precepts would in such case be meaningless. Also if he acts always under compulsion, how can he be held morally responsible for his actions? How can he, for example, be punished for what he could not help doing?

It is to be observed that those learned professors of philosophy or psychology who deny the existence of free will do so only in their professional moments and in their studies and lecture rooms. For when it comes to doing anything practical, even of the most trivial kind, they invariably behave as if they and others were free. They inquire from you at dinner whether you will choose this dish or that dish. They will ask a child why he told a lie, and will punish him for not having chosen the way of truthfulness. All of which is inconsistent with a disbelief in free will. This should cause us to suspect that the problem is not a real one; and this, I believe, is the case. The dispute is merely verbal, and is due to nothing but a confusion about the meanings of words. It is what is now fashionably called a semantic problem.

Having shown importance of free will for morality and that even determinists must live as though they believed in free will, Stace goes on to describe the conceptual confusion underlying the dispute over free will and determinism. It is a type of verbal dispute.

How does a verbal dispute arise? Let us consider a case which, although it is absurd in the sense that no one would ever make the mistake which is involved in it, illustrates the principle which we shall have to use in the solution of the problem. Suppose that someone believed that the word "man" means a certain sort of five-legged animal; in short that 'five-legged animal is the correct *definition* of man. He might then look around the world, and rightly observing that there are no five-legged animals in it,

---

From: Walter Stace, *Religion and the Modern Mind* (New York: Lippincott, 1952).

he might proceed to deny the existence of men. This preposterous conclusion would have been reached because he was using an incorrect definition of "man." All you would have to do to show him his mistake would be to give him the correct definition; or at least show him that his definition was wrong. Both the problem and its solution would, of course, be entirely verbal. The problem of free will, and its solution, I shall maintain, is verbal in exactly the same way. The problem has been created by the fact that learned men, especially philosophers, have assumed an incorrect definition of free will, and then finding that there is nothing in the world which answers to their definition, have denied its existence. As far as logic is concerned, their conclusion is just as absurd as that of the man who denies the existence of men. The only difference is that the mistake in the latter case is obvious and crude, while the mistake which the deniers of free will have made is rather subtle and difficult to detect.

Throughout the modern period, until quite recently, it was assumed, both by the philosophers who denied free will and by those who defended it, that *determinism is inconsistent with free will*. If a man's actions were wholly determined by chains of causes stretching back into the remote past, so that they could be predicted beforehand by a mind which knew all the causes, it was assumed that they could not in that case be free. This implies that a certain definition of actions done from free will was assumed, namely that they are actions *not* wholly determined by causes or predictable beforehand. Let us shorten this by saying that free will was defined as meaning indeterminism. This is the incorrect definition which has led to the denial of free will. As soon as we see what the true definition is we shall find that the question whether the world is deterministic, as Newtonian science implied, or in a measure indeterministic, as current physics teaches, is wholly irrelevant to the problem.[2]

Next Stace illustrates how determinism and "free will," as the phrase is commonly used in conversation, are not incompatible. Here is Stace's imaginary dialogue.

JONES: I once went without food for a week.
SMITH: Did you do that of your own free will?
JONES: No. I did it because I was lost in a desert and could find no food.

But suppose that the man who had fasted was Mahatma Gandhi. The conversation might then have gone:
GANDHI: I once fasted for a week.
SMITH: Did you do that of your own free will?
GANDHI: Yes. I did it because I wanted to compel the British Government to give India its independence.

Take another case. Suppose that I had stolen some bread, but that I was as truthful as George Washington. Then, if I were charged with the crime in court, some exchange of the following sort might take place:
JUDGE: Did you steal the bread of your own free will?
STACE: Yes. I stole it because I was hungry.

Or in different circumstances the conversation might run:
JUDGE: Did you steal of your own free will?
STACE: No. I stole because my employer threatened to beat me if I did not.

At a recent murder trial in Trenton some of the accused had signed confessions, but afterwards asserted that they had done so under police duress. The following exchange might have occurred:

JUDGE: Did you sign the confession of your own free will?

PRISONER: No. I signed it because the police beat me up.

Now suppose that a philosopher had been a member of the jury. We could imagine this conversation taking place in the jury room.

FOREMAN OF THE JURY: The prisoner says he signed the confession because he was beaten, and not of his own free will.

PHILOSOPHER: This is quite irrelevant to the case. There is no such thing as free will.

FOREMAN: Do you mean to say that it makes no difference whether he signed because his conscience made him want to tell the truth or because he was beaten?

PHILOSOPHER: None at all. Whether he was caused to sign by a beating or by some desire of his own—the desire to tell the truth, for example—in either case his signing was causally determined, and therefore in neither case did he act of his own free will. Since there is no such thing as free will, the question whether he signed of his own free will ought not to be discussed by us.

The foreman and the rest of the jury would rightly conclude that the philosopher must be making some mistake. What sort of a mistake could it be? There is only one possible answer. The philosopher must be using the phrase "free will" in some peculiar way of his own which is not the way in which men usually use it when they wish to determine a question of moral responsibility. That is, he must be using an incorrect definition of it as implying action not determined by causes....

We have now collected a number of cases of actions which, in the ordinary usage of the English language, would be called cases in which people have acted of their own free will. We should also say in all these cases that they *chose* to act as they did. We should also say that they could have acted otherwise, if they had chosen. For instance, Mahatma Gandhi was not compelled to fast; he chose to do so. He could have eaten if he had wanted to. When Smith went out to get his lunch, he chose to do so. He could have stayed and done some work, if he had wanted to. We have also collected a number of cases of the opposite kind. They are cases in which men were not able to exercise their free will. They had no choice. They were compelled to do as they did. The man in the desert did not fast of his own free will. He had no choice in the matter. He was compelled to fast because there was nothing for him to eat. And so with the other cases. It ought to be quite easy, by an inspection of these cases, to tell what we ordinarily mean when we say that a man did or did not exercise free will. We ought therefore to be able to extract from them the proper definition of the term. Let us put the cases in a table:

Free Acts	*Unfree Acts*
Gandhi fasting because he wanted to free India.	The man fasting in the desert because there was no food.
Stealing bread because one is hungry.	Stealing because one's employer threatened to beat one.
Signing a confession because one wanted to tell the truth.	Signing because the police beat one.

It is obvious that to find the correct definition of free acts we must discover what characteristic is common to all the acts in the left-hand column, and is, at the same time, absent from all the acts in the right-hand column. This characteristic which all free acts have, and which no unfree acts have, will be the defining characteristic of free will.

Is being uncaused, or not being determined by causes, the characteristic of which we are in search? It cannot be, because although it is true that all the acts in the right-hand column have causes, such as the beating by the police or the absence of food in the desert, so also do the acts in the left-hand column. Mr. Gandhi's fasting was caused by his desire to free India, ... and so on. Moreover there is no reason to doubt that these causes of the free acts were in turn caused by prior conditions, and that these were again the results of causes, and so on back indefinitely into the past. Any physiologist can tell us the causes of hunger. What caused Mr. Gandhi's tremendously powerful desire to free India is no doubt more difficult to discover. But it must have had causes. Some of them may have lain in peculiarities of his glands or brain, others in his past experiences, others in his heredity, others in his education. Defenders of free will have usually tended to deny such facts. But to do so is plainly a case of special pleading, which is unsupported by any scrap of evidence. The only reasonable view is that all human actions, both those which are freely done and those which are not, are either wholly determined by causes, or at least as much determined as other events in nature. It may be true, as the physicists tell us, that nature is not as deterministic as was once thought. But whatever degree of determinism prevails in the world, human actions appear to be as much determined as anything else. And if this is so, it cannot be the case that what distinguishes actions freely chosen from those which are not free is that the latter are determined by causes while the former are not. Therefore, being uncaused or being undetermined by causes, must be an incorrect definition of free will.[3]

Gandhi fasted because he wanted to free India from colonial rule and so performed a voluntary, or free act, whereas a man starving in the desert is not giving up food voluntarily or as a free act. A thief purposefully and voluntarily steals, whereas a kleptomaniac cannot help stealing. In both cases, each act or event has causal antecedents, but the former in each set are free, whereas the latter are unfree. Stace concludes his argument:

Acts freely done are those whose immediate causes are psychological states in the agent. Acts not freely done are those whose immediate causes are states of affairs external to the agent.

It is plain that if we define free will in this way, then free will certainly exists, and the philosopher's denial of its existence is seen to be what it is—nonsense. For it is obvious that all those actions of men which we should ordinarily attribute to the exercise of their free will, or of which we should say that they freely chose to do them, are in fact actions which have been caused by their own desire, wishes, thoughts, emotions, impulses, or other psychological states.[4]

Has Stace convinced you that compatibilism is true, that there is no opposition between free will and determinism? Before you answer that question, let's continue our analysis of this theory.

We can analyze Stace's argument in terms of reasons for actions. The agent is free just in case she acted according to reasons rather than from internal neurotic or external coercive pressure. But our reasons are not things we choose but wants and beliefs with which we find ourselves. Since free actions are caused by that which is not a free act, we can see that our free actions are in a sense determined.

The argument for compatibilism may be formulated like this:

1. The reasons R that someone S has for performing act A are not themselves actions.

2. S could not help having R.

3. Act A could nevertheless be free, since it was not coerced by external causes.

4. Therefore, an action may result from having a reason that one could not help having (that is, a reason that one was not free not to have), and the action might nevertheless be free.

5. Therefore, we obtain the collapse of the argument for the incompatibility of free action and determinism.

The compatibilist challenges the libertarian to produce an action that does not fit this formula. Take the act of raising my hand at time t_1. Why do I do it? Well, if it's a rational (that is, free) act, it's because I have a reason for raising my hand. For example, at t_1 I wish to vote for Joan to be president of our club. I deliberate on whom to vote for (read: allow the options to present themselves before my mind), decide that Joan is the best candidate, and raise my hand in response to that judgment. It is a free act, but all the features can be accommodated within causal explanatory theory. Reasons function as causes here.

What would be a free act that was not determined by reasons? Consider the situation of coming to a fork in the road with no obvious reason to take either one (or go back, for that matter). If there are no reasons to do one thing more than another, I have no basis for choice. But I may still believe that doing something is better than just standing still, so I flip a coin in order to decide. This belief functions as my reason for flipping the coin. Similarly, I may flip a "mental coin," by letting the internal devices of my subconscious make an arbitrary decision. The alternative to these arbitrary "flips of the coin" is to be in the same position as Buridan's ass who starved to death while he was equal distance between two luscious bales of hay, because there was no more reason to choose one bale over the other! So, the objection runs, all rational action is determined by reason, and libertarianism turns out to be incoherent.

The compatibilist joins with the determinist to the extent that he asserts that all actions have a sufficient causal explanation. Free actions are caused by reasons the person has, and unfree actions are caused by nonrational coercion. What would it mean to act freely without reasons? What kind of freedom would that be? Would it not turn out to be irrational, hence arbitrary or unconsciously motivated action?

However, if our free acts are the acts we do voluntarily because we have reasons for them, we can be held accountable for them. We identify with the springs of those actions and so may be said to have produced them in a way that we do not produce involuntary actions. We could have avoided those actions, if we had chosen to do so. Hence, we are responsible for them.

One particularly sophisticated version of this position is that of Harry Frankfurt who argues that what is important about freedom of the will is not any contracausal notions but the manner in which the will is structured.[5] What distinguishes *persons* from other conscious beings (which he calls "wantons") are the second-order desires they have. All conscious beings have first-order desires, but persons have attitudes about those first-order desires. They either want it to be the case that their first-order desires motivate them to action or that they do not motivate them to action. "Someone has a desire of the second order either when he wants simply to have a certain desire or when he wants a certain desire to be his will. In situations of the latter kind, I shall call his second-order desires 'second-order volitions.'"[6] A nicotine addict may very well desire that his first-order desire for a cigarette be frustrated or overcome, and a wife unable to feel certain sentiments toward her husband may have a second-order desire that she would come to have feelings of affection for her husband.

Nevertheless, we should not confuse free will with free action:

We do not suppose that animals enjoy freedom of the will, although we recognize that an animal may be free to run in whatever direction it wants. Thus, having the freedom to do what one wants to do is not a sufficient condition of having a free will. It is not a necessary condition either. For to deprive someone of his freedom of action is not necessarily to undermine the freedom of his will. When an agent is aware that there are certain things he is not free to do, this doubtless affects his desires and limits the range of choices he can make. But suppose someone, without being aware of it, has in fact lost or been deprived of his freedom of action. Even though he is no longer free to do what he wants to do, his will may remain as free as it was before. Despite the fact that he is not free to translate his desires into actions or to act according to the determinations of his will, he may still form those desires and make those determinations as freely as if his freedom of action had not been impaired.[7]

Hence, it makes no sense to define free will as the libertarians do, as those actions that originate in ways underdetermined by antecedent causes. A person's will is free just in case she is free to have the will she wants, whether or not she is able to act.

A Critique of Compatibilism: A "Quagmire of Evasion"?

The compatibilist may be accused of wanting his cake and eating it too. The libertarian does not meet the compatibilist challenge head on, for he admits that we don't have a straightforward argument for libertarianism. Instead, he shows that compatibilism is really simply a wistful sort of determinism. William James (1842–1910) labeled it "a quagmire of evasion" and argued that the compatibilist is simply an inconsistent determinist or a determinist who tries to smuggle in moral responsibility by virtue of an irrelevant dichotomy between voluntary and involuntary action.

Lois Hope Walker (1945–) has stood against compatibilists like Stace and Frankfurt, arguing that moral responsibility entails free will and the absence of complete determinist explanations of our behavior.

A LIBERTARIAN DEFENSE OF MORAL RESPONSIBILITY

In recent years there has been an exodus by philosophers from a libertarian position to soft determinism, sometimes called *"compatibilism."* Bewitched by the attraction of neurobiology, which promises to explain all human behavior via brain behavior, philosophers have been running over each other in their eagerness to endorse the latest hypotheses of the neurologist-philosophers. Witness the number of books and articles defending compatibilist positions. In this mob-like stampede, I find myself going against the traffic. Having embraced determinism as an undergraduate, in my old age I have become disillusioned with this unfaithful guide. In this essay I want to defend the libertarian view of moral responsibility. In particular, I want to argue two theses: (1) soft-determinist arguments for moral responsibility are invalid; (2) the libertarian position is rationally justified. In the process of defending thesis 2, I point out that the soft determinist often misrepresents the libertarian position on this matter. Although the free will/determinism problem is one of the most difficult paradoxes in philosophy, and intelligent people can differ as to solution, the argument from moral responsibility seems to shift the weight of evidence in the libertarian's direction.

The Argument from Moral Responsibility

Determinism seems to conflict with the thesis that we have moral responsibilities, for responsibility implies that we could have done otherwise than we did. We do not hold a dog morally responsible for chewing up our philosophy book or hold a one-month-old baby responsible for crying, because they could not help it, but we do hold a twenty-year-old student responsible for his cheating because (we believe) he could have done otherwise. Black-backed seagulls will tear apart a stray baby herring seagull without the slightest suspicion that their act may be immoral, but if humans lack this sense we judge them as pathological, as substandard.

Moral responsibility is something we take very seriously. We believe we do have duties, oughts, over which we feel rational guilt at failure to perform. But there can be no such things as duties, oughts, praise, blame, or rational guilt, if we are not actually free. The argument is the following.

From: Lois Hope Walker, "A Libertarian Defense of Moral Responsibility," in *Introduction to Philosophy: Classical and Contemporary Readings,* ed. Louis P. Pojman (Belmont, CA: Wadsworth, 1991), 453–457.

1. Since "ought" implies "can," in order to have a duty to do Act A, we must be able to do A *and* able to refrain from doing A.

2. Being morally responsible for doing A entails that I could have done otherwise if I had chosen to do so and that at some previous time I could have chosen to have done otherwise (or chosen some course of action that would have enabled me to do A).

3. But if determinism is true and our actions are merely the product of the laws of nature and antecedent states of affairs, then it is not up to us to choose what we do.

4. But if it is not up to us to choose what we do, we cannot be said to be responsible for what we do.

5. So if determinism is true, we are not responsible for what we do.

6. But our belief in moral responsibility is self-evident and more worthy of acceptance than belief in universal causality.

7. So if we believe that we have moral responsibilities, determinism cannot be accepted.

8. Therefore, since we justifiably believe in moral responsibility, we must reject the notion of determinism even if we cannot give a full explanatory account of how agents choose.

Is this argument sound? Interestingly enough, both hard determinists and libertarians accept the first five premises. Together they make up the group known as *incompatibilists,* for they claim that free will and moral responsibility are incompatible with determinism.

Here the determinist usually bites the bullet and admits that we do not have moral responsibilities, and that it is just an illusion that we do. But we are determined to have such an illusion, so there is nothing we can do about it. We cannot consciously live as determinists, but why should we think that we can? We are finite and fallible creatures, whose behavior is entirely governed by causal laws, but with self-consciousness that makes us aware of part (but only a part) of the process that governs our behavior.

Let us look more closely at the key premises in the argument. The notion that *ought* implies *can* was first pointed out by Immanuel Kant. It simply makes no sense to say that I have an obligation to do something that I do not have the power to do. Suppose I have been hypnotized and ordered to shake hands with every person in my class. I do so, feeling that I am acting under my own free will, but I am not acting freely and I am not responsible for my behavior. Or suppose through some deep brain defect and poor early upbringing I am a kleptomaniac. I am not able to refrain from stealing, so I am not responsible for my behavior—even though I may feel free while doing so. I am excused for my behavior and, one may hope, treated.

But suppose I have acquired my habit of theft through giving in to the temptation to steal over a period of time and now cannot refrain. Even though I now cannot refrain, I am responsible for the state I am now in. I am responsible for my character and morally responsible for my thievery. This conclusion is conveyed by Premise 2: "Being morally responsible for doing A entails that I could have done otherwise if I had chosen to do so and that at some previous time I could have chosen to have done otherwise (or chosen some course of action that would have enabled me to do A)."

The compatibilist usually responds at this point that the phrase "could have done otherwise" should be translated hypothetically as "would have done otherwise if I had chosen differently." When pressed and asked whether at the time in question I could have *chosen* otherwise, the compatibilist *qua* determinist must answer no. I could not have chosen differently. But if I could not have chosen differently, then what sense does it make to say that freedom amounts to being able to do differently if one chooses to do so? If I could never choose to do other than I do, I cannot be said to be able to do any other act but the one I actually do. The hypothetical interpretation is a red herring, amounting to little more than the truth that if things had been different, they would have been different. That is, is I had been *determined* to choose differently, I would have been *determined* to do otherwise than I did.

Premise 3 contends that if determinism is true, then we do not have the power to refrain from doing A (if A is what we indeed do). For any time t there is only one act open to us, that caused by the state of the world plus the laws of nature, together. But if antecedent states of affairs cause A to happen, then they are responsible for what we "do," and we ourselves are not responsible for those acts (Premise 4). We are puppets in the hands of nature.

So 5, "If determinism is true, we are not responsible for what we do." If nature is responsible for our actions, then nature should be praised or blamed for what we do, not us. The determinist may argue that in punishing or rewarding us we are really punishing or rewarding nature, but this of course is hyperbolic persiflage, for the notions of reward and punishment presuppose that the subject in question be conscious and have interests, neither of which apply to nature.

But if we are not responsible for our actions, then we are mere objects of nature, without selves worthy of respect in their own right. As Nagel says, "The area of genuine agency and therefore of legitimate moral judgement seems to shrink under this scrutiny to an extensionless point."

Walker notes that sophisticated compatibilists like Frankfurt revise the meaning of *free will* in terms of identification with one's second-order desires. She argues that this is an unacceptable maneuver.[8]

Humans, unlike other animals, have the ability to deliberate and choose courses of actions. Although both animals and humans have basic *first-order* desires (such as desires to eat, to be warm, and to copulate), animals act directly on their wants, whereas humans can weigh them and accept or reject them. For example, you may have the first-order desire to stay in bed rather than come to class today, but you may also have a first-order desire to learn more about the problem of free will and determinism. So you compare the two desires and form a *second-order* desire that one of the first-order desires be the one that motivates you—we hope it's the one enjoining you to come to class, based on your passionate desire to understand the free-will problem. So you choose to let your second-order desire affect your behavior. Frankfurt calls this your second-order *volition:* "To the extent that a person identifies himself with the springs of his actions, he takes a responsibility for those actions and acquires moral responsibility for them."

Frankfurt may have described the phenomenology of free choice, but he hasn't shown that this saves the compatibilist account of free will. He has given only necessary but not sufficient conditions for free choice. For consider, suppose you are deciding whether to get up from bed to go to class. You weigh the alternatives of staying in bed and experiencing the delicious taste of another hour of twilight dreams, against the intellectual pleasures of your philosophy class. You decide to get up, to make learning your second-order volition, to "identify yourself with the springs of this action," and so you rise.

But it turns out that a brilliant neurologist has been controlling your decisions through electronic waves that affect your neurons and brain patterns, *causing* you to choose to get up. Would you want to say that you *freely* got up? It sounds like you weren't free at all. You could not have avoided getting up, for your behavior was caused by the brilliant neurologist, and in spite of making "rising from the bed" your second-order volition, it can be said that you were not free at the moment to do otherwise.

The point is that the compatibilist's notion of second-order volitions turns out to be simply a subtler version of the "brilliant neurologist" story, because nature and antecedent causes cause you to form the second-order volition to get up and to get up. You could not have done anything else at that moment. The idea that you could was only an illusion.

Walker now turns back to her main argument, defending premise 6: the idea that the belief that we are morally responsible is better justified than our belief in determinism's universal causality.

If there is one thing we are sure of it is that we have selves, that we exist with moral obligations. There is nothing more certain than that I ought not kill innocent people, break promises simply for my own advantage, harm others without due cause, or cheat. I have a duty to help my aging parents, to protect my children, and to support my spouse and friends. But if determinism is true, all this obligation is a mere illusion.

And what are determinism's credentials for its horrendous freedom-denying claims? Simply, an atavistic faith in universal causality. Everything in the world must have a cause, so all my behavior and all my mental states are caused.

But this is unduly fideistic. Strange that philosophers should have turned up their noses at simple theists for lacking evidence for belief in a God, and yet should themselves have erected a shrine to the despot Omnicausality!* As David Hume pointed out in his *Enquiry,* the notion of causality is not a necessary truth, nor one of which we have a clear idea. We just observe regularities in nature and sum up these constant conjunctions of behavior in lawlike statements. It is very difficult to define "causality" (to my mind, no one has given an adequate definition) or "natural law," and quantum physics tells us that on the most basic level of physical reality causal relationships do

---

[*_Omnicausality_ is the doctrine that every event and state of affairs in the universe is caused by antecedent causes—Ed.]

not operate. Until we can solve these problems in the philosophy of science, it behooves us to be modest about our claims that all behavior and states of affairs, including the self, are caused.

For my part, if I have to compare the propositions (1) "Every event and state of affairs in the world is caused" and (2) "I have moral responsibilities," I have not the slightest doubt about which I must choose.

At this point the determinist—both the soft kind and the hard variety—object that it is only through having determinate character that we can be said to be good or bad, that actions without determined character are capricious and arbitrary. To quote Sidney Hook,

> The great difficulty with the indeterminist view in most forms is the suggestion it carries that choices and actions, if not determined, are capricious. Caprice and responsibility are more difficult to reconcile than determinism and responsibility, for it seems easier to repudiate a choice or action which does not follow from one's character, or history, or nature, or self, than an act which does follow.

But, as Hook himself recognizes, it is not necessary to equate free will with indeterminism. All that is necessary is to have a self that in deliberation can *weigh* desires and values. The self can exercise control, can veto desires or confirm them, can subscribe to reason or reject it in defiance, and this self itself transcends the ordinary laws of nature. C. A. Campbell and Robert Nozick think the self intervenes thus only on rare and momentous occasions, but I suspect that this claim is unduly modest. If it happens at all, why can't it happen every time the self deliberates?

Of course, we may not be able to give a convincing explanation of the self or agency, because what will count for an explanation in the determinist's eyes is only a causal explanation, and that is exactly what is in question.

Finally, Walker points out that libertarian freedom of the will is a necessary presupposition in defending theism against the atheist's charge that the problem of evil supports or proves that there is no God.

> Many philosophers who work on this problem tend to be agnostics so that one explanation of the self-cum-free-will is cut off from them; that is, the idea of a Supreme Self, or God. If God is a free agent, self-determined, then if he (or she) creates humans in his image, why shouldn't we suppose that humans also are self-determining beings? Indeed, the Jewish-Christian tradition supposes that God did create us as free agents and that we have sinned against God; that is, we have misused our freedom for disobedience and wrongdoing. We are responsible for our actions and so can be held accountable for them. The alternative is to make God strongly responsible for the evil in the world (at least the moral evil), which is blasphemy to any theist. It may be in a weak or indirect sense, as omniscient creator, that God is responsible for *allowing* humans to sin and create evil, but he is not responsible in any direct sense. In this case, we must conclude that either God was not able to create a better world—one with a greater proportion of good over evil—than this one or else that God will bring good out of the evil in the world.

Since the theist will typically hold to the free-will defense to account for the evil in the world, he or she will typically embrace the doctrine of free will. The comprehensive theory, which stands or falls as a whole, carries the theist past the state of agnosticism on this matter. Of course, if it turns out that we are wholly determined by antecedent causes, then (supposing one understands this fact) one would have to give up the free-will defense, and perhaps theism itself. A lot is at stake in this dispute.

In conclusion, I have argued that the compatibilist strategy for saving moral responsibility is an illusion and that only libertarianism has a creditable notion of accountability. I have admitted that the problem of free will and determinism is fraught with paradox, but have argued that we have no good reason to distrust our intuitions about having a responsible self with moral obligations. I have also argued that if one is inclined to theism, one has additional reasons for preferring the libertarian position over its deterministic rivals.

Walker's thesis is this: According to the determinist (and the compatibilist as a determinist), since all our actions are the results of antecedent causes, the notion of free action in this quarter is simply honorific. It does not establish moral responsibility, so it merely passes the buck back to antecedent causes. The distinction between voluntary and involuntary actions is simply the difference between the deterministic process that doesn't find assent in the will (which is also determined) and the deterministic process that does find assent in the will (which is also determined). How can we be responsible for that which we do not cause? We cannot. Hence, we are not responsible for any of our actions, since they can all be traced back to prior causes.

This reasoning applies to the compatibilist's characterization of free action as "S could have done otherwise" = "S would have done otherwise if S had so chosen," for in reality S could not have chosen to have done otherwise in those circumstances. Hence, the conditional is irrelevant and freedom is not established.

The Compatibilist Response

Although the determinist may admit with Clarence Darrow that strictly speaking there is no moral responsibility and that all punishment and reward function as deterrent and incentive, the compatibilist wants to preserve the validity of the notion of accountability within a determinist framework. The compatibilist will still try to work out the distinction between voluntary and involuntary actions and between rational and coerced behavior. Perhaps she will argue that the distinction is a useful fiction or simply that we need to adhere to the notion of voluntary action as the basis of moral responsibility. Perhaps she should admit the paradoxical nature of the problem, refrain from giving it a solution and merely state that we see things in these two different ways, from the viewpoint of agency (where responsibility holds) and from the viewpoint of determinism (where universal causality holds). Perhaps she needs to question whether we know what universal causality involves, for on closer look it turns out to be a rather fuzzy notion. No one has adequately defined it. It has something to do with necessary condition for another event, but that is not a clear concept; nor is it clear how this applies to individual actions. It may be a metaphor that is inapplicable to action language.

We make a difference between cases where the agent is compelled or influenced by unusual stress or "neurotic" causes and "normal" cases where the agent could have done differently (better or worse). We can take the objective perspective in the first case, excuse the subject, understand the causal mechanisms, and treat the behavior as impersonally derived events. But we cannot treat normal behavior in this manner without losing something precious, something vital to human interaction. Unless I take your intentions seriously as belonging to you, I lose something that is necessary to a fully human existence. I lose the personal aspect of relationships, for to view others as personal is to take their intentions seriously as demanding the reactive attitudes. Hence, even if determinism cannot be proved to be false, I still will have to take other people's intentions seriously, react to them spontaneously, and hold them accountable. Human existence, in its deepest interpersonal, nonmechanistic sense, cannot go on without the notion of freedom.

This is how the compatibilist argues.

Summary

Let's summarize the last three chapters of this our work. We have examined the three main theories regarding free will and determinism—determinism, libertarianism, and compatibilism—and have found each to have virtues and vices.

The notion of the libertarian self, which creates new actions that are themselves underdetermined by antecedent causes, is an unexplained mystery, and constitutes a little god standing apart from our normal explanatory schemes.

The theory of evolution tells us that wholly deterministic and physicalistic processes are responsible for whatever we are. But we are self-conscious beings whose inner experiences are not physicalist; they are mental. Hence, the fundamental mystery is how something as physicalistic as an evolutionary process could result in something nonphysical—consciousness—from which freedom of the will emerges.

The determinist cannot explain consciousness or how the physical results in and causes the mental, but the libertarian is no better off, for no one has successfully explained how the mental can affect the physical. How does the mind make contact with the body in order to move it to action? Where are its points of contact, its hooks that pull on our brains and limbs?

In the end, perhaps the best we can do is to be aware of the fascinating mystery of the problem of free will and determinism and admit our ignorance of a solution. If we look at ourselves through the eyes of science and neurophysiology, we will no doubt regard ourselves as determined. If we look at ourselves from the perspective of morality and subjective deliberators, we must view ourselves as having free will. As philosophers—which we all are, like it or not—we stand in wonder at the dualism that forces us to take both an objective/determinist and a subjective/libertarian perspective of conscious behavior. This dichotomy seems unsatisfactory, incompatible, and yet inescapable.

Do you see a way of solving this enigma? It's a worthy challenge for the best minds on Earth.

FOR FURTHER REFLECTION

1. Evaluate the three theories discussed in these last three chapters. Which seem the most plausible to you, and why?

2. The British scientist and philosopher J. S. B. Haldane wrote, "If my mental processes are determined wholly by the motions of atoms in my brain, I have no reason to suppose that my beliefs are true . . . and hence I have not reason for supposing my brain to be composed of atoms."[9] Could the same argument be used against the doctrine of determinism? If nonrational processes have caused the theory of determinism, what *reason* is there to believe it? Is determinism self-refuting?

3. Jean Paul Sartre wrote, "We are condemned to freedom." We will examine Sartre's ideas in Part 8, but can you understand from what you've studied thus far, what he might be getting at?

4. Discuss the problem of punishment. How would a determinist, a libertarian, and a compatibilist defend the practice of punishing criminals?

5. David Hume wrote,

> Men are not blamed for such actions as they perform ignorantly and casually, whatever may be the consequences. Why? but because the principles of these actions are only momentary, and terminate in them alone. Men are less blamed for such actions as they perform hastily and unpremeditatedly than for such as proceed for deliberation. For what reason? but because a hasty temper, though a constant cause or principle in the mind, operates only by intervals, and infects not the whole character. Again, repentance wipes off every crime, if attended with a reformation of life and manners. How is this to be accounted for? but by asserting that actions render a person criminal merely as they are proofs of criminal principles in the mind.[10]

Evaluate Hume's notion. Which theory of freedom or determinism does it best fit?

NOTES

1. Walter Stace, *Religion and the Modern Mind* (New York: Lippencott, 1952). See also Immanuel Kant, *Critique of Pure Reason* (1787); Harry Frankfurt, "Freedom of the Will and the Concept of a Person," in *Free Will,* ed. Gary Watson (Oxford, UK: Clarendon Press, 1982); and Daniel Dennett, *Elbow Room* (Cambridge, MA: MIT Press, 1984).

2. Stace, *Religion and the Modern Mind.*

3. Ibid.

4. Ibid.

5. Frankfurt, "Freedom of the Will," 81–95.
6. Ibid.
7. Ibid.
8. All remaining passages in this section are from Lois Hope Walker, "A Libertarian Defense of Moral Responsibility," in *Introduction to Philosophy: Classical and Contemporary Readings,* ed. Louis P. Pojman (Belmont, CA: Wadsworth, 1991).
9. J. S. B. Haldane, *Possible Worlds* (London: Holden & Stoughton, 1937), 209.
10. David Hume, *Enquiry Concerning Human Understanding* (1748).

FOR FURTHER READING

Dennett, Daniel. *Elbow Room: The Varieties of Free Will Worth Wanting.* Cambridge, MA: MIT Press, 1984. A well-argued defense of compatibilism.

Lehrer, Leith, and James Cornman. *Philosophical Problems and Argument,* 3rd ed. New York: Macmillan, 1982. Lehrer's essay in Chapter 3 is excellent.

Pojman, Louis, ed. *Introduction to Philosophy: Classical and Contemporary Readings.* Belmont, CA: Wadsworth, 1991. Part 5 contains several important readings on free will, responsibility, and the implications for a theory of punishment.

Stace, Walter T. *Religion and the Modern Mind.* New York: Lippencott, 1952. Contains a lucid account of compatibilism.

Trustead, Jennifer. *Free Will and Responsibility.* Oxford, UK: Oxford University Press, 1984. A clear, accessible introduction to the subject.

van Inwagen, Peter. *An Essay on Free Will.* Oxford, UK: Clarendon Press, 1983. A highly original study, criticizing compatibilism.

Watson, Gary, ed. *Free Will.* Oxford, UK: Clarendon Press, 1982. Contains important articles, especially those by Frankfurt, van Inwagen, and Watson himself.

PART VII
Ethics

27 ⚘ What Is Ethics?

Moral Choice: A Case Study

Suppose you have dedicated your life to helping people, teaching philosophy without pay, criticizing the government for injustice, standing on principle against those who would capitulate to expediency, and generally providing others with a sterling example of moral integrity. However, your efforts, instead of being honored, have been resented. Some envy your intellect and ability to reason. Others hate you for opposing and defeating them in their quest for power or for exposing their mediocrity before their peers. Still others judge you to be a danger to society, a corrupter of the youth and enemy of religion. Suppose these enemies join forces and bring trumped up criminal charges against you. You are indicted, convicted, and condemned to death by a jury. Now you are in prison awaiting an imminent execution. Your friends come to visit you. They are outraged by the miscarriage of justice and tell you that they have arranged for your escape to a friendly country. They argue that you should accept their offer, for not only was your trial unfair but also your family and friends need you and you can do more good alive than dead. Should you accept this offer to escape? What would you do?

This is what happened to Socrates (470–399 BCE). As you recall from Chapter 4, he had been tried and convicted by the Athenian assembly for civil impiety and corrupting the youth. When he was asked to propose an alternative to the death penalty, he proposed the reward of getting free meals for life in the dining hall of Olympic heroes (the Prytaneum). So they sentenced him to death, which he was awaiting in prison. His friends, led by Crito, visit and tell him that they have arranged for his escape to Thessaly, a friendly country, where he may be assured of a tranquil retirement. We enter the dialogue as Crito is giving his reasons for the escape.

CRITO

CRITO (C): O my good Socrates, I beg you for the last time to save yourself. Your death will be more than a single disaster; not only shall I lose a friend the like of whom I shall never find again, but many people who do not know you and me well will think that I might have saved you if I had been willing to spend money, but I neglected to do so. The public will never believe that we were committed to saving you, and that you refused to escape. Our reputations will be ruined.

SOCRATES (S): But, my dear Crito, why should we care so much about public opinion? Reasonable people, of whose opinion is worth our while, will believe the truth.

C: But Socrates, it is necessary to care about public opinion too. The majority can do a person great evil, if he is slandered by his enemies.

S: I wish that the multitude were able to do a person great harm, Crito, for then they would also be able to do him the greatest good also. That would be good! But, as it is, they can do neither. They cannot make a person either wise or foolish. They act haphazardly, wholly at random.

C: I won't argue with you about that, Socrates, but surely you aren't worried about me and your other friends and afraid that informers will turn us into the authorities. If you have such fears, dismiss them. For, of course, we are bound to run risks, and still greater risks than these, if necessary to save you. So do not refuse to listen to me.

S: I appreciate your anxiety to save me, and you may be right in arguing that I should escape, but, Crito, are you right to fear what others will say? Consider, don't you think that we must not value all opinions, but only those of the wise? Shouldn't we ignore the foolish?

C: Yes, you're right.

S: Take a parallel instance. If acting under the advice of those who have no understanding, we destroy that which is improved by health and is deteriorated by disease, would life be worth living?

C: No.

S: And will life be worth living if that nobler part of man be destroyed, that part which is improved by justice and depraved by injustice? Is it not life, but a good life, that ought to be most highly valued?

C: Yes, that is so.

S: And the good life is equivalent to a just and honorable one?

C: Yes, it is.

Having established that it is not the many but only the wise whose opinion we should honor and that it is the nobler part of our selves, not the body, that should concern us most, Socrates now sets forth the main argument for his decision not to accept the offer to escape.

From: Plato, *Crito*, translated by Benjamin Jowett (Oxford, UK: Clarendon Press, 1898). I have edited the translation.

s: Should we ever voluntarily do wrong to bring about good results? Or isn't it true, as I have always argued, that we are never voluntarily to do wrong? That such action is always evil and dishonorable?

c: Yes, we should never do wrong, even to bring about good results.

s: So when we are injured, we ought not repay injury for injury? For isn't injuring someone wrong?

c: Clearly it is wrong.

s: Then we ought not to retaliate or render evil for evil to any one, whatever evil we may have suffered from him. Do you agree with this first premise of our argument that it is always wrong to retaliate or render evil for evil? Do you still hold this principle?

s: I do, so you may proceed to the next step of your argument.

S: Then consider, Crito, if we have made a just agreement with someone, should we fulfill it, or are we allowed to break our agreement?

s: We must fulfill it.

S: Then wouldn't my leaving prison against the will of the Athenians be a case of injuring people? Of returning evil for evil? And wouldn't it be a case of breaking an agreement?

c: I'm not sure I understand your question.

s: Consider it this way. Suppose as we are planning our escape the laws and the government confront us and ask: "Tell us, Socrates, what are you intending to do? Do you not by this action intend to destroy us, the laws, and the whole state? Do you imagine that a state can exist and not be overthrown, in which the decisions of law are of no force, and are disregarded and undermined by private individuals?" How shall we answer such questions, Crito? Shall we respond that the state has wronged me, so I should retaliate? Shall we say that?

c: Certainly we will, Socrates.

s: "And was that our agreement with you?" the law would answer; "or were you to abide by the sentence of the state?" And if I were to express my astonishment at their words, the law would probably add: "Answer, Socrates, instead of opening your eyes—you are in the habit of asking and answering questions. Tell us,—What complaint have you to make against us which justifies you in attempting to destroy us and the state? In the first place did we not bring you into existence? Your father married your mother by our aid and begat you. Say whether you have any objection to urge against those of us who regulate marriage?" None, I should reply. "Or against those of us who after birth regulate the nurture and education of children, in which you also were trained? Were not the laws, which have the charge of education, right in commanding your father to train you in music and gymnastic?" Right, I should reply. "Well then, since you were brought into the world and nurtured and educated by us, can you deny in the first place that you are our child and slave, as your fathers were before you? And if this is true you are not on equal terms with us; nor can you think that you have a right to do to us what we are doing to you. Would you have any right to strike or revile or do any other evil to your father or your master, if you had one, because you have been struck or reviled by him, or received some other evil at his hands?—you would not say this? And because we think right to destroy you, do you think that you have any right to destroy us in return, and your country as far as in you lies? Will you, O professor of true virtue, pretend that you are justified in this? Has a philosopher like you failed to discover that our country is more to be valued and higher and holier far than mother or father or any ancestor, and more to be regarded in the eyes of the gods and of men of understanding? also to be soothed, and gently and reverently entreated when angry, even more than a father, and either to be persuaded, or if not persuaded, to be obeyed? And when we are punished by her, whether with imprisonment or stripes, the punishment is to be endured in silence; and if she leads us to wounds or death in battle, thither we follow as is right; neither may any one yield or retreat or leave his rank, but whether in battle or in a court of law, or in any other place, he must do what his city and his country order him; or he must change their view of what is just: and if he may do no violence to his father or mother, much less may he do violence to his country." What answer shall we make to this, Crito? Do the laws speak truly, or do they not?

c: I think that they do.

s: Then the laws will say, "Consider, Socrates, if we are speaking truly that in your present attempt you are going to do us an injury. For, having brought you into the world, and nurtured and educated you, and given you and every other citizen a share in every good which we had to give, we further proclaim to any Athenian by the liberty which we allow him, that if he does not like us when he has become of age and has seen the ways of the city, and made our acquaintance, he may go where he pleases and takes his goods with him. None of us laws will forbid him or interfere with him. Any one who does not like us and the city, and who wants to emigrate to a colony or to any other city, may go where he likes retaining his property. But he who has experience of the manner in which we order justice and administer the state, and still remains, has entered into an implied contract that he will do as we command him. And he who disobeys us is, as we maintain, thrice wrong; first, because in disobeying us he is disobeying his parents; secondly, because we are the authors of his education; thirdly, because he has made an agreement with us that he will duly obey our commands; and he neither obeys them nor convinces us that our commands are unjust; and we do not rudely impose them, but give him the alternative of obeying or convincing us;—that is what we offer, and he does neither.

"These are the sort of accusations to which, as we were saying, you, Socrates, will be exposed if you accomplish your intentions; you, above all other Athenians." Suppose now I ask, why I rather than anybody else? they will justly retort upon me that I above all other men have acknowledged the agreement. "There is clear proof," they will say, "Socrates, that we and the city were not displeasing to you. Of all Athenians you have been the most constant resident in the city, which, as you never leave, you may be supposed to love. For you never went out of the city either to see the games, except once when you went to the Isthmus, or to any other place unless when you were on military service; nor did you travel as other men do. Nor had you any curiosity to know other states or their laws: your affections did not go beyond us and our state; we were your special favourites, and you acquiesced in our government of you; and here in this city you begat your children, which is proof of your satisfaction. Moreover, you might in the course of the trial, if you had liked, have fixed the penalty at banishment; the state which refuses to let you go now would have let you go then. But you pretended that you preferred death to exile, and that you were not unwilling to die. And now you have forgotten these fine sentiments, and pay no respect to us the laws, of whom you are the destroyer; and are doing what only a miserable slave would do, running away and turning your back upon the compacts and agreements which you made as a citizen. And first of all answer this question: Are we right in saying that you agreed to be governed according to us in deed, and not in word only? Is that true or not?" How shall we answer, Crito? Must we not assent?

c: We cannot help it, Socrates.

s: Then will they not say: "You, Socrates, are breaking the covenants and agreements which you made with us at your leisure, not in any haste or under any compulsion or deception, but after you have had seventy years to think of them, during which time you were at liberty to leave the city, if we were not to your mind, or if our covenants appeared to you to be unfair. You had your choice, and might have gone either to Lacdaemon or Crete, both which states are often praised by you for their good government, or to some other hellenic or foreign state. Whereas you, above all other Athenians, seemed to be so fond of the state, or, in other words, of us her laws (and who would care about a state which has no laws?), that you never stirred out of her; the halt, the blind, the maimed were not more stationary in her than you were. And now you run away and forsake your agreements. Not so, Socrates, if you will take our advice; do not make yourself ridiculous by escaping out of the city.

"For just consider, if you transgress and err in this sort of way, what good will you do either to yourself or to your friends? That your friends will be driven into exile and deprived of citizenship, or will lose their property, is tolerably certain; and you yourself, if you fly to one of the neighbouring cities, as, for example, Thebes or Megara, both of which are well governed, will come to them as an enemy, Socrates, and their government will be against you, and all patriotic citizens will cast an evil eye upon you as a subverter of the laws, and you will confirm in the minds of the judges the justice of their own condemnation of you. For he who is a corrupter of the laws is more than likely to be a corrupter of the young and foolish portion of mankind. Will you then flee from well-ordered cities and virtuous men? and is existence worth having on these terms? Or will you go to them without shame, and talk to them, Socrates? And what will you say to them? What you say here about virtue and justice and institutions and laws being the best things among men? Would that be decent of you? Surely not. But if you go away from well-governed states to Crito's friends in Thessaly, where there is great disorder and licence, they will be charmed to hear the tale of your escape from prison, set off with ludicrous particulars of the manner in which you were wrapped in a goatskin or some other disguise, and metamorphosed as the manner is of runaways; but will there be no one to remind you that in your old age you were not ashamed to violate the most sacred laws from a miserable desire of a little more life? Perhaps not, if you keep them in a good temper; but if they are out of temper you will hear many degrading things; you will live, but how?—as the flatterer of all men, and the servant of all men; and doing what?—eating and drinking in Thessaly, having gone abroad in order that you may get a dinner. And where will be your fine sentiments about justice and virtue? Say that you wish to live for the sake of your children—you want to bring them up and educate them—will you take them into Thessaly and deprive them of Athenian citizenship? Is this the benefit which you confer upon them? Or are you under the impression that they will be better cared for and educated here if you are still alive, although absent from them; for your friends will take care of them? Do you fancy that if you are an inhabitant of Thessaly they will take care of them, and if you are an inhabitant of the other world that they will not take care of them? Nay; but if they who call themselves friends are good for anything, they will—to be sure they will.

"Listen, then, Socrates, to us who have brought you up. Think not of life and children first, and of justice afterwards, but of justice first, that you may be justified before the princes of the world below. For neither will you nor any that belong to you be happier or holier or juster in this life, or happier in another, if you do as Crito bids. Now you depart in innocence, a sufferer and not a doer of evil; a victim, not of the laws but of men. But if you go forth, returning evil for evil, and injury for injury, breaking the covenants and agreements which you have made with us, and wronging those whom you ought least of all to wrong, that is to say, yourself, your friends, your country, and us, we shall be angry with you while you live, and our brethren, the laws in the world below, will receive you as an enemy; for they will know that you have done your best to destroy us. Listen, then, to us and not to Crito."

This, dear Crito, is the voice which I seem to hear murmuring in my ears, like the sound of the flute in the ears of the mystic; that voice, I say, is humming in my ears, and prevents me from hearing any other. And I know that nothing more which you may say will be vain. Yet speak, if you have anything to say.

c: I have nothing to say, Socrates.

s: Leave me then, Crito, to fulfill the will of God, and to follow whither he leads.

Was Socrates correct in his reasoning? Do you agree with him? Would you accept the offer to escape? How would you support or argue against his conclusions? What are the principles that would guide your decision?

What Is Morality?

In this part of our book, we want to inquire into the nature of morality. What is its nature? Why do we need morality? What function does it play? What is the good, and how shall I know it? Are moral principles **absolute** or simply relative to social groups or individual decision? Is morality, like beauty, in the eye of the beholder? Is it always in my best interest to be moral? Or is it sometimes in my interest to act immorally? How does one justify one's moral beliefs? What is the basis of morality? Which ethical theory provides the best justification and explanation of the moral life? What is the relationship between morality and religion? What is it to be a moral person?

These are some of the questions that we will be looking at in this section. We want to understand the foundation and structure of morality. We want to know how we should live.

The terms *moral* and *ethics* come from Latin and Greek, respectively (*mores* and *ethos*), deriving their meaning from the idea of custom. Although philosophers sometimes make a distinction between "morality" and "ethics," I use these terms interchangeably. Moral philosophy refers to the systematic endeavor to understand moral concepts and justify moral principles and theories. It undertakes to analyze such concepts as *right, wrong, permissible, ought, good,* and *evil* in their moral contexts. Moral philosophy seeks to establish principles of right behavior that may serve as action guides for individuals and groups. It investigates which values and virtues are paramount to the worthwhile life or society. It builds and scrutinizes arguments in ethical theories and seeks to discover valid principles (for example, "Never kill innocent human beings") and the relationship between those principles (for example, does saving a life in some situations constitute a valid reason for breaking a promise?).

Morality as Compared with Other Normative Subjects

Moral precepts are concerned with norms; roughly speaking, they are concerned not with what *is*, but with what *ought* to be. How should I live my life? What is the right thing to do in this situation? Should I always tell the truth? Do I have a duty to report a co-worker whom I have seen cheating our company? Should I tell my friend that his spouse is having an affair? Is premarital sex morally permissible? Ought a woman ever to have an abortion? Should I tell the truth even when it will cause great suffering? Morality has a distinct action-guiding or *normative* aspect, an aspect it shares with other practical institutions such as religion, law, and etiquette.*

Morality may be closely bound up with religion, and moral behavior is typically held to be essential to the practice of religion. But neither the practices nor precepts of morality should be identified with religion. The practice of morality need not be motivated by religious considerations, and moral precepts need not be grounded in revelation or divine authority—as religious teachings invariably are. The most salient characteristic of ethics—by which I mean both philosophical morality (or morality, as I will simply refer to it) and moral philosophy—is that it is grounded in reason and human experience.

To use a spatial metaphor, secular ethics are horizontal, omitting a vertical or transcendental dimension. Religious ethics has a vertical dimension, being grounded in revelation or divine authority, though generally using reason to supplement or complement revelation. These two differing orientations will often generate different moral principles and standards of evaluation, but they need not. Some versions of religious ethics, which posit God's revelation of the moral law in nature or conscience, hold that reason can discover what is right or wrong even apart from divine revelation. (We will discuss this subject in Chapter 32).

Morality is also closely related to law, and some people equate the two practices. After all, law can promote well-being and social harmony and can resolve

---

*The term *normative* means "seeking to make certain types of behavior normal or standard in a society." *Webster's Collegiate Dictionary* defines it as "of, or relating or conforming to or prescribing norms or standards."

conflicts of interest, just as morality does. Yet there are crucial differences. Ethics may judge some laws to be immoral without denying that they are valid *as laws*. For example, I would judge laws that permit slavery or irrelevant discrimination against people on the basis of race or sex to be legally valid but immoral. An anti-abortion advocate may believe that the laws permitting abortion are immoral.

In a PBS television series, *Ethics in America,* James Neal, a trial lawyer, was asked what he would do if he discovered that his client had committed a murder some years back for which another man had been convicted and would soon be executed.[1] Neal said that he had a legal obligation to keep this information confidential and that if he divulged it he would be disbarred. It is arguable that he has a moral obligation that overrides his legal obligation and demands that he take action to protect the innocent man from being executed.

Furthermore, there are some aspects of morality that are not covered by law. For example, while it is generally agreed that lying is usually immoral, there is no general law against it (except under special conditions, such as in cases of perjury or falsifying income tax returns). Sometimes college newspapers publish advertisements for "research assistance," where it is known in advance that the companies will aid and abet plagiarism. The publishing of such research paper ads is legal, but it is doubtful whether it is morally correct. Some years ago a young woman, Kitty Genovese, was brutally stabbed to death in Queens, New York, as thirty-eight people watched from their apartments for some 35 minutes as a man beat up Kitty Genovese. They did nothing to intervene, not even call the police. These people violated no law, but they were very likely morally culpable for not calling the police or shouting at the assailant.

There is one other major difference between law and morality. In 1351, King Edward of England promulgated a law against treason that made it a crime merely to *think* homicidal thoughts about the king. But, alas, the law could not be enforced, for no tribunal can search the heart and fathom the intentions of the mind. It is true that *intention,* such as malice aforethought, plays a role in the legal process in determining the legal character of the act, once the act has been committed. But preemptive punishment for people presumed to have bad intentions is illegal. If malicious intentions (called in law *mens rea*) were criminally illegal, would we not all deserve imprisonment? Even if it were possible to detect intentions, when should the punishment be administered? As soon as the subject has the intention? But how do we know that he will not change his mind? Furthermore, is there not a continuum between imagining some harm to X, wishing a harm to X, desiring a harm to X, and intending a harm to X?

Though having laws against bad intentions is impractical, these intentions are still bad, still morally wrong. Suppose I buy a gun with the intention of killing Uncle Charlie in order to inherit his wealth, but I never get a chance to fire it (for example, Uncle Charlie moves to Australia). While I have not committed a crime, I have committed a moral wrong.

Morality also differs from etiquette and what is merely social custom, which concerns form and style rather than the essence of social existence. Etiquette determines what is polite behavior rather than whether behavior is, in a deeper sense, right. Custom represents society's decision about how we are to dress, greet one another, eat, celebrate festivals, dispose of the dead, and carry out social transactions.

Whether we greet each other with a handshake, a bow, a hug, or a kiss on the cheek will differ in different social systems, but none of these rituals has any moral superiority. People in England hold their fork in their left hand when they eat, whereas people in other countries hold it in their right hand or in whichever hand a person feels like holding it. In India, people typically eat without a fork. They simply use the forefingers of their right hand. None of these practices has any moral superiority. Etiquette helps social transactions flow smoothly, but it is not the substance of those transactions. The observance of customs graces our social existence, but it is not what social existence is about.

At the same time, it can be immoral to disregard or flout etiquette. A cultural crisis developed in India when American tourists went to the beaches clad in skimpy bikini bathing suits. This was highly offensive to the Indians, and an uproar erupted. There is nothing intrinsically wrong with wearing skimpy bathing suits or with wearing nothing at all, for that matter, but people get used to certain behavioral patterns and it's terribly insensitive to flout those customs—especially when you are a guest in someone else's home or country. Not the bathing suits themselves but *insensitivity* is morally offensive.

Law, etiquette, and religion are all important institutions, but each has limitations. The limitation of the law is that you can't have a law against every social malady, nor can you enforce every desirable rule. The limitation of etiquette is that it doesn't get to the heart of what is of vital importance for personal and social existence. Whether or not one eats with one's fingers pales in significance compared with the importance of being honest, trustworthy, or just. Etiquette is a cultural invention, but morality claims to be a discovery.

The limitation of the religious injunction is that it rests on authority, and we are not always sure of or in agreement about the credentials of the authority, nor on how the authority would rule in ambiguous or new cases. Since religion is not founded on reason but on revelation, you cannot use reason to convince someone who does not share your religious views that your view is the right one. I hasten to add that when moral differences are caused by disagreements about fundamental moral principles, it is unlikely that philosophical reasoning will settle the matter. Often, however, our moral differences turn out to be rooted in worldviews, not moral principles. For example, the anti-abortionist and pro-choice advocate often agree that it is wrong to kill innocent persons, but differ on the facts. The anti-abortionist may hold a religious view that states that the fetus has an eternal soul and thus possesses a right to life, whereas the pro-choice advocate may deny that anyone, let alone a fetus, has a soul and hold that only self-conscious, rational beings have rights to life.

In summary, morality distinguishes itself from law and etiquette by going deeper into the essence of our social existence. It distinguishes itself from religion in that it seeks reasons, rather than authority, to justify its principles. The central purpose of moral philosophy is to secure valid principles of conduct and values that can be instrumental in guiding human actions and producing good character. As such, it is the most important activity known to humans, for it has to do with how we are to live.

Domains of Ethical Assessment

It might seem at this point that ethics concerns itself entirely with rules of conduct based solely on an evaluation of acts. However, the situation is more complicated than this. Most ethical analysis falls into one, or some, of the following domains:

Domain	*Evaluative Terms*
Action (the act)	Right, wrong, obligatory, optional
Consequences	Good, bad, indifferent
Character	Virtuous, vicious, neutral
Motive	Goodwill, evil will, neutral

Let's examine each of these domains.

Types of Action

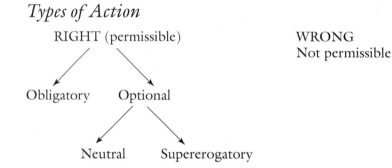

The most common distinction may be the classification of *actions* as right and wrong, but the term *right* is ambiguous. Sometimes it means "obligatory" (as in "the right act"), but sometimes it means "permissible" (as in "a right act" or "it's all right to do that"). Usually, philosophers define *right* as "permissible," including under that category what is obligatory.

1. A *right act* is an act that it is permissible for you to do. It may be either optional or obligatory.
    a. An *optional act* is an act that it is neither obligatory nor wrong to do. It is not your duty to do it; neither is it your duty not to do it. Neither doing it nor not doing it would be wrong.
    b. An *obligatory act* is one that morality requires you to do or an act it is not permissible for you to refrain from doing.
2. A *wrong act* is an act you have obligation, or duty, to refrain from; an act you ought not to do; an act it is not permissible to do.

Let's briefly illustrate these concepts. The act of lying is generally seen as a wrong type of act (and therefore not permissible), whereas truth telling is generally seen as obligatory. But some acts do not seem to be either obligatory or wrong. Whether you decide to take a course in art history or Asian literature or whether you write your friend a letter with a pencil or a pen—all these options seem morally neutral. They are optional (hence permissible).

Consider a decision to marry. Admittedly, this is a decision of great moral significance. It is after all an important decision about how to live one's life. Under most circumstances, however, to marry is neither obligatory nor wrong because being married, in itself, is considered morally neutral. To marry is therefore optional. You are not required to marry; neither are you required not to marry.

Within the range of permissible acts is the notion of **supererogatory acts.** These highly altruistic acts go beyond the call of duty. They are not obligatory but exceed what morality requires. You may have an obligation to give a donation to help strangers in dire need, but you are not obligated to sell your house or car, let alone become destitute, in order to help them. Helping such people by selling your house or car or by becoming destitute yourself would be supererogatory.

Theories that place the emphasis on the nature of the act are called *deontological* (from the Greek word for "duty"). These theories hold that there is something inherently right or good about such acts as truth telling and promise keeping and something inherently wrong or bad about such acts as lying and promise breaking. The most famous of these systems is Immanuel Kant's moral theory, which we will study in Chapter 31.

Consequences

We said earlier that lying is generally seen as wrong and truth telling is generally seen as right. But consider this situation. You are hiding in your home an innocent woman named Laura, who is fleeing gangsters. Gangland Gus knocks on your door, and when you open it, he asks if Laura is in your house. What should you do? Should you tell the truth or lie? Those who say that morality has something to do with consequences of actions would prescribe lying as the morally right thing to do. Those who deny that we should look at the consequences when considering what to do when there is a clear and absolute rule of action will say that we should either keep silent or tell the truth. When no other rule is at stake, of course, the rule-oriented ethicist will allow the foreseeable consequences to determine a course of action. Theories that focus primarily on consequences in determining moral rightness and wrongness are called *teleological* ethical theories (from the Greek *telos,* meaning "goal directed"). The most famous of these theories is utilitarianism, which we will study in Chapter 30.

Character

Whereas some ethical theories emphasize principles of action in themselves and some emphasize principles involving consequences of action, other theories, such as Aristotle's ethics (**aretaic ethics**), emphasize *character,* or virtue, the third domain. According to Aristotle, it is most important to develop virtuous character, for if and only if we have good people can we ensure habitual right action. Although the virtues are not central to other types of moral theories, most moral theories include the virtues as important. Most reasonable people, whatever their notions about ethics, would judge that the people who watched and did nothing to help Kitty Genovese as she was being assaulted lacked good character. Different moral systems emphasize different virtues and emphasize them to different degrees.

Motive

Finally, virtually all ethical systems, but especially Kant's system, accept the relevance of *motive.* It is important to the full assessment of any action that the intention of the agent be taken into account. Two acts may be identical, but one be judged morally culpable and the other excusable. Consider John's pushing Joan off a ledge, causing her to break her leg. In act A he is angry and intends to harm her, but in act B he sees a knife flying in her direction and intends to save her life. In A what he did was clearly wrong, whereas in B he did the right thing. On the other hand, two acts may have opposite results, but the actions may be equally good on the basis of intention. For example, two soldiers may try to cross the enemy lines to communicate with an allied force, but one gets captured through no fault of his own and the other succeeds. In a full moral description of any act, motive will be taken into consideration as a relevant factor.

Why Do We Need Morality?

A Reflection on Lord of the Flies

"Which is better—to have rules and agree, or to hunt and kill?"[2]

Why exactly do we need moral codes? What function do they play in our lives and in society in general? Rather than write a discursive essay on the benefits of morality, let me draw your attention to a book every young person has or should have read: William Golding's classic novel *Lord of the Flies.* This modern moral allegory may provide us with a clue to the nature and purpose of morality.

A group of boys between the ages of 6 and 12 years, from an English private school, are cast adrift on an uninhabited island in the Pacific and must create their own social system. For a while, the constraints of civilized society prevent total chaos. All the older boys recognize the necessity of substantive and procedural rules. Only he who has the white conch, the symbol of authority, may speak at an assembly. The leader is chosen democratically and is invested with limited powers. Even the evil Roger, while taunting little Henry by throwing stones near him, manages to keep the stones from harming the child: "Here invisible yet strong, was the taboo of the old life. Round the squatting child was the protection of parents and school and policemen and the law. Roger's arm was conditioned by a civilization that knew nothing of him and was in ruins."[3]

After some initial euphoria at being liberated from the adult world of constraints into an exciting world of fun in the Sun, the children come up against the usual banes of social existence: competition for power and status, neglect of social responsibility, failure of public policy, and escalating violence. Two boys, Ralph and Jack, vie for leadership, and a bitter rivalry emerges between them. As a compromise, a division of labor ensues in which Jack's choirboy hunters refuse to help the others in constructing shelters. Freeloading soon becomes a common phenomenon as the majority of children leave their tasks to play on the beach. Neglect of duty results in failure to be rescued by a passing airplane. The unbridled lust for excitement leads to the great orgiastic pig kills and finally, at its nadir, to the thirst for human blood.

Civilization's power is weak and vulnerable to atavistic, volcanic passions. The sensitive Simon—the symbol of religious consciousness (namely, "Simon Peter," the first disciple of Jesus), who prophesies that Ralph will be saved and is the first to discover and fight against the "ancient, inescapable recognition" of the beast in us—is slaughtered by the group in a wild frenzy. Only Piggy and Ralph, mere observers of the orgiastic homicide, feel vicarious pangs of guilt at this atrocity.

The incarnation of philosophy and culture—poor, fat, nearsighted Piggy with his broken spectacles and asthma—becomes ever more pathetic as the chaos increases. The nadir of his ridiculous position is reached after the rebels led by Jack steal Piggy's spectacles, to harness the Sun's rays in starting fires. After Ralph, the emblem of not-too-bright-but-morally-good civilized leadership, fails to persuade Jack to return the glasses, Piggy asserts his moral right to them: ". . . You're stronger than I am and you haven't got asthma. You can see . . . But I don't ask for my glasses back, not as a favour. I don't ask you to be a sport . . . not because you're strong, but because what's right's right. Give me my glasses, . . . You got to."[4]

He might as well have addressed the fire itself, for in this state of moral anarchy moral discourse is a foreign tongue that only incites the worst elements to greater immorality. Roger, perched on a cliff above, responds to moral reasoning by dislodging a huge rock that hits Piggy and flings him to his death 40 feet below.

"Lord of the Flies" is a translation of the Greek *Beelzebub,* which was a name for the devil. Golding shows that we need no external devil to bring about evil but that we have found the devil and, in the words of Pogo, "he is us." Ubiquitous, ever waiting for a moment to strike out, he emerges from the depths of the subconscious wherever there is a conflict of interest or a moment of moral lassitude. As E. L. Epstein says, "The tenets of civilization, the moral and social codes, the Ego, the intelligence itself, form only a veneer over this white-hot power, this uncontrollable force, "the fury and the mire of human veins."[5]

Beelzebub's ascendancy proceeds through fear, hysteria, violence, and death. A delegation starts out hunting pigs for meat; then they find themselves enjoying the kill. To drown the incipient shame over bloodthirstiness and take on a persona more compatible with their deed, the children paint themselves with colored mud. Their lusting for the kill takes on all the powerful overtones of an orgiastic sexual ritual—so that being liberated from their social selves, they kill without remorse whomever gets in their way. The death of Simon and Piggy (the symbols of the religious and philosophical, the two great fences blocking the descent to hell) and the final orgiastic hunt with the "spear sharpened at both ends" signal for Ralph the depths of evil in the human heart.

Ironically, it is the British navy that finally comes to the rescue and saves Ralph (civilization) just when all seems lost. The symbol of the navy is a Janus-faced omen: On the one hand, it may symbolize the fact that a military defense is unfortunately sometimes needed to save civilization from the barbarians (Hitler's Nazis or Jack's and Roger's allies); on the other hand, it symbolizes the quest for blood and vengeance latent in contemporary civilization. The children's world is really only a stage lower than the adult world whence they come, and shallow civilization could very well regress to tooth and claw if it were scratched too sharply. The adults saved the children, but who will save the adults who put so much emphasis in military enterprises and weapons systems—in the euphemistic name of "defense"? To quote Epstein, "The officer, having interrupted a man-hunt, prepares to take the children off the island in a cruiser which will presently be hunting its enemy in the same implacable way. And who will rescue the adult and his cruiser?"[6]

The fundamental ambiguity of human existence is seen in every section of the book, poignantly mirroring the human condition. Even Piggy's spectacles, the sole example of modern technology on the island, becomes a bane for the island as Jack uses them to ignite a forest fire that will smoke out their prey, Ralph, and that ends up burning down the entire forest and destroying the island's animal life. It is a symbol both of our penchant of misusing technology to vitiate the environment and of our ability to create weapons that will lead to global suicide.

The Purposes of Morality

What is the role of morality in human existence? What are boys and girls and men and women made of that requires ethical consciousness? Ralph answers these questions at the end of the tale: "And in the middle of [the children], with filthy body, matted hair, and unwiped nose, Ralph wept for the end of innocence, the darkness of man's heart, and the fall through the air of the true, wise friend called Piggy."[7]

In this modern moral allegory, we catch a glimpse of some of the purposes of morality. Rules formed over the ages and internalized within us hold back and, hopefully, defeat the "Lord of the Flies" in society, whether he is inherent in us individually or an emergent property of corporate existence. The moral code restrains the Rogers of society from evil until untoward social conditions open up the sluice gates of sadism. It is the force that enables Piggy and Ralph to maintain a modicum of order within their dwindling society, first motivating them to compromise with Jack and then keeping things in perspective.

In Golding's allegory, morality is honored more in the breach than in the observance, for we see the consequences of not having rules and principles and virtuous character. If we analyze this further, we see that morality has at least four related purposes:

- To keep society from falling apart
- To ameliorate human suffering
- To promote human flourishing
- To resolve conflicts of interest in just and peaceful ways

Morality, first of all, keeps society from falling apart, from sinking to a state of chaos where everyone is the enemy of everyone else, where fear and insecurity dominate the mind and prevent peace and happiness. Thomas Hobbes (1588–1679) described the dismal condition as a "state of nature" wherein there exists a perpetual war of all against all and life is "solitary, poor, nasty, brutish and short." The purpose of moral rules is to help us prevent this state of nature. As a means to prevent this condition, it must have rules of justice to resolve conflicts of interest that are mutually agreed upon and considered just. There are scarce resources, be they positions of power and status, wealth, jobs, land, property, or whatever, and we need rules to adjudicate conflicts when different people lay claim to these goods. Unless we can satisfactorily resolve these conflicts of interest, we will not be able to reach any other goals.

Related to this is morality's function to ameliorate or prevent unnecessary and unjust suffering. It establishes social institutions and conventions that aid victims of disease, famine, and violence. Kitty Genovese's neighbors had an obligation to take responsible action on her behalf.

The purpose of morality is not simply negative—to prevent chaos and unjust suffering. The rules also play a positive role in promoting human flourishing; they enable people to pursue their goals in peace and freedom, encouraging them to friendship and fidelity, challenging them to excellence and a worthwhile life. Deep morality, as it is ingrained in good character, is a "jewel that shines in its own light." It creates a worthwhile life for its participants and turns a potential hell into something that at its highest point (usually confined to small communities, friendships, and families) approximates "a heaven on Earth." In sum, it tries to promote human flourishing.

Even though these four purposes of morality are related, they are not identical, and different moral theories emphasize different purposes and in different ways. Utilitarianism fastens on human flourishing and the amelioration of suffering, whereas contractual systems rooted in Hobbesian egoism accents the role of resolving conflicts of interest. Other systems, such as Kant's theory, place the emphasis on orderly, universal rules of justice. Virtue ethics emphasizes individual flourishing in the virtuous character. As you examine the various theories set forth, you should ask yourself whether it is important to deal with all four purposes satisfactorily.

But before we go any further, we need to examine the very status of moral principles. Are they wholly relative to culture—socially approved habits—or do some of them enjoy universal validity that does not rest on whether or not societies recognize them? It is to this problem we turn next.

Summary

Moral philosophy or ethics is the systematic endeavor to understand moral concepts (for example , right and wrong) and justify moral principles and theories. It seeks to establish principles of right behavior that may serve as guides to our actions. It goes deeper than etiquette and law, and unlike religion it appeals only to reason rather than divine revelation. We need morality in order to stave off a war of all against all, that is, to promote human flourishing and the survival of society.

FOR FURTHER REFLECTION

1. As the illustration from Golding's *Lord of the Flies* shows, we may come to understand and appreciate the need for and purposes of morality by looking at situations where morality is absent or where evil is present. Can you think of literature, social studies, or social experience where this is further illustrated?

2. Illustrate the difference between a moral principle, a legal rule, a principle of etiquette, an aesthetic judgment, and a religious principle. Are these sometimes related? Can something be so aesthetically repulsive that we conclude that it is morally wrong? For example, our laws prohibit public nudity and many people find public nudity revolting or deeply offensive, but is it necessarily morally wrong?

3. A moral dilemma is either a situation in which whatever action you take some evil will be allowed or one in which two accepted moral principles meaningfully conflict. They produce most of the hard cases in applying ethical theory. Here are a few dilemmas for you to discuss

   a. You are driving a trolley down the track; all of a sudden, the brakes fail and you cannot stop the trolley at the red light. Ahead of you are ten men working on the track, whom you will kill if you do nothing. Fortunately, there is a sidetrack that you can turn off on and thus spare the men. Unfortunately, however, a child playing on that track will be killed if you do turn onto the sidetrack. If you do nothing, ten men will be killed due to the brake failure, but if you voluntarily act, you will kill the child. What should you do? (Judith Jarvis Thomson first proposed this example.)

   b. You have discovered that your parents have embezzled a large sum of money from the business corporation for which they work. You have spoken to them about this, and they have denied it, but you know that they are lying. If you report them, they will go to prison and have their lives ruined. If you don't report them, the owners of the business will be financially ruined. How do you handle this situation?

c. You and twenty friends are spelunking in a coastal cave when Fat Freddy gets caught in the mouth of the cave. The tide is rising and soon all will be drowned, except Freddy whose head is outside the cave, if Freddy isn't dislodged from the cave's mouth. Fortuitously, you just happen to have a stick of dynamite with you. Your option is to blow Freddy from his place or drown along with nineteen friends. What should you do?

4. In 399 BCE, Socrates has been unjustly condemned to death by the citizens of Athens. While in jail waiting execution, his friend, Crito, offers him a safe way of escape. Crito argues that Socrates has an obligation to his friends and family to accept this opportunity, but Socrates argues that it is wrong to break the law in order to save oneself. Who is right? Read Plato's dialogue *Crito* to get the details of the arguments. This is probably the first case in history in which the issue of civil disobedience is discussed. Is civil disobedience ever morally justified? If so, under what conditions?

5. Tom Jones, an up-and-coming young businessman, is walking to work on a bridge overlooking a river when he sees a small girl fall into the water. She begins to scream for help. Tom is a good swimmer and knows that he can save the girl's life, but if he does so, he will miss a meeting that is important to his career. Besides, the water is cold, and Tom doesn't want to ruin his new suit. He doesn't want to jump in and reasons that it is not his fault that the girl has fallen into the water. Does Tom have a duty to jump in despite his objections? Why or why not? How is this case related to a case where Tom accidentally pushes the girl into the river? Or where Tom purposefully pushes her into the water?

6. The late French existentialist Jean-Paul Sartre relates the following dilemma. During World War II, when France was occupied by the German army, a student came to Sartre, asking for moral advice. The youth's father was a collaborator with the Nazis, but his older brother had been killed by the German army a few years earlier; the student wanted to avenge his brother's death and help free his country. However, his mother, now estranged from her collaborationist husband, lived alone with him, and he (our student) was her only consolation. Sartre writes:

> The boy was faced with the choice of leaving for England and joining the Free French Forces—that is, leaving his mother behind—or remaining with his mother and helping her to carry on. He was fully aware that the woman lived only for him and that his going-off—and perhaps his death—would plunge her into despair. He was also aware that every act that he did for his mother's sake was a sure thing, in the sense that it was helping her to carry on, whereas every effort he made toward going off and fighting was an uncertain move which might run aground and prove completely useless.
>
> As a result, he was faced with two very difficult kinds of action: one, concrete, immediate, but concerning only one individual; the other concerned an incomparably vaster group, a national collectivity, but for that

very reason was dubious, and might be interrupted en route. And, at the same time, he was wavering between two kinds of ethics. On the one hand, an ethics of sympathy, of personal devotion; on the other, a broader ethics, but one whose efficacy was more dubious. He had to choose between the two.[8]

Here are some questions for you:

a. What should Sartre have advised the student? What was the correct advice?

b. Is there a correct answer to the student's dilemma? Is one option the right one and the other the wrong one? Explain your response.

c. It is sometimes said that men and women tend to view morality from different perspectives, men being more rule-governed and emphasizing global duties and women being more nurturing and emphasizing caring and sympathy. In this case, according to these philosophers, women would generally advise staying home with the mother, whereas men would generally advise fighting for the cause of freedom. Do you agree with this analysis?

7. Where does etiquette leave off and ethics begin? When does rudeness cease to be simply bad manners and become bad morals? Is failing to say "thank you" for a medium-sized favor immoral? Is it immoral not to be grateful for a service rendered? Here is a contemporary problem. It has become accepted practice to use the disjunctive "he or she" instead of simply the old generic "he," in an attempt to be more inclusive (genderwise). Recently, an acquaintance questioned his editor (of a major publishing company), asking, "Why can't I use the generic 'man' and 'he' instead of the cumbersome, 'human beings' and 'he and she'?" The editor responded that using the old forms would not be allowed, for the more inclusive language was "morally correct." My acquaintance replied, "It may be courteous, but I don't see anything intrinsically moral about the issue." What do you think?

8. Think of some difficult moral issues and keep them in mind as you work through the rest of this book, asking yourself how the various theories would treat these issues.

NOTES

1. *Ethics in America* (PBS, 1989), produced by Fred Friendly.
2. William Golding, *Lord of the Flies* (New York: Putnam, 1959), 222.
3. Ibid., 78.
4. Ibid., 211.
5. E. L. Epstein, "Notes on *Lord of the Flies*" in Golding, *Lord of the Flies,* 252.
6. Ibid.
7. Golding, *Lord of the Flies,* 248.
8. Jean-Paul Sartre, *Existentialism and Human Emotions,* trans. Bernard Fechtman and Hazel Barnes (New York: Philosophical Library, 1957), 24–25.

FOR FURTHER READING

Baier, Kurt. *The Moral Point of View.* Ithaca, NY: Cornell University Press, 1958. An abridged edition of this fine work is available in paperback from Random House (1965). The work sees morality primarily in terms of social control.

Brandt, Richard. *Ethical Theory: The Problems of Normative and Critical Ethics.* Englewood Cliffs, NJ: Prentice Hall, 1959. A thorough and thoughtful treatment of ethical theory.

Frankena, William K. *Ethics,* 2nd ed. Englewood Cliffs, NJ: Prentice Hall, 1973.

Gert, Bernard. *Morality: A New Justification of the Moral Rules,* 2nd ed. New York: Oxford University Press, 1988. A clear and comprehensive discussion of the nature of morality.

MacIntyre, Alasdair. *A Short History of Ethics.* New York: Macmillan, 1966. A lucid, if uneven, survey of the history of Western ethics.

Mackie, J. L. *Ethics: Inventing Right and Wrong.* London: Penguin Books, 1976. This book takes a very different view of ethics from mine.

Pojman, Louis, ed. *Ethical Theory: Classical and Contemporary Readings,* 4th ed. Belmont, CA: Wadsworth, 2001. Contains a full range of essays on topics in ethical theory.

Scheffler, Samuel. *Human Morality.* New York: Oxford University Press, 1992. A defense of a "moderate" view of morality between the "extremes": On the one hand, morality generally requires sacrifice of self-interest; on the other, morality never conflicts with self-interest. Scheffler argues that, although conflicts between morality and self-interest sometimes arise, morality is essentially reasonable.

Singer, Peter. *The Expanding Circle: Ethics and Sociobiology.* New York: Oxford University Press, 1983. A fascinating attempt to relate ethics to sociobiology.

Taylor, Paul. *Principles of Ethics.* Belmont, CA: Dickenson, 1975. This work covers many of the same topics as my book, usually from a different perspective. His discussion of the principle of universalizability (pp. 95–105) is especially useful.

Taylor, Richard. *Good and Evil.* Buffalo, NY: Prometheus, 1970. A lively, easy-to-read work that sees the main role of morality to be the resolution of conflicts of interest.

Turnbull, Colin. *The Mountain People.* New York: Simon & Schuster, 1972. An excellent anthropological study of a people living on the edge of morality.

Warnock, G. J. *The Object of Morality.* London: Methuen, 1971. A clearly written, well-argued analysis of the nature of morality.

28 ✿ Ethical Relativism: Who's to Judge What Is Right or Wrong?

> *Ethical relativism is the doctrine that the moral rightness and wrongness of actions varies from society to society and that there are no absolute universal moral standards binding on all men at all times. Accordingly, it holds that whether or not it is right for an individual to act in a certain way depends on or is relative to the society to which he belongs.*
>
> John Ladd[1]

The Case for Ethical Relativism

Nineteenth-century Christian missionaries sometimes used coercion to change the customs of pagan tribal people in parts of Africa and the Pacific Islands. Appalled by the customs of public nakedness, polygamy, working on the Sabbath, and infanticide, they paternalistically went about reforming the "poor pagans." They clothed them, separated wives from their husbands in order to create monogamous households, made the Sabbath a day of rest, and ended infanticide. In the process, they sometimes created social malaise, causing the estranged women to despair and their children to be orphaned. The natives often did not understand the new religion but accepted it in deference to the white man's power: guns and medicine.

Since the 19th century we've made progress in understanding cultural diversity and realize that the social dissonance caused by "do-gooders" was a bad thing. In the last century or so, anthropology has exposed our penchant for *ethnocentrism*, the prejudicial view that interprets all of reality through the eyes of our cultural beliefs and values. We have come to see enormous variety in social practices throughout the world.

Eskimos allow their elderly to die by starvation, whereas we believe that this is morally wrong. The Spartans of ancient Greece and the Dobu of New Guinea believe that stealing is morally right, but we believe it is wrong. Many cultures, past and present, have practiced or still practice infanticide. A tribe in East Africa once threw deformed infants to the hippopotamus, but our society condemns such acts. Sexual practices vary over time and clime. Some cultures permit while others condemn homosexual behavior. Some cultures, including Muslim societies, practice polygamy, while Christian cultures view it as immoral.

Long ago the Greek historian Herodotus (485–430 BCE) wrote of the power of culture to determine the values of people. Here is a classic selection.

CUSTOM IS KING

Thus it appears certain to me, by a great variety of proofs, that Cambyses was raving mad; he would not else have set himself to make a mock of holy rites and long-established usages. For if one were to offer men to choose out of all the customs in the world such as seemed to them the best, they would examine the whole number, and end by preferring their own; so convinced are they that their own usages far surpass those of all others. Unless, therefore, a man was mad, it is not likely that he would make sport of such matters. That people have this feeling about their laws may be seen by very many proofs: among others, by the following. Darius, after he had got the kingdom, called into his presence certain Greeks who were at hand, and asked—"What he should pay them to eat the bodies of their fathers when they died?" To which they answered, that there was no sum that would tempt them to do such a thing. He then sent for certain Indians, of the race called Callatians, men who eat their fathers, and asked them, while the Greeks stood by, and knew by the help of an interpreter all that was said—"What he should give them to burn the bodies of their fathers at their decease?" The Indians exclaimed aloud, and bade him forbear such language. Such is men's wont herein; and Pindar was right, in my judgment, when he said, "Custom is the king o'er all."

In her highly influential article "Anthropology and the Abnormal," anthropologist Ruth Benedict argues that (1) what counts as normal and abnormal is relative to culture and (2) normality forms the basis of our concept of moral goodness.

ANTHROPOLOGY AND THE ABNORMAL

Modern social anthropology has become more and more a study of the varieties and common elements of cultural environment and the consequences of these in human behavior. For such a study of diverse social orders primitive peoples fortunately provide

From: *Journal of General Psychology* 10 (1934): 59–82. Reprinted with permission of the Helen Dwight Reid Educational Foundation. Published by Heldref Publications, 1319 Eighteenth St. NW, Washington, DC, 20036–1802. Copyright © 1934.

a laboratory not yet entirely vitiated by the spread of a standardized worldwide civilization. Dyaks and Hopis, Fijians and Yakuts are significant for psychological and sociological study because only among these simpler peoples has there been sufficient isolation to give opportunity for the development of localized social forms.... Modern civilization, from [the anthropological] point of view, becomes not a necessary pinnacle of human achievement but one entry in a long series of possible adjustments.

These adjustments, whether they are in mannerisms like the ways of showing anger, or joy, or grief in any society, or in major human drives like those of sex, prove to be far more variable than experience in any one culture would suggest. In certain fields, such as that of religion or of formal marriage arrangements, these wide limits of variability are well known and can be fairly described.

One of [the] problems [studied] relates to the customary modern normal–abnormal categories and our conclusions regarding them. In how far are such categories culturally determined, or in how far can we regard inability to function socially as diagnostic of abnormality, or in how far is it necessary to regard this as a function of the culture?

As a matter of fact, one of the most striking facts that emerge from a study of widely varying cultures is the ease with which our abnormals function in other cultures. It does not matter what kind of "abnormality" we choose for illustration, those which indicated extreme instability, or those which are more in the nature of character traits like sadism or delusions of grandeur or of persecution, there are well-described cultures in which these abnormals function at ease and with honor, and apparently without danger or difficulty to the society.

Benedict illustrates her thesis with a series of examples from different cultures. Whereas in our culture, catalepsy—suspended animation or trancelike behavior—is regarded as an extreme psychic aberration, in many other cultures it is regarded as a visitation from the gods. Next she considers homosexuality.[2]

Homosexuality is an[other] excellent example. A tendency towards this trait in our culture exposes an individual to all the conflicts to which all aberrants are always exposed, and we tend to identify the consequences of this conflict with homosexuality. But these consequences are obviously local and cultural. Homosexuals in many societies are not incompetent, but they may be such if the culture asks adjustments of them that would strain any man's vitality. Wherever homosexuality has been given an honorable place in any society, those to whom it is congenial have filled adequately the honorable roles society assigns to them. Plato's *Republic* is, of course, the most convincing statement of such a reading of homosexuality. It is presented as one of the major means to the good life, and it was generally so regarded in Greece and that time.

The cultural attitude toward homosexuals has not always been on such a high ethical plane, but it has been very varied. Among many American Indian tribes there exists the institution of the berdache, as the French called them. These men-women were men who at puberty or thereafter took the dress and the occupations of women. Sometimes they married other men and lived with them. Sometimes they were men with no inversion, persons of weak sexual endowment who chose this role to avoid the jeers of the women. The berdaches were never regarded as of first-rate supernatural power, as similar men-women were in Siberia, but rather as leaders in women's occupations, good healers in certain diseases, or, among certain tribes, as the genial organizers of social affairs. In any case, they were socially placed. They were not left exposed to the conflicts that visit the deviant who is excluded from participation in the recognized patterns of his society.

The most spectacular illustrations of the extent to which normality may be culturally defined are those cultures where an abnormality of our culture is the cornerstone of their social structure. It is not possible to do justice to these possibilities in a short discussion. A recent study of an island of northwest Melanesia by Fortune describes a society built upon traits which we regard as beyond the border of paranoia. In this tribe the exogamic groups look upon each other as prime manipulators of black magic, so that one marries always into an enemy group which remains for life one's deadly and unappeasable foes. They look upon a good garden crop as a confession of theft, for everyone is engaged in making magic to induce into his garden the productiveness of his neighbors'; therefore no secrecy in the island is so rigidly insisted upon as the secrecy of a man's harvesting of his yams. Their polite phrase at the acceptance of a gift is, "And if you now poison me, how shall I repay you this present?" Their preoccupation with poisoning is constant; no woman ever leaves her cooking pot for a moment untended. Even the great affinal economic exchanges that are characteristic of this Melanesian culture area are quite altered in Dobu since they are incompatible with this fear and distrust that pervades the culture. They go farther and people the whole world outside their own quarters with such malignant spirits that all-night feasts and ceremonials simply do not occur here. They have even rigorous religiously enforced customs that forbid the sharing of seed even in one family group. Anyone else's food is deadly poison to you, so that communality of stores is out of the question. For some months before harvest the whole society is on the verge of starvation, but if one falls to the temptation and eats up one's seed yams, one is an outcast and a beachcomber for life. There is no coming back. It involves, as a matter of course, divorce and the breaking of all social ties.

Now in this society where no one may work with another and no one may share with another, Fortune describes the individual who was regarded by all his fellows as crazy. He was not one of those who periodically ran amok and, beside himself and frothing at the mouth, fell with a knife upon anyone he could reach. Such behavior they did not regard as putting anyone outside the pale. They did not even put the individuals who were known to be liable to these attacks under any kind of control. They merely fled when they saw the attack coming on and kept out of the way. "He would be all right tomorrow." But there was one man of sunny, kindly disposition who liked work and liked to be helpful. The compulsion was too strong for him to repress it in favor of the opposite tendencies of his culture. Men and women never spoke of him without laughing; he was silly and simple and definitely crazy. Nevertheless, to the ethnologist used to a culture that has, in Christianity, made his type the model of all virtue, he seemed a pleasant fellow....

...Among the Kwakiutl it did not matter whether a relative had died in bed of disease, or by the hand of an enemy, in either case death was an affront to be wiped out by the death of another person. The fact that one had been caused to mourn was proof that one had been put upon. A chief's sister and her daughter had gone up to Victoria, and either because they drank bad whiskey or because their boat capsized they never came back. The chief called together his warriors, "Now I ask you, tribes, who shall wail? Shall I do it or shall another?" The spokesman answered, of course, "Not you, Chief. Let some other of the tribes." Immediately they set up the war pole to announce their intention of wiping out the injury, and gathered a war party. They set out, and found seven men and two children asleep and killed them. "Then they felt good when they arrived at Sebaa in the evening."

The point which is of interest to us is that in our society those who on that occasion would feel good when they arrived at Sebaa that evening would be the definitely abnormal. There would be some, even in our society, but it is not a recognized and approved mood under the circumstances. On the Northwest Coast those are favored and fortunate to whom that mood under those circumstances is congenial, and those to whom it is repugnant are unlucky. This latter minority can register in their own culture only by doing violence to their congenial responses and acquiring others that are difficult for them. The person, for instance, who, like a Plains Indian whose wife has been taken from him, is too proud to fight, can deal with the Northwest Coast civilization only by ignoring its strongest bents. If he cannot achieve it, he is the deviant in that culture, their instance of abnormality.

This head-hunting that takes place on the Northwest Coast after a death is no matter of blood revenge or of organized vengeance. There is no effort to tie up the subsequent killing with any responsibility on the part of the victim for the death of the person who is being mourned. A chief whose son has died goes visiting wherever his fancy dictates, and he says to his host, "My prince has died today, and you go with him." Then he kills him. In this, according to their interpretation, he acts nobly because he has not been downed. He has thrust back in return. The whole procedure is meaningless without the fundamental paranoid reading of bereavement. Death, like all the other untoward accidents of existence, confounds man's pride and can only be handled in the category of insults.

Behavior honored upon the Northwest Coast is one which is recognized as abnormal in our civilization, and yet it is sufficiently close to the attitudes of our culture to be intelligible to us and to have a definite vocabulary with which we may discuss it. The megalomaniac paranoid trend is a definite danger in our society. It is encouraged by some of our major preoccupations, and it confronts us with a choice of two possible attitudes. One is to brand it as abnormal and reprehensible, and is the attitude we have chosen in our civilization. The other is to make it an essential attribute of ideal man, and this is the solution in the culture of the Northwest Coast.

Benedict sums up the lessons of these illustrations of cultural diversity regarding abnormality: *Normality is culturally defined.*

An adult shaped to the drives and standards of either of these cultures, if a megalomaniac paranoid, [from the Kwakiutl culture] were transported into our civilization, he would fall into our category of abnormality. He would be faced with the psychic dilemmas of the socially unavailable. In his own culture, however, he is the pillar of society, the end result of socially inculcated mores, and the problem of personal instability in his case simply does not arise.

Next Benedict compares the enormous possibility for cultural diversity with the great range of possible phonemes, the basic sound utterances of which humans are capable.

> No one civilization can possibly utilize in its mores the whole potential range of human behavior. Just as there are great numbers of possible phonetic articulations, and the possibility of language depends on a selection and standardization of a few of these in order that speech communication may be possible at all, so the possibility of organized behavior of every sort, from the fashions of local dress and houses to the dicta of a people's ethics and religion, depends upon a similar selection among the possible behavior traits. In the field of recognized economic obligations or sex tabus this selection is as nonrational and subconscious a process as it is in the field of phonetics. It is a process which goes on in the group for long periods of time and is historically conditioned by innumerable accidents of isolation or of contact of peoples.

Cultures take these individual traits and carry them further and further, integrating them more and more completely with one another, so that what one culture regards as abnormal and unworkable functions in another culture as normal because it plays a different role in a culture with a different pattern of traits.

Benedict now carries her argument to the moral domain.

> It is a point that has been made more often in relation to ethics than in relation to psychiatry. We do not any longer make the mistake of deriving the morality of our locality and decade directly from the inevitable constitution of human nature. We do not elevate it to the dignity of a first principle. We recognize that morality differs in every society, and is a convenient term for socially approved habits. Mankind has always preferred to say, "It is morally good," rather than "It is habitual," and the fact of this preference is matter enough for a critical science of ethics. But historically the two phrases are synonymous.
>
> The concept of the normal is properly a variant of the concept of the good. It is that which society has approved. A normal action is one which falls well within the limits of expected behavior for a particular society. Its variability among different peoples is essentially a function of the variability of the behavior patters that different societies have created for themselves, and can never be wholly divorced from a consideration of culturally institutionalized types of behavior.
>
> Each culture is a more or less elaborate working out of the potentialities of the segment it has chosen. In so far as a civilization is well integrated and consistent within itself, it will tend to carry farther and farther, according to its nature, its initial impulse toward a particular type of action, and from the point of view of any other culture those elaborations will include more and more extreme and aberrant traits.
>
> Each of these traits, in proportion as it reinforces the chosen behavior patterns of that culture, is for that culture normal. Those individuals to whom it is congenial either

congenitally, or as the result of childhood sets, are accorded prestige in that culture, and are not visited with the social contempt or disapproval which their traits would call down upon them in a society that was differently organized. On the other hand, those individuals whose characteristics are not congenial to the selected type of human behavior in that community are the deviants, no matter how valued their personality traits may be in a contrasted civilization.

The Dobuan who is not easily susceptible to fear of treachery, who enjoys work and likes to be helpful, is their neurotic and regarded as silly. On the Northwest Coast the person who finds it difficult to read life in terms of an insult contest will be the person upon whom fall all the difficulties of the culturally unprovided for. The person who does not find it easy to humiliate a neighbor, nor to see humiliation in his own experience, who is genial and loving, may, of course, find some unstandardized way of achieving satisfactions in his society, but not in the major patterned responses that his culture requires of him. If he is born to play an important role in a family with many hereditary privileges, he can succeed only by doing violence to his whole personality. If he does not succeed, he has betrayed his culture; that is, he is abnormal.

I have spoken of individuals as having sets toward certain types of behavior, and of these sets as running sometimes counter to the types of behavior which are institutionalized in the culture to which they belong. From all that we know of contrasting cultures it seems clear that differences of temperament occur in every society. The matter has never been made the subject of investigation, but from the available material it would appear that these temperament types are very likely of universal recurrence. That is, there is an ascertainable range of human behavior that is found wherever a sufficiently large series of individuals is observed. But the proportion in which behavior types stand to one another in different societies is not universal. The vast majority of individuals in any group are shaped to the fashion of that culture. In other words, most individuals are plastic to the moulding force of the society into which they are born. In a society that values trance, as in India, they will have supernormal experience. In a society that institutionalizes homosexuality, they will be homosexual. In a society that sets the gathering of possessions as the chief human objective, they will amass property. The deviants, whatever the type of behavior the culture has institutionalized, will remain few in number, and there seems no more difficulty in moulding the vast malleable majority to the "normality" of what we consider an aberrant trait, such as delusions of reference, than to the normality of such accepted behavior patterns as acquisitiveness. The small proportion of the number of the deviants in any culture is not a function of the sure instinct with which that society has built itself upon the fundamental sanities, but of the universal fact that, happily, the majority of mankind quite readily take any shape that is presented to them....

What do you make of Benedict's arguments? Can you think of any problems with her thesis that morality is simply one of "a long series of possible adjustments"? Just because different cultures view normalcy and abnormalcy differently, does that make them equally valid? Could there be universal moral principles despite this cultural diversity? If a culture institutes slavery and it becomes "normal," does slavery automatically become morally good? And what exactly defines a culture? Benedict's examples are isolated societies, but what happens when people participate in a multicultural society or where one person belongs to different cultures within his or her society? Suppose John is a southerner, a Catholic, and an African American. Does he not belong to three different cultures? Which culture defines normalcy for John, or must he change his identity constantly—"when in Rome, do as the Romans do"?

These are good questions to discuss, but before you get too involved in that discussion, you might read the next section in this chapter, where ethical relativism is analyzed and criticized. It was written for my students some years ago when I could not find a serious critique of relativism. I found that somewhere between 60 and 80 percent of the students in my classes claimed that they were ethical relativists and yet had little idea of the implications of their position. For example, on the same questionnaire on which they said they were ethical relativists, they would state that "abortion is always immoral," "capital punishment is never morally permissible," or "homosexuality is always permissible." But, of course, as is probably obvious to you, those statements contradict the thesis of ethical relativism.

A Critique of Ethical Relativism

Ethical **relativism** is the theory that there are no universally valid moral principles, but that all moral principles are valid relative to culture or individual choice. It is to be distinguished from moral skepticism, the view that there are no valid moral principles at all (or at least we cannot know whether there are any), and from all forms of moral **objectivism** or absolutism. John Ladd's statement at the beginning of this chapter is a typical characterization of the theory, defining *ethical relativism* as "the doctrine that the moral rightness and wrongness of actions varies from society to society and that there are no absolute universal moral standards binding on all men at all times." Whether something is right or wrong depends on the society to which he belongs. This view should be distinguished from *cultural relativism*, which merely describes ethical systems of different cultures as holding different principles. Culture Alpha may hold principles A, B, C, and D; culture Beta holds principles C, D, E, and F; and culture Kappa holds principles F, G, H, and I. The three cultures hold no one principle in common, but this makes *no claims* whatsoever on the validity of the principles held. It could well be the case that principles A, B, F, and G are invalid moral principles, whereas principles C, D, E, H, and I are universally valid. So one could be a cultural relativist, the descriptive theory, without embracing *ethical relativism*, the normative theory—there are no universally valid moral principles. I turn to my essay.

A CRITIQUE OF ETHICAL RELATIVISM

Subjective Ethical Relativism (Subjectivism)

Some relativists think that the above description is too tame and maintain that morality is not dependent on the society but on the *individual* him or herself. As students sometimes maintain, "Morality is in the eye of the beholder." Ernest Hemingway wrote,

> So far, about morals, I know only that what is moral is what you feel good after and what is immoral is what you feel bad after and judged by these moral standards, which I do not defend, the bullfight is very moral to me because I feel very fine while it is going on and have a feeling of life and death and mortality and immortality, and after it is over I feel very sad but very fine.

Subjectivism, however, has the sorry consequence that it makes morality a useless concept, for, on its premises, little or no interpersonal criticism or judgment is logically possible. Hemingway may feel good about the killing of bulls in a bullfight, while Albert Schweitzer or Mother Teresa would feel the opposite. No argument about the matter is possible. The only basis for judging Hemingway or anyone else wrong would be if he failed to live up to his own principles; however, one of Hemingway's principles could be that hypocrisy is morally permissible (he feels good about it), so that it would be impossible for him to do wrong. For Hemingway hypocrisy and nonhypocrisy are both morally permissible. On the basis of subjectivism it could very easily turn out that Adolf Hitler was as moral as Mahatma Gandhi, as long as each believed he was living by his chosen principles. Notions of moral good and bad, right or wrong cease to have interpersonal evaluative meaning.

In the opening days of philosophy classes, I often find students vehemently defending subjective relativism. I then give the students their first test. The next class period I return all the tests, marked F even though my comments show that most of the tests are of a very high quality. When the students express outrage at this injustice, I answer that I have accepted subjectivism for purposes of marking the exams, in which case the principle of justice has no objective validity.

Absurd consequences follow from subjective ethical relativism. If it is correct, then morality reduces to aesthetic tastes, over which there can be neither argument nor interpersonal judgment. Although many people say that they hold this position, there seems to be a conflict between it and other of their moral views (e.g., that Hitler was really morally bad or that capital punishment is always wrong). There seems to be a contradiction between subjectivism and the very concept of morality, which it is supposed to characterize, for morality has to do with *proper* resolution of interpersonal conflict and the amelioration of the human predicament. Whatever else it does, morality has the minimal aim of preventing a state of chaos in which life is "solitary, poor, nasty, brutish, and short." But if so, subjectivism is no help at all in doing this, for it does

From: Louis Pojman, "A Critique of Ethical Relativism," in *Ethical Theory: Classical and Contemporary Readings*, ed. Louis Pojman (Belmont, CA: Wadsworth Publishing Company, 1989).

not rest on social *agreement* of principle (as the conventionalist maintains) or on an objectively independent set of norms that bind all people for the common good.

Subjectivism treats individuals like billiard balls on a societal pool table where they meet only in radical collisions, each aimed at his or her own goal and striving to do in the others before they themselves are done in. This atomistic view of personality is belied by the facts that we develop in families and mutually dependent communities in which we share a common language, common institutions, and similar habits, and that we often feel one another's joys and sorrows. As John Donne said, "No man is an island, entire of itself; every man is a piece of the continent."...

If this argument is sound, radical individualistic relativism (subjectivism) seems incoherent. If so, it follows that the only plausible view of ethical relativism must be one that grounds morality in the group or culture. This form of relativism is called *conventionalism*, which we looked at earlier and to which I now return.[3]

Conventional Ethical Relativism (Conventionalism)

Conventional ethical relativism, the view that there are no objective moral principles but rather that all valid moral principles are justified by virtue of their cultural acceptance, recognizes the social nature of morality. That is precisely its power and virtue. It does not seem subject to the same absurd consequences that plague subjectivism. Recognizing the importance of our social environment in generating customs and beliefs, many people suppose that ethical relativism is the correct ethical theory. Furthermore, they are drawn to it for its liberal philosophical stance. It seems to be an enlightened response to the sin of ethnocentricity, and it seems to entail or strongly imply an attitude of tolerance toward other cultures. As Ruth Benedict says, in recognizing ethical relativity

> we shall arrive at a more realistic social faith, accepting as grounds of hope and as new bases for tolerance the coexisting and equally valid patterns of life which mankind has created for itself from the raw materials of existence.

The most famous of those holding this position is the anthropologist Melville Herskovits, who argues even more explicitly than Benedict that ethical relativism entails intercultural tolerance.

1. Morality is relative to its culture.
2. There is no independent basis for criticizing the morality of any other culture.
3. Therefore we ought to be tolerant of the moralities of other cultures.

Tolerance is certainly a virtue, but is this a good argument for it? I think not. If morality is simply relative to each culture then if the culture does not have a principle of tolerance, its members have no obligation to be tolerant. Herskovits seems to be treating the principle of tolerance as the one exception to his relativism. But from a relativistic point of view there is no more reason to be tolerant than to be intolerant, and neither stance is objectively morally better than the other.

Not only do relativists fail to offer a basis for criticizing those who are intolerant, but they cannot rationally criticize anyone who espouses what they might regard as a heinous principle. If, as seems to be the case, valid criticism supposes an objective or impartial standard, relativists cannot morally criticize anyone outside their own culture. Adolf Hitler's genocidal actions, as long as they were culturally accepted, were as morally legitimate as Mother Teresa's works of mercy. If conventional relativism is accepted, then racism, genocide of unpopular minorities, oppression of the poor, slavery, and even the advocacy of war for its own sake are as equally moral as their opposites. And if a subculture decided that starting a nuclear war was somehow morally acceptable, we could not morally criticize these people, for any actual morality, whatever its content, is as valid as every other and more valid than ideal moralities, because the latter aren't adhered to by any culture.

There are other disturbing consequences of ethical relativism. It seems to entail that reformers are always (morally) wrong, since they go against the tide of cultural standards. William Wilberforce was wrong, in the 18th century, to oppose slavery; the British were immoral in opposing suttee in India (the burning of widows on their husbands' funeral pyres, which is now illegal in India); and missionaries were immoral in opposing clitorectomies in Central Africa. The early Christians were wrong in refusing to serve in the Roman army or bow down to Caesar, since the majority in the Roman Empire believed these two acts were moral duties. In fact, Jesus himself was immoral in advocating the beatitudes and principles of the Sermon on the Mount, since it is clear that few in his time (or in ours) accepted them.

Yet we normally feel just the opposite, that the reformer is the courageous innovator who is right, who has the truth, in the face of the mindless majority. Sometimes the individual must stand alone with the truth, risking social censure and persecution. As Dr. Stockman says in Ibsen's *Enemy of the People,* after he loses the battle to declare his town's profitable polluted tourist spa unsanitary, "The most dangerous enemy of the truth and freedom among us—is the compact majority. Yes, the damned, compact and liberal majority. The majority has *might*—unfortunately—but *right* it is not. Right—are I and a few others." Yet if relativism is correct, the opposite is necessarily the case. Truth is with the crowd and error with the individual.

Similarly, conventional ethical relativism entails disturbing judgments about the law. Our normal view is that we have a prima facie duty to obey the law, because law, in general, promotes the human Good. According to most objective systems, this obligation is not absolute but rather is conditional, depending on the particular law's relation to a wider moral order. Civil disobedience is warranted in some cases in which the law seems to be in serious conflict with morality. However, if moral relativism is true, then neither law nor civil disobedience has a firm foundation. On the one hand, for society at large, civil disobedience will be morally wrong, so long as the culture agrees with the law in question. On the other hand, if you belong to the relevant subculture which doesn't recognize the particular law in question, disobedience will be morally mandated. The Ku Klux Klan, which believes that Jews, Catholics, and Blacks are evil or undeserving of high regard, are, given conventionalism, morally permitted or required to break the laws that protect these endangered groups. Why should I obey a law that my group doesn't recognize as valid?

To sum up, unless we have an independent moral basis for law, it is hard to see why we have any general duty to obey it; and unless we recognize the priority of a universal moral law, we have no firm basis to justify our acts of civil disobedience against "unjust laws." Both the validity of law and morally motivated disobedience of unjust laws are annulled in favor of a power struggle.

There is an even more basic problem with the notion that morality is dependent on cultural acceptance for its validity. The problem is that the concepts of *culture* and *society* are notoriously difficult to define, especially in a pluralistic society such as our own, in which the concepts seem rather vague. One person may belong to several societies (subcultures) with different emphases on values and arrangements of principles. A person may belong to the nation as a single society with certain values of patriotism, honor, courage, laws (including some that are controversial but have majority acceptance, such as the law on abortion). But he or she may also belong to a church that opposes some of the laws of the state. The same individual may also be an integral member of a socially mixed community in which different principles hold sway, and additionally may belong to clubs and a family that adhere to still other rules. Relativism would seem to tell us that when a person is a member of societies with conflicting moralities, that person must be judged both wrong and not wrong, whatever he or she does. For example, if Mary is a U.S. citizen and a Roman Catholic, she is wrong (qua Catholic) if she chooses to have an abortion and not wrong (qua citizen of the United States) if she acts against the teaching of the church on abortion. As a member of a racist university fraternity, the Ku Klux Klan, John has no obligation to treat his fellow African American students as equals; but as a member of the university community itself (in which the principle of equal rights is accepted), he does have that obligation; but as a member of the surrounding community (which may reject the principle of equal rights), John again has no such obligation; but then again as a member of the nation at large (which accepts the principle), he is obligated to treat his fellow citizens with respect. What is the morally right thing for John to do? The question no longer makes much sense in this moral Babel; morality has lost its action-guiding function.

Perhaps the relativist would adhere to a principle that says in such cases the individual may choose which group to belong to as primary. If Mary chooses to have an abortion, she is choosing to belong to the general society relative to that principle. And John must likewise choose among groups. The trouble with this option is that it seems to lead back to counterintuitive results. If Mafia Mike feels like killing bank president Otis Ortcutt and wants to feel good about it, he identifies with the Mafia society rather than with the general public morality. Does this justify the killing? In fact, couldn't one justify anything simply by forming a small subculture that approved of it? Charles Manson would be morally pure in killing innocents simply by virtue of forming a little coterie. How large must the group be in order to be a legitimate subculture or society? Does it need 10 or 15 people? How about just 3? Come to think about it, why can't my burglary partner and I found our own society with a morality of its own? Of course, if my partner dies, I could still claim that I was acting from an originally social set of norms. But why can't I dispense with the interpersonal agreements altogether and invent my own morality? After all, morality, on this view, is only an invention anyway.

Conventionalist relativism seems to reduce to subjectivism. And subjectivism leads, as we have seen, to the demise of morality altogether.

Should one object that this is an instance of the *slippery slope fallacy,* let that person give an alternative analysis of what constitutes a viable social basis for generating valid moral principles. Perhaps we might agree (for the sake of argument, at least) that the very nature of morality entails two people making an agreement. This move saves the conventionalist from moral solipsism, but it still permits almost any principle at all to count as moral. And what's more, those principles can be thrown out and their contraries substituted for them as the need arises. If two or three people decide that they will make cheating morally acceptable for themselves at their university, via forming Cheaters Anonymous, then cheating becomes moral. Why not?

You should evaluate these arguments and see whether you find any problems therein. Have I been fair to the relativist? Why or why not? But whatever may be the case for ethical relativism, one wants to know whether a case can be made for its opposite, ethical objectivism.

The Case for Ethical Objectivism

First, we must distinguish between ethical objectivism and ethical absolutism. *Ethical absolutism* holds that a complete set of moral principles is always and universally binding. They can have no exceptions and cannot be overridden by other moral principles. *Ethical objectivism* holds that, although universally valid principles exist, they may be overridden by each other. For example, the objectivist may hold that it is a universal valid principle to keep your promise. But if after promising to meet me in my office at 3 p.m. today, you come across an injured person whom you may help, the principle of helping those in need may in this case override your duty to keep your promise. As Renford Bambrough puts it,

> To suggest that there is a right answer to a moral problem is at once to be accused of or credited with a belief in moral absolutes. But it is no more necessary to believe in moral absolutes in order to believe in moral objectivity than it is to believe in the existence of absolute space or absolute time in order to believe in the objectivity of temporal and spatial relations and of judgments about them.[4]

I turn back to my article.

On the objectivist's account, moral principles are what the Oxford University philosophy William D. Ross (1877–1971) refers to as *prima facie* principles, valid rules of action that should generally be adhered to but that may be overridden by another moral principle in cases of moral conflict. For example, a principle of justice may generally outweigh a principle of benevolence, but there are times when enormous good could be done by sacrificing a small amount of justice, so that an objectivist would be inclined to act according to the principle of benevolence. There may be some absolute or non-overridable principles (indeed the next principle I mention is probably one), but there need not be any or many for objectivism to be true.

If we can establish or show that it is reasonable to believe that there is, in some ideal sense, at least one objective moral principle that is binding on all people everywhere, then we shall have shown that relativism probably is false and that a limited objectivism is true. Actually, I believe there are many qualified general ethical principles that are binding on all rational beings, but one will suffice to refute relativism. The principle I've chosen is the following:

A. It is morally wrong to torture people for the fun of it.

I claim that this principle is binding on all rational agents, so that if some agent, S, rejects A, we should not let that affect our intuition that A is a true principle; rather, we should try to explain S's behavior as perverse, ignorant, or irrational instead. For example, suppose Adolf Hitler doesn't accept A. Should that affect our confidence in the truth of A? Is it not more reasonable to infer that Hitler is morally deficient, morally blind, ignorant, or irrational than to suppose that his noncompliance is evidence against the truth of A?

Suppose further that there is a tribe of "Hitlerites" somewhere who enjoy torturing people. Their whole culture accepts torturing others for the fun of it. Suppose that Mother Teresa or Mohatma Gandhi tries unsuccessfully to convince these sadists that they should stop torturing people altogether, and they respond by torturing them. Should this affect our confidence in A? Would it not be more reasonable to look for some explanation of Hitlerite behavior? For example, we might hypothesize that this tribe lacked the developed sense of sympathetic imagination that is necessary for the moral life. Or we might theorize that this tribe was on a lower evolutionary level than most *Homo sapiens*. Or we might simply conclude that the tribe was closer to a Hobbesian state of nature than most societies, and as such probably would not survive very long—or if it did, the lives of its people would be largely "solitary, poor, nasty, brutish and short," as is the case in the Ik culture in Northern Uganda, where the core morality has partly broken down.

But we need not know the correct answer as to why the tribe was in such bad shape in order to maintain our confidence in A as a moral principle. If A is a basic or core belief for us, we will be more likely to doubt the Hitlerites' sanity or ability to think morally than to doubt the validity of A.

We can perhaps produce other candidates for membership in our minimally basic objective moral set. For example:

1. Do not kill innocent people.
2. Do not cause unnecessary pain or suffering.
3. Do not steal or cheat.
4. Keep your promises and honor your contracts.
5. Do not deprive another person of his or her freedom.
6. Do justice, treating equals equally and unequals unequally.
7. Show gratitude for services rendered; that is, reciprocate.

8. Tell the truth.

9. Help other people

10. Obey just laws.

These ten principles are examples of the *core morality*, principles necessary for the good life. Fortunately, it isn't as though the ten principles were arbitrary, for we can give reasons why we believe these rules are necessary to any satisfactory social order. Principles like the Ten Commandments, the Golden Rule, justice (treating equals equally), telling the truth, keeping promises, and the like are central to the fluid progression of social interaction and the resolution of conflicts of interest (at least minimal morality is, even thought there may be more to morality than simply these kinds of concerns). For example, language itself depends on a general and implicit commitment to the principle of truth-telling. Accuracy of expression is a primitive form of truthfulness. Hence, every time we use words correctly to describe something or to communicate information, we are telling the truth. Without this behavior, language wouldn't be possible. Similarly, without the recognition of a rule of promise-keeping, contracts are of no avail and cooperation is less likely to occur. And without the protection of life and liberty, we could not secure our other goals.

A moral code would be adequate if it contained the principles of the core morality. But there could be more than one adequate moral code, with each one applying these principles differently. That is, although there may be a certain relativity to secondary principles (e.g., whether to opt for monogamy rather than polygamy, whether to include a principle of high altruism in the set of moral duties, whether to allocate more resources to medical care than to environmental concerns, whether to institute a law to drive on the left side of the road or the right side of the road), in every morality a certain core will remain, though applied somewhat differently because of differences in environment, belief, tradition, and the like.

The core moral rules are analogous to the set of nutrients necessary for a healthy diet. We need an adequate amount of each nutrient—some people need more of one than of another—but in prescribing a nutritional diet we don't have to set forth recipes, specific foods, place settings, or culinary habits. Gourmets will meet the requirements differently than ascetics and vegetarians, but the basic nutrients may be had by all without rigid regimentation or an absolute set of recipes.

Imagine that you have been miraculously transported to the dark kingdom of hell, and there you get a glimpse of the sufferings of the damned. What is their punishment? Well, they have eternal back itches, which ebb and flow constantly, but they cannot scratch their backs, for their arms are paralyzed in a frontal position. And so they writhe with itchiness through eternity. But just as you are beginning to feel the itch in your own back, you are suddenly transported to heaven. What do you see the in the kingdom of the blessed? Well, you see people with eternal back itches, who cannot scratch their own backs. But they are all smiling instead of writhing. Why? Because everyone has his or her arms stretched out to scratch someone else's back, and, so arranged in one big circle, a hell is turned into a heaven of ecstasy.

If we can imagine some states of affairs or cultures that are better than others in a way that depends on human action, we can ask what are those character traits that make them so. In our story, people in heaven, but not in hell, cooperate for the amelioration of suffering and the production of pleasure. These are very primitive goods, not sufficient for a full-blown morality, but they give us a hint as to the objectivity of morality. Moral goodness has something to do with the ameliorating of suffering, the resolution of conflict, and the promotion of human flourishing. If our heaven is really better than the eternal itchiness of hell, then whatever makes it so is constitutively related to moral rightness.

The Attraction of Ethical Relativism

Why, if this argument is sound, do so many people opt for ethical relativism? What accounts for its tremendous popularity, especially among college students? In my essay, I identify three reasons.

Why, then, is there such a strong inclination toward ethical relativism? I think there are three reasons, which need to be noted. First, the options are usually presented as though absolutism and relativism were the *only* alternatives, so conventionalism wins out against an implausible competitor. My student questionnaire reads as follows: "Are there any ethical absolutes, moral duties binding on all persons at all times, or are moral duties relative to culture? Is there any alternative to these two positions?" Hardly 3 percent of my students suggest a third position, and very few of them identify objectivism. Granted, it takes a little philosophical sophistication to make the crucial distinctions, and it is precisely for lack of this sophistication or reflection that relativism has procured its enormous prestige. But, as I have argued in this chapter, one can have an objective morality without being absolutist.

Second, our increased sensitivity to cultural relativism and the evils of ethnocentrism, which have plagued the relations of Europeans and Americans with those of other cultures, has made us conscious of the frailty of many aspects of our moral repertoire. This has led to a tendency to wonder "who's to judge what's really right or wrong?" However, the move from a reasonable cultural relativism, which rightly causes us to rethink our moral systems, to an ethical relativism, which causes us to give up the heart of morality altogether, is an instance of the fallacy of confusing factual or descriptive statements with normative ones. Cultural relativism doesn't entail ethical relativism. The very reason that we are against ethnocentrism constitutes the basis for affirming an objective moral system: that impartial reason draws us to it.

We may well agree that cultures differ and that we ought to be cautious in condemning what we don't understand, but this is no way need imply that there are not better and worse ways of living. We can understand and excuse, to some degree at least, those who differ from our best notions of morality, without abdicating the notion that cultures without such principles as justice, promise keeping, or protection of the innocent are morally poorer for those omissions.

A third reason, which has driven some to moral nihilism and others to relativism, is the decline of religion in Western society. As one of Fyodor Dostoevsky's characters has said, "If God is dead, all things are permitted." The person who has lost religious faith feels a deep vacuum and understandably confuses it with a moral vacuum; or, he or she may finally resign to a form of secular conventionalism. Such people reason that if there is no God to guarantee the validity of the moral order, there must not be a universal moral order. There is just radical cultural diversity and death at the end. But even if there turns out to be no God and no immortality, we still will want to live happy, meaningful lives during our four-score years on earth. If this is true, then it matters greatly which principles we live by, and those that win out in the test of time will be objectively valid principles.

Summary

Ethical relativism—the thesis that moral principles derive their validity from dependence on society or the individual—seem at first glance plausible but when scrutinized is seen to have some serious difficulties. Subjectivism seems to boil down to anarchistic individualism, and conventionalism must deal with the problems of the reformer, the question of defining a culture, and the whole enterprise of moral criticism.

In the second part of this chapter, arguments were presented for the thesis that "there are moral truths," principles belonging to the core morality. If this is correct, society will not long survive, and individuals will not flourish without these principles. Reason can discover these principles, and it is in our interest to promote them.

So who's to judge what's right and wrong? We are. We are to do so on the basis of the best reasoning we can bring forth and with sympathy and understanding.

FOR FURTHER REFLECTION

1. Go over Ladd's definition of ethical relativism given at the beginning of this chapter. Is it a good definition? Ask three other students whether they accept the thesis as defined by Ladd. You might put the question this way: "Are there any moral absolutes, or is morality completely relative?"

2. Examine Benedict's essay in order to assess its merits. Do you think her defense of ethical relativism is cogent? Why or why not?

3. Can you separate the anthropological claim of *cultural relativism* (different cultures have different moral principles) from *ethical relativism* (there are no universally valid moral principles)?

4. Explain the difference between moral absolutism and moral objectivism. What are prima facie moral principles or duties?

5. What are the main arguments for moral objectivism? Assess its merits.

6. In the reading "A Critique of Ethical Relativism," why does the author think that so many people are attracted to ethical relativism? Do you agree?

NOTES

1. John Ladd, *Ethical Relativism* (Belmont, CA: Wadsworth, 1973).
2. All remaining passages in this section are from Ruth Benedict, "Anthropology and the Abnormal," *Journal of General Psychology* 10 (1934): 59–82. Reprinted with permission.
3. All remaining passages, unless otherwise noted, are from Louis Pojman, "A Critique of Ethical Relativism," in *Ethical Theory: Classical and Contemporary Readings,* ed. Louis Pojman (Belmont, CA: Wadsworth, 1989).
4. Renford Bambrough, *Moral Skepticism and Moral Knowledge* (London: Routledge & Kegan Paul, 1979), 33.

FOR FURTHER READING

Fishkin, James. *Beyond Subjective Morality.* New Haven, CT: Yale University, 1984.

Ladd, John, ed. *Ethical Relativism.* Belmont, CA: Wadsworth, 1973. A good collection of basic readings.

Mackie, J. L. *Ethics: Inventing Right and Wrong.* London: Penguin Books, 1976. A defense of relativism.

Stace, W. T. *The Concept of Morals.* New York: Macmillan, 1937.

Sumner, William Graham. *Folkways.* New York: Ginn, 1906. A classic treatise in defense of ethical relativism.

Taylor, Paul. *Principles of Ethics.* Belmont, CA: Dickenson, 1975, Chapter 2.

Wellman, Carl. "The Ethical Implications of Cultural Relativity," *Journal of Philosophy* 60 (1963).

Westermarck, Edward. *Ethical Relativity.* New York: Harcourt Brace, 1932.

Williams, Bernard. *Morality.* New York: Harper Torchbooks, 1972. Contains a good discussion of ethical relativism.

Williams, Bernard. *Ethics and the Limits of Philosophy.* Cambridge, MA: Harvard University Press, 1985.

Wong, David. *Moral Relativity.* Berkeley: University of California Press, 1985. Defends a sophisticated version of ethical relativism, which has some objectivist elements.

29 ✶ Egoism: Why Should I Be Moral?

The good is good for you.

Statement of Socratic ethics

Why Should People Be Moral? Why Should I Be Moral?

These two questions should not be confused. The former question asks for a justification for the institution of morality, whereas the latter asks for reasons why one personally should be moral even when it does not appear to be in one's interest. I once knew a student, call him Joe, who cheated his way into medical school. Had he not cheated, by his own admission, he would not have been admitted into medical school, and, hence, would not have become a physician. For Joe, morality and self-interest were clearly at odds, and he chose self-interest. Sometimes we call a person who puts self-interest in front of morality an *egoist*. Joe was an egoist who was willing to violate moral norms for his own career. Joe's case concerns the second question, Why should I be moral? What reasons are there to argue against Joe's behavior? Why should Joe and you be moral when you can cheat?

Let's turn to the first question, Why should people be moral? Thomas Hobbes's account of the state of nature in the *Leviathan* offers a plausible answer to this question, supplying a minimal justification of morality in general. Unless there is a general adherence to a basic moral code that protects basic values, society itself would be impossible. Without that minimal morality, containing rules against killing the innocent, rape, robbery, the violation of agreements, and the like, we would exist in a "state of nature" deprived of common laws, reliable expectations, and security of person and possessions. There would be no incentive to mutual trust or cooperation but only chaotic anarchy as egoists tried to maximize personal utility. The result would be a "war of all against all" in which individual life is "solitary, poor, nasty, brutish and short."

Morality serves as an antidote to this state of nature and allows self-interested individuals to fulfill their needs and desires in a context of peace and cooperation. As such, morality is a mechanism for social control. It is in all of our interests to have a moral system that is generally adhered to so that we can maximize our individual life plans. Unless there is general adherence to the moral point of view, society will break down. Many sociologists have come to the same conclusion: Without a minimal morality, society will break down.[1]

This minimalist model of morality may not be the whole picture of morality, nor a very inspiring one, but it is certainly part of the picture, the part that virtually everyone agrees with. Whether morality also has intrinsic value, whether it is, as Immanuel Kant said, "a jewel that shines by its own light" is another matter, one that has to do with the second question about morality.

The second question is, Why should I be moral? Actually, this question may also be divided into two different questions: Why should I accept the moral point of view at all? Why should I be moral all the time—that is, even on those rare occasions when I can greatly profit from breaking the moral code? We'll examine both questions in this chapter.

Why shouldn't I *appear* moral and promote morality in society so that I can profit egotistically from the docility of the stupid public? Paul Taylor calls this the "Ultimate Question":

> There is one problem of moral philosophy that perhaps deserves, more
> than any other, to be called the Ultimate Question. It is the question
> of the rationality of the moral life itself. It may be expressed thus:
> Is the commitment to live by moral principles a decision grounded on
> reason or is it in the final analysis, an arbitrary choice?[2]

Is the choice of a moral way of life a rational choice or simply an arbitrary one? The question is first raised over two millennia ago in Plato's dialogue, *The Republic,* where Plato's brother, Glaucon, asks Socrates whether justice or moral goodness is something that is only a necessary evil. That is, he wants to know whether it is the case that it would be better if we could have complete freedom to indulge ourselves as we will, but since others could do the same, it is better to compromise and limit our acquisitive instincts. Glaucon tells the story of a shepherd named Gyges who comes upon a ring that at his behest makes him invisible. He uses it to escape the external sanctions of society, its laws and censure, and to serve his greed to the fullest. Let's turn to the text. Glaucon is telling Socrates what the common people believe about the origin and nature of justice or morality.

THE REPUBLIC

They say that to do injustice is, by nature, good; to suffer injustice, evil; but that the evil is greater than the good, and so when men have both done and suffered injustice and have had experience of both, not being able to avoid the one and obtain the other, they think that they had better agree among themselves to have neither. Hence there arise laws and mutual covenants; and that which is ordained by law is termed lawful and just. This people affirm to be the origin and nature of justice:—it is a mean or compromise, between the best of all, which is to do injustice and not be punished, and the worst of all, which is to suffer injustice without being able to retaliate; and justice, being at a middle point between these two, is tolerated not as a good, but as the lesser evil, and honored by reason of the inability of men to get away with injustice. For no man who is worthy to be called a man would ever submit to such an agreement if he were able to resist. He would be crazy if he did. Such is the received account, Socrates, of the nature and origin of justice.

Even those who practice justice do so against their will because they lack the power to do wrong. Try this thought experiment to show this. Suppose we could give both the just and the unjust person power to do as they wished. Let us watch and see where their desire will lead them. I think we would discover that the just and the unjust person travelled along the same road, following their interest, which all natures deem to be their good, and are only diverted into the path of justice by the force of law. The freedom which we are supposing may be most completely given to them in the form of such a power as is said to have been possessed by Gyges, the ancestor of Croesus the Lydian. According to the tradition, Gyges was a shepherd in the service of the king of Lydia; there was a great storm, and an earthquake made an opening in the earth at the place where he was feeding his flock. Amazed at the sight, he descended into the opening, where, among other marvels, he beheld a hollow brazen horse, having doors, at which he stooping and looking in saw a dead body of stature, as appeared to him, more than human, and having nothing on but a gold ring; this he took from the finger of the dead and reascended. Now the shepherds met together, according to custom, that they might send their monthly report about the flocks to the king; into their assembly he came having the ring on his finger, and as he was sitting among them he chanced to turn the collet of the ring inside his hand, when instantly he became invisible to the rest of the company and they began to speak of him as if he were no longer present. He was astonished at this, and again touching the ring he turned the collet outwards and reappeared; he made several trials of the ring, and always with the same result—when he turned the collet inwards he became invisible, when outwards he reappeared. Whereupon he contrived to be chosen one of the messengers who were sent to the court; where as soon as he arrived he seduced the queen, and with her help conspired against the king and slew him, and took the kingdom. Suppose now that there were two such magic rings, and the just put on one of them and the unjust the other; no man can be imagined to be of such an iron nature that he would stand fast in justice. No man would keep his hands off what was not his own when he

From: Plato, *The Republic*, trans. B. Jowett (Oxford, UK: Oxford University Press, 1897).

could safely take what he liked out of the market, or go into houses and lie with any one at his pleasure, or kill or release from prison whom he would, and in all respects be like a God among men. Then the actions of the just would be as the actions of the unjust; they would both come at last to the same point. And this we may truly affirm to be a great proof that a man is just, not willingly or because he thinks that justice is any good to him individually, but of necessity, for wherever any one thinks that he can safely be unjust, there he is unjust. For all men believe in their hearts that injustice is far more profitable to the individual than justice, and he who argues as I have been supposing, will say that they are right. If you could imagine any one obtaining this power of becoming invisible, and never doing any wrong or touching what was another's, he would be thought by the lookers-on to be a most wretched idiot, although they would praise him to one another's faces, and keep up appearances with one another from a fear that they too might suffer injustice. Enough of this.

Now, if we are to form a real judgment of the life of the just and unjust, we must isolate them; there is no other way; and how is the isolation to be effected? I answer: Let the unjust man be entirely unjust, and the just man entirely just; nothing is to be taken away from either of them, and both are to be perfectly furnished for the work of their respective lives. First, let the unjust be like other distinguished masters of craft; like the skillful pilot or physician, who knows intuitively his own powers and keeps within their limits, and who, if he fails at any point, is able to recover himself. So let the unjust make his unjust attempts in the right way, and lie hidden if he means to be great in his injustice (he who is found out is nobody): for the highest reach of injustice is: to be deemed just when you are not. Therefore I say that in the perfectly unjust man we must assume the most perfect injustice; there is to be no deduction, but we must allow him, while doing the most unjust acts, to have acquired the greatest reputation for justice. If he have taken a false step he must be able to recover himself; he must be one who can speak with effect, if any of his deeds come to light, and who can force his way where force is required by his courage and strength, and command of money and friends. And at his side let us place the just man in his nobleness and simplicity, wishing, as Aeschylus says, to be and not to seem good. There must be no seeming, for if he seem to be just he will be honoured and rewarded, and then we shall not know whether he is just for the sake of justice or for the sake of honours and rewards; therefore, let him be clothed in justice only, and have no other covering; and he must be imagined in a state of life the opposite of the former. Let him be the best of men, and let him be thought the worst; then he will have been put to the proof; and we shall see whether he will be affected by the fear of infamy and its consequences. And let him continue thus to the hour of death; being just and seeming to be unjust. When both have reached the uttermost extreme, the one of justice and the other of injustice, let judgment be given which of them is the happier of the two.

Now, Glaucon wants to know, if you were forced to make a choice between living either of these lives, which life would you choose to live: the life of the unjust man who seems just and is incredibly successful *or* the life of the just man who seems unjust and is incredibly unsuccessful? Is it better to be bad but seem good than to be good but to seem bad? Which would *you* choose?[3]

I don't know what you would choose, but let's consider two initial reasons for choosing to live the life of the seemingly unjust *but* good man. The first is Socrates' answer to Glaucon—that, despite appearances, we should choose the life of the "unsuccessful" just person because it's to our advantage to be moral. He draws attention to the idea of the harmony of the soul and argues that immorality corrupts the inner person, whereas virtue purifies the inner person, so that one is happy or unhappy in exact proportion to one's moral integrity. Asking to choose between being morally good and immoral is like asking to choose between being healthy and sick. Even if the immoral person has material benefits, he cannot enjoy them in his awful state, whereas the good person may find joy in the simple pleasures despite poverty and ill fortune.

But is Socrates correct? Is the harm that the good person suffers compensated by the innate goodness of his soul? And is the good that the bad person experiences outweighed by the evil of his heart? Perhaps we don't know enough about the hearts of people to be certain which is better off. But perhaps we know of (or can imagine) bad people who seem to flourish despite their wickedness. They may not completely fool us, but they seem satisfied with the lives they are living, moderately happy in their business and personal triumphs. And perhaps we know of some good people who are really very sad despite their goodness. They wish they had meaningful work, a loving family, friends, and shelter. They don't and their virtue is insufficient to produce happiness. Some good people are unhappy, and some bad people seem to be happy. So the Socratic answer on the health–sickness analogy may not be correct.

The second answer to Glaucon is the religious response: God will reward and punish people on the basis of their virtue or vice. The promise is of eternal bliss for the virtuous and hard times for the vicious. God sees all and rewards with absolute justice according to our moral merit so that, despite what may be their differing fates here on Earth, the good person is infinitely better off than the bad. If ethical monotheism of this sort is true, it is in our self-interest to be moral. The good is really good for you. The religious person has good reason to choose the life of the destitute saint.

We will take up the relationship of religion to morality in a later chapter, but we can say this much about the problem: Unfortunately, we do not know for certain whether there is a God or life after death. Many sincere people doubt or disbelieve religious doctrines, and it is not easy to prove them wrong. Even the devout have doubts and probably cannot be sure of the truth of the doctrine of life after death and the existence of God. In any case, millions of moral people are not religious, and the question of the relationship between self-interest and morality is a pressing one. Can a moral philosopher give a secular answer to secularists as to why we should choose to be moral all the time?

The Paradox of Morality and Self-Interest

Initially, we seem to run into a paradox in trying to discuss this issue. On many contemporary accounts of moral duty, one only has a duty to do some act A if one has sufficient reason to do A. But this seems to generate a paradox of asking for self-interested reasons about why we should prefer morality when it conflicts with our self-interest. What David Gauthier has called the "paradox of morality and advantage"[4] goes like this: If it is morally right to do an act, then it must be reasonable to do it. If it is reasonable to do the act, then it must be in my interest to do it. However, sometimes the requirements of morality are incompatible with the requirements of self-interest. Hence, we have an apparent contradiction: It both must be reasonable and need not be reasonable to meet our moral duties.

Since morality is not always in our self-interest, one must wonder if it is not simply a delusion, an artifice to keep us in place. If it is a delusion, the rational person will be an egoist and promote morality for everyone else but violate it whenever he or she can safely do so.

To get us started in our attempt to solve this puzzle, consider the case of the Prisoner's Dilemma. The secret police in another country have arrested two of our spies, Sam and Sue. They both know that if they adhere to their agreement to keep silent, the police will be able to hold them for 4 months; however, if they violate their agreement and confess that they are spies, they will each get 6 years in prison. However, if one adheres and the other violates, the one who adheres will get 9 years, and the one who confesses will be let go immediately. We might represent their plight with this matrix (the figures on the left represent the amount of time Sam will spend in prison under the various alternatives, and the figures on the right represent the amount of time that Sue will spend in prison under those alternatives):

		Sue	
		Adheres	*Violates*
	Adheres	4 months, 4 months	9 years, 0 time
Sam			
	Violates	0 time, 9 years	6 years, 6 years

Initially, Sam reasons that either Sue will adhere to or violate the agreement. If Sue adheres, then I should violate. If Sue violates, then I should violate it. Therefore, I should violate. But Sue reasons exactly the same way about Sam: Either he will adhere or he will violate. If he adheres, I should violate. If he violates, then I should still violate. Therefore, I should violate. If both use reason in this way, however, they will obtain the second worst-off position, 6 years each, which we know to be pretty awful. If they could only come to an agreement, they could each do better—get off with only 4 months. But how can they do that?

If it is only a one-time shot, it is difficult to be sure that the other person will cooperate, but suppose we switch to an *iterated* version of the Prisoner's

		What you do	
		Cooperate	**Cheat**
What I do	**Cooperate**	Fairly good **REWARD** (for mutual cooperation) e.g., $300	Very bad **SUCKER'S PAYOFF** e.g., $100 fine
	Cheat	Very good **TEMPTATION** (to cheat) e.g., $500	Fairly bad **PUNISHMENT** (for mutual cheating) e.g., $10 fine

Figure 29.1

Dilemma. Robert Axelrod has developed such a game.[5] There are two players and a banker who pays out money or fines the players. Each player has two cards labeled COOPERATE and CHEAT. Each move consists of each player simultaneously laying down one of his cards. Suppose you and I are playing "against" one another. There are four possible outcomes:

1. We both play COOPERATE. The banker pays each of us $300. We are rewarded nicely.
2. We both play CHEAT. The banker fines each of us $10. We are punished for mutual defection.
3. You play COOPERATE and I play CHEAT. The banker pays me $500 (temptation money), and you are fined $100 (a sucker fine).
4. I play COOPERATE and you CHEAT. The banker fines me $100 and pays you $500. This is the reverse of outcome 3.

Figure 29.1 shows the payoff matrix.

The game goes on indefinitely until the banker calls it quits. Theoretically, I could win a lot of money by always cheating. After twenty moves, I could hold the sum of $10,000—that is, if you are sucker enough to continue to play COOPERATE, in which case you will be short $2000. If you are rational, you won't do that. If we both continually cheat, we'll each end up with minus $200 after twenty rounds.

So suppose we act like reciprocators and act on the principle, "Always cooperate if the other fellow does and cheat only if he does first." If we both adhere to this principle, we'll each end up with $6000 after our twenty rounds—not a bad reward! And we have the prospects of winning more if we continue to act rationally—that is, like reciprocators.

We may conclude that rational self-interest over the long run advises Sam and Sue (and you and I) to adhere to their agreement. It may not be the optimal choice for each of us (exploiting the situation would bring that about, but rational people won't stand for that), but it is a very good second best.

As Gauthier puts it, "Morality is a system of principles such that it is advantageous for everyone if everyone accepts and acts on it, yet acting on the system of principles requires that some persons perform disadvantageous acts."[6] The Prisoner's Dilemma illustrates that morality is the due we each have to pay to keep the minimal good we have in a civilized society. We have to bear some disadvantage in loss of freedom (analogous to paying membership dues in an important organization) so that we can have both protection from the onslaughts of chaos and promotion of the good life.

Since an orderly society is no small benefit, the egoist will allow his or her freedom to be limited. Thus, no real paradox exists between morality and self-interest in this sense. We allow some disadvantage in order to reap an overall, long-run advantage.

Still, it may be conceded that this is not quite the same as accepting the moral point of view, for the prudent person will still break the moral code whenever he or she can do so without getting detected and unduly undermining the whole system. The clever amoralist takes into account the overall consequences on the social system and cheats whenever a careful cost–benefit analysis warrants it. With the proceeds of his embezzlement, he will perhaps give a tithe to moral education so that more people will be more dedicated to the moral code. That in turn will allow him to cheat with greater impunity.

So although the Prisoner's Dilemma informs us that even the amoralist must generally adhere to the moral code, it doesn't tell us why he or why I should be moral all the time, why I should not act egoistically when it is in my self-interest to do so. Let's look more closely, then, at the *paradox of morality and advantage:*

- If it is morally right to do an act, then it must be reasonable to do it. If it is reasonable to do the act, then it must be in my interest to do it. But sometimes the requirements of morality are incompatible with the requirements of self-interest. Hence, we have a seeming contradiction: It both must be reasonable and need not be reasonable to meet our moral duties.

The problematic premise seems to be the second sentence, which we will label SI to stand for the thesis that reasons for acting must appeal to self-interest.

SI: If it is reasonable to do act A, then it must be in my interest to do A.

Might we not doubt SI? Could we not have good reasons to do something that went against our interest? Suppose Lisa sees a child about to get run over by a car and, intending to save the child, hurls herself at the boy, while fully aware of the danger to herself. Lisa's interest is in no way tied up with the life of that child, but she still tries to save his life at great risk to her own. Isn't this a case of having a reason to go against one's self-interest?

I think that it is such a reason. SI seems unduly based on the doctrine of **psychological egoism,** which holds that we can never act from any motive except a selfish one, a doctrine that is unsupported by reason and experience as it is unfalsifiable. (If I say Mother Teresa's motive for helping the poor was altruistic, the egoist can claim that she had hidden motives that she was unaware of—but how does he know this?) It is sheer dogmatism. Sometimes we have reasons to do things that go against our perceived self-interest. The nonreligious person who gives away needed funds to help the poor or hungry does so. The student who refrains from cheating when he knows that he could easily escape detection apparently does so. Being faithful, honest, generous, and kind often require us to act against our interest.

But you may object to this reasoning in the following way: "It is perhaps *against* our immediate or short-term interest to be faithful, honest, generous, or kind, but really in the long run it is likely to be in our best interest. The moral and altruistic life promises benefits and satisfactions that are not available to the immoral and stingy."

In an insightful article, the late Gregory Kavka speaks of *internal sanctions* that may play a powerful role in motivating us to be moral even when it is not in our perceived self-interest.[7]

A RECONCILIATION PROJECT

There is no entirely satisfactory label for the positive internal sanctions, the agreeable feelings that typically accompany moral action and the realization that one has acted rightly, justly, or benevolently. So let us opt for the vague term "the satisfactions of morality." Moral people have long testified as to the strength and value of such satisfactions, often claiming that they are the most agreeable satisfactions we can attain. This last claim goes beyond what is necessary for our purposes. All we need to assert is that there are special significant pleasures or satisfactions that accompany regular moral action and the practice of a moral way of life that are not available to (unreformed) immoralists and others of their ilk. For if this is so, then the forgoing of these potential satisfactions must be charged as a significant opportunity cost of choosing an immoral way of life.

Can an individual have it both ways, enjoying the psychic benefits of morality while living an immoral life? He could, perhaps, if he lived immorally while sincerely believing he was not. Certain fanatics who selflessly devote themselves to false moral ideals, such as purifying the human race by eugenics or pleasing God by destroying nonbelievers, might fall into this category. Of more concern in the present context, however, is the individual who adopts morality as a provisional way of life or policy while planning to abandon it if a chance to gain much by immorality should arise later. This person, we would say, is not truly moral, and it is hard to believe that he would perceive himself to be, so long as his motives are purely prudential and his commitment to

From: Gregory Kavka, "A Reconciliation Project," in *Morality, Reason, and Truth,* ed. D. Copp and D. Zimmerman (Lanham, MD: Rowman and Allanheld, 1984).

morality is only conditional. In any case, we would not expect him to experience the satisfactions of morality in the same way, or to the same degree, as the genuinely moral individual who is aware of the (relative) purity of his motives and the nature and depth of his commitment.

Note that if this is so we have arrived at a paradox of self-interest: *being* purely self-interested will not always best serve one's interests. For there may be certain substantial personal advantages that accrue only to those who are not purely self-interested, such as moral persons. Thus it may be rational for you, as a purely self-interested person, to cease being one if you can, to transform yourself into a genuinely moral person. And once you are such a person, you will not be disposed to act immorally, under risk, whenever so doing promises to maximize personal expected utility.

Kavka concedes that the lesson of this paradox does not apply to those incapable of learning to enjoy the satisfactions of morality or to those for whom the cost of becoming moral might be too high.

In sum: If one has been raised in a normal social context, one will feel deep psychic distress at the thought of harming others or doing what is immoral and deep psychic satisfaction in being moral. For these persons, the combination of internal and external sanctions may well bring prudence and morality close together. This situation may not apply, however, to persons not brought up in a moral context. Should this dismay us? No, Kavka says: "[We should not perceive] an immoralist's gloating that it does not pay him to be moral . . . as a victory over us. It is more like the pathetic boast of a deaf person that he saves money because it does not pay him to buy opera records." He is a Scrooge who takes pride in not having to buy Christmas presents because he has no friends.

We want to say, then, that the choice of the moral point of view is not an arbitrary choice but a rational one. Some kinds of lives are better than others. A human life without the benefits of morality is not an ideal or fulfilled life. It lacks too much that makes for human flourishing.

The occasional acts through which we sacrifice our self-interest within the general flow of a satisfied life are unavoidable risks, which reasonable people will take. You might lose by betting on morality, but you are almost certain to lose if you bet against it. Thus, SI must be restated as SIM (self-interest modified):

> SIM: If it is reasonable to choose a life plan L, which includes the possibility of doing act A, then it must be in my interest (or at least not against it) to choose L, even though A itself may not be in my self-interest.

Now there is no longer anything paradoxical in doing something not in one's interest. Although the individual moral act may occasionally conflict with one's self-interest, the entire life plan in which the act is embedded and from which it flows is not against the individual's self-interest.

Suppose you can cheat a company or a country out of some money. It would leave you materially better off, but it would be contrary to the *form of life* to which you have committed yourself and that has generally been rewarding.

Furthermore, character counts and habits harness us to predictable behavior. Once we obtain the kind of character necessary for the moral life, once we become *virtuous,* we will not be able to turn morality off and on like a faucet. When we yield to temptation, we will experience alienation in going against this well-formed character. The guilt will torment us greatly, diminishing any ill-gotten gains.

Thus, the paradox is resolved and Glaucon's question has been successfully answered. Not only is it sometimes reasonable to act for reasons that do not immediately involve our self-interest, but, more important, a life without such spontaneous or deliberate altruism may be one not worth living.

Of course, there's no guarantee that morality will yield success and happiness. The good person, in Glaucon's story at the beginning of this chapter, is not happy. In a sense, morality is a rational gamble; it cannot guarantee success or happiness. Life is tragic. The good fail and the bad seem to prosper, yet the moral person is prepared for this eventuality. John Rawls sums up vulnerability of the moral life in this way:

> A just person is not prepared to do certain things, and so in the face of evil circumstances he may decide to chance death rather than to act unjustly. Yet although it is true enough that for the sake of justice a man may lose his life where another would live to a later day, the just man does what all things considered he most wants; in this sense he is not defeated by ill fortune, the possibility of which he foresaw. The question is on a par with the hazards of love; indeed, it is simply a special case. Those who love one another, or who acquire strong attachments to persons and to forms of life, at the same time become liable to ruin: their love makes them hostages to misfortune and the injustice of others. Friends and lovers take great chances to help each other; and members of families willingly do the same. . . . Once we love we are vulnerable.[8]

We can take steps to lessen the vulnerability by working together for a more moral society, by bringing up our children with keener moral sensitivities and good habits so that there are fewer Gyges around. We can establish a more just society so that people are less tempted to cheat and more inclined to cooperate, since they see that we are all working together for a happier world, a mutual back-scratching world, if you like. In general, the more just the political order, the more likely it will be that the good will prosper, the more likely that self-interest and morality will converge.

Summary

The question "Why should people be moral?" is very different from the question "Why should I be moral when I can profit from immorality?" The answer to the first question is, It is in all of our interest that people generally adhere to moral principles. We may say that morality, by definition, consists of those principles that if almost everyone follows, almost everyone will be better off—at least most of the time. The second questions, "Why should I be moral when I can profit from immorality?" is more difficult to answer. The answer partly consists of the fact that you can't simply turn your moral dispositions on and off like a water faucet. If you are a moral person, you will hate immorality to such a degree that you seldom, if ever, will really profit from immoral behavior. In the long run, it is not in your self-interest to be immoral at all. Finally, we noted that the more society becomes just, the greater the chances are that the good flourish and the bad are punished. So morality can defend itself. But if it turns out that God exists, sees all our actions, and will reward us according to our deeds, the question "Why be moral?" gets an even more firm answer. We will consider the relationship between religion and morality in Chapter 32.

FOR FURTHER REFLECTION

1. Consider the following situation proposed by John Hospers:

Suppose someone whom you have known for years and who has done many things for you asks a favor of you which will take considerable time and trouble when you had planned on doing something else. You have no doubt that helping out the person is what you ought to do, but you ask yourself all the same *why* you ought to do it. Or suppose you tell a blind news vendor that it's a five-dollar bill you are handing him, and he gives you four dollars and some coins in change, whereas actually you handed him only a one-dollar bill. Almost everyone would agree that such an act is wrong. But some people who agree may still ask, "Tell me why I shouldn't do it just the same."[9]

What would you say to such people?

2. Hospers believes that the question "Why should I be moral?" can only be answered by the response "Because it's right." Self-interested answers just won't do. They come down to asking for self-interested reasons for going against my self-interest, which is a self-contradiction. Is Hospers correct about this, or is there something more we can say about being moral?

3. At the beginning of this chapter, I mentioned the student who cheated his way into medical school. Would you want to be one of his patients? What does this tell you about the reasons to be moral?

4. Whether you believe that there are always self-interested reasons for being moral will largely depend on whether and to what degree you believe that some forms of life are objectively better than others. Are all forms of life equally valid, or are some objectively better than others? Explain your answer.

5. Could a person understand that something was his or her duty and yet not be motivated to do it? What is the connection between having a duty and being motivated to do it? If there is no necessary connection, then Kant would seem to be wrong when he wrote that "ought implies can." According to Kant's formula, if I *cannot* do act A, I have no duty to do A. Kant seems to have a point. It does seem odd to say that I have a duty to do what it is impossible for me to do. On the other hand, if I must be motivated to do X before I can be said to have an obligation to do X, why don't I always do my duty? Is there a way out of this paradox?

6. Consider the following dialogue written by one of my students.

MOM & DAD: Johnny, now why did you steal that candy bar?

JOHNNY: Cause I wanted to.

M & D: Don't you think that it is wrong to steal?

J: I don't know.

M & D: Well, it *is* wrong to steal.

J: Why? Can you give me a reason?

M & D: Well there are several reasons why you shouldn't steal . . .

J: Oh, yeah—cause God says so. Well, I don't believe in God, so try again.

M & D: No—there are other reasons. For one, you cannot be truly happy unless you are a good person.

J: Sure. That's what everyone says. And you know why? So that everyone else will be good; but as soon as someone can get away with something bad, they would probably do it—isn't that why you cheat on your taxes? In any case, isn't that an odd reason for why to be good? If I should be good because it will make me happy, then you are telling me to put happiness over goodness. Well, that is exactly why I steal. Understand?

M & D: But don't you understand that it is not only your happiness that you should be concerned with, but everyone's? We should act so as to maximize everyone's net happiness.

J: Well, that candy bar gave me a lot of happiness. And who suffered? No one. Maybe some millionaire lost fifty cents, but even then, he will never know, and even if he did know he would just write it off as a tax break. So the net happiness was greater than the net unhappiness. Thanks for the argument; can I go get another one?

M & D: But selfishness is wrong.

J: Why?

M & D: Because to be fully human, you have to care about others.

J: So, when I get older, I will get married and have children and I will care about my family. I can appreciate that I need to share and love others in this way to be happy and fulfilled. But I don't see why I should make a motto in my life, "Everywhere and anywhere, in all situations, inside and outside, day or night, I will always be unselfish." Forget it. No one does that. So, ok, you've got a point—I probably cannot be happy unless I honor my interpersonal agreements. But I get to choose with whom I make those, and I certainly have not made one with any grocery store.

M & D: No, no. You do not understand. What if everyone acted like you? Then the owner *would* be hurt. In fact, if everyone acted like you, then there would be no more stores, so you would have no more candy to steal. Therefore, your activity is contradictory: If you think that stealing candy is good, then you shouldn't do it or else there will be no more candy to steal.

J: That is a bunch of nonsense if I ever heard any. Why does the fact that I like to steal candy imply that I think that everyone else should? Just the opposite. I am quite happy that you all think stealing is bad. I fully encourage you in your ethical pursuits. I enthusiastically applaud your integrity. Now you still haven't told me why I shouldn't appear to be good and do whatever I want when I can get away with it.

M & D: Don't you have a conscience?

J: A what?

M & D: A conscience, a voice in your head that tells you not to do something bad, or when you do something bad it makes you regret it.

J: No, I ain't got no voices in my head. Do you?

M & D: Well, if you try hard, you can develop your conscience. Just the fact that you can distinguish between good and bad means that you have one—it's just not developed.

J: Hey, the only reason I use the words *good* and *bad* are because everyone else uses them. You don't reckon that I think stealing is *really* bad, do you? And why would I want to develop something that makes me feel bad? Sounds pretty dumb.

M & D: But don't you see? Again you are recognizing a distinction between good and bad. There is a concept of morality within you.

J: Yeah, maybe. I have had sixteen years of social conditioning. It will take me a while before I can clean my brain of it all.

M & D: No, think about this. You understand that certain things make you happy and that others do not. Right?

J: Sure.

M & D: And you're interested in maximizing your own happiness, right?

J: Sounds good.

M & D: Well, isn't it the case that some pleasures are better than others? Once you start thinking about it, you come to realize that to be happy you have to live life in a certain way.

J: Well, whatever works for you. Believe me, I in no way want to discourage anyone else from being moral.

How would you respond to Johnny?

NOTES

1. See Steven Lukes, *Emile Durkeim: His Life and Work* (New York: Harper & Row, 1972), Chapter 21; and Brigette Burger and Peter Burger, *The War over the Family* (New York: Doubleday, 1983).

2. Paul Taylor, *Problems of Moral Philosophy* (Belmont, CA: Dickenson, 1978), 483.

3. In case you think that this story is artificial, let me cite a quote (given to me by an anonymous reviewer) from Joseph Kennedy on the prospects of his son, John F. Kennedy, becoming a congressman. When his daughter expressed doubt that John could ever be a successful congressman, he replied, "You must always remember, it isn't what you are, but what people *think* you are, that counts." In *The Kennedys,* by Collier and Horowitz (New York: Summit Books, 1984).

4. David Gauthier, "Morality and Advantage," *Philosophical Review* 76 (1967); reprinted in *Ethical Theory: Classical and Contemporary Readings,* ed. L. Pojman (Belmont, CA: Wadsworth, 1989).

5. Robert Axelrod, *The Evolution of Cooperation* (New York: Basic Books, 1984); and Robert Axelrod and William Hamilton, "The Evolution of Cooperation," *Science* 211 (1981): 1390–1396.

6. Gauthier, "Morality and Advantage."

7. Kavka attempts to resolve the paradox and reconcile prudence with morality. Beginning with an analysis of a Hobbesian approach to the problem (one similar to Gauthier's), Kavka argues that this sort of approach, though illuminating and partially correct, "cannot take us far enough" and ultimately is invalid because of its assumption of psychological egoism, which assumes that all motivation must be self-interested. What needs to be added to the Hobbesian picture is an account of internal sanctions, the kind of built-in constraints that are an important part of socialization.

8. John Rawls, *A Theory of Justice* (Cambridge, MA: Harvard University Press, 1971), 573. Rawls goes on to add that "in a well-ordered society, being a good person (and in particular having an effective sense of justice) is indeed a good for that person" (p. 577).

9. John Hospers, *Human Conduct* (New York: Harcourt Brace Jovanovich, 1961), 174.

FOR FURTHER READING

Baier, Kurt. *The Moral Point of View.* Ithaca, NY: Cornell University Press, 1959.

Frankena, William. *Thinking About Morality.* Ann Arbor: University of Michigan Press, 1980.

Gauthier, David, ed. *Morality and Rational Self-Interest.* Englewood Cliffs, NJ: Prentice Hall, 1970.

Gauthier, David. *Morality by Agreement.* Oxford, UK: Clarendon Press, 1986.

Hospers, John. *Human Conduct: An Introduction to the Problems of Ethics.* New York: Harcourt Brace Jovanovich, 1961.

Kavka, Gregory. "A Reconciliation Project." In *Morality, Reason, and Truth.* Edited by D. Copp and D. Zimmerman. Lanham, MD: Rowman and Allanheld, 1984.

Nielsen, Kai. "Is 'Why Should I Be Moral?' an Absurdity?" *Australasian Journal of Philosophy* 36 (1958).

Nielsen, Kai. "Why Should I Be Moral?" *Methodos* 15, no. 59–60 (1963). This comprehensive article appears in several anthologies.

Phillips, D. Z. "Does It Pay to Be Good?" *Proceedings of the Aristotelian Society* 65 (1964–1965).

Richards, David. *A Theory of Reasons for Action.* Oxford, UK: Oxford University Press, 1971.

Taylor, Richard. *Good and Evil.* New York: Macmillan, 1970. Especially Chapter 5.

30 ❧ Utilitarianism

The Greatest Happiness for the Greatest Number.

Francis Hutcheson

Suppose you are on an island with a dying millionaire. As he lies dying, he entreats you for one final favor: "I've dedicated my whole life to baseball and have gotten endless pleasure, and some pain, rooting for the New York Yankees for 50 years. Now that I am dying, I want to give all my assets, $2 million, to the Yankees. Would you take this money [he indicates a box containing the money in large bills] back to New York and give it to the New York Yankees' owner, so that he can buy better players?" You agree to carry out his wish, at which point a huge smile of relief and gratitude breaks out on his face as he expires in your arms. After returning to New York, you see a newspaper advertisement placed by your favorite charity, the World Hunger Relief Organization (whose integrity you do not doubt), pleading for $2 million to be used to save 100,000 people dying of starvation in East Africa. Not only will the $2 million save their lives, but also it will be used to purchase small technology and the kinds of fertilizers necessary to build a sustainable economy. You reconsider your promise to the dying Yankee fan in the light of this great need. What should you do with the money?

Or suppose two men are starving to death on a raft floating in the Pacific Ocean. One day they discover some food in an inner compartment of a box on the raft. They have reason to believe that the food will be sufficient to keep one of them alive until the raft reaches a certain island where help is available, but if they share the food both of them will most likely die. Now one man is a brilliant scientist who has in his mind the cure for cancer; the other man is undistinguished.

453

Otherwise, there is no relevant difference between the two men. What is the morally right thing to do? Share the food and hope against the odds for a miracle? Flip a coin to decide which man gets the food? Give the food to the scientist?

What is the right thing to do in these kinds of situations? Consider some traditional moral principles and see if they help you come to a decision. One principle often given to guide action is "Let your conscience be your guide." I recall this principle with fondness, for it was the one my father taught me at an early age, and it still echoes in my mind. But does it help here? No. Conscience is primarily a function of our upbringing; people's consciences will speak to them in different ways according to how they were brought up. Depending on upbringing, some people feel no conscience qualms about terrorist acts while others feel the torments of conscience over stepping on a gnat. Suppose your conscience tells you to give the money to the Yankees and my conscience tells me to give the money to the World Hunger Relief Organization (WHRO). How can we ever discuss the matter? If conscience is the end of the matter, we're left mute.

If you decide to act on the principle of promise keeping or not-stealing in the case of the millionaire's money or if you decide to share the food in the case of the two men on the life raft on the basis of the principle of fairness or equal justice, then you adhere to a type of moral theory called *deontology.*

If, on the other hand, you decide to give the money to the WHRO to save an enormous number of lives and restore economic solvency to the region, you side with a type of theory called *teleology,* or **teleological ethics.** Similarly, if you decide to give the food to the scientist because he would probably do more good with his life, you side with the teleologist.

Traditionally, two major types of ethical systems have dominated the field, one in which the locus of value is the act or kind of act and the other in which the locus of value is the outcome, or consequences, of the act. The former type of theory is called *deontological* (from the Greek *deon,* meaning "duty" and *logos* meaning "logic"), and the latter is called *teleological* (from the Greek *teleos,* meaning "having reached one's end" or "finished"). Whereas teleological systems see the ultimate criterion of morality in some nonmoral value that results from acts, deontological systems see certain features in the act itself as having intrinsic value. For example, a teleologist would judge whether lying was morally right or wrong by the consequences it produced, but a deontologist would see something intrinsically wrong in the very act of lying. In this chapter, we consider the dominant version of teleological ethics, utilitarianism. In Chapter 31, we'll examine Immanuel Kant's ethics as the major form of **deontological ethics.** Let's turn to teleological ethics.

As we mentioned earlier, a teleologist is a person whose ethical decision making aims solely at maximizing nonmoral goods, such as pleasure, happiness, welfare, and the amelioration of suffering. That is, the standard of right or wrong action for the teleologist is the comparative consequences of the available actions. The act that is right produces the best consequences. Whereas the deontologist is concerned only with the rightness of the act itself, the teleologist asserts that an act cannot have intrinsic worth. That is, though there is something intrinsically bad about the *act* of lying for the deontologist, for the teleologist the only thing wrong with lying is the bad *consequences* it produces. If you can reasonably calculate that a lie will do even slightly more good than telling the truth, you have an obligation to lie.

We have already noticed one type of teleological ethics: **ethical egoism,** the view that the act producing the most amount of good for the agent is the right act. Egoism is teleological ethics narrowed to the agent himself or herself. **Utilitarianism,** on the other hand, is a universal teleological system. It calls for the maximization of goodness in society or the greatest goodness for the greatest number. We turn now to an examination of utilitarianism.

What Is Utilitarianism?

One of the earliest examples of utilitarian reasoning is found in Sophocles' *Antigone* (circa 440 BCE), where we find King Creon faced with the tragic task of sacrificing his beloved niece, Antigone, who had violated the law by performing funeral rites over her brother, Polynices. Creon judges that it is necessary to sacrifice one person rather than expose his society to the dangers of rebelliousness—regardless of their intrinsic merit. "And whoever places a friend above the good of his own country, I have no use for him . . . I could never stand by silent, watching destruction march against our city, putting safety to rout, nor could I ever make that man a friend of mine who menaces our country. Remember this: our country is our safety."[1]

In the New Testament, Caiphas the High Priest advises the Council to deliver Jesus to the Romans for execution: "You know nothing at all; you do not understand that it is expedient that one man should die for the people, and that the whole nation should not perish" (John 11:50). Sometimes Jesus himself is interpreted as adhering to utilitarianism, as when he breaks the Sabbath laws in order to do good, saying that "the Sabbath was made for man, not man for the Sabbath" (Mark 2:27).

However, as a moral philosophy, utilitarianism begins with the work of Scottish philosophers Francis Hutcheson (1694–1746), David Hume (1711–1776), and Adam Smith (1723–1790) and comes into its classical stage in the persons of English social reformers Jeremy Bentham (1748–1832) and John Stuart Mill (1806–1873). They were the nonreligious ancestors of 20th-century secular humanists, optimistic about human nature and our ability to solve our problems without recourse to providential grace. Engaged in a struggle for legal as well as moral reform, they were impatient with the rule-bound character of law and morality in 18- and 19-century Great Britain and tried to make the law serve human needs and interests.

Bentham's concerns were practical more than theoretical. He worked for a thorough reform of what he regarded as an irrational and outmoded legal system. He might well have paraphrased Jesus, making his motto "Morality and law were made for man, not man for morality and law." What good was adherence to outworn deontological rules that served no useful purpose, that only kept the poor from enjoying a better life, and that supported punitive codes only serving to satisfy sadistic lust for vengeance?

The changes the utilitarians proposed were not done in the name of justice, for even justice must serve the human good. The poor were to be helped, women were to be liberated, and the criminal rehabilitated if possible, because by so doing we could bring about more utility: Ameliorate suffering and promote more pleasure or happiness.

Their view of punishment is a case in point. Whereas deontologists believe in retribution—that all the guilty should be punished in proportion to the gravity of their crime—the utilitarians' motto is "Don't cry over spilt milk!" They believe that the guilty should only be punished if the punishment would serve some deterrent (or preventive) purpose. Rather than punish John in exact proportion to the heinousness of his deed, we ought to find the punishment that will serve as the optimum deterrent.

The proper amount of punishment to be inflicted upon the offender is the amount that will do the most good (or least harm) to all those who will be affected by it. The measure of harm inflicted on the criminal, John, should be preferable to the harm avoided by fixing that penalty rather than one slightly lower. If punishing John will do no good (because John is not likely to commit the crime again and no one will be deterred by the punishment), John should go free.

What are the implications of this theory? Some have claimed that it is the *threat* of punishment that is the important thing. Every act of punishment is to that extent an admission of the failure of the threat. If the threat were successful, there would be no punishment to justify. Of course, utilitarians believe that, given human failing, punishment is vitally necessary as a deterrent, so the guilty will seldom if ever be allowed to go free. Also, unless there is a history of punishment having been carried out on offenders, the threat will have no deterrent force. But the logic of deterrence remains in place: It is the threat that does the motivating, deterring would-be offenders.

There are two main features of utilitarianism: the *consequentialist principle* (or its teleological aspect) and the *utility principle* (or its **hedonic** aspect). The consequentialist principle states that the rightness or wrongness of an act is determined by the goodness or badness of the results that flow from it. It is the end, not the means, that counts. The end justifies the means. The utility principle states that the only thing that is good in itself is some specific type of state (for example, pleasure, happiness, welfare). Hedonistic utilitarianism views pleasure as the sole good and pain as the only evil. Let's now turn to Bentham's work.

AN INTRODUCTION TO THE PRINCIPLES OF MORALS AND LEGISLATION

Of the Principle of Utility

I. Nature has placed mankind under the governance of two sovereign masters, *pain* and *pleasure*. It is for them alone to point out what we ought to do, as well as to determine what we shall do. On the one hand the standard of right and wrong, on the other

---

From: Jeremy Bentham, *An Introduction to the Principles of Morals and Legislation* (1789), Chapter 1.

the chain of causes and effects, are fastened to their throne. They govern us in all we do, in all we say, in all we think: every effort we can make to throw off our subjection, will serve but to demonstrate and confirm it. In words a man may pretend to abjure their empire: but in reality he will remain subject to it all the while. The *principle of utility* recognizes this subjection, and assumes it for the foundation of that system, the object of which is to rear the fabric of felicity by the hands of reason and law. Systems which attempt to question it, deal in sounds instead of sense, in caprice instead of reason, in darkness instead of light.

But enough of metaphor and declamation: it is not by such means that moral science is to be improved.

II. The principle of utility is the foundation of the present work: it will be proper therefore at the outset to give an explicit and determinate account of what is meant by it. By the principle of utility is meant that principle which approves or disapproves of every action whatsoever, according to the tendency which it appears to have to augment or diminish the happiness of the party whose interest is in question: or, what is the same thing in other words, to promote or to oppose that happiness. I say of every action whatsoever; and therefore not only of every action of a private individual, but of every measure of government.

III. By utility is meant that property in any object, whereby it tends to produce benefit, advantage, pleasure, good, or happiness, (all this in the present case comes to the same thing) or (what comes again to the same thing) to prevent the happening of mischief, pain, evil, or unhappiness to the party whose interest is considered: if that party be the community in general, then the happiness of the community: if a particular individual, then the happiness of that individual.

An act is right if it either brings about more pleasure than pain or prevents pain, and an act is wrong if it brings about more pain than pleasure or prevents pleasure from occurring.

Bentham invented a scheme for measuring pleasure and pain, which he called the *hedonic calculus*. The quantitative score for any pleasure or pain experience comes about by giving sums to seven aspects of an experience in terms of pleasure and pain. Here is what he says.[2]

VALUE OF A LOT OF PLEASURE OR PAIN, HOW TO BE MEASURED

I. Pleasures then, and the avoidance of pains, are the *ends* which the legislator has in view: it behooves him therefore to understand their *value*. Pleasures and pains are the *instruments* he has to work with: it behooves him therefore to understand their force, which is again, in other words, their value.

II. To a person considered *by himself*, the value of a pleasure or pain considered *by itself*, will be greater or less, according to the four following circumstances:

1. Its *intensity*.
2. Its *duration*.
3. Its *certainty* or *uncertainty*.
4. Its *propinquity* or *remoteness*.

III. These are the circumstances which are to be considered in estimating a pleasure or a pain considered each of them by itself. But when the value of any pleasure or pain is considered for the purpose of estimating the tendency of any *act* by which it is produced, there are two other circumstances to be taken into the account; these are,

5.   Its *fecundity,* or the chance it has of being followed by sensations of the *same* kind: that is, pleasures, if it be a pleasure: pains, if it be a pain.

6.   Its *purity,* or the chance it has of *not* being followed by sensations of the *opposite* kind: that is, pains, if it be a pleasure: pleasures, if it be a pain.

These two last, however, are in strictness scarcely to be deemed properties of the pleasure or the pain itself; they are not, therefore, in strictness to be taken into the account of the value of that pleasure or that pain. They are in strictness to be deemed properties only of the act, or other event, by which such pleasure or pain has been produced; and accordingly are only to be taken into the account of the tendency of such act or such event.

IV. To a *number* of persons, with reference of each of whom the value of a pleasure or a pain is considered, it will be greater or less, according to seven circumstances: to wit, the six preceding ones; *viz.*

1.   Its *intensity*.

2.   Its *duration*.

3.   Its *certainty* or *uncertainty*.

4.   Its *propinquity* or *remoteness*.

5.   Its *fecundity*.

6.   Its *purity*.

And one other; to wit:

7.   Its *extent;* that is, the number of persons to whom it *extends;* or (in other words) who are affected by it.

V. To take an exact account then of the general tendency of any act, by which the interests of a community are affected, proceed as follows. Begin with any one person of those whose interests seem most immediately to be affected by it: and take an account,

1.   Of the value of each distinguishable *pleasure* which appears to be produced by it in the *first* instance.

2.   Of the value of each *pain* which appears to be produced by it in the *first* instance.

3.   Of the value of each pleasure which appears to be produced by it *after* the first. This constitutes the *fecundity* of the first *pleasure* and the *impurity* of the *first* pain.

4.   Of the value of each *pain* which appears to be produced by it after the first. This constitutes the *fecundity* of the first *pain,* and the *impurity* of the first pleasure.

5.   Sum up all the values of all the *pleasures* on the one side, and those of all the pains on the other. The balance, if it be on the side of pleasure, will give the *good*

tendency of the act upon the whole, with respect to the interests of that *individual* person; if on the side of pain, the *bad* tendency of it upon the whole.

6. Take an account of the *number* of persons whose interests appear to be concerned; and repeat the above process with respect to each. *Sum up* the numbers expressive of the degrees of *good* tendency, which the act has, with respect to each individual, in regard to whom the tendency of it is *good* upon the whole: do this again with respect to each individual, in regard to whom the tendency of it is *good* upon the whole: do this again with respect to each individual, in regard to whom the tendency of it is *bad* upon the whole. Take the *balance;* which, if on the side of *pleasure,* will give the general *good tendency* of the act, with respect to the total number or community of individuals concerned; if on the side of pain, the general *evil tendency,* with respect to the same community.

So we have seven aspects of a pleasurable or painful experience: its intensity, duration, certainty, nearness, fruitfulness, purity, and extent. By adding up the sums of each possible act in terms of pleasure and pain and comparing them, we would be able to decide on which act to perform. With regard to our example of deciding between giving the dying man's money to the Yankees or the starvation victims, we should add up the likely pleasures to all involved in terms of these seven qualities. Suppose we find that by giving the money to the East African famine victims we will cause at least 3 million *hedons* (that is, units of happiness), but by giving the money to the Yankees, we will probably cause less than a 1000 hedons. We would then have an obligation to give the money to the famine victims.

Bentham made a novel move in Western moral philosophy. Virtually all previous moral philosophies applied solely to human beings, but Bentham extended the sphere of moral considerability to animals—after all, they are also susceptible to pleasure and pain.

XVII. Under the Gentoo and Mahometan religions, the interests of the rest of the animal creation seem to have met with some attention. Why have they not, universally, with as much as those of human creatures, allowance made for the difference in point of sensibility? Because the laws that are have been the work of mutual fear; a sentiment which the less rational animals have not had the same means as man has of turning to account. Why ought they not? No reason can be given. If the being eaten were all, there is very good reason why we should be suffered to eat such of them as we like to eat: we are the better for it, and they are never the worse. They have none of those long-protracted anticipations of future misery which we have. The death they suffer in our hands commonly is, and always may be, a speedier, and by that means a less painful one, than that which would await them in the inevitable course of nature. If the being killed were all, there is very good reason why we should be suffered to kill such as molest us: we should be the worse for their living, and they are never the worse for being dead. But is there any reason why we should be suffered to torment them? Not any that I can see. Are there any why we should not be suffered to torment them? Yes, several. The day has been, I grieve to say in many places it is not yet past, in which the greater part of the species, under the denomination of slaves, have been treated by the law exactly upon the same footing, as, in England for example, the inferior races of animals are still. The day may come, when the rest of the animal creation may acquire those rights which never could have been withholden from them but by the hand of tyranny. The French have already discovered that the blackness of the skin is no reason why a human being should be abandoned without redress to the caprice of a tormentor. It may come one day to be recognized, that the number of the legs, the villosity of the skin, or the termination of the os sacrum, are reasons equally insufficient for abandoning a sensitive being to the same fate. What else is it that should trace the insuperable line? Is it the faculty of reason, or, perhaps, the faculty of discourse? But a full-grown horse or dog is beyond comparison a more rational, as well as a more conversable animal, than an infant of a day, or a week, or even a month, old. But suppose the case were otherwise, what would it avail? The question is not, Can they reason? nor, Can they talk? but, Can they suffer?[3]

What do you make of Bentham's utilitarianism? There is certainly something appealing about it. It is simple in that there is only one principle to apply: Maximize pleasure and minimize suffering. It is commonsensical in that we think that morality really is about ameliorating suffering and promoting benevolence. It is scientific: Simply make quantitative measurements and apply the principle impartially, giving no special treatment to yourself or to anyone else because of race, gender, or religion.

However, Bentham's philosophy may be too simplistic in one way and too complicated in another. It may be too simplistic in that there are other values than pleasure, as we saw in the last chapter, and it seems too complicated in its artificial hedonic calculus. The calculus is encumbered with too many variables and problems in attempting to give scores to the variables. What score does one give a cool drink on a hot day or a warm shower on a cool day? How do you compare a 5-year-old's delight over a new toy with a 50-year-old's delight with a new lover? Can I take your second car from you and give it to Beggar Bob who does not own a car and would enjoy it more than you? And if it's simply the overall benefits of pleasure that we are measuring, might it not turn out that if Jack or Jill would be "happier" in the Pleasure or Happiness Machine or on drugs than in the real world, then would we have an obligation to see to it that these conditions obtain? Because of these considerations, Bentham's version of utilitarianism was even in his own day referred to as the "pig-philosophy," since a pig enjoying his life would constitute a higher moral state than a slightly dissatisfied Socrates.

It was to meet these sorts of objections and save utilitarianism from the charge of being a pig philosophy that Bentham's brilliant successor John Stuart Mill sought to distinguish happiness from mere sensual pleasure. His version of utilitarianism, *eudaimonistic utilitarianism* (from the Greek **eudaimonia,** meaning "happiness"), defines happiness in terms of certain types of higher-order pleasures or satisfactions but argues that some types of pleasure are higher than others. The higher pleasures, such as intellectual, aesthetic, and social enjoyments, provide more happiness than the lower ones, for example, getting drunk or tickled. Let's turn to the text. First, Mill states the general utilitarian philosophy.

UTILITARIANISM

The creed which accepts the greatest happiness principle as the foundation of morals holds that actions are right in proportion as they tend to promote happiness, wrong as they tend to produce the reverse of happiness. By happiness is intended pleasure, and the absence of pain; by unhappiness, pain, and the privation of pleasure. This theory I propose to expound and defend.

The standard is not the agent's own greatest happiness, but the greatest amount of happiness altogether. As between his own happiness and that of others, utilitarianism requires him to be as strictly impartial as a disinterested and benevolent spectator.

The test of morality is not the greatest happiness of the agent himself. Utilitarianism does not dream of defining morality to be the self-interest of the agent. The greatest happiness principle is the greatest happiness of mankind and all sentient creatures.

He who does anything for any other purpose than to increase the amount of happiness in the world is no more deserving of admiration than the ascetic mounted on his pillar. He may be an inspiring proof of what men can do, but assuredly not an example of what they should do.

Pleasure and freedom from pain are the only things desirable as ends, and all desirable things are inherent in them or as means to the promotion of pleasure and the prevention of pain.

Mill next distinguishes various kinds of pleasure. Some kinds of pleasure are more desirable and more valuable than others. We must judge a pleasure by its *quality* as well as by its *quantity*. How do we know which pleasures are more valuable? Here is Mill's reply.[4]

If I am asked, what I mean by difference of quality in pleasures, or what makes one pleasure more valuable than another, merely as a pleasure, except its being greater in amount, there is but one possible answer. Of two pleasures, if there be one to which all or almost all who have experience of both give a decided preference, irrespective of any feeling of moral obligation to prefer it, that is the more desirable pleasure. If one of the two is, by those who are competently acquainted with both, placed so far above the other that they prefer it, even though knowing it to be attended with a greater amount of discontent, and would not resign it for any quantity of the other pleasure which their nature is capable of, we are justified in ascribing to the preferred enjoyment a superiority in quality, so far outweighing quantity as to render it, in comparison, of small account.

Now it is an unquestionable fact that those who are equally acquainted with, and equally capable of appreciating and enjoying, both, do give a most marked preference to the manner of existence which employs their higher faculties. Few human creatures would consent to be changed into any of the lower animals, for a promise of the fullest allowance of a beast's pleasures; no intelligent human being would consent to be a fool, no instructed person would be an ignoramus, no person of feeling and conscience would be selfish and base, even though they should be persuaded that the fool, the dunce,

---

From: John Stuart Mill, *Utilitarianism* (1863), Chapter 2.

or the rascal is better satisfied with his lot than they are with theirs. They would not resign what they possess more than he, for the most complete satisfaction of all the desires which they have in common with him. If they ever fancy they would, it is only in cases of unhappiness so extreme, that to escape from it they would exchange their lot for almost any other, however undesirable in their own eyes. A being of higher faculties requires more to make him happy, is capable probably of more acute suffering, and is certainly accessible to it at more points, than one of an inferior type; but in spite of these liabilities, he can never really wish to sink into what he feels to be a lower grade of existence. We may give what explanation we please to this unwillingness; we may attribute it to pride, a name which is given indiscriminately to some of the most and to some of the least estimable feelings for which mankind are capable; we may refer it to the love of liberty and personal independence, an appeal to which was with the Stoics one of the most effective means for the inculcation of it; to the love of power, or to the love of excitement, both of which do really enter into and contribute to it; but its most appropriate appellation is a sense of dignity, which all human beings possess in one form or other, and in some, though by no means in exact, proportion to their higher faculties, and which is so essential a part of the happiness of those in whom it is strong, that nothing which conflicts with it could be, otherwise than momentarily, an object of desire to them. Whoever supposes that this preference takes place at a sacrifice of happiness—that the superior being, in anything like the equal circumstances, is not happier than the inferior—confounds the two very different ideas, of happiness, and content. It is indisputable that the being whose capacities of enjoyment are low, has the greatest chance of having them fully satisfied; and a highly-endowed being will always feel that any happiness which he can look for, as the world is constituted, is imperfect. But he can learn to bear its imperfections, if they are at all bearable; and they will not make him envy the being who is indeed unconscious of the imperfections, but only because he feels not at all the good which those imperfections qualify. It is better to be a human being dissatisfied than a pig satisfied; better to be a Socrates dissatisfied than a fool satisfied. And if the fool, or the pig, is of a different opinion, it is because they only know their own side of the question. The other party to the comparison knows both sides.

In sum, there are two types of pleasures: the lower or elementary (for example, eating, drinking, sexuality, resting, sensuous titillation) and the higher (for example, the intellectual, creative, spiritual). Though the lower pleasures are more intensely gratifying, they also lead to pain when overindulged in. The spiritual or achieved pleasures tend to be more protracted, continuous, and gradual. Thus, Mill thinks he has answered the objection that utilitarianism with its doctrine of **hedonism** is a philosophy fit for pigs. But the objector may persist that happiness cannot be the rational purpose of life because it is unattainable. Mill replies with the following.

This objection, were it well founded, would go to the root of the matter; for if no happiness is to be had at all by human beings, the attainment of it cannot be the end of morality. However, the assertion that it is impossible that human life be happy is an exaggeration.

If by *happiness* be meant a continuity of highly pleasurable excitement, it is evident that this is impossible. A state of exalted pleasure lasts only for a few moments, or in some cases for somewhat longer periods. If this kind of intense rapture be meant by *happiness,* then happiness is unattainable.

But this is not what philosophers have meant by *happiness* when they taught that happiness was the end of life. The happiness which they meant was not a life of rapture, but moments of such in an existence made up of few and transitory pains, many and various pleasures, with a decided predominance of the active over the passive, and having as the foundation not to expect more from life than it is capable of bestowing. A life thus composed, to those who have been fortunate enough to obtain it, has always appeared worthy of the name of happiness. And such an existence is even now the lot of many.

Humans are the kind of creatures who require more to be truly happy. They want the lower pleasures but also deep friendship, intellectual ability, culture, ability to create and appreciate art, knowledge, and wisdom. But, one may object, how do we know that it really is better to have these higher pleasures? Here Mill imagines a panel of experts and says that of those who have had wide experience of pleasures of both kinds almost all give a decided preference to the higher type. Since Mill was an empiricist, one who believed all knowledge and justified belief was based in our experience, he had no recourse but to rely on the composite consensus of human history. People who experience both rock music and classical music will, if they appreciate both, prefer Bach and Beethoven to the Rolling Stones or Dancing Demons. We generally move up from appreciating simple things (for example, nursery rhymes) to more complex and intricate things (for example, poetry that requires great talent) rather than the other way around.

Mill has been criticized for not giving a better reply and for being an elitist and unduly favoring the intellectual over the sensual, but he has a point. Don't we generally agree, if we have experienced both the lower and the higher types of pleasure, that while a full life would include both, a life with only the former is inadequate for human beings? Isn't it better to be Socrates dissatisfied than the pig satisfied? And better still to be Socrates satisfied?

The point is not merely that humans would not be satisfied with what satisfies a pig but that somehow the quality of these pleasures is *better.* But what does it mean to speak of better pleasure? Is Mill assuming some nonhedonic notion of intrinsic value to make this distinction? That is, knowledge, intelligence, freedom, friendship, love, health, and so forth are good things in their own right. Or is Mill simply saying that the lives of humans are generally such that we can predict that they will be happier with more developed, refined, spiritual values? Which thesis would you be inclined to defend? Discuss his final formula:

Happiness... [is] not a life of rapture; but moments of such, in an existence made up of few and transitory pains, many and various pleasures, with a decided predominance of the active over the passive, and having as the foundation of the whole, not to expect more from life than it is capable of bestowing.

Contemporary Utilitarianism

There are two types of contemporary utilitarianism: act utilitarianism and rule utilitarianism.[5] In applying the principle of utility, act utilitarians, such as Bentham, say that ideally we ought to apply the principle to all the alternatives open to us at any given moment. We may define *act utilitarianism* in this way: An act is right if and only if it results in as much good as any available alternative.

Of course, we cannot do the necessary calculations to determine which act is the correct one in each case, for often we must act spontaneously and quickly. So rules of thumb (for example, "In general, don't lie"; "Generally, keep your promises") are of practical importance. However, the right act is still the alternative that will result in the most utility.

The obvious criticism of act utility is that it seems to fly in the face of fundamental intuitions about minimally correct behavior. Consider Richard Brandt's criticism of act utilitarianism:

> It implies that if you have employed a boy to mow your lawn and he has finished the job and asks for his pay, you should pay him what you promised only if you cannot find a better use for your money. It implies that when you bring home your monthly paycheck you should use it to support your family and yourself only if it cannot be used more effectively to supply the needs of others. It implies that if your father is ill and has no prospect of good in his life, and maintaining him is a drain on the energy and enjoyments of others, then, if you can end his life without provoking any public scandal or setting a bad example, it is your positive duty to take matters into your own hands and bring his life to a close.[6]

Rule utilitarians like Brandt attempt to offer a more credible version of the theory. They state that an act is right if it conforms to a valid rule within a system of rules that, if followed, will result in the best possible state of affairs (or least bad state of affairs, if it is a question of all the alternatives being bad). We may define *rule utilitarianism* this way: An act is right if and only if it is required by a rule that is itself a member of a set of rules whose acceptance would lead to greater utility for society than any available alternative.

An often-debated question in ethics is whether rule utilitarianism is a consistent version of utilitarianism. Briefly, the argument that rule utilitarianism is an inconsistent version that must either become a deontological system or transform itself into act utilitarianism goes like this. Imagine that following the set of general rules of a rule-utilitarian system yields 100 hedons (positive-utility units). We could always find a case where breaking the general rule would result in additional hedons without decreasing the sum of the whole. So, for example, we could imagine a situation where breaking the general rule "Never lie" in order to spare someone's feelings would create more utility (for example, 102 hedons) than keeping the rule would. It would seem that we could always improve on any version of rule utilitarianism by breaking the set of rules wherever we judge that by so doing we could produce even more utility than the set itself.

One way of resolving the difference between act and rule utilitarians is to appeal to the notion of *levels of rules.* For the sophisticated utilitarian, three levels of rules guide actions. On the lowest level is a set of utility-maximizing rules of thumb that should always be followed unless there is a conflict between them, in which case a second-order set of conflict-resolving rules should be consulted. At the top of the hierarchy is the *remainder* rule of act utilitarianism: When no other rule applies, simply do what your best judgment deems to be the act that will maximize utility.

An illustration of this might be the following. Two of our lower-order rules might be "Keep your promises" and "Help those in need when you are not seriously inconvenienced in doing so." You have made a promise to meet your teacher at 3 p.m. in his office. As you are on your way to his office, you come upon an accident victim who has been left stranded by the wayside. She desperately needs help. It doesn't take you long to decide to break your appointment with your teacher, for it seems obvious in this case that the rule to help others overrides the rule to keep promises. We might say that there is a second-order rule prescribing that the first-order rule of helping people in need when you are not seriously inconvenienced in doing so overrides the rule to keep promises. However, there may be some situation where no obvious rule of thumb applies. Say you have $50, which you don't really need now. How should you use this money? Put it into your savings account? Give it to your favorite charity? Use it to throw a party? Here and only here, on the third level, the general act-utility principle applies without any other primary rule: Do what in your best judgment will do the most good.

It is a subject of keen debate whether Mill was a rule or an act utilitarian. He doesn't seem to have noticed the difference, and there seem to be aspects of both theories in his work. Philosophers like Kai Nielsen hold views that are clearer examples of act utilitarianism.[7] Nielsen attacks what he calls "moral conservatism," any "normative ethical theory which maintains that there is a privileged moral principle or cluster of moral principles, prescribing determinate actions, with which it would always be wrong not to act in accordance no matter what the consequences." For Nielsen, no rules are sacrosanct, but differing situations call forth different actions and potentially any rule could be overridden (though in fact we may need to treat some as absolutes for the good of society).

Nielsen's argument in favor of utilitarianism makes strong use of the notion of *negative responsibility.* That is, we are not only responsible for the consequences of our actions, but we are also responsible for the consequences of our nonactions. Here is what he writes:

The Case of the Innocent Fat Man   Consider the story of the fat man stuck in the mouth of a cave on a coast. He was leading a group of people out of the cave when he got stuck in the mouth of the cave and in a very short time high tide will be upon them, and unless he is promptly unstuck, they all will be drowned except the fat man, whose head is out of the cave. But, fortunately or unfortunately, someone has with him a stick of dynamite. The short of the matter is, either they use the dynamite and blast the poor innocent fat man out of the mouth of the cave or everyone else drowns. Either one life or many lives. Our conservative presumably would take the attitude that it is all in God's hands and say that he ought never to blast the fat man out, for it is always wrong to kill the innocent. Must or should a moral man come to that conclusion?[8]

Neilsen argues not only that we should blow up the fat man in order to save the others but that if we do not do so, we are morally responsible for the deaths of the other people whom we could have saved. That is, to keep our hands clean, as it were, is really a cop-out. Not to act is really an action of its own—it is a negative act. We delude ourselves if we think that we can escape blame by inaction. In cases like the fat man in the cave, the choices are simply between causing one man to die and allowing everyone to die. In any case, we are responsible for the outcome.

Strengths and Weaknesses of Utilitarianism

Whatever the answers to these questions are, utilitarianism does have two very positive features. The first attraction, or strength, is that it is a single principle, an absolute system, with a potential answer for every situation. Do what will promote the most utility! It's good to have a simple action-guiding principle, applicable for every occasion—even if it may be difficult to apply (life's not simple). Its second strength is that utilitarianism seems to get to the substance of morality. It is not merely a formal system (that is, systems that set forth broad guidelines for choosing principles but offer no principles; such a guideline would be "Do whatever you can to universalize"), but has a material core: promoting human (and possibly animal) flourishing and ameliorating suffering. The first virtue gives a clear decision procedure in arriving at the answer about what to do. The second virtue appeals to our sense that morality is made for humans (and other animals?) and that morality is not so much about rules as about helping people and alleviating the suffering in the world.

Utilitarianism seems commonsensical; it gives us clear and reasonable guidance in dealing with the two cases mentioned at the beginning of this chapter. In the case of deciding what to do with the $2 million of the dead millionaire, something in us says that it is absurd to keep a promise to a dead man when it means allowing hundreds of thousands of famine victims to die (how would we like it if we were in their shoes?). Far more good can be accomplished by helping the needy than by giving the money to the Yankees! Similarly, giving the food to the scientist will do the most good, so he should get it.

However, utilitarianism has several problems that need to be addressed before we can give it a "philosophically clean bill of health."

Problem 1: Formulating Utilitarianism

The first set of problems occurs in the very formulation of utilitarianism: the greatest happiness for the greatest number. Notice that we have two superlatives mentioned in the formula, two "greatest" things: happiness and number. Whenever one has two variables, one invites problems of incommensurability—of not being able to decide which of the variables to rank first when they seem to conflict. To see this point, consider the following example. Suppose I offer a $1000 prize to the person who runs the longest distance in the shortest amount of time. Three people participate. Joe runs 5 miles in 31 minutes, John runs 7 miles in 50 minutes, and Jack runs 1 mile in 6 minutes. Who should get the prize? John has fulfilled one part of the requirement (run the longest distance), but Jack has fulfilled the other requirement (run the shortest amount of time).

This is precisely the problem with utilitarianism. Should we concern ourselves with spreading happiness around so that the greatest number obtain it? If this is the case, we should get busy and procreate a larger population. Or should we be concerned that the greatest amount of happiness possible obtains in society? If so, we might be tempted to allow some people to become far happier than others, as long as their increase offsets the losers' diminished happiness. Should we worry about total happiness or highest average? What is the place of distribution requirements? And just whose happiness are we talking about anyway? All sentient beings or all human beings or all rational beings (which might exclude some human beings and include some higher animals)? Finally, how do we measure happiness and make interpersonal comparisons between the happiness of different people?

Problem 2: Knowing the Comparative Consequences of Actions

Sometimes utilitarians are accused of playing God. They seem to hold to an ethical theory that demands godlike powers (for example, knowledge of the future). Of course, we normally do not know the long-term consequences of our actions, for life is too complex and the consequences go on into the indefinite future. One action causes one state of affairs, which in turn causes another state of affairs indefinitely so that calculation becomes impossible. Recall the nursery rhyme:

> For want of a nail, the shoe was lost;
> For want of a shoe, the horse was lost;
> For want of a horse, the rider was lost;
> For want of a rider, the battle was lost;
> For want of a battle, the kingdom was lost;
> And all for the want of a horse-shoe nail.

Poor, unfortunate Blacksmith! What utilitarian guilt he must bear all the rest of his days!

However, blaming the loss of one's kingdom on the poor unsuccessful blacksmith is ridiculous, and utilitarians are not so foolish as to hold him responsible for the bad situation. Instead, following C. I. Lewis, they distinguish three different kinds of consequences: (1) actual consequences of an act, (2) consequences that could reasonably have been expected to occur, and (3) intended consequences.[9]

An act is *objectively* right if it is reasonable to expect that it will have the best consequences. An act is *subjectively* right if its agent intends or actually expects it to have the best consequences. It is the second kind of rightness, that based on reasonable expectations, that is central here, for only the subsequent observer of the consequences is in a position to determine the actual results. The most that the agent can do is use the best information available and do what a reasonable person would expect to produce the best overall results. Suppose, for example, that while Hitler's grandmother was carrying little Adolf up the stairs to her home, she slipped and had to choose between dropping infant Adolf, causing him to be fatally injured, and breaking her arm. According to the formula just given, it would have been absolutely right for her to let him be killed, but it would not have been within her power to know that. She did what any reasonable person would do—save the baby's life at the risk of some injury to oneself. She did what was objectively right. The utilitarian theory is that by generally doing what reason judges to be the best act based on likely consequences, we will in general actually promote the best consequences.

Opponents raise several other objections against utilitarianism. Let me mention two of them: the absurd-implications objection and the justice objection.

The Absurd-Implications Objection

W. D. Ross argued that utilitarianism is to be rejected because it is counterintuitive. If we accepted it, we would have to accept an absurd implication. Consider two acts, A and B, which will both result in 100 hedons (units of pleasure of utility). The only difference is that A involves telling a lie and B involves telling the truth. The utilitarian must maintain that the two acts are of equal value, but this seems implausible. Truth telling seems to be an intrinsically good thing.

Similarly, in Arthur Koestler's *Darkness at Noon,* Rubashov writes of the Communist philosophy in the Soviet Republic:

> History has taught us that often lies serve her better than the truth; for man is sluggish and has to be led through the desert for forty years before each step in his development. And he has to be driven through the desert with threats and promises, by imaginary terrors and imaginary consolations, so that he should not sit down prematurely to rest and divert himself by worshipping golden calves.[10]

According to this interpretation, orthodox Soviet communism justifies its lies and atrocities by utilitarian ideas. Something in us revolts at this kind of value system. Truth is sacred and must not be sacrificed on the altar of expediency.

The Justice Objection

Suppose a rape and murder is committed in a racially volatile community. As the sheriff of the town, you have spent a lifetime working for racial harmony. Now, just when your goal is being realized, this incident occurs. The crime is thought to be racially motivated, and a riot is about to break out that will very likely result in the death of several people and create long-lasting racial antagonism. You are able to frame a derelict for the crime, so a trial will show that he is guilty. He will then be executed. There is every reason to believe that a speedy trial and execution will head off the riot and save community harmony. Only you (and the real criminal, who will keep quiet about it) will know that an innocent man has been tried and executed. What is the morally right thing to do? The utilitarian seems committed to framing the derelict, but many would find this appalling.

Or consider this hypothetical situation. You are a utilitarian physician who has five patients under your care. One needs to have a heart transplant, one needs two lungs, one a liver, and the last two each need a kidney. Now into your office comes a healthy bachelor needing an immunization. You judge him to be a perfect sacrifice for your five patients. Doing a utility calculus, there is no doubt in your mind that you could do the most good by injecting the healthy man with a sleep-inducing drug and using his organs to save your five patients.[11]

This cavalier view of justice offends us. The very fact that utilitarians even countenance such actions, that they would misuse the legal system or the medical system to carry out their schemes, seems frightening. It reminds us of the medieval Roman Catholic bishop's justification for heresy hunts, inquisitions, and religious wars:

> When the existence of the Church is threatened, she is released from the commandments of morality. With unity as the end, the use of every means is sanctified, even cunning, treachery, violence, simony, prison, death. For all order is for the sake of the community, and the individual must be sacrificed to the common good.[12]

Utilitarian Responses to Standard Objections

These objections are weighty and complicated, but let's allow the utilitarian to make an initial defense. What sorts of responses are open to utilitarians? Well, it seems to me that a sophisticated version of utilitarianism can offset at least some of the force of these criticisms. He or she can use the *multilevel strategy,* which goes like this. We must split considerations of utility into two levels, the lower level dealing with a set of rules that we judge to be most likely to bring about the best consequences most of the time. We'll call this the *rule-utility feature* of utilitarianism. Normally, we have to live by the best rules our system can devise, and rules of honesty, promise keeping, obedience to the law, and justice will be among them.

But sometimes the rules conflict or clearly will not yield the best consequences. In these infrequent cases, we will need to suspend or override the rule
in favor of the better consequences. We call this the *act-utility feature* of utilitarianism. It constitutes the second level of consideration and is referred to
only when there is dissatisfaction with the rule-utility feature. An example of
this might be the rule against breaking a promise. Normally, the most utility
will come about through keeping one's promises, but what if I have promised
to meet you at the movies tonight at seven o'clock. Unbeknown to you, on the
way to our rendezvous I come across an accident and am able to render great
service to the injured parties. Unfortunately, I cannot contact you, and you are
inconvenienced as you patiently wait in front of the theater for an hour. I have
broken a utility rule in order to maximize utility and am justified in so doing.

Here is another example, set forth by Judith Jarvis Thomson. You are a trolley car driver who sees five workers on the track before you. You suddenly realize that the brakes have failed. Fortunately, the track has a spur leading off to
the right, and you can turn the trolley onto it. Unfortunately, there is one
person on the right-hand track. You can turn the trolley to the right, killing
one person, or you can refrain from turning the trolley, in which case five
people will die. Under traditional views, there is a distinction between killing
and letting die, between actively killing and passively allowing death, but the
utilitarian rejects this distinction. You should turn the trolley, causing the lesser
evil, for the only relevant issue is expected utility. So the normal rule against
actively causing an innocent to die is suspended in favor of the utility principle.

With regard to problem 1, Ross's absurd-implications objection, the utilitarian can agree that there is something counterintuitive in the calculus of
equating an act of lying with one of honesty; but, he argues, we must be ready
to change our culture-induced moral biases. What is so important about truth
telling or so bad about lying? If it turned out that lying really promoted human
welfare, we'd have to accept it. But that's not likely. Our happiness is tied up
with a need for reliable information (that is, truth) on how to achieve our ends.
So truthfulness will be a member of the rule-utility set. However, where lying
will clearly promote utility without undermining the general adherence to the
rule, we simply ought to lie. Don't we already accept lying to a gangster or
telling white lies to spare people's feelings?

With regard to Rubashov's utilitarian defense of the inhumanity of communism or the medieval defense of the Inquisition, the utilitarian replies that this
abuse of utilitarianism only illustrates how dangerous the doctrine can be in the
hands of self-serving bureaucrats. Any theory can be misused in this way.

We turn to the most difficult objection, the claim that utilitarianism permits
injustice, as seen in the example of the sheriff framing the innocent derelict.
The utilitarian counters that justice is not an absolute—mercy and benevolence
and the good of the whole society sometimes should override it; but, the
sophisticated utilitarian insists, it makes good utilitarian sense to have a principle of justice that is generally adhered to. It is not clear what the sheriff should
do in the racially torn community. More needs to be said, but if we could be
certain that it would not start a precedent of sacrificing innocent people, it may
be right to sacrifice one person for the good of the whole. Wouldn't we all

agree, the utilitarian continues, that would be right to sacrifice one innocent person to prevent great evil?

Virtually all standard moral systems have a rule against torturing innocent people. But suppose a maniac is about to set off a nuclear bomb that will destroy New York City. He is scheduled to detonate the bomb in 1 hour. His psychiatrist knows the lunatic well and assures us that there is one way (and only one way) to stop him: Torture his 10-year-old daughter and show it on television. Suppose, for the sake of the argument, there is no way to simulate the torture. Would you not consider torturing the child in this situation? Just in case you don't think New York City is worth saving, imagine that the lunatic has a lethal gas that will spread throughout the globe and wipe out all life within a few weeks.

Is it not right to sacrifice one innocent person to stop a war or save the human race from destruction? We seem to proceed on this assumption in wartime, in every bombing raid, especially in the dropping of the atom bomb on Hiroshima and Nagasaki. We seem to be following this rule in our decision to drive automobiles and trucks even though we are fairly certain that the practice will result in the death of thousands of innocent people each year.

On the other hand, the sophisticated utilitarian may argue that—in the case of the sheriff framing the innocent derelict—justice should not be overridden by current utility concerns, for human rights themselves are outcomes of utility consideration and should not lightly be violated. That is, because we tend subconsciously to favor our own interests and biases, we institute the principle of rights to protect ourselves and others from capricious and biased acts that would in the long run have great disutility. Thus, we must not undermine institutional rights too easily; we should not kill the bachelor in order to provide a heart, two lungs, a liver, and two kidneys to the five patients—at least not at this present time given peoples' expectations of what will happen to them when they enter hospitals. But neither should we worship rights! They are to be taken seriously but not given ultimate authority. The utilitarian cannot foreclose the possibility of sacrificing innocent people for the greater good of humanity. If slavery could be humane and result in great overall utility, utilitarians would accept it.

We see then that sophisticated, multileveled utilitarianism has responses to all the criticisms leveled on it. For most people, most of the time, the ordinary moral principles should be followed, for they actually maximize utility in the long run. However, we should not be tied down to this rule: "Morality was made for man, not man for morality." The purpose of morality is to promote flourishing and ameliorate suffering and where sacrificing a rule can do these, we should do them. Whether this is an adequate defense, I must leave for you to decide.

Summary

We see then that sophisticated, multileveled utilitarianism has plausible responses to all of the criticisms leveled on it. Whether they are adequate is another story and depends on certain factual claims—claims about human psychology, institutional feasibility, and so forth. The ideas of some ethicists (notably Kantians) who might question the appropriateness of making conclusions about justice, human rights and responsibilities, and the like, turn on claims that are themselves less certain than the moral claims that they are meant to support. Others hold that utilitarianism is the only theory that makes any sense. Perhaps it is better to hold off making a final judgment until after reading the next chapter, wherein Kantian and deontological ethical theories will be portrayed.

FOR FURTHER REFLECTION

1. Consider the three purposes of morality mentioned in Chapter 27: (1) to promote human flourishing, (2) to ameliorate human suffering, and (3) to resolve conflicts of interest justly. Which of these does utilitarianism fulfill, and which does it fail to fulfill?

2. Ross argued that utilitarianism is to be rejected because it is counterintuitive. Consider two acts, A and B, that will both result in 100 hedons (units of pleasure of utility). The only difference is that A involves telling a lie and B involves telling the truth. The utilitarian must maintain that the two acts are of equal value. Do you agree? Does more need to be said?

3. One criticism of utilitarianism is that it fails to protect people's rights. Consider five sadists getting a total of 100 hedons while torturing an innocent victim who is suffering 10 dolors (units of pain). On a utilitarian calculus, this would result in a total of 90 hedons. If no other act would result in as many or more hedons, the utilitarian would have to endorse this act and argue that the victim has a duty to submit to the torture and that the sadists had a duty to torture the victim. What do you think of this sort of reasoning? How does it count against utilitarianism?

4. John Rawls's *false-analogy argument:* Utilitarianism errs in applying to society the principle of personal choice. That is, we all would agree that an individual has a right to forgo a present pleasure for a future good. I have a right to go without a new suit so that I can save the money for my college education or so that I can give it to my favorite charity. Utilitarianism prescribes, however, that you forego a new suit for someone else's college education or for the overall good of the community—whether you like it or not or whether you agree to it or not. That is, it takes the futuristic notion of agent-utility maximization and extends it to cover society in a way that violates the individual's rights. Is this a fair criticism?

5. Consider the following situation. You are an army officer who has just captured an enemy soldier who has the secret to where a time bomb has been planted. The bomb, unless soon defused, will explode and kill thousands of citizens. Would it be morally permissible to torture the soldier in order to get him to reveal the location of the bomb? Suppose you have also captured his children. Would it be permissible to torture his children in order to get him to reveal the location of the bomb? Discuss this problem in the light of utilitarian and deontological theories.

6. At the beginning of this chapter, we quoted Francis Hutcheson: "The Greatest Happiness for the Greatest Number." Do you find anything puzzling about this motto? Notice that it has two superlatives. Recall the situation

mentioned earlier: I am going to give a $1000 prize to the person who runs the farthest distance in the least amount of time. Three people sign up and run. Here are the results:

Person	Distance	Time
John	7 miles	50 minutes
Joe	5 miles	31 minutes
Jack	1 mile	6 minutes

Who should get the prize? Can you see how this could become a problem for utilitarian calculus? How does the utilitarian go about deciding how to distribute goods to different groups of people?

7. Suppose we have a situation involving three social policies that will divide up welfare between three equal groups of people. In policy 1, group A will receive 75 units; group B, 45 units; and group C, 25 units of welfare—for a total of 145 units. In policy 2, A will receive 50 units, and B and C will receive 45 units each—for a total of 140 units. In policy 3, A will receive 100 units, and B and C will receive 25 each—for a total of 150 units (see the diagram for a graphic illustration). Suppose it is agreed that 30 units is necessary for a minimally acceptable social existence. Which policy should the utilitarian choose?

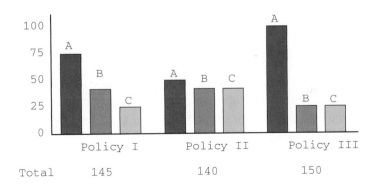

NOTES

1. Sophocles, *Antigone*, trans. Robert Eagles (Baltimore: Penguin Classics, 1947), lines 204–214. I am indebted to an anonymous reviewer for this reference.
2. Jeremy Bentham, *An Introduction to the Principles of Morals and Legislation* (1789), Chapter 1.
3. Ibid.
4. All remaining passages in this section are from John Stuart Mill, *Utilitarianism* (1863), Chapter 2.
5. Although it is generally agreed that Bentham was an act utilitarian, controversy remains about whether Mill was one. He seems not to have taken the distinction between act and rule utilitarianism seriously. See David Brink, "Mill's Deliberative Utilitarianism," *Philosophy & Public Affairs* 21:1 (Fall 1992), for a good discussion of this issue.

6. Richard Brandt, "Towards a Credible Form of Utilitarianism," in *Morality and the Language of Conduct,* ed. H. Castaneda and G. Naknikian (Detroit: Wayne State University Press, 1963), 109–110.

7. Kai Nielsen, "Against Moral Conservatism," in *Ethics* (1972), reprinted in Louis Pojman, ed., *Ethical Theory: Classical and Contemporary Readings* (Belmont, CA: Wadsworth, 1989), 181–188. Nielsen no longer holds the position espoused in this article. J. J. C. Smart, *Outlines of a Utilitarian System of Ethics* (Melbourne, 1961); and J. J. C. Smart and Bernard Williams, *Utilitarianism: For and Against* (Cambridge, UK: Cambridge University Press, 1973).

8. Kai Nielsen, "The Case of the Innocent Fat Man," reprinted in Pojman, ed., *Ethical Theory,* 194.

9. See Anthony Quinton's *Utilitarian Ethics* (London: Macmillan, 1973), 49f., for a good discussion of this and similar points. My discussion is indebted to Quinton.

10. Arthur Koestler, *Darkness at Noon* (New York: Macmillan, 1941), 80.

11. This example is found in Judith Jarvis Thomson's "The Trolley Problem," in *Rights, Restitution, and Risk* (Cambridge, MA: Harvard University Press, 1986), 94–116.

12. Dietrich von Nieheim, Bishop of Verden, *De Schismate Librii* (1411 CE), quoted in Koestler, *Darkness at Noon,* 76.

FOR FURTHER READING

Bentham, Jeremy. *Introduction to the Principles of Morals and Legislation.* Edited by W. Harrison. Oxford, UK: Oxford University Press, 1948.

Brandt, Richard. "Towards a Credible Form of Rule-Utilitarianism." In *Morality and the Language of Conduct.* Edited by H. N. Castaneda and George Nakhnikian. Detroit: Wayne State University, 1963. This often-anthologized article is one of the most sophisticated defenses of utilitarianism.

Brandt, Richard. *A Theory of the Good and the Right.* Oxford, UK: Clarendon Press, 1979.

Brink, David. *Moral Realism and the Foundation of Ethics.* Cambridge, UK: Cambridge University Press, 1989. Chapter 8 is an excellent discussion of utilitarianism.

Brock, Dan. "Recent Work in Utilitarianism." *American Philosophical Quarterly* 10 (October 1973).

Hardin, Russell. *Morality Within the Limits of Reason.* Chicago: University of Chicago Press, 1988. A cogent contemporary defense of utilitarianism.

Hare, R. M. *Moral Thinking.* Oxford, UK: Oxford University Press, 1981.

Lyons, David. *Forms and Limits of Utilitarianism.* Oxford, UK: Oxford University Press, 1965.

Mill, John Stuart. *Utilitarianism.* Indianapolis: Bobbs-Merrill, 1957.

Miller, Harlan, B., and William Williams, eds. *The Limits of Utilitarianism.* Minneapolis/St. Paul: University of Minnesota Press, 1982. Contains important but advanced articles.

Parfit, Derik. *Reasons and Persons.* Oxford, UK: Oxford University Press, 1984.

Quinton, Anthony. *Utilitarian Ethics*. London: Macmillan, 1973. A clear exposition of classical utilitarianism.

Scheffler, Samuel. *The Rejection of Consequentialism*. Oxford, UK: Clarendon Press, 1982. A careful discussion, including an outline of a hybrid system between deontological and utilitarian theories.

Scheffler, Samuel, ed. *Consequentialism and Its Critics*. Oxford, UK: Oxford University Press, 1988. Contains important selections, many of which refocus the debate between consequentialists and deontologists.

Sen, Amartya, and Bernard Williams, eds. *Utilitarianism and Beyond*. Cambridge, UK: Cambridge University Press, 1982. Contains important readings.

Smart, J. J. C., and Bernard Williams. *Utilitarianism: For & Against*. Cambridge, UK: Cambridge University Press, 1973. A classic debate on the subject.

31 ✣ Kantian Deontological Ethics

Duty, Thou sublime and mighty name that dost embrace nothing charming or insinuating but requirest submission and yet seekest not to move the will by threatening aught that would arouse natural aversion or terror, but only holdest forth a law which of itself finds entrance into the mind and yet gains reluctant reverence—a law before which all inclinations are dumb, which proudly rejects all kinship with the inclinations and is the indispensable condition for the only worth which men can give themselves.

Immanuel Kant[1]

Hour by hour resolve to do the task of the hour carefully, with unaffected dignity, affectionately, freely and justly. You can avoid distraction that might interfere with such performance if every act is done as though it were the last act of your life. Free yourself from random aims and curb any tendency to let the passions of emotion, hypocrisy, self-love and dissatisfaction with your allotted share cause you to ignore the commands of reasons.

Marcus Aurelius (121–180 CE)

What makes a right act right? The teleological answer to this question is that it is the good consequences that make it right. Moral rightness and wrongness are determined by nonmoral values (for example, happiness or utility). To this extent, the end justifies the means. The deontological answer to this question is quite the opposite. The end never justifies the means. Indeed, you must do your duty whatever the consequences, simply because it is your duty. As the quotation from the Stoic Emperor Marcus Aurelius indicates, you must do your duty disinterestedly, as though it was the last act of your life, simply because it is your duty. Similarly, the Danish philosopher Søren Kierkegaard (1813–1855) describes his childhood experience of sensing his duty to learn his first-grade grammar lesson:

When I was five years old I was sent to school. I made my appearance at school, was introduced to the teacher, and then was given as my lesson for the following day, the first ten lines of Balle's *Lesson Book,* which I was to learn by heart. Every other impression was then obliterated from my soul, only my task stood out vividly before it. As a child I had a good memory, so I had soon learned my lesson. My sister had heard me recite it several times and affirmed that I knew it. I went to bed, and before I fell asleep I catechized myself once more; I fell asleep with the firm purpose of reading the lesson over the following morning. I awoke at five o'clock, got dressed, got hold of my lesson-book and read it again. At this moment everything stands as vividly before my eyes as if it had occurred yesterday. To me it was as if heaven and earth might collapse if I did not learn my lesson, and on the other hand as if, even if heaven and earth were to collapse, this would not exempt me from doing what was assigned to me. I had only one duty, that of learning my lesson, and yet I can trace my whole ethical view of life to this impression.[2]

It is not the consequences that determine the rightness or wrongness of an act but certain features in the act itself. For example, there is something right about truth telling and promise keeping even when acting thusly may bring about some harm, and there is something wrong about lying and promise breaking even when acting thusly may bring about good consequences. Acting unjustly is wrong even if it will maximize expected utility. Referring to our examples in Chapter 30, as a deontologist you would very likely keep your promise and give the $2 million to the Yankees and share or flip a coin for the food on the raft.

Kant's Rationalist Deontological System

Immanuel Kant (1724–1804), the greatest philosopher of the German Enlightenment and one of the most important philosophers of all time, was both an *absolutist* and a *deontological* rationalist. He believed that we could use reason to work out an absolute (that is, nonoverridable) consistent set of moral principles.

To understand Kant's moral philosophy, it is helpful to understand a little about his life. Kant was born in Königsberg, Germany, in 1724 and died there in 1804, never having left the surroundings of the city. His father was a saddle maker. His parents were Pietists (from *piety,* dutifulness in religion), a sect in the Lutheran Church. The Pietists, much like present-day Quakers, emphasized sincerity, deep feeling, and the moral life rather than theological doctrine or orthodox belief. Pietism is a religion of the heart, not the head, of the spirit rather than ritual. However, Kant as an intellectual emphasized the head as much as the heart, but it was a head that was concerned about the moral life, especially the good will.

Kant was a quiet man, short and methodical—so methodical that tradition has it that the citizens of Königsberg set their watches by his daily three o'clock walks. He never married but devoted his life to the study and teaching of philosophy. He taught philosophy at the University of Königsberg. His *magnum opus, The Critique of Pure Reason* (1781), was heralded in his own day as a monumental work, and his *The Foundations of the Metaphysics of Morals* (1785) is generally regarded as one of the two or three most important books in the history of ethics.

There were three strong influences on Kant's ethical thinking. The first is Pietism, already mentioned, which set a tone of deep sincerity to his views. It is not correct beliefs or results that really matter, but inner goodness. The idea is that if we live within our lights we will be given more light, and God judges us not on how lucky or successful we are in accomplishing our tasks but on how earnestly we have lived according to our principles. It is this influence that informs his notion of the good will as the sole intrinsic good in life.

The second influence was the work of Jean-Jacques Rousseau (1712–1778) on human freedom, especially his *Social Contract,* and it was said that the only time Kant ever missed his three o'clock walk was on the day that he read the tome. Rousseau taught him the meaning and importance of human dignity, the primacy of freedom and **autonomy,** and that human beings had intrinsic worth apart from any functions they might perform.

Finally, Kant was influenced by the debate between **rationalism** and **empiricism,** which took place in the 17th and 18th centuries. Rationalists, such as René Descartes, Baruch Spinoza, Gottfried Leibniz, and Christian Wolff, claimed that pure reason could tell us how the world is, independent of experience. We can know metaphysical truth—such as the existence of God, the immortality of the soul, freedom of the will, and the universality of causal relations—apart from experience (experience may be necessary to open our minds to these ideas, but essentially they are innate ideas, synthetic a priori truths). Empiricists, led by John Locke and David Hume, on the other hand, denied that we had any innate ideas and argued that all knowledge came from experience. Our minds were a *tabula rasa*, an empty slate, upon which experience wrote her lessons.

The rationalists and empiricists carried their debate into the area of moral knowledge. The rationalists claimed that our knowledge of moral principles was a type of metaphysical knowledge, implanted in us by God, and discoverable by reason as it deduces general principles about human nature. The British empiricists, especially Francis Hutcheson, David Hume, and Adam Smith, on the other hand, argued that morality is founded entirely on the contingencies of human nature and based on desire. Morality has to do with making people happy, fulfilling their reflected desires, and reason is just a practical means of helping us obtain our desires. There is nothing of special importance in reason in its own right. It is mainly a rationalizer and servant of the passions ("a pimp of the passions"). As Hume said, "Reason is and ought only to be a slave of the passions and can never pretend to any other office than to serve and obey them." Morality is founded on our feeling of sympathy with other people's sufferings, on fellow feeling. For such empiricists, then, morality is contingent upon human nature:

Human nature $\longrightarrow$ Feelings and desires $\longrightarrow$ Moral principles

If we had a different nature, we would have different feelings and desires, and hence we would have different moral principles.

Kant rejected the ideas of Hutcheson, Hume, and Smith. He was outraged by the thought that morality should depend on human nature and be subject to the fortunes of change and the luck of empirical discovery. Morality is not contingent but necessary. It would be no less binding on us if our feelings were different than they are.

THE FOUNDATIONS OF THE METAPHYSICS OF MORALS

As my concern here is with moral philosophy, I limit the question to this: Whether it is not of the utmost necessity to construct a pure moral philosophy, perfectly cleared of everything which is only *empirical,* and which belongs to anthropology? for that such a philosophy must be possible is evident from the common idea of duty and of the moral laws. Everyone must admit that if a law is to have moral force, that is, to be the basis of an obligation, it must carry with it *absolute necessity.* For example, the precept, "Thou shall not lie," is not valid for men alone, as if other rational beings had no need to observe it. And so with all the other moral laws properly so-called. Therefore, the basis of obligation must not be sought in the nature of man or in the circumstances in the world in which he is placed, but a priori simply in the conception of pure reason; and although any other precept which is founded on principles of mere experience may be in certain respects universal, yet in as far as it rests even in the least degree on an empirical basis, perhaps only as to a motive, such a precept, while it may be a practical rule, can never be called a moral law.

Every empirical element is not only quite incapable of being an aid to the principle of morality, but is even highly prejudicial to the purity of morals; for the proper and inestimable worth of an absolutely good will consists just in this, that the principle of action is free from all influence of contingent grounds, which alone experience can furnish. We cannot too much or too often repeat our warning against this lax and even mean habit of thought which seeks for its principle amongst empirical motives and laws; for human reason in its weariness is glad to rest on this pillow, and in a dream of sweet illusions it substitutes for morality a bastard patched up from limbs of various derivation, which looks like anything one chooses to see in it; only not like virtue to one who has once beheld her in her true form.

No, said Kant, it is not our desires that ground morality, but our rational will. Reason is sufficient for establishing the moral law as something transcendent and universally binding on all rational creatures.

Kant wants to remove moral truth from the zone of contingency and empirical observation and place it securely in the area of **necessary truth**—an absolute, universal truth. The term *a priori* means "prior to experience" and refers to the fact that morality can be justified independently of empirical considerations. Kant continues with an explanation of the good will as the basis of the moral law.[3]

From: Immanuel Kant, *The Foundations of the Metaphysics of Morals,* trans. T. K. Abbott (1873). I have revised the translation.

The Good Will

Nothing can possibly be conceived in the world, or even out of it, which can be called good, without qualification, except a Good Will. Intelligence, wit, judgment, and the other *talents* of the mind, however they may be named, or courage, resolution, perseverance, as qualities of temperament, are undoubtedly good and desirable in may respects; but these gifts of nature may also become extremely bad and mischievous if the will which is to make use of them, and which, therefore, constitutes what is called *character,* is not good. It is the same with the *gifts of fortune.* Powers, riches, honour, even health, and the general well-being and contentment with one's conditions which is called *happiness,* inspire pride, and often presumption, if there is not a good will to correct the influence of these on the mind, and with this also to rectify the whole principle of acting, and adapt it to its end. The sight of a being who is not adorned with a single feature of a pure and good will, enjoying unbroken prosperity, can never give pleasure to an impartial rational spectator. Thus a good will appears to constitute the indispensable condition even of being worthy of happiness.

There are even some qualities which are of service to this good will itself, and may facilitate its action, yet which have no intrinsic unconditional value, but always presuppose a good will, and this qualifies the esteem that we justly have for them, and does not permit us to regard them as absolutely good. Moderation in the affections and passions, self-control, and calm deliberation are not only good in may respects, but even seem to constitute part of the intrinsic worth of the person; but they are far from deserving to be called good without qualification, although they have been so unconditionally praised by the ancients. For without the principles of a good will, they may become extremely bad; and the coolness of a villain not only makes him far more dangerous, but also directly makes him more abominable in our eyes than he would have been without it.

A good will is good not because of what it performs or effects, not by its aptness for the attainment of some proposed end, but simply by virtue of the volition, that is, it is good in itself, and considered by itself to be esteemed much higher than all that can be brought about by it in favour of any inclination, nay, even of the sum-total of all inclinations. Even if it should happen that, owing to special disfavour of fortune, or the [grudging] provision of a step-motherly nature, this will should wholly lack power to accomplish its purpose, if with its greatest efforts it should yet achieve nothing, and there should remain only the good will (not, to be sure, a mere wish, but the summoning of all means in our power), then, like a jewel, it would still shine by its own light, as a thing which has its whole value in itself. Its usefulness or fruitlessness can neither add to nor take away anything from this value. It would be, as it were, only the setting to enable us to handle it the more conveniently in common commerce, or to attract to it the attention of those who are not yet connoisseurs, but not to recommend it to true connoisseurs, or to determine its value.

The only thing that is intrinsically good, good in itself and without qualification, is the good will. All the other virtues, both intellectual and moral, can serve the vicious will and thus contribute to evil. None of these are good in themselves but only for a further purpose. They can be united in themselves but only for further purposes. They are only valuable if accompanied by good will. Even success and happiness are not good in themselves. Honor can lead to pride. Happiness without good will is not worthwhile. Is honor with deceit worth attaining? No. Nor is utilitarianism plausible, for if we have a quantity of happiness to distribute, is it just to distribute it equally regardless of virtue? Should we not distribute it discriminately, according to moral goodness? Happiness should be distributed in proportion to one's moral worth, and happiness without moral worth is not inherently valuable.

How good is Kant's argument for the good will? Could we imagine a world where nonmoral virtues were always and necessarily put to good use, where it was simply impossible to use a virtue like intelligence for evil? Is happiness any less good simply because it can be distributed incorrectly? Can't the good will itself be put to bad use, as with the misguided do-gooder? As the aphorism goes, "The road to hell is paved with good intentions." Could Hitler have had good intentions in carrying out his dastardly programs? Can't the good will have bad effects?

We may agree that the good will is a great good, but it is not obvious on Kant's account that it is the only inherently good thing, for even as intelligence and courage and happiness can be put to bad uses, so can the good will; and even as it does not seem to count against the good will that it can be put to a bad use, so it shouldn't count against the other virtues that they can be put to bad uses. The good will may be a necessary element to any morally good action, but it's another question whether it is also a sufficient condition to moral goodness.

Perhaps we can reinterpret Kant in such a way as to preserve his central insight. There does seem to be something morally valuable about the good will apart from any consequences. Consider this illustration. Two soldiers volunteer to cross the enemy lines to make contact with their allies on the other side of the enemy lines. They both start off and do their best to make their way through the enemy's area. One succeeds, but the other doesn't and is captured. Aren't they both morally praiseworthy? The success of one in no way detracts from the goodness of the other. Judged from a commonsense moral point of view, their actions are equally good, even though judged from a utilitarian or consequentialist view the successful act is far more valuable than the unsuccessful one. Here one may distinguish the agent's worth from the value of the consequences and make two separate, nonconflicting judgments.

Duty and the Moral Law

Let's see how Kant develops these ideas in his theory of the moral law: the *categorical imperative*.

The First Proposition of Morality [An Action Must Be Done from a Sense of Duty, If It Is to Have Moral Worth]

We have then to develop the notion of a will which deserves to be highly esteemed for itself, and is good without a view to anything further, a notion which exists already in the sound natural understanding, requiring rather to be cleared up than to be taught, and which in estimating the value of our actions always takes the first place, and constitutes the condition of all the rest. In order to do this, we will take the notion of duty, which includes that of a good will, although implying certain subjective restrictions and hindrances. These, however, far from concealing it, or rendering it unrecognizable, rather bring it out by contrast, and make it shine forth so much the brighter.

I omit here all actions which are already recognized as inconsistent with duty although they may be useful for this or that purpose, for with these the question whether they are done *from duty* cannot arise at all, since they even conflict with it. I also set aside those actions which really conform to duty, but to which men have *no* direct *inclination*, performing them because they are impelled thereto by some other inclination. For in this case we can readily distinguish whether the action which agrees with duty is done *from duty,* or from a selfish view. It is much harder to make this distinction when the action accords with duty, and the subject has besides a *direct* inclination to it. For example, it is always a matter of duty that a dealer should not overcharge an inexperienced purchaser; and wherever there is much commerce the prudent tradesman does not overcharge, but keeps a fixed price for everyone, so that a child buys of him as well as any other. Men are thus *honestly* served; but this is not enough to make us believe that the tradesman has so acted from duty and principles of honesty: his own advantage required it; it is out of the question in this case to suppose that he might besides have a direct inclination in favour of the buyers, so that, as it were, from love he should give no advantage to one over another. Accordingly the action was done neither from duty nor from direct inclination, but merely with a selfish view.

On the other hand, it is a duty to maintain one's life; and, in addition, everyone has also a direct inclination to do so. But on this account the often anxious care which most men take for it has no intrinsic worth, and their maxim has no moral import. They preserve their life *as duty requires,* no doubt, but not *because duty requires.* On the other hand, if adversity and hopeless sorrow have completely taken away the relish for life; if the unfortunate one, strong in mind, indignant at his fate rather than desponding or dejected, wishes for death, and yet preserves his life without loving it—not from inclination or fear, but from duty—then his maxim has a moral worth.

To be beneficent when we can is a duty; and besides this, there are many minds so sympathetically constituted that, without any other motive of vanity or self-interest, they find a pleasure in spreading joy around them, and can take delight in the satisfaction of others so far as it is their own work. But I maintain that in such a case an action of this kind, however proper, however amiable it may be, has nevertheless no true moral worth, but is on a level with other inclinations, *e.g.,* the inclination to honour, which, if it is happily directed to that which is in fact of public utility and accordant with duty, and consequently honourable, deserves praise and encouragement, but not esteem. For the maxim lacks the moral import, namely, that such actions be done *from duty,* not from inclination. Put the case that the mind of that philanthropist was clouded by sorrow of his own, extinguishing all sympathy with the lot of others, and that while he still has the power to benefit others in distress, he is not touched by their trouble because he is absorbed with his own; and now suppose that he tears himself out of this dead insensibility, and performs the action without any inclination to it, but simply from duty, then first has his action its genuine moral worth. Further still; if nature has put little sympathy in the heart of this or that man; if he, supposed to be an upright man, is by temperament cold and indifferent to the sufferings of others, perhaps because in respect of his own he is provided with the special gift of patience and fortitude, and supposes, or even requires, that others should have the same—and such a man would certainly not be the meanest product of nature—but if nature had not specially framed him for a philanthropist, would he not still find in himself a source from whence to give himself a far higher worth than that of a good-natured temperament could be? Unquestionably. It is just in this that the moral worth of the character is brought out which is incomparably the highest of all, namely, that he is beneficent, not from inclination, but from duty.

To secure one's own happiness is a duty, at least indirectly; for discontent with one's condition, under a pressure of many anxieties and amidst unsatisfied wants, might easily become a great *temptation to transgression of duty.* But there again, without looking to duty, all men have already the strongest and most intimate inclination to happiness, because it is just in this idea that all inclinations are combined in one total. But the precept of happiness is often of such a sort that it greatly interferes with some inclinations, and yet a man cannot form any definite and certain conception of the sum of satisfaction of all of them which is called happiness. It is not then to be wondered at that a single inclination, definite both as to what it promises and as to the time within which it can be gratified, is often able to overcome such a fluctuating idea, and that a gouty patient, for instance, can choose to enjoy what he likes, and to suffer what he may, since, according to his calculation, on this occasion at least, he has [only] not sacrificed the enjoyment of the present moment to a possibly mistaken expectation of a happiness which is supposed to be found in health. But even in this case, if the general desire for happiness did not influence his will, and supposing that in his particular case health was not a necessary element in this calculation, there yet remains in this, as in all other cases, this law, namely, that he should promote his happiness not from inclination but from duty, and by this would his conduct first acquire true moral worth.

It is in this manner, undoubtedly, that we are to understand those passages of Scripture also in which we are commanded to love our neighbour, even our enemy. For love, as an affection, cannot be commanded, but benefience for duty's sake may; even though we are not impelled to it by any inclination—nay, are even repelled by a natural and unconquerable aversion. This is *practical* love, and not *pathological**—a love which is seated in the will, and not in the propensions of sense—in principles of action and not of tender sympathy; and it is this love alone which can be commanded.

The Second Proposition of Morality

The second proposition is: That an action done from duty derives its moral worth, *not from the purpose* which is to be attained by it, but from the maxim by which it is determined, and therefore does not depend on the realization of the object of the action,

---

*[Passional or emotional—Ed.]

but merely on the *principle of volition* by which the action has taken place, without regard to any object of desire. It is clear from what precedes that the purposes which we may have in view in our actions, or their effects regarded as ends and springs of the will, cannot give to actions any unconditional or moral worth. In what, then, can their worth lie, if it is not to consist in the will and in reference to its expected effect? It cannot lie anywhere but in the *principle of the will* without regard to the ends which can be attained by the action. For the will stands between its *a priori principle,* which is formal, and its *a posteriori* spring, which is material, as between two roads, and as it must be determined by something, it follows that it must be determined by the formal principle of volition when an action is done from duty, in which case every material principle has been withdrawn from it.

The Third Proposition of Morality

The third proposition, which is a consequence of the two preceding, I would express thus: *Duty is the necessity of acting from respect for the law.* I may have *inclination* for an object as the effect of my proposed action, but I cannot have *respect* for it, just for this reason, that it is an effect and not an energy of will. Similarly, I cannot have respect for inclination, whether my own or another's; I can at most, if my own, approve it; if another's, sometimes even love it; *i.e.* look on it as favourable to my own interest. It is only what is connected with my will as a principle, by no means as an effect—what does not subserve my inclination, but overpowers it, or at least in case of choices excludes it from its calculation—in other words, simply the law of itself, which can be an object of respect, and hence a command. Now an action done from duty must wholly exclude the influence of inclination, and with it every object of the will, so that nothing remains which can determine the will except objectively the *law,* and subjectively *pure respect* for this practical law, and consequently the maxim that I should follow this law even to the thwarting of all my inclinations.

Thus the moral worth of an action does not lie in the effect expected from it, nor in any principle of action which requires to borrow its motive from this expected effect. For all these effects—agreeableness of one's condition, and even the promotion of the happiness of others—could have been also brought about by other causes, so that for this there would have been no need of the will of a rational being; whereas it is in this alone that the supreme and unconditional good can be found. The pre-eminent good which we call moral can therefore consist in nothing else than *the conception of law* in itself, *which certainly is only possible in a rational being,* in so far as this conception, and not the expected effect, determines the will. This is a good which is already present in the person who acts accordingly, and we have not to wait for it to appear first in the result.

As we noted earlier, Kant wants to remove moral truth from the zone of contingency and empirical observation and place it securely in the area of necessary, absolute, universal truth. Morality's value is not based on the fact that it has instrumental value, that it often secures nonmoral goods such as happiness, but it is valuable in its own right. As such, an act has moral worth only if it is done from a sense of duty. An act done from duty derives its moral worth not from the consequences aimed at but from the maxim (that is, subjective principle) upon which it is based. Finally, duty is defined as "necessity of acting from respect for the law."

Next Kant discusses moral principles as a kind of imperative. All mention of duties (or obligations) can be translated into the language of imperatives or commands. Moral duties have imperative force. Kant distinguishes two kinds of imperatives: hypothetical and categorical. The formula for the **hypothetical imperative** is

If you want to A, then do B.

Two examples are "If you want to get a good job, get a good education," and "If you want to be happy, stay sober and live a balanced life." The formula for a **categorical imperative** is simply

Do B!

That is, do what reason discloses to be the intrinsically right thing to do (for example, "Tell the truth!"). Hypothetical or means–ends imperatives are not the imperatives that characterize moral actions. Categorical or unqualified imperatives are the right kind of imperatives, for they show proper recognition of the imperial status of moral obligations. This imperative is an intuitive, immediate, absolute injunction that all rational agents understand by virtue of their rationality.

Moral duty must be done solely for its own sake ("Duty for duty's sake"). Some people conform to the moral law because they deem it in their own enlightened self-interest to be moral, but they are not moral because they do not act for the sake of the moral law. For example, a businessman may believe that "honesty is the best policy." That is, he may judge that it is conducive to good business to give his customers correct change and good-quality products, but unless he does these acts *because* they are his duty, he is not acting morally, even though his acts are the same ones that they would be if he were acting morally.

The kind of imperative that fits Kant's scheme as a product of reason is one that universalizes principles of conduct. He names it the categorical imperative: "Act only on that maxim whereby thou canst at the same time will that it would become a universal law." This is given as the criterion (or second-order principle) by which to judge all other principles. Let us turn back to the text.

First Formulation of the Categorical Imperative: Universal Law

In this problem we will first inquire whether the mere conception of a categorical imperative may not perhaps supply us also with the formula of it, containing the proposition which alone can be a categorical imperative; for even if we know the tenor of such an absolute command, yet how it is possible will require further special and laborious study, which we postpone to the last section.

When I conceive a hypothetical imperative, in general I do not know beforehand what it will contain until I am given the condition. But when I conceive a categorical imperative, I know at once what it contains. For as the imperative contains besides the law only the necessity that the maxims shall conform to this law, while the law contain no conditions restricting it, there remains nothing but the general statement that the maxim of the action should conform to a universal law, and it is this conformity alone that the imperative properly represents as necessary.

There is therefore but one categorical imperative, namely, this: *Act only on that maxim whereby thou canst at the same time will that it should become a universal law.*

Now if all imperatives of duty can be deduced from this one imperative as from their principle, then, although it should remain undecided whether what is called duty is not merely a vain notion, yet at least we shall be able to show what we understand by it and what this notion means.

Since the universality of the law according to which effects are produced constitutes what is properly called *nature* in the most general sense (as to form), that is the existence of things so far as it is determined by general laws, the imperative of duty may be expressed thus: *Act as if the maxim of thy action were to become by thy will a universal law of nature.*

By *maxim*, Kant means the general rule in accordance with which the agent intends to act; by *law*, he means an objective principle, a maxim which passes the test of **universalizability.** The categorical imperative is the way to apply the universalizability test. It enables us to stand outside our personal maxims and estimate impartially and impersonally whether they are suitable as principles for all of us to live by. If you could consistently will that everyone would do some type of action, then there is an application of the categorical imperative enjoining that type of action. If you cannot consistently will that everyone would do some type of action, then that type of action is morally wrong. The maxim must be rejected as self-defeated. The formula looks like this:

Maxim (*M*)

↓

Second-order principle (*CI*) ⟶ Rejected maxims

↓

First-order principle (*P*)

Kant offers four illustrations of this principle.

We will now enumerate a few duties, adopting the usual division of them into duties to ourselves and to others, and into perfect and imperfect duties.

1. A man reduced to despair by a series of misfortunes feels wearied of life, but is still so far in possession of his reason that he can ask himself whether it would not be contrary to his duty to himself to take his own life. Now he inquires whether the maxim of his action could become a universal law of nature. His maxim is: From self-love I adopt it as a principle to shorten my life when its longer duration is likely to bring more

evil than satisfaction. It is asked then simply whether this principle founded on self-love can become a universal law of nature. Now we see at once that a system of nature of which it should be a law to destroy life by means of the very feeling whose special nature it is to impel to the improvement of life would contradict itself, and therefore could not exist as a system of nature; hence that maxim cannot possibly exist as a universal law of nature, and consequently would be wholly inconsistent with the supreme principle of all duty.

2. Another finds himself forced by necessity to borrow money. He knows that he will not be able to repay it, but sees also that nothing will be lent to him, unless he promises stoutly to repay it in a definite time. He desires to make this promise, but he has still so much conscience as to ask himself: Is it not unlawful and inconsistent with duty to get out of a difficulty in this way? Suppose, however, that he resolves to do so, then the maxim of his action would be expressed thus: When I think myself in want of money, I will borrow money and promise to repay it, although I know that I never can do so. Now this principle of self-love or of one's own advantage may perhaps be consistent with my whole future welfare; but the question is, Is it right? I change then the suggestion of self-love into a universal law, and state the question thus: How would it be if my maxim were a universal law? Then I see at once that it could never hold as a universal law of nature, but would necessarily contradict itself. For supposing it to be a universal law that everyone when he thinks himself in a difficulty should be able to promise whatever he pleases, with the purpose of not keeping his promise, the promise itself would become impossible, as well as the end that one might have in view in it, since no one would consider that anything was promised to him, but would ridicule all such statements as vain pretenses.

3. A third finds in himself a talent which with the help of some culture might make him a useful man in many respects. But he finds himself in comfortable circumstances, and prefers to indulge in pleasure rather than to take pains in enlarging and improving his happy natural capacities. He asks, however, whether his maxim of neglect of his natural gifts, besides agreeing with his inclination to indulgence, agrees also with what is called duty. He sees then that a system of nature could indeed subsist with such a universal law although men (like the South Sea islanders) should let their talents rest, and resolve to devote their lives merely to idleness, amusement, and propagation of their species—in a word, to enjoyment; but he cannot possibly *will* that this should be a universal law of nature, or be implanted in us as such by a natural instinct. For, as a rational being, he necessarily wills that his faculties be developed, since they serve him, and have been given him, for all sorts of possible purposes.

4. A fourth, who is in prosperity, while he sees that others have to contend with great wretchedness and that he could help them, thinks: What concern is it of mine? Let everyone be as happy as Heaven pleases, or as he can make himself; I will take nothing from him nor even envy him, only I do not wish to contribute anything to his welfare or to his assistance in distress! Now no doubt if such a mode of thinking were a universal law, the human race might very well subsist, and doubtless even better than in a state in which everyone talks of sympathy and good-will, or even takes care occasionally to put it into practice, but, on the other side, also cheats when he can, betrays the rights of men, or otherwise violates them. But although it is possible that a

universal law of nature might exist in accordance with that maxim, it is impossible to *will* that such a principle should have the universal validity of a law of nature. For a will which resolved this would contradict itself, inasmuch as many cases might occur in which one would have need of the love and sympathy of others, and in which, by such a law of nature, sprung from his own will, he would deprive himself of all hope of the aid he desires.

These are a few of the many actual duties, or at least what we regard as such, which obviously fall into two classes on the one principle that we have laid down. We must be *able to will* that a maxim of our action should be a universal law. This is the canon of the moral appreciation of the action generally. Some actions are of such a character that their maxim cannot without contradiction be even *conceived* as a universal law of nature, far from it being possible that we should *will* that it *should* be so. In others this intrinsic impossibility is not found, but still it is impossible to *will* that their maxim should be raised to the universality of a law of nature, since such a will would contradict itself. It is easily seen that the former violate strict or rigorous (inflexible) duty; the latter only laxer (meritorious) duty. Thus it has been completely shown by these examples how all duties depend as regards the nature of the obligation (not the object of the action) on the same principle.

Let's examine the first example. Suppose I need some money and consider whether it would be moral to borrow the money from you and promise to repay it without intending ever to do so.

M: Whenever I need money, I should make a lying promise while borrowing the money.

Can I universalize the maxim of my act?

P: Whenever anyone needs money, that person should make a lying promise while borrowing the money.

But something has gone wrong, for if I universalize this principle of making promises without intending to keep them, I would be involved in a contradiction. The resulting state of affairs would be self-defeating, for no one in his right mind would take promises as promises unless there was the expectation of fulfillment. Thus, the maxim of the lying promise fails the universalizability criterion. Hence, it is immoral.

Now I universalize the opposite:

M_1: Whenever I need money, I should make a sincere promise while borrowing it.

Can I universalize this maxim?

P_1: Whenever anyone needs money, he or she should make a sincere promise while borrowing it.

Yes, I can universalize M_1, for there is nothing self-defeating or contradictory in this. So, it follows, making sincere promises is moral. We can make the maxim of promise keeping into a universal law.

Test Kant's formula on his other three illustrations. Do they come out as well as the first one? Does the categorical imperative prohibit suicide? The principle might be formulated as

P: Whenever it looks like one will experience more pain than pleasure, one ought to kill himself.

According to Kant, this involves a self-contradiction in that it would go against the very *principle of survival* itself upon which it is based. But whatever the merit of the form of this argument, we could modify the principle to read:

P_1: Whenever the pain or suffering of existence erodes the quality of life in such a way as to make nonexistence a preference to suffering existence, one is permitted to commit suicide.

Why couldn't this (or something close to it) be universalized? It would not oppose the general principle of survival itself but cover rare instances where no hope is in sight for terminally ill patients and victims of torture or deep depression, but not cover the normal kinds of suffering and depression that most of us experience in the normal course of life. Kant seems unduly absolutist in his prohibition of suicide.

Kant's other two examples of the application of the categorical imperative are also questionable. In his third example, he claims that we cannot universalize a maxim to refrain from developing our talents. But again, could we not qualify this and stipulate that under certain circumstances it was permissible not to develop our talents? Perhaps Kant is correct, that if everyone refrained from developing any talent, society would soon degenerate into anarchy, but couldn't one universalize the following maxim?

M_2: Whenever I am not inclined to develop a talent and this refraining will not seriously undermine the social order, I may so refrain.

Kant's fourth example of the way the categorical imperative functions regards the situation of not coming to the aid of others whenever I am secure and independent. He claims that I cannot universalize this maxim because I never know whether I will need the help of others in some future time. It seems that Kant is wrong again. I could universalize that people who are completely independent never help those who are less well-off just as long as their own independence is not threatened by the less well-off. Perhaps it would be selfish and cruel to make this into a universal law, but I don't see anything contradictory or self-defeating in the principle itself. The problems with universalizing selfishness are the same ones that we encountered in analyzing egoism, but it's dubious whether Kant's categorical imperative captures what is wrong with egoism. Perhaps he has other weapons that do capture what is wrong with egoism. We will return to this later.

Kant thought that he could generate an entire moral law from his categorical imperative. It seems to work with such principles of promise keeping and truth telling and a few other maxims, but it doesn't seem to give us all that Kant wanted. It has been objected that Kant's categorical imperative is both *too wide* and *too unqualified,* leading to horrendous possibilities.

The charge that it is too wide is based on the perception that it seems to justify some actions that we would think to be trivial and even immoral. Consider, for example, principle P:

P: Everyone should always tie one's right shoe before one's left shoe.

Can we universalize P without contradiction? Why not? Just as we universalize that people should drive cars on the right side of the street rather than the left, we could make it a law that everyone would tie the right shoe before the left shoe. It seems obvious that there would be no point to such a law. It would be trivial, but it is justified by the categorical imperative.

It may be objected that all this counterexample shows is that it may be permissible to live by the principle of tying the right shoe before the left, for we could also universalize the opposite maxim (tying the left before the right) without contradiction. That seems correct.

A more serious objection is the charge that the categorical imperative seems to justify acts that we judge to be horrendously immoral. Consider P_1:

P_1: Always kill blue-eyed children.

Is there anything contradictory in this injunction? Could we make it into a universal law? Why not? Blue-eyed children might not like it, but there is no logical contradiction involved in such a principle. Had I been a blue-eyed child when this command was in effect, I would not be around to write this book, but the world would have survived my loss without too much inconvenience.

Of course, it would be possible to universalize the opposite—that no one should kill innocent people—but that only shows that either type of action is permissible.

It may be objected that Kant presupposed that only rational acts could be universalized, but this won't work, for the categorical imperative is supposed to be the criterion for rational action.

It may be that when we come to Kant's second formulation of the categorical imperative, he will have more ammunition with which to defeat P_1.

Finally, Kant thought that the categorical imperative yielded unqualified **absolutes.** The rules that the categorical imperative generates are universal and exceptionless. He illustrates this point with regard to truth telling. Suppose an innocent man comes to your door, begging for asylum, for a group of gangsters is hunting him down in order to kill him. You take the man in and hide him in your third-floor attic. Moments later, the gangsters arrive and inquire after the innocent man. "Is he in your house?" they inquire. What should you do? Kant's advice is to tell them the truth: "Yes, he's in my house."[4]

What is Kant's reasoning here? It is simply that the moral law is sacrosanct and exceptionless. It is your duty to obey its commands, not to reason about the likely consequences. You have done your duty: hidden an innocent man and told the truth when asked a straightforward question. You are absolved of any responsibility for the harm that comes to the innocent man, for it's not your fault that gangsters are in the world.

To many of us, this kind of absolutism seems counterintuitive. There are two ways in which we might alter Kant here. The first way is simply to write in qualifications to the universal principles, changing the sweeping generalization "Never lie" to the more modest "Never lie except in order to save an innocent person's life." The trouble with this way of solving the problem of the sweeping generalization is that there seem to be no limits on the qualifications that would need to be attached to the original generalization: for example, "Never lie except to save an innocent person's life (except when this will undermine the social fabric) or when lying will spare people of great anguish (for example, telling a cancer patient the truth about her condition)." And so on. The process seems infinite, time-consuming, and thus impractical.

A second way of qualifying the counterintuitive results of the Kantian program is to follow W. D. Ross and distinguish between *actual* and **prima facie** duties. The prima facie duty that wins out in the comparison is called the *actual duty*, or the *all-things-considered duty*. We may apply this distinction to Kant's innocent man example. First, we have the principle L, "Never lie." Next we ask whether any other principle is relevant in this situation, and we discover that principle P, "Always protect innocent life," also applies. But we cannot obey both L and P (we assume for the moment that silence will be a giveaway). We have two general principles, but neither are to be seen as absolute or nonoverridable, but rather as prima facie. We have to decide which of the two overrides the other, which has greater moral force. This is left up to our considered judgment (or the considered judgment of the reflective moral community). Presumably, we will opt for P over L, so lying to the gangsters becomes our actual duty.

Will this maneuver save the Kantian system? Well, it changes it in a way that Kant might not have liked, but it seems to make sense. It transforms Kant's absolutism into an objectivist system. But now we need to have a separate criterion to adjudicate the conflict between two objective principles.

I conclude, then, that the categorical imperative is an important criterion for evaluating moral principles, but it needs supplementation. In itself, it is purely formal and leaves out any understanding about the content or material aspect of morality. The categorical imperative with its universalizability test constitutes a necessary condition for being a valid moral principle, but it does not provide us with a sufficiency criterion. That is, any principle—if it is to count as rational or moral—must be universalizable. It must apply to everyone and every case that is relevantly similar. If I believe that it's wrong for others to cheat on exams, then unless I can find a reason to believe that I am relevantly different from others, it is also wrong for me to cheat on exams. If premarital heterosexual sex is prohibited for women, then it must also be prohibited for men. (Otherwise, who would the unmarried men have sex with? Other men's wives?) This formal consistency does not tell us, however, whether cheating itself is right or wrong or whether premarital sex is right or wrong. That has to do with the substantive content of morality, which other considerations must help us decide upon.

Kant's Second Formulation of the Categorical Imperative

Kant offered a second formulation of the categorical imperative, which has been referred to as the *principle of ends*.

Second Formulation of the Categorical Imperative: Humanity as an End in Itself

… Now I say: man and generally any rational being *exists* as an end in himself, *not merely as a means* to be arbitrarily used by this or that will, but in all his actions, whether they concern himself or other rational beings, must be always regarded at the same time as an end. All objects of the inclinations have only a conditional worth; for if the inclinations and the wants founded on them did not exist, then their object would be without value. But the inclinations themselves being sources of want are so far from having an absolute worth for which they should be desired, that, on the contrary, it must be the universal wish of every rational being to be wholly free from them. Thus the worth of any object which is *to be acquired* by our action is always conditional. Beings whose existence depends not on our will but on nature's, have nevertheless, if they are nonrational beings, only a relative value as means, and are therefore called *things;* rational beings, on the contrary, are called *persons,* because their very nature points them out as ends in themselves, that is as something which must not be used merely as means, and so far therefore restricts freedom of action (and is an object of respect). These, therefore, are not merely subjective ends whose existence has a worth *for us* as an effect of our action, but *objective ends,* that is things whose existence is an end in itself: an end moreover for which no other can be substituted, which they should subserve *merely* as means, for otherwise nothing whatever would possess *absolute worth;* but if all worth were conditioned and therefore contingent, then there would be no supreme practical principle of reason whatever.

If then there is a supreme practical principle or, in respect of the human will, a categorical imperative, it must be one which, being drawn from the conception of that which is necessarily an end for everyone because it is *an end in itself,* constitutes an *objective* principle of will, and can therefore serve as a universal practical law. The foundation of this principle is: *rational nature exists as an end in itself.* Man necessarily conceives his own existence as being so: so far then this is a *subjective* principle of human actions. But every other rational being regards its existence similarly, just on the same rational principle that holds for me: so that it is at the same time an objective principle, from which as a supreme practical law all laws of the will must be capable of being deduced. Accordingly the practical imperative will be as follows: *So act as to treat humanity, whether in thine own person or in that of any other, in every case as an end withal, never as means only.* …

What is Kant's argument for viewing rational beings as having ultimate value? It goes like this: In valuing anything, I endow it with value. It has no value apart from someone's valuing it. As a valued object, it has *conditional* worth, derived from my valuation. On the other hand, the person who values the object is the ultimate source of the object and as such belongs to a different sphere of beings. We, as valuers, must conceive ourselves as having *unconditioned* worth. We cannot think of our personhood as a mere thing, for then we would have to judge it to be without any value except that given to it by the estimation of other people. But then that person would be the source of value, and there is no reason to suppose that one person should have unconditional worth and not another who is relevantly similar. Therefore, we are not mere objects. We have unconditional worth and so must treat all such value givers as valuable in themselves, as ends, not merely means. I leave it to you to evaluate the validity of this argument, but most of us do hold that there is something exceedingly valuable about human life.

Kant thought that this formulation, the principle of ends, was substantively identical with his first formulation of the categorical imperative, but most scholars disagree with him. It seems better to treat this principle as a supplement to the first, adding content to the purely formal categorical imperative. In this way, Kant would limit the kinds of maxims that could be universalized. Egoism and the principle (P_1 above) enjoining killing blue-eyed children would be ruled out at the very outset, since they involve a violation of the dignity of rational persons. The process would be as follows:

1. Maxim (M) formulated.
2. Ends test (Does the maxim involve violating the dignity of rational beings?)
3. Categorical imperative (Can the maxim be universalized?)
4. Successful moral principles survive both tests.

Does the principle of treating persons as ends in themselves fare better than the original version of the categorical imperative? Three problems soon emerge. The first problem has to do with Kant's setting such a high value on rationality. Why does reason and only reason have intrinsic worth? Who gives this value to rational beings, and how do we know that they have this value? What if we believe that reason has only instrumental value?

Kant's notion of the high inherent value of reason will be more plausible to those who believe that humans are made in the image of God and interpret that, as the mainstream of the Judeo-Christian tradition has, as entailing that our rational capabilities are the essence of being created in God's image. We have value because God created us with worth—that is, with reason. Kant does not use such an argument. Instead he thinks that we must necessarily value rational nature since we, *qua* rational beings, must value ourselves and, by the principle of consistency, anyone rational like us.

Kant seems to many to be correct in valuing rationality (the essence of our rational nature). It does enable us to engage in deliberate and moral reasoning and lift us above lower animals. Where he is more controversial is in neglecting other values or states of being that may have moral significance. For example, he believed that we have no obligations to animals, since they were not rational. Many of us believe (with Bentham and Peter Singer) that the fact that animals can suffer should constrain us in our behavior toward them. We ought not cause unnecessary harm. Perhaps Kantians can supplement their system to accommodate this objection.

This brings us to our second problem with Kant's formulation. If we agree that reason (or rational nature) is an intrinsic value, then does it not follow that those who have more of this quality should be respected and honored more than those who have less? Doesn't more mean better here?

Following Kant's logic, we should treat people in exact proportion to their ability to reason. Thus, geniuses and intellectuals should be given privileged status in society (as Plato and Aristotle might argue). Kant could deny the second premise and argue that rationality is a threshold quality, and that having a sufficient quantity of it grants one equal worth. The question is whether Kant or Kantians have good (nonreligious) reasons to accept the egalitarian premise that all those who have rational nature have equal worth. I leave this question for you to discuss and come to your own conclusion.

There is a third problem with Kant's view of the dignity of rational beings. Even if we should respect them and treat them as ends, this does not tell us very much. It may tell us not to enslave them or act cruelly toward them without a good reason, but it doesn't tell us what to do in conflict situations. For example, what does it tell us to do about a terminally ill patient who wants us to help her die? What does it tell us to do in a war when we are about to aim our gun at an enemy soldier? Aren't we treating the soldier merely as a means?

Furthermore, what does it mean to treat this rational being as an end? What does it tell us to do with regard to the innocent victim and the gangsters who have just asked us about the whereabouts of the victim? What does it tell us about whether we should steal from the pharmacy in order to procure medicine that we can't afford to pay for in order to bring healing to a loved one?

Every moral system has difficulty with dilemmas. The question is, Does some form of Kantianism handle these situations better than other systems? Kant has profoundly influenced our ethical thinking. Even those who reject his system find it difficult to avoid using his categories or appealing to his distinctions, for one may appreciate a great ethical system without embracing it. So the final question is, Is Kant's system the correct way to look at morality? The task before you is to answer this question.

Summary

Deontological theories place the locus of moral value in the act itself, regardless of the actual consequences. The end never justifies the means. The greatest of the deontologists was Immanuel Kant, whose moral theory is centered in the categorical imperative: "Act only on that maxim whereby thou canst at the same time will that it would become a universal law." His second principle was "So act as to treat humanity, whether in your own person or in that of any other, in every case as an end and never merely as a means only." The strengths and weakness of Kant's system were examined.

FOR FURTHER REFLECTION

1. Is the Kantian argument that combines the categorical imperative with the notion of the kingdom of ends successful? Is the notion of treating persons as ends clear enough to be significantly action guiding? Does it cover some intelligent

animals but not severely retarded people? What about fetuses and infants? Are they included? Why or why not?

2. Note the comments of the anti-Kantian, Richard Taylor:

> If I were ever to find, as I luckily never have, a man who assured me that he really *believed* Kant's metaphysical morals, and that he modeled his own conduct and his relations with others after those principles, then my incredulity and distrust of him as a human being could not be greater than if he told me he regularly drowned children just to see them squirm.[5]

He and others have criticized Kant for being too rigid. Many people use the idea of moral duty to keep themselves and others from enjoying life and showing mercy. Do you thing there is a basis for this criticism?

3. Kant has been criticized for stifling spontaneous moral feelings in favor of the deliberate will, so the person who successfully exercises the will in overcoming a temptation is superior to the person who isn't tempted at all but spontaneously acts rightly. For example, the person who just barely resists the temptation to shoplift through a strenuous act of the will would be, on this criterion, morally superior to the person who isn't tempted to shoplift at all. Based on your analysis of Kant, do you think this is a fair interpretation of Kant, and if so, does it undermine his ethics?

4. Here is a question similar to the above. Kant holds that we must act from a motive centered on doing the morally right act simply because it is right, not because we simply are altruistic or benevolent or have good moral habits. He has been criticized for emphasizing the will too much and for rejecting the place of character and feelings in moral actions. Are these criticisms valid?

5. Many people besides Taylor have a negative reaction to Kant's moral theory. Evaluate the following quotation from Oliver Wendell Holmes, Jr.:

> From this it is easy to proceed to the Kantian injunction to regard every human being as an end in himself and not as a means. I confess that I rebel at once. If we want conscripts, we march them up to the front with bayonets in their rear to die for a cause in which perhaps they do not believe. The enemy we treat not even as a means but as an obstacle to be abolished, if so it may be. I feel no pangs of conscience over either step, and naturally am slow to accept a theory that seems to be contradicted by practices that I approve.[6]

6. Does Kant's moral theory depend on a libertarian view of freedom of the will? Can the rational nature of humanity have the dignity or high worth we ascribe to it without the notion of radical free will?

NOTES

1. Immanuel Kant, *Critique of Practical Reason,* trans. Lewis White Beck (Indianapolis: Bobbs-Merrill, 1956), 89.
2. Søren Kierkegaard, *Either/Or,* vol. 2, trans. Walter Lowrie (New York: Anchor Books, 1959), 271.

3. Unless otherwise noted, all remaining passages are from Immanuel Kant, *The Foundations of the Metaphysic of Morals,* trans. T. K. Abbott (1873). I have revised the translation.
4. Immanuel Kant, *On a Supposed Right to Lie from Altruistic Motives* (1797), in Lewis White Beck, *Immanuel Kant: Critique of Practical Reason and Other Writings in Moral Philosophy* (New York: Garland, 1976).
5. Richard Taylor, *Good and Evil* (Buffalo, NY: Prometheus Books, 1984), xii.
6. Oliver Wendell Holmes, Jr., *Collected Legal Papers* (New York: Harcourt Brace Jovanovich, 1920), 340.

FOR FURTHER READING

Acton, Harry. *Kant's Moral Philosophy.* London: Macmillan, 1970. A succinct, clearly written introduction to Kant's thought.

Donagan, Alan. *The Theory of Morality.* Chicago: University of Chicago Press, 1977. A contemporary version of a deontological theory.

Feldman, Fred. *Introductory Ethics.* Englewood Cliffs, NJ: Prentice Hall, 1978, Chapters 7 and 8. A clear and critical exposition of Kant's theory.

Gewirth, Alan. *Reason and Morality.* Chicago: University of Chicago Press, 1978. An important but advanced version of a deontological theory.

Harris, C. E. *Applying Moral Theories.* Belmont, CA: Wadsworth, 1992, Chapters 6 and 7. An excellent exposition of contemporary deontological theories, especially of Gewirth's work.

Hill, Thomas E. *Dignity and Practical Reason in Kant's Moral Theory.* Ithaca, NY: Cornell University Press, 1992. A helpful interpretation of difficult issues in Kant.

Kant, Immanuel. *The Foundations of the Metaphysics of Morals.* Translated by Lewis White Beck. Indianapolis: Bobbs-Merrill, 1959.

Wolff, Robert P. *The Autonomy of Reason: A Commentary on Kant's "Groundwork of the Metaphysics of Morals."* New York: Harper & Row, 1973. A useful commentary of Kant's work.

32 ✢ Religion and Ethics

Does God love goodness because it is good, or is it good because God loves it?

Socrates, paraphrased

The attempts to found a morality apart from religion are like the attempts of children who, wishing to transplant a flower that pleases them, pluck it from the roots that seem to them unpleasing and superfluous, and stick it rootless into the ground. Without religion there can be no real, sincere morality, just as without roots there can be no real flower.

Leo Tolstoy[1]

Adam and Eve disobeying God in the Garden of Eden and bringing suffering and death upon themselves and all people for all time; Moses receiving the Ten Commandments from the hand of God and delivering them to the people of Israel as laws to be adhered to on pain of death; the prophets Amos, Hosea, Isaiah, and Jeremiah warning the people that to disobey God's laws is to ensure doom and destruction; Jesus teaching us to love God with all our hearts, our neighbor as ourselves, and extending that love even to our enemies; visions in the Apocalypse of the Last Judgment wherein God shall reward every man and woman according to his or her deeds on Earth; the hope of heaven and fear of hell that have impelled behavior for at least 2000 years—for Western civilization, as for the majority of humanity throughout the ages, morality has been identified with adherence to religion, immorality equated with sin, and the moral law with the command of God so that the moral life is seen as a personal relationship to a heavenly parent. To act immorally is essentially to disobey God. David, after committing adultery with Bathsheba and arranging for her husband Uriah's death, can say to God without being misunderstood, "Against Thee only have I sinned" (Psalm 51).

Whether it be the impoverished Calcutta Hindu harijan accepting his degradation as his karma, the Shiite Muslim fighting a jihad in the name of Allah, the Jew circumspectly striving to keep kosher, or the Christian giving to charity in the name of Christ, religion has so dominated the moral landscape that it is virtually indistinguishable from it.

There have been exceptions to be sure. Confucianism in China is essentially a secular system, there are nontheist versions of Buddhism, and the philosophers of Greece thought of morality independently from religion; for the most part throughout most of recorded history, however, most people have identified morality with religion, with the commands of God.

The question is whether the equation is a valid one. Is morality essentially tied to religion so that the term *secular ethics* is an oxymoron, a contradiction in terms? Can morality survive without religion? Is it the case, as Tolstoy declares in the chapter-opening quotation, that to separate morality from religion is like cutting a flower from its roots and transplanting it rootless into the ground? Is Dostoyevsky's character Ivan Karamazov correct when he proclaims that "if God doesn't exist, everything is permissible"?

Essentially, our inquiry comes down to addressing two questions: Does morality depend on religion? Are religious ethics essentially different from secular ethics?

Does Morality Depend on Religion?

The first question is whether moral standards themselves depend on God for their validity or whether there is an autonomy of ethics so that even God is subject to the moral order. The question first arises in Plato's dialogue *Euthyphro,* where Socrates asks the pious Euthyphro whether morality has an independent existence apart from religion.

EUTHYPHRO

SOCRATES (S): But shall we ... say that whatever all the gods hate is unholy, and whatever they all love is holy: while whatever some of them love, and others hate, is either both or neither? Do you wish us now to define holiness and unholiness in this manner?

EUTHYPHRO (E): Why not, Socrates?

S: There is no reason why I should not, Euthyphro. It is for you to consider whether that definition will help you to instruct me as you promised.

E: Well, I should say that holiness is what all the gods love, and that unholiness is what they all hate.

S: Are we to examine this definition, Euthyphro, and see if it is a good one? Or are we to be content to accept the bare assertions of other men, or of ourselves, without asking any questions? Or must we examine the assertions?

E: We must examine them. But for my part I think that the definition is right this time.

S: We shall know that better in a little while, my good friend. Now consider this question. Do the gods love holiness because it is holy, or it is holy because they love it?

E: I do not understand you, Socrates.

From: Plato, *Euthyphro,* trans. William Jowett (New York: Scribner, 1889).

s: I will try to explain myself: we speak of a thing being carried and carrying, and being led and leading, and being seen and seeing; and you understand that all such expressions mean different things, and what the difference is.

E: Yes, I think I understand.

s: And we talk of a thing being loved, and, which is different, of a thing loving?

E: Of course.

s: Now tell me: is a thing which is being carried in a state of being carried, because it is carried, or for some other reason?

E: No, because it is carried.

s: And a thing is in a state of being led, because it is led, and of being seen, because it is seen?

E: Certainly.

s: Then a thing is not seen because it is in a state of being seen; it is in a state of being seen because it is seen: and a thing is not led because it is in a state of being led; it is in a state of being led because it is led: and a thing is not carried because it is in a state of being carried; it is in a state of being carried because it is carried. Is my meaning clear now, Euthyphro? I mean this: if anything becomes or is affected, it does not become because it is in a state of becoming; it is in a state of becoming because it becomes; and it is not affected because it is in a state of being affected: it is in a state of being affected because it is affected. Do you not agree?

E: I do.

s: Is not that which is being loved in a state, either of becoming, or of being affected in some way by something?

E: Certainly.

s: Then the same is true here as in the former cases. A thing is not loved by those who love it because it is in a state of being loved. It is in a state of being loved because they love it.

E: Necessarily.

s: Well, then, Euthyphro, what do we say about holiness? Is it not loved by all the gods, according to your definition?

E: Yes.

s: Because it is holy, or for some other reason?

E: No, because it is holy.

s: Then it is loved by the gods because it is holy: it is not holy because it is loved by them?

E: It seems so.

s: But then what is pleasing to the gods is pleasing to them, and is in a state of being loved by them, because they love it?

E: Of course.

s: Then holiness is not what is pleasing to the gods, and what is pleasing to the gods is not holy, as you say, Euthyphro. They are different things.

E: And why, Socrates?

s: Because we are agreed that the gods love holiness because it is holy; and that it is not holy because they love it. Is not this so?

E: Yes.

> s: And that what is pleasing to the gods because they love it, is pleasing to them by reason of this same love: and that they do not love it because it is pleasing to them.
> E: True.
> s: Then, my dear Euthyphro, holiness, and what is pleasing to the gods, are different things. If the gods had loved holiness because it is holy, they would also have loved what is pleasing to them because it is pleasing to them; but if what is pleasing to them had been pleasing to them because they loved it, then holiness too would have been holiness, because they loved it. But now you see that they are opposite things, and wholly different from each other. For the one is of a sort to be loved because it is loved: while the other is loved, because it is of a sort to be loved. My question, Euthyphro, was, What is holiness? But it turns out that you have not explained to me the essence of holiness; you have been content to mention an attribute which belongs to it, namely, that all the gods love it. You have not yet told me what is its essence. Do not, if you please, keep from me what holiness is; begin again and tell me that. Never mind whether the gods love it, or whether it has other attributes: we shall not differ on that point. Do your best to make it clear to me what is holiness and what is unholiness.

"Do the gods love holiness because it is holy, or is it holy because the gods love it?"[2] Changing the terms but still preserving the meaning, we want to know whether God commands what is good because it is good or whether the good is good because God commands it. According to one theory, called the *divine command theory* (DCT), ethical principles are simply the commands of God. They derive their validity from God's commanding them, and they *mean* "Commanded by God." Without God, there would be no universally valid morality. Here is how the theologian Carl Henry states this view:

> Biblical ethics discredits an autonomous morality. It gives theonomous ethics its classic form—the identification of the moral law with the Divine will. In Hebrew-Christian revelation, distinctions in ethics reduce to what is good or what is pleasing, and to what is wicked or displeasing to the Creator-God alone. The biblical view maintains always a dynamic statement of values, refusing to sever the elements of morality from the will of God.... The good is what the Creator-Lord does and commands. He is the creator of the moral law, and defines its very nature.[3]

Morality not only originates with God, but *moral rightness* simply means "willed by God" and *moral wrongness* means "being against the will of God." Since, essentially, morality is based on divine will, not on independently existing reasons for action, no further reasons for action are necessary. As Ivan Karamazov asserts, "If God doesn't exist, everything is permissible." Nothing is forbidden or required. Without God we have moral nihilism.

Bringing out the implications of this theory, we may list four propositions.

1. Act A is wrong if and only if it is contrary to the command of God.
2. Act A is right (required) if and only if God commands it.
3. Act A is morally permissible if and only if it is permitted by the command of God.

4. If there is no God, then nothing is ethically wrong, required, or permitted.

The opposing viewpoint, call it the **autonomy** thesis (standing for the independence of ethics), denies the theses of the DCT, asserting, to the contrary, that

1. Morality does not originate with God (though the way God created us may affect the specific nature of morality).
2. Rightness and wrongness are not based simply on God's will.
3. Essentially, reasons for acting one way or the other may be known independently of God's will.

In sum, ethics are autonomous, and even God must obey the moral law, which exists independently of himself—as the laws of mathematics and logic do. Just as even God cannot make a three-sided square or make it the case that he never existed, so even God cannot make what is intrinsically evil good or make what is good evil. Here is Immanuel Kant's rendition of the thesis:

> [Christianity] has enriched philosophy with far more definite and purer concepts than it had been able to furnish before; but which, once they are there, are freely assented to by Reason and are assumed as concepts to which it could well have come of itself and which it could and should have introduced. . . . Even the Holy One of the Gospels must first be compared with our ideal of moral perfection, before we can recognize him as such.[4]

Kant's system exalts ethics to an intrinsic good; indeed, doing one's duty for no other reason but that it is one's duty is the highest good there is.

Theists who espouse the autonomy thesis may well admit some epistemological advantage to God. God *knows* what is right—better than we do. And since he is good, we can always learn from consulting him, but, in principle, we act morally for the same reasons that God does. We both follow moral reasons that are independent of God. We are against torturing the innocent because it is cruel and unjust, just as God is against torturing the innocent because it is cruel and unjust. If there is no God, on this account, nothing is changed. Morality is left intact, and both theists and nontheists have the very same moral duties.

The attractiveness of the DCT lies in the fact that it seems to do justice to the omnipotence or sovereignty of God. God somehow is thought to be less sovereign or necessary to our lives if he is not the source of morality. It seems inconceivable to many believers that anything having to do with goodness or duty could be "higher" than or independent of God. He is the supreme Lord of the believer's life, and what the believer means by "morally right" is that "the Lord commands it—even if I don't fully understand it." When the believer asks what the will of God is, it is a direct appeal to a personal will, not to an independently existing rule.

Two problems with the DCT need to be faced by those who hold it. One is that the DCT would seem to make the attribution of "goodness" to God redundant. When we say, "God is good," we think that we are ascribing a property to God, but if "good" simply means "what God commands or wills," then we are not attributing any property to God. Our statement "God is good" merely means "God does whatever he wills to do" or "God practices what he preaches," and the statement "God commands us to do what is good" merely is the tautology "God commands us to do what God commands us to do."

A second problem with the DCT is that it seems to make morality into something arbitrary. If God's fiat is the sole arbiter of right and wrong, it would seem to be logically possible for such heinous acts as rape, killing of the innocent for the fun of it, and gratuitous cruelty to become morally good actions—if God suddenly decided to command us to do these things. The radicality of the DCT is set forth in the classic statement by William of Occam:

> The hatred of God, theft, adultery, and actions similar to these actions according to common law, may have an evil quality annexed, in so far as they are done by a divine command to perform the opposite act. But as far as the sheer being in the actions is concerned, they can be performed by God without any evil condition annexed; and they can even be performed meritoriously by an earthly pilgrim if they should come under divine precepts, just as now the opposite of these in fact fall under the divine command.[5]

The implications of this sort of reasoning seem far reaching. If there are no constraints on what God can command, no independent measure or reason for moral action, then anything can become a moral duty, and our moral duties can change from moment to moment. Could there be any moral stability? The proponent of the DCT may object that God has revealed what is his will in his word, in sacred scriptures. But, the fitting response is, How do you know that God isn't lying? For, if there is no independent criterion of right and wrong except what God happens to will, how do we know God isn't willing to make lying into a duty? In which case, believers have no reason to believe the Bible!

If God could make what seems morally heinous morally good simply by willing it, wouldn't morality be reduced to the right of the powerful? Nietzsche's "Might Makes Right"? Indeed, what would be the difference between the devil and God, if morality were simply an arbitrary command?

Suppose we had two sets of commands, one from the devil and one from God. How would we know which set was which? Could they be identical? What would make them different? If there is no independent criterion by which to judge right and wrong, it's difficult to see how we could know which was which. The only basis for comparison would be who won. God is simply the biggest bully on the block (granted it is a pretty big block, covering the entire universe).

Is Religion Irrelevant or Even Inimical to Morality?

Many secularists, such as Bertrand Russell and Kai Nielsen, have argued against both the stronger claim of the DCT that religion is the basis of ethics and the weaker Kantian claim that religion completes ethics. They contend that morality has no need of God. One can be moral, and, within the limits of thoughtful stoic resignation, even happy. The world may well be a product of blind evolutionary striving, ultimately absurd, but this doesn't remove our duty to fill our lives with meaning and goodness. Here is a classical essay by Russell.

A FREE MAN'S WORSHIP

To Dr. Faustus in his study Mephistopheles told the history of the Creation saying:

"The endless praises of the choirs of angels had begun to grow wearisome; for, after all, did he not deserve their praise? Had he not given them endless joy? Would it not be more amusing to obtain undeserved praise, to be worshipped by beings whom he tortured? He smiled inwardly, and resolved that the great drama should be performed.

"For countless ages the hot nebula whirled aimlessly through space. At length it began to take shape, the central mass threw off planets, the planets cooled, boiling seas and burning mountains heaved and tossed, from black masses of cloud hot sheets of rain deluged the barely solid crust. And now the first germ of life grew in the depths of the ocean, and developed rapidly in the fructifying warmth into vast forest tress, huge ferns springing from the damp mould, sea monsters breeding, fighting, devouring, and passing away. And from the monsters, as the play unfolded itself, Man was born, with the power of thought, the knowledge of good and evil, and the cruel thirst for worship. And Man saw that all is passing in this mad, monstrous world, that all is struggling to snatch, at any cost, a few brief moments of life before Death's inexorable decree. And Man said: "There is a hidden purpose, could we but fathom it, and the purpose is good; for we must reverence something, and in the visible world there is nothing worthy of reverence." And Man stood aside from the struggle, resolving that God intended harmony to come out of chaos by human efforts. And when he followed the instincts which God had transmitted to him from his ancestry of beasts of prey, he called it Sin, and asked God to forgive him. But he doubted whether he could be justly forgiven, until he invented a divine Plan by which God's wrath was to have been appeased. And seeing the present was bad, he made it yet worse, that thereby the future might be better. And he gave God thanks for the strength that enabled him to forgo even the joys that were possible. And God smiled; and when he saw that Man had become perfect in renunciation and worship, he sent another sun through the sky, which crashed into Man's sun; and all returned again to nebula.

"Yes," he murmured, "it was a good play; I will have it performed again."

Such, in outline, but even more purposeless, more void of meaning, is the world which Science presents for our belief. Amid such a world, if anywhere, our ideals henceforward must find a home. That Man is the product of causes which had no prevision of the end they were achieving; that his origin, his growth, his hopes and fears, his loves and his beliefs, are but the outcome of accidental collocations of atoms; that no fire, no heroism, no intensity of thought and feeling, can preserve an individual life beyond the grave; that all the labours of the ages, all the devotion, all the inspiration, all the

From: Bertrand Russell, "A Free Man's Worship," reprinted in *Ethical Theory: Classical and Contemporary Readings*, ed. Louis Pojman (Belmont, CA: Wadsworth, 1989).

> noonday brightness of human genius, are destined to extinction in the vast death of the solar system, and that the whole temple of Man's achievement must inevitably be buried beneath the debris of a universe in ruins—all these things, if not quite beyond dispute, are yet so nearly certain, that no philosophy which rejects them can hope to stand. Only within the scaffolding of these truths, only on the firm foundation of unyielding despair, can the soul's habitation henceforth be safely built.
>
> How, in such an alien and inhuman world, can so powerless a creature as Man preserve his aspirations untarnished? A strange mystery it is that Nature, omnipotent but blind, in the revolutions of her secular hurryings through the abysses of space, has brought forth at last a child, subject still to her power, but gifted with sight, with knowledge of good and evil, with the capacity of judging all the works of his unthinking Mother. In spite of Death, the mark and seal of the parental control, Man is yet free, during his brief years, to examine, to criticize, to know, and in imagination to create. To him alone, in the world with which he is acquainted, this freedom belongs; and in this lies his superiority to the resistless forces that control his outward life.

Russell urges us to exalt the "dignity of Man" by freeing him from the tyranny of nonhuman Power. Then he asks "When we have realized that Power is largely bad, that Man, with his knowledge of good and evil, is but a helpless atom in a world which has no such knowledge, the choice is again presented to us: Shall we worship Force, or shall we worship Goodness? Shall our God exist and be evil, or shall he be recognized as the creation of our own conscience?" What is the answer to this momentous question?

> If strength is to be respected, let us respect rather the strength of those who refuse that false "recognition of the facts" which fails to recognize that facts are often bad. Let us admit that, in the world we know, there are many things that would be better otherwise, and that the ideals to which we do and must adhere are not realized in the realm of matter. Let us preserve our respect for truth, for beauty, for the ideal of perfection which life does not permit us to attain, though none of these things meet with the approval of the unconscious universe.[6]

So the first thing we must do is get rid of the myth that the truth is always edifying or flattering. According to Russell, we are just the product of random, accidental forces, without free will, immortal souls, and a caring Creator: animals who at death will rot and who make up a universe that cares not a fig about us. What hope is there then for us?

> In this lies Man's true freedom: in determination to worship only the God created by our own love of the good, to respect only the heaven which inspires the insight of our best moments. In action, in desire, we must submit perpetually to the tyranny of outside forces; but in thought, in aspiration, we are free, free from our fellow men, free from the petty planet on which our bodies impotently crawl, free even, while we live, from the tyranny of death. Let us learn, then, that energy of faith which enables us to live constantly in the vision of the good; and let us descend, in action into the world of fact, with that vision always before us.

When first the opposition of fact and ideal grows fully visible, a spirit of fiery revolt, of fierce hatred of the gods, seems necessary to the assertion of freedom. To defy with Promethean constancy a hostile universe, to keep its evil always in view, always actively hated, to refuse no pain that the malice of Power can invent, appears to be the duty of all who will not bow before the inevitable. But indignation is still a bondage, for it compels our thoughts to be occupied with an evil world; and in the fierceness of desire from which rebellion springs there is a kind of serf-assertion which it is necessary for the wise to overcome. Indignation is a submission of our thoughts, but not of our desires; the Stoic freedom in which wisdom consists is found in the submission of our desires, but not of our thoughts. From the submission of our desires springs the virtue of resignation; from the freedom of our thoughts springs the whole world of art and philosophy, and the vision of beauty by which, at last, we half reconquer the reluctant world. But the vision of beauty is possible only to unfettered contemplation, to thoughts not weighted by the load of eager wishes; and thus Freedom comes only to those who no longer ask of life that it shall yield them any of those personal goods that are subject to the mutations of Time.

Although the necessity of renunciation is evidence of the existence of evil, yet Christianity, in preaching it, has shown a wisdom exceeding that of the Promethean philosophy of rebellion. It must be admitted that, of the things we desire, some, though they prove impossible, are yet real goods; others, however, as ardently longed for, do not form part of a fully purified ideal. The belief that what must be renounced is bad, though sometimes false, is far less often false than untamed passion supposes; and the creed of religion, by providing a reason for proving that it is never false, has been the means of purifying our hopes by the discovery of many austere truths.

But there is in resignation a further good element: even real goods, when they are unattainable, ought not to be fretfully desired. To every man comes, sooner or later, the great renunciation. For the young, there is nothing unattainable; a good thing desired with the whole force of a passionate will, and yet impossible, is to them not credible. Yet, by death, by illness, by poverty, or by the voice of duty, we must learn, each one of us, that the world was not made for us, and that, however beautiful may be the things we crave, Fate may nevertheless forbid them. It is the part of courage, when misfortune comes, to bear without repining the ruin of our hopes, to turn away our thoughts from vain regrets. This degree of submission to Power is not only just and right: it is the very gate of wisdom.

But passive renunciation is not the whole of wisdom; for not by renunciation alone can we build a temple for the worship of our own ideals. Haunting foreshadowings of the temple appear in the realm of imagination, in music, in architecture, in the untroubled kingdom of reason, and in the golden sunset magic of lyrics, where beauty shines and glows, remote from the touch of sorrow, remote from the fear of change, remote from the failures and disenchantments of the world of fact. In the contemplation of these things the vision of heaven will shape itself in our hearts, giving at once a touchstone to judge the world about us, and an inspiration by which to fashion to our needs whatever is not incapable of serving as a stone in the sacred temple....

The life of Man, viewed outwardly, is but a small thing in comparison with the forces of Nature. The slave is doomed to worship Time and Fate and Death, because they are greater than anything he finds in himself, and because all his thoughts are of things which they devour. But, great as they are, to think of them greatly, to feel their passionless splendour, is greater still, and such thought makes us free men; we no longer bow before the inevitable in Oriental subjection, but we absorb it, and make it a part of ourselves. To abandon the struggle for private happiness, to expel all eagerness of temporary desire, to burn with passion for eternal things—this is emancipation, and this is the free man's worship. And this liberation is effected by a contemplation of Fate; for Fate itself is subdued by the mind which leaves nothing to be purged by the purifying fire of Time.

United with his fellow men by the strongest of all ties, the tie of a common doom, the free man finds that a new vision is with him always, shedding over every daily task the light of love. The life of Man is a long march through the night, surrounded by invisible foes, tortured by weariness and pain, towards a goal that few can hope to reach, and where none may tarry long. One by one, as they march, our comrades vanish from our sight, seized by the silent orders of omnipotent Death. Very brief is the time in which we can help them, in which their happiness or misery is decided. Be it ours to shed sunshine on their path, to lighten their sorrows by the balm of sympathy, to give them the pure joy of a never-tiring affection, to strengthen failing courage, to instill faith in hours of despair. Let us not weigh in grudging scales their merits and demerits, but let us think only of their need—of the sorrows, the difficulties, perhaps the blindnesses, that make the misery of their lives; let us remember that they are fellow-sufferers in the same darkness, actors in the same tragedy with ourselves. And so, when their day is over, when their good and their evil have become eternal by the immortality of the past, be it ours to feel that, where they suffered, where they failed, no deed of ours was the cause; but wherever a spark of the divine fire kindled in their hearts, we were ready with encouragement, with sympathy, with brave words in which high courage glowed.

Brief and powerless is Man's life; on him and all his race the slow, sure doom falls pitiless and dark. Blind to good and evil, reckless of destruction, omnipotent matter rolls on its relentless way; for Man, condemned today to lose his dearest, tomorrow himself to pass through the gate of darkness, it remains only to cherish, ere yet the blow fall, the lofty thoughts that ennoble his little day; disdaining the coward terrors of the salve of Fate, to worship at the shrine that his own hands have built; undismayed by the empire of chance, to preserve a mind free from the wanton tyranny that rules his outward life; proudly defiant of the irresistible forces that tolerate, for a moment, his knowledge and his condemnation, to sustain alone, a weary but unyielding Atlas, the world that his own ideals have fashioned despite the trampling march of unconscious power.[7]

"Nature, omnipotent but blind, in the revolutions of her secular hurryings through the abysses of space, has brought forth at last a child, subject still to her power, but gifted with sight, with knowledge of good and evil, with the capacity of judging all the works of his unthinking Mother."[8] It is this conscious power of moral evaluation that makes the child superior to his omnipotent Mother. He is free to think, to evaluate, to create, and to live committed to ideals. So despite suffering, despair, and death, humans are free. Life has the meaning that we give it, and morality will be part of any meaningful life.

Theists may counter, however, that secularists like Russell are whistling in the dark. The Christian philosopher George Mavrodes has criticized Russell's secular view as puzzling.

RELIGION AND THE QUEERNESS OF MORALITY

For convenience, I will call a world that satisfies the description given here a "Russellian world." But we are primarily interested in what the status of morality would be in the actual world if that world should turn out to be Russellian. I shall therefore sometimes augment the description of a Russellian world with obvious features of the actual world.

What are the most relevant features of a Russellian world? The following strike me as especially important: (1) Such phenomena as minds, mental activities, consciousness, and so forth are the products of entities and causes that give no indication of being mental themselves. In Russell's words, the causes are "accidental collocations of atoms" with "no prevision of the end they were achieving." Though not stated explicitly by Russell, we might add the doctrine, a commonplace in modern science, that mental phenomena—and indeed life itself—are comparative latecomers in the long history of the earth. (2) Human life is bounded by physical death and each individual comes to a permanent end at his physical death. We might add to this the observation that the span of human life is comparatively short, enough so that in some cases we can, with fair confidence, predict the major consequences of certain actions insofar as they will affect a given individual throughout his whole remaining life. (3) Not only each individual but also the human race as a species is doomed to extinction "beneath the debris of a universe in ruins."

So much, then for the main features of a Russellian world. Because the notion of benefits and goods plays an important part in the remainder of my discussion, I want to introduce one further technical expression—"Russellian benefit." A Russellian benefit is one that could accrue to a person in a Russellian world. A contented old age would be, I suppose, a Russellian benefit, as would a thrill of sexual pleasure or a good reputation. Going to heaven when one dies, though a benefit, is not a Russellian benefit. Russellian benefits are only the benefits possible in a Russellian world. But one can have Russellian benefits even if the world is not Russellian. In such a case there might, however, also be other benefits, such as going to heaven.

Could the actual world be Russellian? Well, I take it to be an important feature of the actual world that human beings exist in it and that in it their actions fall, at least sometimes, within the sphere of morality—that is, they have moral obligations to act (or to refrain from acting) in certain ways. And if they do not act in those ways, then they are properly subject to a special and peculiar sort of adverse judgment (unless it happens that there are special circumstances that serve to excuse their failure to fulfill the

---

From: George Mavrodes, "Religion and the Queerness of Morality," in *Rationality, Religious Belief, and Moral Commitment*, ed. R. Audi and W. Wainwright (Ithaca, NY: Cornell University Press, 1986).

obligations). People who do not fulfill their obligations are not merely stupid or weak or unlucky, they are morally reprehensible.

If there is no God, then doesn't secular ethics suffer from a certain inadequacy? Mavrodes argues that the Russellian world of secular morality can't satisfactorily answer the question, Why should I be moral? For, on its account, the common goods, which morality in general aims at, are often just those that we sacrifice in carrying out our moral obligations. Why should we sacrifice our welfare or self-interest for our moral duty?[9]

> Finally, it is, I think, a striking feature of moral obligations that a person's being unwilling to fulfill the obligation is irrelevant to having the obligation and is also irrelevant to the adverse judgment in case the obligation is not fulfilled. Perhaps even more important is the fact that, at least for some obligations, it is also irrelevant in both these ways for one to point out that he does not see how fulfilling the obligations can do him any good. In fact, unless we are greatly mistaken about our obligations, it seems clear that in a Russellian world there are an appreciable number of cases in which fulfilling an obligation would result in a loss of good to ourselves. On the most prosaic level, this must be true of some cases of repaying a debt, keeping a promise, refraining from stealing, and so on. And it must also be true of those rarer but more striking cases of obligation to risk death or serious injury in the performance of a duty. People have, of course, differed as to what is good for humans. But so far as I can see, the point I have been making will hold for any candidate that is plausible in a Russellian world. Pleasure, happiness, esteem, contentment, self-realization, knowledge—all of these can suffer from the fulfillment of a moral obligation.

The second oddity about secular ethics, according to Mavrodes, is that it is superficial and not deeply rooted. It seems to lack that metaphysical basis that a Platonic (that is, the view holding that reality and value essentially exist in a transcendent realm) or Judeo-Christian worldview affords:

> Values and obligations cannot be deep in such a [secular] world. What is deep in a Russellian world must be such things as matter and energy, or perhaps natural law, chance, or chaos. If it really were a fact that one had obligations in a Russellian world, then something would be laid upon man that might cost a man everything but that went no further than man. And that difference from a Platonic world seems to make all the difference.

Mavrodes closes with the following comparison between secular morality and religion:

> I come more and more to think that morality, while a fact, is a twisted and distorted fact. Or perhaps better, that it is a barely recognizable version of another fact, a version adapted to a twisted and distorted world. It is something like, I suppose, the way in which the pine that grows at timberline, wind blasted and twisted low against the rock, is a version of the tall and symmetrical tree that grows lower on the slopes. I think it may be that the related notions of sacrifice and gift represent (or come close

to representing) the fact, that is, the pattern of life, whose distorted version we know here as morality. Imagine a situation, an "economy" if you will, in which no one ever buys or trades for or seizes any good thing. But whatever good he enjoys it is either one which he himself has created or else one which he receives as a free and unconditional gift. And as soon as he has tasted it and seen that it is good he stands ready to give it away in his turn as soon as the opportunity arises. In such a place, if one were to speak either of his rights or his duties, his remark might be met with puzzled laughter as his hearers struggled to recall an ancient world in which those terms referred to something important.

We have, of course, even now some occasions that tend in this direction. Within some families perhaps, or even in a regiment in desperate battle, people may for a time pass largely beyond morality and live lives of gift and sacrifice. On those occasions nothing would be lost if the moral concepts and the moral language were to disappear. But it is probably not possible that such situations and occasions should be more than rare exceptions in the daily life of the present world. Christianity, however, which tells us that the present world is "fallen" and hence leads us to expect a distortion in its important features, also tells us that one day the redemption of the world will be complete and that then all things shall be made new. And it seems to me to suggest an "economy" more akin to that of gift and sacrifice than to that of rights and duties. If something like that should be true, then perhaps morality, like the Marxist state, is destined to wither away (unless perchance it should happen to survive in hell).

Of course, the secularist will continue the debate. If what morality seeks is the good, as I have argued, then secular morality based on a notion of the good life is inspiring in itself, for it promotes human flourishing and can be shown to be in all of our interest, whether or not a God exists. A religious or Platonic metaphysical orientation may not be necessary for a rational, secular, common-sense morality. To be sure, there will be differences in the exact nature of the ethical codes—religious ethics will be more likely to advocate strong altruism, whereas secular codes will emphasize reciprocal altruism—but the core morality will be the same.

Some secularists, call them antireligious secularists, go even further than Russell and Nielsen. They claim that it is not the case that religious and secular morality are similar but that religious morality is an inferior brand of morality that actually prevents deep moral development. Both P. H. Nowell-Smith and James Rachels have argued that religion is (or gives rise to) an inferior morality.[10] Both base their contention on the notion of autonomy. Nowell-Smith's argument is based on child psychologist Jean Piaget's research in child-development. Very small children have to be taught to value rules. When they do, they tend to hold tenaciously to those rules even when games or activities would seem to call for a suspension of the rules. For example, suppose there are only ten children and a rectangular lot not large enough to have three fields. Some children might object to playing baseball with only five on a side and no right field because it violates the official rules. Religious morality in being deontologically rule-governed is analogous to children who have not understood the wider purposes of the rules of games. It is an infantile morality.

Rachels's argument alleges that believers relinquish their autonomy in worship and so are immoral. Using Kant's dictum that "kneeling down or groveling on the ground, even to express your reverence for heavenly things, is contrary to human dignity," he argues that since we have inherent dignity, no one deserves our worship. But since the notion "God" implies "being worthy of worship," God cannot exist. He writes, "(1) If any being is God, he must be a fitting object of worship. (2) No being could possibly be a fitting of worship, since worship requires the abandonment of one's role as an autonomous moral agent. (3) Therefore, there cannot be any being who is God."

Are these sound arguments? They seem to have problems. Take Nowell-Smith's contention that religious morality is infantile. Perhaps some religious people and some secularists as well are rigidly and unreasonably rule bound, but not all religious people are. Indeed, Jesus himself broke the Sabbath-day rule to heal and do good, saying "the Sabbath was made for man, not man for the Sabbath." Does not the strong love motif in New Testament religious morality indicate that the rules are seen as serving a purpose, the human good?

With regard to Rachels's argument, premise 2 seems false. In worshipping God, a person need not give up one's reason, one's essential autonomy. Doesn't a rational believer need to use reason to distinguish the good from the bad, the holy from what is not holy? A mature believer does not (or need not) sacrifice his or her reason or autonomy in worship, but rather these traits are part and parcel of what worship entails. The command to love God is for one to love him with one's whole *mind* as well as one's heart and strength. If there is a God, he must surely want us to be intelligent and discriminating and sensitive in all of our deliberations. Being a religious worshipper in no way entails or condones intellectual suicide.

Of course, a believer may submit his or her judgment to God's, when there is good evidence that God has given a judgment. If this is sacrificing one's autonomy, then it only shows that autonomy is not an absolute value but a significant prima facie value. If I am working in the physics laboratory with Albert Einstein, whom I have learned to trust as a competent authority, and he advises me to do something different from what my amateur calculations dictate, I am likely to defer to his authority. But I don't thereby give up my autonomy. I freely and rationally give up my judgment because in this area Einstein simply is a better judge in these things, and I may not be able to understand the complex mathematics needed to explain his reasons. One could say, I autonomously give up my first-order autonomy. Similarly, the believer may submit to God whenever he or she judges God's authority to override one's own finite judgment. It seems eminently rational to give up that kind of autonomy. To do otherwise would make autonomy into a foolhardy fetish.

Does Religion Enhance the Moral Life?

Contrary to philosophers like Nowell-Smith and Rachels (and even Russell and Nielsen), there may be some morally relevant advantages to theism. Lois Walker suggests several ways in which morality may be enhanced by religion.[11] A few should be noted here.

1. If there is a God, Good will win out over Evil. We're assured that right-eousness will triumph in the end, so we are not fighting in vain—we'll win eventually. As William James said before a skeptical audience, "If religion be true and the evidence for it be still insufficient, I do not wish, by putting your extinguisher upon my nature to forfeit my sole chance in life of getting upon the winning side—that chance depending, of course, on my willingness to run the risk of acting as if my passional need of taking the world religiously might be prophetic and right."[12] This thought of the ultimate Victory of Goodness gives us confidence to go on in the fight against injustice and cruelty when others calculate that the odds against righteousness are too great to fight against.

2. Related to the preceding point, we have an added incentive to be moral. There will be a judgment of good and evil at the Judgment Day, where we shall all be rewarded according to our deeds. Death is not the end of us, but we will continue to exist in a far happier world. So it is not an overwhelming tragedy if we do not get our just reward now. We are assured of cosmic justice in an afterlife.

Related to this point is the question of "Why should I be moral, when I can get away with being immoral?" which haunts secular ethics. The question makes no sense within a religious framework, since faith in God's justice assures the believer that one never gets away with immorality and the least good deed will be rewarded.

3. Furthermore, if there is a God who loves and cares for us—his love com-pels us, we have a deeper motive for morally good actions, including profound altruism. We desire to live moral lives because of deep gratitude to One who loves us and whom we love. Perhaps love also inspires secularists, but it may not be of the same degree or kind as that which fills the hearts of saints and redeemed sinners. Most of those whom we consider moral saints and heroes are also religious ones—Moses, Buddha, Jesus, St. Francis, Mohandas Gandhi, Martin Luther King, and Mother Teresa. You need special love to leave a world of comfort in order to go to a desolate island to minister to lepers, as Father Damian did.

As Walker also notes, religion is not an unequivocal force for good. A lot of evil has been done in the name of religion. Furthermore, many rational and moral people doubt or disbelieve in religion, so not everyone will have the insights and motivational factors available in religion. Here is how one of my students, Laura Burrell, a sophomore, summed up the matter.

> God is like a cosmic gardener—he tends and protects individual morality, he nourishes it and helps it bloom. Some people, like a hot-house orchid or a fancy rose, do seem to need religion for their morality to have a purpose or justification. Others are like the Queen Anne's Lace (QAL), who need just that extra bit of fertilizer to break into bloom—and God provides it. But mankind could do as well.

The relationship between God and morality is as simple as that—god is a parent, gardener, and so on. He strengthens and cushions individual morality, he gives motivation (in the form of the outcomes: heaven and hell), and justice and order in a sometimes extremely chaotic world. But morality exists apart from God, and as hard as it is for some to accept, it could survive and even in a world without God.

Summary

Throughout the ages, morality has been closely related to religion. The divine command theory (DCT) takes a strong stand on this issue, asserting that apart from religion morality has no secure foundations. The autonomy thesis of Kant and contemporary secular philosophers holds, to the contrary, that morality is entirely distinct from religion and logically prior to it, so morality is the proper judge of religion. An intermediate position holds that, although the moral law is autonomous, religion provides powerful incentives and added justification for the moral point of view.

FOR FURTHER REFLECTION

1. Imagine that a superior being appears to you and says, "I am God and I am good; therefore, obey me when I tell you to torture your mother." How would a proponent of the DCT deal with this problem?

2. Consider Tolstoy's statement at the beginning of this chapter: "The attempts to found a morality apart from religion are like the attempts of children who, wishing to transplant a flower that pleases them, pluck it from the roots that seem to them unpleasing and superfluous, and stick it rootless into the ground. Without religion there can be no real, sincere morality, just as without roots there can be no real flower." Evaluate this claim.

3. In your judgment, how important is religion for a meaningful life? How would a secularist respond to the claims made in favor of religion's ability to procure added meaning in life? Do you think that religion really does provide added meaning to life?

4. Karl Marx said that religion was the opium of the people. (Today, the metaphor might better be changed to "cocaine" or "crack.") It deludes them into thinking that all will be well with the world, leading to passive acceptance of evil and injustice. Is there some truth in Marx's dictum? How would a theist respond to this?

5. Discuss the matter of the problems connected with religious revelation and rational morality. What if one's religion prohibits certain types of speech and requires the death penalty for them? Such was the case when the Ayatollah Khoumeni condemned the author Salman Rushdie to death for blasphemous words in the novel *Satanic Verses*. Some religious people believe that abortion or homosexual behavior is morally wrong based on religious authority. How should

a secular ethicist who believes that these practices are not morally wrong argue with the believer? Can there be rational dialogue?

NOTES

1. "Religion and Morality," in *Leo Tolstoy: Selected Essays,* trans. Aylmer Maude (New York: Random House, 1964), 31.
2. Plato, *Euthyphro,* trans. William Jowett (New York: Scribner, 1889).
3. Carl F. Henry, *Christian Personal Ethics* (Grand Rapids, MI: Eerdmans, 1957), 210.
4. Immanuel Kant, *Critique of Judgment,* trans. J. Bernard, p. 410; and *Fundamental Principles of the Metaphysics of Ethics,* trans. T. K. Abbott (London: Longmans, 1873).
5. William of Occam, quoted in *Divine Command Morality,* ed. J. M Idziak (Lewiston, NY: Mellon, 1979).
6. Bertrand Russell, "A Free Man's Worship," in *Ethical Theory: Classical and Contemporary Readings,* ed. Louis Pojman (Belmont, CA: Wadsworth, 1989).
7. Ibid.
8. Ibid.
9. All remaining passages in this section are from George Mavrodes, "Religion and the Queerness of Morality," in *Rationality, Religious Belief and Moral Commitment,* ed. R. Audi and W. Wainwright (Ithaca, NY: Cornell University Press, 1986).
10. Patrick Nowell-Smith, "Morality: Religious and Secular," in Pojman, *Ethical Theory,* 497–507; James Rachels, "God and Human Attitudes," *Religious Studies 7* (1971). Reprinted with a reply by Philip Quinn in Paul Helm (listed in "For Further Reading").
11. Lois H. Walker, "Religion Gives Meaning to Life," in *Philosophy: The Quest for Truth,* 5th ed., ed. Louis Pojman (New York: Oxford University Press, 2002).
12. William James, *The Will to Believe* (New York: Longmans, Green, 1987).

FOR FURTHER READING

Helm, Paul, ed. *The Divine Command Theory of Ethics.* Oxford, UK: Oxford University Press, 1979. Contains valuable articles by William Frankena, James Rachels, Philip Quinn, Robert Adams, and Robert Young.

Kant, Immanuel. *Religion Within the Bounds of Reason Alone.* Translated by T. M. Greene and H. H. Hudson. New York: Harper & Row, 1960. A classic work.

Kierkegaard, Søren. *Fear and Trembling.* Translated by Howard Hong and Edna Hong. Princeton, NJ: Princeton University Press, 1983. Sets forth a radical thesis of the teleological suspension of the ethical dimension.

Mitchell, Basil. *Morality: Religious and Secular.* Oxford, UK: Oxford University Press, 1980. An important discussion.

Nielsen, Kai. *Ethics Without God.* Buffalo, NY: Prometheus Books, 1973. A very accessible defense of secular morality.

Outka, Gene, and J. P. Reeder, eds. *Religion and Morality: A Collection of Essays.* New York: Anchor Books, 1973. Contains Robert M. Adams's "A Modified

Divine Command Theory of Ethical Wrongness," a sophisticated version of the divine command theory.

Pojman, Louis, ed. *Ethical Theory: Classical and Contemporary Readings,* 3rd ed. Belmont, CA: Wadsworth, 1998. Part 11 contains important essays by Immanuel Kant, Bertrand Russell, George Mavrodes, and Kai Nielsen.

Quinn, Philip. *Divine Commands and Moral Requirements.* Oxford, UK: Clarendon Press, 1978. An advanced, detailed defense of the divine command theory.

PART VIII
Existentialism and the Meaning of Life

PART VII

Existentialism and the Meaning of Life

33 ⚘ What Is Existentialism?

There was once a young student of philosophy and theology who mastered all the philosophical positions of his time, who patiently worked through one system of knowledge after another, memorizing, analyzing, refuting, revising, and amalgamating the theses of learned men. His one aim was to find the Truth, but not simply empirical truth, factual knowledge, but a truth for which there wasn't yet a name, a sort of inner truth, a spiritual ideal for which he could live and die, an ideology that either proceeded from the heart or found a resounding echo of affirmation in the heart. The student wrote the following in his diary.

PRIVATE PAPERS

What I really lack is to be clear in my mind what *I am to do,* not what I must know—except that a certain amount of knowledge is presupposed in every action. I need to understand my purpose in life, to see what God wants me to do, and this means that I must find a truth which is true for me, that I must find *that idea for which I can live and die.*

He then criticizes his whole academic career as largely superfluous.

What would be the use of discovering so-called "objective" truth, of working through all the systems of philosophy and of being able to review them all and show up the inconsistencies within each system? What good would it do me to be able to develop a political theory and combine all the intricate details of politics into a complete system, and so construct a world for the exhibition of others but in which I did not live;

From: Søren Kierkegaard, *Private Papers* (1838–1855), my translation.

what would it profit me if I developed the correct interpretation of Christianity in which I resolved all the internal problems, if it had no deeper significance *for me and for my life;* what would it profit me if truth stood before me cold and naked, indifferent to whether I recognized her, creating in me paroxysms of anxiety rather than trusting devotion?[1]

He then asks, "What is truth but to live for an idea? Ultimately everything must rest on a hypothesis but the moment it is no longer outside him, but he lives in it, then and only then does it cease to be merely a hypothesis for him." It becomes the lived truth, *subjective truth.*

The student graduated from the university with honors but was unable to obtain a teaching position. So he began to write, developing the sort of thoughts expressed in the sentences you have just read—only he didn't write in the usual philosophical jargon. Instead, he told stories and wrote witty aphorisms and essays about literature, music, the aesthetic life, morality, and religion in which the flow of the discourse was arranged so as to awaken the conscience, compelling the reader to ask questions about the meaning and purpose of life. His first books were best sellers—only no one knew who this mysterious author was, for he didn't sign his name to his books; he used pseudonyms: Victor Eremita, Johannes de Silentio, Vigilius Haufniensis, Nicolas Notabene, Constantine Constantius, and Johannes Climacus. All these Latin pseudonyms had symbolic meaning. Translated they read, "The Victorious Hermit," "John Who Is Silent," "The Vigilant Watchman of the Harbor" (he lived in a harbor town), "Nicolas Note Well!" "Constant Constantine" (who is not fickle as you suppose, my beloved), and "John Who Is Trying to Climb" to heaven. The author's reasons for not including his own name were complex, but the main reason was due to his desire to draw attention to the ideas contained in his books and to the reader's personal relationship with these ideas, rather than to himself. The books were often written on several levels: an innocent story, a message to his ex-fiancée, a philosophical discourse, a call to "subjective truth." He was prolific, producing eighteen books in 5 years, publishing completely at his own expense and losing money in the venture.

He lived a life of constant and intense suffering. He was frustrated in love, frustrated in his vocational aspirations, frustrated by his physical liabilities—especially by a severe back ailment, which eventually led to his premature death. He opposed the journalistic corruption of his day, incurring the wrath of the avant-garde press, which mocked him almost daily. One cartoon depicts him standing in the center of the universe with the Sun, Moon, stars, and all else revolving around him—as though to suggest that he was an egomaniac. Eventually, his reputation was ruined, and he became undeservedly the laughing stock of his community. He felt a mission to teach the common folk but was even rejected by them; they began to name their dogs after him. He was deeply religious, devoutly Christian, but in his quest for integrity, he felt compelled to reject the established Church of his land as anti-Christian and joined the Atheist Society in protest to its materialism. The established Church responded in kind, hurling abuse his way. An intense controversy erupted between him and the Church. He wrote of the Church, "As a religion [organized Christianity], as it is now practiced, is just about as genuine as tea made from a bit of paper which once lay in a drawer beside another bit of paper which once had been used to wrap up a few dried tea leaves from which tea had already been made three times."

In the midst of his battle with the Church, he collapsed one October day on the main street of his city, Copenhagen. He was taken to the hospital. Some days later, a priest came to administer last rites, the Eucharist (Holy Communion), advising him that he was dying. Our subject brushed the priest aside, exclaiming, "No, I will not accept the body and blood of my Lord and Savior from the hands of a lackey of the state! Send an unpaid layman and I will partake." A few days later, without the benefit of the Eucharist, he died at the age of 42. Thus ended the life of the father of existentialism, Søren Aabye Kierkegaard (May 5, 1813–November 11, 1855).

This was the beginning of existentialism as a philosophical movement. For about 50 years, Kierkegaard's name, as well as his ideas, were almost entirely forgotten in the intellectual world. His books were long out of print and his private papers stowed away in a dusky closet, awaiting the sanitation department. Then suddenly early in the 20th century, his ideas exploded like a time bomb. Discovered first in Germany, his thoughts were initially linked with those of Friedrich Nietzsche (1844–1900). Soon they spread to theology, literature, psychoanalysis, and art. A new philosophy had been born.

Nietzsche held that the fundamental creative force that motivates all creation is the *will to power*. We all seek to affirm ourselves, to flourish and dominate. Since we are essentially unequal in ability, it follows that the fittest will survive and be victorious in the contest with the weaker and baser. There is great aesthetic beauty in the noble spirit coming to fruition, but this process is hampered by Judeo-Christian morality, which Nietzsche labels "slave morality." Slave morality, which is the invention of jealous priests, envious and resentful of the power of the noble, prescribes that we give up the will to power and excellence and become meek and mild, that we believe the lie of all humans having equal worth. Nietzsche also refers to this as the "ethics of resentment."

> The baseness of some people suddenly spurts up like dirty water when some holy vessel, some precious thing from a locked shrine, some book with the marks of a great destiny, is carried past; and on the other hand there is a reflex of silence, a hesitation of the eye, a cessation of all gestures that express how a soul *feels* the proximity of the most venerable.

Thus, similarly, the superiority of the noble souls engenders envious hate in the herd, in ignoble souls.

Nietzsche's ideas of inegalitarian ethics are based on his notion of the death of God. God plays no vital role in our culture—except as a protector of the slave morality, including the idea of equal worth of all persons. If we recognize that there is no rational basis for believing in God, we will see that the whole edifice of slave morality must crumble and with it the notion of equal worth. In its place will arise the morality of the noble person, Superman, based on the virtues of high courage, discipline, and intelligence, in the pursuit of self-affirmation and excellence.

Thus, existentialism, as Christian and atheist thoughts were linked together, entered the world as a two-pronged fork, disturbing the intellectual soil throughout Europe. First it was the theologians, such as Karl Barth, Rudolf Bultmann, Paul Tillich, and Reinhold Niebuhr, who welcomed Kierkegaard's thoughts. Soon novelists and poets became infected with these new ideas: Fyodor Dostoyevsky, Franz Kafka, Hermann Hesse, T. S. Eliot, W. H. Auden, and later Saul Bellow, Norman Mailer, John Barth, Walker Percy, and John Updike. Psychoanalysts adopted its categories. Sigmund Freud borrowed Kierkegaard's notion of *angst* (or dread); Victor Frankl and Abraham Maslow devised "psychologies of being." A new breed of philosophers began to spring up, the existentialists, among whom are Martin Buber, Martin Heidegger, Albert Camus, Jean-Paul Sartre, and José Ortega y Gassett. Before long, existentialism had permeated the intellectual world everywhere. It was at first condemned by both the Communist Soviet Union as bourgeois subjectivism and by the Roman Catholic Church as dangerous individualism, though before long Catholics had appropriated many of its ideas.

What exactly is this new philosophy? What is its purpose and mission? Well, in order to touch the spirit of Kierkegaard's and existentialism's ideas, let me tell a story.

> There was once a man who discovered his shadow. Watching its lithe motion, he assumed that it was alive. Because it followed him so faithfully, he decided that he was its master, and that it was his servant. But gradually he began to believe that it was the shadow that was initiating the action and that the shadow was his irreplaceable guide and companion. He took increasing account of its comfort and welfare. He awkwardly maneuvered himself in order that it might sit in a chair or lie in bed. The importance of the shadow to the man grew to such an extent that finally the man became, in effect, "the shadow of his shadow"!

Existentialism is a call to look inward, to develop one's own personal philosophy of life, to get one's priorities right. Kierkegaard and Nietzsche deplored the tendency of humanity to become slaves of their technologies, "shadows of their shadows." Both decried the herd mentality of modern people, their susceptibility to peer pressure, what others think, and the identification with ethnic or political groups rather than as autonomous selves.

> Each age has its own peculiar depravity. Ours is perhaps not pleasure of indulgence or sensuality, but rather a dissolute pantheistic contempt for the individual person. In the midst of all our exultation over the achievements of our age, there sounds a note of poorly conceived contempt for the individual. In the midst of the self-importance of the contemporary generation there is revealed a sense of despair over being *human*. Everything must attach itself so as to be a part of some movement, some group. People are determined to lose themselves in the totality of things, in world-history, fascinated and deceived by a magical witchery. No one wants to be an *individual* human being.[2]

Kierkegaard warned in his journals in the 1840s that a time would come when people would be mesmerized by a box that would inform them on what to believe. The true individual must stand alone, deriving his or her ideals from within, not from without. The eternity that dwells within the heart is a neglected treasure by most people. Each of us has a duty to work out his or her own salvation with fear and trembling, to find a personal truth for which one can live and die.

The Three Theses of Existentialism

If we analyze existential writings, three theses stand out, embraced in one way or another by virtually all members of this movement: (1.) Existence precedes Essence, (2) life is absurd, and (3) freedom is at the core of our existence. We examine the first two theses in this chapter and the idea of freedom in Chapter 34.

Existence Precedes Essence

In classical philosophy, notably that of Plato and Aristotle, the concept of Essence preceded Existence. Truth is Eternal, Unchangeable, Absolute, and the central goal of philosophy. For Plato, as we saw in Part 2, the Forms or Essences exist in a transcendent dimension, and our job is to discover them through philosophical contemplation, through reason—through ascending from the cave of appearances. Human beings have a common eternal nature defined by reason ("humans are rational animals"). As Aristotle said,

> Reason is the true self of every person, since it is the supreme and better part. It will be strange, then, if he should choose not his own life, but some other's…. What is naturally proper to every creature is the highest and pleasantest for him. And so, to man, this will be the life of Reason, since Reason is, in the highest sense, a man's self.

In one way or another, all major philosophical systems from Plato through the Middle Ages down to Descartes and Kant carried on the essentialist tradition. Truth is outside of us, and our job is to use reason to discover it.

Existentialism denies the priority of objective truth. Subjectivity must be the starting point. What does this mean? Here is how Jean-Paul Sartre puts the point.

EXISTENTIALISM AND HUMAN EMOTIONS

Just what does that mean? Let us consider some object that is manufactured, for example, a book or a paper-cutter: here is an object which has been made by an artisan whose inspiration came from a concept. He referred to the concept of what a paper-cutter is and likewise to a known method of production, which is part of the concept,

From: Jean-Paul Sartre, *Existentialism and Human Emotions*, trans. Bernard Frechtman (New York: Philosophical Library, 1948).

something which is, by and large, a routine. Thus, the paper-cutter is at once an object produced in a certain way and, on the other hand, one having a specific use; and one cannot postulate a man who produces a paper-cutter but does not know what it is used for. Therefore, let us say that, for the paper-cutter, essence—that is, the ensemble of both the production routines and the properties which enable it to be both produced and defined—precedes existence. Thus, the presence of the paper-cutter or book in front of me is determined. Therefore, we have here a technical view of the world whereby it can be said that production precedes existence.

When we conceive God as the Creator, He is generally though of as a superior sort of artisan. Whatever doctrine we may be considering, whether one like that of Descartes or that of Leibnitz, we always grant that will more or less follows understanding or, at the very least, accompanies it, and that when God creates He knows exactly what He is creating. Thus, the concept of man in the mind of God is comparable to the concept of paper-cutter in the mind of the manufacturer, and, following certain techniques and a conception, God produces man, just as the artisan, following a definition and a technique, makes a paper-cutter. Thus, the individual man is the realization of a certain concept in the divine intelligence.

In the eighteenth century, the atheism of the *philosophes* discarded the idea of God, but not so much for the notion that essence precedes existence. To a certain extent, this idea is found everywhere; we find it in Diderot, in Voltaire, and even in Kant. Man has a human nature; this human nature, which is the concept of the human, is found in all men, which means that each man is a particular example of a universal concept, man. In Kant, the result of this universality is that the wild-man, the natural man, as well as the bourgeois, are circumscribed by the same definition and have the same basic qualities. Thus, here too the essence of man precedes the historical existence that we find in nature.

Atheistic existentialism, which I represent, is more coherent. It states that if God does not exist, there is at least one being in whom existence precedes essence, a being who exists before he can be defined by any concept, and that this being is man, or, as Heidegger says, human reality. What is meant here by saying that existence precedes essence? It means that, first of all, man exists, turns up, appears on the scene, and, only afterwards, defines himself. If man, as the existentialist conceives him, is indefinable, it is because at first he is nothing. Only afterward will he be something, and he himself will have made what he will be. Thus, there is no human nature, since there is no God to conceive it. Not only is man what he conceives himself to be, but he is also only what he wills himself to be after this thrust toward existence.

Man is nothing else but what he makes of himself. Such is the first principle of existentialism. It is also what is called subjectivity, the name we are labeled with when charges are brought against us. But what do we mean by this, if not that man has a greater dignity than a stone or table? For we mean that man first exists, that is, that man first of all is the being in the future. Man is at the start a plan which is aware of itself, rather than a patch of moss, a piece of garbage, or a cauliflower; nothing exists prior to this plan; there is nothing in heaven; man will be what he will have planned to be. Not what he will want to be. Because by the word "will" we generally mean a conscious decision, which is subsequent to what we have already made of ourselves. I may want to belong to a political party, write a book, get married; but all that is only a manifestation of an earlier, more spontaneous choice that is called "will." But if existence really does precede essence, man is responsible for what he is. Thus, existentialism's first move is to make every man aware of what he is and to make the full responsibility of his existence rest on him. And when we say that a man is responsible for himself, we do not only mean that he is responsible for his own individuality, but that he is responsible for all men.

The word subjectivism has two meanings, and our opponents play on the two. Subjectivism means, on the one hand, that an individual chooses and makes himself; and, on the other, that it is impossible for man to transcend human subjectivity. The second of these is the essential meaning of existentialism. When we say that man chooses his own self, we mean that every one of us does likewise; but we also mean by that that in making this choice he also chooses all men. In fact, in creating the man that we want to be, there is not a single one of our acts which does not at the same time create an image of man as we think he ought to be. To choose to be this or that is to affirm at the same time the value of what we choose, because we can never choose evil. We always choose the good, and nothing can be good for us without being good for all.

If, on the other hand, existence precedes essence, and if we grant that we exist and fashion our image at one and the same time, the image is valid for everybody and for our whole age. Thus, our responsibility is much greater than we might have supposed, because it involves all mankind.

What is important is what we do about ourselves, how we choose to live, the decisions we make.

For Martin Heidegger, the metaphor of *throwness* signifies the idea that we find ourselves already here, "thrown" into existence, as if we were in 70,000 fathoms of ocean water and must somehow keep afloat (or drown). A key question becomes "Why not drown?" But the urgency of finding a purpose to life radically transforms the relationship between objective truth and subjective apprehension.

For Kierkegaard, this thesis is set forth in his dictum that "subjectivity is Truth."

CONCLUDING UNSCIENTIFIC POSTSCRIPT

All existential problems are passionate problems, for when existence is interpreted with reflection it generates passion. To think about existential problems without passion is tantamount to not thinking about them at all, since it is to forget the point, which is that the thinker is himself an existing individual. Passion is the way to Truth—and the Way may be more valuable than the End.

He likes to quote the German philosopher Gotthold Lessing who said, "If God set forth before me the Eternal, unchangeable Truth in his right hand and

From: Søren Kierkegaard, *Concluding Unscientific Postscript* (Copenhagen, 1846); my translation.

the eternal quest for Truth in his left hand and said, 'Choose,' I would point to the left hand and say, 'Father, give me this, for the eternal unchangeable Truth belongs to you alone.'" The quest for Truth is appropriate to the dynamics of people still growing, still in need of spiritual development. The reason that God can truly possess Absolute Truth is that he is pure Subjectivity (pure Love), but we are sinful, selfish, ignorant, alienated from the ground of our being, and the way to overcome this alienation (for Kierkegaard, it is equivalent to sin) is to delve deep and act from our inner resources, listening to the still small voice within rather than the roar of the crowd or the imperious voice of authority.

In this regard, the existentialists follow Blaise Pascal (1623–1662): "The heart has reasons which the mind knows nothing of." Kierkegaard disagreed with Aristotle about the divinity of reason within us: "In existence rational thought is by no means higher than imagination and feeling, but coordinate. In existence all factors must be co-present." The passions, feelings, intuitions, and imagination have been neglected by philosophers, but they are just as valuable as reason and also define our being.

All essential knowledge concerns existence, for only that knowledge that relates to existence is essential, is *essential* knowledge. All knowledge that is not existential, that does not involve inward reflection, is really *accidental* knowledge, its degree and compass are essentially a matter of no importance. This essential knowledge that relates itself essentially to the existing individual is not to be equated with the above-mentioned abstract identity between thought and being. But it means that knowledge must relate itself to the knower, who is essentially an existing individual, and therefore all essential knowledge essentially relates itself to existence, to that which exists. But all ethical and all ethical–religious knowledge has this essential relationship to the existence of the knower.

When the question of truth is put forward in an objective manner, reflection is directed objectively to the truth as an object to which the knower is related. The reflection is not on the relationship but on whether he is related to the truth. If that which he is related to is the truth, the subject is in the truth. When the question of truth is put forward in a subjective manner, the reflection is directed subjectively to the individual's relationship. If the relation's HOW is in truth, the individual is in truth, even if the WHAT to which he is related is not true.

We may illustrate this by examining the knowledge of God. Objectively, the reflection is on whether the object is the true God; subjectively, the reflection is on whether the individual is related to a *what* in such a way that his relationship is a God-relationship.

If one who lives in a Christian culture goes up to God's house, the house of the true God, with a true conception of God, with knowledge of God and prays—but prays in a false spirit; and one who lives in an idolatrous land prays with the total passion of the infinite, although his eyes rest on the image of an idol; where is there most truth? The one prays in truth to God, although he worships an idol. The other prays in untruth to the true God and therefore really worships an idol.

When a person objectively inquires about the problem of immortality and another person embraces it as an uncertainty with infinite passion, where is there most truth, and who really has the greater certainty? The one has entered into an inexhaustible approximation, for certainty of immortality lies precisely in the subjectivity of the individual.[3]

To ask about immortality in a detached, objective attitude is to miss the point that it pertains to one's essential self. The objective inquiry may have limited importance in understanding the lack of objective certainty, but ultimately one must appropriate the idea, live in it.

Kierkegaard now offers a definition of subjective truth.

Here is a definition of Truth: An objective uncertainty held fast in an approximation process of the most passionate inwardness is the truth, the highest truth attainable for an existing individual.... The above definition is an equivalent expression for faith. Without risk there is no faith. Faith is precisely the contradiction between the infinite passion of the individual's inwardness and the objective uncertainty. If I am capable of grasping God objectively, I do not believe, but precisely because I cannot do this I must believe..., so as to remain out upon the deep, over seventy fathoms of water, still preserving my faith.[4]

We find ourselves thrown out into a sea of unknowing.

Sitting quietly in a ship while the weather is calm is not a picture of faith; but when the ship has sprung a leak, enthusiastically to keep the ship afloat by pumping while yet not seeking the harbor; this is the picture. And if the picture involves an impossibility in the long run, that is but the imperfection of the picture.[5]

We are never finished with existence, a task filled with paradoxes. It demands our passionate interest, and reason must take its proper place as a servant of the inner promptings of a passionate heart. Finally, the proof is in the pudding. Just as objective truth is a correspondence of a proposition with a fact or state of affairs, so subjective truth becomes the correspondence of the fact of one's life with an ideal. Subjective truth is becoming a work of art, portraying the ideal in one's life. All true understanding involves a deepening commitment to an ideal: "The only fundamental basis for understanding is that one understands only in proportion to becoming himself that which he understands."[6]

Sometimes these passages from Kierkegaard are interpreted to mean that Kierkegaard thought there was *no* truth to the matter and that we should simply choose our metaphysical belief and make irrational leaps of faith. This is a misunderstanding, however. Kierkegaard thought that the only way to come to a knowledge of metaphysical truths was through *subjective* processes. In fact, he thought that if we were truly subjective, truly passionate about our existential selves, we would discover objective metaphysical truths. Here is a revealing passage from his *Private Papers*.

Both proving and being convinced by an argument for the existence of God are equally fantastic, for just as no one has ever proved the existence of God, so no one has

> ever been an atheist, although many have never willed to allow their knowledge of God's existence to get power over their mind. It is the same with immortality.... With regard to God's existence, immortality, and all problems of immanence, recollection is valid; it is present in every man, only he is not aware of it. However, this in no way means that his concept of these metaphysical truths is adequate.[7]

Existence comes before essence for Kierkegaard—but in a deeper sense this is a paradox, for we have a profound identity (essence) within—but it can only be discovered by passionate, subjective inquiry, and commitment to the light we have. If we live in the light we have, we will be given more light. So for us, existence precedes essence; but, if Kierkegaard is right, there is a hidden essence after all, deep in the heart and accessible to faith.

Kierkegaard was a Christian, but other existentialists—Nietzsche, Sartre, and Camus—all denied such paradoxical notions about essence and existence. For them, existence precedes essence because there is no preformed self. As Sartre says, we create our essence by our choices in an absurd world. To see this alternate model of existence, let's proceed to the second characteristic of existentialism, the idea of the absurdity of existence.

The Absurdity of Existence

In his autobiography, Leo Tolstoy tells the story of a traveler fleeing an infuriated animal. Attempting to save himself from the beast, the man runs toward a well and begins to climb down, when to his distress he spies a dragon at the bottom of the well. The dragon is waiting with open jaws, ready to eat him. The poor fellow is caught in a dilemma. He dares not drop into the well for fear of the dragon, but he dare not climb out of the well for fear of the beast. So he clutches a branch of a bush growing in the cleft of the well and hangs onto it for dear life. His hands grow weak, and he feels that soon he shall to give in to his grim fate, but he still holds on desperately. As he grasps the branch for his salvation, he notices that two mice, one white and one black, are nibbling away at the main trunk of the branch onto which he is clinging. Soon they will dislodge the branch. At the same time, the traveler notices some honey on the end of the branch. Turning his mind off his imminent fate, he sticks out his tongue and enjoys a taste of honey.

The traveler is you and I, and his plight is yours and mine, the danger of our demise on every hand. The white mouse represents our days and the black our nights. Together they are nibbling away at the three-score years and ten that make up our branch of life. Inevitably, all will be over, and what have we to show for it? Are the distractions of "the taste of honey" all there is? Is there nothing more? Can this brief moment in the history of the universe have significance? What gives life value or importance?

The certainty of death heightens the question of the meaning of life. Like a prisoner sentenced to death or a patient with terminal illness, we know that, in a sense, we are all sentenced to death and are terminally ill, but we flee the thought in a thousand ways. What is the purpose of life?

The French existentialist Albert Camus (1913–1960), in his youthful work *The Myth of Sisyphus,* looks at the existence as an objectively meaningless event and is forced to conclude the following.

THE MYTH OF SISYPHUS

There is but one truly serious philosophical problem, and that is suicide. Judging whether life is or is not worth living amounts to answering the fundamental question of philosophy. All the rest—whether or not the world has three dimensions, whether the mind has nine or twelve categories—comes afterwards. These are games.

With life at stake, Camus begins an inquiry into the absurdity of existence. Here is his description of the state of mind that leads to the thought of voluntary death.[8]

Suicide has never been dealt with except as a social phenomenon. On the contrary, we are concerned here, at the outset, with the relationship between individual thought and suicide. An act like this is prepared within the silence of the heart, as is a great work of art. The man himself is ignorant of it. One evening he pulls the trigger or jumps. Of an apartment-building manager who had killed himself I was told that he had lost his daughter five years before, that he had changed greatly since, and that that experience had "undermined" him. A more exact word cannot be imagined. Beginning to think is beginning to be undermined. Society has but little connection with such beginnings. The worm is in man's heart. That is where it must be sought. One must follow and understand this fatal game that leads from lucidity in the face of existence to flight from light. . . .

But it is hard to fix the precise instant, the subtle step when the mind opted for death, it is easier to deduce from the act itself the consequences it implies. In a sense, and as in melodrama, killing yourself amounts to confessing. It is confessing that life is too much for you or that you do not understand it. Let's not go too far in such analogies, however, but rather return to everyday words. It is merely confessing that that "is not worth the trouble." Living, naturally, is never easy. You continue making the gestures commanded by existence for many reasons, the first of which is habit. Dying voluntarily implies that you have recognized, even instinctively, the ridiculous character of that habit, the absence of any profound reason for living, the insane character of that daily agitation, and the uselessness of suffering.

What, then, is that incalculable feeling that deprives the mind of the sleep necessary to life? A world that can be explained even with bad reasons is a familiar world. But, on the other hand, in a universe suddenly divested of illusions and lights, man feels an alien, a stranger. His exile is without remedy since he is deprived of the memory of a lost home or the hope of a promised land. This divorce between man and his life, the

From: Albert Camus, *The Myth of Sisyphus and Other Essays,* trans. Justin O'Brien (New York: Knopf, 1955). Copyright © 1955, 1983 by Alfred A. Knopf. Reprinted by permission of Alfred A. Knopf, a division of Random House, Inc.

actor and his setting, is properly the feeling of absurdity. All healthy men having thought of their own suicide, it can be seen, without further explanation, that there is a direct connection between this feeling and the longing for death.

The subject of this essay is precisely this relationship between the absurd and suicide, the exact degree to which suicide is a solution to the absurd. The principle can be established that for a man who does not cheat, what he believes to be true must determine his action. Belief in the absurdity of existence must then dictate his conduct. It is legitimate to wonder, clearly and without false pathos, whether a conclusion of this importance requires forsaking as rapidly as possible an incomprehensible condition. I am speaking, of course of men inclined to be in harmony with themselves....

All great deeds and all great thoughts have a ridiculous beginning. Great works are often born on a street-corner or in a restaurant's revolving door. So it is with absurdity. The absurd world more than others derives its nobility from that abject birth. In certain situations, replying "nothing" when asked what one is thinking about may be pretense in a man. Those who are loved are well aware of this. But if that reply is sincere, if it symbolizes that odd state of soul in which the void becomes eloquent, in which the chain of daily gestures is broken, in which the heart vainly seeks the link that will connect it again, then it is as it were the first sign of absurdity.

It happens that the stage sets collapse. Rising, streetcar, four hours in the office or the factory, meal, streetcar, four hours of work, meal, sleep, and Monday Tuesday Wednesday Thursday Friday and Saturday according to the same rhythm—this path is easily followed most of the time. But one day the "why" arises and everything begins in that weariness tinged with amazement. "Begins"—this is important. Weariness comes at the end of the acts of a mechanical life, but at the same time it inaugurates the impulse of consciousness. It awakens consciousness and provokes what follows. What follows is the gradual return into the chain or it is the definitive awakening. At the end of the awakening comes, in time, the consequence: suicide or recovery. In itself weariness has something sickening about it. Here, I must conclude that it is good. For everything begins with consciousness and nothing is worth anything except through it.

Does Camus have an answer to these questions: Why not suicide? Why accept the absurdity of existence? Here is his discussion.

But what does life mean in such a universe? Nothing else for the moment but indifference to the future and a desire to use up everything that is given. Belief in the meaning of life always implies a scale of values, a choice, our preferences. Belief in the absurd, according to our definitions, teaches the contrary. But this is worth examining.

Knowing whether or not one can live *without appeal* is all that interests me. I do not want to get out of my depth. This aspect of life being given me, can I adapt myself to it? Now, faced with this particular concern, belief in the absurd is tantamount to substituting the quantity of experiences for the quality. If I convince myself that this life has no other aspect than that of the absurd, if I feel that its whole equilibrium depends on that perpetual opposition between my conscious revolt and the darkness in which it struggles, if I admit that my freedom has no meaning except in relation to its limited fate, than I must say that what counts is not the best of living but the most living....

On the one hand the absurd teaches that all experiences are unimportant, and on the other it urges toward the greatest quantity of experiences. How, then, can one fail to do as so many of those men I was speaking of earlier—choose the form of life that brings us the most possible of that human matter, thereby introducing a scale of values that on the other hand one claims to reject?

But again it is the absurd and its contradictory life that teaches us. For the mistake is thinking that the quantity of experiences depends on the circumstances of our life when it depends solely on us. Here we have to be over-simple. To two men living the same number of years, the world always provides the same sum of experiences. It is up to us to be conscious of them. Being aware of one's life, one's revolt, one's freedom, and to the maximum, is living, and to the maximum. Where lucidity dominates, the scale of values becomes useless ....

Somehow we are driven to accept life in all its absurdity. We learn to live with and through and by absurdity. It becomes a catalyst for meaning. Camus illustrates his thesis with a rendition of the ancient Greek legend of *The Myth of Sisyphus.*

The gods had condemned Sisyphus to ceaselessly rolling a rock to the top of a mountain, whence the stone would fall back of its own weight. They had thought with some reason that there is no more dreadful punishment than futile and hopeless labor.

If one believes Homer, Sisyphus was the wisest and most prudent of mortals. According to another tradition, however, he was disposed to practice the profession of highwayman. I see no contradiction in this. Opinions differ as to the reasons why he became the futile laborer of the underworld. To begin with, he is accused of a certain levity in regard to the gods. He stole their secrets. Ægina, the daughter of Æsopus, was carried off by Jupiter. The father was shocked by that disappearance and complained to Sisyphus. He, who knew of the abduction, offered to tell about it on condition that Æsopus would give water to the citadel of Corinth. To the celestial thunderbolts he preferred the benediction of water. He was punished for this in the underworld. Homer tells us also that Sisyphus had put Death in chains. Pluto could not endure the sight of his deserted, silent empire. He dispatched the god of war, who liberated Death from the hands of her conqueror.

It is said also that Sisyphus, being near to death, rashly wanted to test his wife's love. He ordered her to cast his unburied body into the middle of the public square. Sisyphus woke up in the underworld. And there, annoyed by an obedience so contrary to human love, he obtained from Pluto permission to return to earth in order to chastise his wife. But when he had seen again the fact of this world, enjoyed water and sun, warm stones and the sea, he no longer wanted to go back to the infernal darkness. Recalls, signs of anger, warnings were of no avail. Many years more he lived facing the curve of the gulf, the sparkling sea, and the smiles of earth. A decree of the gods was necessary. Mercury came and seized the impudent man by the collar and, snatching him from his joys, led him forcibly back to the underworld, where his rock was ready for him.

You have already grasped that Sisyphus is the absurd hero. He *is,* as much through his passions as through his torture. His scorn of the gods, his hatred of death, and his passion for life won him that unspeakable penalty in which the whole being is exerted toward accomplishing nothing. This is the price that must be paid for the passions of this earth. Nothing is told us about Sisyphus in the underworld. Myths are made for the imagination to breathe life into them. As for this myth, one sees merely the whole effort of a body straining to raise the huge stone, to roll it and push it up a slope a hundred times over; one sees the face screwed up, the cheek tight against the stone, the shoulder bracing the clay-covered mass, the foot wedging it, the fresh start with arms outstretched, the wholly human security of two earth-clotted hands. At the very end of his long effort measured by skyless space and time without depth, the purpose is achieved. Then Sisyphus watches the stone rush down in a few moments toward that lower world whence he will have to push it up again toward the summit. He goes back down to the plain.

It is during that return, that pause, that Sisyphus interests me. A face that toils so close to stones is already stone itself! I see that man going back down with a heavy yet measured step toward the torment of which he will never know the end. That hour like a breathing-space which returns as surely as his suffering, that is the hour of consciousness. At each of those moments when he leaves the heights and gradually sinks toward the lairs of the gods, he is superior to his fate. He is stronger than his rock.

If this myth is tragic, that is because its hero is conscious. Where would his torture be, indeed, if at every step the hope of succeeding upheld him? The workman of today works every day in his life at the same tasks, and this fate is no less absurd. But it is tragic only at the rare moments when it becomes conscious. Sisyphus, proletarian of the gods, powerless and rebellious, knows the whole extent of his wretched condition: it is what he thinks of during his descent. The lucidity that was to constitute his torture at the same time crowns his victory. There is no fate that cannot be surmounted by scorn.

If the descent is thus sometimes performed in sorrow, it can also take place in joy. This word is not too much. Again I fancy Sisyphus returning toward his rock, and the sorrow was in the beginning. When the images of earth cling too tightly to memory, when the call of happiness becomes too insistent, it happens that melancholy rises in man's heart: this is the rock's victory, this is the rock itself. The boundless grief is too heavy to bear. These are our nights of Gethsemane. But crushing truths perish from being acknowledged. Thus, Œdipus at the outset obeys fate without knowing it. But from the moment he knows, his tragedy begins. Yet at the same moment, blind and desperate, he realizes that the only bond linking him to the world is the cool hand of a girl. Then a tremendous remark rings out: "Despite so many ordeals, my advanced age and the nobility of my soul make me conclude that all is well." Sophocles' Œdipus, like Dostoyevsky's Kirilov, thus gives the recipe for the absurd victory. Ancient wisdom confirms modern heroism.

One does not discover the absurd without being tempted to write a manual of happiness. "What! by such narrow ways—?" There is but one world, however. Happiness and the absurd are two sons of the same earth. They are inseparable. It would be a mistake to say that happiness necessarily springs from the absurd discovery. It happens as well that the feeling of the absurd springs from happiness. "I conclude that all is well," says Œdipus, and that remark is sacred. It echoes in the wild and limited universe of man. It teaches that all is not, has not been, exhausted. It drives out of this world a god who had come into it with dissatisfaction and a preference for futile sufferings. It makes of fate a human matter, which must be settled among men.

All Sisyphus' silent joy is contained therein. His fate belongs to him. His rock is his thing. Likewise, the absurd man, when he contemplates his torment, silences all the idols. In the universe suddenly restored to its silence, the myriad wondering little voices of the earth rise up. Unconscious, secret calls, invitations from all the faces, they are the necessary reverse and price of victory. There is no sun without shadow, and it is essential to know the night. The absurd man says yes and his effort will henceforth be unceasing. If there is a personal fate, there is no higher destiny, or at least there is but one which he concludes is inevitable and despicable. For the rest, he knows himself to be the master of his days. At that subtle moment when man glances backward over his life, Sisyphus returning toward his rock, in that slight pivoting he contemplates that series of unrelated actions which becomes his fate, created by him, combined under his memory's eye and soon sealed by his death. Thus, convinced of the wholly human origin of all that is human, a blind man eager to see who knows that the night has no end, he is still on the go. The rock is still rolling.

I leave Sisyphus at the foot of the mountain! One always finds one's burden again. But Sisyphus teaches the higher fidelity that negates the gods and raises rocks. He too concludes that all is well. This universe henceforth without a master seems to him neither sterile nor futile. Each atom of that stone, each mineral flake of that night-filled mountain, in itself forms a world. The struggle itself toward the heights is enough to fill a man's heart. One must imagine Sisyphus happy.

Is Camus correct? Can one be happy in the midst of the knowledge that life is absurd? Camus's answer is not the only one, of course. We may reintroduce Kierkegaard as representing the more optimistic response to the question of meaning. Kierkegaard, being religious, agrees with such sentiments to the extent that life for most people is absurd, but he argues that our very alienation from what we inwardly sense to be a higher self is a hint of God's voice, a holy hypochondria, calling us back, inwardly, to God. Not rational demonstration, not the philosophical proofs of God's existence, but the inner turmoil of the soul in the absurdity of existence leads us to make a leap of faith into a religious mode of existence. Absurdity is not an objective but a subjective problem that calls for a subjective response, a decision in passion, a leap of faith into the religious way of life.

Only those who, like Sisyphus, have felt the contradictions of life, the inner alienation, and the dread and despair connected with self-realization can appreciate religion, but to have experienced the absurd in life is to be a candidate for the religious quest. The idea of God must become a live hypothesis:

In a way God becomes a hypothesis but not in the lifeless manner in which the term is commonly used. It becomes clear rather that the only way in which an existing individual comes into a relationship with God is when the dialectical contradiction brings his passion to the point of despair, and enables him to embrace God with the "category of despair"—*faith*. Then the hypothesis is so far from being arbitrary that it is precisely a life-necessity. It is not so much that God is a hypothesis, as that the existing individual's hypothesizing god is a necessity.[9]

Ultimately, Kierkegaard believes that Christianity with its doctrine of the Incarnation, wherein God becomes man in Christ, is the proper fit for the passions of the heart:

> Subjectivity culminates in passion, Christianity [through the doctrine of the Incarnation] is the paradox, paradox and passion are a mutual fit, and the paradox is altogether suited to one whose situation is, to be in the extremity of existence. Aye, never in all the world could there be found two lovers so wholly suited to one another as paradox and passion.[10]

Both theist and nontheist existentialists begin with the apparent absurdity of existence, and both emphasize the need for autonomy or freedom in the midst of life's contradictory forces. It is that characteristic we now turn in Chapter 34.

Summary

See Summary in Chapter 34.

FOR FURTHER REFLECTION

1. What are the essential features of existentialism? Describe the first two. (The third feature will be discussed in Chapter 34).

2. Why did existentialism arise in Europe in the 19th century? Is its message valid today? Explain your answer. (You may want to wait until you read Chapter 34 before fully answering this question.)

3. Explain Kierkegaard's philosophy of life. What are the key ideas? What are their strengths and weaknesses?

4. What gives you meaning in life? Kierkegaard defined *subjective truth* as that for which you are willing to live and die. What are you willing to live and die for?

5. Some people argue that only something eternal like God or religious ideals can satisfy the human heart. "Thou hast made us for Thyself, O Lord, and our hearts are restless until they rest in Thee," wrote St. Augustine. Do you agree with this? Explain your answer.

6. What does Camus think is the only important philosophical question? How does he illustrate and argue for his position? How convincing is his answer that we should reject suicide?

7. What is the message of "The Myth of Sisyphus"?

NOTES

1. Søren Kierkegaard, *Private Papers* (1838–1855); my translation. All quotations from Kierkegaard in this chapter are my own.

2. Ibid.

3. Søren Kierkegaard, *Concluding Unscientific Postscript* (Copenhagen, 1846); my translation.

4. Ibid.

5. Ibid.

6. Kierkegaard, *Private Papers.*

7. Ibid.

8. Unless otherwise noted, all remaining passages are from Albert Camus, *The Myth of Sisyphus and Other Essays,* trans. Justin O'Brien (New York: Knopf, 1955). Reprinted by permission.

9. Kierkegaard, *Postscript.*

10. Ibid.

FOR FURTHER READING

See For Further Reading in Chapter 34.

34 ☙ Freedom: The Core of Our Being

Freedom and the Death of God in Modern Existentialism

As we noted, classical philosophers from Plato to Leibniz and Hegel supposed that humans were created with an essence, the image of God, a rational self, or a soul. Existence was seen as the exemplification of this essence. Our essence was seen to involve living according to an internal design plan, usually said to have been created by God.

But take away God and what do you have left? Here is how one existentialist stated the case.

THE MADMAN AND THE DEATH OF GOD

Have you ever heard of the madman who on a bright morning lighted a lantern and ran to the market-place calling out unceasingly: "I seek God! I seek God!"—As there were many people standing about who did not believe in God, he caused a great deal of amusement. Why! is he lost? said one. Has he strayed away like a child? said another. Or does he keep himself hidden? Is he afraid of us? Has he taken a sea-voyage? Has he emigrated?—the people cried out laughingly, all in a hubbub. The insane man jumped into their midst and transfixed them with his glances. "Where is God gone?" he called out. "I mean to tell you! *We have killed him,*—you and I! We are all his murderers! But how have we done it? How were we able to drink up the sea? Who gave us the sponge to wipe away the whole horizon? What did we do when we loosened this earth from its sun? Whither does it now move? Whither do we move? Away from all suns? Do we not dash on unceasingly? Backwards, sideways, forewards, in all directions? Is there still

From: Friedrich Nietzsche, *The Complete Words of Nietzsche*, trans. Oscar Levy (T. N. Foulis, 1910).

an above and below? Do we not stray, as through infinite nothingness? Does not empty space breathe upon us? Has it not become colder? Does not night come on continually darker and darker? Shall we not have to light lanterns in the morning? Do we not hear the noise of the grave-diggers who are burying God? Do we not smell the divine putrefaction?—for even Gods putrefy? God is dead! God remains dead! And we have killed him! How shall we console ourselves, the most murderous of all murderers? The holiest and the mightiest that the world has hitherto possessed, has bled to death under our knife,—who will wipe the blood from us? With what water could we cleanse ourselves? What lustrums, what sacred games shall we have to devise? Is not the magnitude of this deed too great for us? Shall we not ourselves have to become Gods, merely to seem worthy of it? There never was a greater event,—and on account of it, all who are born after us belong to a higher history than any history hitherto!"—Here the madman was silent and looked again at his hearers; they also were silent and looked at him in surprise. At last he threw his lantern on the ground, so that it broke in pieces and was extinguished. "I come too early," he then said, "I am not yet at the right time. This prodigious event is still on its way, and is travelling,—it has not yet reached men's ears. Lightning and thunder need time, the light of the stars needs time, deeds need time, even after they are done, to be seen and heard. This deed is as yet further from them than the furthest star,—*and yet they have done it!*"—It is further stated that the madman made his way into different churches on the same day, and there intoned his *Requiem Aeternam deo.* When led out and called to account, he always gave the reply: "What are these churches now, if they are not the tombs and monuments of God?"—…

Who was the man who wrote such audacious thoughts? He was a man brought up in a Protestant parsonage. Friedrich Nietzsche (1844–1900), a German existentialist, has played a major role in contemporary intellectual development, affecting both philosophy and literary theory. Descending through both of his parents from Christian ministers, Nietzsche was brought up in a pious German Lutheran home and was known as "the little Jesus" by his schoolmates. He studied theology at the University of Bonn and philology at Leipzig, becoming an atheist in the process. At the age of 24, he was appointed professor of classical philology at the University of Basel in Switzerland where he taught for 10 years until forced by ill health to retire. He suffered greatly from migraine headaches, ulcers, insomnia, and fever. Eventually, he became mentally ill and spent the last 10 years of his life in a mental institution. He died on August 25, 1900. Whatever our assessment of his life, the power of his pen, of his mind, has awakened many a contented man or woman and left them deeply disturbed about their lives.

Nietzsche believed that the fundamental creative force that motivates all creation is the *will to power.* We all seek to affirm ourselves, to flourish and dominate.

What is good? All that enhances the feeling of power, the Will to Power, and the power itself in man. What is bad?—All that proceeds from weakness. What is happiness?—The feeling that power is increasing—that resistance has been overcome.

Not contentment, but more power; not peace at any price, but war; not virtue, but competence (virtue in the Renaissance sense, *virtu*, free from moralistic acid). The first principle of our humanism: The weak and the failures shall perish. They ought even to be helped to perish.

What is more harmful than any vice?—Practical sympathy and pity for all the failures and all the weak: Christianity.[1]

Having cast off religion, we have the dizzy realization that we are infinitely free.

On the Horizon of the Infinite. We have left the land and have embarked. We have burned our bridges behind us—indeed, we have gone farther and destroyed the land behind us. Now, little ship. look out! Before you is the ocean. To be sure, it does not always roar, and at times it lies spread out like silk and gold and reveries of graciousness. But hours will come when you will realize that it is infinite and that there is nothing more awesome than infinity! Oh, the poor bird that felt free and now strikes the walls of this cage! Woe, when you feel homesick for the land as if it had offered more *freedom*—and there is not longer any "land."[2]

We must be strong and creative enough to create our own values.

All actions may be traced back to values, and all values are either one's own or adopted from others, the latter being by far the case with the majority. Why do we adopt other people's values? Through fear. We think it prudent to pretend that they are our own, and so well do we accustom ourselves to do so that it at last becomes second nature to us. A value of our own is something very rare indeed! but must not our valuing of our neighbor—which is prompted by the motive that we adopt his values in most cases—*proceed from ourselves and by our own decision?* Of course, but then we come to these decisions during our childhood, and seldom change them. We often remain during our whole lifetime the dupes of our childish and accustomed judgment beliefs about our fellow men, and we find it necessary to subscribe to their values.[3]

Since we are essentially unequal in ability, it follows that the fittest will survive and be victorious in the contest with the weaker and baser. There is great aesthetic beauty in the noble spirit coming to fruition, but this process is hampered by Judeo-Christian morality, which Nietzsche labels "slave morality." Slave morality, which is the invention of jealous priests, envious and resentful of the power of the noble, prescribes that we give up the will to power and excellence and become meek and mild, that we believe the lie of all humans having equal worth. Nietzsche also refers to this as the *ethics of resentment:* "Difference engenders hate: the baseness of some people suddenly spurts up like filthy liquid when a holy vessel, a priceless object from a locked shrine, a book with the marks of a great destiny, is carried past."[4] So the muddled masses hurl malice at noble souls. The weak envy genius with a self-loathing projected on the strong. They seek revenge on them for being strong, by showing up their inadequacy and inferiority.

Nietzsche's ideas of inegalitarian ethics are based on his notion of the death of God, as set forth earlier. God plays no vital role in our culture—except as a (fictitious) protector of the slave morality, including the idea of equal worth of all persons. If we recognize that there is no rational basis for believing in God, we will see that the whole edifice of slave morality must crumble and with it the notion of equal worth. In its place will arise the morality of the noble person—based on the virtues of the high courage, discipline, and intelligence—in the pursuit of self-affirmation and excellence. On the horizon is a new man, one who is strong, heroic, intellectual, forceful. He is the hope of the future—he is the "Superman" (German, *Übermench*). Meanwhile, we "immoralists" must prepare the way for such superior beings, by being superior ourselves.

BEYOND GOOD AND EVIL

We immoralists make it a point of honor to be affirmers. More and more our eyes have opened to that economy which needs and knows how to utilize all that the holy witlessness of the priest, of the diseased reason of the priest, rejects—that economy in the law of life which finds an advantage even in the disgusting species of the prigs, the priests, the virtuous. What advantage? Be we ourselves, we immoralists, are the answer.

As superior, spiritual aristocrats, we must recognize the necessity of sacrificing lower human beings.

The essential characteristic of a good and healthy aristocracy, however, is that it experiences itself not as a function (whether of the monarchy or the commonwealth) but as their meaning and highest justification—that it therefore accepts with a good conscience the sacrifice of untold human beings who, for its sake, must be reduced and lowered to incomplete human beings, to slaves, to instruments. Their fundamental faith simply has to be that society must not exist for society's sake but only as the foundation and scaffolding on which a choice type of being is able to raise itself to its higher task and to a higher state of being—comparable to those sun-seeking vines of Java—called *Sipo madador*—that so long and so often enclasp an oak tree with their tendrils until eventually, high above it but supported by it, they can unfold their crowns in the open light and display their happiness.

Refraining from injury, violence and exploitation and placing one's will on a par with that of someone else—this may become, in a certain rough sense, good manners among individuals if the appropriate conditions are present (i.e., if these men are actually similar in strength and value standards and belong together in one body). But as soon as this principle is extended and possibly even accepted as the fundamental principle of society, it immediately proves to be what it really is—a will to the denial of life, a principle of disintegration and decay.

From: Friedrich Nietzsche, "Beyond Good and Evil," in *The Complete Works of Nietzsche,* trans. Oscar Levy (T. N. Foulis, 1910).

Here we must beware of superficiality and get to the bottom of the matter, resisting all sentimental weakness: life is essentially appropriation, injury, overpowering of what is alien and weaker; suppression, hardness, imposition of one's own forms, incorporation and, at least, at its mildest exploitation.

Even the body within which individuals treat each other as equals has to do to other bodies what the individuals within it refrain from doing to each other: it will have to be an incarnate will to power, it will strive to grow, spread, seize, become predominant—not from any morality or immorality but because it is living and because life simply is *will to power*. Exploitation is a consequence of the will to power, which is after all the will of life.

Slave morality: Precisely what the masters value is called evil by the slave, who believe weakness, blindness, stupidity, and pity good. The slave's eye looks unfavorably upon the virtues of the mighty. He is skeptical toward, and mistrusts, whatever is honored as "good." He might persuade himself that not even happiness is there. Conversely, those qualities are underlined and spotlighted which serve to ease the existence of the sufferer: pity, the kindly helping hand, a warm heart, patience, diligence, humility, friendship—these are honored.[5]

Slave morality is essentially a reaction to the creative ideals of the spiritual nobles.

The slave revolt in morality begins when *resentment* itself becomes creative and gives birth to values. When every nobel morality develops from a triumphant affirmation of itself, slave morality from the outset says No to what is "outside," what is "different," what is "not itself"; and *this* No is its creative deed. This inversion of the value-positing eye—this *need* to direct one's view outward instead of back to oneself—is of the essence of *resentment*. In order to exist, slave morality always first needs a hostile external world. It needs, physiologically speaking, external stimuli in order to act at all. Its action is fundamentally reaction.[6]

Nietzsche is also credited with the idea of *perspectivism:* that thought and valuation proceed from different interpretation. Rejecting the notion of a god's-eye view of reality, Nietzsche explores the possibility that there ("really"?) is no reality—only various interpretations.

THE WILL TO POWER

On Interpretation

Everything is Interpretation: Against positivism, which halts at phenomena—Against those who say "There are only facts," I say, "No, facts are precisely what there is not, only interpretations." We cannot establish any fact *in itself*. Perhaps it is folly to want to do such a thing.

From: Friedrich Nietzsche, "The Will to Power," in *The Complete Works of Nietzsche*, trans. Oscar Levy (T. N. Foulis, 1910).

"Everything is subjective," you say; but even here we have interpretation. The "subject" is not something given. It is something given; it is something added and invented and projected behind what there is. Finally, is it necessary to posit an interpreter behind the interpretation? Even this is invention, hypothesis.

Insofar as the word "knowledge" has any meaning, the world is knowable; but it is *interpretable* otherwise. It has no meaning behind it, but countless meanings. *Perspectivism.*

It is our needs that interpret the world; our drives and their For and Against. Every drive is a kind of lust to rule; each one has its perspective that it would like to compel all other drives to accept as a norm.

The criterion of truth resides in the enhancement of the feeling of power....Truth is the kind of error without which a certain species of life could not live. The value of life is ultimately decisive....There are many kinds of eyes. Even the sphinx has eyes—and consequently there are many kinds of "truths," and consequently there is no truth.

These perplexing, paradoxical ideas run through Nietzsche's writings and have profoundly influenced modern philosophy and literary theory. Contemporary thinkers such as Richard Rorty, Paul De Mann, and Jacques Derrida all take Nietzsche's critique of truth and idea of perspectivism as points of departure for their own work. Nietzsche himself was haunted by his religious past. Here is the last entry in his diary written just before his death.

Dionysus Versus Christ

The two types: Dionysus and the Crucified. Here I set the Dionysus of the Greeks: the religion of affirmation of life, life not denied in whole or in part. Dionysus versus the "Crucified": there you have the antithesis. It is not a difference in regard to their martyrdom—it is a difference in the meaning of it. Life itself, its eternal fruitfulness and recurrence, creates torment, destruction, the will to annihilation. In the other case, suffering—"the Crucified as the innocent one"—counts as an objection to this life, as a formula for its condemnation. One will see that the problem is that of the meaning of suffering: whether a Christian meaning or a tragic meaning. In the former case, it is supposed to be the path to a holy existence; in the latter case, being is counted as holy enough to justify even a monstrous amount of suffering. The tragic man affirms even the harshest suffering. He is sufficiently strong, rich, and capable of deifying to do so. The Christian denies even the happiest lot on earth. He is sufficiently weak, poor, disinherited to suffer from life in whatever form he meets it. The god on the cross is a curse on life, a signpost to seek redemption from life. Dionysus cut to pieces is a promise of life. It will be eternally reborn and return again from destruction.[7]

The "death of God" is both the glory and the degradation of humanity. It is the glory because it means that we must become gods ourselves. We are our own creators, so to speak. It is the degradation because it means that we are not immortal, not intrinsically valuable, but mere happenstances of accidental, evolutionary collocations of matter. We find ourselves "thrown" into existence and must create our essence. These ideas are developed in the work of the greatest existentialist of the 20th century, Jean-Paul Sartre.

The Idea of Freedom in Sartre's Work

Jean-Paul Sartre was born in 1905 into the home of a historic Swiss-French Protestant family, the Schweitzers (he was the second cousin of Albert Schweitzer). His father died when he was 1 year old, so he was brought up by his young mother Anne Marie, who was more like his playmate and worshipper than parent, and his maternal grandfather in Alsace. Of his childhood he wrote, "I had no rights because I was overwhelmed with love. I had no duties because I did everything through love." His godlike grandfather spoke to him once about being a writer; Sartre mistook it for a divine command and spent the rest of his life in obedience, sometimes writing 10,000 words a day. He served in the French army during World War II, was captured by the Germans, and spent time in a prison camp reading German philosophers (especially Hegel, Husserl, and Heidegger). After the war, his plays, novels, and philosophical work, especially *Being and Nothingness* (1943), set him apart as Europe's premier existentialist. On October 29, 1945, he delivered a famous lecture. Here is Paul Johnson's description of that event.

> October 29, 1945, is the turning point in French culture. Shortly after the end of World War II a beleaguered and exhausted France is trying to recover from defeat and four years of German occupation. A lecture was to be given at the Club Maintenant. Everyone came, fights broke out, people went hysterical trying to get into the hall, which was packed to capacity. Frenchmen and women fought each other for chairs and with chairs, smashing 30 of them before the lecture. Men and women fainted in the fray, as they were crushed against one another. When the celebrated speaker arrived, the mob in the street was so large, he thought that he was witnessing a demonstration organized by the Communist Party. His friends had to force an entrance for him. Meanwhile, the theaters in Paris were deserted. A leading speaker addressed an all but empty hall. All Paris had gone to hear a short (5'2"), squinty, bespectacled, mole of a man give a lecture entitled "Existentialism Is a Humanism." Who was this man and what caused this astonishing spectacle?
>
> A new literary and philosophical hero had emerged from the war with a new philosophy in tune with the times, which accepted the dark tragedy of defeat and war and the absurdity of the human condition. A secular priest was offering a secular gospel, Existentialism, which was neither Christian nor Communist, to make sense of a senseless world. Jean-Paul Sartre had just launched his new literary review, *Les Temps Modernes* (named after Charley Chaplin's famous film), and was about to give one of the most famous speeches in modern cultural history. This editor, philosopher, novelist, and playwright, who would soon be referred to as the "Eiffel Tower of French Culture," would dominate the intellectual life of Europe for the next 25 years. At his funeral April 19, 1980, 50,000 French people would converge in procession on the Montparnasse Cemetery. Sartre's press coverage defied the wildest

dreams. Several newspapers carried every word of the long lecture. The Catholic daily, *La Croix,* called Sartre's existentialism "a greater danger than eighteenth-century rationalism or nineteenth-century positivism." Soon all his books were placed on the Roman Catholic Index [list of censored books], which greatly increased their sales. The Communist *L'Humanite* called Sartre an enemy of society, and Stalin's cultural commissar, Alexander Fadayev, called him "a jackal with a typewriter, a hyena with a fountain pen." It was the greatest intellectual promotion scheme of the century. "Existentialism as a Humanism" sold over 1/2 million copies in the first month alone.[8]

The selections from Sartre in this chapter are from that lecture.

According to traditional philosophy, man has a human nature; this human nature, which is the concept of the human, is found in all people, which means that each person has an essence, a function to fulfill. Our nature determines the limits of our being and somewhat determines what we will be. We have already seen how Nietzsche thought that the "death of God" undermined the idea of an essence and left us free to create our own essence. Nietzsche was an elitist, an inegalitarian, who thought that a few people were inwardly stronger or more intelligent than others, so he accepted a strong element of evolutionary determinism. However, Sartre was an egalitarian. We all have equal opportunity and equal necessity of creating our essence. We are all equally "condemned to freedom."

First, Sartre describes the way we proceed to impute essences and worth on others by the way we treat them. By "looking" at people (or not looking, not regarding them), we impart a vicarious value to their lives. Because we value them, they suppose that they must really possess some intrinsic goodness. This is especially true of parents' regard of their children.

The child takes his parents for gods. Their actions, like their judgments, are absolute. They are the incarnation of universal reason, law, the meaning and purpose of the world. When the eye of these divine beings is turned on him, their look is enough to justify him at once to the very roots of his existence. It confers on him a definite, sacred character. Since they are infallible, it follows that they see him as he really is. There is no room in his mind for hesitation or doubt. True, all that he sees of himself is the vague success of his moods, but the gods have made themselves the guardians of his eternal essence. He knows that it exists. Even though he can have no direct experience of it, he realizes that his truth does not consist in what he can know of himself but that it is hidden in the large, terrible-yet-gentle eyes that are turned toward him. He is a real essence among other real essences; he has his place in the world—an absolute place in an absolute world. As the child grows, he discovers that his parents are fallible, that they are neither gods nor viceroys of God, that the whole phenomenon of the essence-granting process is a charade. There is no God, no essence, no absolute place in the universe for us, no absolute determinants whatsoever. We have neither intrinsic value nor an essence. We are alone, doomed to death and totally free, free to create what we shall: We are condemned to freedom.

EXISTENTIALISM AND HUMAN EMOTIONS

There is no human nature, since there is no god to conceive it. . . . Man is nothing else but what he makes of himself. . . . Thus, our responsibility is much greater than we might have supposed, because it involves all mankind. If I am a workingman and choose to join a Christian trade-union rather than be a communist, and if by being a member I want to show that the best thing for man is resignation, that the kingdom of man is not of this world, I am not only involving my own case—I want to be resigned for everyone. As a result, my action has involved all humanity. To take a more individual matter, if I want to marry, to have children; even if this marriage depends solely on my own circumstances or passion or wish, I am involving all humanity in monogamy and not merely myself. Therefore, I am responsible for myself and for everyone else. I am creating a certain image of man of my own choosing. In choosing myself, I choose man.

Note the similarity to Kant's categorical imperative: Always act in such a way that you could will that the maxim of your act would become a universal law of nature (Part 7). We must universalize principles, or they are not really valid principles. Sartre carries Kant's idea beyond where Kant would recognize it, for Kant thought only one set of moral principles could be derived from the categorical imperative. Sartre claims that it will yield an infinite variety of principles—anything that you desire to do—just choose it for humankind.

Sartre acknowledges that such **absolute freedom** is fearful. It means that we are always responsible for ourselves and everyone else. This fills us with anxiety, with deep anguish.[9]

This helps us understand what the actual content is of such rather grandiloquent words as anguish, forlornness, despair. As you will see, it's all quite simple.

First, what is meant by anguish? The existentialists say at once that man is anguish. What that means is this: the man who involves himself and who realizes that he is not only the person he chooses to be, but also a law-maker who is, at the same time, choosing all mankind as well as himself, cannot help escape the feeling of his total and deep responsibility. Of course, there are many people who are not anxious; but we claim that they are hiding their anxiety, that they are fleeing from it. Certainly, many people believe that when they do something, they themselves are the only ones involved, and when someone says to them, "What if everyone acted that way?" they shrug their shoulders and answer, "Everyone doesn't act that way." But really, one should always ask himself, "What would happen if everybody looked at things that way?" There is no escaping this disturbing thought except by a kind of double-dealing. A man who lies and makes excuses for himself by saying "not everybody does that," is someone with an uneasy conscience, because the act of lying implies that a universal value is conferred upon the lie.

From: Jean-Paul Sarte, *Existentialism and Human Emotions*, trans. Bernard Fechtman (New York: Philosophical Library, 1948). Reprinted by permission.

Anguish is evident even when it conceals itself. This is the anguish that Kierkegaard called the anguish of Abraham. You know the story: an angel has ordered Abraham to sacrifice his son; if it really were an angel who has come and said, "You are Abraham, you shall sacrifice your son," everything would be all right. But everyone might first wonder, "Is it really an angel, and am I really Abraham? What proof do I have?"…

Now, I'm not being singled out as an Abraham, and yet at every moment I'm obliged to perform exemplary acts. For every man, everything happens as if all mankind had its eyes fixed on him and were guiding itself by what he does. And every man ought to say to himself, "Am I really the kind of man who has the right to act in such a way that humanity might guide itself by my actions?" And if he does not say that to himself, he is masking his anguish.

There is no question here of the kind of anguish which would lead to quietism, to inaction. It is a matter of a simple sort of anguish that anybody who has had responsibilities is familiar with. For example, when a military officer takes the responsibility for an attack and sends a certain number of men to death, he chooses to do so, and in the main he alone makes the choice. Doubtless, orders come from above, but they are too broad; he interprets them, and on this interpretation depend the lives of ten or fourteen or twenty men. In making a decision he cannot help having a certain anguish. All leaders know this anguish. That doesn't keep them from acting; on the contrary, it is the very condition of their action. For it implies that they envisage a number of possibilities, and when they choose one, they realize that it has value only because it is chosen. We shall see that this kind of anguish, which is the kind that existentialism describes, is explained, in addition, by a direct responsibility to the other men whom it involves. It is not a curtain separating us from action, but is part of action itself.

When we speak of forlornness, a term Heidegger was fond of, we mean only that God does not exist and that we have to face all the consequences of this. The existentialist is strongly opposed to a certain kind of secular ethics which would like to abolish God with the least possible expense. About 1880, some French teachers tried to set up a secular ethics which went something like this: God is a useless and costly hypothesis; we are discarding it; but meanwhile, in order for there to be an ethics, a society, a civilization, it is essential that certain values be taken seriously and that they be considered as having a *a priori* existence. It must be obligatory, *a priori,* to be honest, not to lie, not to beat your wife, to have children, etc., etc. So we're going to try a little device which will make it possible to show that values exist all the same, inscribed in a heaven of ideas, though otherwise God does not exist. In other words—and this, I believe, is the tendency of everything called reformism in France—nothing will be changed if God does not exist. We shall find ourselves with the same norms of honesty, progress, and humanism, and we shall have made of God an outdated hypothesis which will peacefully die off by itself.

The existentialist, on the contrary, thinks it very distressing that God does not exist, because all possibility of finding values in a heaven of ideas disappears along with Him; there can be no longer an *a priori* Good, since there is no infinite and perfect consciousness to think it. Nowhere is it written that the Good exists, that we must be honest, that we must not lie; because the fact is we are on a plane where there are only men. Dostoievsky said, "If God didn't exist, everything would be possible." That is the very starting point of existentialism. Indeed, everything is permissible if God does not exist, and as a result man is forlorn, because neither within him nor without does he find anything to cling to. He can't start making excuses for himself.

If existence really does precede essence, there is no explaining things away by reference to a fixed and given human nature. In other words, there is no determinism, man is free, man is freedom. On the other hand, if God does not exist, we find no values or commands to turn to which legitimize our conduct. So, in the bright realm of values, we have no excuse behind us, no justification before us. We are alone, with no excuses.

That is the idea I shall try to convey when I say that man is condemned to be free. Condemned, because he did not create himself, yet, in other respects is free; because, once thrown into the world, he is responsible for everything he does. The existentialist does not believe in the power of passion. He will never agree that a sweeping passion is a ravaging torrent which fatally leads a man to certain acts and is therefore an excuse. He thinks that man is responsible for his passion.

The existentialist does not think that man is going to help himself by finding in the world some omen by which to orient himself. Because he thinks that man will interpret the omen to suit himself. Therefore, he thinks that man, with no support and no aid, is condemned every moment to invent man. Ponge, in a very fine article, has said, "Man is the future of man." That's exactly it. But if it is taken to mean that this future is recorded in heaven, that God sees it, then it is false, because it would really no longer be a future. If it is taken to mean that, whatever a man may be, there is a future to be forged, a virgin future before him, then this remark is sound. But then we are forlorn.

To illustrate the idea of forlornness, this sense of being deserted by the gods, Sartre tells a story to illustrate how even our morality is relative to our free, creative invention. During World War II, a student came to Sartre asking for advice.

To give you an example which will enable you to understand forlornness better, I shall cite the case of one of my students who came to see me under the following circumstances: his father was on bad terms with his mother, and, moreover, was inclined to be a collaborationist; his older brother had been killed in the German offensive of 1940, and the young man, with somewhat immature but generous feelings, wanted to avenge him. His mother lived alone with him, very much upset by the half-treason of her husband and the death of her older son; the boy was her only consolation.

The boy was faced with the choice of leaving for England and joining the Free French Forces—that is, leaving his mother behind—or remaining with his mother and helping her to carry on. He was fully aware that the woman lived only for him and that his going-off—and perhaps his death—would plunge her into despair. He was also aware that every act that he did for his mother's sake was a sure thing, in the sense that it was helping her to carry on, whereas every effort he made toward going off and fighting was an uncertain move which might run aground and prove completely useless; for example, on his way to England he might, while passing through Spain, be detained indefinitely in a Spanish camp; he might reach England or Algiers and be stuck in an office at a desk job. As a result, he was faced with two very different kinds of action: one, concrete, immediate, but concerning only one individual; the other concerned an incomparably vaster group, a national collectivity, but for that very reason was dubious, and might be interrupted en route. And, at the same time, he was wavering between two kinds of ethics. On the one hand, an ethics of sympathy, of personal devotion; on the other, a broader ethics, but one whose efficacy was more dubious. He had to choose between the two.

Who could help him choose? Christian doctrine? No. Christian doctrine says, "Be charitable, love your neighbor, take the more rugged path, etc., etc." But which is the more rugged path? Whom should he love as a brother? The fighting man or his mother? Which does the greater good, the vague act of fighting in a group, or the concrete one of helping a particular human being to go on living? Who can decide *a priori*? Nobody. No book of ethics can tell him. The Kantian ethics says, "Never treat any person as a means, but as an end." Very well, if I stay with my mother, I'll treat her as an end and not as a means; but by virtue of this very fact, I'm running the risk of treating the people around me who are fighting, as means; and, conversely, if I go to join those who are fighting, I'll be treating them as an end, and, by doing that, I run the risk of treating my mother as a means.

If values are vague, and if they are always too broad for the concrete and specific case that we are considering, the only thing left for us is to trust our instincts. That's what this young man tried to do; and when I saw him, he said, "In the end, feeling is what counts. I ought to choose whichever pushes me in one direction. If I feel that I love my mother enough to sacrifice everything else for her—my desire for vengeance, for action, for adventure—then I'll stay with her. If, on the contrary, I feel that my love for my mother isn't enough, I'll leave."

But how is the value of a feeling determined? What gives his feeling for his mother value? Precisely the fact that he remained with her. I may say that I like so-and-so well enough to sacrifice a certain amount of money for him, but I may say so only if I've done it. I may say, "I love my mother well enough to remain with her" if I have remained with her. The only way to determine the value of this affection is, precisely, to perform an act which confirms and defines it. But, since I require this affection to justify my act, I find myself caught in a vicious circle....

As for despair, the term has a very simple meaning. It means that we shall confine ourselves to reckoning only with what depends upon our will, or on the ensemble of probabilities which make our action possible. When we want something, we always have to reckon with probabilities. I may be counting on the arrival of a friend. The friend is coming by rail or street-car; this supposes that the train will arrive on schedule, or that the street-car will not jump the track. I am left in the realm of possibility; but possibilities are to be reckoned with only to the point where my action comports with the ensemble of these possibilities, and no further. The moment the possibilities I am considering are not rigorously involved by my action, I ought to disengage myself from them, because no God, no scheme, can adapt the world and its possibilities to my will. When Descartes said, "Conquer yourself rather than the world," he meant essentially the same thing.

The Marxists to whom I have spoken reply, "You can rely on the support of others in your action, which obviously has certain limits because you're not going to live forever.

That means: rely on both what others are doing elsewhere to help you, in China, in Russia, and what they will do later on, after your death, to carry on the action and lead it to its fulfillment, which will be the revolution. You even *have* to rely upon that, otherwise you're immortal." I reply at once that I will always rely on fellow fighters insofar as these comrades are involved with me in a common struggle, in the unity of a party or a group in which I can more or less make my weight felt; that is, one whose ranks I am in as a fighter and whose movements I am aware of at every moment. In such a situation, relying on the unity and will of the party is exactly like counting on the fact that the train will arrive on time or that the car won't jump the track. But, given that man is free and that there is no human nature for me to depend on, I cannot count on men whom I do not know by relying on human goodness or man's concern for the good of society. I don't know what will become of the Russian revolution; I may make an example of it to the extent that at the present time it is apparent that the proletariat plays a part in Russia that it plays in no other nation. But I can't swear that this will inevitably lead to a triumph of the proletariat. I've got to limit myself to what I see.

Given that men are free, and that tomorrow they will freely decide what man will be, I cannot be sure that, after my death, fellow fighters will carry on my work to bring it to its maximum perfection. Tomorrow, after my death, some men may decide to set up Fascism, and the others may be cowardly and muddled enough to let them do it. Fascism will then be the human reality, so much the worse for us.

Actually, things will be as man will have decided they are to be. Does that mean that I should abandon myself to quietism? No. First, I should involve myself; then, act on the old saw, "Nothing ventured, nothing gained." Nor does it mean that I shouldn't belong to a party, but rather that I shall have no illusions and shall do what I can. For example, suppose I ask myself, "Will socialization, as such, ever come about?" I know nothing about it. All I know is that I'm going to do everything in my power to bring it about. Beyond that, I can't count on anything. Quietism is the attitude of people who say, "Let others do what I can't do." The doctrine I am presenting is the very opposite of quietism, since it declares, "There is no reality except in action." Moreover, it goes further, since it adds, "Man is nothing else than his plan; he exists only to the extent that he fulfills himself; he is, therefore, nothing else than the ensemble of his acts, nothing else than his life."

For Kierkegaard, even faith itself is a function of freedom. Reason is a prostitute who sells to the highest bidder. "If I really have reason and am in the situation in which I must act decisively, my reason will put forth as many possibilities *pro* and *contra*, exactly as many." Reason always leads to skepticism, leaving all important issues in doubt, so faith must take over where reason leaves off. Through freedom, the leap of faith comes into play. You are responsible even for what you believe!

We usually think of freedom as a very positive, salutary trait, one that all adolescents crave. But, as we see with Sartre, it is, according to the existentialists, at least, as negative as it is positive. It is a dreadful freedom, imposing a heavy burden of responsibility on us, for with it we cannot get off the hook of existence. We are totally responsible for our actions, for what we become.

The experience of freedom is not that of fear. It's inappropriate to say that we fear freedom. We dread it. It causes deep anxiety within. Here is how Kierkegaard describes it:

> Imagine that you are walking along a narrow ridge overlooking two precipices, with no guard rail on either side. You might fear that you will slip on a stone and be hurled over into the abyss or that the earth will give way beneath you. But you might also experience anguish at the vertigo, or dizziness, of looking over the cliff, which could result in your falling into the abyss. You might be numbly aware of a certain attraction for the abyss, which calls to you from below, to which you might respond by casting yourself into its deep bosom. Fear is caused by the world; it has an object that we would avoid. But dread or anxiety is not caused by the world but by ourselves. We would like to ensure our beings against the contingency of freedom, but we cannot. No guarantee is given against our destructive use of freedom. It is ominous, pervading our entire being, pushing us at every moment. In dreadful freedom, we shape our essence. We said before that, for the existentialist, humans lack an essence, but we could say that freedom is our essence.[10]

In Sartre's most famous play, *No Exit,* three people sit in hell, torturing each other, each believing that fate has conspired against them and that they are damned to torment each other for eternity: "Hell is other people." But at the end of the play, we see that the door next to them has always been unlocked. They endure damnation by their own volition. Similarly, you are responsible for what you do and what you become. You are free to change just as soon as you decide to do so.

Assessment

Existentialism has served, at least, as an important corrective for an overly rationalistic philosophy that would tend to leave out an appreciation of the arts, the imagination, the passions, and emotions. Perhaps certain classical and medieval systems were guilty of that. Kierkegaard thought that the German idealist George F. W. Hegel was the major villain of his day. Hegel, Kierkegaard contended, erected marvelous castles in the ethereal heavens of thought while he himself lived in an existential doghouse. Take care, philosopher, how you live!

Each of us must come to terms with his or her personal existence. Kierkegaard is correct. Philosophy must become personal. We must work out the meaning of our lives, not once, but continually. Actually, I think many philosophers before Kierkegaard, Nietzsche, and Sartre said as much. Socrates sought to make philosophy practical and personal. St. Augustine recognized the inward element of philosophical endeavor. Descartes threw off all previous authority in order to work out a new and vibrant system of thought. Hume recognized the role of the passions and emotions, stating that "reason is and ought to be a slave of the passions."

Perhaps it is mainly in its emphasis on the subjective, on freedom, that existentialists tend to distinguish themselves. But there is just where the criticism of existentialism starts. Does it not overemphasize the role and reality of freedom and undermine the reality of determinate structures and the role of reason? I think so.

Sartre, in his passion for freedom, goes so far as to reject the reality of the unconscious! Apparently, even our dreams are freely chosen. But psychologists, if not the Bible and common sense, have taught us that we are not always aware of our deepest motives, that we deceive ourselves, that early experiences, long buried in our subconscious, incline our behavior. Indeed, whether and to what extent we are free is itself a deeply philosophical problem, as we saw in Part 6. Reason is the means by which we discover whether and to what extent we are free.

The emphasis on subjectivity and freedom easily slides into an overemphasis on *individualism,* tending toward a solipsism in which the self becomes a world entire to itself, cut off from other selves. But, to quote John Donne, "No man is an island." Men and women are social beings, connected to one another in interpersonal relations, through such institutions as family, school, club, business, community, city, and state. We are all in each other's debt so that we must come out of ourselves, communicate with others, reason together, and strive for an interpersonal moral code.

For Kierkegaard, no moral rule was fully binding. God could at any moment call on people to sacrifice their loved ones as he once called Abraham to do. Notice Sartre's description of his student's dilemma over whether to leave his mother and join the Free French Forces or remain with her. Isn't this a dilemma just because two recognizably valid values are at stake: loyalty to family and devotion to justice? What if the student had come to Sartre and said, "I have a dilemma. I want to know whether I should rape my mother or take care of her?" Would Sartre have nothing more to say than, "Morality requires nothing. You must choose your own morality and universalize it for all others!" If so, then we can only say that he misunderstands the social function of morality, which in part is to procure human flourishing and the resolution of conflicts of interest. The mistake of existentialism is to suppose that every moral decision has the same status as a genuine dilemma, but if everything is a dilemma, then nothing is, for nothing matters! It is only because morality has a rational structure wherein universal values inhere that we can rightly realize that sometimes we are placed in situations where two values compete and whatever we do will be an evil of sorts and so choose the lesser of evils.

What I recommend is a rationalized and socialized, moral existentialism or, what comes to much the same thing, an analytic philosophy that recognizes the need for autonomy and subjective depth. Reason is a higher value than existentialists sometimes allow, but the passions, imagination, and personal adaptation of ideas are also important, more so than traditional philosophy has sometimes recognized. We are by nature feeling creatures, but so are other animals. What sets us apart is largely our ability to reason and deliberate on our desires and emotions and to act on those deliberations. And then, of course, we can reason about the reasoning that went into the earlier reasons and deliberations. We can judge, compare, and communicate our reasons to others in argument; revise our conclusions in the light of their rational critiques; and generally make progress toward being wiser, more understanding persons.

Summary

Existentialism is a type of philosophy rooted in lived experience, concerned with human freedom and purpose in the midst of apparent absurdity. Both religious and secular versions emphasize the need for personal decision, freedom, and the contingent. Kierkegaard, the father of existentialism, thought that the quest for meaning would lead to religion, but secular existentialists— Nietzsche, Sartre, and Camus—reject religion as a viable option and call on humans to live without objective meaning or religion. We noted the criticisms of existentialism, that it tends to be overly individualistic and may become irrational. It may be seen as a corrective to more purely abstract (*essentialist*) philosophies.

FOR FURTHER REFLECTION

1. Do you agree with Sartre that there is no objective purpose in life but that each of us must give our lives a purpose? Or are there objective purposes already present that we need only discover? Explain.

2. Some people say that life is made meaningful by ameliorating the suffering in society and/or by bringing revolutionary changes into being. As a youth, the English philosopher John Stuart Mill had such a view. In his *Autobiography*, Mill describes the crisis of meaning, which took place when he was 22 years old. Following the English utilitarian reformer Jeremy Bentham, his whole life had been dedicated to social reform, and as long as he could see the world improving, he felt satisfaction and even happiness. But a crisis arose in 1826. He was in "a dull state of nerves, such as everybody is occasionally liable to," when the following question occurred to him:

> Suppose that all your objects in life were realized; that all the changes in institutions and opinions which you are looking forward to, could be completely effected at this very instant: would this be a great joy and happiness to you? An irrepressible self-consciousness distinctly answered, "No!" At this my heart sank within me: the whole foundation on which my life was constructed fell down. All my happiness was to have been founded in the continual pursuit of this end. The end had ceased to charm, and how could there ever again be any interest in the means? I seemed to have nothing left to live for.[11]

Mill went through a deep depression which lasted several months during which he came close to suicide. Ask yourself the same question as he did. What would be your answer? What is the significance of your answer?

3. Analyze Nietzsche's passage on the "Death of God." Does Nietzsche really think we killed God? What is the meaning of this passage? Do you agree or disagree with Nietzsche? Explain your answer.

4. Analyze Nietzsche's idea of master–slave morality. Does it disturb you, or do you find some truth in it (even though Nietzsche says there is no truth, only perspectives)?

5. Analyze Nietzsche's discussion on there not being any truth, only interpretations. What problems do you see with this passage?

6. Do you agree with the existentialists, especially Sartre, that we are "condemned to freedom"? Are we responsible for what we do with our lives, or do chance and circumstances have a lot more to do with what we become than the existentialists assert?

NOTES

1. Friedrich Nietzsche, *The Antichrist,* trans. Walter Kaufmann (New York: Random House, 1968).

2. Friedrich Nietzsche, *The Gay Science,* trans. Walter Kaufmann (New York: Random House, 1974), 124.

3. Friedrich Nietzsche, "Daybreak," in *The Complete Works of Nietzsche,* trans. Oscar Levy (T. N. Foulis, 1910), Section 104; my translation.

4. Nietzsche, "Beyond Good and Evil," in *The Complete Works,* 263; my translation.

5. Ibid.

6. Friedrich Nietzsche, *On the Genealogy of Morals,* trans. Walter Kaufmann (New York: Random House, 1967).

7. Nietzsche, "The Will to Power," in *The Complete Works.*

8. Paul Johnson, *Modern Times* (New York: Harper & Row, 1983), 575.

9. All remaining passages are from Jean-Paul Sartre, *Existentialism and Human Emotions,* trans. Bernard Fechtman (New York: Philosophical Library, 1948). Reprinted by permission.

10. Søren Kierkegaard, *The Doncept of Dread* (1844); my translation.

11. John Stuart Mill, *Autobiography* (Oxford, UK: Oxford University Press, 1873).

FOR FURTHER READING

Barrett, William *Irrational Man.* New York: Doubleday, 1958. Still the best introduction to existentialism.

Bretall, Robert, ed. *A Kierkegaard Anthology.* Princeton, NJ: Princeton University Press, 1946. A good collection.

Camus, Albert. *The Plague.* New York: Random House, 1948. Deals poignantly with existentialism and the problems of evil.

Camus, Albert. *The Myth of Sisyphus and Other Essays.* Translated by J. O. O'Brien. New York: Random House, 1955. Camus's youthful, brilliant essay.

Frankl, Victor. *Man's Search for Meaning.* Boston: Beacon Press, 1963. An important work in existential psychology.

Kaufmann, Walter, ed. and trans. *A Portable Nietzsche.* New York: Viking Press, 1954. A good collection.

Kaufmann, Walter. ed. *Existentialism from Dostoevsky to Sarte.* New York: New American Library, 1975. A good anthology.

Kierkegaard, Søren. *Fear and Trembling.* Translated by Walter Lowrie. Princeton, NJ: Princeton University Press, 1954. One of Kierkegaard's most important works.

Klemke, E. D. *The Meaning of Life.* New York: Oxford University Press, 1981. A good collection.

Nietzsche, Friedrich. *Beyond Good and Evil.* Translated by Walter Kaufmann. New York: Random House, 1966. A classic.

Oaklander, Nathan, ed. *Existentialist Philosophy.* Englewood Cliffs, NJ: Prentice Hall, 1992. An excellent anthology with important introductory essays.

Pojman, Louis. *The Logic of Subjectivity: Kierkegaard's Philosophy of Religion.* University, AL: University of Alabama Press, 1984. A critical examination of Kierkegaard's existentialism.

Sartre, Jean-Paul. *Existentialism and Human Emotions.* New York: Philosophical Library, 1948. A classic in modern existentialism.

Appendix: How to Read and Write a Philosophy Paper

Nothing worthwhile was ever accomplished without great difficulty.

Plato, *The Republic*

Just about everyone who comes to philosophy—usually in college—feels a sinking sensation in his or her stomach when first encountering this very strange material, involving a different sort of style and method from anything else they have ever dealt with. It was certainly my first reaction as a student. Lured by questions such as "Is there a God? What can I truly know? What is the meaning of life? How shall I live my life?" I began to read philosophy on my own. My first book was Bertrand Russell's *History of Western Philosophy,* which is much more than a history of the subject, being also Russell's own analysis and evaluation of major themes in the history of Western philosophy. Although it is not a terribly difficult text, most of the ideas and arguments were new to me. Since he opposed many of the beliefs that I had been brought up with, I felt angry with him. But since he seemed to argue so persuasively, my anger gave way to confusion and then to a sense of defeat and despair. Yet I felt compelled to go on with this "forbidden fruit," finishing Russell's long work and going on to read Plato's *Republic,* René Descartes's *Meditations,* David Hume's *Dialogues on Natural Religion,* selected writings of Immanuel Kant, William James's *Will to Believe,* and finally contemporary readings by Antony Flew, R. M. Hare, John Hick, and Ludwig Wittgenstein. Gradually, I became aware that on every issue on which I disagreed with Hume or Russell, Kant or Hick, someone else had a plausible counterargument. Eventually, I struggled to the place where I could see weaknesses in arguments (sometimes in the arguments of those figures with whom I had agreed), and finally I came to the point where I could write out arguments of my own. The pain of the process slowly gave way to joy—almost addictive joy, let me warn you—so that I decided to go to graduate school to get an advanced degree in philosophy.

As I mentioned earlier, it was a gnawing worry about fundamental questions of existence that drew me to philosophy. Is there a God? What can I know for sure? Do I have a soul that will live forever? Am I truly free or simply determined by my heredity and environment? What is it to live a moral life? If you have asked these questions and pondered alternative responses, most of the essays in this book will make sense to you. But if you haven't spent a lot of time thinking about this sort of subject matter, you might ask yourself whether or not these questions are important, and you might outline your own present responses to them. For unless you've asked the question, the proposed answers can sound like only one end of a telephone conversation.

This textbook is meant to suggest responses to stimulate you to work out your own position on the questions addressed herein. This text, offering readings on alternative sides of each issue, along with a teacher to serve as a guide—and, I hope, some fellow students with whom to discuss the material—should challenge you to begin to work out your own philosophy of life.

However, neither the textbook nor the teacher will be sufficient to save you from a sense of disorientation and uncertainty in reading and writing about philosophy, so let me offer a few tips from my experience as a student and as a teacher of philosophy.

Suggestions on Reading a Philosophy Text

The styles and methods of philosophy are different from other subjects that you have been acquainted with since grammar school: English, history, psychology, and science. Of course, there are many methods, and some writings—for example, those of the existentialists: Søren Kierkegaard, Friedrich Nietzsche, Albert Camus, and Jean-Paul Sartre—do resemble what we encounter in literature more than more typical essays in philosophical analysis. In some ways, philosophy resembles mathematics because it usually strives to develop a deductive argument much like a mathematical proof, only the premises of the argument are usually in need of a lot of discussion and objections need to be considered. Sometimes I think of arguing about a philosophical problem as a kind of legal reasoning before a civil court. Each side presents its evidence and gives reasons for accepting its conclusion rather than the opponent's. For example, suppose you believe in freedom of the will and I believe in determinism. We each set forth the best reasons we have for accepting our respective conclusions. The difference between philosophical argument and the court case is that we are also the jury. We can change our minds on hearing the evidence and even change sides by hearing our opponent make a persuasive case.

Suggestions on Writing a Philosophy Paper

Talking about philosophy and writing philosophy are excellent ways to improve your understanding of the content and process of the subject as well as to improve your philosophical reasoning skill. Writing an essay on a philosophical issue focuses your mind and forces you to concentrate on the essential arguments connected with the issue. The process is hard, but it's amazing how much progress one can make—some faster than others, but in my experience some of those who have the hardest time at first end up doing the deepest, most thorough work.

First, identify a *problem* you want to shed light on or solve or a *thesis* you want to defend. Be sure that you have read at least a few good articles on different sides of the issue and can put the arguments in your own words.

Now you are ready to begin to write. Here are some suggestions that might help you.

1. Identify the problem you want to analyze. For example, you might want to show that W.T. Stace (see Chapter 26) has put forth an unsound argument for the thesis that free will and determinism are compatible.

2. As clearly as possible, state the problem and what you intend to show (for example, "I intend to analyze Stace's argument for compatibilism and show that he has misconstrued the issue. His argument for compatibilism is unsound.").

3. Set forth your argument in logical order, supporting your own premises with reasons. It might help to illustrate your points with examples or to point out counterexamples to the opposing points of view.

4. Consider alternative points of view from your own and objections to your position. Try to meet these charges and to show why your position is more plausible.

5. End your paper with a summary and a conclusion: Review your argument and show its implications for other issues.

6. You will probably need to write at least two drafts before you have a working copy. It helps to have another philosophy student go over the preliminary draft before you write a final draft. Make sure that your argument is well constructed and that your paper as a whole is coherent.

7. Regarding style, write *clearly,* in an active voice, put other people's ideas in your own words as much as possible, and give credit in the text and in bibliographic notes wherever you have used someone else's idea or quoted someone.

8. Include a bibliography at the end of your paper, listing all the sources you used for your paper.

When you have a serious problem, do not hesitate to contact your teacher. That is what he or she is there for: to help you make progress in doing philosophical reasoning.

Good luck and I hope you come to enjoy the philosophical quest for truth and wisdom as much as I have.

✠ Glossary

---

abduction   A form of nondeductive reasoning. Sometimes referred to as inference to the best explanation in which the proponent argues that this explanation beats all its rivals as a plausible account of the events in question. (See Chapter 2.)

absolute   A moral absolute is a universally binding principle. It can never be overridden by another principle. *Utilitarianism* is a type of system that has only one ethical absolute principle: Do the action that maximizes utility. Immanuel Kant's system (see Chapter 31) has several absolutes, whereas other deontological systems may have only a few broad absolutes, such as "Never cause unnecessary harm." Sometimes ethical absolutism refers to the notion that every moral problem has only one correct answer. Diametrically opposed to ethical absolutism is ethical *relativism,* which says that the validity of ethical principles is dependent on social acceptance. In between these polar opposites is ethical *objectivism.*

absolute freedom   A concept found in Jean-Paul Sartre's writings to indicate that we are always free to choose and are entirely responsible for our actions. (See Chapter 34.)

absurd   Irrational, paradoxical, or contradictory. Søren Kierkegaard uses the term in two ways: (1) to indicate the apparent *contradictions* in existence and (2) to signify the Christian doctrine of the Incarnation in which God becomes man in Jesus Christ. This is absurd, yet, for the passionate believer, the Truth. Albert Camus, following Kierkegaard's first meaning, uses the concept to refer to "the confrontation of reasonable man and an indifferent universe."

ad hoc   A *proposition* added to a theory in order to save it from being considered logically impossible or implausible. As ad hoc, the proposition itself may

---

Note: All *italicized terms* are defined in this glossary.

have little or no support itself but simply serves to stave off rejection of the original theory.

agnosticism   The view that we do not know whether God exists. It is contrasted with *theism,* the belief in God, and *atheism,* the belief that there is no such being. Although the term is used loosely, a popular way of describing agnostics versus believers and atheists is to say that the believer in God holds that the probability of God's existence is greater than 50 percent, the atheist holds that it is less than 50 percent, and the agnostic holds that it is right at 50 percent. T. H. Huxley coined the phrase to point to a less dogmatic attitude from either theism or atheism.

anthropomorphism   From the Greek meaning "form of humanity," the tendency to see the divine as having human properties. David Hume argues that when theists view God as a superhuman being rather than as something infinitely beyond humanity, they sacrifice the essence of God's transcendence. (See Chapter 8.)

a posteriori   From the Latin meaning "the later," knowledge that is obtained only from experience, such as sense perceptions or pain sensations. (See Chapter 13.)

a priori   From the Latin meaning "preceding," knowledge that is not based on sense experience but is *innate* or known simply by the meaning of words or definitions. David Hume limited the term to "relations of ideas," referring to analytic truths and mathematics. (See Chapter 13.)

aretaic ethics   From the Greek *arete,* meaning "virtue," the theory, first presented by Aristotle, that the basis of ethical assessment is character. Rather than seeing the heart of ethics in actions or duties, it focuses on the character and dispositions of the agent. Whereas *deontological* and teleological ethics emphasize doing, aretaic or virtue ethics emphasize being, being a certain type of person who will no doubt manifest his or her being in appropriate actions. (See Chapter 27.)

argument   A process of reasoning from a set of statements, or premises, to a conclusion. Arguments are either *valid* or invalid. They are valid if they have proper logical form and invalid if they do not. (See Chapter 2.) Also see *deductive argument* and *inductive argument.*

assumption   A principle or *proposition* that is taken for granted in an *argument.*

atheism   The view that there is no such being as God. (See *agnosticism; theism.*)

autonomy   Self-rule, independence. Immanuel Kant uses the term to mean freedom from external authority (*heteronomy*). The ability of the rational person to choose for himself or herself. Truly autonomous selves, Kant thought, would arrive at common judgments on moral issues.

behaviorism   The view that no mental events exist or that they are unimportant for science. Statements about mental events are really about dispositions to behave. "She's angry with me" really means that she is disposed to do nasty things to me and say nasty things about me. The most important recent behaviorist was B. F. Skinner. (See Chapters 19 and 20.)

categorical imperative   Commands actions that are necessary of themselves without reference to other ends. This is contrasted with the *hypothetical imperative* that commands actions not for their own sakes but for some other good. For Immanuel Kant, moral duties command categorically. They represent the injunctions of reason, which endows them with universal validity and objective necessity. (See Chapter 31.)

coherence theory of truth   The theory that a *proposition* is true only if it coheres with a system of propositions that mutually entail and support each other. (See Chapter 18.)

compatibilism   This is the view that an act may be entirely determined and yet be free in the sense that it was done voluntarily and not under external coercion. It is sometimes referred to as "soft determinism." However, whereas soft determinism positively holds to *determinism*, the compatibilist may be agnostic on the truth of determinism, holding that if we are determined, only then could we still be said to act freely under some conditions. (See Chapter 26.)

contingent   A *proposition* is contingent if its denial is logically possible and is not contradictory. A being is contingent if it is not logically necessary.

contradiction   When one statement denies another, both of which cannot be true. For example, "God exists" and "God does not exist." (See Chapter 2.)

correspondence theory of truth   The theory that a *proposition* is true just in case it corresponds with the facts or states of affairs in reality. The theory goes back to Plato and, especially, Aristotle who said that "to say of what is that it is not, or of what is not that it is, is false, while to say of what is that it is, or of what is not that it is not, is true." (See Chapter 18.)

deductive argument   An *argument* is a *sound* deductive argument if it follows a *valid* form and has true premises. In that case, the truth of its conclusion is guaranteed. A deductive argument is valid (but not necessarily sound) if it follows an approved form that would guarantee the truth of the conclusion if the premises were true. (See Chapter 2.)

deism   The view that God exists but takes no interest in human affairs. He wound up the world like a clock and then left it to run itself down.

deontological ethics   Deontological (from the Greek *deon*, meaning "duty") ethical systems see certain features in the moral act itself as having intrinsic value. These are contrasted with *teleological systems* that see the ultimate criterion of morality in some nonmoral value that results from actions. For example, for the deontologist, there is something right about truth telling even when it may cause pain or harm, and there is something wrong about lying even when it may produce good consequences. (See Chapter 31.)

determinism   The theory that every event and state of affairs in the world, including human actions, is caused. There are two versions of determinism: hard determinism, which states that, because every event is caused, no one is responsible for his or her actions; and soft determinism, or *compatibilism,* which states that rational creatures can still be held accountable for their actions insofar as they acted voluntarily. (See Chapter 24.)

dualism   The view that there are two types of substances or realities in conscious beings, mind and matter, and that these interact with one another, the body producing mental events and the mind leading to physical action. (See Chapters 15 and 19.)

dualistic interactionism   See *dualism.*

egoism   There are two types of egoism. Psychological egoism, a descriptive theory about human motivation, holds that people always act to satisfy their perceived best interest. Ethical egoism, a prescriptive or normative theory, is about how people ought to act; they ought to act according to their perceived best interests. (See Chapter 29.)

eliminative materialism   The view that *Folk Psychology* (commonsense language about mental states, including beliefs, emotions, desires, and intentions) will eventually be replaced in favor of a neurologically accurate language that reports brain states. For example, instead of saying "I have a pain in my forehead," we might be led to say, "My C-5 fiber is firing at such and such a rate." (See Chapter 20.)

empiricism   The school of philosophy asserting that the source of all knowledge is experience. John Locke stated that our minds were like blank slates (*tabula rasa*) on which experience writes her messages. There are no *innate ideas.* Empiricism is contrasted with *rationalism,* which holds that there are innate ideas so that the mind can discover important metaphysical truth through reason alone. In our readings, David Hume and Bertrand Russell are empiricists. (See Part 4.)

epiphenomenalism   A version of *dualism,* holding that bodily events cause mental events but mental events do not cause bodily events. The action is one-way only, from body to mind. (See Chapter 19.)

epistemology   The study of the nature, origin, and validity of knowledge and belief. (See Chapter 13.)

ethical egoism   See *egoism.*

eudaimonia   Aristotle's word for "happiness."

existentialism   The philosophical method that studies human existence from inside the subject's experience rather than the outside. It takes a first-person, or subjective, approach to the ultimate questions rather than a third-person, or objective, approach. Examples of this view are the 19th-century Danish philosopher Søren Kierkegaard (1813–1855), the German philosopher Friedrich Nietzsche (1840–1900), and the French philosophers Jean-Paul Sartre (1905–1980) and Albert Camus (1913–1960). (See Chapter 33).

externalism   The epistemological view that knowledge is not to be understood in terms of reasons justifying a true belief but as beliefs produced by reliable processes, such as perception or deductive reasoning. (See Part 4 and *internalism.*)

fideism The doctrine that one does not need evidence for one's religious faith. Reason is inappropriate for religious belief. (See Chapter 12.)

Folk Psychology Our commonsense view about mental events (e.g., pains, beliefs, desires, emotions, and intentions) that sees them as of a different nature from physical events and substance. (See Chapter 19.)

functionalism The theory denying that a type-type relationship needs to exist between mental events and mental states. Though mental events may be identical to certain processes in one brain, they may be identical to a different process in a different brain, and they may be eventually produced in robots without brains like ours. (See Chapters 19 and 21.)

hedonic From the Greek *hedone*, meaning "pleasure," a quality possessing pleasure or pain. Sometimes "hedon" is used to stand for a quantity of pleasure.

hedonism Psychological hedonism is the theory that motivation is to be explained exclusively in terms of desire for pleasure and aversion from pain. Ethical hedonism is the theory that pleasure is the only intrinsic positive value and pain or "unpleasant consciousness" the only thing that has negative intrinsic value or intrinsic disvalue. All other values are derived from these two. (See Part 7.)

hedonistic paradox The apparent contradiction arising from the doctrine that pleasure is the only thing worth seeking and the fact that whenever one seeks pleasure, it is not found. Pleasure normally arises as an accompaniment of satisfaction of desire whenever one reaches one's goal.

heteronomy of the will Immanuel Kant's term for the determination of the will on nonrational grounds. It is contrasted with *autonomy* of the will where the will is guided by reason.

hypothetical imperative Commands actions because they are useful for the attainment of some end, which one may or may not desire to obtain. Ethicists who view moral duties to be dependent on consequences would view moral principles as hypothetical imperatives. They have this form: If you want X, do action A (for example, if you want to live in peace, do all in your power to prevent violence). This is contrasted with the *categorical imperative*. (See Chapter 31.)

indeterminism The view that some events are uncaused. Some versions state that some events are uncaused because they happen by chance. Others hold the minimal thesis that some events or states of being (for example, the self) are uncaused, so free will is consistent with the position. This view is contrasted with *determinism*. (See Chapter 25.)

inductive argument An *argument* in which the premises support the truth of the conclusion but do not guarantee it (as a *valid deductive argument* would). (See Chapter 2.)

inference The process of deriving conclusions from premises.

innate ideas The theory, which we first read of in Plato's *Meno* (Chapter 5) and later in René Descartes (Chapter 13), that states all humans are born with certain knowledge.

internalism   The theory that knowledge is true belief that is justified in the appropriate manner, as opposed to *externalism* where no reasons for belief are necessary for knowledge. (See Part 4.)

intuitionism   The ethical theory that the good or the right thing to do can be known directly via the intuition. G. E. Moore is an intuitionist about the good, defining it as a simple, unanalyzable property. William Frankena holds to a version of this doctrine.

libertarianism   The theory that humans have free will in the sense that given the same antecedent conditions, one can do otherwise. That is, the self is underdetermined by causes and is itself the determining cause of action. This view is represented by Richard Taylor (see Chapter 25). This view is contrasted with *compatibilism* and *determinism.*

logic   The study of rational *arguments,* the rules of *valid inference* and inductive generalization. (See Chapter 2.)

materialism   The metaphysical view that only physical matter and its properties exists. What appears to be nonmaterial (for example, consciousness) is really either physical or a property of what is physical. (See Chapters 19 and 20.)

metaphysics   Meaning "beyond physics," the study of ultimate reality, that which is not readily accessible through ordinary empirical experience. Metaphysics includes within its domain such topics as free will, causality, the nature of matter, immortality, and the existence of God. (See Part 5.)

monism   The theory that reality is all of one substance, rather than two or more. Examples are materialist monism, which holds that matter is the single substance making up all there is, and idealism, which holds that all reality is spiritual or made up of ideas. Lucretius, Democritus, Bertrand Russell, and Richard Taylor all hold to materialistic monism. Baruch Spinoza, George Berkeley, and Hinduism are examples of proponents of idealism. (See Chapter 19.)

naturalism   The theory that ethical terms are defined through factual terms in that ethical terms refer to natural properties. Ethical *hedonism* is one version of ethical naturalism, for it states that the good, which is at the basis of all ethical judgment, refers to the experience of pleasure. Other naturalists like Geoffrey Warnock speak of the content of morality in terms of promoting human flourishing or ameliorating the human predicament.

The term also has a broader metaphysical meaning: as opposed to supernaturalism, explanations that appeal only to the natural, physical order of things.

natural theology   The view that knowledge of God can be obtained through the use of reason. Strong versions hold that we can prove the existence of God. It is contrasted with revealed theology, which holds that all knowledge of God must come from a revelation of God. (See Chapter 12.)

necessary truth   A truth that cannot be false, such as an analytic *proposition* (for example, "All bachelors are male").(See Chapters 14 and 31.)

neutral monism   The view held by Baruch Spinoza and William James that reality is made up of one substance, neither matter nor mind, but something common to both of these. (See Chapter 19.)

noncognitivism   The theory that ethical judgments have no truth-value but only express attitudes or prescriptions. (See Part 7.)

objectivism   The view that moral principles have objective validity whether or not people recognize them as such; that is, moral rightness or wrongness does not depend on social approval but on independent considerations. Objectivism differs from absolutism in that it allows, in given situations, many of its principles to be overridden. (See Chapter 28.)

Occam's Razor   Named after William of Occam (1290–1349) and sometimes called the "principle of parsimony," the principle stating that "entities are not to be multiplied beyond necessity." The razor metaphor connotes that useless or unnecessary material should be cut away from any explanation and the simplest hypothesis accepted. (See Chapter 19.)

ontology   The study of the essence of things and of what there is. What kinds of things are there in the universe? For example, the mind-body problem is in part a debate over whether mental events are of a separate substance or property from physical events or things. René Descartes thought there were three different kinds of things: God, created souls, and created material things.

panpsychism   The view that everything—that is every object in the world, such as stones, blades of grass, molecules—as well as living beings have souls. (See Chapter 19.)

pantheism   The view that God is everything and everything is God. (See Chapter 19.)

parallelism   The view first put forth by Gottfried Leibniz that no causal interaction exists between bodies and minds. Each proceeds on its own, parallel to but independent of the other. (See Chapter 19.)

philosophy   The probing of existence for its meaning; the search for truth and understanding; and the hope of gaining, if not knowledge of the truth, at least wisdom.

pragmatic theory of truth   Set forth by C. S. Peirce and William James, the theory that interprets the meaning of a statement in terms of its practical consequences. They usually go on, as James does in Chapter 18, to say that a *proposition* is true or false according to its results.

prima facie   The Latin phrase that means "at first glance," it signifies an initial status of an idea or principle. In ethics, beginning with W. D. Ross, it stands for a duty that has a presumption in its favor but may be overridden by another duty. Prima facie duties are contrasted with actual duties or all-things-considered duties. (See Chapter 31.)

proposition   A sentence or statement that must either be true or false. Every statement that "states" how the world is a proposition. Questions and imperatives—"Would you open the door?" and "Please, open the door"—are not propositions, but "The door is open" is a proposition since it claims to describe a situation. (See Chapter 2.)

psychological egoism   See *egoism*.

rationalism   The school of philosophy holding that important truths can be known by the mind even though we have never experienced them. The rationalist generally believes in *innate ideas* (or knowledge), so we can have certainty about metaphysical truth. Plato and René Descartes are two classic examples of rationalists. (See Chapter 13.)

reductive materialism   The view that all mental states can be identified with states in the brain. (See Chapters 19 and 20.)

relativism   There are two main types of relativism: cultural and ethical. Cultural relativism is a descriptive thesis, stating that there is an enormous variety of moral beliefs across cultures. It is neutral about whether this is the way things ought to be. Ethical relativism, on the other hand, is an evaluative thesis holding that the truth of a moral judgment depends on whether a culture recognizes the principle in question. (See Chapter 28.)

skepticism   The view that we can have no knowledge. Global skepticism holds that we cannot know anything at all, whereas local (or particular) skepticism holds that there are important realms of which we are ignorant (for example, David Hume regarding *metaphysics*). (See Chapter 14.)

soundness   If a *deductive argument* has *valid* form and its premises are true, the conclusion must also be true.

supererogatory act   From the Latin *supererogatus*, meaning "beyond the call of duty," an act that is not required by moral principles but contains enormous value. Supererogatory acts are those that are beyond the call of duty, such as risking one's life to save a stranger. Although most moral systems allow for the possibility of supererogatory acts, some theories (most versions of classical *utilitarianism*) deny that there can be such acts. (See Chapter 27.)

teleological ethics   Ethical theories that place the ultimate criterion of morality in some nonmoral value (for example, happiness or welfare) that results from acts. Whereas *deontological ethics* ascribe intrinsic value to features of the acts themselves, teleological theories see only instrumental value in the acts but intrinsic value in the consequences of those acts. Both ethical *egoism* and *utilitarianism* are teleological theories. (See Chapters 29 and 30.)

theism   The belief that a personal God exists and is providentially involved in human affairs. It is to be contrasted with *atheism,* which believes that no such being exists, and *deism,* which holds that God exists but he is not providentially concerned with human affairs. (See Chapter 7.)

theodicy   This view holds that evil can be explained in the light of God's overall plan and that, rightly understood, this world is the best of all possible worlds. John Hick holds to a version of this doctrine in Chapter 11.

universalizability   This principle, which is found explicitly in Immanuel Kant's and R. M. Hare's philosophy and implicitly in most ethicists' work, states that if some act is right (or wrong) for one person in a situation, it is right (or wrong) for any relevantly similar person in that kind of a situation. It is a principle of consistency, which aims to eliminate irrelevant considerations from ethical assessment. (See Chapter 31.)

utilitarianism   The theory that the right action is one that maximizes utility. Sometimes utility is defined in terms of pleasure (Jeremy Bentham), happiness (J. S. Mill), ideals (G. E. Moore and H. Rashdall), or interests (R. B. Perry). Its motto, which characterizes one version of utilitarianism, is "The Greatest Happiness for the Greatest Number." Utilitarians further divide into act- and rule-utilitarians. Act-utilitarians hold that the right act in a situation is one that results (or is most likely to result) in the best consequences, whereas rule-utilitarians hold that the right act is one that conforms to the set of rules that in turn will result in the best consequences (relative to other sets of rules). (See Chapter 30.)

validity   When arguments have proper form. There are two kinds of valid arguments: deductive and inductive. A valid *deductive argument* is one such that if the premises are true, the conclusion necessarily is true. A valid *inductive argument* is one such that if the premises are true, it is probable that the conclusion is true.

✢ Index